Volume 1 Fourth Edition

PATTERNS IN
Western Civilization

Sarah Chappell Trulove • James Woelfel • Stephen Auerbach • Rachel Epp Buller

PEARSON
Custom Publishing

PEARSON CUSTOM PUBLISHING
75 Arlington Street, Suite 300, Boston, MA 02116
A Pearson Education Company

CONTENTS

INTRODUCTION TO THE FOURTH EDITION, VOLUME ONE

Patterns in Western Civilization was first published in 1991 as a large single volume with a miscellany of chapters contributed by twenty-five scholars, most of them faculty of the University of Kansas. A second edition appeared in 1998, incorporating a number of revisions in response to criticisms and suggestions and to changes in the primary sources, but retaining the essential structure of the first edition. With the third edition, published in 2002, we substantially altered the format and content, dividing *Patterns* into two volumes corresponding to the two semesters of the Western Civilization curriculum, with fourteen "streamlined" chapters in each volume correlated to the fourteen weeks of assigned primary source readings, periodically interspersed with general background sections on certain historical periods. The third edition proved popular with both students and instructors because of the shorter chapters each dedicated to providing historical background to and guidance in reading the primary text for the week.

In the fourth edition we wanted to maintain the essential structure of the previous edition, but were not happy with the inconsistencies in the handling of historical background, which was sometimes in the weekly chapter and sometimes added as extra material. Thus we decided to create separate historical background sections covering periods appropriate to the chapters that follow them. Volume One includes six such sections.

Historical background sections. The first of the background sections introduces the three oldest civilizations influencing the West: Egypt, Mesopotamia, and the Hebrews. This is followed by the chapter providing guidance to the Tanakh (the Hebrew Scriptures). The second background section

is on ancient Greece, after which there are three chapters: Greek Drama, Plato, and Aristotle. There are two motives for this. The background material leads into the chapters that focus on the primary text or texts. Instructors are then at liberty to use these secondary sources as they like. The background material may simply be assigned with the expectation that the student reads it on her own, with the text-focused chapter lectured on and discussed.

The third background section covers the Roman world and is followed by chapters on Roman literature (Virgil) and Roman philosophy (Seneca). Background section four concludes the story of the Roman Empire, when Christianity became an institution, and introduces the first half of the Middle Ages. There are three primary text-related chapters following this section on the topics: Early Christianity, Movement to Institution (which includes a full discussion of Augustine), and Islam. Section five completes the story of the Middle Ages and is followed by a chapter on Aquinas and the intellectual life of the later Middle Ages and one on Chaucer and medieval literature. The final section leads us through the Renaissance and the Reformation. It is followed by three concluding chapters: new political thought and Machiavelli, Luther and the Reformation, and finally the Scientific Revolution and Galileo.

Throughout this book, when we refer to time periods and dates we use the abbreviations "BCE" (Before the Common Era) and "CE" (Common Era) rather than the more familiar "BC" (Before Christ) and "AD" (*Anno Domini*, Latin for "in the year of the Lord"). This has become standard usage among scholars in many fields. "BCE" and "CE," unlike "BC" and "AD," are inclusive rather than specifically

Christian designations and thus more appropriate for general use in a religiously pluralistic world.

Art and music. Two additions to the textbook are separate sections on art and on music. We are delighted to be able to have color plates and more images throughout the text than we had in previous editions. There is also a CD with selections of music from each historical period, and there are commentaries on the pieces at the end of each music section.

Changes in the primary sources assigned. The fourth edition, like the previous editions, has been prepared to correspond with changes in the primary sources that accompany and are supported by this textbook. The changes in the reading list are few, but important. We think you will find the new selections interesting and enjoyable. Here are some highlights of the changes in volume I:

Homer's *Iliad* has been replaced by Virgil's *Aeneid*. Like the *Iliad*, it is translated by Stanley Lombardo, who is now quite well known for his translations as well as his performances of classical Greek and Roman works. Readers like his lively contemporary translations, which lend themselves very well to being read aloud. Sappho's poems—also translated by Professor Lombardo—have been quite popular with students, so several have been added, which perhaps goes in a small way toward "compensation" for the absence of Homer.

With the *Aeneid* we now have two chapters on Roman authors. The first one talks about the development of Roman literature and Virgil as one of its best-known representatives. A second chapter discusses Roman philosophy. All that the Romans knew they learned from the Greeks, but they also made a considerable contribution to philosophy through their own additions and emphases. It was the Romans who shaped the philosophical tradition and vocabulary in the West, which for centuries knew Greek thinkers like Plato and Aristotle only in Latin translations.

The best-known Roman philosophy is Stoicism, and as in past editions it is here represented by Seneca. We are no longer assigning "Scipio's Dream," by the statesman and philosopher Cicero. This was not very popular with students and, although intended to represent the Stoic ideal of duty, tended to confuse readers because of Cicero's eclecticism—his mixing in elements of Platonism along with Stoicism.

Editorial group. Our staff has been smaller than ever before. We have been fortunate to have Stephen Auerbach, a European historian, who has written the historical sections. Evan Kreider revised the Aristotle chapter and wrote a new Plato chapter. We have been delighted to be able to work with two art historians for the first time. Elissa Anderson made the selections of images for Volume I but was unable to complete the project. Rachel Epp Buller came on board and wrote the art history essays and the captions. She has already begun work on Volume II.

We have long talked about adding music to the curriculum and we finally persuaded Jim Woelfel, who is well known for his musical introductions to his lectures, to compile period music with the assistance of staff of the publisher. The essays that he has written and the CD provided with the text will give you an opportunity to hear Hebrew psalms sung in Jewish worship, processional music for Roman gladiators, Islamic chanting of the surahs from the Qur'an, Gregorian chant, music by Martin Luther, and an aria from an early opera, among other selections.

In the final few weeks before our absolute deadline date Carrie McDonald agreed to "read through" the manuscript. She did more than read through. She found grammatical errors, noted inconsistencies, and made many phrasing suggestions that ultimately improved the text. Whatever else was done to the text I did, so at this point I must follow the usual path and assume full editorial responsibility: all other errors are my own, or at least the result of my own decision.

As readers or previous editions of this text know, since its inception a lot of people have contributed material to it. We are grateful for their knowledge and expertise. Those who have been resources for *Patterns* are listed after the editorial staff biographies.

Sarah Chappell Trulove

THE STUDY OF WESTERN CIVILIZATION

What is Western civilization, and why study it? Western civilization, like all human civilizations, is not a single thread or even a weave of many strands, but something more like the varied patterns in a quilt of complex design. There are diverse basic colors and designs, continuities and discontinuities, harmonies and disharmonies, dominant and subordinate themes. "Western civilization" is a very broad term intended to designate the common features of the human cultures that have dominated Europe and been transplanted to the Americas and other parts of the world. Those common features have their roots in ancient Mesopotamia and Egypt, Israel, Greece, and Rome—all very different cultures whose heritages came to be woven together and transmitted by the Christian European civilization of the Middle Ages. That original diversity was further enriched by native European populations such as the Franks, Goths, Saxons, Lombards, and Celts, and later by races and peoples from other parts of the world.

Furthermore, from their origins to the present day the cultures that have contributed to the shaping of Western civilization, like almost all human cultures, have not existed in isolation but in the context of and in interaction with other cultures. This pattern of mutual influence and conflict has been a continuous one. The ancient Hebrews were influenced by and struggled with surrounding Middle Eastern and North African cultures such as Mesopotamia (Iraq), Syria, Persia (Iran), Egypt, and Ethiopia, and for long the Jews were subject to the Romans. In the fourth century BCE Alexander the Great conquered and brought Greek culture to lands as far away as India, and today one can see ancient Indian statues of the Buddha showing Greek influence. The Roman Empire included an enormous variety of peoples, religions, and cultural traditions stretching from Spain and Britain in the west to Syria in the east. Throughout the Middle Ages Christian Europe and the empire of Islam engaged in centuries of struggle with each other for control over parts of Europe and the Middle East, a contact which at the same time opened up trade for Europe and bequeathed to Europe a rich legacy of learning that included the ideas of Muslim philosophers, theolo-

gians, physicians, and scientists and the works of Aristotle they had preserved. Because of this intimate, albeit contested, history between Christian and Islamic civilizations, one that has continued to the present day, it is vitally important for students of Western civilization to gain a basic knowledge of the Qur'an and the formative history of Islam. Intercultural conflict and exchange between the West and the non-Western world generally have momentously shaped the modern world, on the one hand through the global dominance of Western imperialism, colonialism, capitalism, warfare, science, technology, and communications; and on the other hand by immigration to Western countries and the reaffirmation by other cultures of their distinctive heritage and contributions.

The culturally diverse richness of Western civilization, and its ongoing interaction with other cultures are facts the student of Western Civilization needs always to keep in mind. A number of our chapters provide reminders of these facts within the context of a focus on the distinctive development and character of that heritage we call Western. At the same time, in a course emphasizing Western thought we are centrally concerned with those distinctive ideas, values, and institutions that have become the common property of the Western world. That common property is itself a plurality of different and often conflicting responses to the fundamental and perennial human questions. Every human civilization asks these questions and comes up with answers that show both great variety and also overlap and similarity. In Western Civilization courses we learn about and critically examine the answers that have taken shape over millennia in one complex world civilization, while recognizing that these Western answers take their place within a larger human conversation on the great questions and have their counterparts and alternatives in other civilizations.

But it has also become essential to recognize that the characteristically Western responses to the great human questions are even more richly pluralistic than we used to think. Through a wealth of research in areas such as African and African-American and other ethnic and world area studies, Judaic studies, and women's studies over the past thirty years, we are now acutely aware of voices in the Western conversation that have not been heard because historically they have been marginalized and suppressed. We have tried to incorporate some of that research into this textbook, offering glimpses, explanations, and sometimes sustained treatments of the historic situation and the achievements of women in various Western societies, the modern phenomenon of Western racism and the response to it of Africans and African-Americans, and the story of the Jewish people and of anti-Semitism in the Western world.

We now realize, for example, that because of their historic subordination—which has often meant exclusion from educational opportunity and public life as well as legal disabilities—women's experience and outlooks have been seriously under-represented in the influential writings of the Western world. Those women who have managed to contribute publicly, as political and religious leaders, writers, artists, scientists, and philosophers, have often had their contributions neglected, denigrated, and denied—not because of the quality of their work but because of their sex. This recognition makes the study of the influential writings of Western civilization more complex and also more stimulating and rewarding.

People used to read the "great books of the Western world"—written almost entirely by Caucasian European men—as definitive statements on various aspects of the human condition. Now we recognize the need to balance a continuing recognition of their greatness and enduring insights with what some scholars call a "hermeneutics of suspicion." What this means, first, is that we must examine closely their assumptions about the roles of women and men and about sexuality generally. Secondly, we must consider their assumptions about human groups other than their own—other social classes, races, and cultures. Thirdly, we must ask how these assumptions affect their ideas about humans and the world and their claims to universality. At the same time, we must become aware of how women and other marginalized and oppressed groups in Western civilization have based their struggles for dignity and equality precisely on ideas and values that are enshrined in the "great works" of Western religion, philosophy, and art, seeing in

those ideas and values universal implications that their authors often did not see. In addition, we have the task, in today's Western Civilization courses, of including some of these hitherto suppressed voices in the Western heritage alongside the "classic texts," to enrich and make more fully "whole" the Western world's discussion of the great human issues.

And what are those great human issues? There are various ways we might formulate the basic questions that all human cultures ask, but they include the following: What can we know about the world and ourselves, and what is true and false? What is the meaning of our brief existence in the world, and is it to be found in nature and ourselves or in higher powers? What is the good life for the individual, and what are our responsibilities toward one another? Do humans choose freely, or are we determined by fate, divine will, or heredity and environment? What is the good society, and how is justice to be defined? What is the meaning of being male and female and in other ways diverse as humans? What are the roles of love and work in our lives? What is beauty, and why do we enjoy it and create it? Is the realm of human events a history with a meaning and a goal, or repeating cycles? Why do we suffer and inflict suffering? What is the significance of death for human life? Is there a destiny beyond death, and if so what is it? At the bottom of all these questions is the most fundamental question of all: What are we human beings, these strange creatures who ask so many questions of life?

Now of course cultures and individuals have asked and answered these questions implicitly and explicitly, inchoately and articulately, simply and sophisticatedly. They have also typically asked and answered them quite concretely and not in the general way indicated above. Humans have lived in families and tribes, democracies and monarchies; they have worshipped gods and goddesses; they have created songs and pictures and stories; they have toiled in fields and towns; they have struggled to get along with one another; they have observed the movement of the planets and stars. That is to say that humans raise the great issues of human life and grapple with them largely through the realities of human community, religious faith and tradition, politics and law, artistic expression, intellectual curiosity, the customs and mores of society, work and family.

Out of this concrete matrix emerge some individuals who quite consciously and single-mindedly ponder the foundational questions and try to give expression to the best answers they can. Among these men and women are prophets and mystics, poets and artists, philosophers and theologians, scientists and historians. They are the main sources of the oral traditions, writings, and works of art that have shaped and interpreted the common ideas and values of civilizations. In this book and in a course on the civilization of the West our interest is in those who have played such a role in the Western world, looking at them and their achievements against the background of the social, economic, political, religious, and cultural life of their time and place.

But *why* study Western civilization, and particularly its ideas, values, and institutions? The most obvious answer is that most of us who learn and teach in colleges and universities in the United States are children of and participants in that civilization, and one of the marks of a well-educated human being is knowledge of the roots and development of her or his own cultural heritage. Those students who also claim another cultural legacy—Native Americans, African-Americans, Latin Americans and Latinos, Asian-Americans, Arab-Americans— have been profoundly shaped by Western civilization even as it has often tried to reject or suppress their other cultural traditions. Similarly, in a world that has come to be heavily influenced by so many things European and American, it is important for students from non-Western nations and cultures to learn of the history, ideas, and values of this civilization that has had such an impact—in both positive and negative ways—on their own lives and the lives of their people.

But the study of Western civilization alone is not nearly enough. It is equally important for American and European students to learn of civilizations other than their own. Indeed, in our ever-shrinking "global village" knowledge of other human cultures has become imperative for informed persons, and in international relations we continue to make serious mistakes even at the highest levels of diplomacy out of ignorance of other countries and peoples. Courses in the language, geography, politics, history, religion, philosophy, and arts of other civilizations should be an integral part of one's education together with courses in Western civilization.

To be human is to have a personal story and to be part of a larger story, and the past—history—is everything about me and the larger world in which I live up to the moment I am telling the story. When I "open up" to another person about who I am, I inevitably begin to tell a story—to be a historian in miniature. I talk about the place or places I came from, where I went to school, something about my parents and siblings. If I really ponder in depth who I am, I realize that my story includes not only my immediate family but also a wider family (aunts, uncles, and cousins) and earlier generations of family (grandparents and great-grandparents). I become aware that I am a link in a chain of human generations stretching back through time and forward through the children and grandchildren I may have.

Probing still further, I come to recognize that my personal identity is inseparable from the fact that I am, say, black rather than white, female rather than male, middle-class rather than working-class, and what it means to be one or the other in the society in which I grew up. Then I come to all the things that I simply take for granted in my self-definition because they are part of the very fabric of my society: democratic ideas and institutions, religious freedom together with the dominance of Christianity, characteristically American customs and prejudices, capitalism and consumerism, science and advanced technology, colleges and universities, certain traditions and tastes in music and literature. I begin to grasp that the story of who I am is part of a much larger story going back generations without number and encompassing a whole civilization. I may begin to wonder how all these things that I have always taken for granted started, how they came to be in the form in which I know them, and how they compare to other alternatives. That kind of curiosity is what the study of Western civilization tries to help stimulate and satisfy.

A Western Civilization program is part of a liberal education. A basic assumption of liberal education is that people can be liberated from the tyranny of attitudes controlled entirely by custom and convention and can make informed and independent choices concerning those questions of fundamental human concern about which we spoke earlier. The root of the word "liberal" is the Latin word meaning "free," and we may think of a liberal education as one designed to enlarge human freedom. Free choices can only be informed choices, made in the context of the knowledge of alternative possible answers to the questions and in view of a careful study of the arguments and evidence that are relevant to evaluating the worth of those answers.

The role of a Western Civilization program within a liberal education is to acquaint us with the history, variety, and content of the responses that some of the influential and representative authors of the Western world have given to those perennial human questions. We in the present enter thereby into a dialogue with them in a great conversation through the ages—learning from them, questioning them, weighing the strengths and weaknesses of the alternatives they present, discovering their impact on issues of our day and how we think about those issues. The perspectives we develop personally from our dialogue with the past may be other than those which the ancient, medieval, and modern shapers of Western civilization have forged. But in the process of our study we discover that we cannot develop our own views in an informed manner without their aid. We find that our views—whether unconscious, half-formed, or really thought out—are inescapably indebted to traditions of thought those men and women have created, carried forward, built on, revised, and criticized.

The ancient Greek philosopher Socrates is famous for his exhortation, "Know yourself." For the liberally educated person an important part of acquiring self-knowledge is learning and coming seriously to grips with the sources and history of the ideas and institutions that have molded the modern Western world and all who grow up in it or are affected by it.

James Woelfel

BIOGRAPHIES

MANAGING EDITOR

Sarah Chappell Trulove has an M.A. in Religious Studies from the University of Kansas. She has been involved in the Humanities and Western Civilization Program for over twenty years. She co-authored a 1984 NEH grant that inaugurated significant changes in the Western Civilization program. She helped develop the program's Semester Abroad in Florence and Paris in 1995 and has been a Lecturer in the Program since 1997. She co-directed the Semester Abroad in 2001. In addition to her work in developing the 4th edition of *Patterns* she is the instructor for the Western Civilization Independent Study course.

SENIOR EDITOR

James Woelfel has a Ph.D. from the University of St. Andrews, Scotland, and is Professor of Philosophy and Professor and Director of the Humanities and Western Civilization Program at the University of Kansas. He has done extensive teaching and research in modern European philosophical and religious thought. He recently published the *Legacy of Existentialism and Other Essays on Philosophy and Religion* (University Press of America, 2006).

EDITOR

Stephen Auerbach received his Ph.D. in 2001 from Louisiana State University and is currently an Assistant Professor of History at Georgia College and State University. He specializes in intellectual and cultural history and his primary area of research examines the origins of the French Revolution. He is currently working on a book entitled *Bordeaux and the End of the Old Regime in France, 1750-1789*.

ART HISTORY EDITOR

Rachel Epp Buller has a Ph.D. in art history from the University of Kansas. She works in the area of twentieth century art history and has specific interests in German art, feminist art, and photomontage/collage. She was a visiting assistant professor of art history at Bethel College and currently works as a freelance writer, editor, and curator.

Evan Kreider, who authored the chapters on Plato and Aristotle, was a graduate teaching assistant in Philosophy and Humanities and Western Civilization for five years. He received his Ph.D. in philosophy from the University of Kansas in 2005, and is now an assistant professor of philosophy at the University of Wisconsin-Fox Valley.

LIST OF CONTRIBUTORS

S. Daniel Breslauer	Oliver Phillips
SunHee Kim Gertz	James Seaver
Richard Jeske	Michael Shaw
Scott Hendrix	Jerry Stannard
Stanley Lombardo	Susan Warden
Susan Noakes	

SECTION ONE

THE ANCIENT WORLD:
MESOPOTAMIA, EGYPT, AND THE HEBREWS

7000–2000 BCE Rise of Kingdoms

7000 BCE Earliest evidence of civilization in the West

3500 BCE Rise of cities in Egypt and Mesopotamia

3100 BCE Kingdoms of Egypt are united

3000 BCE Development of cuneiform and hieroglyphic writing

2700 BCE Building of the Great Pyramids begins
Epic of Gilgamesh

2000–1200 BCE

2000 BCE Beginning of Egypt's Golden Age

1800 BCE Dating of stories of the Hebrew Patriarchs

1750 BCE Code of Hammurabi

1350 BCE Promulgation of Egyptian monotheism

1200–700 BCE Emergence of Judaism

1200 BCE Dating of story of Hebrew exodus from Egypt
Assyrians dominate Mesopotamia

1000 BCE Reign of the House of David

950 BCE Written evidence of earliest Hebrew Scriptures

922 BCE Hebrew kingdom divides: Israel and Judah

780 BCE Collapse of Kingdom of Israel

700–200 BCE Empire Building

650 BCE Library at Nineveh

586 BCE Sacking of Jerusalem and "Babylonian Captivity"

539 BCE Persians capture Babylon
Some Jews return to Israel

332 BCE Alexander the Great conquers Persians

295 BCE Founding of great library at Alexandria

250 BCE Tanakh translated into Greek *Septuagint*

Dates given are approximate

THE ANCIENT WORLD:
MESOPOTAMIA, EGYPT, AND THE HEBREWS

Scholars locate the earliest beginnings of Western civilization in the cultures of Mesopotamia in the Near East and Egypt in the Nile Delta region. Humans, of course, had already occupied these regions for thousands of years, but from the evidence we have to date it was in these two areas—near great waterways—where civilized societies, as we define them, began to develop. For our purposes we define "civilization" as *humans living in settled societies, based on agriculture and centered in cities, with a written language and a complex social structure.*

The word "civilization" is itself an "urban" word, derived from the Latin *civis*, citizen, and *civitas*, city. Civilization is the urbanization of a formerly scattered rural population. The resulting urban center, the city, remains intimately related to and dependent upon a surrounding agricultural base and rural community. Beware of thinking of the earliest civilizations as being "simple" or "primitive." While they did lack scientific knowledge in the modern sense, their religious, economic, political, social, and familial structures were often highly developed and complex. Written language constitutes the demarcation between *prehistory* and *history*, and both Mesopotamia and Egypt produced written records dating as far back as 3500 BCE.

Little was known about Mesopotamia or Egypt until archaeologists began excavating in those areas in the nineteenth century. Since then we have learned much about these two civilizations. Archaeologists have been able to mostly recreate the towns (if not literally, in diagrams and drawings), cities, and monuments of these societies. They have collected a variety of artifacts that tell us about human life at this time: their clothing, diet, personal habits, and religious rituals. Roads have been uncovered and machinery has provided us with evidence of their economy, but most importantly, the discovery of written languages has enabled scholars to compose a history of these peoples. We now know that both Mesopotamia and Egypt substantially influenced the development of Western civilization. Approximately two millennia later a tribe identified as the Hebrews or "Hapiru" appeared in the coastal region of what is now Palestine. They, too, would substantially influence the development of Western civilization, but in a very different way.

MESOPOTAMIA

The region we call Mesopotamia refers to the land surrounding and between the Tigris and Euphrates Rivers, running from the region of Nineveh in the north to the Persian Gulf in the south. It is roughly the area of modern-day Iraq. The name *Mesopotamia* is a Greek word that means "between the rivers." Thus "Mesopotamia" is a geographical and not a political designation of the region. The Mesopotamian region makes up the main part of what is called the *Fertile Crescent*, a large crescent-shaped area of rich farmland extending from Mesopotamia in the east to Syria in the north to southern Palestine in the south. The soil of the Tigris and Euphrates valleys was good for agriculture, but by contrast to the Nile River in Egypt, the flooding of the two Mesopotamian rivers was unpredictable and sometimes destructive. As a result, controlling the water source for crops through irrigation, especially in the southern regions was important. It may have been this need of flood control that brought the inhabitants together into urban communities. Northern Mesopotamia, on the other hand, was less affected, since there was sufficient rainfall and natural wells for agricultural development.

The earliest civilization in the region of Mesopotamia is called Sumer or Sumeria, and dates from around 3500–2300 BCE. It consisted of some fifteen to twenty city-states with peak populations of 20,000–30,000 each, encompassing as much as one hundred square miles, and concentrated in the southern portion of Mesopotamia. These city-states were enclosed by walls and had at their centers a great stair-stepped structure called a *ziggurat*, or temple, dedicated to a specific god or goddess. The villages surrounding the city were responsible for providing food, grain, fish, and meat. These provisions were stored within the walls and distributed among the inhabitants.

Social structure was hierarchical. The king, or *lugul*, who also served as the spiritual leader, was at the top. The priests and scribes who functioned as the bureaucrats and ran the city-state followed him in line of importance. Craftsmen such as stonemasons, copper workers, and weavers, lived and performed their tasks within the city walls. Landowners and merchants made up one class, and peasants and slaves fell at the bottom of the class structure.

Trading was an integral part of Sumerian life. It may have been a for-profit-industry with the administration based at the temples. They imported timber and precious metals, which it lacked, and sold grain in return. The Sumerians combined copper and tin to make bronze. This brought about improvements in irrigation techniques and weaponry and the development of the metal-tipped plow, which so improved the levels of production that Sumeria became a "breadbasket" to the greater region. These advances led to an ever-expanding network of trade routes along the Euphrates River, linking the north to the south, and along caravan routes from the Persian Gulf across the Arabian Desert to the Mediterranean Sea. In this way the Sumerians laid the foundations for economic interdependence that would encompass the entire Middle East by the end of the third millennium (2000 BCE).

Sumerians created a script that has been given the name cuneiform from the Latin *cuneus* meaning "wedge." It was composed of pictographs which combine into wedge-shaped forms that represented the particular sounds of the spoken language. A stick with a wedge-shaped end that we call a stylus was used to impress the writing on soft clay tablets. The clay was allowed to dry or was baked for greater permanence. The earliest written records are lists, inventories, and economic and legal transactions. A professional class called scribes arose and because of their skills in writing and record keeping became influential in the running of government bureaucracies and business enterprises. They were the first governmental clerks.

The Sumerians were the first people to use the wheel for transportation. They invented a water clock to measure time and divided the circle into 360 degrees and the hour into sixty minutes. They developed a lunar calendar, adding a third month every three years. They mapped the night sky, identifying planets, stars, and constellations and invented a number system based on multiples of six and twelve.

We learn a great deal about the life of a people through their myths (*muthos* in Greek means "stories"), and so it is with the Sumerians. The stories they tell are not necessarily meant to convey literal meaning, but to communicate messages that have significance beyond the literal meaning of the story. They tell stories about the gods and their relationships with one another and with human beings, how the universe and the earth came to be, what human beings are, the role of that community in the world, how society should be organized and how individuals should live their lives, and what destiny awaits human beings. Some mythical stories seem to explain the origin of some cultural or religious phenomenon. Others purport to narrate the origins of the institutions of marriage, various human handicrafts, and religious shrines. Myths typically include elements that have political and religious implications. Through the myths of different societies we receive insight into the actual conditions that people faced in those communities and their outlook on the world. The key to understanding the stories is to read them symbolically rather than literally. We will be looking at the creation myths for each of the three civilizations we are discussing in this section.

Like other peoples of the ancient world, those who inhabited Mesopotamia were *polytheists*: they believed in many gods. Among the various gods, rulers of Mesopotamian cities selected one of the gods from the pantheon to be chief god of their city. The cities and their gods would compete with each other to determine which divine being would receive universal praise. The buildings—the walls and palaces of the city—measured the city's greatness and were inscribed in honor of the favored deity. Vanquished nations were forced to acknowledge the superiority of the god of the conqueror, who was housed in the city temple. Rituals of feeding, clothing, and washing the god were carried out in its sanctuary. Gods typically "lived with" a spouse and sometimes children.

Religion dominated human life and provided the people with a worldview that gave human life meaning. There was little distinction between the sacred and the secular. The king and the official priesthood were closely connected. The Mesopotamian kings ruled their cities both as political leaders and as officiants in major religious rites. Exorcists and diviners played a key role in Mesopotamian religion, and their skills were highly regarded throughout the ancient world. Exorcists cast out evil spirits, Diviners interpreted the meaning of various omens, from the entrails of sacrificed animals to patterns or unusual events in the sky.

Ordinary people attached themselves to a particular god or goddess, offering prayers and sacrifices in which they asked their personal deity to intercede with other deities, to protect them from evil spirits, or to insure a good harvest. A popular Sumerian goddess was Ishtar also known as Innana. Their identities merge as do what they represent. Both are goddesses of love and fertility, but they also serve as the goddess of war. They resemble the goddesses Aphrodite and Venus in Greek and Roman culture. Through religious practice people were able to avail themselves of a large body of spells and incantations. Common people were not allowed into the inner sanctuaries of the temples, but they watched the great religious processions outside them.

Among the Mesopotamian religious texts there are some that tell about the creation of the world. Such writings are called *cosmologies*, because they tell stories about how the cosmos or universe began and what it is like. The "Enuma Elish," a Babylonian hymn of creation, describes a great war among the gods. The mother goddess, Tiamat, created the world. She and her consort are slain by a rebel god, Marduk, who with the blood of the slain gods created human beings. Humans were to be servants of the gods, but because the rebel Marduk created them, they, too, have a tendency to rebellion. Humans attempt to keep their own chaos under control and help the gods maintain an ordered universe. As a token of their servitude, humans are to bring sacrifices before the gods at the great towers that link heaven and earth: the *ziggurats*. Like the pyramids in Egypt and in Mayan civilization, these were human-constructed "holy mountains." They were the gateway to the divine and their construction and preservation provided the Mesopotamians with their true purpose—obedience to the divine beings. The "Tower of Babel" story in Genesis 11 in the Hebrew Bible is a satire on the ziggurat of Babylon. ("Babel" was the Hebrew name for Babylon, which is from the Akkadian *Bab-ilu*, "gate of the god.") It is interesting that in both stories, human beings are co-creators with the divine in structuring the world.

Mesopotamians saw themselves as working with the gods to transform the world order. Therefore, death, after which a person no longer acts as a self-conscious agent for change, is the greatest defeat possible. We find the idea that immortality belongs only to the gods expressed powerfully in the *Epic of Gilgamesh*, a rare example of Mesopotamian literature. (This text will be discussed in Chapter One.) Humans are thoroughly mortal, and whatever lies beyond death is not a fulfillment of life on earth and certainly not something to welcome. In this view the peoples of Mesopotamia were similar to ancient Hebrews and Greeks and, as we shall see, completely different from the very positive beliefs of the Egyptians about life after death.

Sumerian political dominance in Southern Mesopotamia began to wane around 2300 BCE. The Akkadians, a Semitic people from the north with their capital city of Akkad, succeeded them. Their leader was Sargon, who was one of history's earliest empire builders. "Semitic" refers to a family of languages having a common root. (The modern term "anti-Semitism" is not based in language, but was created in the twentieth century and applied to the a group of people who followed the Jewish religion. It was meant to define them as a race which they are not.) Akkadian, Phoenician, Assyrian, Hebrew, and Arabic all belong to the Semitic language family. For the most part the Akkadians assimilated into the Sumerian culture. The language changed from Sumerian to Akkadian and was written in the cuneiform alphabet. Some texts found from this period suggest that the Akkadians emphasized individualism and personal rights and created an economic system that encouraged private enterprise.

The Amorites, from the central region of Mesopotamia, took control in 2000 BCE and are known as the Old Babylonian Kingdom after their capital city of Babylon. Their most illustrious leader was King Hammurabi (ruled 1792–1750 BCE), remembered for the Code of Hammurabi. We know that law codes had existed since earlier times, but Hammurabi's was influential from the Persian Gulf to the Mediterranean Sea. His laws were inscribed on a *stele*, or pillar, some seven feet tall and set in the center of the city. On it Hammurabi proclaims authority from the gods, and identifies himself as a "guardian shepherd" who will bring both security and justice to the land. Included in the code are laws governing family life, ownership of land, and commerce—all aspects of Babylonian life. The code glorifies the god Marduk as Babylon's supreme god. This enabled Hammurabi to portray his personal political aims as a divinely appointed task.

Whether the Code of Hammurabi actually functioned as legislation or served a symbolic purpose is not known. The content suggests a particular understanding of social order and human life that was hierarchical in structure but nevertheless advanced individual enterprise. Such a system continued to have appeal for later rulers of the Mesopotamian region. The Assyrian king Assurbanipal in the seventh century BCE used the code to reinforce a hierarchical social structure that helped preserve the "peace" of the city-state. The story of the symbolic influence of this code actually comes

down to the present day. When Iraq's former leader, Saddam Hussein, wanted to justify his opposition to the West in general, and to the United States in particular, he called attention to Hammurabi's laws as proof that ancient Iraq had a higher and nobler view of society than "promiscuous" Western liberalism and democracy.

The Old Babylonian Kingdom fell under the pressures of both internal unrest and periodic invasions from warring tribes. Most prominent among the latter were the Hittites from the region of Anatolia (modern-day Turkey) and the Kassites, nomads from the east in the Zagros Mountain area. The Hittites were probably responsible for the sacking of Babylon in 1600 BCE. They plundered and withdrew, but the Kassites remained, were assimilated into the existing culture and held power for over three hundred years.

In the thirteenth century BCE a great power arose from Assyria, in the north of Mesopotamia. Under a succession of powerful and ruthless kings, the Assyrians soon dominated a vast empire. For the Assyrians war was a way of life, and they are remembered for their excessive cruelty. At the height of their power the Assyrians made conquests in Syria, Egypt, Israel, and Mesopotamia, setting up *suzerains*, overlords, to rule the regions. As the Babylonians had elevated Marduk to supremacy among the gods, so the Assyrians exalted their divinity Assur (Ashur). The Hebrew Bible tells how in 721 the army of the Assyrian ruler Sargon II (ruled 722–706 BCE) destroyed the northern kingdom of Israel and sent all its inhabitants into exile. This created the so-called "Ten Lost Tribes" of Israel. The biblical account of the invasion (2 Kings 17) blames the faithlessness of the leaders and people of the kingdom of Israel for this catastrophe. By contrast, the Assyrians saw themselves as champions of religious truth. Assyria's last great leader was Assurbanipal (ruled 668–627 BCE), who is remembered favorably only in modern times because of the great library that he established in his capital at Nineveh. Since its discovery in the last century this royal library has been the source of many of the texts, both literary and administrative, that give us vital information on the life and thought of ancient Mesopotamia.

We bring our historical narrative of ancient Mesopotamia to a close with a brief look at the last political powers that controlled the region in ancient times. A military alliance of smaller states ended Assyrian dominance in the seventh century BCE. Out of this arose a group called the Chaldeans to form what is known as the New Babylonian Empire. Nineveh was sacked and abandoned, which is the reason Assurbanipal's library was left unknown and relatively undisturbed. The greatest Chaldean ruler, Nebuchadnezzar (ruled 604–562 BCE), restored the city of Babylon and made it legendary for its opulence and beauty. It was Nebuchadnezzar also who brought about a key event in the history of the Jewish people when he destroyed Jerusalem and carried a large portion of the Judean population to Babylonia. This is known as the period of the "Babylonian Exile." King Cyrus of Persia captured Babylon in 539 BCE and united all of the Middle East into a great Persian empire. The Persian Empire in its turn was overthrown by the Greek empire-builder, Alexander the Great, in 331 BCE.

Among the written texts of Mesopotamia recovered by archaeologists only a small portion can be characterized as literature. The best-known literary survivor is the *Epic of Gilgamesh*. *Gilgamesh* is the earliest example of epic literature known to us in the Western world. An *epic* is a long narrative poem that tells the story of a human or semi-divine hero whose actions are of fateful significance for his tribe or nation, or perhaps for the whole human race. Among the great epics in the history of Western civilization are Homer's *Iliad* and *Odyssey* and Virgil's *Aeneid*. *Gilgamesh* originated in the form of separate poems. As a connected narrative *Gilgamesh* may have intended to express the ideal of good kingship and good citizenship.

When studied together one can find a number of similarities among the themes in the literature of Mesopotamia, Egypt, and the Hebrew scriptures. For this reason you will read the flood story from the *Epic of Gilgamesh* as part of the lesson in Chapter One. Among other examples of ancient Mesopotamian literature the following are also of interest: "Letters to the God" are royal inscriptions typically celebrating victory in battle in highly poetic and exaggerated language. "Dialogue Texts" were a form of popular entertainment. The "Dialogue of Pessimism" is an ancient version of a comic situation that is still used today: the servant who outwits his master. The "Poor Man of Nippur" tells the tale of a poor man who takes revenge on the mayor of Nippur for taking his last goat. The poor man plays three clever tricks on the mayor. All these forms of literature were initially presented orally.

The "Babylonian Theodicy" is a dialogue between a skeptic and a pious man who politely debate their views of life. This has certain similarities to the Book of Job. Both are in dialogue form and both question divine justice. (A theodicy is an argument defending the reality and benevolence of God or the gods in the face of the evils of life.) Like Job, the speaker lives an exemplary ethical life. Yet this suffering hero notes that those who sin and act unethically still succeed. The friend seeks to justify the God. Questioning divinity, the friend remarks, is irrational and unhelpful. Such emotional outpouring is blasphemy and a forsaking of justice. The divine plan, the friend comments, "is remote." The conclusion is that the gods are inscrutable. Humanity cannot look to the divine for an explanation of what happens in the world. The individual must assume the responsibility for giving meaning to the world.

EGYPT

Egyptian history and civilization have been shaped and dominated by the Nile, one of the great waterways of the world. The ancient Greek historian Herodotus famously and aptly called Egypt "the gift of the Nile." The Nile River flows over seven hundred miles from its source in central Africa north to the Mediterranean Sea, creating a narrow strip of green and fertile land where ninety-nine percent of the population lives, flanked by vast stretches of desert on either side. In prehistoric times the area was divided into Lower Egypt, the Nile delta in the north, and Upper Egypt that consisted of settlements on the higher ground in the south. The recorded history of Egypt begins with the union of Lower and Upper Egypt into one nation.

Egypt was rich in stone—limestone, porphyry, and granite. Their first tools were made of wood or stone. The use of copper emerged in the middle of the third millennium. The basic diet included barley, beer, onions, and fish. To this was added wild vegetables and eventually the meat from cattle, goats, sheep and pigs. The Nile provided a trade link between settlements, which facilitated the uniting of the two kingdoms under a central administration.

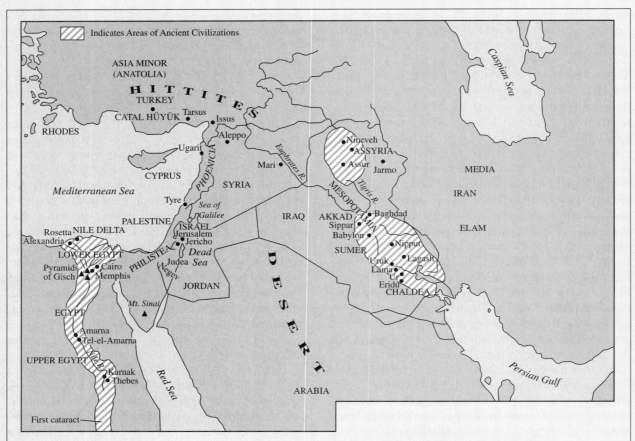

Cradles of Civilization. Reprinted from *A History of Civilization,* Ninth Edition, by Robin W. Winks, (1996), Prentice-Hall, Inc.

The division of Egyptian society fell into the following categories: the royal family, priests, nobles, a "middle class" of scribes, merchants, and wealthy farmers, and finally peasants and urban workers. During the period of the New Kingdom a professional army and slaves brought back from foreign conquests added two further social categories. Marriage laws and customs permitted polygamy, but monogamy was the standard marital unit. The king had many wives and concubines, but one chief wife. Women were not secluded, as they later were in Greek society, and could inherit property, and engage in business. Evidence supports that a woman named Hatshepsut ruled as a powerful pharaoh of the eighteenth dynasty during the fifteenth century BCE, and it is possible that there were one or two other women who ruled as well.

The ancient Egyptian form of writing is called *hieroglyphics* (literally "sacred carving"), which was first developed in the early dynastic period. Hieroglyphics was based on three types of characters: pictographic, syllabic, and alphabetic. The alphabetic characters represented twenty-four single consonant sounds. The Egyptians wrote on *papyrus,* a kind of paper made from the pith of papyrus reeds that grew abundantly in Lower Egypt. Papyrus paper was certainly more convenient to use than the clay tablets of the Mesopotamians, but it had the disadvantage of being less durable.

The meaning of hieroglyphics was lost to the world for centuries. In 1799 the discovery of a stone tablet by a soldier in the army of Napoleon enabled scholars to decipher the ancient script. Known as the *Rosetta Stone,* the tablet contains a text in three forms: the hieroglyphic script of the priests, the demotic script of everyday Egyptians, and Greek. Working from the Greek text, scholars found the key to translating hieroglyphics.

The Egyptians practiced medicine with some success. They recognized the importance of hygiene, performed some surgery, and sought natural causes for disease. In mathematics the Egyptians, like the Mesopotamians, marked off 360 degrees to a circle and noticed that the circumference of a circle to its diameter, the "pi" ratio, is the same for all circles. They developed a calendar based on the sun that was much more accurate than the Mesopotamian moon calendar. It became the basis for the Julian calendar developed by the Romans.

Generally speaking, Egyptian art and architecture were inseparable from Egyptian religion. Painted and sculpted figures were highly stylized, not naturalistic: they were icons and symbols by which the divine world manifested itself in the human. The monumental statues and temples of the New Kingdom were expressions of the pharaoh's divine power. The "picture writing" of hieroglyphics was also artistic and iconographic in character, and carved texts such as we find on pyramid and tomb walls were integral parts of the artistic and religious presentation. We will examine Egyptian religion and Egyptian literature separately below. The history of ancient Egypt is traditionally divided into three major periods—the Old, Middle, and New Kingdoms—preceded by what is called the "early dynastic period" and interrupted by two Intermediate Periods. In about 3100 BCE a king of Upper Egypt named Menes or Narmer conquered the Lower Kingdom and united the two regions. He established his capital at the new kingdom's geographical center, Memphis (near modern Cairo). This remained the royal capital through many dynasties. The kings of Egypt were often portrayed wearing the tall, cone-like crown that combined the red crown of Lower Egypt and the white crown of Upper Egypt. This was meant to emphasize that the king was a ruler of "Two Lands." ("Pharaoh" is a term applied to the Egyptian rulers in the Hebrew Bible, not the term used by the ancient Egyptians themselves.) '

The Old Kingdom, ca. 2705–2250, was the period of pyramid building. Over eighty were built.

An aspect of the pyramid building that remains puzzling to engineers today is how such huge stone structures were created without the wheel and pulley. Excavation of the areas around the pyramids continues in an effort to learn more about both the method of the construction of the pyramids and the daily life of the builders.

The pyramids were royal tombs, symbolic depictions in stone of the sun's rays shining through the clouds and a stairway for the pharaoh to ascend and take his place with the sun god in his journey through the heavens. They show dramatically the centrality to Egyptian religion of the divine status of the pharaohs and life after death. It was the Egyptian belief that toiling for the king, who was viewed as a sacred person, was a religious duty and those who did so would benefit in the afterworld. Politically and socially, the pyramids attest to the high degree of centralized state authority and bureaucracy that Egypt had achieved in the early centuries as a united kingdom.

Around 2250 BCE the central authority of the monarchy crumbled, although dynasties of pharaohs continued. The country essentially broke up into a group of city-states each vying for control. Eventually one of these local chieftains consolidated his power, took over the dynasty, and moved the capital to Thebes. This inaugurates the Middle Kingdom, ca. 2061–1750, that is considered Egypt's "Golden Age." Temples, as suitable resting places for the god-kings, replaced pyramids. Public works projects, such as irrigation and drainage systems, were undertaken. Commercial development along the African shore of the Mediterranean expanded trade to include the Phoenician city-states to the east. There was something of a "flowering" in literature. Archaeologists have uncovered adventure tales, poetry in the form of religious hymns and songs, and a special type of poetry celebrating the goodness of life. Religious belief and practice, which had previously offered the promise of afterlife only to the pharaoh and his family, were "democratized" to include everyone, resulting in a greater emphasis on the importance of moral conduct in establishing one's worthiness to be granted life beyond death.

A second Intermediate Period, 1750–1570, was again caused by a breakdown of central authority, but also a factor was a rivalry between Upper and

Lower Egypt. In addition this was a time when a desert people from western Asia whom the Egyptians called "Hyksos"—"rulers of foreign lands"—invaded Egypt. They held power for nearly two centuries when a Theban, Ahmose, defeated them and founded the eighteenth dynasty. It was from the Hyksos that the Egyptians adopted the use of the war chariot in battle.

The New Kingdom, 1570–1070, was led by a series of pharaohs—such as Thutmose III, Amenhotep II, Sety I, and Ramses II—who carried Egyptian power to new heights of imperialism and military might. Egypt became an aggressor nation, and its kings conquered territory extending south into Nubia and as far east as the Euphrates River. These wars of conquest created a professional army and an expanded bureaucracy, and increased the power of the priestly class. A slave class comprised of foreign captives became part of Egyptian society. Commercial and cultural exchange accelerated, and foreign influence in Egyptian art became evident.

The Egyptian kings of this period had colossal temples and statues of themselves built, including the great temple complexes at Luxor and Karnak. One of the most architecturally brilliant of these structures was the Mortuary Temple of Queen Hatshepsut (ruled 1477–59), a huge terraced structure in Deir-el-Bahri, the "Beautiful Desert Valley," that looks as though it has been carved out of the cliffs that rise behind it. The New Kingdom pharaohs also adopted new burial customs: their mummies were buried in tombs cut out of the rock in the Valley of Kings, a desolate area west of the Nile near Thebes.

Perhaps the greatest pharaoh of the New Kingdom was Ramses II, whose long rule spanned the period 1290–1224 BCE. He was a powerful military leader as well as a great builder. He left a legacy of monumental structures, among which are his mortuary temple at Thebes and four colossal statues of himself. Another popularly-known ruler from this time is "King Tut," Tutankhamun, whose undisturbed tomb was discovered by archaeologists in 1922 CE. It revealed the fabulous wealth of the Egyptian royal court during the New Kingdom.

By the end of the twelfth century Egypt had fallen prey to renewed foreign invasion. A weakened Egypt came under the rule of the Libyans to the north, the Nubians from the south, the Assyrians, the Persians, and finally the Greeks under Alexander the Great in the latter part of the fourth century BCE. Although pharaohs continued to rule (dynasties 26–30), they were either foreign-born or mere puppets installed by foreign rulers.

Alexander founded the seaport city of Alexandria in Egypt. With its famous library, Alexandria became the major center of learning in the ancient world. Egyptian culture merged with the Hellenistic culture that had spread across the Mediterranean world by Alexander's conquests. Egypt became a part of the Roman world when Octavian Augustus Caesar defeated Mark Antony, a Roman general, and Cleopatra, the last pharaoh. Modern-day Egypt is profoundly stamped with the culture and language of its final conquerors, the Arabs, who in 641 CE brought them the new religion of Islam.

The pharaoh was the focal point of both political and religious life; he was a god as well as the king. His power over the people, institutions, and wealth of Egypt was absolute. The king was treated with reverence and awe, as were his queen and their children. Elaborate rituals characterized every aspect of the royal family's everyday life. Just below the king and his family in the social hierarchy were the priests of the temple, who not only presided over the religious rites but were also the administrators, scholars, and educators. The vast temple complexes in the great Egyptian capitals such as Memphis and Thebes were centers not only of worship but also of government administration; in addition, they were archives, schools, and storehouses. The pharaoh or his priestly representatives led the rituals in the temple. As with the Sumerians ordinary people were not allowed into the temple, although they could be a part of the festivals held outside the temple.

Central to Egyptian religion was the principle of cosmic order, harmony, and justice, personified as the goddess *Ma'at*, which made the universe and human life possible. The pharaoh in his very person embodied the principle of Ma'at; law was simply his will and decrees, although pharaohs always built upon the legal precedents of their predecessors.

Egypt had two creation myths: The "Cosmology of Heliopolis" was found in the religious texts inscribed in hieroglyphics in the tombs of the pharaohs of the fifth dynasty, ca. 2465–2325 BCE. In this myth the creator is Atum, the one supreme reality. He contains all the elements and forces of nature, and his seed alone brings forth the cosmos, the other gods, and humankind. Atum was associated with the sun, *Re* in Egyptian, and so was often called "*Re-Atum.*" A large eye—an all-seeing eye—is the symbol that represents Atum. Look on a U.S. treasury one-dollar bill for an example of this.

The "Memphite Theology" promotes the god Ptah, who precedes and is superior to Atum. He brings the other gods and the universe into being, not through a sexual act, but by means of the thoughts in his heart (the Egyptians located the roots of thought in the heart, not the head) and the words of his tongue. This idea of an intellectual principle behind everything is called the "logos doctrine" (the Greek word *logos* means both reason and speech), and has interesting similarities both to the story of God's creating everything by his word in Genesis 1 and the story in John's Gospel of Jesus as the embodiment of the Word (*Logos*) of God through which everything was created.

The myth of Osiris was very popular in ancient Egypt. It became associated with Egypt's kings and queens, thus endowing them with divine status. There are various versions and many elaborations of the story. We will present it in its barest outline. Osiris was one of the four children of the gods (Osiris, Isis, Set, Nephthys), and as a ruler of Egypt teaches his people agriculture and other practical arts. He is slain by his jealous brother Set (Seth), who cuts his body into pieces and scatters them far and wide. Osiris' loyal sister-wife, Isis, assisted by Nephthys, collects these pieces and miraculously restores him to life. Osiris impregnates her and she bears a son, Horus. Osiris regains his kingdom, but he eventually descended to the underworld to serve as a judge of the dead. Later his son, Horus, avenges his murder by challenging his uncle Set for the throne and destroying him.

Originally this death and resurrection story may have been simply a nature myth, representing the drying of the Nile in the autumn and the coming of the flood in the spring. But eventually it took on deeper significance, showing the paternal solicitude of Osiris for his subjects and the devotion of his wife and son. More importantly, the death and resurrection of Osiris conveyed a promise of personal immortality, and the victory of Horus over

Set foreshadowed the ultimate ascendancy of good over evil.

What modern scholars find fascinating is that the religion of Osiris lacked association with any particular center of worship or official priesthood. Worship of this god transcended any single political group. Several times in Egyptian religious history the worship of Osiris would displace the official cult sponsored by the pharaoh. Some scholars think of the religion of Osiris as more "democratic" and "popular" than other cults, because all Egyptians could identify with this divinity. Joining his worship did not require that a person belong to a particular elite group, whether defined by particular skill, wealth, or status. Eventually pharaohs incorporated Osiris into their own story. The dead Pharaoh was the incarnation of Osiris, the reigning queen was Isis, and the reigning Pharaoh was Horus.

The goddess Isis—sister and wife of Osiris—came to play a prominent role in Egyptian religion and beyond. She is often depicted in stone and on papyri in the role of loyal and supportive wife as well as a tender and loving mother. The worship of Isis spread throughout the Mediterranean world. Among some Semitic peoples Isis was identified with the ancient Mesopotamian goddess Ishtar or Ashtoreth, whose cult was associated with ritual prostitution. Among a plurality of religions during the period of the Roman Empire, the cult of Isis was quite strong; some scholars have suggested that it was Christianity's primary contender. There are interesting parallels between the cult of Isis and the cult surrounding the Virgin Mary that developed in medieval Christianity. Like Mary, the Mother of God in Catholic and Orthodox Christian tradition, Isis was often pictured with the divine child Horus in her lap, or as a grieving mother whose divine son dies but is later resurrected.

Both Egypt and Mesopotamia are regarded as *polytheistic,* that is, they emphasized a plurality of deities. Every natural force seems to have had a particular divine being animating it. Each city had its special god, which frequently spawned religious rivalry. We usually understand *monotheism,* on the other hand, as requiring the denial that any more than one god exists. All other divine beings are rejected in the name of one God who is said to be the only true divinity. Even the early Hebrews were polytheistic until they emerged into monotheism during the Babylonian Captivity. Nevertheless, another type of belief often occurred in polytheistic societies that might be called another type of monotheism. It claims that divinity takes many forms, and that different gods are simply various manifestations of a single divine power. Several religious texts in both places acknowledge the names of many gods, only to go on to say that these are simply aspects of a single, comprehensive deity. (This sort of monotheism can also be seen in aspects of the indigenous religious traditions of India.) If we define monotheism in this way, both Egypt and Mesopotamia did indeed include monotheism as an aspect of their religions. The interplay between this type of monotheism, the exaltation of a single God as the supreme deity, and a more polytheistic affirmation of the value of many deities, can be seen as reflecting certain social and political realities at different times and places.

Egyptians had long believed in an afterlife, but initially they held that it existed only for kings and their families. By the time of the Middle Kingdom, the possibility of an afterlife was believed open to everyone. As a result, furnishing the dead for immortality became a general concern. Since the pharaoh was a manifestation of the divine, at death he was believed to ascend directly to heaven and be united with Osiris. Everyone else, however, was subject to a more elaborate procedure for gaining access to the afterworld that included judgment by Osiris and assignment either to bliss or to hell.

Historians and archaeologists have been able to learn much about ancient Egyptian life and culture from their often elaborate funerary remains. It was important to equip the deceased with everything necessary for a comfortable eternity, believed to be a literal continuation of life on earth but on a higher plane. The preservation of the body through mummification was important. The Egyptians believed that humans have a soul, which consists of the *ba,* or life force, and the *ka,* the personality, which survive death, and it was essential to preserve the dead body to provide a continuing seat of "life" for the soul. The mummified body was placed in a coffin with food, clothing, tools, weapons and a *shabti* figurine. The *shabti* was essential because it would be a servant in the next world and do all the work, leaving the "dead" free to enjoy

a realm of physical delights. But before achieving the paradise of the next world, every individual must stand before Osiris, judge of the underworld, and have his or her heart "weighed." Failure to pass the moral test meant eternal torment in the afterlife, described in graphically dreadful terms in Egyptian texts. Concern over this impending judgment is the subject of the Egyptian *Book of the Dead,* which we will examine in more detail below.

An Experiment with Monotheism

A shift to a monotheistic religious belief and practice occurred during the reign of Pharaoh Amenhotep IV (ruled 1367–1350 BCE), who took the name Akhenaten ("it pleases Aten"). Akhenaten's queen was Nefertiti, who is immortalized in the beautiful bust displayed in the Egyptian Museum in Berlin. There is some evidence that Nefertiti was as deeply involved in leading Akhenaten's religious revolution as he was, and some scholars believe she was actually the primary impetus behind the reforms. As we examine the historical and literary evidence of this period, we see indications of major social and political changes taking place. Egypt had grown into a diverse and complex society. International expansion introduced innovations in thought and custom, which demanded a more universal perspective. To a society that had always emphasized its unchanging status, this developing internationalism seemed to Akhenaten to demand a new worldview, a belief system in a deity that transcended any single divine force and created a greater unity and cooperation.

As divine representative on earth, the pharaoh Akhenaten symbolized this new universalism by presenting himself as the human link to a single divine being which contained within itself all divinities. All the former deities were now incorporated as aspects of the sole true divinity—Aten, the Sun God. Akhenaten moved the center of worship to a new city he had built, Akhetaten, and suppressed alternative creeds and rituals. This strategy had the disadvantage of angering and alienating many of the powerful priests in the various cities, not only denying the power and reality of those cities' patron deities but also threatening the priests' status and livelihood. Akhenaten's actions and the texts surviving from his revolution suggest a vigorous monotheism.

One of the most important texts associated with Akhenaten is the *Hymn to Aten* found at Tel El Amarna. It is very similar to parts of Psalm 104 in the Hebrew Bible. Some scholars have thought that it may have influenced the writing of the psalm, while others have suggested that a common influence lies behind both. The hymn expresses a radical monotheism: all creation in its bewildering diversity springs from a single source. Aten—God—is represented as the one controlling influence unifying the apparent confusion of reality. The seeming differences among humanity, domesticated and wild animals, and flying things disappear in the oneness of the divine.

Beyond attributing unity where diversity seems to reign, the hymn also attributes a value to all things. God acts compassionately toward his creatures. Life from birth through its various stages testifies to a divine grace. Not only the natural world but the distinctively human world finds order through this single deity. Each individual depends upon Aten for existence. But God controls more than just the fate of individuals; God also sets the destiny of nations. Aten has established the separate identity of the foreign nations. The different languages arise from divine command. God is "the Lord of All" who is busied with all humanity, "The Lord of every land, arising for all nations." This monotheistic deity transcends parochial boundaries, making national distinctions irrelevant to the true unity binding humanity in an international community. This radical monotheism produced an equally radical negative response. At Akhenaten's death a counter-revolution removed all traces of his innovation. The local shrines regained their power and the traditional gods once again became supreme.

Literary Remains

The Egyptians were a writing people, and the picture-quality of their hieroglyphic script invested especially their religious writings with a kind of iconic quality. Egyptian writing included many types of literature we can recognize today: myths, chants, spells, rituals, hymns, prayers, and theological texts, folk tales, short stories, dialogues, fairy tales, and poetry. Broadly speaking, Egyptian literature, whatever the type, is "religious" in the sense that it expresses the Egyptian worldview and values, including belief in the gods, the pharaoh, and the afterlife, and it typically has a lesson to teach. Didactic stories, containing a moral lesson, were especially popular, somewhat like Aesop's fables in ancient Greece or Horatio Alger stories for American children a hundred years ago. Folk and fairy tales had themes that recur in such stories throughout the world—enchanted princes, two brothers in competition, betrayed husbands. At the same time, we can find among these writings satire, humor, irony, and theological criticism such as protests against the gods.

The Egyptian *Book of the Dead* is a collection of some two hundred different chants, incantations, spells, and supplications written in hieroglyphics on the walls of tombs and coffins of the dead. The oldest is called the "Pyramid Texts" because some of the texts are found inscribed on the walls of the pyramids. A later group is called "Coffin Texts," from the period after the pyramid building was over and when the belief in a general afterlife was common. Many of the extant examples of these manuscripts, sometimes referred to as chapters or spells, are elaborately illustrated and personalized.

A typical example of a text from the *Book of the Dead* is "Spell 125" from the "Papyrus of Ani," the most complete of all the extant manuscripts, which contains one hundred ninety of the known texts. Spell 125 is what is called a "negative confession" or "declaration of innocence," in which the one pleading his case before Osiris enumerates aspects of his good behavior. So, for example, we read the following:

> . . . I have not defrauded the humble man of his property. I have not done what the gods abominate. I have not vilified a slave to his master. I have not inflicted pain. I have not caused anyone to go hungry. I have not made any man to weep. I have not committed murder. . . .

The reference to slaves is one way in which a document such as this informs us about the social situation at the time it was written. There are also varied agricultural references, as well as indications of permitted and forbidden sexual practices. Biblical scholars have long noted Egyptian phrases and allusions in the Book of Job in the Hebrew Bible, and Chapter 31 of Job has the form of an Egyptian "negative confession."

The purpose of these writings was to win acquittal before the court of the underworld. Consequently the demand for them was great. Soon they were mass-produced and could even be purchased with a favorable verdict already given! One is tempted here to draw a comparison between Egyptian "spells for sale" to the selling of indulgences in early sixteenth century Catholicism, a practice which sparked the Reformation.

THE HEBREWS

The origins and early history of the Hebrews are clouded in mist. Many people believe they know the history of ancient Israel, because they assume the Bible provides a reliable historical account. According to modern archaeological and historical methods historical reconstruction is impossible at this time. The approach taken in this historical summary is the same as that which is taken to establish the histories of Mesopotamia and Egypt: it is based upon what is known through scholarly evidence.

No evidence has been produced to substantiate the existence of Abraham, Isaac and Jacob, Joseph, the Exodus or a conquest of Canaan as historical persons and events. There is even confusion about the name applied to the people we identify as the ancestors of the Jews.

Both "Hebrew" and "Hapiru" are terms denoting a type of status—that of a landless group of wandering people. "Israel" was also known to have been a personal name, one of the many personal names that have the ending "El," a Canaanite name for "god." It is of the late thirteenth century BCE that historians and archaeologists find evidence and can speak with confidence of Hebrews or Israelites as an identifiable people within the land we now identify as Palestine. But, based on scholarly criteria, who these people were and where they came from is not verifiable. The biblical narrative is supported by archaeological discoveries dated 1200–1000 BCE and evidence increases in later excavations dated 1000–55 BCE.

Before we move to the discussion of the credible historical evidence, let us review the biblical account of the founding of an Israelite monarchy as told in the biblical books, 1 and 2 Samuel. (We will begin at this point to speak of the previously identified "Hebrew tribes" as the Israelites.)

The Israelites are under attack by the Philistines and the tribal heads call for a leader, a king, to unite them in fighting their enemy. Samuel, a priest, is reluctant to take this action, because he believes that it was God's intent that there should be no earthly king. With warnings to the people about the dangers that might arise from a monarchy (1 Sam 12), Samuel anoints the warrior Saul as king. Saul's reign is a troubled one and he is eventually killed in battle. David, said to be the son of Jesse a Bethlehemite, succeeds him, an identification that later Christians would find significant. David, as anointed king of the Israelites, leads the Israelites to victory over the Philistines. (There is certainly much more to this story, but our purpose is to summarize the biblical account in order to compare it with the historical evidence.)

The biblical narrative tells us that David's son Solomon succeeded him. Solomon is reputed to have ruled a large kingdom, been a wise ruler and built a magnificent temple in Jerusalem. (1 Kings 1–11) To date there is no historical or archaeological evidence for a king named Solomon. Nor is there any non-controversial archaeological evidence for the temple. Jerusalem is an especially difficult location for excavation because of its many levels of previous habitation and because it is still a fully occupied city. There have been structures identified that are considered "palaces" but nothing of the magnitude of what is described in the Scriptures. The temple as described in the biblical texts is elaborately decorated, with cherubims, palm trees, pomegranates, and *lily-work*. It is noteworthy that no remains representing such artistic work have ever been found. Since the last editors of the biblical texts wrote following the destruction of the temple in the seventh century BCE, they would have to have had some sort of blueprint either from the original building or another similar one. They certainly never saw it.

The first archaeological evidence to support the existence of Israel as a nation was discovered in 1868. It is a stone from the ancient site of Moab, southeast of the Dead Sea, in modern-day Jordan. It is named the Mesha Stele for the king during that period, but is also referred to as the Moabite Stone. The stone is dated in the mid-ninth century BCE. This would correspond with the kingship of Ahab and his Phoenician queen Jezebel in Israel (1 Kings

16). The inscription on the stele records the story of conflicts with the Israelites and refers to both "Israel" and the "King of Israel."

An exciting discovery at Tel Dan in northern Israel in the last decade offers more conclusive evidence for not only the nation of Israel but for the "House of David." Excavation began in the early 1990s in a location near the headwaters of the Jordan River in the area of Galilee. The area was found to have been heavily fortified during the ninth and eighth centuries BCE, probably for protection against the Assyrians. Of particular interest to archaeologists is the elaborate system of bronze gates. Entrance to the city was made by way of a stone path first through a gate in the outside wall

and then through another gate in another wall. Once inside there were narrow walkways leading to other gates and finally into a courtyard. A large ceremonial area complete with podium was also uncovered. Objects found in the area indicate that the religious practices performed there were cultic in nature. Archaeological evidence reveals a relatively high degree of literacy, attested to by the high number of fragments with inscriptions.

What these artifacts establish is that a monarchy did arise ca. 1000 BCE, and that it probably was a monarchy named for David, or from the House of David, but the reign of Solomon and his achievements is thus far unverifiable. The biblical narration tells us that the monarchy split shortly after Solomon's death. In the south was the kingdom of Judah with its center in Jerusalem. In the north was the kingdom of Israel with Samaria as its royal city. There is ample archaeological evidence beginning in the ninth century BCE to support a large Israelite population spread throughout the area of Palestine. Therefore we can consider the biblical narrative as providing us with broadly historical information regarding the two nations of Israelites in the area of Palestine.

Both the Bible and archaeological evidence support the intermingling of the worship of *Baal* with early Israelite religious practice. Baalism was a Canaanite polytheistic faith with origins in what we not know as Syria. Ritual prostitution was practiced and the gods demanded propitiation in this religion as well as they did in similar polytheistic societies in the larger region. Some of the sayings of the Major Hebrew prophets—social reformers such as Hosea, Amos, Isaiah, and Jeremiah—portray the Israelites as often bordering on *apostasy* by worshipping false gods. A pantheon of gods was headed by the creator god, El. But Baal was the chief god. A consort, Asherah (also Athirat) has been associated with both Baal and El. There is considerable archaeological evidence that Yahweh, the God of Israel, had a female consort. It has been argued that a tenth-century religious object known as the Ta'naach cult stand (table) represents Yahweh and his divine consort Asherah.

Late in the eighth century BCE the great power of Assyria invaded the area of Palestine and brought down the northern kingdom of Israel and scattered its people. Excavations at the ancient city of Lachish

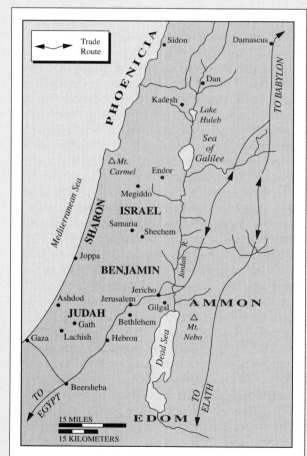

Ancient Palestine. Reprinted from *The Western Heritage*, Combined Edition, Sixth Edition, by Donald Kagan, et al., (1998), Prentice-Hall, Inc.

testify to the devastation wrought by the Assryians. This event is also mentioned in the Bible (2 Kings 18) as well as in Assyrian texts. According to archaeologist, A. Mazor, this may be the "best documented event from the period of the Monarchy." At this time the southern kingdom of Judeans paid tribute to Assyria and were left alone, but little more than a century later Nebuchadnezzar, king of the Babylonians, sacked Jerusalem and deported many of the Jews to Babylon, which came to be called the "Babylonian Captivity" or "Babylonian Exile." This marks the beginning of the dispersion or scattering of Jews throughout the world, called the *Diaspora*, that has continued down to the present day.

It is at this point that we can begin to speak of Judaism, the religious tradition that emerged from these Judean exiles, and of Jews, which means "descendants of the Judeans." Jews became productive citizens within the society of Babylonia as farmers and in a variety of skilled occupations, but they did not assimilate into the society. Without the Jerusalem Temple, the Jews of Babylonia had to develop a new, more "portable" and universal version of their religion. They gathered in groups to celebrate the holy days, sing hymns, and offer the prescribed sacrifices. This was the beginning of the synagogue. Their leaders were the first rabbis ("teachers" or "masters"), who devoted themselves to the study and interpretation of Torah, the first five books of the Hebrew Bible, and the writings of the prophets. The rabbis in Babylonia laid the foundation of the rich tradition of rabbinic discussion and interpretation of the meaning of the Hebrew Bible, and formed a community of religious learning and a Jewish culture that became renowned throughout the Diaspora. Centuries later the traditions of the rabbinic scholars of Babylonia would be compiled and written down as the Talmud (a term meaning study and learning), the definitive body of Jewish teaching.

Within five decades after the beginning of the Babylonian Captivity the Persian king Cyrus conquered Babylon. He allowed Jews to return to Judea. Several thousand returned but many remained in Babylonia. The Persians controlled Palestine but allowed the inhabitants freedom to practice their religion. The returning Jews were intent on rebuilding the Temple, but the society they found in Jerusalem had changed. Those who had been left behind had developed their own way of life and worship and there had been intermarriage between Jews and other Judean inhabitants. The resident Judeans were fearful that they would be excluded from the new Temple and resented the intrusion of the returnees. The rebuilding of the Temple was delayed until the period of the leadership of Nehemiah and Ezra in the mid-fifth century BCE. Proper religious practice was revived and the Temple rebuilt. All of this began to raise nationalistic feelings among the Jews.

In the fourth century BCE Alexander of Macedonia and his great army swept into Asia and defeated the Persians. Following his untimely death the Ptolemies of Egypt assumed rule of Palestine. The first several decades of Ptolemaic rule were favorable to the Jews. Many Jews emigrated to Egypt and the city of Alexandria, which was a great center of learning and had the largest and finest library in the ancient world. It was here that over the course of the third century BCE a group of Jewish scholars translated the Jewish Scriptures into Greek. It was called the *Septuagint* in recognition of the seventy-two scholars who were commissioned by the Ptolemaic king. It was the Septuagint that was used by the early Christians. Another distinguished Jewish scholar from Alexandria was Philo, a contemporary of Jesus of Nazareth. Philo, who was thoroughly Hellenized, sought to make a synthesis of Judaism and Greek philosophy. He viewed Moses as the first philosopher and the teacher of all the Greek philosophers. Philo ultimately had more influence on Christians than on Jews.

The other successor of Alexander's conquest, the Seleucids, had long wanted to take Palestine from the Ptolemies. In ca. 200 BCE they succeeded. At first they followed the previous policy of toleration to the Jews. The Jews themselves were divided. The priesthood was in the hands of a few wealthy families who were a more Hellenized group of Jews and they angered the stricter Jews, the Hasidim. Their quarrels did not please the new ruler, Antiochus IV, who held a more negative view of their religion anyway. Eventually the Temple was desecrated. This insult stirred up the bubbling nationalist feelings and a rebellion broke out under a group of brothers known as the Maccabees. The Maccabees, from the family of the Hasmoneans, were motivated by both political and religious issues. After a conflict that went on for a period of thirty years, 166–134, the Maccabees gained control and an independent Israel came into being once again. It would last for less than a century ending when the Roman armies ejected the Seleucids from Palestine and took control.

What we have learned about the history of the Jewish people is that until the period of the monarchy beginning around 1000 BCE there is virtually no historical evidence for the people, events, and institutions found in the earlier books of the Hebrew Bible. They narrate myths, legends, stories, folkways, and laws not written down until centuries later. From about 1000 BCE forward independent evidence of Israel's existence and monarchy begins to appear, and biblical narratives describing these later centuries that purport to be historical may be considered broadly reliable. It is important always to keep in mind, however, that even the later narratives are told from the standpoint of representatives of the monotheistic faith that eventually triumphed. From that standpoint the meaning of the history of

Israel's kings and the disasters of the Assyrian and then the Babylonian conquests was the story of the struggle of Yahwist faith against the polytheism of Baal worship and the faithfulness or faithlessness of Israel's rulers. In their protest against injustice the prophets were seen as spokesmen for God, who through them was guiding, warning, and punishing his people. With the final destruction of the Kingdom of Judea in 586 BCE and the Babylonian Captivity, the Judean exiles had to learn to "sing the Lord's song in a strange land"—to transform the monotheistic faith and traditions they had inherited into something new. With them began the universal religion called Judaism. While remaining and returning Jews in Israel would once again enjoy a brief period of independence through the Maccabean Revolt, the destiny of Judaism and the Jewish people for many centuries to come would be as communities scattered throughout the world. Not until the twentieth century would Judaism be connected with nationhood and Israel exist as a political entity.

We are indebted for archaeological scholarship on biblical times to John C. Laughlin, *Archaeology and the Bible*. London: Routledge, 2000.

ART OF THE ANCIENT WORLD

Much art of Egypt and of the ancient Near East functions simultaneously as art object and as a form of historical documentation. Sumerian temples, or ziggurats, give insight into the economic wealth of Sumer's rulers and into the religious culture of its inhabitants. Stone tablets filled with cuneiform writing record not only religious myths and heroic tales but also histories and codes of law. By including figural representations as well, such tablets effectively blend Mesopotamian art, literature, and history. In ancient Egypt, we see a similar fusion. The most beloved Egyptian form, the pyramid, signifies economic prosperity and architectural achievement in addition to serving as a funerary temple, whose contents tell us much of Egyptian society and religious beliefs. Like the Mesopotamians, the Egyptians combined their own written form, hieroglyphs, with figural representations of their rulers, recording both histories and artistic styles in the process.

The history of the ancient Hebrews is much less thoroughly documented in visual form. A few art objects from Mesopotamia make passing reference to events in Jewish history. Early Jewish art, however, is almost non-existent. In order to prevent idolatry, Jewish law forbade the representation of living creatures particularly in synagogues. Despite this prohibition, the use of imagery first appeared in Jewish art during the second century CE, visually documenting and commemorating some famous scenes from the Hewbrew Bible or Tanakh.

MESOPOTAMIA

King Hammurabi preserved his place in history through some significant achievements. Known as the first great king of Babylon, Hammurabi ruled from 1792 to 1750 BCE and successfully unified the warring Sumerian and Akkadian city-states. Even more important for posterity, however, was Hammurabi's code of law, a document engraved in stone whose stated goal was "to cause justice to prevail in the land and to destroy the wicked and the evil, that the strong might not oppress the weak nor the weak the strong." Thirty six hundred lines of cuneiform writing are engraved onto the seven-foot upright stone slab known as the *Stele of Hammurabi* (Plate 1). Hammurabi's code contained 282 articles of law, organized into six categories: personal property, land, trade and commerce, family, maltreatment, and labor. In his quest for justice, Hammurabi set forth a nearly all-encompassing body of law that addressed a host of potential disputes as well as possible penalties and retributions. The code proclaimed "an eye for an eye," the principle of a punishment equivalent to the crime, although the severity of punishments largely depended upon the gender and social standing of the offender.

Not simply a legal document, however, the Stele of Hammurabi also functions as a work of art, providing further insight into Hammurabi's reign. Made of basalt, a hard medium difficult to carve, the stele combines the written code of law with figural representations of King Hammurabi and the sun god, Shamash. The figures are smoothly rounded with a modicum of detail. The visible adornments of Shamash clearly mark him as a god: a four-tiered headdress; sunrays rising from his shoulders; a measuring rod and ring, symbols of justice and power; and his ziggurat-throne. Hammurabi's close proximity to and relative intimacy with the god suggests a divine element to the king's rule. The hierarchical representation of the figures, however, guarantees that they are not perceived as equals. In what is known as a hieratic composition, the more important figure is elevated, enlarged, and generally given greater prominence through attention to detail. The earthly Hammurabi, clearly the smaller of the two figures, stands below the divine Shamash, who sits upon his royal throne with feet raised above the ground. The combination of this artistic representation with the legal code below perhaps suggested Shamash's heavenly endorsement of Hammurabi's law enforcement on earth.

EGYPT

Egyptian art and ideology often espoused a similar connection between earthly and heavenly rulers. King Akhenaten, who ruled from 1367–1350 BCE (alternatively, 1352–1335 BCE) changed his name from Amenhotep IV to reflect his worship of the god Aten. Akhenaten is most remembered for exchanging polytheism for monotheism: the worship of a single god, Aten, symbolized by the sun disk. The king regarded himself as Aten's son, endowing himself and his family with divine status.

The sunken relief of *Akhenaten and His Family* (Figure I-1), likely part of a household altar in the palace at Amarna, depicts the importance of Aten to Akhenaten's reign. In the relief, both Akhenaten and Queen Nefertiti commune with the sun god. Although elevated above the king and queen in a hierarchical composition, Aten's proximity nonetheless implicates them as the god's living counterparts on earth. Aten's sunrays extend the *ankh*, or breath of life, to the noses of both king and queen. Such a representation on a household altar suggests a common acceptance of the idea that Aten bestowed his blessing and even his divinity upon the Egyptian rulers.

Figure I–1   Akhenaten and His Family, (city of) Akhetaten (modern Tell el-Amarna). Dynasty 18, ca. 1348–1336 BCE. Painted limestone relief, 12½ × 15½ (31.1 × 38.7 cm). Staatliche Museen zu Berlin, Preussischer Kulturbesitz, Ägyptisches Museum. Courtesy of Vanni/Art Resource, NY.

Other elements of the composition provide further insight into aspects of Akhenaten's reign. Hieroglyphs and cartouches (Egyptian symbols that are outlined in the background) are interspersed throughout the composition. The addition of text to the descriptive images ensures that the work is read at least in part as an historical document. Nefertiti is rendered in the same scale and as an equal partner of Akhenaten, denoting her importance to his rule. The base of her throne contains the symbol of a unified Egypt, understood by some scholars to mean that Nefertiti acted as co-ruler with her husband. The figural depictions of the king and queen illustrate the new artistic style promoted by Akhenaten. In stressing the principle of *ma'at*, or divine truth, Akhenaten encouraged his artists to portray the royal family with candor, rather than as idealized figures, and in informal settings. In following his directive, artists did not hide the king's protruding stomach or elongated neck. This newfound artistic naturalism included informal poses and even playful actions. In the relief seen here, Akhenaten's gesture of kissing one of the three child princesses is a new public display of affection and testifies to the importance Akhenaten placed on his family. As a household image, it also suggests that Egyptians venerated the royal family as much as Aten or other families of gods.

The artistic and religious changes instituted under Akhenaten were short-lived. Following his reign, previous beliefs were revived and Egypt returned to a polytheistic culture. Artistic naturalism, too, fell by the wayside, as the more traditional blocky and geometric style returned to favor. In the most extreme maneuvers, some later rulers attempted to erase all traces of Akhenaten's religion and artistic style.

THE HEBREWS

There are no known art objects that date from the earliest histories of the ancient Israelites. As with extant historical documentation, the first evidence of art the Hebrew people dates from the ninth century BCE. The *Black Obelisk of Shalmaneser III* (Plate 2), discovered in 1846 in northern Iraq by archeologist Henry Layard, includes the earliest known picture of an Israelite, a representation of King Jehu.

The Obelisk, made of black limestone, glorifies the military campaigns of the Assyrian king Shalmaneser III (reigned 858–824 BCE). Much like other objects we have discussed, the obelisk is a combination of image and text, art and historical documentation. Cuneiform writing identifies the subjects in each panel of carving. In addition to scenes of military conquest, the obelisk features five panels in which representatives of neighboring regions pay tribute to the Assyrian king. In one of these panels, the biblical King Jehu of Israel bows down before Shalmaneser. The accompanying cuneiform text reads, "The tribute of Jehu, son of Omri: I received from him silver, gold, a golden bowl, a golden vase with pointed bottom, golden tumblers, golden buckets, tin, a staff for a king and spears." This scene and scenes of Israelite slaves on the obelisk correspond to events related in 1 and 2 Kings. As such, they are the earliest known artistic depictions of biblical figures and occurrences.

While few art objects exist from the time period of the ancient Israelites, Jewish art flourished during the third century CE. One example is a house-synagogue from Dura-Europos in Syria, whose walls are covered with narrative mural scenes from Jewish tradition. Uncovered in 1920, the location of the synagogue represents a unique find. Dura-Europos was a naturally fortified city (*Dura* meaning fortress), surrounded by deep ravines, huge cliff walls, and the Euphrates River. Its unusual placement made it a highly sought after location over the centuries, inhabited first by the Assyrians and later by the Macedonians. Dura-Europos eventually became an ethnic melting pot of Greeks, Byzantines, Persians, Christians, and Jews, living and working side by side. The city was destroyed by the Sassanians in the third century CE, covered by mud and desert for over sixteen hundred years. Twentieth-century archaeologists discovered not only the Jewish synagogue but also temples to Greek and Roman gods, as well as the earliest dated Christian church.

The synagogue itself is remarkable for the murals illustrating scenes from the Hebrew Scriptures. The abstracted paintings surround a niche in the western wall, intended for housing the Torah scrolls and facing in the direction of Jerusalem. The sanctuary's figural decorations seem in direct violation of Jewish law, whose prohibitions strove to prevent idolatry. The iconography, however, is still sparse; only main characters such as Moses are represented. The detail seen here, "Moses Gives Water to the Tribes" (Plate 3), highlights his central role in Jewish tradition and relates a specific biblical scene. According to the story in Numbers 21:16–18, a well was dug after God told Moses to "gather the people together, and I will give them water." Several of the mural images from Dura-Europos highlight the importance of the covenant between God and the Israelites. This particular scene's proximity to the wall niche further underscores the importance of Moses: attributed to Moses, the books of Torah contain the basic rules of Jewish faith, including the Ten Commandments given to Moses by God on Mount Sinai.

MUSIC OF ANCIENT ISRAEL AND EARLY JUDAISM

Ancient Israel had a rich tradition of both vocal and instrumental music going back to its earliest times. Hebrew vocal music was inseparable from Hebrew poetry; as in most ancient cultures, poems were meant to be sung. Our main source of knowledge of music in ancient Israel is, not surprisingly, the Hebrew Bible. There we find singing and dancing associated with family and harvest festivals, welcoming home victorious generals, and the coronation and marriage of kings. But above all we find detailed biblical accounts of the important role of music in Hebrew worship and particularly in the Temple in Jerusalem.

Both vocal and instrumental music were an essential part of Temple worship from early times, but our knowledge of the role music played in the liturgy comes largely from the post-exilic period (after 586 BCE), beginning with the building of the Second Temple by exiles who returned to Jerusalem and Judah and its consecration in 515 BCE. From that time there were professional musicians—choral singers (both men and women) and instrumentalists—who provided the music for the daily and Sabbath services and high holy days. Among the instruments were ten- and twelve-string harps, trumpets, drums, cymbals, bells, flutes, and the *shofar*, a hollowed-out ram's horn. The Book of Psalms in the Hebrew Bible is a collection of Hebrew poems that were hymns sung in Temple worship; Psalms has been called the "hymnbook of the Second Temple." Even certain of the "cues" or instructions to the musicians are still included in the texts of the Psalms, such as *selah*, which may have indicated a cymbal-stroke; and also congregational responses, such as *hallelujah* and *amen*. A feature of the Temple choral music was *antiphonal* singing, in which two choirs alternated singing lines of the psalms.

As with music in other ancient cultures, we don't know what the music of ancient Israel sounded like. Music historians and musicologists, applying knowledge of the instruments used and the words sung and some guesswork, try to reconstruct how it might have been performed. We do know that both the singing and the instrumental music would have been entirely melody, without harmony. That is still characteristic of the music of Arab countries, which perhaps exhibits the closest historical links.

With the fall of Jerusalem and the destruction of the Temple by the Romans in 70 CE, the Pharisees, representing the rabbinic tradition of Torah interpretation, took over the direction of Jewish life and created what would come to be the normative or Rabbinic Judaism we know today: a religion centered in study of Torah and worship in the synagogue. The rabbis had long been critical of the music in Jewish worship on both religious and moral grounds, and when there could be no more Temple worship and they were in charge, they banned instrumental music entirely and frowned on men and women singing together. Among instruments only the shofar was permitted, precisely because it was not considered a musical instrument but, as it had primarily been in ancient Israel, a means of signaling or announcing something. Today the shofar is blown only on Rosh Hashanah, the Jewish New Year, to herald the beginning of the high holy days. So the synagogue music that has come down through the centuries was, until the nineteenth century, entirely vocal and *a capella*, with a male cantor chanting biblical texts and prayers and male congregants singing the musical responses. Outside of worship, popular forms of Jewish music developed more freely and variously, with instruments, and with the participation of both sexes. Since Jewish history for the past two thousand years has been a history of Diaspora or dispersion among many different countries and cultures, Jewish music of the Common Era has also been influenced by many musical traditions—Greek, Spanish, Arabic, Russian, German, Hungarian, and others.

CD SELECTIONS

Two examples of traditional Jewish liturgical music are represented, from *Greek-Jewish Musical Traditions* (recordings and notes by Ammon Shiloah of the Hebrew University in Jerusalem, Folkways Records, 1978). Professor Shiloah visited a number of Jewish communities in Greece and recorded several different musical traditions reflecting various immigrations of Jews to Greece over the centuries. One of the oldest such traditions comes from Ioanina, from which our selections are taken. The first selection, *Adonay malakh* ("The Lord reigns"), on track #1, is an example of the singing of the Psalms in the synagogue service, in this case Psalm 93. It is sung in Hebrew by men and unaccompanied. Track #2, *Kamti be-ashmoret* ("I got up early"), is the opening hymn of a penitential ceremony held at dawn a month before Rosh Hashanah by communities of Sephardic Jews. Like many hymns for the religious holidays, it is sung in a slow and plaintive manner.

CHAPTER ONE

THE TANAKH

Tanakh is the name for the sacred scriptures of the Jewish religion. It is also referred to as the Hebrew Bible or Jewish Bible and these terms will be used interchangeably throughout the chapter. The Jewish religion is the first of the world's three great monotheistic faiths and the Tanakh has been one of the foundational documents in framing the ideas of Western civilization. When the early Christians composed their foundational documents, they adopted the Tanakh and referred to it as the Old Testament.

The Tanakh is not a unified book; rather it is a collection of books from different time periods, having different authors, and written to convey different messages. The kinds of literature represented are: creation myths, so-called historical narrative, laws, prophetic discourse, psalms (or songs), proverbs, genealogies, and apocalyptic narratives. However, all of these texts together tell us many things about a people originally identified as Hebrew, or Hapiru, whose distant origins remain a mystery. They tell us how they organized their family, social, and political institutions, about their ethical expectations for their followers, and how they worshipped. They reveal that their faith was initially polytheistic, or rather *henotheistic* (primary belief in one god, but acknowledging the existence of others), and how it evolved into monotheism. We know that these beliefs existed side by side with other ancient peoples in Asia and Asia Minor and were influenced by them.

APPROACHING THE SCRIPTURES
The approach to our study of the Tanakh is an academic one, and we will use the same tools the scholars use to examine and interpret other ancient

texts. This approach is referred to as the *Historical-Critical Method* and was developed in Germany in the late eighteenth century. It is a system of analysis that investigates the texts from different points of view. We will list the standard categories and explain the approach they take to their work.

Textual Criticism Textual scholars determine the earliest texts and thus convey the most accurate intended meaning. They work with texts that have originated in different locations, confirm their dating as closely as possible, and attempt to identify authorship. Then they do a comparison of the content.

Form Criticism Here the scholars look back to the pre-written stage to uncover as closely as possible the oral tradition that stands behind the text. Most biblical texts were first transmitted orally, and the investigators try to recreate the human situations out of which they emerged. Form critics investigate the genre of the texts.

Tradition Criticism Religious traditions varied from location to location and this inevitably would have some effect on the texts that were used. Scholars who work in this area analyze the variants in traditions and how they alter the texts.

Redaction Criticism A redaction critic is someone who studies the work of the editors of a text. Editors of all sorts of written material inevitably put their stamp on their work. This method sometimes comes under the heading of "Source Criticism," since the editors compile different sources into a whole.

Canonical Criticism Both Judaism and Christianity have a collection of scriptures they consider authoritative. This is referred to as their *canon,* from the Greek word for "rule." The Tanakh is the Jewish canon, but there were other writings that could have been selected. Canon critics study the various texts and try to determine why certain texts were chosen and not others.

Literary Criticism Literary criticism looks at the texts as literature. Similar to form critics, literary scholars identify and classify different literary genres, for example, hymns, prayers, and blessings such as we have listed in the introduction to this chapter.

There is admittedly much crossover among the approaches used in the Historical-Critical Method. Biblical scholars from a variety of disciplines including anthropology, linguistics, psychology, sociology, and gender studies use the approach that is appropriate to their discipline.

All scholars propose hypotheses and historical reconstructions based on the best evidence available and the most plausible interpretations of that evidence. However, since additional evidence can come to light, as has happened especially during the last century with the discovery of the Dead Sea Scrolls and the Qumran texts (discussed in Chapter Seven), the conclusions reached are open to revision.

Jews have never believed in the inerrancy of scripture. Jewish tradition has insisted that the Tanakh tells us truths, but that these truths are not to be equated with a literal reading of the text. Tanakh must be interpreted anew by every generation, in the light of post-biblical Jewish teachings and the new insights that we are given with the passing of the years. Thus other books have been created that are sacred to Jews. Commentary on the scriptures, that is, offering explanation and interpretation, is referred to as *midrash* and dates from 400 to 1000 CE. *Mishnah* applies specifically to the collection and interpretation of different law codes, the definitive version of which was made in 210 CE. Various materials of *midrash* and *mishnah* became codified in a single massive volume called the *Talmud*. The long history of Jewish religious life has involved study and interpretation of these books.

Some may wonder why we cannot use the Tanakh as fact. In addition to the scarcity of archaeological evidence, internal inconsistencies, legendary and mythological elements, and theological agendas, literary critics have determined that the composition of the Tanakh is much later than the events described. The stories of the patriarchs, for example—Abraham, Isaac and Jacob—were not written down earlier than the ninth century BCE, although they are reported as having lived in the sixteenth and seventeenth centuries BCE. Another editor added new material a century later, and a third editor added more in the seventh century. All of this was brought together by a fourth editor/author in the sixth century. This "four-document hypothesis" will be explained later in this chapter. To further compromise the accuracy of the biblical text, the earliest surviving manuscripts date from the third century BCE.

In the background chapter on ancient Mesopotamia, Egypt, and Israel, we summarized the historically credible evidence regarding the ancient Hebrews, comparing it with the biblical account of the origins and development of the monarchy. Here, similarly, we will briefly review the early chapters of the Hebrew Bible that purport to give the history and origins of the Hebrew people. You are reading most of the first two books of the Bible, Genesis and Exodus. The story they tell begins with the creation of the world and continues with the story of the alienation between God and the first humans. This is followed by the worldwide destruction in a great flood. Following the flood God pledges a covenant with Noah promising not to destroy the world again and then spreads people across the world. God singles out Abraham, a nomadic herdsman in Mesopotamia, and makes a second covenant with him. Abraham and his descendants found the Hebrew nation and the mark of membership is circumcision of the males. The first Hebrews establish themselves in Canaan but eventually flee to Egypt because of famine. They are at first welcomed in Egypt, but 400 years later they are nothing more than forced laborers. A man named Moses arises and leads them out of Egypt into Sinai where they wander for forty years. It is here that God makes a third covenant with Moses. In the books of Joshua and Judges, we learn that under the leadership of Joshua, successor to Moses, the Hebrews conquer the land of Canaan and occupy it. The land is divided among tribal leaders. Some time later a united monarchy is formed to fight the Philistines.

While these narratives do not fulfill the requirements for historicity or factual occurrence according to modern historical criteria, they can still communicate faith. Let us consider this statement.

The faith that they express is one that begins as polytheistic, which was the norm as we have seen in our discussion of the Mesopotamians and Egyptians, and evolves into a monotheistic faith. These stories tell of human behavior that, as we know, is fraught with contradictions. The biblical characters are good and evil, compassionate and cruel, honest and dishonest, wise and stupid. They stumble and they pick themselves up. In other words, they are human like us. God expects even the "People of the Covenant" to fall, but God also expects them to recover and commit themselves to better behavior. And if they do, God will guide them. God, in these chapters, is a God of history, not a God of future glory (that idea will come later) but a God who rewards in this lifetime if the Hebrews as a people will follow God's demands. The prophet is a spokesman for God, and it is his duty to call all people, rulers and commoners alike, to account for their behavior. He warns of God's wrath and insists upon radical obedience to God's commandments.

We explained earlier that the scriptures were written much later than the events they purport to narrate and cannot be understood as history. These stories and myths first circulated orally and were transmitted from generation to generation until the Hebrews decided that it was important to have them written down. This point in time seems to correspond to the establishment of the monarchy, ca. 1000 BCE. This move to written texts could also represent a growing literacy among the people, as was noted in our discussion of the excavation at Tel Dan in the historical section that precedes this chapter.

A common theory about the authorship of these first texts is that there were two main authors, one using *YHVH* and the other using *Elohim* for the name of God. These narratives appear prominently in Genesis and Exodus. A more sophisticated and widely-held theory posits four different authors or sources whose writings were more or less woven together by priestly editors in the fifth century BCE. The following is an outline of this theory, called the *four-document hypothesis*.

(1) The earliest contributor is the *"J" writer*, so called because this author typically refers to the divine as *Yahweh*. (The German scholars who developed this theory named the writer "J" because in the German language there is no "y," but "j" has the sound of "y" as in "ja!") Yahweh became the

"ineffable" name—a name that should not be pronounced—because of its sacredness. Whenever the name YHVH was encountered in the scriptures, Jews would substitute the generic term *Adonai*, "Lord," in their worship. That remains Jewish practice. Inserting the vowels in "Adonai" in between the consonants "YHVH" created the word Jehovah, a substitution that became popular in medieval times. This was popular among Reforming Protestants and explains why we encounter this translation in some Christian Bibles.

(2) Another of the four authors refers to God with the generic designation Elohim, and thus is called the *E writer*. J, writing probably during the height of the united monarchy, ca. 1000 BCE, and E, perhaps writing a hundred years later in the northern kingdom of Israel, make up the two oldest strands in the Bible. They were responsible for the first collection of the narrative stories and myths that comprise the Tanakh.

(3) The third editor, referred to as D, emerged in the time of the "reformation" under King Josiah in 621 BCE (2 Kings 22). As the story is told, King Josiah and his chief priest discovered in the Temple in Jerusalem a previously unknown scroll that they proclaimed were chapters 12–26 of the Book of Deuteronomy, also called the second covenant of Moses. This scroll described the exact reforms that Josiah was imposing on the people. One of these reforms was a new edition of scripture.

(4) The fourth editor or editors is designated by the letter P, which stands for the *priestly history*. This edition was probably the effort of a group of priests beginning during the Babylonian exile and completed in Jerusalem subsequent to their return and the rebuilding of the Temple in the late sixth century BCE. They brought together the strands of the older traditions, producing the version that stands behind the version we read today. This edition was written in what is referred to as classical Hebrew. Some portions of this sixth century BCE text came to light with the discovery of the Dead Sea Scrolls in 1945.

To explain what we mean by the term "stands behind" we must speak about what survives of this "fourth edition." We cannot simply open a box and pull out a sixth century BCE version of the Tanakh and translate it into English and print it in this book. There is no such text. The oldest versions of the

Tanakh come to us from the third century BCE in two translations. The first is the Septuagint that is in Greek, and the second is in Aramaic. Beginning in the third century BCE the Hebrew language had faded from use, so the Jews of Palestine used the Aramaic language.

Following the fall of Jerusalem in 70 CE the rabbis gathered the surviving manuscripts and over time produced what is called the Massoretic text, after the word *massorah* which means tradition. However, the oldest surviving copies of this translation are from the ninth to the eleventh centuries CE. Over the centuries the Tanakh has been translated into many languages, including Ethiopic, Syriac, and Arabic for the many Jews who lived in Muslim countries. The English translation you are reading took into consideration all of the best surviving manuscripts. It was produced through the efforts of widely respected scholars and rabbis from the three main branches of Judaism in the U.S.: Orthodox, Conservative, and Reform.

THE THREEFOLD DIVISION OF THE HEBREW BIBLE

The first section of the Bible, from Genesis through Deuteronomy, is priestly guidance called *Torah*. Although often translated as "law," the word *torah* really means "teaching" intended to instruct individuals and the entire community in a basic way of life. The second section, which

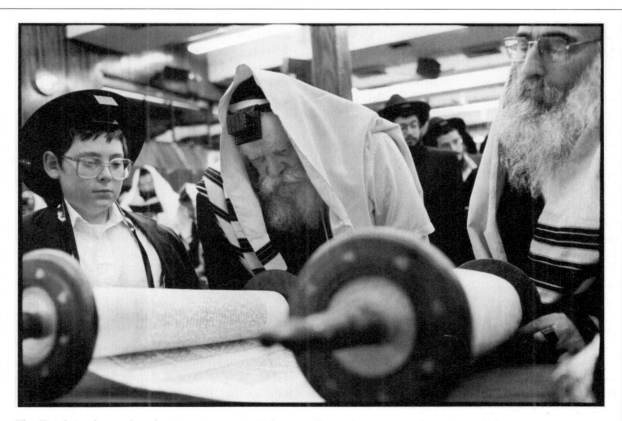

The Torah is always handwritten in ornate Hebrew calligraphy on a parchment scroll for use in synagogue services. Here, an Orthodox rabbi, another scholar, and a young boy read a large Torah scroll. The practice of reading the Torah aloud has long been a tradition in Jewish worship. During readings of the Torah, at least three people are present on the raised platform, or *bimah*, as seen here.

Figure I-2 Rabbi Menachem Schneerson Reading the Torah. Early 1990s. Lubavitch world headquarters, Crown Heights, Brooklyn, New York. Courtesy of Marc Asnin/Corbis Saba.

includes histories such as Joshua and Judges and books of prophetic sayings such as Isaiah and Jeremiah, is entitled the *Prophets* (*Nevi'im*). The stories and the sayings in this section are meant as instruments by which God's word penetrates human history. The concluding section is called the *Writings* (*Ketuvah*) and consists of poetry, stories, and sayings intended to educate and to inspire. The Writings include such books as Psalms, Proverbs, Job, Ecclesiastes, and Ruth. Thus the culture that produced the Tanakh looked for knowledge from three sources: priestly teaching, prophetic pronouncements, and sage advice from the wise. Tanakh, the word for the Jewish Bible, is an acronym formed from the first letters of the Hebrew names of the three divisions: *Torah, Nevi'im,* and *Ketuvah.*

Torah   Torah is a collection of stories—myths and legends—and laws. The religion of Judaism claims that within this diverse group of writings are contained the foundational teachings for religious living. While Muslims, Orthodox Jews, and conservative Christians consider Torah solely the work of Moses, our view, as outlined above in the four-source document hypothesis, is that it needs to be seen as the weaving together of several different authors reflecting different historical periods and different social and religious perspectives. A helpful way of reading Torah is to approach it as if reading an anthology of stories. On one level the stories are interesting literary narratives with plots and characters. On another level they express different ways of interpreting the world through the diverse ways in which they talk about God, human nature, and the world humans inhabit. Torah is also referred to as the *Pentateuch,* Greek for "five books."

The first book, Genesis (Greek for "beginning"), offers two stories of creation and is followed by a narrative about Israel's early leaders. This is referred to as the period of the Patriarchs (Abraham, Isaac, Jacob, and Joseph), although a few women are featured prominently as wives or concubines (Sarah, Hagar, Rebecca, Rachel). The second book, Exodus (from the Greek *exodos,* a going out), tells how God took a group of Hebrew slaves out of Egypt and made a contract, or covenant, with them, in the wilderness under the leadership of a man named Moses. Leviticus, the third book, is a continuation of the details of the contract, with spe-

cial reference to priestly regulations. Book four, Numbers, begins with a census—hence its name—and includes narratives about the wanderings of the people in the wilderness (the place resembles the Sinai Peninsula, between the Gulf of Suez and the Gulf of Aqabah). This book expands on details of the rules of the covenant with Yahweh. The fifth book, Deuteronomy, reviews both the stories and the rules that preceded it; thus it is a "second law" (the meaning of the Greek word deuteronomos) or the "sermons" of Moses.

In Torah we read of special covenants with God. A *covenant* in its general sense simply means a binding agreement between two or more persons. "Covenant" is used in all sorts of non-religious contexts, for example, legal contracts are covenants. Thus, we want to remind you that the word is not exclusively a religious term. In its biblical use it describes God's plan, the role humans play, and the consequences of their obedience or disobedience to that plan. Modern biblical scholars often find a similarity between these contractual sections of the Hebrew Bible and other ancient Near Eastern legal forms. They point, in particular, to treaty formulae that stipulated the relations between two political groups, the consequences of abiding by the stipulations, and the consequences of transgressing those stipulations. There are several covenantal passages in the Hebrew Bible, but the important ones to recognize are: the covenant with Noah (Gen. 6–9), the covenant with Abraham (Gen. 17), and the covenant with Moses (Ex. 20).

The Prophets, Nevi'im   The second section of Tanakh is the *Prophets.* It includes books that in the Christian tradition are considered "historical books" as well as the stories and sayings of the prophets. The "historical books" are grouped under the heading of the "Former Prophets," and include Joshua, Judges, 1 and 2 Samuel, and 1 and 2 Kings. These books follow up on the Exodus stories in telling how the Hebrew people crossed over into the land of Palestine and what followed. Scholars who question their historicity suggest that these books have been "written backwards," or very much after the fact. Reading the stories of the succession of monarchs in the divided monarchies of Israel and Judah, one is struck by the ongoing corruption of these leaders, who are frequently called to reform by one of the prophets. What are we to make of this? Perhaps the authors wish to cast doubt on the ability of human institutions to maintain and further an ethical and just society.

The "Latter Prophets" includes a list of the books that tradition has long labeled "major" and "minor" prophets. The major prophets are Isaiah, Jeremiah, and Ezekiel. There are twelve minor or shorter prophets. The purpose of prophets in the Hebrew Scriptures differs somewhat from the prophets one encounters in Greek literature, who are often thought to predict the future. The Hebrew prophets are viewed as interpreters, "forthtellers," not "foretellers." (You will want to compare the Hebrew prophets with Tiresias, the prophet in *Antigone*.) Their purpose is to promote an ethics of social justice. They condemn the emptiness of sacrifice and ritual that does not lead to moral action.

Some scholars interpret the message of the prophets as varied according to three periods in the history of Israel: *pre-exilic* (from the emergence of Israel as a nation), *exilic* (the period of the Babylonian exile), and *post-exilic* (the return of Jews to Jerusalem and the rebuilding of the Temple). The message of the pre-exilic prophets is to call the Hebrews to "personal commitment and social responsibility." They repeatedly warn about the shallowness evident in ritual and demand sincere ethical behavior. They continually express their skepticism about the ability of human institutions to act morally; they affirm the justice of God in punishing a society that has become corrupted. Emerging out of the condemnation of an unjust leader arises the image of a just leader, one that would be anointed with oil as a symbol of kingship. These prophecies or imaginings become the source of what came to be called the messianic prophecies.

Exilic and post-exilic prophets exhibit a new *"universalism"*—religion not merely as a national ideology but as a universal human expression. It is in this period, ca. 600--500 BCE, when we can begin to speak of an emergence of Judaism (descendants of the Judeans), a religion that will not be tied to a political entity but instead will serve as a "light to the nations" (Isaiah 42.6). Out of this period the characteristic institutions that have continued through the centuries and define what it is to be a Jew emerged: kosher laws, the synagogue tradition, and the commitment to study and learning. Jews never had a preoccupation with the after-

life, but during the exilic and post-exilic periods emerged a belief in the resurrection of the dead. Not all modern-day Jews accept this belief. Jews as a whole have never held a belief in a heaven as described in Christian and Islamic faiths.

The Writings, Ketuvah   This third division of the Hebrew Scriptures is a miscellany of literature that emphasizes "advice" or practical wisdom. The "advice" literature consists of poetry (e.g., Psalms, Song of Songs, Lamentations), aphorisms (e.g. Proverbs and Ecclesiastes), dramatic dialogue (Job), and historical romances (e.g. Ruth, Daniel). An example of practical wisdom is found in the Book of Daniel. It appears among the *Writings* in the Jewish Bible because it teaches loyalty and fidelity to Jewish customs. Daniel remains true to the dietary laws, ritual performances, and theological injunctions, despite temptations and threats from Babylonian kings and officials. The stories demonstrate that while following tradition may at times seem to be perilous, such devotion leads to ultimate triumph and victory. The Book of Daniel in the Christian Bible is placed among the Prophets so as to call attention to its inclusion of apocalyptic visions of the end of time.

The Book of Psalms, traditionally ascribed to King David, is actually an anthology of public and private poetry. Other books ascribed to royalty are the Song of Songs, and Proverbs (Solomon). The significance of these ascriptions could lie in the association of power and literacy. Some of the Writings provide images of women who hold power. The Book of Esther shows both how men fear the power of women and how that fear leads to foolish behavior that gives women even more power than they had before. Even the wise "King Lemuel" is made to recapitulate the "proverbs his mother taught him" in Proverbs 31. The erotic element in the Song of Songs also shows how men necessarily follow after their beloved.

Other texts are pessimistic in nature. The conclusion of the Book of Ecclesiastes makes this ideology clear: ". . . the use of books is endless, and much study is wearisome" (Ecclesiastes 12:12). The Bible, therefore, includes within it a caution against taking itself too seriously. Even books are deceptive and misleading. Do not trust what you read in these pages, the Bible announces to its readers! This is why some scholars see a recurring theme throughout the

Wisdom literature of withdrawal into a private world of personal morality, in the belief that there is little hope of great social change such as the prophets had envisioned.

GOD THE "FATHER"

One issue that has become increasingly important in contemporary Jewish and Christian thought is the extent to which God is described in masculine imagery in the biblical literature. Recent writers subject the scriptural texts to "gender analysis" to discover how the use of masculine and feminine images for God shapes the meaning and significance communicated. These studies range from socio-political analysis to literary interpretation, uncovering potential messages in apparently commonplace descriptions.

When God appears as a warrior or hero in battle, masculine language prevails as well as when God appears as a judge. But while its texts make extensive use of masculine images, the Hebrew Bible also employs clearly feminine ways of describing the divine. Thus the parental metaphor in the Book of Hosea applies as easily to a mother as well as a father.

Usually Yahweh is compared to a woman when the author wants to emphasize God's unconditional love for and faithfulness to the people, compassion and forgiveness. Significantly, the root word for the words for compassion and mercy is *rechem*, the Hebrew word for womb. This "feminizing" of Yahweh appears in what is called the "wisdom tradition" of early Judaism. The Book of Proverbs not only extols moral wisdom as the highest human virtue, it personifies wisdom in feminine imagery as a mediating principle by which God creates the universe and guides humanity.

Later wisdom literature, including Ecclesiasticus and the Wisdom of Solomon, which were omitted from the final canon of Hebrew Scripture but are found in the Catholic Bible and Protestant Bibles that include the Apocrypha, speak in even more exalted terms of *sophia* (the Greek word for "wisdom" in its feminine form). Normative rabbinic Judaism that emerged in the first centuries of the Common Era replaced the "wisdom" image with that of "presence." The Hebrew word is *Shekinah*, which now became a new feminine image of God's mediating presence. Shekinah later became a central

image and idea in Jewish mysticism. The Shekinah both reveals God's will to his people and also reconciles them with God. Each Sabbath (worship) is a symbol of God's embrace of his "bride," Shekinah, which anticipates the final reconciliation of God with the Jewish people and with the whole creation in the messianic age.

WOMEN'S PLACE

Although we cannot speak for the authenticity of the stories in the Bible we can draw some conclusions about social roles. We want particularly to look at the status of women in Hebrew/Israelite/Jewish society. These stories can offer insights into the treatment of women in Jewish society.

That the Hebrew Scriptures are patriarchal is without question. However, it is useful to look at the images of women and the laws pertaining to women in order to understand fully their positions in the community. Primarily women are viewed as wives and mothers, but even in this role they are sometimes singled out as being powerful personalities. Sarah and Rebecca, as wives of the first two patriarchs, are strong women with considerable influence on their husbands. Even among "bad" women, such as Jezebel and Delilah, we see examples of feminine strength. In law women are sometimes considered as property of their husbands, but on the other hand there are codes that establish marriage as binding on men. There are verses in Exodus (21:22-25) that prescribe differing penalties for injury to a fetus and towards the woman carrying the fetus, suggesting the greater value placed on the life of the woman. But scholars warn against generalizing concerning the actual practice of these laws. As in other cultures of this time the significance of the laws may be more symbolic than practical. Feminist scholars, such as Phyllis Trible, Mieke Bal, Rosemary Radford Reuther, and others, however, affirm that women in Israelite society were respected within their assigned place.

CREATION STORIES

Genesis 1-4:16 contains two distinctly different creation stories. The first is considered to come from the editor P (1-2:4a). It is a stately, "cosmic" portrayal of the stages of God's creating after the pattern of the seven-day Jewish week, with the repeated pronouncement that it was "good." Notice that the divine creating consists of bringing order out of a primeval, watery chaos. The language about the creation of an "expanse" ("firmament" in older translations) expresses ancient Hebrew cosmology. The expanse or firmament (the heavens) is a translucent dome by which God divides the chaotic waters to make a space for earth and life (that is why the sky is blue). Then God creates the earth as a disk floating on the waters below the firmament.

The fourth day of creation (Gen. 14–19) is noteworthy, because here sun and moon are clearly creatures of God rather than deities in their own right, in contrast to neighboring cultures like Mesopotamia and Egypt in which sun and moon were worshipped. Humans are created last, on the sixth day, male and female together suggesting an equality of roles as compared with Genesis 2:4, and given "dominion" as stewards over the rest of nature. Worth calling attention to are verses 29–30, which portray an original vegetarianism that is modified

in the kosher laws in the chapters in Leviticus (*kosher* refers to the dietary laws of Judaism).

J's creation story (2:4b-4:16), by contrast, is earthy and very anthropomorphic. A useful exercise is to put the first and second stories side by side and list all the differences in both content and form. Notice J's characteristic use of "the Lord" (*Yahweh*) to refer to God, the single day it takes Yahweh to create, the creation of the man (*adam* = man) before the creation of plants and other animals, and the familiar Garden of Eden setting (traditionally located in Mesopotamia, since the Tigris and Euphrates are mentioned). The woman (Eve = mother of all living) is created after all the other animals, from a rib of Adam, in a reversal of the biological fact that all men are born of women. And Adam names Eve just as he names everything else, thus asserting his authority over her as well.

The story of the two humans disobediently eating fruit (not identified as an apple) from the tree of

Dürer's print of Adam and Eve depicts the first biblical man and woman just at the moment of their temptation. A German Renaissance master, Dürer not only shows a virtuoso handling of the burin, or engraving tool, but also sets forth a scene of iconographic complexity. Dürer uses animals to represent the four classical temperaments: the elk for the melancholic or depressed, the ox for the phlegmatic or impassive, the cat for the choleric or angry, and the rabbit for the sanguine or confident. To further underscore Adam and Eve's imminent expulsion from Eden, Dürer juxtaposed the predatory cat with the vulnerable mouse in the foreground; in the background, a goat teeters symbolically on the edge of a cliff. Dürer cleverly signed the print by hanging a placard from the Tree of Life that reads, "Albrecht Dürer of Nuremberg made this in 1504."

Figure I-3 Albrecht Dürer. *Adam and Eve.* 1504. Engraving, 9⅞ × 7⅝" (25.1 × 19.4 cm). Victoria and Albert Museum, London, Great Britain. Courtesy of Victoria & Albert Museum, London/Art Resource, NY.

the knowledge of good and evil, with the serpent (not identified as Satan) as a voice of temptation, came many centuries later to have an importance in Christianity that it has never had in Judaism. The story came to be interpreted as the fall of the human race and the beginning of original sin and indeed of all evil. When we come in a later lesson to study the life and thought of Augustine (354–430 CE), we will see how his very "dark" interpretation of the fall and original sin, based on some passages in Paul's letters in the Christian scriptures, came to dominate Western Christianity.

TWO FLOOD STORIES

Genesis 6-9:17 tells of a universal flood that is God's punishment on the human race for their sinfulness and disobedience. The story of Noah and the ark is woven together from J and P versions, both of which in turn probably derive from Mesopotamian originals such as the flood story found in many versions of the *Epic of Gilgamesh*. The biblical flood story is familiar to you. In this reading note the covenant God establishes with Noah in 9:1-17. The covenant, known as the Noahide covenant, is especially important to the Jewish tradition. Since there is not yet a Hebrew people (they were, like all peoples, among the descendants of Noah's sons), the covenant God makes with Noah after the flood is with the whole human race, and the moral code that is part of it is seen as God's commandments to all of humanity. God's post-diluvian (after the flood) commandments are modifications of the original commandments in Genesis 1: meat-eating is now permitted, but not the blood of the animal; the penalty for killing another human is the forfeiting of one's own life; and the injunction to "be fruitful and multiply" is repeated. Occasionally the biblical flood story is interpreted as a creation story. This is not a correct understanding of this text.

The *Epic of Gilgamesh,* a Mesopotamian story, is one of the oldest known texts in Western literature and predates Hebrew Scripture by at least one thou-

This enormous lion-taming spirit, an ornament from the palace throne room of Sargon II, symbolized divine and royal power. Traditionally identified as the hero Gilgamesh, also an ancient king of Uruk, the figure embodies the omnipotence of kingship as he effortlessly overpowers the lion. The contrast between the roaring lion and the hero's calm strength underscores the magical power and divinity of the royal ruler. The figure's large eyes, once brightly colored, were meant to mesmerize the viewer and impart the supernatural supremacy of the king.

Figure I-4 Hero Choking a Small Lion, from the palace complex of Sargon II, King of Assur, Dur Sharrukin (modern Khorsabad, Iraq). ca. 721–705 BCE gypseous alabaster, height 18" x 11" (5.52 m). Louvre, Paris. Courtesy of Erich Lessing/Art Resource, NY.

sand years. It was found written in cuneiform on stone tablets in the mid-nineteenth century. Its existence seems to support the idea that the flood story in Genesis is not unique. There may well have been others. That archaeologists have found evidence of devastating floods both in the regions of the Tigris and Euphrates Rivers and in Egypt bears out the possibility that these flood stories were based in fact. In order to understand such devastation, the victims of these tragedies quite naturally would want to explain them in mythological or religious ways. We will make some comparisons as we conclude this discussion, but first let us summarize the plot of *Gilgamesh*.

Gilgamesh is the young king of Uruk, one of the Sumerian city states bordering the Tigris and Euphrates valley (ca. 3500 BCE). Like Achilles in Homer's *Iliad*, he is a larger-than-life hero, son of a goddess and a human father. The story begins when the gods create a companion for him, Enkidu, who matches his strength, and they become close friends and "brothers." They have various adventures together. Finally they offend the goddess, Ishtar, and the result is Enkidu's death. Gilgamesh is devastated at the loss of his friend, and mourns him for seven days and seven nights. He is also fearful because he now realizes he too will die. He has heard of a man named Utnapishtim, who survived the great flood and was granted everlasting life by the gods. He seeks out Utnapishtim in order to obtain everlasting life. His quest is unsuccessful, but through the experiences of the journey he comes to learn to value life while he has it. *Carpe diem!*

The story as told in the Old Babylonian version of the *Gilgamesh* epic emphasizes the arbitrary and unforeseeable nature of divine displeasure. The gods need human beings to participate in the life of the world. At the very least they need the sacrifices that people offer. Yet the gods are driven by whim, and therefore humans have little to guide them as they seek to anticipate divine actions. By contrast the story as it is told in Genesis clearly has a moral message.

LEGENDS OF THE PATRIARCHS

Genesis 12–25 contains the cycle of legends about Abraham, the eponymous father of the people Israel (he is also looked to by Christianity and Islam as the beginning of their traditions). These are part of the "patriarchal stories," tales of the traditional "fathers" of the nation: Abraham, Isaac, Jacob, and Joseph. The geographical and cultural setting of much in the earlier stories is Mesopotamia around 1800 BCE, and of course we are told in chapter 12 that Abraham originally came from "Ur of the Chaldees," a city in Babylonia. Chapter 17 tells about the origin of circumcision as the initiation and physical sign of membership in the divine covenant for Israelite males. It is from the priestly writer (P), who is characteristically interested in recounting how Jewish rituals and holy days began. The practice of circumcision can be dated back to at least 3000 BCE in Egypt, and probably goes back much farther, perhaps originally as a rite of passage for adolescent boys. Chapter 21 relates the birth of Isaac, the "son of the promise," and the rivalry between Sarah and the slave Hagar, mother of Abraham's son Ishmael, which leads to the latter's expulsion. This story provides an explanation of the origins of the Ishmaelites, who lived south of the Negev in southern Palestine, and much later Ishmael came to be seen as the father of the Arab peoples generally.

The E story of Abraham's would-be sacrifice of his son Isaac in chapter 22 is one of the most famous and perplexing stories in the Hebrew Bible, immortalized in painting and sculpture through the centuries and used by the modern "father of existentialism," Søren Kierkegaard, as the basis for one of his most provocative books (*Fear and Trembling*). Human sacrifice was by no means uncommon in the ancient world, and there is some biblical evidence that the Hebrews may have practiced it at some periods; but the main point of the story is that this is the supreme test or trial of Abraham's trust in God, and it is followed by God's reiteration of his promise that Abraham will be the father of a great nation.

You have not been assigned the remaining chapters in Genesis, but a summary of these chapters has been provided following the reading of the assigned Genesis readings, pages 39–58.

THE STORY OF MOSES

The readings from Exodus tell the story of Moses, Israel's and Judaism's greatest figure, according to tradition the one through whom God made of the Hebrews a people, reaffirmed his covenant with them, gave them Torah, and brought them to the promised land of Canaan. The Joseph stories at the end of Genesis brought a group of Hebrews to Egypt; the Moses stories tell the dramatic tale of their exodus or escape from the power of pharaoh. Take a very close look at the story of Moses' call by God in chapter 3, one of the great theophanies or "divine appearances" in the history of religions. Here is where God discloses his name Yahweh, a play on the Hebrew word for "to be" (see Gen. 13–15). Chapters 7–14 recount the pharaoh's refusal to allow the Hebrew people to leave Egypt, and the seven plagues God sends upon the Egyptians. The last plague (chaps. 11–12), in which God kills all the first-born among the Egyptians but "passes over" the Hebrews, is the basis of the Feast of Passover, and the story is recounted in such a way as to tell in detail how and when this holy day is to be observed. Chapter 19 sets the stage for God's giving to Moses the holiest part of the covenant law, the Ten Commandments or "ten words" (Greek *decalogue*) in chapter 20. The Decalogue also appears in Deuteronomy 5. Notice the explicit link made in the fourth commandment in verses 8–11 between the six days of labor and one of rest and the days of God's creation of the universe.

To conclude the book: "The Book of the Covenant" (Exod. 20:22–23:33) is a compilation of laws covering specific institutions, such as slavery, and specific actions such as harming and killing other persons. While there are certain similarities between these laws and the Mesopotamian Code of Hammurabi, we find here and in other legal portions of Torah a remarkably humane and "egalitarian" body of social legislation.

Chapter 24 combines two accounts of the making of the covenant between Yahweh and the Hebrew people, one of them P's version of the story. Chapters 25–31 are a large interpolation into the narrative by the priestly writer, who gives instructions for the building of the "tabernacle." The tabernacle is to house the Ark of the Covenant, a large chest about the size of a coffin, containing the tablets on which the Ten Commandments are written. This reading probably describes an earlier shrine, perhaps in a tent, that housed the Ark. Chapters 32–34 return to the story of the giving of Torah to Moses on Mt. Sinai, telling the tale of the golden calf that the people make and worship while Moses is on the

mountain. In his wrath Moses breaks the stone tablets containing the commandments and the calf is destroyed. Chapter 33 includes a very different description of the tabernacle or "tent of meeting" from the earlier P account. A series of laws called the Ritual Code having to do with the ritual obligations of the Israelites under the covenant are found in chapter 34. Exodus concludes with six chapters (35–40) containing instructions for the sanctuary of the tabernacle and the worship of Yahweh.

WHY DO GOOD PEOPLE SUFFER?

The Book of Job is perhaps one of the most misinterpreted among the scriptures, particularly by Christian readers who have been influenced for centuries by an obscure reference in the Book of James 5:11 referring to the "steadfastness of Job," which has frequently been quoted as "the patience of Job." If, however, you read the book objectively and with an open mind, you will realize that "patience" is not a word that can legitimately be applied to Job, "steadfast" perhaps, but not because Job was "happy" as the verse states.

We must first look at the Book of Job as two separate literary documents. Perhaps you might want to stop here and refer to the diagram at the end of this section. The first part of the book is an ancient legend or folk tale, Job 1–2:10, 42:7–17, probably known throughout the Middle East, and may have been Persian in origin. It circulated orally as far back as 2000 BCE and was written down as part of the Hebrew Scriptures for the first time during the period of the monarchy. The legend provides a "frame" for the long philosophical and poetic dialogue that forms the central portion of the text (Job 3:1–42:6). We suggest that you read first the Legend separately from the poem. The poem, by an unknown author, was added some centuries later in either the sixth or fifth century BCE. In the Tanakh, Job follows the Book of Proverbs and is a narrative example of wisdom teachings.

The Legend begins by introducing Job, a perfect man who fulfills all ritual and ethical obligations. Job is identified as a non-Israelite from Uz, and his experiences are those of "everyman," an everyman to whom the unthinkable, the illogical, occurs. The predicament of Job reveals the inadequacy of ritual and ethics. Although Job fulfills every religious requirement, God toys with his life and happiness. The story opens upon a conversation between God and the Adversary. The Adversary is a member of God's "heavenly court" who, it appears, has the job of checking up on God's creatures. He introduces Job as a "man [who] was blameless and upright; he feared God and shunned evil" (Job 1:1). In the conversation that follows God brags about Job. The Adversary responds with a challenge, saying that if Job lost all of God's "blessings" he would curse God. The two of them make a bet and the plot is set. For what appears to be no more than amusement God permits the loss of all Job's possessions and the destruction of his family. When Job does not bend to this dreadful misfortune God permits the Adversary to afflict Job's person. Job remains "steadfast" even when coached by his wife to "curse God and die." The Adversary throughout acts only at God's direct instruction.

(In most translations of the Bible the Adversary is called "Satan" or "the Satan." The idea of Satan developed and changed over a long period of history. At the time the Prologue and Epilogue to Job were written, Satan was a member of the heavenly court of angels—not the cosmic enemy of God he became in much later Jewish writings and in early Christianity. The role of Satan or the Adversary in the first and last parts of Job is simply that of a kind of prosecuting attorney in the service of God.)

This is where the legend is interrupted and the text moves into a series of poetic passages that are loosely construed as a dialogue between Job, his friends, and God (Job 4–42). At first Job cries out in agony, describing eloquently the suffering he is experiencing, regretting the day of his birth, and yearning for death. Gradually he pulls himself together and begins to question his affliction, asking of God "Tell me where I am wrong" (Job 6:24). By contrast, his friends all presume to have knowledge of God when they suggest that Job is suffering because of some sin that he, or possibly members of his family, have committed. But Job continues his protestation of innocence, and accuses God of "[destroying] the blameless and guilty" and "[mocking] as the innocent fail" (Job 9:22–23). Job is following the practice of Israelite law courts in which the accused had a right to be confronted by the accuser. He is characteristic of Jewish tradition in his frank expression of anger and calling God to account.

The long poetic section of Job ends with God's announcement that Job was right: no human being can understand the deity. Righteousness and love should never be expected from the divine. God challenges Job to compete with him in creative power and intellectual achievement. The text never hides the brutality of this divinity who uses force to browbeat a mortal creature. It offers no apologies for God, but neither does it disguise the divine nature. The reader cannot help but notice the *non sequitur* in Job 40:8–9, where God says:

> Would you impugn My justice?
> Would you condemn Me that you may
> be right?
> Have you an arm like God's?
> Can you thunder with a voice like His?

Here, certainly, is a case where "might makes right." The proverbial wisdom of human sages cannot hope to approximate the arbitrary, self-justifying tyranny of divine power. Job recognizes the futility of seeking justice from such a force. He admits, "Therefore, I recant and relent, Being but dust and ashes" (Job 42:6). That admission merely reaffirms his statements from the beginning of the dialogue. Already in Job 3 the themes of despising his life and recognizing that God cannot be counted upon for justice have been established.

A final irony of the story occurs in an epilogue, the second half of the legend, returning from poetry to prose (Job 42:7–17). The prediction in Job 13 comes true: God is angry with Job's friends, vindicates Job, commands them to let Job offer a sacrifice for them, and says he won't be harsh with them but only for Job's sake. Job is correct; even God admits that the conventional wisdom is false! The author deliciously leaves the Adversary's and God's testing of Job back in chapters 1 and 2 and concentrates instead on the ludicrous whimsy of the divine. God's treatment of Job has demonstrated that sacrifices are ineffective, yet he insists that only if Job offers sacrifices for his friends can they be forgiven. God rewards Job by restoring all his wealth and giving him a new set of children—as if children possess no inherent worth but are valuable only as pawns in a divine game. The text's main point seems to be that speculation about the why and wherefore of life is futile and irrelevant.

The outline below may be helpful in understanding the composition of the Book of Job. It indicates the division between the legend and the poem. Structurally one can identify three rounds of conversations among Job and his friends, Eliphaz, Bildad, and Zophar. You are assigned only the first round and subsequent rounds are incomplete. The "Hymn to Wisdom" may be a later addition into the text and bears some similarity to an Egyptian text dedicated to a pharaoh. The text shows other evidence of possible Egyptian influence through the inclusion of Egyptian loan words. You can see from the outline that you have only been assigned a portion of Elihu's speech, the opening chapter and the end. The "Voice from the Whirlwind" is a theophany (god appearance) and, like Moses and the burning bush, is one of the great theophanies in religious literature. Another is the disclosure of Lord Krishna to Prince Arjuna in the *Bhagavad Gita*, one of the sacred texts of Hinduism.

SUGGESTED DIVISIONS OF JOB

The Legend: 1–2:11
The Poem:
> The Curse: Chap. 3
> Round 1, Chaps. 4–14:22
> Round 2, Chaps. 15–21:34
> Round 3, Chaps. 22–27:23
> Hymn to Wisdom: Chap. 28
> Job's Summation: Chaps. 29–31:40
> Elihu Interpolation: Chaps. 32–37
> The theophany: Chaps. 38–42:6

The Legend, concluded: 42:7–10

QUESTIONS FOR STUDY AND DISCUSSION

1. What is meant by the Historical-Critical Method? List at least four of the different approaches.

2. What is the threefold division of the Tanakh? Name and describe the content of each division.

3. Describe what is meant by the four-source hypothesis.

4. What was the role of the prophets in ancient Israel?

5. What are the various images for God in the Tanakh?

6. What can we say about the role and position of women in Hebrew society? Where are our sources?

7. Explain how we know there are two creation stories.

8. Why do you suppose you have been asked to read the flood story from the ancient *Epic of Gilgamesh*? How is it similar to the Flood Story in the Book of Genesis and how is it different?

9. What does the Book of Job reveal about the relationship between humankind and the divine?

SUGGESTIONS FOR FURTHER READING

Alter, Robert. *The Art of Biblical Narrative*. New York: Basic Books, Inca., 1981.
> The first of Professor Alter's many books on the Hebrew Bible, this work provides the theoretical basis for his literary approach to the Bible, a wealth of detailed analysis of biblical stories, and a good sense of what can occur when an author looks beyond literal historical fact when studying the Bible.

Bal, Mieke, ed. *Anti-Covenant: Counter-Reading Women's Lives in the Hebrew Bible*. Bible and Literature Series 22. Sheffield: Sheffield Academic Press, 1989.
> Mieke Bal's many studies show her to be at the forefront of both literary and feminist investigations of the Bible. In this anthology she collects many essays by outstanding biblical scholars who demonstrate how stories, taken as literary expressions, use feminine images to convey more general ideas.

Cantor, Norman F. *The Sacred Chain*. New York: HarperCollins Publishers, Inca., 1994.
> Described as the most comprehensive, readable, and up-to-date history of the Jews in the English language. Cantor's focus on how the Jews created their identity over three millennium will engender much debate.

Davies, Phillip R. *In Search of Ancient Israel*. Journal for the Study of the Old Testament Supplement Series 148. Sheffield: Sheffield Academic Press, 1992.
> This book, written for Professor Davies' students rather than his colleagues, provides both a sum-

mary of recent studies concerning the "history of Israel" and a wealth of supporting evidence. Professor Davies makes the case that the Bible as we have it is a late literary invention and cannot be used as a reliable source of history.

Knight, Douglas A. and Gene M. Tucker, eds. *The Hebrew Bible and Its Modern Interpreters*. Philadelphia and Chico, CA: Fortress and Scholars Press, 1985.

The essays collected in this anthology survey the history of biblical scholarship, by historical period, genre, and theological topica. Each essay provides a review of the scholarly literature in the field and offers a good point of departure for future study.

Neusner, Jacob. *The Judaism the Rabbis Take for Granted*. Atlanta: Scholars Press, 1994.

Neusner is the foremost contemporary interpreter of rabbinic Judaism. All his books are worth reading. This one focuses on the religious aspects of rabbinic Judaism and may well be the best place for students to begin their study of his approach.

Russell, Letty M., ed. *Feminist Interpretation of the Bible*. Philadelphia: Fortress Press, 1985.

This useful anthology includes methodological studies, examples of interpretation of stories from the Hebrew Scriptures, and a general consideration of the feminist consciousness.

Trible, Phyllis. *Texts of Terror: Literary-Feminist Readings of the Biblical Narratives*. Philadelphia: Fortress Press, 1984.

Professor Trible is one of the best-known feminist scholars of the Hebrew Scriptures, and her work is frequently referred to by other scholars.

Tcherikover, Victor. *Hellenistic Civilization and the Jews*. Philadelphia: Jewish Publication Society of America, 1959.

This valuable study surveys the relationship between Persians, Greeks, and Jews during the period when the Bible took shape. The author provides provocative analysis of biblical and early post-biblical Jewish texts.

Zeitlin, Solomon. *The Rise and Fall of the Judean State*. 3 vols. Philadelphia: Jewish Publication Society of America, 1965, 1969, 1978.

These three volumes give detailed descriptions of post-exilic Jewish life and culture. Specific chapters analyze the later biblical books—especially those in the Writings—and the development of Judaism.

THE FORMATION OF THE TANAKH

You are reading a widely used modern English translation of *Tanakh* done by scholars and rabbis from the three main branches of Judaism in the U. S. (Orthodox, Conservative, and Reform) under the auspices of the Jewish Publication Society. They began working on the translation in 1955, publishing the *Torah* in 1962, the *Prophets* in 1978, and the *Writings* in 1982. In 1985 the three divisions were published together as the whole Tanakh.

Translation of Tanakh from the original Hebrew into other languages began in the third century BCE. By that time the large Jewish community in Alexandria, Egypt, were Greek-speakers and often no longer understood the Hebrew text of the Bible. A translation into Greek called the *Septuagint* was made for the Alexandrian Jews. Around the same time Tanakh was also translated into Aramaic, the spoken language of Jews (including Jesus) who lived in the northern and eastern parts of Palestine. The Aramaic translations were called the *Targums*. Both the Greek and the Aramaic translations had a lasting influence on all later biblical translation. The Bible of the early Christians was the Septuagint, which was the basis for the translation of Tanakh into other languages. Christian translators followed the methods and word choices of the Jewish scholars who had translated the Septuagint. They were also influenced by the interpretations of the Hebrew texts by the scholars who had done the Targums. The development of a body of distinctively Christian literature beginning with Paul's letters resulted in the fourth century CE in an official canon of Christian writings that Christians would call the "New Testament," with Tanakh, now called the "Old Testament," the two parts together making up the Christian Bible.

In the fourth century the Church Father Jerome produced a Latin translation of the Old and New Testaments called the *Vulgate,* which became the official translation of the Roman Catholic Church and thus of Western Christianity for many centuries. In translating the Hebrew tests Jerome drew on Jewish tradition and consulted Jewish scholars. Saadia Gaon, a tenth-century Jewish philosopher and philologist, translated the Hebrew Bible into Arabic for the many Jews who by then were living in Muslim countries. Christian reformers William Tyndale in England and Martin Luther in Germany, both of whom wrote influential Bible translations, were guided in their work on the Old Testament by Latin translations of the important medieval Jewish biblical interpreters Rashi, Ibn Ezra, and Kimhi, all of whom worked from the Targums.

The King James version of the Bible, an English translation carried out under royal authority in England in 1611, has had a profound impact on English-speaking cultures. Its use and influence were so pervasive that it was an important guide for most modern English-language version, including the Jewish Publication Society's *The Holy Scriptures* in 1917 and the widely used *Revised Standard Version,* published under the auspices of the National Council of Churches in 1952. After World War II the Jewish Publication Society decided to produce a completely new translation of Tanakh, the version you are reading. The aim of the translators, in the words of the Preface, was to "reproduce the Hebrew idiomatically and reflect contemporary scholarship, thus laying emphasis on intelligibility and correctness."

GENESIS

1 When God began to create heaven and earth—
²the earth being unformed and void, with darkness over the surface of the deep and a wind from God sweeping over the water—³God said, "Let there be light"; and there was light. ⁴God saw that the light was good, and God separated the light from the darkness. ⁵God called the light Day, and the darkness He called Night. And there was evening and there was morning, a first day.

⁶God said, "Let there be an expanse in the midst of the water, that it may separate water from water." ⁷God made the expanse, and it separated the water which was below the expanse from the water which was above the expanse. And it was so. ⁸God called the expanse Sky. And there was evening and there was morning, a second day.

⁹God said, "Let the water below the sky be gathered into one area, that the dry land may appear." And it was so. ¹⁰God called the dry land Earth, and the gathering of waters He called Seas. And God saw that this was good. ¹¹And God said, "Let the earth sprout vegetation: seed-bearing plants, fruit trees of every kind on earth that bear fruit with the seed in it." And it was so. ¹²The earth brought forth vegetation: seed-bearing plants of every kind, and trees of every kind bearing fruit with the seed in it. And God saw that this was good. ¹³And there was evening and there was morning, a third day.

¹⁴God said, "Let there be lights in the expanse of the sky to separate day from night; they shall serve as signs for the set times—the days and the years; ¹⁵and they shall serve as lights in the expanse of the sky to shine upon the earth." And it was so. ¹⁶God made the two great lights, the greater light to dominate the day and the lesser light to dominate the night, and the stars. ¹⁷And God set them in the expanse of the sky to shine upon the earth, ¹⁸to dominate the day and the night, and to separate light from darkness. And God saw that this was good. ¹⁹And there was evening and there was morning, a fourth day.

²⁰God said, "Let the waters bring forth swarms of living creatures, and birds that fly above the earth across the expanse of the sky." ²¹God created the great sea monsters, and all the living creatures of every kind that creep, which the waters brought forth in swarms, and all the winged birds of every kind. And God saw that this was good. ²²God blessed them, saying, "Be fertile and increase, fill the waters in the seas, and let the birds increase on the earth." ²³And there was evening and there was morning, a fifth day.

²⁴God said, "Let the earth bring forth every kind of living creature: cattle, creeping things, and wild beasts of every kind." And it was so. ²⁵God made wild beasts of every kind and cattle of every kind, and all kinds of creeping things of the earth. And God saw that this was good. ²⁶And God said, "Let us make man in our image, after our likeness. They shall rule the fish of the sea, the birds of the sky, the cattle, the whole earth, and all the creepings that creep on earth." ²⁷And God created man in His image, in the image of God He created him; male and female He created them. ²⁸God blessed them and God said to them, "Be fertile and increase, fill the earth and master it; and rule the fish of the sea, the birds of the sky, and all the living things that creep on earth."

²⁹God said, "See, I give you every seed-bearing plant that is upon all the earth, and every tree that has seed-bearing fruit; they shall be yours for food. ³⁰And to all the animals on land, to all the birds of the sky, and to everything that creeps on earth, in which there is the breath of life, [I give] al the green plants for food." And it was so. ³¹And God saw all that He had made, and found it very good. And there was evening and there was morning, the sixth day.

2 The heaven and the earth were finished, and all their array. ²On the seventh day God finished the work that He had been doing, and He ceased on the seventh day from all the work that He had done. ³And God blessed the seventh day and declared it holy, because on it God ceased from all the work of creation that He had done. ⁴Such is the story of heaven and earth when they were created.

When the Lord God made earth and heaven—
⁵when no shrub of the field was yet on earth and no grasses of the field had yet sprouted, because the Lord God had not sent rain upon the earth and

there was as no man to till the soil, 6but a flow would well up from the ground and water the whole surface of the earth—7the Lord God formed man from the dust of the earth. He blew into his nostrils the breath of life, and man became a living being.

8The Lord God planted a garden in Eden, in the east, and placed there the man whom He had formed. 9and from the ground the Lord God caused to grow every tree that was pleasing to the sight and good for food, with the tree of life in the middle of the garden, and the tree of knowledge of good and bad.

10A river issues from Eden to water the garden, and it then divides and becomes four branches. 11The name of the first is Pishon, the one that winds through the whole land of Havilah, where the gold is. 12(The gold of that land is good; bdellium is there, and lapis lazuli.) 13The name of the second river is Gihon, the one that winds through the whole land of Cush. 14The name of the third river is Tigris, the one that flows east of Asshur. And the fourth river is the Euphrates.

15The Lord God took the man and placed him in the garden of Eden, to till it and tend it. 16And the Lord God commanded the man, saying, "Of every tree of the garden you are free to eat; 17but as for the tree of knowledge of good and bad, you must not eat of it; for as soon as you eat of it, you shall die."

18The Lord God said, "It is not good for man to be alone; I will make a fitting helper for him." 19And the Lord God formed out of the earth all the wild beasts and all the birds of sky, and brought them to the man to see what he would call them; and whatever the man called each living creature, that would be its name. 20And the man gave names to all the cattle and to the birds of the sky and to all the wild beasts; but for Adam no fitting helper was found. 21So the Lord God cast a deep sleep upon the man; and, while he slept, He took one of his ribs and closed up the flesh at that spot. 22And the Lord God fashioned the rib that He had taken from the man into a woman; and He brought her to the man. 23Then the man said,

"This one at last
Is bone of my bones
And flesh of my flesh.

This one shall be called Woman,
For from man was she taken."

24Hence a man leaves his father and mother and clings to his wife, so that they become one flesh.

25The two of them were naked, the man and his wife, yet they felt no shame. 3 1Now the serpent was the shrewdest of all the wild beasts that the Lord God had made. He said to the woman, "Did God really say: You shall not eat of any tree of the garden?" 2The woman replied to the serpent, "We may eat of the fruit of the other trees of the garden. 3It is only about fruit of the tree in the middle of the garden that God said: 'You shall not eat of it or touch it, lest you die.'" 4And the serpent said to the woman, "You are not going to die, 5but God knows that as soon as you eat of it your eyes will be opened and you will be like divine beings who know good and bad." 6When the woman saw that the tree was good for eating and a delight to the eyes, and that the tree was desirable as a source of wisdom, she took of its fruit and ate. She also gave some to her husband, and he ate. 7Then the eyes of both of them were opened and they perceived that they were naked; and they sewed together fig leaves and made themselves loincloths.

8They heard the sound of the Lord God moving about in the garden at the breezy time of day; and the man and his wife hid from the Lord God among the trees of the garden. 9The Lord God called out to the man and said to him, "Where are you?" 10He replied, "I heard the sound of You in the garden, and I was afraid because I was naked, so I hid." 11Then He asked, "Who told you that you were naked? Did you eat of the tree from which I had forbidden you to eat?" 12The man said, "The woman You put at my side—she gave me of the tree, and I ate." 13And the Lord God said to the woman, "What is this you have done!" The woman replied, "The serpent duped me, and I ate." 14Then the Lord God said to the serpent,

"Because you did this,
More cursed shall you be
Than all cattle
And all the wild beasts:
On your belly shall you crawl
And dirt shall you eat
All the days of your life.
15I will put enmity

Between you and the woman,
And between your offspring and hers;
They shall strike at your head.
And you shall strike at their heel."

16And to the woman he said,

"I will make most severe
Your pangs in childbearing;
In pain shall you bear children.
Yet your urge shall be for your husband,
And he shall rule over you."

17To Adam He said, "Because you did as your wife said and ate of the tree about which I commanded you, 'You shall not eat of it,'

Cursed be the ground because of you;
By toil shall you eat of it
All the days of your life:
18Thorns and thistles shall it sprout for you.
But your food shall be the grasses of the field;
19By the sweat of your brow
Shall you get bread to eat,
Until you return to the ground—
For from it you were taken.
For dust you are,
And to dust you shall return."

20The man named his wife Eve, because she was the mother of all the living. 21And the Lord God made garments of skins for Adam and his wife, and clothed them.

22And the Lord God said, "Now that the man has become like one of us, knowing good and bad, what if he should stretch out his hand and take also from the tree of life and eat, and live forever!" 23So the Lord God banished him from the garden of Eden, to till the soil from which he was taken. 24He drove the man out, and stationed east of the garden of Eden the cherubim and the fiery ever-turning sword, to guard the way to the tree of life.

4 Now the man knew his wife Eve, and she conceived and bore Cain, saying, "I have gained a male child with the help of the Lord." 2She then bore his brother Abel. Abel became a keeper of sheep, and Cain became a tiller of the soil. 3In the course of time, Cain brought an offering to the Lord from the fruit of the soil; 4and Abel, for his part, brought the choicest of the firstlings of his flock. The Lord paid heed to Abel and his offering, 5but to Cain and his offering He paid no heed. Cain was much distressed and his face fell. 6And the Lord said to Cain,

"Why are you distressed,
And why is your face fallen?
7Surely, if you do right,
There is uplift.
But if you do not do right
Sin couches at the door;
Its urge is toward you,
Yet you can be its master."

8Cain said to his brother Abel . . . and when they were in the field, Cain set upon his brother Abel and killed him. 9The Lord said to Cain, "Where is your brother Abel?" And he said, "I do not know. Am I my brother's keeper?" 10Then He said, "What have you done? Hark, your brother's blood cries out to Me from the grounds! 11Therefore, you shall be more cursed than the ground, which opened its mouth to receive your brother's blood from your hand. 12If you till the soil, it shall no longer yield its strength to you. You shall become a ceaseless wanderer on earth."

13Cain said to the Lord, "My punishment is too great to bear! 14Since You have banished me this day from the soil, and I must avoid Your presence and become a restless wanderer on earth—anyone who meets me may kill me!" 15The Lord said to him, "I promise, if anyone kills Cain, sevenfold vengeance shall be taken on him." And the Lord put a mark on Cain, lest anyone who met him should kill him. 16Cain left the presence of the Lord and settled in the land of Nod, east of Eden.

17Cain knew his wife, and she conceived and bore Enoch. And he then founded a city, and named the city after his son Enoch. 18To Enoch was born Irad, and Irad begot Mehujael, and Mehujael begot Methusael, and Methusael begot Lamech. 19Lamech took to himself two wives: the name of the one was Adah, and the name of the other was Zillah. 20Adah bore Jabal; he was the ancestor of those who dwell in tents and amidst herds. 21And the name of his brother was Jubal; he was the ancestor of all who play the lyre and the pipe. 22As for Zillah, she bore Tubal-cain, who forged all implements of copper and iron. And the sister of Tubal-cain was Naamah.

23And Lamech said to his wives,

"Adah and Zillah, hear my voice;
O wives of Lamech, give ear to my speech.
I have slain a man for wounding me,
And a lad for bruising me.
24If Cain is avenged sevenfold,
Then Lamech seventy-sevenfold."

25Adam knew his wife again, and she bore a son and named him Seth, meaning, "God has provided me with another offspring in place of Abel," for Cain had killed him. 26And to Seth, in turn, a son was born, and he named him Enosh. It was then that men began to invoke the Lord by name.

5 This is the record of Adam's line.—When God created man, He made him in the likeness of God; 2male and female He created them. And when they were created, He blessed them and called them Man.—3When Adam had lived 130 years, he begot a son in his likeness after his image, and he named him Seth. 4After the birth of Seth, Adam lived 800 years and begot sons and daughters. 5All the days that Adam lived came to 930 years; then he died.

6When Seth had lived 105 years, he begot Enosh. 7After the birth of Enosh, Seth lived 807 years and begot sons and daughters. 8All the days of Seth came to 912 years; then he died.

9When Enosh had lived 90 years, he begot Kenan. 10After the birth of Kenan, Enosh lived 815 years and begot sons and daughters. 11All the days of Enosh came to 905 years; then he died.

12When Kenan had lived 70 years, he begot Mahalalel. 13After the birth of Mehalalel, Kenan lived 840 years and begot sons and daughters. 14All the days of Kenan came to 910 years; then he died.

15When Mahalalel had lived 65 years, he begot Jared. 16After the birth of Jared, Mahalalel lived 830 years and begot sons and daughters. 17All the days of Mahalalel came to 895 years; then he died.

18When Jared had lived 162 years, he begot Enoch. 19After the birth of Enoch, Jared lived 800 years and begot sons and daughters. 20All the days of Jared came to 962 years; then he died.

21When Enoch had lived 65 years, he begot Methuselah. 22After the birth of Methuselah, Enoch walked with God 300 years; and he begot sons and daughters. 23All the days of Enoch came to 365

years. 24Enoch walked with God; then he was no more, for God took him.

25When Methuselah had lived 187 years, he begot Lamech. 26After the birth of Lamech, Methuselah lived 782 years and begot sons and daughters. 27All the days of Methuselah came to 969 years; then he died.

28When Lamech had lived 182 years, he begot a son. 29And he named him Noah, saying, "This one will provide us relief from our work and from the toil of our hand, out of the very soil which the Lord placed under a curse." 30After the birth of Noah, Lamech lived 595 years and begot sons and daughters. 31All the days of Lamech came to 777 years; then he died.

32When Noah had lived 500 years, Noah begot Shem, Ham, and Japheth.

6 When men began to increase on earth and daughters were born to them, 2the divine beings saw how beautiful the daughters of men were and took wives from among those that pleased them.—3The Lord said, "My breath shall not abide in man forever, since he too is flesh; let the days allowed him be one hundred and twenty years."—4It was then, and later too, that the Nephilim appeared on earth—when the divine beings cohabited with the daughters of men, who bore them offspring. They were heroes of old, the men of renown.

5The Lord saw how great was man's wickedness on earth, and how every plan devised by his mind was nothing but evil all the time. 6And the Lord regretted that He had made man on earth, and His heart was saddened. 7The Lord said, "I will blot out from the earth the men whom I created—men together with beasts, creeping things, and birds of the sky; for I regret that I made them." 8but Noah found favor with the Lord.

9This is the line of Noah.—Noah was a righteous man; he was blameless in his age; Noah walked with God.—10Noah begot three sons: Shem, Ham, and Japheth.

11The earth became corrupt before God; the earth was filled with lawlessness. 12When God saw how corrupt the earth was, for all flesh had corrupted its ways on earth, 13God said to Noah, "I have decided to put an end to all flesh, for the earth is filled with lawlessness because of them: I am about to destroy them with the earth. 14Make yourself an ark of gopher wood; make it an ark with compartments, and cover it inside and out with pitch. ¹⁵This is how you shall make it: the length of the ark shall be three hundred cubits, its width fifty cubits, and its height thirty cubits. ¹⁶Make an opening for daylight in the ark, and terminate it within a cubit of the top. Put the entrance to the ark in its side; make it with bottom, second, and third decks.

¹⁷"For my part, I am about to bring the Flood—waters upon the earth—to destroy all flesh under the sky in which there is breath of life; everything on earth shall perish. ¹⁸But I will establish My covenant with you, and you shall enter the ark, with your sons, your wife, and your sons' wives. ¹⁹And of all that lives, of all flesh, you shall take two of each into the ark to keep alive with you; they shall be male and female. ²⁰From birds of every kind, cattle of every kind, every kind of creeping thing on earth, two of each shall come to you to stay alive. ²¹For your part, take everything that is eaten and store it away, to serve as food for you and for them." ²²Noah did so; just as God commanded him, so he did.

7 Then the Lord said to Noah, "Go into the ark, with your household, for you alone have I found righteous before Me in this generation. ²Of every clean animal you shall take seven pairs, males and their mates, and of every animal that is not clean, two, a male and its mate; ³of the birds of the sky also, seven pairs, male and female, to keep seed alive upon all the earth. ⁴For in seven days' time I will make it rain upon the earth, forty days and forty nights, and I will blot out from the earth all existence that I created." ⁵And Noah did just as the Lord commanded him.

⁶Noah was six hundred years old when the Flood came, waters upon the earth. ⁷Noah, with his sons, his wife, and his sons' wives, went into the ark because of the waters of the Flood. ⁸Of the clean animals, of the animals that are not clean, of the birds, and of everything that creeps on the ground, ⁹two of each, male and female, came to Noah into the ark, as God had commanded Noah. ¹⁰And on the seventh day the waters of the Flood came upon the earth.

¹¹In the six hundredth year of Noah's life, in the second month, on the seventeenth day of the month, on that day.

All the fountains of the great deep burst apart,
And the floodgates of the sky broke open.

¹²(The rain fell on the earth forty days and forty nights.) ¹³That same day Noah and Noah's sons, Shem, Ham and Japheth, went into the ark, with Noah's wife and the three wives of his sons—¹⁴they and all beasts of every kind, all cattle of every kind, all creatures of every kind that creep on the earth, and all birds of every kind, every bird, every winged thing. ¹⁵They came to Noah into the ark, two each of all flesh in which there was breath of life. ¹⁶Thus they that entered comprised male and female of all flesh, as God had commanded him. And the Lord shut him in.

¹⁷The Flood continued forty days on the earth, and the waters increased and raised the ark so that it rose above the earth. ¹⁸The waters swelled and increased greatly upon the earth, and the ark drifted upon the waters. ¹⁹When the waters had swelled much more upon the earth, all the highest mountains everywhere under the sky were covered. ²⁰Fifteen cubits higher did the waters swell, as the mountains were covered. ²¹And all flesh that stirred on earth perished—birds, cattle, beasts, and all the things that swarmed upon the earth, and all mankind. ²²All in whose nostrils was the merest breath of life, all that was on dry land, died. ²³All existence on earth was blotted out—man, cattle, creeping things, and birds of the sky; they were blotted out from the earth. Only Noah was left, and those with him in the ark.

²⁴And when the waters had swelled on the earth 8 one hundred and fifty days, ¹God remembered Noah and all the beasts and all the cattle that were with him in the ark, and God caused a wind to blow across the earth, and the waters subsided. ²The fountains of the deep and the floodgates of the sky were stopped up, and the rain from the sky was held back; ³the waters then receded steadily from the earth. At the end of one hundred and fifty days the waters diminished, ⁴so that in the seventh month, on the seventeenth day of the month, the ark came to rest on the mountains of Ararat. ⁵The waters went on diminishing until the tenth month; in the tenth month, on the first of the month, the tops of the mountains became visible.

⁶At the end of forty days, Noah opened the window of the ark that he had made ⁷and sent out the raven; it went to and from until the waters had dried up from the earth. ⁸Then he sent out the dove

to see whether the waters had decreased from the surface of the ground. 9But the dove could not find a resting place for its foot, and returned to him to the ark, for there was water over all the earth. So putting out his hand, he took it into the ark with him. 10He waited another seven days, and again sent out the dove from the ark. 11The dove came back to him toward evening, and there in its bill was a plucked-off olive leaf! Then Noah knew that the waters had decreased on earth. 12He waited still another seven days and sent the dove forth; and it did not return to him anymore.

13In the six hundred and first year, in the first month, on the first of the month, the waters began to dry from the earth; and when Noah removed the covering of the ark, he saw that the surface of the ground was drying. 14And in the second month, on the twenty-seventh day of the month, the earth was dry.

15God spoke to Noah, saying, 16"Come out of the ark, together with your wife, your sons, and your sons' wives. 17Bring out with you every living thing of all flesh that is with you: birds, animals, and everything that creeps on earth; and let them swarm on the earth and be fertile and increase on earth." 18So Noah came out, together with his sons, his wife, and his sons' wives. 19Every animal, every creeping thing, and every bird, everything that stirs on earth came out of the ark by families.

20Then Noah built an altar to the Lord and, taking of every clean animal and of every clean bird, he offered burnt offerings on the altar. 21The Lord smelled the pleasing odor, and the Lord said to Himself: "Never again will I doom the earth because of man, since the devisings of man's mind are evil from his youth; nor will I ever again destroy every living being, as I have done.

22So long as the earth endures,
Seedtime and harvest,
Cold and heat,
Summer and winter,
Day and night
Shall not cease."

9 God blessed Noah and his sons, and said to them, "Be fertile and increase, and fill the earth. 2The fear and the dread of you shall be upon all the beasts of the earth and upon all the birds of the sky—everything with which the earth is astir—and upon all the fish of the sea; they are given into your hand. 3Every creature that lives shall be yours to eat; as with the green grasses, I give you all these. 4You must not, however, eat flesh with its life-blood in it. 5But for your own life-blood I will require a reckoning: I will require it of every beast; of man, too, will I require a reckoning for human life, of every man for that of his fellow man!

6Whoever sheds the blood of man,
By man shall his blood be shed;
For in His image
Did God make man.

7Be fertile, then, and increase; abound on the earth and increase on it."

8And God said to Noah and to his sons with him, 9"I now establish My covenant with you and your offspring to come, 10and with every living thing that is with you—birds, cattle, and every wild beast as well—all that have come out of the ark, every living thing on earth. 11I will maintain My covenant with you: never again shall all flesh be cut off by the waters of a flood, and never again shall there be a flood to destroy the earth."

12God further said, "This is the sign that I set for the covenant between Me and you, and every living creature with you, for all ages to come. 13I have set My bow in the clouds, and it shall serve as a sign of the covenant between Me and the earth. 14When I bring clouds over the earth, and the bow appears in the clouds, 15I will remember My covenant between Me and you and every living creature among all flesh, so that the waters shall never again become a flood to destroy all flesh. 16When the bow is in the clouds, I will see it and remember the everlasting covenant between God and all living creatures, all flesh that is on earth. 17That," God said to Noah, "shall be the sign of the covenant that I have established between Me and all flesh that is on earth."

18The sons of Noah who came out of the ark were Shem, Ham and Japheth—Ham being the father of Canaan. 19These three were the sons of Noah, and from these the world would branch out.

20Noah, the tiller of the soil, was the first to plant a vineyard. 21He drank of the wine and became drunk, and he uncovered himself within his tent. 22Ham, the father of Canaan, saw his father's nakedness and told his two brothers outside. 23But Shem and Japheth took a cloth, placed it against both their backs and, walking backward, they covered their father's nakedness; their faces were turned the other way so that they did not see their father's nakedness. 24When Noah woke up from his wine and learned what his youngest son had done to him, 25he said,

"Cursed be Canaan;
The lowest of slaves
Shall he be to his brothers."

26And he said,

"Blessed be the Lord,
The God of Shem;
Let Canaan be a slave to them.
27May God enlarge Japheth,
And let him dwell in the tents of Shem;
And let Canaan be a slave to them."

28Noah lived after the Flood 350 years. 29And all the days of Noah came to 950 years; then he died.

10 These are the lines of Shem, Ham, and Japheth, the sons of Noah: sons were born to them after the Flood.

2The descendants of Japheth: Gomer, Magog, Madai, Javan, Tubal, Meshech, and Tiras. 3The descendants of Gomer Ashkenaz, Riphath, and Togarmah. 4The descendants of Javan: Elishah and Tarshish, the Kittim and the Dodanim. 5From these the maritime nations branched out. [These are the descendants of Japheth] by their lands—each with its language—their clans and their nations.

6The descendants of Ham: Cush, Mizraim, Put, and Canaan. 7The descendants of Cush: Seba, Havilah, Sabtah, Raamah, and Sabteca. The descendants of Raamah: Sheba and Dedan.

8Cush also begot Nimrod, who was the first man of might on earth. 9He was a mighty hunter by the grace of the Lord; hence the saying, "Like Nimrod a mighty hunter by the grace of the Lord." 10The mainstays of his kingdom were Babylon, Erech, Accad, and Calneh in the land of Shinar. 11From that land Asshur went forth and built Nineveh, Rehoboth-ir,

Calah, 12and Resen between Nineveh and Calah, that is the great city.

13And Mizraim begot the Ludim, the Anamim, the Lehabim, the Naphtuhim, 14the Pathrusim, the Casluhim, and the Caphtorim, whence the Philistines came forth.

15Canaan begot Sidon, his first-born, and Heth; 16and the Jebusites, the Amorites, the Girgashites, 17the Hivites, the Arkites, the Sinites, 18the Arvadites, the Zemarites, and the Hamathites. Afterward the clans of the Canaanites spread out. 19(The [original] Canaanite territory extended from Sidon as far as Gerar, near Gaza, and as far as Sodom, Gomorrah, Admah, and Zeboiim, near Lasha.) 20These are the descendants of Ham, according to their clans and languages, by their lands and nations.

21Sons were also born to Shem, ancestor of all the descendants of Eber and older brother of Japheth. 22The descendants of Shem: Elam, Asshur, Arpachshad, Lud, and Aram. 23The descendants of Aram: Uz, Hul, Gether, and Mash. 24Arpachshad begot Shelah, and Shelah begot Eber. 25Two sons were born to Eber: the name of the first was Peleg, for in his days the earth was divided; and the name of his brother was Joktan. 26Joktan begot Almodad, Sheleph, Hazarmaveth, Jerah, 27Hadoram, Uzal, Diklah, 28Obal, Abimael, Sheba, 29Ophir, Havilah, and Jobab; all these were the descendants of Joktan. 30Their settlements extended from Mesha as far as Sephar, the hill country to the east. 31These are the descendants of Shem according to their clans and languages, by their lands, according to their nations.

32These are the groupings of Noah's descendants, according to their origins, by their nations; and from these the nations branched out over the earth after the Flood.

11 Everyone on earth had the same language and the same words. 2And as they migrated from the east, they came upon a valley in the land of Shinar and settled there. 3They said to one another, "Come, let us make bricks and burn them hard."—Brick served them as stone, and bitumen served them as mortar.—4And they said, "Come, let us build us a city, and a tower with its top in the sky, to make a name for ourselves; else we shall be scattered all over the world." 5The Lord came down to look at the city and tower that man had built, 6and the Lord said, "If, as one people with one language for all, this is how they have begun to act, then nothing that they may propose to do will be out of their reach. 7Let us, then, go down and confound their speech there, so that they shall not understand one another's speech." 8Thus the Lord scattered them from there over the face of the whole earth; and they stopped building the city. 9That is why it was called Babel, because there the Lord confounded the speech of the whole earth; and from there the Lord scattered them over the face of the whole earth.

10This is the line of Shem. Shem was 100 years old when he begot Arpachshad, two years after the Flood. 11After the birth of Arpachshad, Shem lived 500 years and begot sons and daughters.
12When Arpachshad had lived 35 years, he begot Shelah. 13After the birth of Shelah, Arpachshad lived 403 years and begot sons and daughters.
14When Shelah had lived 30 years, he begot Eber. 15After the birth of Eber, Shelah lived 403 years and begot sons and daughters.
16When Eber had lived 34 years, he begot Peleg. 17After the birth of Peleg, Eber lived 430 years and begot sons and daughters.
18When Peleg had lived 30 years, he begot Reu. 19After the birth of Reu, Peleg lived 209 years and begot sons and daughters.
20When Reu had lived 32 years, he begot Serug. 21After the birth of Serug, Reu lived 207 years and begot sons and daughters.
22When Serug lived 30 years, he begot Nahor. 23After the birth of Nahor, Serug lived 200 years and begot sons and daughters.
24When Nahor lived 29 years, he begot Terah. 25After the birth of Terah, Nahor lived 119 years and begot sons and daughters.
26When Terah had lived 70 years, he begot Abram, Nahor, and Haran. 27Now this is the line of Terah: Terah begot Abram, Nahor, and Haran; and Haran begot Lot. 28Haran died in the lifetime of his father Terah, in his native land, Ur of the Chaldeans. 29Abram and Nahor took to themselves wives, the name of Abram's wife being Sarai and that of Nahor's wife Milcah, the daughter of Haran, the father of Milcah and Iscah. 30Now Sarai was barren, she had no child.
31Terah took his son Abram, his grandson Lot the son of Haran, and his daughter-in-law Sarai, the wife of his sons Abram, and they set out together from Ur of the Chaldeans for the land of Canaan; but when they had come as far as Haran, they settled there. 32The days of Terah came to 205 years; and Terah died in Haran.

12 The Lord said to Abram, "Go forth from your native land and from your father's house to the land that I will show you.

2I will make of you a great nation,
And I will bless you;
I will make your name great,
And you shall be a blessing.
3I will bless those who bless you
And curse him that curses you;
And all the families of the earth
Shall bless themselves by you."

4Abram went forth as the Lord had commanded him, and Lot went with him. 5Abram was seventy-five years old when he left Haran. Abram took his wife Sarai and his brother's son Lot, and all the wealth that they had amassed, and the persons that they had acquired in Haran; and they set out for the land of Canaan. When they arrived in the land of Canaan, 6Abram passed through the land as far as the site of Shechem, at the terebinth of Moreh. The Canaanites were then in the land.
7The Lord appeared to Abram and said, "I will assign this land to your offspring." And he built an altar there to the Lord who had appeared to him. 8From there he moved on to the hill country east of Bethel and pitched his tent, with Bethel on the west and Ai on the east; and he built there an altar to the Lord and invoked the Lord by name. 9Then Abram journeyed by stages toward the Negeb.
10There was a famine in the land, and Abram went down to Egypt to sojourn there, for the famine was severe in the land. 11As he was about to enter Egypt, he said to his wife Sarai, "I know what a beautiful woman you are. 12If the Egyptians see you, and think, 'She is his wife,' they will kill me and let you live. 13Please say that you are my sister, that it may go well with me because of you, and that I may remain alive thanks to you."
14When Abram entered Egypt, the Egyptians saw how very beautiful the woman was. 15Pharaoh's courtiers saw her and praised her to Pharaoh, and

the woman was taken into Pharaoh's palace. [16]And because of her, it went well with Abram; he acquired sheep, oxen, asses, male and female slaves, she-asses, and camels.

[17]But the Lord afflicted Pharaoh and his household with mighty plagues on account of Sarai, the wife of Abram. [18]Pharaoh sent for Abram and said, "What is this you have done to me! Why did you not tell me that she was your wife? [19]Why did you say, 'She is my sister,' so that I took her as my wife? Now, here is your wife; take her and begone!" [20]And Pharaoh put men in charge of him, and they sent him off with his wife and all that he possessed.

13 From Egypt, Abram went up into Negeb, with his wife and all that he possessed, together with Lot. [2]Now Abram was very rich in cattle, silver, and gold. [3]And he proceeded by stages from the Negeb as far as Bethel, to the place where his tent had been formerly, between Bethel and Ai, [4]the site of the altar that he had built there at first; and there Abram invoked the Lord by name.

[5]Lot, who went with Abram, also had flocks and herds and tents, [6]so that the land could not support them staying together; for their possessions were so great that they could not remain together. [7]And there was quarreling between the herdsmen of Abram's cattle and those of Lot's cattle.—The Canaanites and Perizzites were then dwelling in the land.—[8]Abram said to Lot, "Let there be no strife between you and me, between my herdsmen and yours, for we are kinsmen. [9]Is not the whole land before you? Let us separate: if you go north, I will go south; and if you go south, I will go north." [10]Lot looked about him and saw how well watered was the whole plain of the Jordan, all of it—this was before the Lord had destroyed Sodom and Gomorrah—all the way to Zoar, like the garden of the Lord, like the land of Egypt. [11]So Lot chose for himself the whole plain of the Jordan, and Lot journeyed eastward. Thus they parted from each other; [12]Abram remained in the land of Canaan, while Lot settled in the cities of the Plain, pitching his tents near Sodom. [13]Now the in habitants of Sodom were very wicked sinners against the Lord.

[14]And the Lord said to Abram, after Lot had parted from him, "Raise your eyes and look out from where you are, to the north and south, to the east and west, [15]for I give all the land that you see to you and your offspring forever. [16]I will make your offspring as the dust of the earth, so that if one can count the dust of the earth, then your offspring too can be counted. [17]Up, walk about the land, through its length and its breadth, for I give it to you." [18]And Abram moved his tent, and came to dwell at the terebinths of Mamre, which are in Hebron; and he built an altar there to the Lord.

14 Now, when King Amraphel of Shinar, King Arioch of Ellasar, King Chedorlaomer of Elam, and King Tidal of Goiim [2]made war on King Bera of Sodom, King Birsha of Gomorrah, King Shinab of Admah, King Shemeber of Zeboiim, and the king of Bela, which is Zoar, [3]all the latter joined forces at the Valley of Siddim, now the Dead Sea. [4]Twelve years they served Chedorlaomer, and in the thirteenth year they rebelled. [5]In the fourteenth year Chedorlaomer and the kings who were with him came and defeated the Rephaim at Ashterothkarnaim, the Zuzim at Ham, the Emim at Shavehkiriathaim, [6]and the Horites in their hill country of Seir as far as El-paran, which is by the wilderness. [7]On their way back they came to En-mishpat, which is Kadesh, and subdued all the territory of the Amalekites, and also the Amorites who dwelt in Hazazon-tamar. [8]Then the king of Sodom, the king of Gomorrah, the king of Admah, the king of Zeboiim, and the king of Bela, which is Zoar, went forth and engaged them in battle in the Valley of Siddim: [9]King Chedorlaomer of Elam, King Tidal of Goiim, King Amraphel of Shinar, and King Arioch of Ellasar—four kings against those five.

[10]Now the Valley of Siddim was dotted with bitumen pits; and the kings of Sodom and Gomorrah, in their flight, threw themselves into them, while the rest escaped to the hill country. [11][The invaders] seized all the wealth of Sodom and Gomorrah and all their provisions, and went their way. [12]They also took Lot, the son of Abram's brother, and his possessions, and departed; for he had settled in Sodom.

[13]A fugitive brought the news to Abram the Hebrew, who was dwelling at the terebinths of Mamre the Amorite, kinsman of Eshkol and Aner, these being Abram's allies. [14]When Abram heard that his kinsman had been taken captive, he mustered his retainers, born into his household, numbering three hundred and eighteen, and went in

pursuit as far as Dan. ¹⁵At night, he and his servants deployed against them and defeated them; and he pursued them as far as Hobah, which is north of Damascus. ¹⁶He brought back all the possessions; he also brought back his kinsman Lot and his possessions, and the women and the rest of the people.

¹⁷When he returned from defeating Chedorlaomer and the kings with him, the king of Sodom came out to meet him in the Valley of Shaveh, which is the Valley of the King. ¹⁸And King Melchizedek of Salem? brought out bread and wine; he was a priest of God Most High. ¹⁹He blessed him saying,

"Blessed be Abram of God Most High,
Creator of heaven and earth.
²⁰And blessed be God Most High,
Who has delivered your foes into your hand."

And [Abram] gave him a tenth of everything.

²¹Then the king of Sodom said to Abram, "Give me the persons, and take the possessions for yourself." ²²But Abram said to the king of Sodom, "I swear to the Lord, God Most High, Creator of heaven and earth: ²³I will not take so much as a thread or a sandal strap of what is yours; you shall not say, 'It is I who made Abram rich.' ²⁴For me, nothing but what my servants have used up; as for the share of men who went with me—Aner, Eshkol, and Mamre—let them take their share."

15 Some time later, the word of the Lord came to Abram in a vision. He said,

"Fear not, Abram,
I am a shield to you;
Your reward shall be very great."

²But Abram said, "O Lord God, what can You give me, seeing that I shall die childless, and the one in charge of my household is Dammesek Eliezer!" ³Abram said further, "Since You have granted me no offspring, my steward will be my heir." ⁴The word of the Lord came to him in reply, "That one shall not be your heir; none but your very own issue shall be your heir." ⁵He took him outside and said, "Look toward heaven and count the stars, if you are able to count them." And He added, "So

shall your offspring be." ⁶And because he put his trust in the Lord, He reckoned it to his merit.

⁷Then He said to him, "I am the Lord who brought you out from Ur of the Chaldeans to assign this land too as a possession." ⁸And he said, "O Lord God, how shall I know that I am to possess it?" ⁹He answered, "Bring Me a three-year-old heifer, a three-year-old she-goat, a three-year-old ram, a turtledove, and a young bird." ¹⁰He brought Him all these and cut them in two, placing each half opposite the other; but he did not cut up the bird. ¹¹Birds of prey came down upon the carcasses, and Abram drove them away. ¹²As the sun was about to set, a deep sleep fell upon Abram, and a great dark dread descended upon him. ¹³And He said to Abram, "Know well that your offspring shall be strangers in a land not theirs, and they shall be enslaved and oppressed four hundred years; ¹⁴but I will execute judgment on the nation they shall serve, and in the end they shall go free with great wealth. ¹⁵As for you,

You shall go to your fathers in peace;
You shall be buried at a ripe old age.

¹⁶And they shall return here in the fourth generation, for the iniquity of the Amorites is not yet complete."

¹⁷When the sun set and it was very dark, there appeared a smoking oven, and a flaming torch which passed between those pieces. ¹⁸On that day the Lord made a covenant with Abram, saying, "To your offspring I assign this land, from the river of Egypt to the great river, the river Euphrates: ¹⁹the Kenites, the Kenizzites, the Kadmonites, ²⁰the Hittites, the Perizzites, the Rephaim, ²¹the Amorites, the Canaanites, the Girgashites, and the Jebusites."

16 Sarai, Abram's wife, had borne him no children. She had an Egyptian maidservant whose name was Hagar. ²And Sarai said to Abram, "Look, the Lord has kept me from bearing. Consort with my maid; perhaps I shall have a son through her." And Abram heeded Sarai's request. ³So Sarai, Abram's wife, took her maid, Hagar the Egyptian—after Abram had dwelt in the land of Canaan ten years—and gave her to her husband Abram as concubine. ⁴He cohabited with Hagar and she conceived; and when she saw that she had conceived, her mistress was lowered in her esteem. ⁵And Sarai

said to Abram, "The wrong done me is your fault! I myself put my maid in your bosom; now that she sees that she is pregnant, I am lowered in her esteem. The Lord decide between you and me!" [6]Abram said to Sarai, "Your maid is in your hands. Deal with her as you think right." Then Sarai treated her harshly, and she ran away from her.

[7]An angel of the Lord found her by a spring of water in the wilderness, the spring on the road to Shur, [8]and said, "Hager, slave of Sarai, where have you come from, and where are you going?" And she said, "I am running away from my mistress Sarai."

[9]And the angel of the Lord said to her, "Go back to your mistress, and submit to her harsh treatment." [10]And the angel of the Lord said to her,

"I will greatly increase your offspring,
And they shall be too many to count."

[11]The angel of the Lord said to her further,

"Behold, you are with child
And shall bear a son;
You shall call him Ishmael,
For the Lord has paid heed to your suffering.
[12]He shall be a wild ass of a man;
His hand against everyone,
And everyone's hand against him;
He shall dwell alongside of all his kinsmen."

[13]And she called the Lord who spoke to her, "You Are El-roi," by which she meant, "Have I not gone on seeing after He saw me!" [14]Therefore the well was called Beer- lahai-roi; it is between Kadesh and Bered.— [15]Hagar bore a son to Abram, and Abram gave the son that Hagar bore him the name Ishmael. [16]Abram was eighty-six years old when Hagar bore Ishmael to Abram.

17 When Abram was ninety-nine years old, the Lord appeared to Abram and said to him, "I am El Shaddai. Walk in My ways and be blameless. [2]I will establish My covenant between Me and you, and I will make you exceedingly numerous."

[3]Abram threw himself on his face; and God spoke to him further, [4]"As for Me, this is My covenant with you: You shall be the father of a multitude of nations. [5]And you shall no longer be called Abram, but your name shall be Abraham, for I make you the father of a multitude of nations. [6]I will make you exceedingly fertile, and make

nations of you; and kings shall come forth from you. [7]I will maintain My covenant between Me and you, and your offspring to come, as an everlasting covenant throughout the ages, to be God to you and to your offspring to come. [8]I assign the land you sojourn in to you and your offspring to come, all the land of Canaan, as an everlasting holding. I will be their God."

[9]God further said to Abraham, "As for you, you and your offspring to come throughout the ages shall keep My covenant. [10]Such shall be the covenant between Me and you and your offspring to follow which you shall keep: every male among you shall be circumcised. [11]You shall circumcise the flesh of your foreskin, and that shall be the sign of the covenant between Me and you. [12]And throughout the generations, every male among you shall be circumcised at the age of eight days. As for the home-born slave and the one bought from an outsider who is not of your offspring, [13]they must be circumcised, home born, and purchased alike. Thus shall My covenant be marked in your flesh as an everlasting pact. [14]And if any male who is uncircumcised fails to circumcise the flesh of his foreskin, that person shall be cut off from his kin; he has broken My covenant."

[15]And God said to Abraham, "As for your wife Sarai, you shall not call her Sarai, but her name shall be Sarah. [16]I will bless her; indeed, I will give you a son by her. I will bless her so that she shall give rise to nations; rulers of peoples shall issue from her." [17]Abraham threw himself on his face and laughed, as he said to himself, "Can a child be born to a man a hundred years old, or can Sarah bear a child at ninety?" [18]And Abraham said to God, "O that Ishmael might live by Your favor!" [19]God said, "Nevertheless, Sarah your wife shall bear you a son, and you shall name him Isaac; and I will maintain My covenant with him as an everlasting covenant for his offspring to come. [20]As for Ishmael, I have heeded you. I hereby bless him. I will make him fertile and exceedingly numerous. He shall be the father of twelve chieftains, and I will make of him a great nation. [21]But My covenant I will maintain with Isaac, whom Sarah shall bear to you at this season next year." [22]And when He was done speaking with him, God was gone from Abraham.

[23]Then Abraham took his son Ishmael, and all his homeborn slaves and all those he had bought,

every male in Abraham's household, and he circumcised the flesh of their foreskins on that very day, as God had spoken to him. ²⁴Abraham was ninety-nine years old when he circumcised the flesh of his foreskin, ²⁵and his son Ishmael was thirteen years old when he was circumcised in the flesh of his foreskin. ²⁶Thus Abraham and his son Ishmael were circumcised on that very day; ²⁷and all his household, his homeborn slaves and those that had been bought from outsiders, were circumcised with him.

18 The Lord appeared to him by the terebinths of Mamre; he was sitting at the entrance of the tent as the day grew hot. ²Looking up, he saw three men standing near him. As soon as he saw them, he ran from the entrance of the tent to greet them and, bowing to the ground, ³he said, "My lords, if it please you, do not go on past your servant. ⁴Let a little water be brought; bathe your feet and recline under the tree. ⁵And let me fetch a morsel of bread that you may refresh yourselves; then go on—seeing that you have come your servant's way." They replied, "Do as you have said."

⁶Abraham hastened into the tent to Sarah, and said, "Quick, three *seahs of* choice flour! Knead and make cakes!" ⁷Then Abraham ran to the herd, took a calf, tender and choice, and gave it to a servant-boy, who hastened to prepare it. ⁸He took curds and milk and the calf that had been prepared and set these before them; and he waited on them under the tree as they ate.

⁹They said to him, "Where is your wife Sarah?" And he replied, "There, in the tent." ¹⁰Then one said, "I will return to you next year, and your wife Sarah shall have a son!" Sarah was listening at the entrance of the tent, which was behind him. ¹¹Now Abraham and Sarah were old, advanced in years; Sarah had stopped having the periods of women. ¹²And Sarah laughed to herself, saying, "Now that I am withered, am I to have enjoyment—with my husband so old?" ¹³Then the Lord said to Abraham, "Why did Sarah laugh, saying, 'Shall I in truth bear a child, old as I am?' ¹⁴Is anything too wondrous for the Lord? I will return to you at the time next year, and Sarah shall have a son." ¹⁵Sarah lied, saying, "I did not laugh," for she was frightened. But He replied, "You did laugh."

¹⁶The men set out from there and looked down toward Sodom, Abraham walking with them to see them off. ¹⁷Now the Lord had said, "Shall I hide from Abraham what I am about to do, ¹⁸since Abraham is to become a great and populous nation and all the nations of the earth are to bless themselves by him? ¹⁹For I have singled him out, that he may instruct his children and his posterity to keep the way of the Lord by doing what is just and right, in order that the Lord may bring about for Abraham what He promised him." ²⁰Then the Lord said, "The outrage of Sodom and Gomorrah is so great, and their sin so grave! ²¹I will go down to see whether they have acted altogether according to the outcry that has reached Me; if not, I will take note."

²²The men went on from there to Sodom, while Abraham remained standing before the Lord. ²³Abraham came forward and said, "Will You sweep away the innocent along with the guilty? ²⁴What if there should be fifty innocent within the city; will You then wipe out the place and not forgive it for the sake of the innocent fifty who are in it? Far be it from You to do such a thing, to bring death upon the innocent as well as the guilty, so that innocent and guilty fare alike. ²⁵Far be it from You! Shall not the Judge of all the earth deal justly?" ²⁶And the Lord answered, "If I find within the city of Sodom fifty innocent ones, I will forgive the whole place for their sake." ²⁷Abraham spoke up, saying, "Here I venture to speak to my Lord, I who am but dust and ashes: ²⁸What if the fifty innocent should lack five? Will You destroy the whole city for want of the five?" And He answered, "I will not destroy if I find forty-five there." ²⁹But he spoke to Him again, and said, "What if forty should be found there?" And He answered, "I will not do it, for the sake of the forty." ³⁰And he said, "Let not my Lord be angry if I go on: What if thirty should be found there?" And He answered, "I will not do it if I find thirty there." ³¹And he said, "I venture again to speak to my Lord: What if twenty should be found there?" And He answered, "I will not destroy, for the sake of the twenty." ³²And he said, "Let not my Lord be angry if I speak but this last time: What if ten should be found there?" And He answered, "I will not destroy, for the sake of the ten."

³³When the Lord had finished speaking to Abraham, He departed; and Abraham returned to his place.

19 The two angels arrived in Sodom in the evening, as Lot was sitting in the gate of Sodom. When Lot saw them, he rose to greet them and, bowing low with his face to the ground, [2]he said, "Please, my lords, turn aside to your servant's house to spend the night, and bathe your feet; then you may be on your way early." But they said, "No, we will spend the night in the square." [3]But he urged them strongly, so they turned his way and entered his house. He prepared a feast for them and baked unleavened bread, and they ate.

[4]They had not yet lain down, when the townspeople, the men of Sodom, young and old—all the people to the last man—gathered about the house. [5]And they shouted to Lot and said to him, "Where are the men who came to you tonight? Bring them out to us, that we may be intimate with them." [6]So Lot went out to them to the entrance, shut the door behind him, [7]and said, "I beg you, my friends, do not commit such a wrong. [8]Look, I have two daughters who have not known a man. Let me bring them out to you, and you may do to them as you please; but do not do anything to these men, since they have come under the shelter of my roof." [9]But they said, "Stand back! The fellow," they said, "came here as an alien, and already he acts the ruler! Now we will deal worse with you than with them." And they pressed hard against the person of Lot, and moved forward to break the door. [10]But the men stretched out their hands and pulled Lot into the house with them, and shut the door. [11]And the people who were at the entrance of the house, young and old, they struck with blinding light, so that they were helpless to find the entrance.

[12]Then the men said to Lot, "Whom else have you here? Sons-in-law, your sons and daughters, or anyone else that you have in the city—bring them out of the place. [13]For we are about to destroy this place; because the outcry against them before the Lord has become so great that the Lord has sent us to destroy it." [14]So Lot went out and spoke to his sons-in-law, who had married his daughters, and said, "Up, get out of this place, for the Lord is about to destroy the city." But he seemed to his sons-in-law as one who jests.

[15]As dawn broke, the angels urged Lot on, saying, "Up, take your wife and your two remaining daughters, lest you be swept away because of the iniquity of the city." [16]Still he delayed. So the men seized his hand, and the hands of his wife and his two daughters—in the Lord's mercy on him—and brought him out and left him outside the city. [17]When they had brought them outside, one said, "Flee for your life! Do not look behind you, nor stop anywhere in the Plain; flee to the hills, lest you be swept away." [18]But Lot said to them, "Oh no, my lord! [19]You have been so gracious to your servant, and have already shown me so much kindness in order to save my life; but I cannot flee to the hills, lest the disaster overtake me and I die. [20]Look, that town there is near enough to flee to; it is such a little place! Let me flee there—it is such a little place—and let my life be saved." [21]He replied, "Very well, I will grant you this favor too, and I will not annihilate the town of which you have spoken. [22]Hurry, flee there, for I cannot do anything until you arrive there." Hence the town came to be called Zoar.

[23]As the sun rose upon the earth and Lot entered Zoar, [24]the Lord raised upon Sodom and Gomorrah sulfurous fire from the Lord out of heaven. [25]He annihilated those cities and the entire Plain, and all the inhabitants of the cities and the vegetation of the ground. [26]Lot's wife looked back, and she thereupon turned into a pillar of salt.

[27]Next morning, Abraham hurried to the place where he had stood before the Lord, [28]and, looking down toward Sodom and Gomorrah and all the land of the Plain, he saw the smoke of the land rising like the smoke of a kiln.

[29]Thus it was that, when God destroyed the cities of the Plain and annihilated the cities where Lot dwelt, God was mindful of Abraham and removed Lot from the midst of the upheaval.

[30]Lot went up from Zoar and settled in the hill country with his two daughters, for he was afraid to dwell in Zoar; and he and his two daughters lived in a cave. [31]And the older one said to the younger, "Our father is old, and there is not a man on earth to consort with us in the way of all the world. [32]Come, let us make our father drink wine, and let us lie with him, that we may maintain life through our father." [33]That night they made their father drink wine, and the older one went in and lay with her father; he did not know when she lay down or when she rose. [34]The next day the older

one said to the younger, "See, I lay with Father last night; let us make him drink wine tonight also, and you go and lie with him, that we may maintain life through our father." [35]That night also they made their father drink wine, and the younger one went and lay with him; he did not know when she lay down or when she rose.

[36]Thus the two daughters of Lot came to be with child by their father. [37]The older one bore a son and named him Moab; he is the father of the Moabites of today. [38]And the younger also bore a son, and she called him Ben-ammi; he is the father of the Ammonites of today.

20 Abraham journeyed from there to the region of the Negeb and settled between Kadesh and Shur. While he was sojourning in Gerar, [2]Abraham said of Sarah his wife, "She is my sister." So King Abimelech of Gerar had Sarah brought to him. [3]But God came to Abimelech in a dream by night and said to him, "You are to die because of the woman that you have taken, for she is a married woman." [4]Now Abimelech had not approached her. He said, "O Lord, will You slay people even though innocent? [5]He himself said to me, 'She is my sister!' And she also said, 'He is my brother.' When I did this, my heart was blameless and my hands were clean." [6]And God said to him in the dream, "I knew that you did this with a blameless heart, and so I kept you from sinning against Me. That was why I did not let you touch her. [7]Therefore, restore the man's wife—since he is a prophet, he will intercede for you—to save your life. If you fail to restore her, know that you shall die, you and all that are yours."

[8]Early next morning, Abimelech called his servants and told them all that had happened; and the men were greatly frightened. [9]Then Abimelech summoned Abraham and said to him, "What have you done to us? What wrong have I done that you should bring so great a guilt upon me and my kingdom? You have done to me things that ought not to be done. [10]What, then," Abimelech demanded of Abraham, "was your purpose in doing this thing?" [11] "I thought," said Abraham, "surely there is no fear of God in this place, and they will kill me because of my wife. [12]And besides, she is in truth my sister, my father's daughter though not my mother's; and she became my wife. [13]So when God

made me wander from my father's house, I said to her, 'Let this be the kindness that you shall do me: whatever place we come to, say there of me: He is my brother.'"

[14]Abimelech took sheep and oxen, and male and female slaves, and gave them to Abraham; and he restored his wife Sarah to him. [15]And Abimelech said, "Here, my land is before you; settle wherever you please." [16]And to Sarah he said, "I herewith give your brother a thousand pieces of silver; this will serve you as vindication before all who are with you, and you are cleared before everyone." [17]Abraham then prayed to God, and God healed Abimelech and his wife and his slave girls, so that they bore children; [18]for the Lord had closed fast every womb of the household of Abimelech because of Sarah, the wife of Abraham.

21 The Lord took note of Sarah as He had promised, and the Lord did for Sarah as He had spoken. [2]Sarah conceived and bore a son to Abraham in his old age, at the set time of which God had spoken. [3]Abraham gave his newborn son, whom Sarah had borne him, the name of Isaac. [4]And when his son Isaac was eight days old, Abraham circumcised him, as God had commanded him. [5]Now Abraham was a hundred years old when his son Isaac was born to him. [6]Sarah said, "God has brought me laughter; everyone who hears will laugh with me." [7]And she added,

"Who would have said to Abraham
That Sarah would suckle children!
Yet I have borne a son in his old age."

[8]The children grew up and was weaned, and Abraham held a great feast on the day that Isaac was weaned.

[9]Sarah saw the son whom Hagar the Egyptian had borne to Abraham playing. [10]She said to Abraham, "Cast out the slave-woman and her son, for the son of that slave shall not share in the inheritance with my son Isaac." [11]The matter distressed Abraham greatly, for it concerned a son of his. [12]But God said to Abraham, "Do not be distressed over the boy or your slave; whatever Sarah tells you, do as she says, for it is through Isaac that offspring shall be continued for you. [13]As for the son of the slave-woman, I will make a nation of him, too, for he is your seed."

14Early next morning Abraham took some bread and a skin of water, and gave them to Hagar. He placed them over her shoulder, together with the child, and sent her away. And she wandered about in the wilderness of Beer-sheba. 15When the water was gone from the skin, she left the child under one of the bushes, 16and went and sat down at a distance, a bowshot away; for she thought, "Let me not look on as the child dies." And sitting thus afar, she burst into tears.

17God heard the cry of the boy, and an angel of God called to Hagar from heaven and said to her, "What troubles you, Hagar? Fear not, for God has heeded the cry of the boy where he is. 18Come lift up the boy and hold him by the hand, for I will make a great nation of him." 19Then God opened her eyes and she saw a well of water. She went and filled the skin with water, and let the boy drink. 20God was with the boy and he grew up; he dwelt in the wilderness and became a bowman. 21He lived in the wilderness of Paran; and his mother got a wife for him from the land of Egypt.

22At that time Abimelech and Phicol, chief of his troops, said to Abraham, "God is with you in everything that you do. 23Therefore swear to me here by God that you will not deal falsely with me or with my kith and kin, but will deal with me and with the land in which you have sojourned as loyally as I have dealt with you." 24And Abraham said, "I swear it."

25Then Abraham reproached Abimelech for the well of water which the servants of Abimelech had seized. 26But Abimelech said, "I do not know who did this; you did not tell me, nor have I heard of it until today." 27Abraham took sheep and oxen and gave them to Abimelech, and the two of them made a pact. 28Abraham then set seven ewes of the flock by themselves, 29and Abimelech said to Abraham, "What mean these seven ewes which you have set apart?" 30He replied, "You are to accept these seven ewes from me as proof that I dug this well." 31Hence that place was called Beersheba, for there the two of them swore an oath. 32When they had concluded the pact at Beer-sheba, Abimelech and Phicol, chief of his troops, departed and returned to the land of the Philistines. 33[Abraham] planted a tamarisk at Beer-shebaa, and invoked there the name of the Lord, the Everlasting God. 34And Abraham resided in the land of the Philistines a long time.

22 Some time afterward, God put Abraham to the test. He said to him, "Abraham," and he answered, "Here I am." 2And He said, "Take your son, your favored one, Isaac, whom you love, and go to the land of Moriah, and offer him there as a burnt offering on one of the heights that I will point out to you." 3So early next morning, Abraham saddled his ass and took with him two servants and his son Isaac. He split the wood for the burnt offering, and he set out for the place of which God had told him. 4On the third day Abraham looked up and saw the place from afar. 5Then Abraham said to his servants, "You stay here with the ass. The boy and I will go up there; we will worship and we will return to you."

6Abraham took the wood for the burnt offering and put it on his son Isaac. He himself took the firestone and the knife; and the two walked off together. 7Then Isaac said to his father Abraham, "Father!" And he answered, "Yes, my son." And he said, "Here are the firestone and the wood; but where is the sheep for the burnt offering?" 8And Abraham said, "God will see to the sheep for His burnt offering, my son." And the two of them walked on together.

9They arrived at the place of which God had told him. Abraham built an altar there; he laid out the wood; he bound his son Isaac; he laid him on the altar, on top of the wood. 10And Abraham picked up the knife to slay his son. 11Then an angel of the Lord called to him from heaven; "Abraham! Abraham!" And he answered, "Here I am." 12And he said, "Do not raise your hand against the boy, or do anything to him. For now I know that you fear God, since you have not withheld your son, your favored one, from Me." 13When Abraham looked up, his eye fell upon a ram, caught in the thicket by its horns. So Abraham went and took the ram and offered it up as a burnt offering in place of his son. 14And Abraham named that site Adonai-yireh, whence the present saying, "On the mount of the Lord there is vision."

15The angel of the Lord called to Abraham a second time from heaven, 16and said, "By Myself I swear, the Lord declares: Because you have done this and have not withheld your son, your favored one, 17I will bestow My blessing upon you and make your descendants as numerous as the stars of heaven and the sands on the seashore; and your descendants shall seize the gates of their foes. 18All the nations of the earth shall bless themselves by your descendants, because you have obeyed My command." 19Abraham then returned to his servants, and they departed together for Beer-sheba; and Abraham stayed in Beer-sheba.

20Some time later, Abraham was told, "Milcah too has borne children to your brother Nahor: 21Uz the first-born, and Buz his brother, and Kemuel the father of Aram; 22and Chesed, Hazo, Pildash, Jidlaph, and Bethuel"—23Bethuel being the father of Rebekah. These eight Milcah bore to Nahor, Abraham's brother. 24And his concubine, whose name was Reumah, also bore children: Tebah, Gaham, Tahash, and Maacah.

23 Sarah's lifetime—the span of Sarah's life—came to one hundred and twenty-seven years. 2Sarah died in Kiriath-arba—now Hebron—in the land of Canaan; and Abraham proceeded to mourn for Sarah and to bewail her. 3Then Abraham rose from beside his dead, and spoke to the Hittites, saying, 4"I am a resident alien among you; sell me a burial site among you, that I may remove my dead for burial." 5And the Hittites replied to Abraham, saying to him, 6"Hear us, my lord: you are the elect of God among us. Bury your dead in the choicest of our burial places; none of us will withhold his burial place from you for burying your dead." 7Thereupon Abraham bowed low to the people of the land, the Hittites, 8and he said to them, "If it is your wish that I remove my dead for burial, you must agree to intercede for me with Ephron son of Zohar. 9Let him sell me the cave of Machpelah that he owns, which is at the edge of his land. Let him sell it to me, at the full price, for a burial site in your midst."

10Ephron was present among the Hittites; so Ephron the Hittite answered Abraham in the hearing of the Hittites, all who entered the gate of his town, saying, 11"No, my lord, hear me: I give you the field and I give you the cave that is in it; I give it to you in the presence of my people. Bury your dead." 12Then Abraham bowed low before the people of the land, 13and spoke to Ephron in the hearing of the people of the land, saying, "If only you would hear me out! Let me pay the price of the land; accept it from me, that I may bury my dead there." 14And Ephron replied to Abraham, saying to him, 15"My lord, do hear me! A piece of land worth four hundred shekels of silver—what is that between you and me? Go and bury your dead." 16Abraham accepted Ephron's terms. Abraham paid out to Ephron the money that he had named in the hearing of the Hittites—four hundred shekels of silver at the going merchants' rate.

17So Ephron's land in Machpelah, near Mamre—the field with its cave and all the trees anywhere within the confines of that field—passed 18to Abraham as his possession, in the presence of the Hittites, of all who entered the gate of his town. 19And then Abraham buried his wife Sarah in the cave of the field of Machpelah, facing Mamre—now Hebron—in the land of Canaan. 20Thus the field with its cave passed from the Hittites to Abraham, as a burial site.

24 Abraham was now old, advanced in years, and the Lord had blessed Abraham in all things. 2And Abraham said to the senior servant of his household, who had charge of all that he owned, "Put your hand under my thigh 3and I will make you swear by the Lord, the God of heaven and the God of the earth, that you will not take a wife for my son from the daughters of the Canaanites among whom I dwell, 4but will go to the land of my birth and get a wife for my son Isaac." 5And the servant said to him, "What if the woman does not consent to follow me to this land, shall I then take your son back to the land from which you came?" 6Abraham answered him, "On no account must you take my son back there! 7The Lord, the God of heaven, who took me from my father's house and from my native land, who promised me on oath, saying, 'I will assign this land to your offspring'—He will send His angel before you, and you will get a wife for my son from there. 8And if the woman does not consent to follow you, you shall then be clear of this oath to me; but do not take my son back there." 9So the servant put his hand under the thigh of his master Abraham and swore to him as bidden.

10Then the servant took ten of his master's camels and set out, taking with him all the bounty of his master; and he made his way to Aramnaharaim, to the city of Nahor. 11He made the camels kneel down by the well outside the city, at evening time, the time when women come out to draw water. 12And he said, "Oh Lord, God of my master Abraham, grant me good fortune this day, and deal graciously with my master Abraham: [13]Here I stand by the spring as the daughters of the townsmen come out to draw water; [14]let the maiden to whom I say, 'Please, lower your jar that I may drink,' and who replies, 'Drink, and I will also water your camels'—let her be the one whom You have decreed for Your servant Isaac. Thereby shall I know that You have dealt graciously with my master."

[15]He had scarcely finished speaking, when Rebekah, who was born to Bethuel, the son of Milcah the wife of Abraham's brother Nahor, came out with her jar on her shoulder. [16]The maiden was very beautiful, a virgin whom no man had known. She went down to the spring, filled her jar, and came up. [17]The servant ran toward her and said, "Please, let me sip a little water from your jar." [18]"Drink, my lord," she said, and she quickly lowered her jar upon her hand and let him drink. [19]When she had let him drink his fill, she said, "I will also draw for your camels, until they finish drinking." [20]Quickly emptying her jar into the trough, she ran back to the well to draw, and she drew for all his camels.

[21]The man, meanwhile, stood gazing at her, silently wondering whether the Lord had made his errand successful or not. [22]When the camels had finished drinking, the man took a gold nose-ring weighing a half-shekel, and two gold bands for her arms, ten shekels in weight. [23]"Pray tell me," he said, "whose daughter are you? Is there room in your father's house for us to spend the night?" [24]She replied, "I am the daughter of Bethuel the son of Milcah, whom she bore to Nahor." [25]And she went on, "There is plenty of straw and feed at home, and also room to spend the night." [26]The man bowed low in homage to the Lord [27]and said, "Blessed be the Lord, the God of my master Abraham, who has not withheld His steadfast faithfulness from my master. For I have been guided on my errand by the Lord, to the house of my master's kinsmen."

[28]The maiden ran and told all this to her mother's household. [29]Now Rebekah had a brother whose name was Laban. Laban ran out to the man at the spring—[30]when he saw the nose-ring and the bands on his sister's arms, and when he heard his sister Rebekah say, "Thus the man spoke to me." He went up to the man, who was still standing beside the camels at the spring. [31]"Come in, O blessed of the Lord," he said, "why do you remain outside, when I have made ready the house and a place for the camels?" [32]So the man entered the house, and the camels were unloaded. The camels were given straw and feed, and water was brought to bathe his feet and the feet of the men with him. [33]But when food was set before him, he said, "I will not eat until I have told my tale." He said, "Speak, then."

[34]"I am Abraham's servant," he began. [35]"The Lord has greatly blessed my master, and he has become rich: He has given him sheep and cattle, silver and gold, male and females slaves, camels and asses. [36]And Sarah, my master's wife, bore my master a son in her old age, and he has assigned to him everything he owns. [37]Now my master made me swear, saying, 'You shall not get a wife for my son from the daughters of the Canaanites in whose land I dwell; [38]but you shall go to my father's house, and my kindred, and get a wife for my son.' [39]And I said to my master, 'What if the woman does not follow me?' [40]He replied to me, 'The Lord, whose ways I have followed, will send His angel with you and make your errand successful; and you will get a wife for my son from my kindred, from my father's house. [41]Thus only shall you be freed from my adjuration: if, when you come to my kindred, they refuse you—only then shall you be freed from my adjuration.'

[42]"I came today to the spring, and I said: O Lord, God of my master Abraham, if You would indeed grant success to the errand on which I am engaged! [43]As I stand by the spring of water, let the young woman who comes out to draw and to whom I say, 'Please, let me drink a little water from your jar,' [44]and who answers, 'You may drink, and I will also draw for your camels'—let her be the wife whom the Lord has decreed for my master's son.' [45]I had scarcely finished praying in my heart, when Rebekah came out with her jar on her shoulder, and went down to the spring and drew. And I said to her, 'Please give me a drink.' [46]She quickly lowered her jar and said, 'Drink, and I will also water your camels.' So I drank, and she also watered the camels. [47]I inquired of her, 'Whose daughter are you?' And she said, 'The daughter of Bethuel, son of Nahor, whom Milcah bore to him.' And I put the ring on her nose and the bands on her arms. [48]Then I bowed low in homage to the Lord and blessed the Lord, the God of my master Abraham, who led me on the right way to get the daughter of my

master's brother for his son. [49]And now, if you mean to treat my master with true kindness, tell me; and if not, tell me also, that I may turn right or left."

[50]Then Laban and Bethuel answered, "The matter was decreed by the Lord; we cannot speak to you bad or good. [51]Here is Rebekah before you; take her and go, and let her be a wife to your master's son, as the Lord has spoken." [52]When Abraham's servant heard these words, he bowed low to the ground before the Lord. [53]The servant brought out objects of silver and gold, and garments, and gave them to Rebekah; and he gave presents to her brother and her mother. [54]Then he and the men with him ate and drank, and they spent the night. When they arose next morning, he said, "Give me leave to go to my master." [55]But her brother and her mother said, "Let the maiden remain with us some ten days; then you may go." [56]He said to them, "Do not delay me, now that the Lord has made my errand successful. Give me leave that I may go to my master." [57]And they said, "Let us call the girl and ask for her reply." [58]They called Rebekah and said to her, "Will you go with this man?" And she said, "I will." [59]So they sent off their sister Rebekah and her nurse along with Abraham's servant and his men. [60]And they blessed Rebekah and said to her,

"O sister!
May you grow
Into thousands of myriads;
May your offspring seize
The gates of their foes."

[61]Then Rebekah and her maids arose, mounted the camels, and followed the man. So the servant took Rebekah and went his way.

[62]Isaac had just come back from the vicinity of Beer-lahai-roi, for he was settled in the region of the Negeb. [63]And Isaac went out walking in the field toward evening and, looking up, he saw camels approaching. [64]Raising her eyes, Rebekah saw Isaac. She alighted from the camel [65]and said to the servant, "Who is that man walking in the field toward us?" And the servant said, "That is my master." So she took her veil and covered herself. [66]The servant told Isaac all the things that he had done. [67]Isaac then brought her into the tent of his mother Sarah, and he took Rebekah as his wife. Isaac loved her, and thus found comfort after his mother's death.

25 Abraham took another wife, whose name was Keturah. [2]She bore him Zimran, Jokshan, Medan, Midian, Ishbak, and Shuah. [3]Jokshan begot Sheba and Dedan. The descendants of Dedan were the Asshurim, the Letushim, and the Leummim. [4]The descendants of Midian were Ephah, Epher, Enoch, Abida, and Eldaah. All these were descendants of Keturah. [5]Abraham willed all that he owned to Isaac; [6]but to Abraham's sons by concubines Abraham gave gifts while he was still living, and he sent them away from his son Isaac eastward, to the land of the East.

[7]This was the total span of Abraham's life: one hundred and seventy-five years. [8]And Abraham breathed his last, dying at a good ripe age, old and contented; and he was gathered to his kin. [9]His sons Isaac and Ishmael buried him in the cave of Machpelah, in the field of Ephron son of Zohar the Hittite, facing Mamre, [10]the field that Abraham had bought from the Hittites; there Abraham was buried, and Sarah his wife. [11]After the death of Abraham, God blessed his son Isaac. And Isaac settled near Beer-lahai-roi.

[12]This is the line of Ishmael, Abraham's son, whom Hagar the Egyptian, Sarah's slave, bore to Abraham. [13]These are the names of the sons of Ishmael, by their names, in order of their birth: Nebaioth, the first-born of Ishmael, Kedar, Adbeel, Mibsam, [14]Mishma, Dumah, Massa, [15]Hadad, Tema, Jetur, Naphish, and Kedmah. [16]These are the sons of Ishmael and these are their names by their villages and by their encampments: twelve chieftains of as many tribes.—[17]These were the years of the life of Ishmael: one hundred and thirty-seven years; then he breathed his last and died, and was gathered to his kin.—[18]They dwelt from Havilah, by Shur, which is cose to Egypt, all the way to Asshur; they camped alongside all their kinsmen.

[19]This is the story of Isaac, son of Abraham. Abraham begot Isaac. [20]Isaac was forty years old when he took to wife Rebekah, daughter of Bethuel the Aramean of Paddan-aram, sister of Laban the Aramean. [21]Isaac pleaded with the Lord

on behalf of his wife, because she was barren; and the Lord responded to his plea, and his wife Rebekah conceived. 22But the children struggled in her womb, and she said, "If so, why do I exist?" She went to inquire of the Lord, 23and the Lord answered her,

> "Two nations are in your womb,
> Two separate peoples shall issue from your body;
> One people shall be mightier than the other,
> And the older shall serve the younger."

24When her time to give birth was at hand, there were twins in her womb. 25The first one emerged red, like a hairy mantle all over; so they named him Esau. 26Then his brother emerged, holding on to the heel of Esau; so they named him Jacob. Isaac was sixty years old when they were born.

27When the boys grew up, Esau became a skillful hunter, a man of the outdoors; but Jacob was a mild man who stayed in camp. 28Isaac favored Esau because he had a taste for game; but Rebekah favored Jacob. 29Once when Jacob was cooking a stew, Esau came in from the open, famished. 30And Esau said to Jacob, "Give me some of that red stuff to gulp down, for I am famished"—which is why he was named Edom. 31Jacob said, "First sell me your birthright." 32And Esau said, "I am at the point of death, so of what use is my birthright to me?" But Jacob said, "Swear to me first." 33So he swore to him, and sold his birthright to Jacob. 34Jacob then gave Esau bread and lentil stew; he ate and drank, and he rose and went away. Thus did Esau spurn the birthright.

We have included in here a summary of the intervening chapters so you may follow the story line.

SUMMARY OF GENESIS 26–50

The story of **Isaac,** son of Abraham, begins with verse 17 of chapter 25. Isaac's wife, Rebekah, is at first barren but finally gives birth to twin sons, Jacob and Esau. The order in which these two boys emerge from the womb becomes important. Esau is the "first born." We learn that Isaac favors Esau and Rebekah favors Jacob. The chapter closes with the story of Esau selling his birthright to Jacob for a pot of stew!

Chapter 26 tells of Isaac moving his people to the land of the Philistines where he initially passes Rebekah off as his sister. He prospers there and the Philistines become jealous, but a peaceful covenant is negotiated. When Isaac is old and blind, Jacob, at the suggestion of his mother, Rebekah, pretends to be Esau and receives the blessing of the first born from his father (27:28). When Esau finds out about this he is enraged. Subsequently Jacob is told to "go east" (back to the land of Ur) to Rebekah's brother, Laban, where he should find a wife. We now move on to the story of **Jacob.**

Enroute to the East Jacob has a dream in which he receives a promise from God. When he awakes he declares the place holy, renames it Bethel, and sets up a pillar (28:10). Chapters 29–32 tell of Jacob's life and "adventures" in the east. He is welcomed by his uncle and agrees to work for him for seven years to win the hand of his daughter, Rachel. When the wedding night arrives, he finds he has been tricked into marrying the older sister, Leah. He works another seven years and is finally given Rachel as wife. There is competition between the two women as to who will bear Jacob the most sons. Leah produces six sons and one daughter, Dinah. Rachel has difficulty conceiving but finally gives birth to **Joseph,** who will be the featured player in the story of the next generation. Jacob also has two concubines, Bilah and Zilphah.

Finally, Jacob tells his father-in-law that he wishes to return to his family in Canaan. They seem to arrive at a fair settlement regarding the distribution of property, but in the end Laban tries again to trick Jacob. Finally, Jacob, with his herds and family, departs.

Jacob sends ahead messages to his brother Esau announcing his return and sending peace offerings. Before they meet, Jacob, has another dream (32:23) in which he wrestles with "a man" all night. Jacob's hip socket is wrenched. From that time forward he walks with a limp, which earns him the name "Israel." This means he has striven with God and prevailed. Esau and Jacob are reunited and all is well, but Jacob with his tribe goes his own way , which is to Bethel. The question is raised as to whether they are fleeing contamination from alien gods. Rachel gives birth to her second son, Benjamin and dies. Together with his sons by Leah, Jacob has twelve sons. Jacob is reunited with his father Isaac (35:27), who soon dies (he is 180 years old) and is buried by both sons. Chapter 36 gives us the line of Esau, who is the father of the Edomites.

Chapter 37 begins the story of **Joseph** who is his father Jacob's favorite son and therefore causes jealousy among the brothers. They sell him into slavery in Egypt and bring home to Joseph his cloak stained with animal blood to convince him that Joseph is dead.

In Egypt Joseph is first favored by the Egyptian, Potiphar, who takes him into his household and puts him in charge of all his goods. But he runs afoul of Potiphar's wife when he refuses her sexual advances. He is thrown in prison. While in prison he demonstrates his ability to know the future through his dreams. This eventually takes him out of prison and into the house of the Pharaoh where he interprets the Pharaoh's dreams. He predicts seven years of great abundance followed by seven years of great famine. The Pharaoh puts him in charge of planning for this and hence avoiding disaster in Egypt. He manages this quite well and in the years of the famine Egypt is well fed. But the rest of the world is not, and this brings his brothers to Egypt in search of famine relief. They naturally appeal to Joseph, whom they do not recognize. He "toys" with them for awhile, but he insists that they return to Canaan and bring back his brother Benjamin. They are reluctant to do so because he is the only remaining comfort to the elderly Jacob. The Hebrews immigrate to Egypt because the Pharaoh has offered them land in Goshen because "all shepherds are abhorrent to Egyptians." Jacob lives seventeen more years in Egypt, dies, and is embalmed. The brothers return the body to Canaan, where he is buried with great pomp and ceremony. Genesis concludes with Joseph's death. He too is embalmed but is not taken to Canaan immediately, but makes his (older) brothers promise to take him "When God has taken notice of you. . . ." 50:25.

EXODUS

1 These are the names of the sons of Israel who came to Egypt with Jacob, each coming with his household: [2]Reuben, Simeon, Levi, and Judah; [3]Issachar, Zebulun, and Benjamin; [4]Dan and Naphtali, Gad and Asher. [5]The total number of persons that were of Jacob's issue came to seventy, Joseph being already in Egypt. [6]Joseph died, and all his brothers, and all that generation. [7]But the Israelites were fertile and prolific; they multiplied and increased very greatly, so that the land was filled with them.

[8]A new king arose over Egypt who did not know Joseph. [9]And he said to his people, "Look, the Israelite people are much too numerous for us. [10]Let us deal shrewdly with them, so that they may not increase; otherwise in the event of war they may join our enemies in fighting against us and rise from the ground." [11]So they set taskmasters over them to oppress them with forced labor; and they built garrison cities for Pharaoh: Pithom and Raamses. [12]But the more they were oppressed, the more they increased and spread out, so that the [Egyptians] came to dread the Israelites.

[13]The Egyptians ruthlessly imposed upon the Israelites [14]the various labors that they made them perform. Ruthlessly they made life bitter for them with harsh labor at mortar and bricks and with all sorts of tasks in the field.

[15]The king of Egypt spoke to the Hebrew midwives, one of whom was named Shiphrah and the other Puah, [16]saying, "When you deliver the Hebrew women, look at the birthstool: if it is a boy, kill him; if it is a girl, let her live." [17]The midwives, fearing God, did not do as the king of Egypt had told them; they let the boys live. [18]So the king of Egypt summoned the midwives and said to them, "Why have you done this thing, letting the boys live?" [19]The midwives said to Pharaoh, "Because the Hebrew women are not like the Egyptian women: they are vigorous. Before the midwife can come to them, they have given birth." [20]And God dealt well with the midwives; and the people multiplied and increased

greatly. [21]And because the midwives feared God, He established households for them. [22]Then Pharaoh charged all his people, saying, "Every boy that is born you shall throw into the Nile, but let every girl live."

2 A certain man of the house of Levi went and married a Levite woman. [2]The woman conceived and bore a son; and when she saw how beautiful he was, she hid him for three months. [3]When she could hide him no longer, she got a wicker basket for him and caulked it with bitumen and pitch. She put the child into it and placed it among the reeds by the bank of the Nile. [4]And his sister stationed herself at a distance, to learn what would befall him.

[5]The daughter of Pharaoh came down to bathe in the Nile, while her maidens walked along the Nile. She spied the basket among the reeds and sent her slave girl to fetch it. [6]When she opened it, she saw that it was a child, a boy crying She took pity on it and said, "This must be a Hebrew child." [7]Then his sister said to Pharaoh's daughter, "Shall I go and get you a Hebrew nurse to suckle the child for you?" [8]And Pharaoh's daughter answered, "Yes." So the girl went and called the child's mother. [9]And Pharaoh's daughter said to her, "Take this child and nurse it for me, and I will pay your wages." So the woman took the child and nursed it. [10]When the child grew up, she brought him to Pharaoh's daughter, who made him her son. She named him Moses, explaining, "I drew him out of the water."

[11]Some time after that, when Moses had grown up, he went out to his kinfolk and witnessed their labors. He saw an Egyptian beating a Hebrew, one of his kinsmen. [12]He turned this way and that and, seeing no one about, he struck down the Egyptian and hid him in the sand. [13]When he went out the next day, he found two Hebrews fighting; so he said to the offender, "Why do you strike your fellow?" [14]He retorted, "Who made you chief and ruler over us? Do you mean to kill me as you killed the Egyptian?" Moses was frightened, and thought: Then the matter is known! [15]When Pharaoh learned of the matter, he sought to kill Moses; but Moses fled from Pharaoh. He arrived in the land of Midian, and sat down beside a well.

[16]Now the priest of Midian had seven daughters. They came to draw water, and filled the troughs to water their father's flock; [17]but shepherds came and drove them off. Moses rose to their defense, and he watered their flock. [18]When they returned to their father Reuel, he said, "How is it that you have come back so soon today?" [19]They answered," An Egyptian rescued us from the shepherds; he even drew water for us and watered the flock." [20]He said to his daughters, "Where is he then? Why did you leave the man? Ask him in to break bread." [21]Moses consented to stay with the man, and he gave Moses his daughter Zipporah as wife. [22]She bore a son whom he named Gershom, for he said, "I have been a stranger in a foreign land."

[23]A long time after that, the king of Egypt died. The Israelites were groaning under the bondage and cried out; and their cry for help from the bondage rose up to God. [24]God heard their moaning, and God remembered His covenant with Abraham and Isaac and Jacob. God looked upon the Israelites, and God took notice of them.

3 Now Moses, tending the flock of his father-in-law Jethro, the priest of Midian, drove the flock into the wilderness, and came to Horeb, the mountain of God. [2]An angel of the Lord appeared to him in a blazing fire out of a bush. He gazed, and there was a bush all aflame, yet the bush was not consumed. [3]Moses said, "I must turn aside to look at this marvelous sight; why doesn't the bush burn up?" [4]When the Lord saw that he had turned aside to look, God called to him out of the bush: "Moses! Moses!" He answered, "Here I am." [5]And He said, "Do not come closer. Remove your sandals from your feet, for the place on which you stand is holy ground. [6]I am," He said, "the God of your father, the God of Abraham, the God of Isaac, and the God of Jacob." And Moses hid his face, for he was afraid to look at God.

[7]And the Lord continued, "I have marked well the plight of My people in Egypt and have heeded their outcry because of their taskmasters; yes, I am mindful of their sufferings. [8]I have come down to rescue them from the Egyptians and to bring them out of that land to a good and spacious land, a land flowing with milk and honey, the region of the Canaanites, the Hittites, the Amorites, the Perizzites, the Hivites, and the Jebusites. [9]Now the cry of the Israelites has reached Me; moreover, I have seen how the Egyptians oppress them. [10]Come,

therefore, I will send you to Pharaoh, and you shall free My people, the Israelites, from Egypt."

[11]But Moses said to God, "Who am I that I should go to Pharaoh and free the Israelites from Egypt?" [12]And He said, "I will be with you; that shall be your sign that it was I who sent you. And when you have freed the people from Egypt, you shall worship God at this mountain."

[13]Moses said to God, "When I come to the Israelites and say to them 'The God of your fathers has sent me to you,' and they ask me, 'What is His name?' whet shall I say to them?" [14]And God said to Moses, "Ehyeh-Asher-Ehyeh." He continued, "Thus shall you say to the Israelites, 'Ehyeh sent me to you.'" [15]And God said further to Moses, "Thus shall you speak to the Israelites: The Lord, the God of your fathers, the God of Abraham, the God of Isaac, and the God of Jacob, has sent me to you:

This shall be My name forever,
This My appellation for all eternity.

[16]"Go and assemble the elders of Israel and say to them: the Lord, the God of your fathers, the God of Abraham, Isaac, and Jacob, has appeared to me and said, 'I have taken note of you and of what is being done to you in Egypt, [17]and I have declared: I will take you out of the misery of Egypt to the land of the Canaanites, the Hittites, the Amorites, the Perizzites, the Hivites, and the Jebusites, to a land flowing with milk and honey.' [18]They will listen to you; then you shall go with the elders of Israel to the king of Egypt and you shall say to him, 'The Lord, the God of the Hebrews, manifested Himself to us. Now therefore, let us go a distance of three days into the wilderness to sacrifice to the Lord our God.' [19]Yet I know that the king of Egypt will let you go only because of a greater might. [20]So I will stretch out My hand and smite Egypt with various wonders which I will work upon them; after that he shall let you go. [21]And I will dispose the Egyptians favorably toward this people, so that when you go, you will not go away empty-handed. [22]Each woman shall borrow from her neighbor and the lodger in her house objects of silver and gold, and clothing, and you shall put these on your sons and daughters, thus stripping the Egyptians."

4 But Moses spoke up and said, "What if they do not believe me and do not listen to me, but say: The Lord did not appear to you?" [2]The Lord said to him, "What is that in your hand?" And he replied, "A rod." [3]He said, "Cast it on the ground." He cast it on the ground and it becarme a snake; and Moses recoiled from it. [4]Then the Lord said to Moses, "Put out your hand and grasp it by the tail"—he put out his hand and seized it, and it became a rod in his hand—[5]"that they may believe that the Lord, the God of their fathers, the God of Abraham, the God of Isaac, and the God of Jacob, did appear to you."

[6]The Lord said to him further, "Put your hand into your bosom." He put his hand into his bosom; and when he took it out, his hand was encrusted with snowy scales! [7]And He said, "Put your hand back into your bosom." He put his hand back into his bosom; and when he took it out of his bosom, there it was again like the rest of his body.—[8]"And if they do not believe you or pay heed to the first sign, they will believe the second. [9]And if they are not convinced by both these signs and still do not heed you, take some water from the Nile and pour it on the dry ground, and it—the water that you take from the Nile—will turn to blood on the dry ground."

[10]But Moses said to the Lord, "Please, O Lord, I have never been a man of words, either in times past or now that You have spoken to Your servant; I am slow of speech and slow of tongue." [11]And the Lord said to him, "Who gives man speech? Who makes him dumb or deaf, seeing or blind? Is it not I, the Lord? [12]Now go, and I will be with you as you speak and will instruct you what to say." [13]But he said, "Please, O Lord, make someone else Your agent." [14] The Lord became angry with Moses, and He said, "There is your brother Aaron the Levite. He, I know, speaks readily. Even now he is setting out to meet you, and he will be happy to see you. [15]You shall speak to him and put the words in his mouth—I will be with you and with him as you speak, and tell both of you what to do—[16]and he shall speak for you to the people. Thus he shall serve as your spokesman, with you playing the role of God to him, [17]And take with you this rod, with which you shall perform the signs."

[18]Moses went back to this father-in-law Jether and said to him, "Let me go back to my kinsmen in Egypt and see how they are faring." And Jethro said to Moses, "Go in peace."

[19]The Lord said to Moses in Midian, "Go back to Egypt, for all the men who sought to kill you are dead." [20]So Moses took his wife and sons, mounted them on an ass, and went back to the land of Egypt; and Moses took the rod of God with him.

[21]And the Lord said to Moses, "When you return to Egypt, see that you perform before Pharaoh all the marvels that I have put within your power. I, however, will stiffen his heart so that he will not let the people go [22]Then you shall say to Pharaoh, 'Thus says the Lord: Israel is My first-born son. [23]I have said to you, "Let My son go, that he may worship Me," yet you refuse to let him go. Now I will slay your first-born son.'"

[24]At a night encampment on the way, the Lord encountered him and sought to kill him. [25]So Zipporah took a flint and cut off her son's foreskin, and touched his legs with it, saying, "You are truly a bridegroom of blood to me!" [26]And when He let him alone, she added, "A bridegroom of blood because of the circumcision."

[27]The Lord said to Aaron, "Go to meet Moses in the wilderness." He went and met him at the mountain of God, and he kissed him. [28]Moses told Aaron about all the things that the Lord had committed to him and all the signs about which He had instructed him. [29]Then Moses and Aaron went and assembled all the elders of the Israelites. [30]Aaron repeated all the words that the Lord had spoken to Moses, and he performed the signs in the sight of the people, [31]and the people were convinced. When they heard that the Lord had taken note of the Israelites and that He had seen their plight, they bowed low in homage.

5 Afterward Moses and Aaron went and said to Pharaoh, "Thus says the Lord, the God of Israel: Let My people go that they may celebrate a festival for Me in the wilderness." [2]But Pharaoh said, "Who is the Lord that I should heed Him and let Israel go? I do not know the Lord, nor will I let Israel go." [3]They answered, "The God of the Hebrews has manifested Himself to us. Let us go, we pray, a dis-

tance of three days into the wilderness to sacrifice to the Lord our God, lest He strike us with pestilence or sword." [4]But the king of Egypt said to them, "Moses and Aaron, why do you distract the people from their tasks? Get to your labors!" [5]And Pharaoh continued, "The people of the land are already so numerous, and you would have them cease from their labors!"

[6]That same day Pharaoh charged the taskmasters and foremen of the people, saying, [7]"You shall no longer provide the people with straw for making bricks as heretofore; let them go and gather straw for themselves. [8]But impose upon them the same quota of bricks as they have been making heretofore; do not reduce it, for they are shirkers; that is why they cry, 'Let us go and sacrifice to our God!' [9]Let heavier work be laid upon the men; let them keep at it and not pay attention to deceitful promises."

[10]So the taskmasters and foremen of the people went out and said to the people, "Thus says Pharaoh: I will not give you any straw. [11]You must go and get the straw yourselves wherever you can find it; but there shall be no decrease whatever in your work." [12]Then the people scattered throughout the land of Egypt to gather stubble for straw. [13]And the taskmasters pressed them, saying, "You must complete the same work assignment each day as when you had straw." [14]And the foremen of the Israelites, whom Pharaoh's taskmasters had set over them, were beaten. "Why," they were asked, "did you not complete the prescribed amount of bricks, either yesterday or today, as you did before?"

[15]Then the foremen of the Israelites came to Pharaoh and cried: "Why do you deal thus with your servants? [16]No straw is issued to your servants, yet they demand of us: Make bricks! Thus your servants are being beaten, when the fault is with your own people." [17]He replied, "You are shirkers, shirkers! That is why you say, 'Let us go and sacrifice to the Lord.' [18]Be off now to your work! No straw shall be issued to you, but you must produce your quota of bricks!"

[19]Now the foremen of the Israelites found themselves in trouble because of the order, "You must not reduce your daily quantity of bricks." [20]As they left Pharaoh's presence, they came upon Moses and Aaron standing in their path, [21]and they said to them, "May the Lord look upon you and punish you for

making us loathsome to Pharaoh and his courtiers—putting a sword in their hands to slay us." 22Then Moses returned to the Lord and said, "O Lord, why did You bring harm upon this people? Why did You send me? 23Ever since I came to Pharaoh to speak in Your name, he has dealt worse with this people; and still You have not delivered Your people."

6 Then the Lord said to Moses, "You shall soon see what I will do to Pharaoh: he shall let them go because of a greater might; indeed, because of a greater might he shall drive them from his land."

2God spoke to Moses and said to him, "I am the Lord. 3I appeared to Abraham, Isaac, and Jacob as El Shaddai, but I did not make myself known to them by My name [YHWH]. 4I also established My covenant with them, to give them the land of Canaan, the land in which they lived as sojourners. 5I have now heard the moaning of the Israelites because the Egyptians are holding them in bondage, and I have remembered My covenant. 6Say, therefore, to the Israelite people: I am the Lord. I will free you from the labors of the Egyptians and deliver you from their bondage. I will redeem you with an outstretched arm and through extraordinary chastisements. 7And I will take you to be My people, and I will be your God. And you shall know that I, the Lord, am your God who freed you from the labors of the Egyptians. 8I will bring you into the land which I swore to give to Abraham, Isaac, and Jacob, and I will give it to you for a possession, I the Lord." 9But when Moses told this to the Israelites, they would not listen to Moses, their spirits crushed by cruel bondage.

10The Lord spoke to Moses, saying, 11"Go and tell Pharaoh king of Egypt to let the Israelites depart from his land." 12But Moses appealed to the Lord, saying, "The Israelites would not listen to me; how then should Pharaoh heed me, a man of impeded speech!" 13So the Lord spoke to both Moses and Aaron in regard to the Israelites and Pharaoh king of Egypt, instructing them to deliver the Israelites from the land of Egypt.

14The following are the heads of their respective clans.

The sons of Reuben, Israel's first-born: Enoch and Pallu, Hezron and Carmi; those are the families of Reuben. 15The sons of Simeon: Jemuel, Jamin, Ohad, Jachin, Zohar, and Saul the son of a Canaan-ite woman; those are the families of Simeon. 16These are the names of Levi's sons by their lineage: Gershon, Kohath, and Merari; and the span of Levi's life was 137 years. 17The sons of Gershon: Libni and Shimei, by their families. 18The sons of Kohath: Amram, Izhar, Hebron, and Uzziel; and the span of Kohath's life was 133 years. 19The sons of Merari: Mahli and Mushi. These are the families of the Levites by their lineage.

20Amram took to wife his father's sister Jochebed, and she bore him Aaron and Moses; and the span of Amram's life was 137 years. 21The sons of Izhar: Korah, Nepheg, and Zichri. 22The sons of Uzziel: Mishael, Elzaphan, and Sithri. 23Aaron took to wife Elisheba, daughter of Amminadab and sister of Nahshon, and she bore him Nadab and Abihu, Eleazar and Ithamar. 24The sons of Korah: Assir, Elkanah, and Abiasaph. Those are the families of the Korahites. 25And Aaron's son Eleazar took to wife one of Putiel's daughters, and she bore him Phinehas. Those are the heads of the fathers' houses of the Levites by their families.

26It is the same Aaron and Moses to whom the Lord said, "Bring forth the Israelites from the land of Egypt, troop by troop." 27It was they who spoke to Pharaoh king of Egypt to free the Israelites from the Egyptians; these are the same Moses and Aaron. 28For when the Lord spoke to Moses in the land of Egypt 29and the Lord said to Moses, "I am the Lord; speak to Pharaoh king of Egypt all that I will tell you," 30Moses appealed to the Lord, saying, "See, I am of impeded speech; how then should Pharaoh heed me!"

7 The Lord replied to Moses, "See, I place you in the role of God to Pharaoh, with your brother Aaron as your prophet. 2You shall repeat all that I command you, and your brother Aaron shall speak to Pharaoh to let the Israelites depart from his land. 3But I will harden Pharaoh's heart, that I may multiply My signs and marvels in the land of Egypt. 4When Pharaoh does not heed you, I will lay My hand upon Egypt and deliver My ranks, My people the Israelites, from the land of Egypt with extraordinary chastisements. 5And the Egyptians shall know that I am the Lord, when I stretch out My hand over Egypt and bring out the Israelites from their midst." 6This Moses and Aaron did; as the Lord commanded them, so they did. 7Moses was

eighty years old and Aaron eighty-three, when they made their demand on Pharaoh.

8The Lord said to Moses and Aaron, 9"When Pharaoh speaks to you and says, 'Produce your marvel,' you shall say to Aaron, 'Take your rod and cast it down before Pharaoh.' It shall turn into a serpent." 10So Moses and Aaron came before Pharaoh and did just as the Lord had commanded: Aaron cast down his rod in the presence of Pharaoh and his courtiers, and it turned into a serpent. 11Then Pharaoh, for his part, summoned the wise men and the sorcerers; and the Egyptian magicians, in turn, did the same with their spells; 12each cast down his rod, and they turned into serpents. But Aaron's rod swallowed their rods. 13Yet Pharaoh's heart stiffened and he did not heed them, as the Lord had said.

14And the Lord said to Moses, "Pharaoh is stubborn; he refuses to let the people go. 15Go to Pharaoh in the morning, as he is coming out to the water, and station yourself before him at the edge of the Nile, taking with you the rod that turned into a snake. 16And say to him, 'The Lord, the God of the Hebrews, sent me to you to say, "Let My people go that they may worship Me in the wilderness." But you have paid no heed until now. 17Thus says the Lord, "By this you shall know that I am the Lord." See, I shall strike the water in the Nile with the rod that is in my hand, and it will be turned into blood; 18and the fish in the Nile will die. The Nile will stink so that the Egyptians will find it impossible to drink the water of the Nile.'"

19And the Lord said to Moses, "Say to Aaron: Take your rod and hold out your arm over the waters of Egypt—its rivers, its canals, its ponds, all its bodies of water—that they may turn to blood; there shall be blood throughout the land of Egypt, even in vessels of wood and stone." 20Moses and Aaron did just as the Lord commanded: he lifted up the rod and struck the water in the Nile in the sight of Pharaoh and his courtiers, and all the water in the Nile was turned into blood 21and the fish in the Nile died. The Nile stank so that the Egyptians could not drink water from the Nile; and there was blood throughout the land of Egypt. 22But when the Egyptian magicians did the same with their spells, Pharaoh's heart stiffened and he did not heed them—as the Lord had spoken. 23Pharaoh turned and went into his palace, paying no regard even to this. 24And all the Egyptians had to dig round about the Nile for drinking water, because they could not drink the water of the Nile.

25When seven days had passed after the Lord struck the Mile, 26the Lord said to Moses, "Go to Pharaoh and say to him, "Thus says the Lord: Let My people go that they may worship Me. 27If you refuse to let them go, then I will plague your whole country with frogs. 28The Nile shall swarm with frogs, and they shall come up and enter your palace, your bedchamber and your bed, the houses of your courtiers and your people, and your ovens and your kneading bowls. 29The frogs shall come up on you and on your people and on all your courtiers.'"

8 And the Lord said to Moses, "Say to Aaron: Hold out your arm with the rod over the rivers, the canals, and the ponds, and bring up the frogs on the land of Egypt." 2Aaron held out his arm over the waters of Egypt, and the frogs came up and covered the land of Egypt. 3But the magicians did the same with their spells, and brought frogs upon the land of Egypt.

4Then Pharaoh summoned Moses and Aaron and said, "Plead with the Lord to remove the frogs from me and my people, and I will let the people go to sacrifice to the Lord." 5And Moses said to Pharaoh, "You may have this triumph over me: for what time shall I plead in behalf of you and your courtiers and your people, that the frogs be cut off from you and your houses, to remain only in the Nile?" 6"For tomorrow," he replied. And [Moses] said, "As you say—that you may know that there is none like the Lord our God; 7the frogs shall retreat from you and your courtiers and your people; they shall remain only in the Nile." 8Then Moses and Aaron left Pharaoh's presence, and Moses cried out to the Lord in the matter of the frogs which He had inflicted upon Pharaoh. 9And the Lord did as Moses asked; the frogs died out in the houses, the courtyards, and the field. 10And they piled them up in heaps, till the land stank. 11But when Pharaoh saw that there was relief, he became stubborn and would not heed them, as the Lord had spoken.

12Then the Lord said to Moses, "Say to Aaron: Hold out your rod and strike the dust of the earth, and it shall turn to lice throughout the land of Egypt." 13And they did so. Aaron held out his arm with the rod and struck the dust of the earth, and vermin came upon man and beast; all the dust of the earth turned to lice throughout the land of Egypt. [14]The magicians did the like with their spells to produce lice, but they could not. The vermin remained upon man and beast; [15]and the magicians said to Pharaoh, "This is the finger of God!" But Pharaoh's heart stiffened and he would not heed them, as the Lord had spoken.

[16]And the Lord said to Moses, "Early in the morning; present yourself to Pharaoh, as he is coming out to the water, and say to him, 'Thus says the Lord: Let My people go that they may worship Me. [17]For if you do not let My people go, I will let loose swarms of insects against you and your courtiers and your people and your houses; the houses of the Egyptians, and the very ground they stand on, shall be filled with swarms of insects. [18]But on that day I will set apart the region of Goshen, where My people dwell, so that no swarms of insects shall be there, that you may know that I the Lord am in the midst of the land. [19]And I will make a distinction between My people and your people. Tomorrow this sign shall come to pass.'" [20]And the Lord did so. Heavy swarms of insects invaded Pharaoh's palace and the houses of his courtiers; throughout the country of Egypt the land was ruined because of the swarms of insects.

[21]Then Pharaoh summoned Moses and Aaron and said, "Go and sacrifice to your God within the land." [22]But Moses replied, "It would not be right to do this, for what we sacrifice to the Lord our God is untouchable to the Egyptians. If we sacrifice that which is untouchable to the Egyptians before their very eyes, will they not stone us! [23]So we must go a distance of three days into the wilderness and sacrifice to the Lord our God as He may command us." [24]Pharaoh said, "I will let you go to sacrifice to the Lord your God in the wilderness; but do not go very far. Plead, then, for me." [25]And Moses said, "When I leave your presence, I will plead with the Lord that the swarms of insects depart tomorrow from Pharaoh and his courtiers and his people; but let not Pharaoh again act deceitfully, not letting the people go to sacrifice to the Lord."

[26]So Moses left Pharaoh's presence and pleaded with the Lord. [27]And the Lord did as Moses asked: He removed the swarms of insects from Pharaoh, from his courtiers, and from his people; not one

remained. [28]But Pharaoh became stubborn this time also, and would not let the people go.

9 The Lord said to Moses, "Go to Pharaoh and say to him, 'Thus says the Lord, the God of the Hebrews: Let My people go to worship Me. [2]For if you refuse to let them go, and continue to hold them, [3]then the hand of the Lord will strike your livestock in the fields—the horses, the asses, the camels, the cattle, and the sheep—with a very severe pestilence. [4]But the Lord will make a distinction between the livestock of Israel and the livestock of the Egyptians, so that nothing shall die of all that belongs to the Israelites. [5]The Lord has fixed the time: tomorrow the Lord will do this thing in the land.'" [6]And the Lord did so the next day: all the livestock of the Egyptians died, but of the livestock of the Israelites not a beast died. [7]When Pharaoh inquired, he found that not a head of the livestock of Israel had died; yet Pharaoh remained stubborn, and he would not let the people go.

[8]Then the Lord said to Moses and Aaron, "Each of you take handfuls of soot from the kiln, and let Moses throw it toward the sky in the sight of Pharaoh. [9]It shall become a fine dust all over the land of Egypt, and cause an inflammation breaking out in boils on man and beast throughout the land of Egypt." [10]So they took soot of the kiln and appeared before Pharaoh; Moses threw it toward the sky, and it caused an inflammation breaking out in boils on man and beast. [11]The magicians were unable to confront Moses because of the inflammation, for the inflammation afflicted the magicians as well as all the other Egyptians. [12]But the Lord stiffened the heart of Pharaoh, and he would not heed them, just as the Lord had told Moses.

[13]The Lord said to Moses, "Early in the morning present yourself to Pharaoh and say to him, 'Thus says the Lord, the God of the Hebrews: Let My people go to worship Me. [14]For this time I will send all My plagues upon your person, and your courtiers, and your people, in order that you may know that there is none like Me in all the world. [15]I could have stretched forth My hand and stricken you and your people with pestilence, and you would have been effaced from the earth. [16]Nevertheless I have spared you for this purpose: in order to show you My power, and in order that My fame may resound

throughout the world. ¹⁷Yet you continue to thwart My people, and do not let them go! ¹⁸This time tomorrow I will rain down a very heavy hail, such as has not been in Egypt from the day it was founded until now. ¹⁹Therefore, order your livestock and everything you have in the open brought under shelter; every man and beast that is found outside, not having been brought indoors, shall perish when the hail comes down upon them!'" ²⁰Those among Pharaoh's courtiers who feared the Lord's word brought their slaves and livestock indoors to safety; ²¹But those who paid no regard to the word of the Lord left their slaves and livestock in the open.

²²The Lord said to Moses, "Hold out your arm toward the sky that hail may fall on all the land of Egypt, upon man and beast and all the grasses of the field in the land of Egypt." ²³So Moses held out his rod toward the sky, and the Lord sent thunder and hail, and fire streamed down to the ground, as the Lord rained down hail upon the land of Egypt. ²⁴The hail was very heavy—fire flashing in the midst of the hail—such as had not fallen on the land of Egypt since it had become a nation. ²⁵Throughout the land of Egypt the hail struck down all that were in the open, both man and beast; the hail also struck down all the grasses of the field and shattered all the trees of the field. ²⁶Only in the region of Goshen, where the Israelites were, there was no hail.

²⁷Thereupon Pharaoh sent for Moses and Aaron and said to them, "I stand guilty this time. The Lord is in the right, and I and my people are in the wrong. ²⁸Plead with the Lord that there may be an end of God's thunder and of hail. I will let you go; you need stay no longer." ²⁹Moses said to him, "As I go out of the city, I shall spread out my hands to the Lord; the thunder will cease and the hail will fall no more, so that you may know that the earth is the Lord's. ³⁰But I know that you and your courtiers do not yet fear the Lord God."—³¹Now the flax and barley were ruined, for the barley was in the ear and the flax was in the bud; ³²but the wheat and the emmer were not hurt, for they ripen late.—³³Leaving Pharaoh, Moses went outside the city and spread out his hands to the Lord: the thunder and the hail ceased, and no rain came pouring down upon the earth. ³⁴But when Pharaoh saw that the rain and the hail and the thunder had ceased, he became stubborn and reverted to his guilty ways, as did his courtiers. ³⁵So Pharaoh's heart stiffened and

he would not let the Israelites go, just as the Lord had foretold through Moses.

10 Then the Lord said to Moses, "Go to Pharaoh. For I have hardened his heart and the hearts of his courtiers, in order that I may display these My signs among them, ²and that you may recount in the hearing of your sons and of your sons' sons how I made a mockery of the Egyptians and how I displayed My signs among them—in order that you may know that I am the Lord." ³So Moses and Aaron went to Pharaoh and said to him, "Thus says the Lord, the God of the Hebrews, 'How long will you refuse to humble yourself before Me? Let My people go that they may worship Me. ⁴For if you refuse to let My people go, tomorrow I will bring locusts on your territory. ⁵They shall cover the surface of the land, so that no one will be able to see the land. They shall devour the surviving remnant that was left to you after the hail; and they shall eat away all your trees that grow in the field. ⁶Moreover, they shall fill your palaces and the houses of all your courtiers and of all the Egyptians—something that neither your fathers nor fathers' fathers have seen from the day they appeared on earth to this day.'" With that he turned and left Pharaoh's presence.

⁷Pharaoh's courtiers said to him, "How long shall this one be a snare to us? Let the men go to worship the Lord their God! Are you not yet aware that Egypt is lost?" ⁸So Moses and Aaron were brought back to Pharaoh and he said to them, "Go, worship the Lord your God! Who are the ones to go?" ⁹Moses replied, "We will all go, young and old: we will go with our sons and daughters, our flocks and herds; for we must observe the Lord's festival." ¹⁰But he said to them, "The Lord be with you the same as I mean to let your children go with you! Clearly, you are bent on mischief. ¹¹No! You menfolk go and worship the Lord, since that is what you want." And they were expelled from Pharaoh's presence.

¹²Then the Lord said to Moses, "Hold out your arm over the land of Egypt for the locusts, that they may come upon the land of Egypt and eat up all the grasses in the land, whatever the hail has left." ¹³So Moses held out his rod over the land of Egypt, and the Lord drove an east wind over the land all that day and all night; and when morning came, the east wind had brought the locusts. ¹⁴Locusts invaded all

the land of Egypt and settled within all the territory of Egypt in a thick mass; never before had there been so many, nor will there ever be so many again. [15]They hid all the land from view, and the land was darkened; and they ate up all the grasses of the field and all the fruit of the trees which the hail had left, so that nothing green was left, of tree or grass of the field, in all the land of Egypt.

[16]Pharaoh hurriedly summoned Moses and Aaron and said, "I stand guilty before the Lord your God and before you. [17]Forgive my offense just this once, and plead with the Lord your God that He but remove this death from me." [18]So he left Pharaoh's presence and pleaded with the Lord. [19]The Lord caused a shift to a very strong west wind, which lifted the locusts and hurled them into the Sea of Reeds; not a single locust remained in all the territory of Egypt. [20]But the Lord stiffened Pharaoh's heart, and he would not let the Israelites go.

[21]Then the Lord said to Moses, "Hold out your arm toward the sky that there may be darkness upon the land of Egypt, a darkness that can be touched." [22]Moses held out his arm toward the sky and thick darkness descended upon all the land of Egypt for three days. [23]People could not see one another, and for three days no one could get up from where he was; but all the Israelites enjoyed light in their dwellings.

[24]Pharaoh then summoned Moses and said, "Go, worship the Lord! Only your flocks and your herds shall be left behind; even your children may go with you." [25]But Moses said, "You yourself must provide us with sacrifices and burnt offerings to offer up to the Lord our God; [26]our own livestock, too, shall go along with us—not a hoof shall remain behind: for we must select from it for the worship of the Lord our God; and we shall not know with what we are to worship the Lord until we arrive there." [27]But the Lord stiffened Pharaoh's heart and he would not agree to let them go. [28]Pharaoh said to him, "Be gone from me! Take care not to see me again, for the moment you look upon my face you shall die." [29]And Moses replied, "You have spoken rightly. I shall not see your face again!"

11 And the Lord said to Moses, "I will bring but one more plague upon Pharaoh and upon Egypt; after that he shall let you go from here; indeed, when he lets you go, he will drive you out of here one and all. [2]Tell the people to borrow, each man from his neighbor and each woman from hers, objects of silver and gold." [3]The Lord disposed the Egyptians favorably toward the people. Moreover, Moses himself was much esteemed in the land of Egypt, among Pharaoh's courtiers and among the people.

[4]Moses said, "Thus says the Lord: Toward midnight I will go forth among the Egyptians, [5]and every first-born in the land of Egypt shall die, from the first-born of Pharaoh who sits on his throne to the first-born of the slave girl who is behind the millstones; and all the first-born of the cattle. [6]And there shall be a loud cry in all the land of Egypt, such as has never been or will ever be again; [7]but not a dog shall snarl at any of the Israelites, at man or beast—in order that you may know that the Lord makes a distinction between Egypt and Israel. [8]Then all these courtiers of yours shall come down to me and bow low to me, saying, 'Depart, you and all the people who follow you!' after that I will depart." And he left Pharaoh's presence in hot anger.

[9]Now the Lord had said to Moses, "Pharaoh will not heed you, in order that My marvels may be multiplied in the land of Egypt." [10]Moses and Aaron had performed all these marvels before Pharaoh, but the Lord had stiffened the heart of Pharaoh so that he would not let the Israelites go from his land.

12 The Lord said to Moses and Aaron in the land of Egypt: [2]This month shall mark for you the beginning of the months; it shall be the first of the months of the year for you. [3]Speak to the whole community of Israel and say that on the tenth of this month each of them shall take a lamb to a family, a lamb to a household. [4]But if the household is too small for a lamb, let him share one with a neighbor who dwells nearby, in proportion to the number of persons: you shall contribute for the lamb according to what each household will eat. [5]Your lamb shall be without blemish, a yearling male; you may take it from the sheep or from the goats. [6]You shall keep watch over it until the fourteenth day of this month; and all the assembled congregation of the Israelites shall slaughter it at twilight. [7]They shall take some of the blood and put it on the two doorposts and the lintel of the houses in which they are to eat it. [8]They shall eat the flesh that same night; they shall eat it roasted over the fire, with unleavened bread and with bitter herbs. 9Do not eat any of it raw, or cooked in any way with water, but roasted—head, legs, and entrails—over the fire. 10You shall not leave any of it over until morning; if any of it is left until morning, you shall burn it.

11This is how you shall eat it: your loins girded, your sandals on your feet, and your staff in your hand; and you shall eat it hurriedly: it is a passover offering to the Lord. 12For that night I will go through the land of Egypt and strike down every first-born in the land of Egypt, both man and beast; and I will mete out punishments to all the gods of Egypt, I the Lord. 13And the blood on the houses where you are staying shall be a sign for you: when I see the blood I will pass over you, so that no plague will destroy you when I strike the land of Egypt.

14This day shall be to you one of remembrance: you shall celebrate it as a festival to the Lord throughout the ages; you shall celebrate it as an institution for all time. 15Seven days you shall eat unleavened bread; on the very first day you shall remove leaven from your houses, for whoever eats leavened bread from the first day to the seventh day, that person shall be cut off from Israel.

16You shall celebrate a sacred occasion on the first day, and a sacred occasion on the seventh day; no work at all shall be done on them; only what every person is to eat, that alone may be prepared for you. 17You shall observe the [Feast of] Unleavened Bread, for on this very day I brought your ranks out of the land of Egypt; you shall observe this day throughout the ages as an institution for all time. 18In the first month, from the fourteenth day of the month at evening, you shall eat unleavened bread until the twenty-first day of the month at evening. 19No leaven shall be found in your houses for seven days. For whoever eats what is leavened, that person shall be cut off from the community of Israel,whether he is a stranger or a citizen of the country. 20You shall eat nothing leavened; in all your settlements you shall eat unleavened bread.

21Moses then summoned all the elders of Israel and said to them, "Go, pick out lambs for your families, and slaughter the passover offering. 22Take a bunch of hyssop, dip it in the blood that is in the basin, and apply some of the blood that is in the basin to the lintel and to the two doorposts. None of you shall go outside the door of his house until

morning. 23For when the Lord goes through to smite the Egyptians, He will see the blood on the lintel and the two doorposts, and the Lord will pass over the door and not let the Destroyer enter and smite your home.

24"You shall observe this as an institution for all time, for you and for your descendants. 25And when you enter the land that the Lord will give you, as He has promised, you shall observe this rite. 26And when your children ask you, 'What do you mean by this rite?' 27you shall say, 'It is the passover sacrifice to the Lord, because He passed over the houses of the Israelites in Egypt when He smote the Egyptians, but saved our houses.'"

The people then bowed low in homage. 28And the Israelites went and did so; just as the Lord had commanded Moses and Aaron, so they did.

29In the middle of the night the Lord struck down all the first-born in the land of Egypt, from the first-born of Pharaoh who sat on the throne to the first-born of the captive who was in the dungeon, and all the first-born of the cattle. 30And Pharaoh arose in the night, with all his courtiers and all the Egyptians—because there was a loud cry in Egypt; for there was no house where there was not someone dead. 31He summoned Moses and Aaron in the night and said, "Up, depart from among my people, you and the Israelites with you! Go, worship the Lord as you said! 32Take also your flocks and your herds, as you said, and begone! And may you bring a blessing upon me also!"

33The Egyptians urged the people on, impatient to have them leave the country, for they said, "We shall all be dead." 34So the people took their dough before it was leavened, their kneading bowls wrapped in their cloaks upon their shoulders. 35The Israelites had done Moses' bidding and borrowed from the Egyptians objects of silver and gold, and clothing. 36And the Lord had disposed the Egyptians favorably toward the people, and they let them have their request; thus they stripped the Egyptians.

37The Israelities journeyed from Raamses to Succoth, about six hundred thousand men on foot, aside from children. 38Moreover, a mixed multitude went up with them, and very much livestock, both flocks and herds. 39And they baked unleavened cakes of the dough that they had taken out of Egypt, for it was not leavened, since they had been driven out of Egypt and could not delay; nor had they prepared any provisions for themselves.

⁴⁰The length of time that the Israelites lived in Egypt was four hundred and thirty years; ⁴¹at the end of the four hundred and thirtieth year, to the very day, all the ranks of the Lord departed from the land of Egypt. ⁴²That was for the Lord a night of vigil to bring them out of the land of Egypt; that same night is the Lord's, one of vigil for all the children of Israel throughout the ages.

⁴³The Lord said to Moses and Aaron: This is the law of the passover offering: No foreigner shall eat of it. ⁴⁴But any slave a man has bought may eat of it once he has been circumcised. ⁴⁵No bound or hired laborer shall eat of it. ⁴⁶It shall be eaten in one house: you shall not take any of the flesh outside the house; nor shall you break a bone of it. ⁴⁷The whole community of Israel shall offer it. ⁴⁸If a stranger who dwells with you would offer the passover to the Lord, all his males must be circumcised; then he shall be admitted to offer it; he shall then be as a citizen of the country. But no uncircumcised person may eat of it. ⁴⁹There shall be one law for the citizen and for the stranger who dwells among you.

⁵⁰And all the Israelites did so; as the Lord had commanded Moses and Aaron, so they did.

⁵¹That very day the Lord freed the Israelites from the land of Egypt, troop by troop.

13 The Lord spoke further to Moses, saying, ²"Consecrate to Me every first-born; man and beast, the first issue of every womb among the Israelites is Mine."

³And Moses said to the people,

"Remember this day, on which you went free from Egypt, the house of bondage, how the Lord freed you from it with a mighty hand: no leavened bread shall be eaten. ⁴You go free on this day, in the month of Abib. ⁵So, when the Lord has brought you into the land of the Canaanites, the Hittites, the Amorites, the Hivites, and the Jebusites, which He swore to your fathers to give you, a land flowing with milk and honey, you shall observe in this month the following practice:

⁶"Seven days you shall eat unleavened bread, and on the seventh day there shall be a festival of the Lord. ⁷Throughout the seven days unleavened

bread shall be eaten; no leavened bread shall be found with you, and no leaven shall be found in all your territory. ⁸And you shall explain to your son on that day, 'It is because of what the Lord did for me when I went free from Egypt.'

⁹"And this shall serve you as a sign on your hand and as a reminder on your forehead—in order that the Teaching of the Lord may be in your mouth—that with a mighty hand the Lord freed you from Egypt. ¹⁰You shall keep this institution at its set time from year to year.

¹¹"And when the Lord has brought you into the land of the Canaanites, as He swore to you and to your fathers, and has given it to you, ¹²you shall set apart for the Lord every first issue of the womb: every male firstling that your cattle drop shall be the Lord's. ¹³But every firstling ass you shall redeem with a sheep; if you do not redeem it, you must break its neck. And you must redeem every first-born male among your children. ¹⁴And when, in time to come, your son asks you, saying, 'What does this mean?' you shall say to him, 'It was with a mighty hand that the Lord brought us out of Egypt, the house of bondage. ¹⁵When Pharaoh stubbornly refused to let us go, the Lord slew every first-born in the land of Egypt, the first-born of both man and beast. Therefore I sacrifice to the Lord every first male issue of the womb, but redeem every first-born among my sons.'

¹⁶"And so it shall be as a sign upon your hand and as a symbol on your forehead that with a mighty hand the Lord freed us from Egypt."

¹⁷Now when Pharaoh let the people go, God did not lead them by way of the land of the Philistines, although it was nearer; for God said, "The people may have a change of heart when they see war, and return to Egypt." ¹⁸So God led the people roundabout, by way of the wilderness at the Sea of Reeds.

Now the Israelites went up armed out of the land of Egypt. ¹⁹And Moses took with him the bones of Joseph, who had exacted an oath from the children of Israel, saying, "God will be sure to take notice of you: then you shall carry up my bones from here with you."

²⁰They set out from Succoth, and encamped at Etham, at the edge of the wilderness. ²¹The Lord went before them in a pillar of cloud by day, to

guide them along the way, and in a pillar of fire by night, to give them light, that they might travel day and night. 22The pillar of cloud by day and the pillar of fire by night did not depart from before the people.

14 The Lord said to Moses: 2Tell the Israelites to turn back and encamp before Pi-hahiroth, between Migdol and the sea, before Baal-zephon; you shall encamp facing it, by the sea. 3Pharaoh will say of the Israelites, "They are astray in the land; the wilderness has closed in on them." 4Then I will stiffen Pharaoh's heart and he will pursue them, that I may gain glory through Pharaoh and all his host; and the Egyptians shall know that I am the Lord.

And they did so.

5When the king of Egypt was told that the people had fled, Pharaoh and his courtiers had a change of heart about the people and said, "What is this we have done, releasing Israel from our service?" 6He ordered his chariot and took his men with him; 7he took six hundred of his picked chariots, and the rest of the chariots of Egypt, with officers in all of them. 8The Lord stiffened the heart of Pharaoh king of Egypt, and he gave chase to the Israelites. As the Israelites were departing defiantly, boldly, 9the Egyptians gave chase to them, and all the chariot horses of Pharaoh, his horsemen, and his warriors overtook them encamped by the sea, near Pi-hahiroth, before Baal-zephon.

10As Pharaoh drew near, the Israelites caught sight of the Egyptians advancing upon them. Greatly frightened, the Israelites cried out to the Lord. 11And they said to Moses, "Was it for want of graves in Egypt that you brought us to die in the wilderness? What have you done to us, taking us out of Egypt? 12Is this not the very thing we told you in Egypt, saying, 'Let us be, and we will serve the Egyptians, for it is better for us to serve the Egyptians than to die in the wilderness'?" 13But Moses said to the people, "Have no fear! Stand by, and witness the deliverance which the Lord will work for you today; for the Egyptians whom you see today you will never see again. 14The Lord will battle for you; you hold your peace!"

15Then the Lord said to Moses, "Why do you cry out to Me? Tell the Israelites to go forward. 16And you lift up your rod and hold out your arm over the sea and split it, so that the Israelites may march into the sea on dry ground. 17And I will stiffen the hearts of the Egyptians so that they go in after them; and I will gain glory thorough Pharaoh and all his warriors, his chariots and his horsemen. 18Let the Egyptians know that I am Lord, when I gain glory through Pharaoh, his chariots, and his horsemen."

19The angel of God, who had been going ahead of the Israelite army, now moved and followed behind them; and the pillar of cloud shifted from in front of them and took up a place behind them, 20and it came between the army of the Egyptians and the army of Israel. Thus there was the cloud with the darkness, and it cast a spell upon the night, so that the one could not come near the other all through the night.

21Then Moses held out his arm over the sea and the Lord drove back the sea with a strong east wind all that night, and turned the sea into dry ground. The waters were split, 22and the Israelites went into the sea on dry ground, the waters forming a wall for them on their right and on their left. 23The Egyptians came in pursuit after them into the sea, all of Pharaoh's horses, chariots, and horsemen. 24At the morning watch, the Lord looked down upon the Egyptian army from a pillar of fire and cloud, and threw the Egyptian army into panic. 25He locked the wheels of their chariots so that they moved forward with difficulty. And the Egyptians said, "Let us flee from the Israelites, for the Lord is fighting for them against Egypt."

26Then the Lord said to Moses, "Hold out your arm over the sea, that the waters may come back upon the Egyptians and upon their chariots and upon their horsemen." 27Moses held out his arm over the sea, and at daybreak the sea returned to its normal state, and the Egyptians fled at its approach. But the Lord hurled the Egyptians into the sea. 28The waters turned back and covered the chariots and the horsemen—Pharaoh's entire army that followed them into the sea; not one of them remained. 29But the Israelites had marched through the sea on dry ground, the waters forming a wall for them on their right and on their left.

³⁰Thus the Lord delivered Israel that day from the Egyptians. Israel saw the Egyptians dead on the shore of the sea. ³¹And when Israel saw the wondrous power which the Lord had wielded against the Egyptians, the people feared the Lord; they had faith in the Lord and His servant Moses.

15 Then Moses and the Israelites sang this song to the Lord. They said:

> I will sing to the Lord, for He has triumphed
>   gloriously;
> Horse and driver He has hurled into the sea.
> ²The Lord is my strength and might;
> He is become my deliverance.
> This is my God and I will enshrine Him;
> The God of my father, and I will exhalt Him.
> ³The Lord, the Warrior—
> Lord is His name!
> ⁴Pharaoh's chariots and his army
> He has cast into the sea;
> And the pick of his officers
> Are drowned in the Sea of Reeds.
> ⁵The deeps covered them;
> They went down into the depths like a
>   stone.
> ⁶Your right hand, O Lord, glorious in power,
> Your right hand, O Lord, shatters the foe!
> ⁷In Your great triumpth You break Your
>   opponents;
> You send forth Your fury, it consumes them
>   like straw.
> ⁸At the blast of Your nostrils the waters piled
>   up,
> The floods stood straight like a wall;
> The deeps froze in the heart of the sea.
> ⁹The foe said,
> "I will pursue, I will overtake,
> I will divide the spoil;
> My desire shall have its fill of them.
> I will bare my sword—
> My hand shall subdue them."
> ¹⁰You made Your wind blow, the sea covered
>   them;
> They sank like lead in the majestic waters.
>
> ¹¹Who is lfike You, O Lord, among the
>   celestials;

> Who is like You, majestic in holiness,
> Awesome in splendor, working wonders!
> ¹²You put out Your right hand,
> The earth swallowed them.
> ¹³In Your love You lead the people You
>   redeemed;
> In Your strength You guide them to Your holy
>   abode.
> ¹⁴The peoples hear, they tremble;
> Agony grips the dwellers in Philistia.
> ¹⁵Now are the clans of Edom dismayed;
> The tribes of Moab—trembling grips them;
> All the dwellers in Canaan are aghast.
> ¹⁶Terror and dread descend upon them;
> Through the might of Your arm they are still
>   as stone—
> Till Your people cross over, O Lord,
> Till Your people cross whom You have
>   ransomed.
> ¹⁷You will bring them and plant them in Your
>   own mountain,
> The place You made to dwell in, O Lord,
> The sanctuary, O Lord, which Your hands
>   established.
> ¹⁸The Lord will reign for ever and ever!

¹⁹For the horses of Pharaoh, with his chariots and horsemen, went into the sea; and the Lord turned back on them the waters of the sea; but the Israelites marched on dry ground in the midst of the sea.

²⁰Then Miriam the prophetess, Aaron's sister, took a timbrel in her hand, and all the women went out after her in dance with timbrels. ²¹And Miriam chanted for them:

> Sing to the Lord, for He has triumphed glori-
>   ously;
> Horse and drive He has hurled into the sea.

²²Then Moses caused Israel to set out from the Sea of Reeds. They went on into the wilderness of Shur; they traveled three days in the wilderness and found no water. ²³They came to Marah, but they could not drink the water of Marah because it was bitter; that is why it was named Marah. ²⁴And the people grumbled against Moses, saying, "What shall we drink?" ²⁵So he cried out to the Lord, and the Lord showed him a piece of wood; he threw it into the water and the water became sweet.

There He made for them a fixed rule, and there He put them to the test. [26]He said, "If you will heed the Lord your God diligently, doing what is upright in His sight, giving ear to His commandments and keeping all His laws, then I will not bring upon you any of the diseases that I brought upon the Egyptians, for I the Lord am your healer."

[27]And they came to Elim, where there were twelve springs of water and seventy palm trees; and they encamped there beside the water.

16 Setting out from Elim, the whole Israelite community came to the wilderness of Sin, which is between Elim and Sinai, on the fifteenth day of the second month after their departure from the land of Egypt. [2]In the wilderness, the whole Israelite community grumbled against Moses and Aaron. [3]The Israelites said to them, "If only we had died by the hand of the Lord in the land of Egypt, when we sat by the fleshpots, when we ate our fill of bread! For you have brought us out into this wilderness to starve this whole congregation to death."

[4]And the Lord said to Moses, "I will rain down bread for you from the sky, and the people shall go out and gather each day that day's portion—that I may thus test them, to see whether they will follow My instructions or not. [5]But on the sixth day, when they apportion what they have brought in, it shall prove to be double the amount they gather each day." [6]So Moses and Aaron said to all the Israelites, "By evening you shall know it was the Lord who brought you out from the land of Egypt; [7]and in the morning you shall behold the Presence of the Lord, because He has heard your "rumblings against the Lord. For who are we that you should grumble against us? [8]Since it is the Lord," Moses continued, "who will give you flesh to eat in the evening and bread in the morning to the full, because the Lord has heard the "grumblings you utter against Him, what is our part? Your grumbling is not against us, but against the Lord!"

[9]Then Moses said to Aaron, "Say to the whole Israelite community: Advance toward the Lord, for He has heard your grumbling." [10]And as Aaron spoke to the whole Israelite community, they turned toward the wilderness, and there, in a cloud, appeared the Presence of the Lord.

[11]The Lord spoke to Moses: [12]"I have heard the grumbling of the Israelites. Speak to them and say: By evening you shall eat flesh, and in the morning you shall have your fill of bread; and you shall know that I the Lord am your God."

[13]In the evening quail appeared and covered the camp; in the morning there was a fall of dew about the camp. [14]When the fall of dew lifted, there, over the surface of the wilderness, lay a fine flaky substance, as fine as frost on the ground. [15]When the Israelites saw it, they said to one another, "What is it?"—for they did not know what it was. And Moses said to them, "That is the bread which the Lord has given you to eat.[16] This is what the Lord has commanded: Gather as much of it as each of you requires to eat, an *omer* to a person for as many of you as there are; each of you shall fetch for those in his tent."

[17]The Israelites did so, some gathering much, some little. [18]But when they measured it by the *omer*, he who had gathered much had no excess, and he who had gathered little had no deficiency: they had gathered as much as they needed to eat. [19]And Moses said to them, "Let no one leave any of it over until morning." [20]But they paid no attention to Moses; some of them left of it until morning, and it became infested with maggots and stank. And Moses was angry with them.

[21]So they gathered it every morning, each as much as he needed to eat; for when the sun grew hot, it would melt. [22]On the sixth day they gathered double the amount of food, two *omers* for each; and when all the chieftains of the community came and told Moses, [23]he said to them, "This is what the Lord meant: Tomorrow is a day of rest, a holy sabbath of the Lord. Bake what you would bake and boil what you would boil; and all that is left put aside to be kept until morning." [24]So they put it aside until morning, as Moses had ordered; and it did not turn foul, and there were no maggots in it. [25]Then Moses said, "Eat it today, for today is a sabbath of the Lord; you will not find it today on the plain. [26]Six days you shall gather it; on the. seventh day, the sabbath, there will be none."

[27]Yet some of the people went out on the seventh day to gather, but they found nothing. [28]And the Lord said to Moses, "How long will you men refuse to obey My commandments and My teach-

ings? [29]Mark that the Lord has given you the sabbath; therefore He gives you two days' food on the sixth day. Let everyone remain where he is: let no man leave his place on the seventh day." [30]So the people remained inactive on the seventh day.

[31]The house of Israel named it manna; it was like coriander seed, white, and it tasted like wafers in honey. [32]Moses said, "This is what the Lord has commanded: Let one *omer* of it be kept throughout the ages, in order that they may see the bread that I fed you in the wilderness when I brought you out from the land of Egypt." [33]And Moses said to Aaron, "Take a jar, put one *omer* of manna in it, and place it before the Lord, to be kept throughout the ages." [34]As the Lord had commanded Moses, Aaron placed it before the Pact, to be kept. [35]And the Israelites ate manna forty years, until they came to a settled land; they ate the manna until they came to the border of the land of Canaan. [36]The *omer is a* tenth of an *ephah.*

17 From the wilderness of Sin the whole Israelite community continued by stages as the Lord would command. They encamped at Rephidim, and there was no water for the people to drink. [2]The people quarreled with Moses. "Give us water to drink," they said; and Moses replied to them, "Why do you quarrel with me? Why do you try the Lord?" [3]But the people thirsted there for water; and the people grumbled against Moses and said, "Why did you bring us up from Egypt, to kill us and our children and livestock with thirst?" [4]Moses cried out to the Lord, saying, "What shall I do with these people? Before long they will be stoning me!" [5]Then the Lord said to Moses, "Pass before the people; take with you some of the elders of Israel, and take along the rod with which you struck the Nile, and set out. [6]I will be standing there before you on the rock at Horeb. Strike the rock and water will issue from it, and the people will drink." And Moses did so in the sight of the elders of Israel. [7]The place was named Massah and Meribah, because the Israelites quarreled and because they tried the Lord, saying, "Is the Lord present among us or not?"

[8]Amalek came and fought with Israel at Rephidim. [9]Moses said to Joshua, "Pick some men for us, and go out and do battle with Amalek. Tomorrow I will station myself on the top of the hill,

with the rod of God in my hand." [10]Joshua did as Moses told him and fought with Amalek, while Moses, Aaron, and I Hur went up to the top of the hill. [11]Then, whenever Moses held up his hand, Israel prevailed; but whenever he let down his hand, Amalek prevailed. [12]But Moses' hands grew Heavy; so they took a stone and put it under him and he sat on it, while Aaron and Hur, one on each side, supported his hands; thus his hands remained steady until the sun set. [13]And Joshua overwhelmed the people of Amalek with the sword.

[14]Then the Lord said to Moses, "Inscribe this in a document as a reminder, and read it aloud to Joshua: I will utterly blot out the memory of Amalek from under heaven!" [15]And Moses built an altar and named it Adonai-nissi. [16]He said, "It means, 'Hand upon the throne of the Lord!' The Lord will be at war with Amalek throughout the ages."

18 Jethro priest of Midian, Moses' father-in-law, heard all that God had done for Moses and for Israel His people, how the Lord had brought Israel out from Egypt. [2]So Jethro, Moses' father-in-law, took Zipporah, Moses' wife, after she had been sent home, [3]and her two sons—of whom one was named Gershom, that is to say, "I have been a stranger in a foreign land"; [4]and the other was named Eliezer, meaning, "The God of my father was my help, and He delivered me from the sword of Pharaoh." [5]Jethro, Moses' father-in-law, brought Moses' sons and wife to him in the wilderness, where he was encamped at the mountain of God. [6]He sent word to Moses, "I, your father-in-law Jethro, am coming to you, with your wife and her two sons." [7]Moses went out to meet his father-in-law; he bowed low and kissed him; each asked after the other's welfare, and they went into the tent.

[8]Moses then recounted to his father-in-law everything that the Lord had done to Pharaoh and to the Egyptians for Israel's sake, all the hardships that had befallen them on the way, and how the Lord had delivered them. [9]And Jethro rejoiced over all the kindness that the Lord had shown Israel when He delivered them from the Egyptians. [10]"Blessed be the Lord," Jethro said, "who delivered you from the Egyptians and from Pharaoh, and who delivered the people from under the hand of the Egyptians. [11]Now I know that the Lord is greater than all gods, yes, by the result of their very

schemes against [the people]." [12]And Jethro, Moses' father-in-law, brought a burnt offering and sacrifices for God; and Aaron came with all the elders of Israel to partake of the meal before God with Moses' father-in-law.

[13]Next day, Moses sat as magistrate among the people, while the people stood about Moses from morning until evening. [14]But when Moses' father-in-law saw how much he had to do for the people, he said, "What is this thing that you are doing to the people? Why do you act alone, while all the people stand about you from morning until evening?" [15]Moses replied to his father-in-law, "It is because the people come to me to inquire of God. [16]When they have a dispute, it comes before me, and I decide between one person and another, and I make known the laws and teachings of God."

[17]But Moses' father-in-law said to him, "The thing you are doing is not right; [18]you will surely wear yourself out, and these people as well. For the task is too heavy for you; you cannot do it alone. [19]Now listen to me. I will give you counsel, and God be with you! You represent the people before God: you bring the disputes before God, and [20]enjoin upon them the laws and the teachings, and make known to them the way they are to go and the practices they are to follow. [21]You shall also seek out from among all the people capable men who fear God, trustworthy men who spurn illgotten gain. Set these over them as chiefs of thousands, hundreds, fifties, and tens, [22]and let them judge the people at all times. Have them bring every major dispute to you, but let them decide every minor dispute themselves. Make it easier for yourself by letting them share the burden with you. [23]If you do this—and God so commands you—you will be able to bear up; and all these people too will go home unwearied."

[24]Moses heeded his father-in-law and did just as he had said. [25]Moses chose capable men out of all Israel, and appointed them heads over the people—chiefs of thousands, hundreds, fifties, and tens; [26]and they judged the people at all times: the difficult matters they would bring to Moses, and all the minor matters they would decide themselves. [27]Then Moses bade his father-in-law farewell, and he went his way to his own land.

19 On the third new moon after the Israelites had gone forth from the land of Egypt, on that very day, they entered the wilderness of Sinai. [2]Having journeyed from Rephidim, they entered the wilderness of Sinai and encamped in the wilderness. Israel encamped there in front of the mountain, [3]and Moses went up to God. The Lord called to him from the mountain, saying, "Thus shall you say to the house of Jacob and declare to the children of Israel: [4]'You have seen what I did to the Egyptians, how I bore you on eagles' wings and brought you to Me. [5]Now then, if you will obey Me faithfully and keep My covenant, you shall be My treasured possession among all the peoples. Indeed, all the earth is Mine, [6]but you shall be to Me a kingdom of priests and a holy nation.' These are the words that you shall speak to the children of Israel.

[7]Moses came and summoned the elders of the people and put before them all that the Lord had commanded him. [8]All the people answered as one, saying, "All that the Lord has spoken we will do!" And Moses brought back the people's words to the Lord. [9]And the Lord said to Moses, "I will come to you in a thick cloud, in order that the people may hear when I speak with you and so trust you ever after." Then Moses reported the people's words to the Lord, [10]and the Lord said to Moses, "Go to the people and warn them to stay pure today and tomorrow. [11]Let them wash their clothes. Let them be ready for the third day; for on the third day the Lord will come down, in the sight of all the people, on Mount Sinai. [12]you shall set bounds for the people round about, saying, 'Beware of going up the mountain or touching the border of it. Whoever touches the mountain shall be put to death: [13]no hand shall touch him, but he shall be either stoned or shot; beast or man, he shall not live' When the ram's horn sounds a long blast, they may go up on the mountain."

[14]Moses came down from the mountain to the people and warned the people to stay pure, and they washed their clothes. [15]And he said to the people, "Be ready for the third day: do not go near a woman."

[16]On the third day, as morning dawned, there was thunder, and lightning, and a dense cloud upon the mountain, and a very loud blast of the horn; and all the people who were in the camp trembled. [17]Moses led the people out of the camp toward God, and they took their places at the foot of the mountain.

[18]Now Mount Sinai was all in smoke, for the Lord had come down upon it in fire; the smoke rose like the smoke of a kiln, and the whole mountain trembled violently. [19]The blare of the horn grew louder and louder. As Moses spoke, God answered him in thunder. [20]The Lord came down upon Mount Sinai, on the top of the mountain, and the Lord called Moses to the top of the mountain and Moses went up. [21]The Lord said to Moses, "Go down, warn the people not to break through to the Lord to gaze, lest many of them perish. [22]The priests also, who come near the Lord, must stay pure, lest the Lord break out against them." [23]But Moses said to the Lord, "The people cannot come up to the Mount Sinai, for You warned us saying, 'Set bounds about the mountain and sanctify it.'" [24]So the Lord said to him, "Go down, and come back together with Aaron; but let not the priests or the people break through to come up to the Lord, lest He break out against them." [25]And Moses went down to the people and spoke to them.

20 God spoke all these words, saying:

[2]I the Lord am your God who brought you out of the land of Egypt, the house of bondage: [3]You shall have no other gods besides Me.

[4]You shall not make for yourself a sculptured image, or any likeness of what is in the heavens above, or on the earth below, or in the waters under the earth. [5]You shall not bow down to them or serve them. For I the Lord your God am an impassioned God, visiting the guilt of the parents upon the children, upon the third and upon the fourth generations of those who reject Me, [6]but showing kindness to the thousandth generation of those who love Me and keep My commandments.

[7]You shall not swear falsely by the name of the Lord your God; for the Lord will not clear one who swears falsely by His name.

[8]Remember the sabbath day and keep it holy. [9]Six days you shall labor and do all your work, [10]but the seventh day is a sabbath of the Lord your God: you shall not do any work—you, your son or daughter, your male or female slave, or your cattle, or the stranger who is within your settlements. [11]For in six days the Lord made heaven and earth and sea, and all that is in them, and He rested on the seventh day; therefore the Lord blessed the sabbath day and hallowed it.

[12]Honor your father and your mother, that you may long endure on the land that the Lord your God is assigning to you.

[13]You shall not murder.

You shall not commit adultery.

You shall not steal.

You shall not bear false witness against your neighbor.

[14]You shall not covet your neighbor's house: you shall not covet your neighbor's wife, or his male or female slave, or his ox or his ass, or anything that is your neighbor's.

[15]All the people witnessed the thunder and lightning, the blare of the horn and the mountain smoking; and when the people saw it, they fell back and stood at a distance. [16]"You speak to us," they said to Moses, "and we will obey; but let not God speak to us, lest we die." [17]Moses answered the people, "Be not afraid; for God has come only in order to test you, and in order that the fear of Him may be ever with you, so that you do not go astray." [18]So the people remained at a distance, while Moses approached the thick cloud where God was.

[19]The Lord said to Moses:

Thus shall you say to the Israelites: You yourselves saw that I spoke to you from the very heavens: [20]With Me, therefore, you shall not make any gods of silver, nor shall you make for yourselves any gods of gold. [21]Make for Me an altar of earth and sacrifice on it your burnt offerings and your sacrifices of well-being, your sheep and your oxen; in every place where I cause My name to be mentioned I will come to you and bless you. [22]And if you make for Me an altar of stones, do not build it of hewn stones; for by wielding your tool upon them you have profaned them. [23]Do not ascend My altar by steps, that your nakedness may not be exposed upon it.

JOB CHAPTERS 1–14, 32 AND 36–42

1 There was a man in the land of Uz named Job. That man was blameless and upright; he feared God and shunned evil. [2]Seven sons and three daughters were born to him; [3]his possessions were seven thousand sheep, three thousand camels, five hundred yoke of oxen and five hundred she-asses, and a very large household. That man was wealthier than anyone in the East.

[4]It was the custom of his sons to hold feasts, each on his set day in his own home. They would invite their three sisters to eat and drink with them. [5]When a round of feast days was over, Job would send word to them to sanctify themselves, and, rising early in the morning, he would make burnt offerings, one for each of them; for Job thought, "Perhaps my children have sinned and blasphemed God in their thoughts." This is what Job always used to do.

[6]One day the divine beings presented themselves before the Lord, and the Adversary came along with them. [7]The Lord said to the Adversary, "Where have you been?" The Adversary answered the Lord, "I have been roaming all over the earth." [8]The Lord said to the Adversary, "Have you noticed My servant Job? There is no one like him on earth, a blameless and upright man who fears God and shuns evil!" [9]The Adversary answered the Lord, "Does Job not have good reason to fear God? [10]Why, it is You who have fenced him round, him and his household and all that he has. You have blessed his efforts so that his possessions spread out in the land. [11]But lay Your hand upon all that he has and he will surely blaspheme You to Your face." [12]The Lord replied to the Adversary, "See, all that he has is in your power; only do not lay a hand on him." The Adversary departed from the presence of the Lord.

[13]One day, as his sons and daughters were eating and drinking wine in the house of their eldest brother, [14]a messenger came to Job and said, "The oxen were plowing and the she-asses were grazing alongside them [15]when Sabeans attacked them and carried them off, and put the boys to the sword; I alone have escaped to tell you." [16]This one was still speaking when another came and said, "God's fire fell from heaven, took hold of the sheep and the boys, and burned them up; I alone have escaped to tell you." [17]This one was still speaking when another came and said, "A Chaldean formation of three columns made a raid on the camels and carried them off and put the boys to the sword; I alone have escaped to tell you." [18]This one was still speaking when another came and said, "Your sons and daughters were eating and drinking wine in the house of their eldest brother [19]when suddenly a mighty wind came from the wilderness. It struck the four corners of the house so that it collapsed upon the young people and they died; I alone have escaped to tell you."

[20]Then Job arose, tore his robe, cut off his hair, and threw himself on the ground and worshiped. [21]He said, "Naked came I out of my mother's womb, and naked shall I return there; the Lord has given, and the Lord has taken away; blessed be the name of the Lord."

[22]For all that, Job did not sin nor did he cast reproach on God.

2 One day the divine beings presented themselves before the Lord. The Adversary came along with them to present himself before the Lord. [2]The Lord said to the Adversary, "Where have you been?" The Adversary answered the Lord, "I have been roaming all over the earth." [3]The Lord said to the Adversary, "Have you noticed My servant Job? There is no one like him on earth, a blameless and upright man who fears God and shuns evil. He still keeps his integrity; so you have incited Me against him to destroy him for no good reason." [4]The Adversary answered the Lord, "Skin for skin—all that a man has he will give up for his life. [5]But lay a hand on his bones and his flesh, and he will surely blaspheme You to Your face." [6]So the Lord said to the Adversary, "See, he is in your power; only spare his life." [7]The Adversary departed from the presence of the Lord and inflicted a severe inflammation on Job from the sole of his foot to the crown of his head. [8]He took a potsherd to scratch himself as he sat in ashes. [9]His wife said to him, "You still keep your integrity! Blaspheme God and die!" [10]But he said to her, "You talk as any shameless woman might talk! Should we accept only good from God

and not accept evil?" For all that, Job said nothing sinful.

¹¹When Job's three friends heard about all these calamities that had befallen him, each came from his home—Eliphaz the Temanite, Bildad the Shuhite, and Zophar the Naamathite. They met together to go and console and comfort him. ¹²When they saw him from a distance, they could not recognize him, and they broke out into loud weeping; each one tore his robe and threw dust into the air onto his head. ¹³They sat with him on the ground seven days and seven nights. None spoke a word to him for they saw how great was his suffering.

3 Afterward, Job began to speak and cursed the day of his birth. ²Job spoke up and said:

³Perish the day on which I was born,
And the night it was announced,
"A male has been conceived!"
⁴May that day be darkness;
May God above have no concern for it;
May light not shine on it;
⁵May darkness and deep gloom reclaim it;
May a pall lie over it;
May what blackens the day terrify it.
⁶May obscurity carry off that night;
May it not be counted among the days of the
    year;
May it not appear in any of its months;
⁷May that night be desolate;
May no sound of joy be heard in it;
⁸May those who cast spells upon the day
    damn it,
Those prepared to disable Leviathan;
⁹May its twilight stars remain dark;
May it hope for light and have none;
May it not see the glimmering of the dawn—
¹⁰Because it did not block my mother's
    womb,
And hide trouble from my eyes.

¹¹Why did I not die at birth,
Expire as I came forth from the womb?
¹²Why were there knees to receive me,
Or breasts for me to suck?
¹³For now would I be lying in repose, asleep
    and at rest,
¹⁴With the world's kings and counselors who
    rebuild ruins for themselves,

¹⁵Or with nobles who possess gold and
who
    fill their houses with silver.
¹⁶Or why was I not like a buried stillbirth,
Like babies who never saw the light?
¹⁷There the wicked cease from troubling;
There rest those whose strength is spent.
¹⁸Prisoners are wholly at ease;
They do not hear the taskmaster's voice.
¹⁹Small and great alike are there,
And the slave is free of his master.

²⁰Why does He give light to the sufferer And
    life to the bitter in spirit;
²¹To those who wait for death but it does not
    come,
Who search for it more than for treasure,
²²Who rejoice to exultation, And are glad to
    reach the grave;
²³To the man who has lost his way,
Whom God has hedged about?

²⁴My groaning serves as my bread;
My roaring pours forth as water.
²⁵For what I feared has overtaken me;
What I dreaded has come upon me.
²⁶I had no repose, no quiet, no rest.
And trouble came.

4 Then Eliphaz the Temanite said in reply:

²If one ventures a word with you, will it be
    too much?
But who can hold back his words?
³See, you have encouraged many;
You have strengthened failing hands.
⁴Your words have kept him who stumble
    from falling;
You have braced knees that gave way.
⁵But now that it overtakes you, it is too much;
It reaches you, and you are unnerved.
⁶Is not your piety your confidence,
Your integrity your hope?
⁷Think now, what innocent man ever
    perished?
Where have the upright been destroyed?
⁸As I have seen, those who plow evil
And sow mischief reap them.
⁹They perish by a blast from God,

Are gone at the breath of His nostrils.
¹⁰The lion may roar, the cub may howl,
But the teeth of the king of beasts are
    broken.
¹¹The lion perishes for lack of prey,
And its whelps are scattered.

¹²A word came to me in stealth;
My ear caught in a whisper of it.
¹³In thought-filled visions of the night,
When deep sleep falls on men,
¹⁴Fear and trembling came upon me,
Causing all my bones to quake with fright.
¹⁵A wind passed by me,
Making the hair of my flesh bristle.
¹⁶It halted; its appearance was strange to
me;
A form loomed before my eyes;
I heard a murmur, a voice,
¹⁷"Can mortals be acquitted by God?
Can man be cleared by his Maker?
¹⁸If He cannot trust His own servants,
And casts reproach on His angels,
¹⁹How much less those who dwell in houses
    of clay,
Whose origin is dust,
Who are crushed like the moth,
²⁰Shattered between daybreak and evening,
Perishing forever, unnoticed.
²¹Their cord is pulled up
And they die, and not with wisdom."

5 Call now! Will anyone answer you?
To whom among the holy beings will you
    turn?
²Vexation kills the fool;
Passion slays the simpleton.
³I myself saw a fool who had struck roots;
Impulsively, I cursed his home:
⁴May his children be far from success;
May they be oppressed in the gate with none
    to deliver them;
⁵May the hungry devour his harvest,
Carrying it off in baskets;
May the thirsty swallow their wealth.
⁶Evil does not grow out of the soil,
Nor does mischief spring from the ground;
⁷For man is born to [do] mischief,
Just as sparks fly upward.

⁸But I would resort to God;
I would lay my case before God,
⁹Who performs great deeds which cannot be
    fathomed,
Wondrous things without number;
¹⁰Who gives rain to the earth,
And sends water over the fields;
¹¹Who raises the lowly up high,
So that the dejected are secure in victory;
¹²Who thwarts the designs of the crafty,
So that their hands cannot gain success;
¹³Who traps the clever in their own wiles;
The plans of the crafty go awry.
¹⁴By day they encounter darkness,
At noon they grope as in the night.
¹⁵But He saves the needy from the sword of
    their mouth,
From the clutches of the strong.
¹⁶So there is hope for the wretched;
The mouth of wrongdoing is stopped.

¹⁷See how happy is the man whom God
    reproves;
Do not reject the discipline of the Almighty.
¹⁸He injures, but He binds up;
He wounds, but His hands heal.
¹⁹He will deliver you from six troubles;
In seven no harm will reach you:
²⁰In famine He will redeem you from death,
In war, from the sword.
²¹You will be sheltered from the scourging
    tongue;
You will have no fear when violence comes.
²²You will laugh at violence and starvation,
And have no fear of wild beasts.
²³For you will have a pact with the rocks in
    the field,
And the beasts of the field will be your allies.
²⁴You will know that all is well in your tent;
When you visit your wife you will never fail.
²⁵You will see that your offspring are many,
Your descendants like grass of the earth.
²⁶You will come to the grave in ripe old age,
As shocks of grain are taken away in their
    season.
²⁷See, we have inquired into this and it is so;
Hear it and accept it.

6 Then Job said in reply:

²If my anguish were weighed,
My full calamity laid on the scales,
³It would be heavier than the sand of the sea;
That is why I spoke recklessly.
⁴For the arrows of the Almighty are in me;
My spirit absorbs their poison;
God's terrors are arrayed against me.
⁵Does a wild ass bray when he has grass?
Does a bull bellow over his fodder?
⁶Can what is tasteless be eaten without salt?
Does mallow juice have any flavor?
⁷I refuse to touch them;
They are like food when I am sick.

⁸Would that my request were granted,
That God gave me what I wished for;
⁹Would that God consented to crush me,
Loosed His hand and cut me off.
¹⁰Then this would be my consolation,
As I writhed in unsparing pains:
That I did not suppress my words against the
    Holy One.
¹¹What strength have I, that I should endure?
How long have I to live, that I should be
    patient?
¹²Is my strength the strength of rock?
Is my flesh bronze?
¹³Truly, I cannot help myself;
I have been deprived of resourcefulness.

¹⁴A friend owes loyalty to one who fails,
Though he forsakes the fear of the Almighty;
¹⁵My comrades are fickle, like a wadi,
Like a bed on which streams once ran.
¹⁶They are dark with ice;
Snow obscures them;
¹⁷But when they thaw, they vanish;
In the heat, they disappear where they are.
¹⁸Their course twists and turns;
They run into the desert and perish.
¹⁹Caravans from Tema look to them;
Processions from Sheba count on them.
²⁰They are disappointed in their hopes;
When they reach the place, they stand aghast.
²¹So you are as nothing:
At the sight of misfortune, you take fright.
²²Did I say to you, "I need your gift;
Pay a bribe for me out of your wealth;

²³Deliver me from the clutches of my enemy;
Redeem me from violent men"?
²⁴Teach me; I shall be silent;
Tell me where I am wrong.
²⁵How trenchant honest words are;
But what sort of reproof comes from you?
²⁶Do you devise words of reproof,
But count a hopeless man's words as wind?
²⁷You would even cast lots over an orphan,
Or barter away your friend.
²⁸Now be so good as to face me;
I will not lie to your face.
²⁹Relent! Let there not be injustice;
Relent! I am still in the right.
³⁰Is injustice on my tongue?
Can my palate not discern evil?

Truly man has a term of service on earth;
His days are like those of a hireling—
7 ²Like a slave who longs for [evening's]
    shadows,
Like a hireling who waits for his wage.
³So have I been allotted months of futility;
Nights of misery have been apportioned to
    me.
⁴When I lie down, I think,
"When shall I rise?"
Night drags on,
And I am sated with tossings till morning
    twilight.
⁵My flesh is covered with maggots and clods
    of earth;
My skin is broken and festering.
⁶My days fly faster than a weaver's shuttle,
And come to their end without hope.
⁷Consider that my life is but wind;
I shall never see happiness again.
⁸The eye that gazes on me will not see me;
Your eye will seek me, but I shall be gone.
⁹As a cloud fades away,
So whoever goes down to Sheol does not
    come up;
¹⁰He returns no more to his home;
His place does not know him.

¹¹On my part, I will not speak with restraint;
I will give voice to the anguish of my spirit;
I will complain in the bitterness of my soul.
¹²Am I the sea or the Dragon,
That You have set a watch over me?

13When I think, "My bed will comfort me,
My couch will share my sorrow,"
14You frighten me with dreams,
And terrify me with visions,
15Till I prefer strangulation,
Death, to my wasted frame.
16I am sick of it.
I shall not live forever;
Let me be, for my days are a breath.

17What is man, that You make much of him,
That You fix Your attention upon him?
18You inspect him every morning,
Examine him every minute.
19Will You not look away from me for a
    while,
Let me be, till I swallow my spittle?
20If I have sinned, what have I done to You,
Watcher of men?
Why make me Your target,
And a burden to myself?
21Why do You not pardon my transgression
And forgive my iniquity?
For soon I shall lie down in the dust;
When You seek me, I shall be gone.

8 Bildad the Shuhite said in reply:

2How long will you speak such things?
 Your utterances are a mighty wind!
3Will God pervert the right?
Will the Almighty pervert justice?
4If your sons sinned against Him,
He dispatched them for their transgression.
5But if you seek God
And supplicate the Almighty,
6If you are blameless and upright,
He will protect you,
And grant well-being to your righteous
    home.
7Though your beginning be small,
In the end you will grow very great.

8Ask the generation past,
Study what their fathers have searched out
9—For we are of yesterday and know nothing;
Our days on earth are a shadow—
10Surely they will teach you and tell you,
Speaking out of their understanding.

11Can papyrus thrive without marsh?
 Can rushes grow without water?
12While still tender, not yet plucked,
They would wither before any other grass.
13Such is the fate of all who forget God;
The hope of the impious man comes to
    naught—
14Whose confidence is a thread of gossamer,
Whose trust is a spider's web.
15He leans on his house—it will not stand;
He seizes hold of it, but it will not hold.
16He stays fresh even in the sun;
His shoots spring up in his garden;
17His roots are twined around a heap,
They take hold of a house of stones.
18When he is uprooted from his place,
It denies him, [saying,]
"I never saw you."
19Such is his happy lot;
And from the earth others will grow.
20Surely God does not despise the blameless;
He gives no support to evildoers.
21He will yet fill your mouth with laughter,
And your lips with shouts of joy.
22Your enemies will be clothed in disgrace;
The tent of the wicked will vanish.

9 Job said in reply:

2Indeed I know that it is so:
Man cannot win a suit against God.
3If he insisted on a trial with Him,
He would not answer one charge in a
    thousand.
4Wise of heart and mighty in power—
Who ever challenged Him and came out
    whole?—
5Him who moves mountains without their
    knowing it,
Who overturns them in His anger;
6Who shakes the earth from its place,
Till its pillars quake;
7Who commands the sun not to shine;
Who seals up the stars;
8Who by Himself spread out the heavens,
And trod on the back of the sea;
9Who made the Bear and Orion,
Pleiades, and the chambers of the south
    wind;

¹⁰Who performs great deeds which cannot be
    fathomed,
And wondrous things without number.
¹¹He passes me by—I do not see Him;
He goes by me, but I do not perceive Him.
¹²He snatches away—who can stop Him?
Who can say to Him, "What are You doing?"
¹³God does not restrain His anger;
Under Him Rahab's helpers sink down.
¹⁴How then can I answer Him,
Or choose my arguments against Him?
¹⁵Though I were in the right, I could not
    speak out,
But I would plead for mercy with my judge.
¹⁶If I summoned Him and He responded,
I do not believe He would lend me His ear.
¹⁷For He crushes me for a hair;
He wounds me much for no cause.
¹⁸He does not let me catch my breath,
But sates me with bitterness.
¹⁹If a trial of strength—He is the strong one;
If a trial in court—who will summon Him
    for me?
²⁰Though I were innocent,
My mouth would condemn me;
Though I were blameless, He would prove
    me crooked.
²¹I am blameless—I am distraught;
I am sick of life.
²²It is all one; therefore I say,
"He destroys the blameless and the guilty."
²³When suddenly a scourge brings death,
He mocks as the innocent fail.
²⁴The earth is handed over to the wicked one;
He covers the eyes of its judges.
If it is not He, then who?

²⁵My days fly swifter than a runner;
They flee without seeing happiness;
²⁶They pass like reed-boats,
Like an eagle swooping onto its prey.
²⁷If I say, "I will forget my complaint;
Abandon my sorrow and be diverted,"
²⁸I remain in dread of all my suffering;
I know that You will not acquit me.
²⁹It will be I who am in the wrong;
Why then should I waste effort?
³⁰If I washed with soap,
Cleansed my hands with lye,

³¹You would dip me in muck
Till my clothes would abhor me.
³²He is not a man, like me, that I can answer
    Him,
That we can go to law together.
³³No arbiter is between us
To lay his hand on us both.
³⁴If He would only take His rod away
    from me
And not let His terror frighten me,
³⁵Then I would speak out without fear
    of Him;
For I know myself not to be so.

10 ¹I am disgusted with life;
I will give rein to my complaint,
Speak in the bitterness of my soul.
²I say to God, "Do not condemn me;
Let me know what You charge me with.
³Does it benefit You to defraud,
To despise the toil of Your hands,
While smiling on the counsel of the wicked?
⁴Do You have the eyes of flesh?
Is Your vision that of mere men?
⁵Are Your days the days of a mortal,
Are Your years the years of a man,
⁶That You seek my iniquity
And search out my sin?
⁷You know that I am not guilty,
And there is none to deliver from Your hand.

⁸"Your hands shaped and fashioned me,
Then destroyed every part of me.
⁹Consider that You fashioned me like clay;
Will You then turn me back into dust?
¹⁰You poured me out like milk,
Congealed me like cheese;
¹¹You clothed me with skin and flesh
And wove me of bones and sinews;
¹²You bestowed on me life and care;
Your providence watched over my spirit.
¹³Yet these things You hid in Your heart;
I know that You had this in mind:
¹⁴To watch me when I sinned
And not clear me of my iniquity;
¹⁵Should I be guilty—the worse for me!
And even when innocent, I cannot lift my
    head;
So sated am I with shame,

And drenched in my misery.
¹⁶It is something to be proud of to hunt me
    like a lion,
To show Yourself wondrous through me time
    and again!
¹⁷You keep sending fresh witnesses against
    me,
Letting Your vexation with me grow.
I serve my term and am my own
    replacement.
¹⁸"Why did You let me come out of the womb?

Better had I expired before any eye saw me,
¹⁹Had I been as though I never was,
Had I been carried from the womb to the
    grave.
²⁰My days are few, so desist!
Leave me alone, let me be diverted a while
²¹Before I depart—never to return—
For the land of deepest gloom;
²²A land whose light is darkness,
All gloom and disarray,
Whose light is like darkness."

11 Then Zophar the Naamathite said in reply:

²Is a multitude of words unanswerable?
Must a loquacious person be right?
³Your prattle may silence men;
You may mock without being rebuked,
⁴And say, "My doctrine is pure,
And I have been innocent in Your sight."
⁵But would that God might speak,
And talk to you Himself.
⁶He would tell you the secrets of wisdom,
For there are many sides of sagacity;
And know that God has overlooked for you
    some of your iniquity.
⁷Would you discover the mystery of God?
Would you discover the limit of the
    Almighty?
⁸Higher than heaven—what can you do?
Deeper than Sheol—what can you know?
⁹Its measure is longer than the earth
And broader than the sea.
¹⁰Should He pass by, or confine,
Or call an assembly, who can stop Him?
¹¹For He knows deceitful men;
When He sees iniquity, does He not
    discern it?
¹²A hollow man will get understanding,

When a wild ass is born a man.

¹³But if you direct your mind,
And spread forth your hands toward Him—
¹⁴If there is iniquity with you, remove it,
And do not let injustice reside in your tent—
¹⁵Then, free of blemish, you will hold your
    head high,
And when in straits, be unafraid.
¹⁶You will then put your misery out of mind,
Consider it as water that has flowed past.
¹⁷Life will be brighter than noon;
You will shine, you will be like the morning.
¹⁸You will be secure, for there is hope,
And, entrenched, you will rest secure;
¹⁹You will lie down undisturbed;
The great will court your favor.
²⁰But the eyes of the wicked pine away;
Escape is cut off from them;
They have only their last breath to look
    forward to.

12 Then Job said in reply:

²Indeed, you are the [voice of] the people,
And wisdom will die with you.
³But I, like you, have a mind,
And am not less than you.
Who does not know such things?
⁴I have become a laughingstock to my
    friend—
"One who calls to God and is answered,
Blamelessly innocent"—a laughingstock.
⁵In the thought of the complacent there is
    contempt for calamity;
It is ready for those whose foot slips.
⁶Robbers live untroubled in their tents.
And those who provoke God are secure,
Those whom God's hands have produced.

⁷But ask the beasts, and they will teach you;
The birds of the sky, they will tell you,
⁸Or speak to the earth, it will teach you;
The fish of the sea, they will inform you.
⁹Who among all these does not know
That the hand of the Lord has done this?
¹⁰In His hand is every living soul
And the breath of all mankind.
¹¹Truly, the ear tests arguments
As the palate tastes foods.
¹²Is wisdom in the aged

And understanding in the long-lived?
¹³With Him are wisdom and courage;
His are counsel and understanding.
¹⁴Whatever He tears down cannot be rebuilt;
Whomever He imprisons cannot be set free.
¹⁵When He holds back the waters, they
    dry up;
When He lets them loose, they tear up the
    land.
¹⁶With Him are strength and resourcefulness;
Erring and causing to err are from Him.
¹⁷He makes counselors go about naked
And causes judges to go mad.
¹⁸He undoes the belts of kings,
And fastens loincloths on them.
¹⁹He makes priests go about naked,
And leads temple-servants astray.
²⁰He deprives trusty men of speech,
And takes away the reason of elders.
²¹He pours disgrace upon great men,
And loosens the belt of the mighty.
²²He draws mysteries out of the darkness,
And brings obscurities to light.
²³He exalts nations, then destroys them;
He expands nations, then leads them away.
²⁴He deranges the leaders of the people,
And makes them wander in a trackless
    waste.
²⁵They grope without light in the darkness;
He makes them wander as if drunk.

13 My eye has seen all this;
My ear has heard and understood it.
²What you know, I know also;
I am not less than you.
³Indeed, I would speak to the Almighty;
I insist on arguing with God.
⁴But you invent lies;
All of you are quacks.
⁵If you would only keep quiet
It would be considered wisdom on your part.
⁶Hear now my arguments,
Listen to my pleading.
⁷Will you speak unjustly on God's behalf?
Will you speak deceitfully for Him?
⁸Will you be partial toward Him?
Will you plead God's cause?
⁹Will it go well when He examines you?

Will you fool Him as one fools men?
¹⁰He will surely reprove you
If in your heart you are partial toward Him.
¹¹His threat will terrify you,
And His fear will seize you.
¹²Your briefs are empty platitudes;
Your responses are unsubstantial.
¹³Keep quiet; I will have my say,
Come what may upon me.
¹⁴How long! I will take my flesh in my teeth;
I will take my life in my hands.
¹⁵He may well slay me; I may have no hope;
Yet I will argue my case before Him.
¹⁶In this too is my salvation:
That no impious man can come into His
    presence.
¹⁷Listen closely to my words;
Give ear to my discourse.
¹⁸See now, I have prepared a case;
I know that I will win it.
¹⁹For who is it that would challenge me?
I should then keep silent and expire.
²⁰But two things do not do to me,
So that I need not hide from You:
²¹Remove Your hand from me,
And let not Your terror frighten me.
²²Then summon me and I will respond,
Or I will speak and You reply to me.
²³How many are my iniquities and sins?
Advise me of my transgression and sin.
²⁴Why do You hide Your face,
And treat me like an enemy?
²⁵Will You harass a driven leaf,
Will You pursue dried-up straw,
²⁶That You decree for me bitter things
And make me answer for the iniquities of my
    youth,
²⁷That You put my feet in the stocks
And watch all my ways,
Hemming in my footsteps?
²⁸Man wastes away like a rotten thing,
Like a garment eaten by moths.

14 Man born of woman is short-lived and sated
    with trouble.
²He blossoms like a flower and withers;
He vanishes like a shadow and does not
    endure.

³Do You fix Your gaze on such a one?
Will You go to law with me?
⁴Who can produce a clean thing out of an
    unclean one? No one!
⁵His days are determined;
You know the number of his months;
You have set him limits that he cannot pass.
⁶Turn away from him, that he may be at ease
Until, like a hireling, he finishes out his day.

⁷There is hope for a tree;
If it is cut down it will renew itself;
Its shoots will not cease.
⁸If its roots are old in the earth,
And its stump dies in the ground,
⁹At the scent of water it will bud
And produce branches like a sapling.
¹⁰But mortals languish and die;
Man expires; where is he?
¹¹The waters of the sea fail,
And the river dries up and is parched.
¹²So man lies down never to rise;
He will awake only when the heavens are
    no more,
Only then be aroused from his sleep.
¹³O that You would hide me in Sheol,
Conceal me until Your anger passes,
Set me a fixed time to attend to me.
¹⁴If a man dies, can he live again?
All the time of my service I wait
Until my replacement comes.
¹⁵You would call and I would answer You;
You would set Your heart on Your
    handiwork.
¹⁶Then You would not count my steps,
Or keep watch over my sin.
¹⁷My transgression would be sealed up in a
    pouch;
You would coat over my iniquity.
¹⁸Mountains collapse and crumble;
Rocks are dislodged from their place.
¹⁹Water wears away stone;
Torrents wash away earth;
So you destroy man's hope,
²⁰You overpower him forever and he
    perishes;
You alter his visage and dispatch him.
²¹His sons attain honor and he does not
    know it;

They are humbled and he is not aware of it.
²²He feels only the pain of his flesh,
And his spirit mourns in him.

• • •

32 These three men ceased replying to Job, for he considered himself right. ²Then Elihu son of Barachel the Buzite, of the family of Ram, was angry—angry at Job because he thought himself right against God. ³He was angry as well at his three friends, because they found no reply, but merely condemned Job. ⁴Elihu waited out Job's speech, for they were all older than he. ⁵But when Elihu saw that the three men had nothing to reply, he was angry.
⁶Then Elihu son of Barachel the Buzite said in reply:

I have but few years, while you are old;
Therefore I was too awestruck and fearful
To hold forth among you.
⁷I thought, "Let age speak;
Let advanced years declare wise things."
⁸But truly it is the spirit in men,
The breath of Shaddai, that gives them
    understanding.
⁹It is not the aged who are wise,
The elders, who understand how to judge.
¹⁰Therefore I say, "Listen to me;
I too would hold forth."
¹¹Here I have waited out your speeches,
I have given ear to your insights,
While you probed the issues;
¹²But as I attended to you,
I saw that none of you could argue with Job,
Or offer replies to his statements.
¹³I fear you will say, "We have found the wise
    course;
God will defeat him, not man."
¹⁴He did not set out his case against me,
Nor shall I use your reasons to reply to him.
¹⁵They have been broken and can no longer
    reply;
Words fail them.
¹⁶I have waited till they stopped speaking,
Till they ended and no longer replied.
¹⁷Now I also would have my say;
I too would like to hold forth,

18For I am full of words;
The wind in my belly presses me.
19My belly is like wine not yet opened,
Like jugs of new wine ready to burst.
20Let me speak, then, and get relief;
Let me open my lips and reply.
21I would not show regard for any man,
Or temper my speech for anyone's sake;
22For I do not know how to temper my
    speech—
My Maker would soon carry me off!

• • •

36 Then Elihu spoke once more.

2Wait a little and let me hold forth;
There is still more to say for God.
3I will make my opinions widely known;
I will justify my Maker.
4In truth, my words are not false;
A man of sound opinions is before you.

5See, God is mighty; He is not contemptuous;
He is mighty in strength and mind.
6He does not let the wicked live;
He grants justice to the lowly.
7He does not withdraw His eyes from the
    righteous;
With kings on thrones
He seats them forever, and they are exalted.
8If they are bound in shackles
And caught in trammels of affliction,
9He declares to them what they have done,
And that their transgressions are excessive;
10He opens their understanding by discipline,
And orders them back from mischief.
11If they will serve obediently,
They shall spend their days in happiness,
Their years in delight.
12But if they are not obedient,
They shall perish by the sword,
Die for lack of understanding.
13But the impious in heart become enraged;
They do not cry for help when He afflicts
    them.
14They die in their youth;
[Expire] among the depraved.
15He rescues the lowly from their affliction,
And opens their understanding through
    distress.

16Indeed, He draws you away from the brink
    of distress
To a broad place where there is no constraint;
Your table is laid out with rich food.
17You are obsessed with the case of the
    wicked man,
But the justice of the case will be upheld.
18Let anger at his affluence not mislead you;
Let much bribery not turn you aside.
19Will your limitless wealth avail you,
All your powerful efforts?
20Do not long for the night
When peoples vanish where they are.
21Beware! Do not turn to mischief;
Because of that you have been tried by
    affliction.
22See, God is beyond reach in His power;
Who governs like Him?
23Who ever reproached Him for His conduct?
Who ever said, "You have done wrong"?
24Remember, then, to magnify His work,
Of which men have sung,
25Which all men have beheld,
Men have seen, from a distance.
26See, God is greater than we can know;
The number of His years cannot be counted.
27He forms the droplets of water,
Which cluster into rain, from His mist.
28The skies rain;
They pour down on all mankind.
29Can one, indeed, contemplate the expanse
    of clouds,
The thunderings from His pavilion?
30See, He spreads His lightning over it;
It fills the bed of the sea.
31By these things He controls peoples;
He gives food in abundance.
32Lightning fills His hands;
He orders it to hit the mark.
33Its noise tells of Him.
The kindling of anger against iniquity.

37 Because of this, too, my heart quakes,
And leaps from its place.
2Just listen to the noise of His rumbling,
To the sound that comes out of His mouth.
3He lets it loose beneath the entire heavens—
His lightning, to the ends of the earth.
4After it, He lets out a roar;

He thunders in His majestic voice.
No one can find a trace of it by the time His
    voice is heard.
⁵God thunders marvelously with His voice;
He works wonders that we cannot
    understand.
⁶He commands the snow, "Fall to the
    ground!"
And the downpour of rain, His mighty
    downpour of rain,
⁷Is a sign on every man's hand,
That all men may know His doings.
⁸Then the beast enters its lair,
And remains in its den.
⁹The storm wind comes from its chamber,
And the cold from the constellations.
¹⁰By the breath of God ice is formed,
And the expanse of water becomes solid.
¹¹He also loads the clouds with moisture
And scatters His lightning-clouds.
¹²He keeps turning events by His stratagems,
That they might accomplish all that He
    commands them
Throughout the inhabited earth,
¹³Causing each of them to happen to His
    land,
Whether as a scourge or as a blessing.
¹⁴Give ear to this, Job;
Stop to consider the marvels of God.
¹⁵Do you know what charge God lays upon
    them
When His lightning-clouds shine?
¹⁶Do you know the marvels worked upon the
    expanse of clouds]
By Him whose understanding is perfect,
¹⁷Why your clothes become hot
When the land is becalmed by the south wind?
¹⁸Can you help him stretch out the heavens,
Firm as a mirror of cast metal?
¹⁹Inform us, then, what we may say to Him;
We cannot argue because [we are in]
    darkness.
²⁰Is anything conveyed to Him when I speak?
Can a man say anything when he is
    confused?
²¹Now, then, one cannot see the sun,
Though it be bright in the heavens,
Until the wind comes and clears them [of
    clouds!.

²²By the north wind the golden rays emerge;
The splendor about God is awesome.
²³Shaddai—we cannot attain to Him;
He is great in power and justice
And abundant in righteousness, He does
    not torment.
²⁴Therefore, men are in awe of Him
Whom none of the wise can perceive.

38 Then the Lord replied to Job out of the tempest
and said:

²Who is this who darkens counsel,
Speaking without knowledge?
³Gird your loins like a man;
I will ask and you will inform Me.

⁴Where were you when I laid the earth's
    foundations?
Speak if you have understanding.
⁵Do you know who fixed its dimensions
Or who measured it with a line?
⁶Onto what were its bases sunk?
Who set its cornerstone
⁷When the morning stars sang together
And all the divine beings shouted for joy?

⁸Who closed the sea behind doors
When it gushed forth out of the womb,
⁹When I clothed it in clouds,
Swaddled it in dense clouds,
¹⁰When I made breakers My limit for it,
And set up its bar and doors,
¹¹And said, "You may come so far and no
    farther;
Here your surging waves will stop"?

¹²Have you ever commanded the day to
    break,
Assigned the dawn its place,
¹³So that it seizes the corners of the earth
And shakes the wicked out of it?
¹⁴It changes like clay under the seal
Till [its hues] are fixed like those of a
    garment.
¹⁵Their light is withheld from the wicked,
And the upraised arm is broken.

¹⁶Have you penetrated to the sources of the
    sea,
Or walked in the recesses of the deep?

¹⁷Have the gates of death been disclosed to
      you?
Have you seen the gates of deep darkness?
¹⁸Have you surveyed the expanses of the
      earth?
If you know of these—tell Me.

¹⁹Which path leads to where light dwells,
And where is the place of darkness,
²⁰That you may take it to its domain
And know the way to its home?
²¹Surely you know, for you were born then,
And the number of your years is many!

²²Have you penetrated the vaults of snow,
Seen the vaults of hail,
²³Which I have put aside for a time of
      adversity,
For a day of war and battle?
²⁴By what path is the west wind
      dispersed,
The east wind scattered over the earth?
²⁵Who cut a channel for the torrents
And a path for the thunderstorms,
²⁶To rain down on uninhabited land,
On the wilderness where no man is,
²⁷To saturate the desolate wasteland,
And make the crop of grass sprout forth?
²⁸Does the rain have a father?
Who begot the dewdrops?
²⁹From whose belly came forth the ice?
Who gave birth to the frost of heaven?
³⁰Water congeals like stone,
And the surface of the deep compacts.

³¹Can you tie cords to Pleiades
Or undo the reins of Orion?
³²Can you lead out Mazzaroth in its season,
Conduct the Bear with her sons?
³³Do you know the laws of heaven
Or impose its authority on earth?

³⁴Can you send up an order to the clouds
For an abundance of water to cover you?
³⁵Can you dispatch the lightning on a
      mission
And have it answer you, "I am ready"?
³⁶Who put wisdom in the hidden parts?
Who gave understanding to the mind?

³⁷Who is wise enough to give an account of
      the heavens?
Who can tilt the bottles of the sky,
³⁸Whereupon the earth melts into a mass,
And its clods stick together.

³⁹Can you hunt prey for the lion,
And satisfy the appetite of the king of
      beasts?
⁴⁰They crouch in their dens,
Lie in ambush in their lairs.

39 ⁴¹Who provides food for the raven
When his young cry out to God
And wander about without food?

Do you know the season when the
mountain goats give birth?
Can you mark the time when the hinds
      calve?
²Can you count the months they must
      complete?
Do you know the season they give birth,
³When they couch to bring forth their
      offspring,
To deliver their young?
⁴Their young are healthy; they grow up in
      the open;
They leave and return no more.

⁵Who sets the wild ass free?
Who loosens the bonds of the onager,
⁶Whose home I have made the wilderness,
The salt land his dwelling-place?
⁷He scoffs at the tumult of the city,
Does not hear the shouts of the driver.
⁸He roams the hills for his pasture;
He searches for any green thing.

⁹Would the wild ox agree to serve you?
Would he spend the night at your crib?
¹⁰Can you hold the wild ox by ropes to the
      furrow?
Would he plow up the valleys behind you?
¹¹Would you rely on his great strength
And leave your toil to him?
¹²Would you trust him to bring in the seed
And gather it in from your threshing floor?

¹³The wing of the ostrich beats joyously;
Are her pinions and plumage like the
      stork's?
¹⁴She leaves her eggs on the ground,
Letting them warm in the dirt,
¹⁵Forgetting they may be crushed underfoot,
Or trampled by a wild beast.
¹⁶Her young are cruelly abandoned as if
      they were not hers;
Her labor is in vain for lack of concern.
¹⁷For God deprived her of wisdom,
Gave her no share of understanding,
¹⁸Else she would soar on high,
Scoffing at the horse and its rider.

¹⁹Do you give the horse his strength?
Do you clothe his neck with a mane?
²⁰Do you make him quiver like locusts,
His majestic snorting [spreading] terror?
²¹He paws with force, he runs with vigor,
Charging into battle.
²²He scoffs at fear; he cannot be frightened;
He does not recoil from the sword.
²³A quiverful of arrows whizzes by him,
And the flashing spear and the javelin.
²⁴Trembling with excitement, he swallows
      the land;
He does not turn aside at the blast of the
      trumpet.
²⁵As the trumpet sounds, he says, "Aha!"
From afar he smells the battle,
The roaring and shouting of the officers.

²⁶Is it by your wisdom that the hawk grows
      pinions,
Spreads his wings to the south?
²⁷Does the eagle soar at your command,
Building his nest high,
²⁸Dwelling in the rock,
Lodging upon the fastness of a jutting rock?
²⁹From there he spies out his food;
From afar his eyes see it.
³⁰His young gulp blood;
Where the slain are, there is he.

40 The Lord said in reply to Job.

²Shall one who should be disciplined
      complain against Shaddai?

He who arraigns God must respond.

³Job said in reply to the Lord:

⁴See, I am of small worth; what can I answer
      You?
I clap my hand to my mouth.
⁵I have spoken once, and will not reply;
Twice, and will do so no more.

⁶Then the Lord replied to Job out of the
      tempest and said:

⁷Gird your loins like a man;
I will ask, and you will inform Me.
⁸Would you impugn My justice?
Would you condemn Me that you may be
      right?
⁹Have you an arm like God's?
Can you thunder with a voice like His?
¹⁰Deck yourself now with grandeur and
      eminence;
Clothe yourself in glory and majesty
¹¹Scatter wide your raging anger;
See every proud man and bring him low.
¹²See every proud man and humble him,
And bring them down where they stand.
¹³Bury them all in the earth;
Hide their faces in obscurity.
¹⁴Then even I would praise you
For the triumph your right hand won you.

¹⁵Take now behemoth, whom I made as I
      did you;
He eats grass, like the cattle.
¹⁶His strength is in his loins,
His might in the muscles of his belly.
¹⁷He makes his tail stand up like a cedar;
The sinews of his thighs are knit together.
¹⁸His bones are like tubes of bronze,
His limbs like iron rods.
¹⁹He is the first of God's works;
Only his Maker can draw the sword against
      him.
²⁰The mountains yield him produce,
Where all the beasts of the field play.
²¹He lies down beneath the lotuses,
In the cover of the swamp reeds.
²²The lotuses embower him with shade;

The willows of the brook surround him.
23He can restrain the river from its rushing;
He is confident the stream will gush at his
    command.
24Can he be taken by his eyes?
Can his nose be pierced by hooks?
25Can you draw out Leviathan by a fish-
    hook?
Can you press down his tongue by a rope?
26Can you put a ring through his nose,
Or pierce his jaw with a barb?
27Will he plead with you at length?
Will he speak soft words to you?
28Will he make an agreement with you
To be taken as your lifelong slave?
29Will you play with him like a bird,
And tie him down for your girls?
30Shall traders traffic in him?
Will he be divided up among merchants?
31Can you fill his skin with darts

41 Or his head with fish-spears?

32Lay a hand on him,
And you will never think of battle again.

See, any hope [of capturing] him must be
    disappointed;
One is prostrated by the very sight of him.
2There is no one so fierce as to rouse him;
Who then can stand up to Me?
3Whoever confronts Me I will requite,
For everything under the heavens is Mine.
4I will not be silent concerning him
Or the praise of his martial exploits.
5Who can uncover his outer garment?
Who can penetrate the folds of his jowls?
6Who can pry open the doors of his face?
His bared teeth strike terror.
7His protective scales are his pride,
Locked with a binding seal.
8One scale touches the other;
Not even a breath can enter between them.
9Each clings to each;
They are interlocked so they cannot be
    parted.
10His sneezings flash lightning,
And his eyes are the glimmerings of dawn.
11Firebrands stream from his mouth;
Fiery sparks escape.

12Out of his nostrils comes smoke
As from a steaming, boiling cauldron.
13His breath ignites coals;
Flames blaze from his mouth.
14Strength resides in his neck;
Power leaps before him.
15The layers of his flesh stick together;
He is as though cast hard; he does not tot-
    ter.
16His heart is cast hard as a stone,
Hard as the nether millstone.
17Divine beings are in dread as he rears up;
As he crashes down, they cringe.
18No sword that overtakes him can prevail,
Nor spear, nor missile, nor lance.
19He regards iron as straw,
Bronze, as rotted wood.
20No arrow can put him to flight;
Slingstones turn into stubble for him.
21Clubs are regarded as stubble;
He scoffs at the quivering javelin.
22His underpart is jagged shards;
It spreads a threshing-sledge on the mud.
23He makes the depths seethe like a caul-
    dron;
He makes the sea [boil] line an ointment-
    pot.
24His wake is a luminous path;
He makes the deep seem white-haired.
25There is no one on land who can dominate
    him.
Made as he is without fear.
26He sees all that is haughty;
He is king over all proud beasts.

42 Job said in reply to the Lord:

2I know that You can do everything,
That nothing you propose is impossible
    for You.
3Who is this who obscures counsel without
    knowledge?
Indeed, I spoke without understanding
Of things beyond me, which I did not know.
4Hear now, and I will speak;
I will ask, and You will inform me.
5I had heard You with my ears,
But now I see You with my eyes;
 6Therefore, I recant and relent,
Being but dust and ashes.

[7]After the Lord had spoken these words to Job, the Lord said to Eliphaz the Temanite, "I am incensed at you and your two friends, for you have not spoken the truth about Me as did My servant Job. [8]Now take seven bulls and seven rams and go to My servant Job and sacrifice a burnt offering for yourselves. And let Job, My servant, pray for you; for to him I will show favor and not treat you vilely, since you have not spoken the truth about Me as did My servant Job." [9]Eliphaz the Temanite and Bildad the Shuhite and Zophar the Naamathite went and did as the Lord had told them, and the Lord showed favor to Job. [10]The Lord restored Job's fortunes when he prayed on behalf of his friends, and the Lord gave Job twice what he had before.

[11]All his brothers and sisters and all his former friends came to him and had a meal with him in his house. They consoled and comforted him for all the misfortune that the Lord had brought upon him. Each gave him one *kesitah* and each one gold ring. [12]Thus the Lord blessed the latter years of Job's life more than the former. He had fourteen thousand sheep, six thousand camels, one thousand yoke of oxen, and one thousand she-asses. [13]He also had seven sons and three daughters. [14]The first he named Jemimah, the second Keziah, and the third Keren-happuch. [15]Nowhere in the land were women as beautiful as Job's daughters to be found. Their father gave them estates together with their brothers. [16]Afterward, Job lived one hundred and forty years to see four generations of sons and grandsons. [17]So Job died old and contented.

"Genesis," "Exodus," and excerpts from "Job," reprinted from *Tanakh: A New Translation of the Holy Scriptures According to the Traditional Hebrew Test*, (1985), the Jewish Publication Society.

The Story of the Flood
from *THE EPIC OF GILGAMESH*

Utnapishtin relates the story of the flood to Gilgamesh:

'You know the city Shurrupak, it stands on the banks of Euphrates? That city grew old and the gods that were in it were old. There was Anu, lord of the firmament, their father, and warrior Enlil their counsellor, Ninurta the helper, and Ennugi watcher over canals; and with them also was Ea. In those days the world teemed, the people multiplied, the world bellowed like a wild bull, and the great god was aroused by the clamour. Enlil heard the clamour and he said to the gods in council, "The uproar of mankind is intolerable and sleep is no longer possible by reason of the babel." So the gods agreed to exterminate mankind. Enlil did this, but Ea because of his oath warned me in a dream. He whispered their words to my house of reeds, "Reed-house, reed-house! Wall, O wall, hearken reed-house, wall reflect; O man of Shurrupak, son of Ubara-Tutu; tear down your house and build a boat, abandon possessions and look for life, and despise worldly goods and save your soul alive. Tear down your house, I say, and build a boat. These are the measurements of the barque as you shall build her: let her beam equal her length, let her deck be roofed like the vault that covers the abyss; then take up into the boat the seed of all living creatures."

'When I had understood I said to my lord, "Behold, what you have commanded I will honour and perform, but how shall I answer the people, the city, the elders?" Then Ea opened his mouth and said to me, his servant, "Tell them this: I have learnt that Enlil is wrathful against me, I dare no longer walk in his land nor live in his city; I will go down to the Gulf to dwell with Ea my lord. But on you he will rain down abundance, rare fish and shy wild-fowl, a rich harvest-tide. In the evening the rider of the storm will bring you wheat in torrents."

'In the first light of dawn all my household gathered round me, the children brought pitch and the men whatever was necessary. On the fifth day I laid the keel and the ribs, then I made fast the planking. The ground-space was one acre, each side of the deck measured one hundred and twenty cubits, making a square. I built six decks below, seven in all, I divided them into nine sections with bulkheads between. I drove in wedges where needed, I saw to the punt-poles, and laid in supplies. The carriers brought oil in baskets, I poured pitch into the furnace and asphalt and oil; more oil was consumed in caulking, and more again the master of the boat took into his stores. I slaughtered bullocks for the people and every day I killed sheep. I gave the shipwrights wine to drink as though it were river water, raw wine and red wine and oil and white wine. There was feasting then as there is at the time of the New Year's festival; I myself anointed my head. On the seventh day the boat was complete.

'Then was the launching full of difficulty; there was shifting of ballast above and below till two thirds was submerged. I loaded into her all that I had of gold and of living things, my family, my kin, the best of the field both wild and tame, and all the craftsmen. I sent them on board, for the time that Shamash had ordained was already fulfilled when he said, "In the evening, when the rider of the storm sends down the destroying rain, enter the boat and batten her down." The time was fulfilled, the evening came, the rider of the storm sent down the rain. I looked out at the weather and it was terrible, so I too boarded the boat and battened her down. All was now complete, the battening and the caulking; so I handed the tiller to Puzur-Amurri the steersman, with the navigation and the care of the whole boat.

'With the first light of dawn a black cloud came from the horizon; it thundered within where Adad, lord of the storm was riding. In front over hill and plain Shullat and Hanish, heralds of the storm, led on. Then the gods of the abyss rose up; Nergal pulled out the dams of the nether waters, Ninurta the war-lord threw down the dykes, and the seven judges of hell, the Annunaki, raised their torches, lighting the land with their livid flame. A stupor of despair went up to heaven when the god of the storm turned daylight to darkness, when he smashed the land like a cup. One whole day the tempest raged, gathering fury as it went, it poured over the people like the tides of battle; a man could not see his brother nor the people be seen from heaven. Even the gods were terrified at the flood, they fled to the highest heaven, the firmament of Anu; they crouched against the walls, cowering like curs. Then Ishtar the sweet-voiced Queen of Heaven cried out like a woman in travail: "Alas the days of old are turned to dust because I commanded evil; why did I command this evil in the council of all the gods? I commanded wars to destroy the people, but are they not my people, for I brought them forth? Now like the spawn of fish they float in the ocean." The great gods of heaven and of hell wept, they covered their mouths.

'For six days and six nights the winds blew, torrent and tempest and flood overwhelmed the world, tempest and flood raged together like warring hosts. When the seventh day dawned the storm from the south subsided, the sea grew calm, the flood was stilled; I looked at the face of the world and there was silence, all mankind was turned to clay. The surface of the sea stretched as flat as a rooftop; I opened a hatch and the light fell on my face. Then I bowed low, I sat down and I wept, the tears streamed down my face, for on every side was the waste of water. I looked for land in vain, but fourteen leagues distant there appeared a mountain, and there the boat grounded; on the mountain of Nisir the boat held fast, she held fast and did not budge. One day she held, and a second day on the mountain of Nisir she held fast and did not budge. A third day, and a fourth day she held fast on the mountain and did not budge; a fifth day and a sixth day she held fast on the mountain. When the seventh day dawned I loosed a dove and let her go. She flew away, but finding no resting-place she returned. Then I loosed a swallow, and she flew away but finding no resting-place she returned. I loosed a raven, she saw that the waters had retreated, she ate, she flew around, she cawed, and she did not come back. Then I threw everything open to the four winds, I made a sacrifice and poured out a libation on the mountain top. Seven and again seven cauldrons I set up on their stands, I heaped up wood and cane and cedar and myrtle. When the gods smelled the sweet savour, they gathered like flies over the sacrifice. Then, at last, Ishtar also came, she lifted her necklace with the jewels of heaven that once Anu had made to please her. "O you gods here present, by the lapis lazuli round my neck I shall remember these days as I remember the jewels of my throat; these last days I shall not forget. Let all the gods gather round the sacrifice, except Enlil. He shall not approach this offering, for without reflection he brought the flood; he consigned my people to destruction."

'When Enlil had come, when he saw the boat, he was wrath and swelled with anger at the gods, the host of heaven, "Has any of these mortals escaped? Not one was to have survived the destruction." Then the god of the wells and canals Ninurta opened his mouth and said to the warrior Enlil, "Who is there of the gods that can devise without Ea? It is Ea alone who knows all things." Then Ea opened his mouth and spoke to warrior Enlil, "Wisest of gods, hero Enlil, how could you so senselessly bring down the flood?

Lay upon the sinner his sin,
Lay upon the transgressor his transgression,
Punish him a little when he breaks loose,
Do not drive him too hard or he perishes;
Would that a lion had ravaged mankind
Rather than the flood,
Would that a wolf had ravaged mankind
Rather than the flood,
Would that famine had wasted the world
Rather than the flood,
Would that pestilence had wasted mankind
Rather than the flood.

It was not I that revealed the secret of the gods; the wise man learned it in a dream. Now take your counsel what shall be done with him."

'Then Enlil went up into the boat, he took me by the hand and my wife and made us enter the boat and kneel down on either side, he standing between us. He touched our foreheads to bless us saying, "In time past Utnapishtim was a mortal man; henceforth he and his wife shall live in the distance at the mouth of the rivers." Thus it was that the gods took me and placed me here to live in the distance, at the mouth of the rivers.'

N. K. Sanders, (1972), Penguin Books, Ltd.

SECTION TWO

ANCIENT GREECE

3000–800 BCE

2200 BCE Rise of Minoan culture on Crete

        1800 BCE Mycenaen Age on Greek mainland

1400 BCE Minoan civilization falls

        1184 BCE Legendary date of end of Trojan War

1100 BCE End of Mycenean civilization

        Dark Age of Greece begins

800–500 BCE

776 BCE First Olympic Games

        700 BCE Homer, Iliad and Odyssey

600 BCE Sappho born on Island of Lesbos

        540 BCE Fall of Ionian city-states to Persia

510 BCE Establishment of democracy in Athens

500–400 BCE

490 BCE Battle of Marathon

        480 BCE Golden Age of Greek art and architecture begins

461 BCE Athens "Age of Pericles" begins

        440 BCE Sophocles and Euripides, great tragedians

432 BCE Parthenon is completed

        431 BCE Peloponnesian War waged until 404 BCE

400–300 BCE

399 BCE Death of Socrates

        387 BCE Plato founds the Academy, writes Apology, Republic

359 BCE Philip of Macedonia conquers Greece
Greek influence spreads

        336 BCE Aristotle founds Lyceum

331 BCE Death of Alexander the Great

        300 BCE Greek influence spreads through "Hellenistic" world

Dates given are approximate

ANCIENT GREECE

For centuries, many have considered the civilization of ancient Greece to be one of the chief foundations of Western civilization, and certainly its role in shaping Western ideas, values, and institutions has been enormous. The nineteenth-century English poet Percy Bysshe Shelley expressed this indebtedness in the introduction to his lyric drama *Hellas:* "We are all Greeks. Our laws, our literature, our arts have their root in Greece." But the Greeks are not of interest to us simply because they are in some respects the culture out of which we evolved. They continue to influence us in both visible and invisible ways, says Shelley, and their achievements in thought, the arts, and politics are still admired.

When Shelley says that our "laws" have their roots in Greece, he refers to the development of the main forms of government in the Western world—democracy (rule of the many), oligarchy (rule of the few), and monarchy (rule of one)—and indeed of the very concept of a "constitution." Greek poets, dramatists, historians, and philosophers explored other ideas essential to political life, such as "equality" and "justice." On the practical level, the Greeks invented trial by jury and the manner of argumentation that goes with it (juridical rhetoric).

In literature, it is not too much of an exaggeration to say that the Greeks developed most of the types or *genres* of Western literature and produced at least one recognized masterpiece in each type. Homer's *Iliad* and *Odyssey* are considered the greatest epic poems. Greek "lyric," originally poetry to be recited with a lyre accompanying, was produced by such great names as Anacreon and Sappho. (The tune to which the national anthem of the United States is sung is entitled "Anacreon ascends into heaven.") The Athenians produced the three writers who defined tragic drama in the West: Aeschylus, Sophocles, and Euripides. The fifth century comic playwright Aristophanes, who attacked Athenian politics and politicians and his neighbors with gusto and who mocked tragedy while writing his own fantastic poetry, is still produced today. The later comedian Menander, whose plays today only exist in fragmentary form, was freely adapted by the Roman comic writers and thus became a major influence on all the comedy that followed Roman comedy. To this list could be added Demosthenes in oratory, Herodotus and Thucydides in historical writing, Plato and Aristotle in philosophy, and many others.

In the fine arts the ancient Greeks have set the standard in sculpture, producing such masterpieces as the "Venus de Milo," the "Apollo Belvedere," "Laöcoon," and others that are familiar to many people today. Greek architecture is constantly before us. Whether we can identify them by name or not, we recognize the Parthenon, and we live among many modern "neo-classical" buildings with their classical facades, Corinthian capitals on the columns, and decorative motifs such as the "meander pattern" of winding or crisscrossing lines.

The Greeks also pioneered in science and mathematics. Thales is considered the first of the Greek philosophers and the founder of natural science. The first great Greek name in mathematics is Pythagoras, he of the "Pythagorean theorem," who was philosopher, mathematician, and mystic. A later Greek famous for his mathematical achievements was Euclid, whose book, *The Elements*, was for two thousand years the standard textbook of mathematics. Archimedes, the greatest Greek mathematician and inventor, is perhaps most famous for his exclamation, "Eureka," the Greek word for "I have found it," when making one of his scientific discoveries. The astronomer Ptolemy is remembered for the "Ptolemaic system" of explaining the movements of the stars and planets, which dominated Western science for almost 1,500 years.

The Greek word for "art" is *techne,* a word that is at the root of "technique" and related words. One such "art" is the art of medicine. There have been immense advances in medicine in the modern period, but our debt to Greek medicine can be seen in the survival of such Greek words as "symptom," "diagnosis," "prognosis," "diet," and "pharmacy." One of the first great Greek medical men was Hippocrates. In the writings of Hippocrates and his followers we can see the roots of modern scientific thought: careful collection of evidence, testing of hypotheses, and the rejection of supernatural causation. Today all new physicians still take the Hippocratic oath.

From these examples we can readily see why it is so important to understand the heritage of the ancient Greeks if we are to understand Western civilization. Along with the Jewish and Christian heritage, the Greeks provide the foundation on which so much familiar to us is constructed. If Moses on Mt. Sinai receiving the law is one enduring symbol of Western civilization, then Socrates in the market square, arguing about goodness and beauty, is the other enduring image upon which the idea of the West would be constructed.

THE MINOANS (ca. 2000–ca. 1400 BCE)

Scholars typically trace the origins of Greek civilization to about 2200 BCE and the island of Crete in the Aegean Sea. There, a Bronze Age civilization developed that used metals, particularly bronze, in the construction of tools and weapons. The civilization of Minoan Crete was first discovered at the end of the nineteenth century by the English archeologist Arthur Evans (1851–1941), who named it *Minoan* after Minos, the legendary king of Crete. According to Greek mythology, it was on Minos that Perseus defeated the Minotaur, a half man, half bull creature.

In the early part of the twentieth century, excavations revealed an enormous palace complex at Knossus near the modern city of Iraklion. Historians have been able to piece together only fragmen-

tary evidence about the daily life, social structure, and political system of the Minoan civilization largely because their language, today called Linear A, remains undecipherable. As a result, it is uncertain whether to count the Minoans as ancestors of the Greeks. It simply is not known if the Minoan language is related to Greek.

We do know that the Minoans, over a period of about 800 years, created a sophisticated palace society. Minoan palaces were massive buildings that served as the centerpiece for most political, economic, and religious activity. The palace at Knossos, for example, was five stories tall, divided up into hundreds of rooms, and possessed indoor plumbing including showers and flush toilets. Minoan palaces were not only places of work and business, but also served as a residence for the rulers and their families.

Built around and adjacent to the palaces were the living quarters for much of the population. These dwellings too possessed indoor plumbing. Many Minoans decorated their walls with elaborate frescoes depicting scenes from daily life, landscapes, sporting events, and domesticated pets. The frescoes also suggest that women played an important role in Minoan religious life.

The Minoans possessed a complex agricultural and urban existence. Archeologists have discovered the remains of typical Mediterranean dietary staples such as grapes, olives and olive oil, wine, and other grains. There is some evidence to suggest an economic system for the redistribution of goods. Minoan farmers donated portions of their crops to the government as part of a tax system. These yields were stored in hundreds of enormous clay jars in the palace. The surpluses would either be given to those in need, or held for distribution during economic downturns. Archeologists have also unearthed stores such as bakeries and pottery shops. Finally, Minoan overseas merchants and sailors engaged in trade around the Mediterranean.

Minoan society and culture thrived and prospered until about 1400 BCE. Then, the Minoans suffered a sudden and catastrophic collapse. The reason for the destruction is unknown and fiercely debated. Some believe the end of Minoan society was caused by a massive volcanic explosion on a nearby island. A more likely theory is that Crete was invaded and pillaged by Greeks from the mainland known as Mycenaeans. Unlike other settlements scattered around the Mediterranean basin, the Minoans did not fortify their settlements with defensive walls. This would have made them a particularly appealing and vulnerable target for the warrior-like Mycenaeans.

THE MYCENAEANS (ca. 1800–ca. 1100 BCE)

While it is unclear if the Minoans should be counted as ancestors of the Greeks, there is no doubt that the Mycenaeans represent the first Greek-speaking civilization to take root on the mainland of Greece. The term "Mycenaean" is a general term applied to a host of cities that developed in the fertile valleys and along the coastlines of Greece beginning around 1800 BCE. Historians refer to these early Greeks as Mycenaeans because of the city of Mycenae, the most prominent and powerful of the cities.

Linguists have had much greater success in translating the written language of the Mycenaean Greeks, called Linear B. This is fortunate as the Mycenaeans were avid record keepers. The result is that we know a great deal more about the Mycenaean civilization than we do about the Minoan.

Excavations have revealed the remnants of a wealthy and sophisticated civilization. The Mycenaean Greeks were predominantly a seafaring people who had grown wealthy from overseas trade. It was not uncommon for the leading families of a city to be buried with gold jewelry and masks, cups, necklaces, pendants, rings and pottery. Moreover, the accumulated wealth and power of the Mycenaean cities was demonstrated by massive buildings, fortified palaces, and sturdy defensive walls.

Unlike the Minoans, the Mycenaean Greeks were a warrior culture. Each of the mainland cities was ruled by powerful and ambitious kings who continually sought to project their power and influence on the peninsula and among their closest neighbors. Pottery and other remnants of Mycenaean Greek culture have been found in such disparate places as modern-day Italy, Turkey, Egypt, and Crete. This has led to the conclusion that the Greeks were not just participating in commercial trade, but were actively engaged in military campaigns of conquest.

War was an important organizing principle for mainland Greek society. Written records of the period reveal that the Greek social hierarchy was arranged with kings and warrior-aristocrats at the top, followed by common soldiers, artisans, and peasants. At the bottom of the hierarchy were slaves–those taken as prisoners of war.

This emphasis on war and conquest can be seen throughout the culture. Mycenaean kings and nobles prided themselves on and celebrated heroic deeds performed in battle. Members of the upper class were frequently buried with their protective armor and weapons. Frescoes on the walls of their living spaces depicted scenes of sporting contests, hunting expeditions and, not surprisingly, battles.

Mycenaean civilization loomed large in the collective imaginations of succeeding Greeks, and indeed, for a large portion of the Western world. Some four hundred years after the collapse of the Mycenaean civilization, the great epic poet Homer forever immortalized this period in his famous work the *Iliad*. The poem tells the story of the Trojan War and the attack on the city of Troy (which the Greeks also called *Ilion*; hence *Iliad*, a story of Ilion) by a league of Mycenaean city-states. For centuries experts believed that the epic was pure myth, but in the nineteenth century a German-Russian-American entrepreneur and self-made scholar, Heinrich Schliemann, discovered and excavated the ruins of ancient Troy, verifying its existence.

One mystery still remaining is exactly how Mycenaean civilization met its end. Records reveal that the city of Mycenae was destroyed sometime around 1200–1100 BCE, though historians do not know how or why this destruction took place. By 1100, other cities on mainland Greece suffered similar fates as Mycenae—again, with no clear consensus on how or why. The scholarly community is deeply divided on these issues. Some believe that it was unceasing and brutal civil war which ultimately led to the demise of the Mycenaean Greek kingdoms. Others believe the Greeks succumbed to widespread famine. Another group believes the Greeks were invaded from the north by a group of Greek-speaking peoples called the Dorians. A final group believes that a massive earthquake destroyed all civilization on the mainland. Ongoing archeological research is shedding new light on this important question. Whatever the causes, by around 1100 BCE, Mycenaean Greek civilization had fallen. Its demise ushered in a period known as the Dark Age.

THE DARK AGE (ca. 1100–800 BCE)

Historians refer to the next four-hundred-year period as the Dark Age because the Greeks lost virtually all of the distinguishing characteristics of civilization. No longer were there heavily populated communities or political and economic organization. Amazingly, the Greeks even lost the ability to write, reverting back to a pre-literate society. They no longer depicted people or animals in their artwork. The Greeks also ceased to engage in overseas commerce and contact with peoples living outside the mainland dwindled to almost nothing.

The Greek peninsula suffered massive depopulation during this period. Less land was cultivated and less food produced. As a result, only a small population could be sustained. Large numbers of Greeks left home in search of more hospitable living circumstances. New Greek communities were established on the islands of Crete and Lesbos, as well as in Ionia (along the coast of present-day Turkey). These new communities proved invaluable in helping to preserve Greek cultural traditions as well as infusing them into new areas around the Mediterranean basin.

Those Greeks who survived on the mainland eked out an existence living in tiny communities, working at subsistence farming and sheep herding sheep. The shadow of darkness would hang over Greece until about 800 BCE and would not be completely lifted until the Greeks learned to read and write again.

THE ARCHAIC AGE AND THE REBIRTH OF CIVILIZATION (ca. 800–ca. 500 BCE)

By about 800 BCE Greek civilization had begun to experience a renaissance. Historians call this period the Archaic Age, which became one of the most vibrant and important epochs in Greek history. A rebirth of literacy led to literary inventions such as Homer's great epic poems and the lyrical poetry of Sappho. Over the ensuing three centuries the Greek economy was revived, leading to rising prosperity and massive population growth. This period also witnessed the birth of the Greek *polis* (city-state) and the rise to prominence of Athens and Sparta.

The leading factor in helping to bring the Greeks out of the Dark Age was a remarkable rebound in economic production and overseas trade. Contact with peoples like the Phoenicians (from present-day Israel) revived economic activity on mainland Greece and even helped restore Greek literacy.

Two important innovations also aided the transformation of the Greek economy. First, coined money was invented in Lydia (modern-day Turkey). The introduction of small, standardized pieces of gold or silver spread quickly among the Greeks and transformed a barter economy into a more sophisticated, efficient, and unified economic system. The second innovation was the invention of iron metallurgy invented in the eastern Mediterranean. The Greeks became acquainted with this new technology through their contacts from overseas trade. Iron had many advantages over bronze. It was more plentiful and therefore cheaper. It was also much more durable. The Greeks soon began to fashion iron farming tools. As a result, they were able to cultivate more land, grow more food, and ultimately feed a large population.

While the population on the mainland was rising, many Greeks took to the sea in search of economic advancement, adventure, and a new home. The expansion of Greek settlements around the Mediterranean was truly remarkable. By the end of the Archaic period, Greek settlements had been established in Sicily, southern France and Italy, Spain, North Africa, and the Black Sea. Major European cities such as Naples and Marseilles began as Greek colonies. By the end of the sixth century BCE the dominant culture of the Western Mediterranean world was Greek.

Perhaps the surest sign the Greeks had emerged from the Dark Age was the appearance of one of the greatest poets of all time, Homer. Composed early in the eight century, Homer's *Iliad* is the oldest surviving literary work of the Greeks and of Western civilization. In the *Iliad*, Homer tells the tale of a ten-year war between the Mycenaeans and the Trojans instigated by the abduction of Helen, wife of the Greek prince Menelaus, by the Trojan prince Paris. The story begins in the later stages of the war, when King Agamemnon and one of his commanders, Achilles, have a bitter quarrel. Agamemnon, commander-in-chief of the Greeks, is forced by the god Apollo to give up a woman who is his warprize. To avoid losing face, he takes the woman of Achilles, a powerful prince and by far the best warrior. They quarrel and Achilles withdraws to his hut. It is clear the tide is turning against the Greeks, but Achilles' pride will not allow him to fight. His stubbornness leads to the death of his close friend Patroclus. To avenge the death of his friend, Achilles rejoins the Greek army and drives the Trojans back into their city. Achilles then kills Hector, the son of the Trojan King Priam, and desecrates the body. Priam risks his life by personally asking for the return of his son's body. The *Iliad* ends with the burial of Hector.

Homer's poetry became standard learning for generations of educated Greeks. Homer's heroes, especially Achilles, became role models and guides to masculine behavior for nearly a millennium. In these tales, the Greeks learned of aristocratic values such as honor, courage, and excellence. They also learned about fate and the interaction between gods and mortals. In the *Iliad*, the gods offered Achilles a choice between a long life without honor or a short life with honor. For Achilles, the choice was clear. As the great Greek tragedian Sophocles noted, "time has no value; each day we may live, or we may die. Live well; die well. That is the noble life" (*Ajax*, ll. 479–480)

Unlike the God of the Hebrews, Greek gods did not insist on moral behavior on the part of their followers. In the *Iliad*, the Olympian gods and goddesses, chief among them Zeus, Hera, Athena, Apollo, Poseidon, Hermes, and Hephaestus, are depicted as aristocratic Greek rulers who have the added advantage of being freed from the constraints of mortality. They possessed the same desire for power and recognition humans did and had endless opportunities to realize their desire because they did not die. Unlike Achilles, they possessed both great glory and a long life.

Greek gods expected honors, gifts, and services, and in return they would bestow rewards in this life. The gods were celebrated in festivals held throughout the year. They differed from city to city. We know the most about those in Athens. Ritual sacrifice was another way of honoring the gods. There was no religious literature—sacred scriptures—such as we commonly identify with religious groups. Communication between the gods and humans was done through divination and the interpretation of omens. The most famous place to seek out the advice of the gods or to make a request

was the oracle of Apollo at Delphi. The Delphic Oracle represented the ultimate in wisdom for the Greeks for centuries. "The god in Delphi neither speaks, nor does he hide; instead he gives a sign"— one of the first sentences we have from the Greek philosopher Heraclitus. As his remark explains, the god's reply, revealed by an inspired priestess, was often enigmatic. However, for the Greeks, priests and priestesses were not necessarily figures of authority, even on religious affairs, which were overseen by the secular authorities. The priests and priestesses were mere functionaries.

Homer was not the only renowned poet of the Archaic age. Other famous Greek poets came from this period as well. A century after Homer, on the Aegean island of Lesbos, Sappho in one poem declared audaciously that "whatever one wants" is more important than military power; she imagined that Aphrodite, goddess of love, was consoling her in another poem; and she described in detail her physical sensations when in the presence of the woman she loved. The Greeks always considered Sappho one of their greatest lyric poets and her poems became well known throughout the Greek world and influenced later Roman poets. A selection of readings from Sappho's poetry can be found following Chapter Two.

Beginning in the Archaic period, Greek philosophers began seeking explanations of the origin and nature of the universe in rational rather than in traditionally mythological ways. They are the first of what are called the "Pre-Socratic" philosophers: those philosophers who came before Socrates. Thinkers such as Thales and Anaximander, both from Ionia, believed that unchanging natural laws governed the universe and not the will of the gods. Their inquiries began with an interest in *change*, as in the human life cycle and the cycles of nature. The Pre-Socratics reasoned that if there is change (becoming) there must be something that undergoes change (being), something that takes different forms but persists in and through time. This was the idea of *unity in difference or plurality*, the notion of a primary universal substance underlying and producing this infinitely varied and changing universe.

Among the pre-Socratics was a group called the Atomists who posited that the universe is made up of an infinite number of indivisible units called atoms

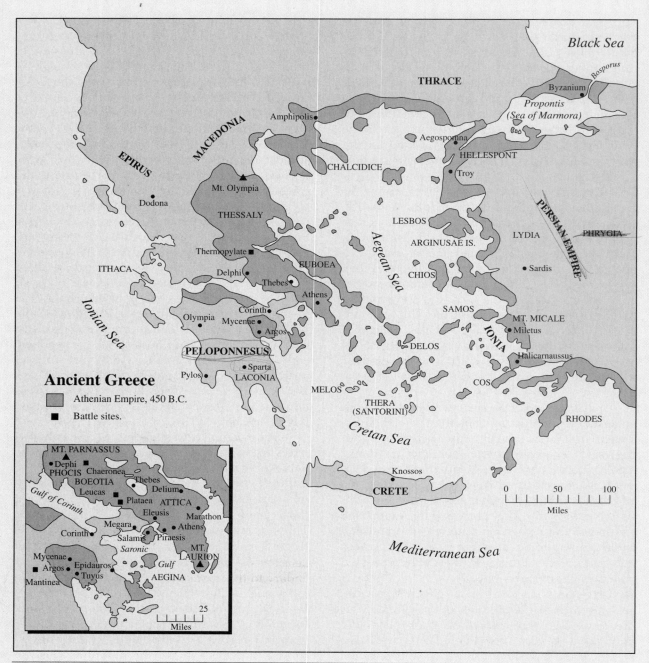

Ancient Greece

🟦 Athenian Empire, 450 B.C.

■ Battle sites.

Ancient Greece. Reprinted from *A History of Civilization*, Ninth Edition, by Robin W. Winks, (1996), Prentice-Hall, Inc.

(from a-tome, meaning uncuttable) which are elements too small to be perceived by the senses. According to the Atomists, everything is made up of collisions and clusters of atoms, including the human mind or soul, and ceases to be when its atoms separate. This idea was revived many centuries later by Galileo, Newton, and other pioneers of the Scientific Revolution of the seventeenth century.

Perhaps the most distinctive and important feature of Greek civilization to emerge during the Archaic age was the polis or city-state. During the earlier Mycenaean Greek civilization, all political, social, and economic life of a city revolved around the king. To live in a city meant to subject oneself to the will of the king. In the polis of the Archaic age, relationships between and among people in the cities were conceived of quite differently. Rather than being subjects, certain people who lived in the city-state were citizens with both rights and obligations.

Because of the rugged, mountainous terrain of mainland Greece, most of the city-states that developed during this period did so in isolation, separate and independent from each other. As a result, the *poleis* (plural of polis) developed different types of political leadership. Some were ruled by a monarchy, meaning "rule of one man." The city-state of Thebes, for example, was ruled by a king. Yet even kings were constrained by laws and expected to recognize the rights of the citizens. Other poleis were ruled by an oligarchy, which literally meant "rule of the few." Sparta, for example, was an oligarchy governed by a small, wealthy, and powerful group of elite families. Finally, a polis could be run as a democracy ("rule of the people"). In democratic poleis, like Athens, all citizens, regardless of wealth or social position, participated in every level of government.

However, only a very circumscribed group of people was able to partake in the rights, benefits, and responsibilities of a citizen of the polis. Foreigners, even Greek-born, could never become a citizen of the polis. Nor could women or slaves become full citizens (although women were allowed some measure of participation in civic and religious life). At its peak, Athens had a total population of about 300,000. Only 43,000 men, however, held the rights of citizenship.

Undoubtedly, the two most prominent and well-known city-states to emerge during this period were Athens and Sparta. Until the middle of the sixth century BCE, Athens was ruled by a series of *tyrants*. A tyrant, as the Greeks defined the term, was a person who came to power by unconstitutional means. Some of the Greek tyrants were remembered for their cruelty or their great wealth, as we might expect, but several of them were famous for their wisdom. Tyrants often were responsible for major public works and supported the arts. By 510, Athenians had come to embrace democracy. That is, every free male Athenian was a citizen and member of the governing assembly. This assembly was aided by a "Council of Five Hundred" which was chosen by lot and which debated matters before presenting them to the assembly. The courts were also in the hands of the citizens. Cases were decided by juries chosen by lot which could be very large, usually in the hundreds. The effective leadership of the state was in the hands of the man who was the most persuasive speaker in the assembly on any given occasion. If someone was persuasive over a period of time, he might be called a *demagogue* or "leader of the people," but he held no official office. To the Greeks, the term demagogue simply meant "leader of the people" and it held none of the negative connotations that it does in the modern age.

Sparta developed quite differently. That city was under the military control of a small, ruling elite. While all Spartan citizens were legally equal, actual leadership of the city was in the hands of two kings who were primarily military leaders. The kings, in conjunction with a small body of warriors, made all decisions for the city. Individual rights were secondary to the interests of the state. Boys after the age of seven were taken from their families and trained under harsh conditions. Men were organized into clubs that took precedence over family life. For their entire lives, Spartan men were soldiers and remained constantly prepared for warfare. Women also played an integral part in Spartan society. They were expected to be just as fit, strong, and courageous as the men. Though they did not serve as soldiers, Spartan women fulfilled their obligations to the city by producing healthy children, raising them as sturdy warriors, and inculcating in them patriotism and morality. Women were viewed as crucial to the survival of the city and as a result enjoyed a large measure of autonomy and equality. The Spartan soldier was considered to be the best-trained soldier in the Greek world. We still use the adjective "Spartan" to refer to persons and conditions of life that are austere or highly disciplined.

THE CLASSICAL PERIOD (ca. 500–ca. 400 BCE)

The classical period began with a great military victory over the Persians and ended in civil war among the Greeks. The period between the wars was perhaps the most creative and productive period in art, architecture, literature, and philosophy the Western world has ever experienced. As a result historians call this period the Classical age of Greek history and the period between the wars as the Golden Age of Athens.

By the middle of the sixth century BCE, the wealthy city-states of Greece made an appealing target for the Persian Empire. Cyrus the Great, leader of Persia, moved against the Greek cities of Ionia and by 540 had successfully brought them under Persian control. Persia now represented a major threat to the Greek mainland.

In 499, the Greek cities of Ionia rebelled against Persian rule. Athens sent a naval fleet to aid in the uprising. Despite Athenian support, the Persians were able to put down the rebellion relatively quickly. Seeking to punish the Athenians for meddling in Persian affairs, Darius, the son of Cyrus, sent a large Persian fleet across the Aegean. Athenian forces met the much larger Persian force at Marathon and defeated them there. After the battle of Marathon, the Greek forces hurried the twenty-six miles back to Athens to guard the city from the Persian navy. The Athenian victory at Marathon is regarded as one of the greatest in all of military history and today's marathons are a commemoration of one Athenian's sprint back to Athens to announce the victory.

The Persians, however, were not to be deterred. In 480 BCE, the Persian King, Xerxes, Darius's successor, launched a full-scale invasion of the Greek mainland. Landing with a massive invasion force numbering about 100,000 soldiers in northern Greece, the Persians methodically began to make their way down the peninsula. In response, the Greek city-states united to face the challenge. This was unprecedented in Greek history. Thirty-one city-states put their deep mistrust of each other and their love of their own independence on hold to unite to face the Persian threat. The Athenians were in charge of naval forces while the Spartans gained command of the Greek army.

The alliance proved decisive, yet victory over the Persians was no foregone conclusion. The Persians continued their march south and in 480 BCE reached Athens. The Athenians, realizing they could not defend themselves, evacuated the city. Persian forces occupied and then burned Athens. That summer, the Greeks turned the tides of war when Athenian naval forces met and destroyed the Persian armada at Salamis, an island just off the coast of Athens. Without naval support, the Persians were finished. The final battle in the Persian wars came in 479 when a combined Spartan and Athenian force defeated the remnants of the Persian army at Plataea. Greece was victorious.

The alliance between Athens and Sparta immediately broke down following the victory over Persia. Cooperation gave way to mistrust and fear. Both cities organized competing alliances in hopes of maintaining a balance of power. Athens became the leader of the Delian League. This league was made up of coastal and island states, most of them relatively small, and many of them formerly dominated by Persia. Through its naval power and threat of force Athens controlled the League in a heavy-handed fashion. Allies were forced to pay financial tribute to Athens in return for protection. Though unpopular, Athens was able to create what historians have called the Athenian Empire.

At home, the victory over the Persians led to increased self-confidence among the Athenians and the burgeoning empire provided the city with the funds necessary to rebuild in a grand fashion. During the next thirty years, from 460 to 430 BCE, Athens would reach the pinnacle of her wealth, power, and prestige.

No political figure was more important to this process than Pericles (ca. 494–429 BCE). A member of one of Athens' leading families, Pericles emerged as the leading demagogue during the Golden Age. Once in power, Pericles set Athens on an ambitious and far-reaching renewal project with the goal of making the city the political, artistic and cultural capital of the Greek world. In a famous speech, Pericles articulates what sets Athenians and their city apart from all other cities:

> Let me say that our system of government [democracy] does not copy the institutions of our neighbours. It is more the case of our being a model to others, than of our imitating anyone else . . . No one, so long as he has it in him to be of service to the state, is kept in political obscurity because of poverty. And, just as our political life is free and open, so is our day-to-day life in our relations with each other . . .
>
> . . . Our city is open to the world, and we have no periodical deportations. . . .
>
> . . . Mighty indeed are the marks and monuments of our empire which we have left. Future ages will wonder at us, as the present age wonders at us now. We do not need the praises of a Homer . . .

[Thucydides, *History of the War Fought Between Athens and Sparta*, translated by Rex Warner. London: Penguin Books, 1954, 117–122.]

During Pericles's reign, construction of most of the buildings and monuments we tend to associate with ancient Athens began. Religious shrines, theatres, and public buildings were constructed, including the Acropolis and Parthenon and other temples on the Acropolis, the great hill that dominates Athens.

In addition to undergoing a physical transformation Athens would also experience a remarkable flowing of its intellectual, cultural, and philosophical life. Athenian drama grew out of the city's religious festivals, particularly the festival to the god Dionysus. Both comedies and tragedies were written and performed, and prizes were awarded to the best ones. It is mainly the tragedies that have come down to us over the centuries because the themes that they dealt with represented the conflict between the will of the gods and human free will, inherent flaws of humanity,

and the limits of human agency. This subject will be dealt with more thoroughly in Chapter Two.

In the realm of philosophical inquiry, the invention of democracy in Athens gave rise to an interest in the problem of living successfully in a political society. The theorists and teachers who first took up the question of humans as "political animals" (as Aristotle was to phrase it) were known as *Sophists*. The Sophists were professional educators and their clients were Athenian citizens who wanted to improve their chances of political success. Their curriculum was based on rhetoric, the art of persuasive speaking. The goal was to produce an informed, well-rounded citizen who could hold his own in the assembly and in the law courts.

The most famous philosopher to emerge from this period was Socrates (469–399 BCE). Socrates rejected the relativism of the popular Sophists ("Man is the measure of all things"), and instead sought universal, objective truths. Socrates would spend his day (indeed his life) in conversation with anyone who would talk to him, questioning their beliefs about, for example, the nature of love, beauty, truth and justice in an effort to arrive at the essence of the concept being discussed. Socrates' emphasis on ethics was profoundly influential on the Western world. For us, Socrates, along with his student Plato, and Plato's student Aristotle, have come to personify philosophy, the love of wisdom, and the pursuit of truth. The philosophy of the classical period will be the subject of Chapters Three and Four.

Another distinctive characteristic of the Golden Age of Athens was the emergence of history as a major field of human inquiry. Herodotus (ca. 485–425 BCE), generally considered to be the father of history, emphasized a critical approach to studying the past. Herodotus's chronicle of the Persian wars entitled *The Histories* was based on massive research including eye-witness accounts of the key events. Unlike Homer and previous story-tellers, Herodotus de-emphasized the role of the gods in the unfolding of human events. Another Athenian historian, Thucydides (ca. 460-ca. 400 BCE), rivaled Herodotus as the Greeks' most influential historian. His *History of the Peloponnesian War* became the definitive work on the most famous war in all of Greek history. It is to that conflict that we now turn our attention.

The Peloponnesian War, fought from 431 to 404 BCE between Athens and her allies and Sparta and hers, would ultimately bring an end to the Golden Age of Greece and deal a severe blow to Greek civilization. According to Thucydides, by the middle of the fifth century, Sparta feared the growing economic and political might of the Athenian Empire. The trigger for war came when Athens fell into trade disputes with two of Sparta's allies. Sparta issued an ultimatum. The Spartan ambassador to Athens warned the Athenians that war between the two city-states would be disastrous for all the Greeks. Unfortunately, Pericles rejected both the Spartan ultimatum and the prophetic words of the ambassador. The war would consume the Greeks for a generation.

Pericles soon recognized that the Athenian army was no match for the larger and more powerful Spartan forces. Athenian hopes for victory rested with her navy. His strategy was to abandon the countryside surrounding Athens and bring the farmers and peasants inside the defensive walls of the city. While perhaps a sound military strategy, Pericles' decision proved disastrous. As a direct result of the overcrowded conditions in the city, in 430 BCE a horrific plague broke out in Athens. The disease spread rapidly and indiscriminately throughout the city, killing thousands. Thucydides painted a grim picture of life in Athens during the plague, describing piles of corpses on the streets and in the temples. Thucydides himself caught the disease but survived. Pericles was less fortunate. He died the following year.

Pericles was replaced by Alcibiades, an aristocrat, a relative of Pericles and a student of Socrates. One of his first acts as commander was to convince the Athenian assembly to reject a Spartan peace offer. Alcibiades persuasively argued that a more aggressive strategy could win the war. To that end, in 418 BCE he led the Athenians in a successful military campaign against the small and insignificant city-state of Melos, an ally of Sparta. According to Thucydides, the Athenians executed all the Melian men and sold the women and children into slavery in order to send a message to the Spartans.

After the Athenian victory at Melos, Alcibiades convinced the assembly to launch an invasion of the island of Sicily off the coast of present-day Italy. Sicily's greatest city, Syracuse, was an important ally of Sparta. The campaign turned out to be a fiasco. Before the military encounter Alicibiades was removed as commander by his political enemies within Athens. He then defected to the enemy. The Athenians pressed on with their plan of attack. It was a disaster. Nearly the entire Athenian naval fleet was destroyed. The military loss triggered a temporary collapse of Athenian democracy. For one year Athens was under the rule of a small group of aristocrats until a popular revolution restored democracy.

The war, however, would not go on much longer. With Persian financing, Sparta constructed a vast navy and proceeded to win a string of important sea battles against the Athenians. In 404 BCE, after twenty-seven years of near-continuous warfare, Athens surrendered. The Athenians could only stand by and watch as Spartan forces tore down the massive walls encircling their city. The Spartans moved quickly to install a puppet regime in Athens. This new anti-democratic government was made up of Athenian collaborators and is known as the Thirty Tyrants. The reign of the Thirty Tyrants was marked by brutality, corruption, and greed. In 403 a group of pro-democratic Athenian citizens rose up and overthrew the tyrants in a series of bloody battles. Democracy was restored to Athens but neither the city nor its government ever completely recovered. The following decades saw Athenians struggling to deal with the issues of military defeat, occupation, and collaboration. It was in this environment that Socrates was tried, convicted, and executed for corrupting the youth of Athens and introducing new gods.

The end of the Peloponnesian War did not bring about the end of warfare. After her victory over Athens, Sparta sought to gain military control over all of Greece. The city-state of Thebes, however, thwarted Sparta's dreams of dominance by defeating the Spartan army in 371 BCE. Though both Athens and Sparta were humbled by defeat, Thebes was too weak to project its power across the peninsula.

Philip of Macedonia (ruled 359–336 BCE) was perfectly poised to exploit this power vacuum. Macedonians, a fierce part-Greek tribe to the north occupying part of modern-day Greece and Serbia, were a divided band until Philip imposed unity upon them. In 354 BCE Philip easily led his forces

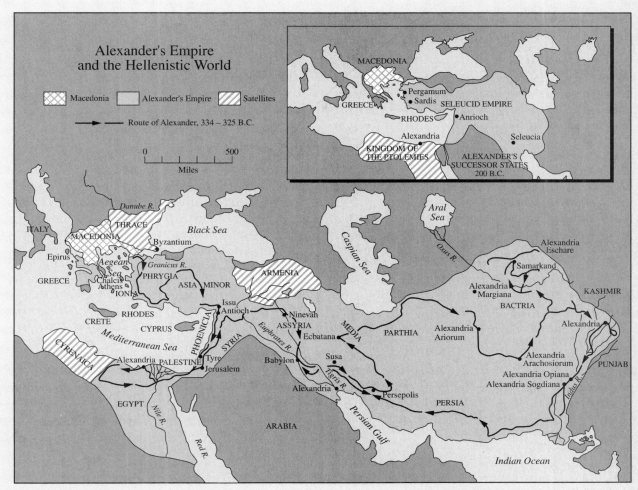

Alexander's Empire. Reprinted from *A History of Civilization*, Ninth Edition, by Robin W. Winks, (1996), Prentice-Hall, Inc.

into northern Greece. A coalition between Athens and Thebes was unable to defeat Philip, and in 338, Philip was able to do what no Greek city-state had accomplished. He had conquered Greece and imposed unity on all Greeks. While Athens would remain an important cultural center for hundreds of years to come, mainland Greece would never be a major power again.

THE HELLENISTIC PERIOD AND ALEXANDER THE GREAT

In 336 BCE Philip was assassinated by a Macedonian and succeeded by his twenty-year old son Alexander. Over the next twelve years Alexander amassed a huge Macedonian-Greek Empire that

extended from the mainland of Greece to modern-day India. His exploits on the battlefield and the empire he created earned him the title Alexander the Great.

Historians are divided on Alexander's impact and legacy. Some view him as a bloodthirsty tyrant interested only in self-aggrandizement and power. Others argue that Alexander's goal was to create a unified, multi-ethnic empire that benefited all of its citizens. The one point scholars do agree upon is that Alexander was one of the greatest military geniuses of all time. Alexander viewed himself in terms no less bold. Educated by Aristotle, Alexander claimed to be a new Achilles, even sleeping with a copy of the *Iliad* under his pillow. Alexander believed he was descended from gods, and by the end of his life claimed to be the son of Zeus.

Once in power young Alexander moved quickly to make real Philip's dream of conquering the Persian Empire. In 334 BCE, he led a combined Macedonian-Greek military force into Asia Minor. By the end of the year he had defeated Persian King Darius' forces in the western part of the Persian Empire (modern-day Turkey). The following year Alexander set his sights on Egypt. In 333 Alexander defeated the Egyptians and took claim to the title pharaoh of Egypt. By the end of that year Syria and Palestine had also fallen to Alexander.

From there, Alexander pushed east into the heart of the Persian Empire. In the summer of 331 BCE, the combined Macedonian-Greek forces routed the much larger Persian army at Gaugamela. Though Darius escaped the battlefield alive he was later assassinated by one of his own men. Alexander entered the city of Babylon (in modern-day Iraq) and declared himself Great King of the Persians.

Not satisfied with his victories over the Persians and Egyptians, Alexander pushed further east. Riding his warhorse Bucephalus, Alexander led his forces through the modern nations of Iran, Uzbekistan, Afghanistan and finally into India. There, his men revolted. Alexander had taken his men past the boundaries of the known world. Scared, tired of fighting for so many years and far from home, his forces refused to go any further. Bowing to the demands of his troops, Alexander headed back. Upon reaching Babylon in 323 BCE, tired, wounded, and sick with a fever, Alexander the Great died at the age of thirty-three.

Scholars call this era the Hellenistic period (literally "to imitate Greeks") because Alexander's military victories helped spread Greek culture and learning throughout the Middle East. After his military conquests Alexander frequently built cities along the way and established Greek colonies. Perhaps the most famous and successful of these new cities was Alexandria, built in Northern Egypt and named after Alexander. The city became a leading center of Greek culture and learning and its library was famous throughout the world. For the next eight hundred years throughout the Mediterranean and Middle East local elites embraced the Greek language, literature, art, and architecture. Historians attribute one final legacy to Alexander. His overriding preoccupation with Persia and the east quite likely opened the door for a Roman invasion from the west.

ART OF ANCIENT GREECE

The Greeks have left us a lasting legacy in many areas, and in none more spectacularly than in art. They set the standard against which all other art is compared, and the name we have given their art is "classical." While the Greeks emphasized the development of the intellect or reason, as in their pioneering studies in early philosophy and science, they also celebrated the perfection of the physical body in their preoccupation with athletic training and competition, famously expressed in the Olympic games that began in the eighth century BCE. Perfection of mind and body are central aspects of ancient Greek "humanism," an absorption in and affirmation of human beings and their values, possibilities, and achievements. It was these two ideals (perfection of mind and body) that the artists of the Classical Age so beautifully portrayed in their art. They articulated this idealism in the recurring visual motifs of balance, control, and stability. In sculpture, they primarily sought to perfect the depiction of the anatomically correct human form, creating artistic representations of human beings that are examples of what is called "naturalism." In architecture, they mathematically ordered spaces and controlled the viewer's interaction with those spaces in ways that far surpassed the accomplishments of earlier cultures.

The Archaic period is dated 800–500 BCE. In ca. 620 art, society, and politics began to thrive under Athens, which dominated the Greek city-states as a cultural hub. Trade flourished in the western Mediterranean; the concept of the citizen was developed; and the identity of Greece as being something altogether different from and superior to its neighbors was cultivated. New and distinct forms of art and ways of describing the world

The Acropolis (high city) looms high over the city of Athens at 512 feet above sea level. Ancient Greek visitors to the massive Parthenon temple on the peak of the Acropolis began their long procession down below in the city streets. They trekked up the rocky hill, followed along the ramp, and entered through the Sacred Way into the Propylaia (gateway). To the left was a building used to exhibit works of art, which was the earliest known art museum in the Western world. The other buildings on the Acropolis were dedicated to major deities like Nike, the goddess of Victory. The Parthenon was the largest structure of them all and was situated on the highest point at the end of the Acropolis, which was meant to inspire worshippers spiritually, emotionally, and intellectually.

Figure II-1 Model of the Acropolis, Athens. ca. 400 BCE. View from the northwest. Royal Ontario Museum, Toronto. Courtesy of the Royal Ontario Museum.

emerged in this period that devoted attention to the study of the human form in its most realistic and perfect form. Greek artists broke from the abstract, strictly symmetrical and geometric styles favored by earlier Egyptians and Mesopotamians, which had been up until this point the predominant artistic influence for the Greeks.

BLACK-FIGURE POTTERY

Pottery was one of the primary modes of artistic creation in the Archaic period. In Athens, the Greek center for the production and international trade of pottery, artists depicted historical narratives and scenes of everyday life on the broad surfaces of large storage vessels like the two-handled amphora that was used to hold oil, wine, and other liquids. The role of the artist in Greek society became so important by the Archaic period that artists, like Exekias, began signing their works for the first time. Exekias inscribed on this amphora (Plate 4) "Exekias painted me and made me," which indicates the pride he took in building and decorating this vessel. Exekias is considered the most superb potter and painter of black-figure designs in sixth century BCE Athens.

Black-figure is a style where the decoration appears in black against a red background. The decoration is painted on using a mixture of clay containing iron oxide, rain water, and wood ash. Under appropriate firing conditions the area that was decorated changes from red to black while the rest of the pot remains red. The scene depicted on this vase is of Achilles and Ajax, two Greek heroes in Homer's *Iliad*, playing draughts, an ancient form of checkers. It is not an actual scene from *Iliad* but imagined by the artist. Achilles dominates the scene with his more decorative armor and a helmet with an elaborate crest that contrasts with Ajax's bare head and less ornate garments. Perhaps this is intended to indicate Achilles' superiority on the battlefield? The inscription on the vase has Achilles announcing the number four, with Ajax admitting defeat in responding with the number three.

Exekias' skill is exemplified in the way he conforms his painted design to the shape of the amphora. The shields and armor resting behind the two men define the vertical borders of the image while the sloping bodies of the men reverberate the slight swell and tapering of the vessel. An implied X shape centers the viewer's focus on the cubed playing surface where their spears intersect at sharp

> ### The Golden Age
>
> Early Classical period: 480–450 BCE
>   Begins with Athenian defeat of Persia
>
> Classical period: 450–400
>   Construction of Parthenon: 447–438
>   Marks the glory of Athens and
>   Its supremacy in the Mediterranean
>
> Late Classical period: 400–323
>
> Death of Alexander the Great

diagonals. An added sense of immediacy and tension is infused in this image through the placement of the players' hands that simultaneously touch the game table to move their pieces. Exekias' work exemplifies the seamless equilibrium and careful observation of the human form.

PARTHENON

One of the greatest artistic accomplishments of ancient Greece is the Parthenon (Plate 5), the largest and most impressive structure on the Athenian Acropolis. Overseen by political leader Pericles, this temple embodies the classical ideals of harmony and balance that signify the Greek Golden Age.

When the Persians sacked Athens and burned the buildings that stood on the Acropolis in 480 BCE, the Athenians left the Acropolis in ruins for thirty years as a memorial. Later, Pericles envisioned a new Acropolis that would represent the great power and wealth of Athens and honor the city's patron goddess, Athena (whom they credited with their victory over Persia). With the full support of the Athenians, he hired the most skilled architects, artists, and craftsmen at great cost.

The architects were Iktinos and Kallikrates and the decorations were under the direction of the sculptor Pheidias. Iktinos and Kallikrates designed it in order to achieve visual perfection in balance, control, and stability. The adjustments made to the structure, which the unaided human eye cannot detect from a distance, make its parts appear to be perfectly vertical and horizontal from a distance.

These modifications include the arching of the base and the entablature over the columns, the swelling of the columns, the spacing of the corner columns closer together than the others in the colonnades, and the inward tilt of the columns and temple walls. Some scholars suggest that these refinements were made to compensate for optical illusions; others posit that the proportions simply control the space aesthetically and add to its beauty.

The structure is made entirely of white marble. It is surrounded by a peristyle of columns and triangular pediments decorated with sculpture in the round over the entrances at each end. A long relief frieze runs around the building inside the colonnade. The structure is designed in the Doric order on the exterior and the Ionic order along the interior—two standard Greek architectural styles that describe the column capitals and the horizontal structural element above the columns called the entablature.

All of the sculpture was painted in bright colors to reflect the intense Mediterranean light and enable the viewer to easily read all of the reliefs from the ground below. The paint wore off over time, which deceived later artists like Michelangelo in the Renaissance who witnessed sculpture like this being unearthed in archaeological digs. Renaissance artists faithfully copied the ancient sculpture and revived the classical style but without color, such as Michelangelo's *David*. They did not realize that the original Greek sculptors covered their gleaming white marble surfaces with paint. The Parthenon's harmonious proportions make this the quintessential example of Greek Classical architecture.

The temples and sculpture on the Acropolis were each dedicated to several deities, and they were a testimony to the religious and civic pride of the Athenians. The Parthenon is dedicated to Athena Parthenos (meaning "virgin"). Inside the two-room rectangular temple was a colossal gold and ivory statue of Athena that stood over forty feet tall. Religious ceremonies took place at an outdoor altar in front of the building.

Every four years, a large-scale celebration called the Panathenaic procession was held when the Athenians marched through the city and up to the Acropolis to worship at the altar of Athena before the Parthenon.

APHRODITE OF KNIDOS

The sculptor Praxiteles was known for his numerous figures devoted to Aphrodite, the Greek goddess of love (Plate 6). He had an extraordinary ability to transform the appearance of hard marble into soft, supple flesh. Praxiteles created the original of this Roman copy of Aphrodite for the city of Knidos in Asia Minor. It was installed in an open shrine that permitted viewers to admire it from all sides. The popularity of the sculpture was so great that this figure of Aphrodite in its particularly erotic pose made it one of the most often copied works in all of Western art.

Praxiteles' representation of a Greek goddess is the earliest known representation in the nude. Her nudity is enhanced by the smoothly carved surfaces of flesh that evenly reflect light and contrasts with the rich texture of her crumpled garments covering the decorated vessel propped on a pedestal at her side. The vessel is an attribute of Aphrodite because this type of object would have typically contained water, which is symbolic of Aphrodite's birth from the sea. Aphrodite stands in a natural *contrapposto* (S-curve) pose in which her weight is placed on one leg, her other leg is bent and her hips and shoulders tilt slightly in opposite directions. The figure's off-balance pose necessitates the use of a support that stabilizes her hip with the marble drapery and jug. She leans forward with her knees held closely together and feet slightly separated in a relaxed pose. The complex, shifting focal points in this object invite the viewer to walk around this freestanding sculpture and examine it from every angle. The tantalizing erotic pose of this figure is a key signature of Praxiteles. Aphrodite draws her right arm across her body in a seeming gesture of modesty, yet it actually attracts attention to her nakedness as does the slim bracelet she wears on her left arm. Her head is directed off to one side, offering the viewer an uninterrupted glimpse at her soft, sinuous curves.

This figure is designed with a Greek canon (meaning "measure" or "rule") of proportions. That is, the Greeks used a set of calculated mathematical ratios to determine the height of the body and its parts. The defining unit of measure is usually eight times the height of the head in Greek Classical sculpture. Thus, the entire body can be divided into eight equal parts from heel to head. The canon was a convenient vehicle for artists to create an ideal human form with precise rules and a commitment to anatomical accuracy. It was made popular by Egyptian artists as early as the early Dynastic period (3100 BCE), before it was later revised and used extensively by the Greek Classical sculptors. The Greeks appropriated the canon in their work to attain balance and simplicity. By controlling the form of the human body, which is a product of nature, Greek artists took pride in the fact that they could conquer the chaos of nature through reason.

THE GALLIC WARRIOR

The Greek Golden Age ended with the death of Alexander in 323 BCE. In the Hellenistic Period that followed (323–31 BCE) the political and cultural center shifted from mainland Greece to other areas in Syria and Egypt. One of the strongest cultural centers in this time was Pergamon (Pergamum) in Turkey. These were tumultuous times and artists responded to the mood. Hellenistic artists preferred dramatic subjects that captured intense emotions of pathos and melodrama, as opposed to the calm and serene forms depicted by the artists of the Golden Age. Heroes and deities that were popular subjects for the Greeks were replaced with individualized representations of mortals. Through an emphasis on the diagonal line, lively surfaces and high contrasts of light and dark in sculpture, Hellenistic artists infused in their work dynamic energy, drama, and theatricality. The sedate and harmonious visual aesthetic of Greek Classical models is supplanted with Hellenistic works that elicit strong emotional responses from the viewer.

One of the most vivid expressions of emotional conflict is demonstrated in a sculpted group called the Gallic Warrior. It records the moment of a murder-suicide of a wife and her husband. (Plate 7). This work commemorates the victory in ca. 230 BCE of the king of Pergamon, Attalus I, over the Gauls, a Celtic group. It was originally in bronze and strikingly honors the noble heroism of the Gauls, the enemies of Pergamon. The Gallic chieftain protects the honor of his family by killing his wife and himself in order to prevent their capture by an enemy in battle. The immediacy of the moment draws the viewer in through the woman's limp body and parted lips suggest that she died only moments ago. Meanwhile, the chieftain drives his sword forcefully into his chest—an act made more powerful by the blood seeping from his wound. This horrific scene is made more potent by the individualized facial features, body types, and the sense of a photographic instant recorded in sculpture.

The figures' twisting and contorted poses that radiate and engage with the three-dimensional space around it enliven the drama of this complex group. The chieftain hangs onto his wife with his left arm that creates a strong diagonal line that contrasts another diagonal formed by the slope of her bent elbow through her right arm that hangs toward the pedestal. Diagonal lines imply movement that is furthered by the deep carving and undercutting in the figures' garments, wiry hair, and facial features. The juxtaposition of solids and voids create stunning contrasts of light and dark. Such contrasts and emphasized diagonals add to the overall emotional impact of the group, which are central to the expressive stylistic traits of the Hellenistic period.

MUSIC OF ANCIENT GREECE

Music was an important aspect of Greek life and, characteristically, even had a role to play in Greek thought and ethics. From the time of Homer on, music was an integral part of both public events and private enjoyment—from festivals, banquets, marriages, and funerals to intimate occasions. In the *Iliad* Homer mentions Achilles playing a lyre, or harp, in his tent, and when bards publicly recited Homer's epics they chanted them to instrumental accompaniment. Music was essential to Greek drama, with the chorus doing both singing and dancing in the theatrical circle called the *orchestra* (which comes from the Greek word for "dance"); the nearest modern equivalent to ancient Greek drama is opera. Even the Olympic games featured contests for musicians as well as athletes, awarding similar prizes for the best performances.

The Greeks believed that music originated with the gods. The goddess who inspired music was Euterpe, one of the Nine Muses (the word "music" is from "muse"). The Greeks also made music an object of study, understanding it in mathematical terms. An important early Greek musical theorist was the philosopher Pythagoras. For Pythagoras and the Pythagoreans, numbers were the key to understanding the universe, and one of the expressions of numbers was music with precise arithmetical intervals between notes. They could even speak of the "music of the spheres," the musical sounds created by the movement of the heavenly bodies. Pythagoras invented a diatonic or eight-tone scale, with each note determined by its numerical ratio to the lowest tone.

Greek composers also devised a series of scales called *modes,* each with a different sequence of intervals. Unlike modern Western musical scales, the Greek modes, with their unequal intervals, sounded more like Arabic, Chinese, and Indian music. Each mode was believed to produce a certain emotional and ethical effect on the listener. All the philosophers discussed music. Plato and Aristotle were concerned with what role music should play in developing character or the inner life, and praised some modes and criticized others on that basis.

Greek music was essentially *monophonic:* there was no harmony such as we understand it, although there is evidence from Plato and other sources that professional musicians sometimes had accompanying voices or instruments on a different pitch from the melody. In addition to the human voice, the chief musical instruments were a variety of lyres (small harps) such as the *kithara* and the *pandoura;* the *aulos* or reed pipe, a wind instrument something like an oboe; the *syrinx* or panpipe, made of several cane tubes joined together; the *salpinx,* a kind of trumpet; and several percussion instruments including drums, bells, and cymbals. What knowledge we have of Greek music is reconstruction based on classical Greek musical theory, depictions of instruments in art and literature, scraps of melody on papyrus or stone, and writings on Greek music dating from a much later period.

CD SELECTIONS

Three selections have been chosen from *Music of the Ancient Greeks* (Pandourion Records, 1997) recorded by an instrumental ensemble named De Organographia, playing reconstructed Greek instruments, together with singer Gayle Stuwe Neuman and additional musicians. Two of the three pieces (tracks #3 and #5) are among the very small number from ancient Greece for which we have the full musical "score." The words to the two vocal songs give us a glimpse of Greek attitudes toward life. Track #3, "Song, Seikilos," was inscribed on a burial monument in the first century CE, and features a female singer, a lyre, and two aulos pipes. The words to the song, from the inscription, say: "As long as you live, be cheerful, do not grieve at all. For life is short, and time collects its tribute."

Track #4 is a surviving example of the sort of music that the chorus would sing in ancient Greek tragedies. This is a choral ode from Euripides' play *Orestes*, accompanied by double pipes, dating from the late fifth century BCE. According to the legend, Orestes, the son of Agamemnon and Clytemnestra, avenged his mother's murder of his father by

killing his mother in turn. In the choral ode the chorus sings to Orestes: "I lament, I lament; because of your mother's blood that drives you mad. Great fortune among mortals does not endure: a god upsets it like the sail of a fast boat overwhelmed in the rough frightful waves of dreadful calamity, as in the sea."

The final selection, on track #5, is especially for everyone who has taken lessons for voice or instrument and had to do various exercises, such as "playing the scale" or "Do-re-mi." It is actually six short exercises for music students, from the second century CE, that have come down to us. The instruments are different types of lyres, a syrinx, and a "time-tapping" percussion instrument called a *kroupeza*, which was a shoe with a clapper attached.

CHAPTER TWO

GREEK DRAMA AND A POET

One of the outstanding achievements of the Golden Age of Greece is Greek drama. As in other civilizations, drama emerges out of religious observances. And so it was in Greece fifth century BCE. The religious festivals honoring the god Dionysus (*Dionysos*) were the seedbed for the development of Greek drama.

Dionysus was not one of the Homeric gods, those gods of the pantheon. He was probably adopted from Thrace (modern-day Bulgaria) but awarded a Greek ancestry. Born of a fiery copulation between Zeus and Semele, Princess of Thebes, he was raised by nymphs in the wild. As a man he wandered the countryside spreading the cultivation of vine. He was considered something of a nature god and was thought to have the power of fertility, and sometimes interpreted as the god of suffering, death, and resurrection. In both cases Dionysus represented joy and exultation—an affirmation of life—whether it was the grape appearing from the seed or the dead risen. The nineteenth-century philosopher Friedrich Nietzsche ends his book *Twilight of the Idols* using Dionysus as the example of his philosophy of "will to life." "For it is only in the Dionysian mysteries, in the psychology of the Dionysian condition, that the *fundamental fact* of the Hellenic instinct expresses itself—its 'will to life'" [*Twilight of the Idols*. Translated by R. J. Hollingdale. London: Penguin, 1968, 119.]

There were actually three festivals to Dionysus over the course of the year. The "Lesser Dionysia" were several small festivals that were held in rural areas in the springtime. These featured the performance of older plays that would otherwise not receive a viewing since only new plays were presented in Athens. The "Lenaea" was held in sacred precincts in Athens in January and its dramatic presentations were mostly comedies. But the most important festival was the "Great Dionysia" held in Athens in March, the season of planting. There is no evidence of when the festivals first began, but we do know that they took place in the mid-fifth century during the reign of the good tyrant, Peristratus. The festivals served both a religious and a patriotic function, were sponsored by the city at its expense, and lasted four to five days. Normal life ceased: offices of government closed, business transactions were suspended. It is known that "everyone" in the city attended, although it is not known if women actually were included. But it seems to be taken for granted in Greek comedy that Athenian women knew a lot about the tragedies of the day.

So much in Greek society seems to have been framed as a contest. It is recorded that in 534 BCE, a poet by the name of Thespis received a first prize. At this time performance was a mixture of poetry in song and dance performed by a group. This was called a *dithyramb*, which is "action" and "doing." Thespis is the first poet to introduce a separate actor, thus moving performance to drama: an opportunity for interaction between an individual and the chorus. Thespis also lends his name to a word we still apply to actors: thespians.

Where did these festivals take place and what were the events? They opened with a procession of city officials and priests followed by young men and young girls escorting the statue of Dionysus into the theater. The first "theater" of Dionysus was little more than a hillside, where the people sat overlooking a flat area where the action took place. In their earliest form these celebrations were more religious than later, when they took on a patriotic theme. By the mid-fourth century Athens had built the Dionysus Eleuthereus (Dionysius the Liberator might be a good translation): a structure, mostly of wood, that seated 14,000–15,000 people. The Theater of Epidaurus, which still survives, closely resembles this theater. What survives in Athens was built in stone in the Hellenistic era and completely rebuilt in Roman times in the first century CE.

The performance area consisted of a semi-circular orchestra (or "dancing area") behind which was the *skene* (from which we get "scene"), a wooden building that was fronted by a wooden platform. The enclosed building served as a backdrop but also was the actors' changing room. It had a single door and entries and exits were either through this door or down the *parodoi*, "side entrances." Other modifications were made over time but it is not necessary for our purposes to go any further. Some study of the image of the theater of Epidaurus will help you fill out the picture.

COMEDY AND TRAGEDY

Drama began, as we explained above, with the separation of one character from the chorus. Soon the playwrights added a second actor and finally a third. With these changes the role of the chorus also changed. The actors became the center of the action while the chorus served to comment on the action, or as representatives of the audience. There was also something called satyric drama, plays that featured human-like creatures called satyrs with pointed ears, short horns, and legs resembling a goat. Some scholars connect satyric drama with tragedy and others view them as comic relief. Whichever is true, satyric drama does seem to relate well to the myth of Dionysus, with its stories of ecstatic celebrations related to worship.

Comedy   We know less about the origins of comedy than we do of tragedy because there are fewer surviving examples. By definition a comedy is a story that ends happily, and by contrast tragedies end unhappily. Aristotle states that comedy was related to cultic processions in which the participants wore a large leather phallus on their persons and directed abusive language to the crowd. Certainly the wearing of an external phallus was common to comedy throughout its history. Aristophanes' comedy *Lysistrata*, set in Athens, is

perhaps the best-known comedic play from this period. It places great emphasis on this particular costume device. Typically comedic actors were also heavily padded. They were supposed to be funny because they were rotund.

Comedies were often parodies of contemporary politics. ("The Daily Show" with Jon Stewart is one contemporary example of political parody.) After the presentation of three tragic dramas, the day ended with no-holds-barred comedies that mercilessly satirized Athenian politics, politicians, objectionable individuals, and Greek tragedy with a farrago of scenes that ranged from the sublimely fanciful to the explicitly physical.

Comedy is grouped for study and by time period into Old Comedy, Middle Comedy, and New Comedy. Old Comedy prevailed during Greece's Golden Age, and the only playwright for whom we have complete plays is Aristophanes. His plays emphasized social and political satire. Very little survives of the Middle Comedy period, from 400 to 320 BCE, but it seems from fragmentary evidence that there was a lessening of emphasis on politics. This may have been the result of the suspicious attitude that arose regarding loyalty to the city-state following the end of the Peloponnesian War. New Comedy emerged at the end of the fourth century and is represented by the dramatist Menander. We know that he wrote nearly a hundred plays, but only one full play survives. New Comedy avoided political commentary entirely and focused on romantic plots using stock characters who encountered many obstacles in their progress toward the inevitable happy ending.

Tragedy   Tragic plots were based on myths well known to the audiences. These are what have survived over centuries because tragedies deal with issues that are timeless. By contrast, the success of comedy depends on its timeliness.

When we use the word "tragic," we usually refer to people experiencing undeserved or excessive suffering, as when a person dies young; or to human passions and mistakes that seem at least partly "destined" and result in suffering that appears to be out of all proportion. One characteristic theme of Greek tragedy is the depiction of humans facing powers either from the inexorability of fate or their own destructive passions—which they cannot fully understand or control—and being destroyed by them. Oedipus does not deserve his fate. He is a tool that the god Apollo uses to punish his father Laius. When Oedipus learns the truth about himself, he gouges his eyes out. Creon is guilty of an error of judgment or of arrogance that unleashes extraordinary suffering on himself and the persons closest to him.

In his *Poetics* Aristotle, familiar with the whole tradition of Greek drama, formulated this influential definition of tragedy:

> A Tragedy . . . is an artistic imitation of an action that is serious, complete in itself, and of an adequate magnitude . . . in language embellished in more than one way . . . the imitation is itself in the form of an action directly presented, not narrated . . . the proper function [of the action presented] is to arouse the emotions of pity and fear in the audience . . . in such a way as to effect that special purging off and relief (*catharsis*) of these two emotions which is the characteristic of Tragedy.

[Aristotle, *On the Art of Poetry.* Translated by Lane Cooper. Ithaca, NY: Cornell University Press, 1947, 17.]

"Pity," says Aristotle, "is what we feel at a misfortune that is out of proportion to the faults of a man; and fear is what we feel when misfortune comes upon one like ourselves" (39). The aim of tragedy, the arousal and "purging" of these emotions, is best achieved by the portrayal of "a fall from happiness to misery; and this fall must come about, not through depravity, but through a serious defect in judgment, or shortcoming in conduct, in a person either as good as the average of mankind, or better than that rather than worse" (41).

According to Aristotle, it was Aeschylus (525–456 B.C.E.) who introduced *seriousness* into tragedy. This means, first, that tragedy portrays plausible human situations, and second, that the situations it portrays raise fundamental human issues related to the lives of the play's audience. Homer had possessed this kind of seriousness, and the tragic poets saw themselves as part of a tradi-

tion begun and dominated by him. Aeschylus, for example, said that his plays were "slices of Homer."

Aristotle's statements about pity and fear and catharsis are part of a debate between him and Plato that seems quite "modern." In his great dialogue *The Republic,* in which he envisioned the ideal state, Plato argued that in politics the masses must learn to control their passions. Literature, especially tragedy, arouses the passions instead of controlling them. Therefore the poets must be banished from the ideal state. Aristotle replied that the tragic art does indeed arouse the passions of pity and fear, but instead of making those passions stronger in the masses it effects a "purification" or *catharsis* of them. Unfortunately, Aristotle does not spell out this psychological process. Catharsis means "cleansing" and is used to refer to the act of purging or cleansing the body of impurities, and to the purification of the soul in religious ceremonies. In the context of tragedy, it may refer to purging unhealthy passions by transferring them to the tragic situation being enacted on the stage. If so, then tragedy is not only about serious matters, it is a serious way of treating those matters.

There is another kind of tragic situation that arises in ancient Greece from the tension between "Dionysian and Apollonian values." In his influential book *The Birth of Tragedy,* Nietzsche identifies two elements in Greek culture, which he calls the *Apollonian* and the *Dionysian.* The Greek god Apollo was associated with two great commandments that were written on his temple at Delphi: "nothing too much" and "know thyself." Nietzsche associates with Apollo the mind's enjoyment in seeing things clearly. By contrast, the god Dionysus was associated with wine and with the forces of nature. Worshippers of Dionysus formed groups that would be "filled with the god" (the literal meaning of "enthusiastic"), and their activities included roaming in the mountains and tearing apart live wild animals. Nietzsche interpreted the tragic dramas performed at the annual festival of Dionysus at Athens as creatively synthesizing the Dionysian (seen in the chorus and its music) and the Apollonian (embodied in the plot structure and dialogue). His insight is harmonious with early Greek thought and serves to complement it, mainly because he depicts the structure of reality in terms of two opposite qualities in eternal conflict with each other. It is tempting to say that his "Apollonian" and "Dionysian" represent reason and passion, but this would be too precise and abstract. The concept "Apollonian" not only includes reason but also the aristocratic way of life and, in rarefied form, the contemplative life of the philosopher. Likewise, the "Dionysian" is a group of feelings associated not only with enthusiasm and undisciplined nature but also with the natural instincts humans share that bind them together in society.

The poet Homer's primary characters in the *Iliad* are often cited as depicting these oppositional attributes. Achilles the hero of the *Iliad* is Dionysian in Nietzsche's terms, but Odysseus, one of the warriors in the *Iliad* and the hero of the *Odyssey*, is identified as having Apollonian characteristics. Repeatedly, Greek tragedy presents the values represented in the Homeric epics in conflict with the way of looking at the world characteristic of the polis. The "Apollonian" ideas associated with the polis are moderation, self-restraint, success, persuasiveness, flexibility, and modesty. The "Dionysian" ideas associated with the Homeric hero are excess, self-willedness, honor, courage, integrity, and glory. In short, *civic virtue* conflicts with *heroic virtue*. Between our Homeric heroes, Odysseus represents the polis or civic virtue; Achilles the heroic virtue. These two sets of qualities are presented in Homer as complementary parts of the human soul. Achilles is great in one way, Odysseus in another. In Greek tragedy, however, these two sets of qualities are often set in direct opposition to each other. Accommodation is not possible. One side or the other will be defeated in the end, and this defeat will endanger either society or the individual. Centuries after Homer, the Roman poet Virgil wrote an epic called the *Aeneid*, which was deeply influenced by and tells part of the same story as Homer's two epics. When we read the *Aeneid* we may want to ask to what extent its hero, Aeneas, exemplifies either heroic or civic virtue.

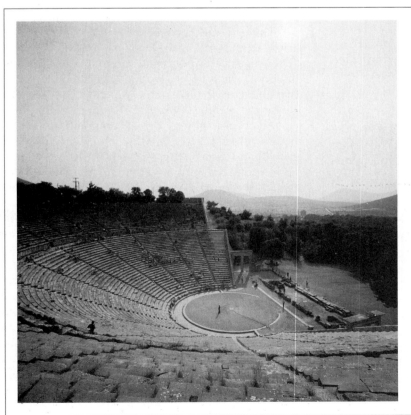

Ancient Greek plays were staged facing a steep hillside like this one at Epidauros. Its fifty-five tiers of seats made of local limestone rise above a circular orchestra where the performances took place. Behind the orchestra was a skene, a wooden building used as a backdrop and changing area, as well as a proskenion, which was a raised platform over the orchestra. The theatre at Epidauros is the best-preserved in Greece and boasts some of the finest acoustics of these early theatrical spaces.

Figure II-2 Theatre, Epidauros, Greece. Early third century BCE and later. Limestone. Courtesy of Roger Wood/Corbis.

THE GREAT PLAYWRIGHTS

At the Dionysian festival three playwrights presented their plays on three successive days. At the end of the festival, ten judges, elected by lot on the opening day, awarded the prizes. The great tragedians were Aeschylus, Sophocles, and Euripides. Sophocles won the first prize eighteen times, and never placed a mere third. Each dramatist wrote a trilogy, or three plays, to be performed successively in the course of the day beginning at sunrise. Only one complete trilogy is extant: Aeschylus' *Oresteia*. It is not clear how often the trilogies were on a single connected theme.

Greek tragedies were composed over a long period, from 534 BCE to the second century CE. The plays that survive, however, come from a rather limited period, 472–404, which we consequently think of as the most important period of Greek tragedy. If, for those sixty-eight years, twelve plays (an approximate figure) were produced each year, there must have been a total of about 816 plays. The three major playwrights, Aeschylus, Sophocles, and Euripides, account for about 280 of those plays, or slightly less than a third. Of those 280 or so tragedies by the three major playwrights, only thirty-two survive.

When we look at the lists of lost plays, it is clear that the Greek tragedians largely took their themes and plots from a wide range of Greek myths and legends that were familiar to their audiences as central to their religion and their past. Only two tragedies (one of which, Aeschylus' *Persians*, survives) were on historical topics. Many of the plots of these lost dramas survive only in retellings of the stories by later authors, such as the Roman writer Ovid (43 BCE–17 CE). However, some stories from Greek mythology were more popular than others, both to the playwrights themselves and to later generations, who selected which plays were to be preserved. Out of the thirty-two surviving tragedies, sixteen are about the war against Troy and related events, including nine about Agamemnon and his family. Of the remaining sixteen dramas six are about Oedipus and his sons and daughters, three of them by Sophocles. Sophocles' plays about the Oedipus story have given Western civilization some of its enduring images and ideas. (Sigmund Freud, for example, drew on the Oedipus story in naming one of his key ideas the "Oedipus complex.")

THE STORY OF OEDIPUS

By way of introducing you to the play *Antigone* we present here a summary of the story of Oedipus. Three of Sophocles' plays deal with the Oedipus legend, which is based on the saga of Thebes, the seven-gated city. *Oedipus Tyrannus* (often referred to by the Latin rendering *Oedipus Rex* or, in English, *Oedipus the King*), *Oedipus at Colonus*, and *Antigone* portray three successive episodes in the saga, although Sophocles wrote them at different times and out of chronological sequence. Two of these dramas are quite famous: *Oedipus Tyrannus* is usually taken as the example of the most perfect tragedy, while *Antigone* is frequently invoked in discussions of history, politics, and philosophy.

The story of *Oedipus Tyrannus* begins with something that happened long before the play begins. When Laius, the king of Thebes, was at Delphi, Apollo warned him that if he had a son, that son would murder his father. A child was born to him and his wife Jocasta, and they gave the child to a shepherd and commanded him to leave the baby, his ankles pierced with metal pins, in the wilderness to die. The shepherd lacked the heart to do this, and gave the child to a fellow shepherd who was from another city, Corinth, who in turn took him to Polybus and Merope, the childless king and queen of Corinth. They adopted him and named him "Oedipus" (in Greek the name suggests "swell-foot," because of the condition of his feet).

When Oedipus is a man, an offhand remark makes him suspicious about his origins, and he goes to Delphi to ask the Oracle who his real parents are. The Oracle does not tell him, but instead declares that he is fated to kill his father and sleep with his mother. In horror, the young man determines never to return to Corinth again. After leaving Delphi, Oedipus encounters an older man in a chariot, attended by servants, who tries to force him off the road. In the altercation that follows, Oedipus kills the old man and all but one of the servants.

Continuing his journey, Oedipus comes to the land of the Thebans, where a Sphinx, a part-human, part-animal monster, is devastating the land. The Sphinx poses a riddle to whoever approaches it. It kills those who cannot give the right answer. The riddle is "What creature goes on four legs in the morning, two legs at noon, and three legs at evening?" Oedipus has the correct answer:

"Humans." For humans crawl as children, walk upright as adults, and use a stick in old age. The Sphinx kills itself and the land is saved. In gratitude, the Thebans award the kingship and their Queen, Jocasta, to Oedipus. It seems that King Laius had gone to Delphi some time earlier and has never returned.

Oedipus and Jocasta live as man and wife for a number of years. They have two sons, Eteocles and Polynices, and two daughters, Antigone and Ismene. Later, a plague visits Thebes, and while Oedipus is trying to learn why this has happened he discovers that the man he killed on the road was his father and that Jocasta is his mother. In the action of the play, Jocasta realizes the truth of the matter first and she dashes from the stage. Once Oedipus has seen everything clearly, he follows her into the palace and finds that she has hanged herself. After he has taken her down, he takes the pins from her robe and drives them into his eye sockets. He returns to the stage in this gruesome condition, where he insists that he has done the only thing he could do, and then laments the future of his helpless daughters. His two sons, he says, can take care of themselves. The play ends with Oedipus being led back into the palace.

Oedipus at Colonus begins some years later. After Oedipus has blinded himself, Jocasta's brother, Creon, becomes king of Thebes, probably serving as regent for the two sons. Oedipus lives in the palace for some years, before the Thebans force him to go into exile. The sons do not stand up for him; they are both more interested in becoming king. After wandering for some time, Oedipus comes to Colonus, a suburb of Athens, where the Athenians accept him as an exile.

During the time of Oedipus's wandering, the sons agree to a scheme of sharing power. First Eteocles will serve for a year, then Polynices will serve for a year, and so on. But at the end of the first year Eteocles refuses to give up the throne. Polynices goes south to Argos into exile. There he marries the daughter of the king. This king raises an army led by seven captains in order to enforce his new son-in-law's "legitimate" claim to the throne of Corinth.

At this point, both brothers learn of a prophecy from Delphi that says that the side that Oedipus supports will win. Eteocles sends Creon to Athens to persuade Oedipus to his cause. Polynices comes himself. Oedipus rejects them with a curse, saying that the only Theban property either of them will ever possess will be a burial plot. After delivering his curse, Oedipus enters a sacred grove of trees and dies in a mysterious fashion. What happens next provides the plot for another play, *Seven Against Thebes*, by Aeschylus. Polynices leads his Argive army to Thebes, where he and the other six captains attack Thebes' seven gates. Polynices charges the seventh gate where his opponent is Eteocles. The brothers kill each other. At the other six gates the Argive captains are killed.

THE STORY OF ANTIGONE

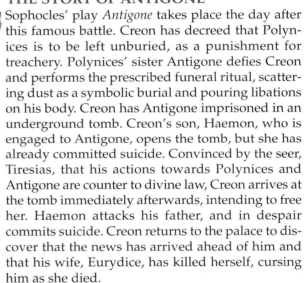

Sophocles' play *Antigone* takes place the day after this famous battle. Creon has decreed that Polynices is to be left unburied, as a punishment for treachery. Polynices' sister Antigone defies Creon and performs the prescribed funeral ritual, scattering dust as a symbolic burial and pouring libations on his body. Creon has Antigone imprisoned in an underground tomb. Creon's son, Haemon, who is engaged to Antigone, opens the tomb, but she has already committed suicide. Convinced by the seer, Tiresias, that his actions towards Polynices and Antigone are counter to divine law, Creon arrives at the tomb immediately afterwards, intending to free her. Haemon attacks his father, and in despair commits suicide. Creon returns to the palace to discover that the news has arrived ahead of him and that his wife, Eurydice, has killed herself, cursing him as she died.

There is a hint in *Antigone* about what happened next, from what we know from other sources. Tiresias mentions that Creon has also refused burial to the other six captains, and that their cities will seek revenge, and that is what happens. The sons of the seven captains, as soon as they reach manhood, return to Thebes and capture it.

The central conflict is, of course, between Antigone and Creon and raises many questions. In their first encounter what are the issues at stake? Is one right and the other wrong? Are both right? Are both wrong? Is there *ate* (moral blindness) that gives rise to *hubris* (unbridled arrogance) on either side? Upon whom does *nemesis* (divine retribution) fall? How do Creon's and Antigone's positions compare with those of Haemon and Tiresias? By the end of the play, in what ways has Antigone's action has been vindicated? She is clearly the heroine of the play; does that mean that Sophocles thinks she was entirely justified in her actions?

Sophocles seems to find it important to show us that Antigone knows what death means. A human being does not meet death "like a god." There is a curious passage in *Antigone* that turns on this kind of mortal knowledge. When the chorus tells Antigone that "she shares a destiny equal to the gods, during life and later, once she's dead," she replies:

> O you mock me!
> Why, in the name of all my fathers' gods
> why can't you wait till I am gone—
> must you abuse me to my face?

[*Antigone.* Translated by Robert Fagles in *The Three Theban Plays.* New York: Penguin, 1984, lines 931–935.]

Antigone goes on to describe the things she will be deprived of—marriage and children. (We moderns would like for her also to mention her love for her fiancé, Haemon). Here and in other plays Sophocles makes it clear that his heroes are not confusing mortal and immortal behavior. Although it is a sign of one's sanity to show that one appreciates life, it is an error to love life too much. The second effect of mortal knowledge is to value highly the only "immortality" available to human creatures. This is the fame (*kleos*) or glory that men win in battle and poets like Homer celebrate and preserve. This fame is granted by society and by poets, but it often seems to be more a family affair than a social one. A warrior wants to be better than his father, and he wants his son to be better than himself. To paraphrase what Sophocles' Ajax says, in the tragedy of that name, to his son: "Time has no value; each day we may live, or we may die. Live well; die well. That is the noble life." For persons to "live well" it must be possible to say of them after their death: "They got what they wanted." This was said of Sophocles' Ajax, but it could be said of his Antigone as well.

Antigone also reveals to us expressions of Greek attitudes and institutions at this time. The preparation of a dead family member's body for burial and making sure the rites were properly performed was the religious and familial duty of the women of the family in ancient Greece—as they still are in traditional societies even today. How does Antigone differ from her sister Ismene, and in what ways does Ismene embody the traditional role of women? In the light of the chorus's role of commenting on the action and representing the audience, notice the fickleness of the chorus—like the fickleness of the "public" anywhere—as they change their opinions through the play. Notice too the role of the gods in the play, and especially the hymn to Dionysus, the patron of Greek tragedy. The gods are never "onstage," but they are powerful forces manipulating things behind the scenes. In that connection, Tiresias, who—be it noted—is a "blind seer," describes Greek augury: interpreting the will of the gods by inspecting the entrails of sacrificed animals.

The reader should observe the shift in Creon's arguments: from the good of the state in a time of emergency to his absolute power as its ruler. Keep this in mind when you come to read Aristotle on the good and bad forms of government. Don't overlook a touch of comedy in the play, as in the character of the Sentry who talks too much. The chorus's praise of human achievement (lines 376–416) is, along with some of Shakespeare's characters' speeches about human nature, a famous dramatic speech. Notice here the human power for both good and evil and the inescapability of death. Finally, compare Antigone's appeal to an ancient, eternal, unwritten law higher than the law of the state to the later development of a very important idea in the Western world: the concept of natural law. This is the universal moral law that all humans know simply by virtue of their reason. We will see this idea later in the philosophy of Stoicism and of Thomas Aquinas, and in the second course in Western Civilization its modern expressions in the concept of natural rights.

WOMEN'S POSITION IN THE "GOLDEN AGE"

Athenian drama produced a remarkable series of portrayals of powerful, intelligent women—some good, some bad, but all impressive. There is a certain pattern to their appearance. They all are literally forced out-of-doors by some outrage committed against them by a man, usually their husband or protector. This outrage violates the sanctity and values of the household in one way or another. Aeschylus' Agamemnon, in the tragedy of the same name, has sacrificed his daughter Iphigenia to the gods to win the Trojan war. This ultimately leads to his death at the hands of his wife, Clytemnestra. In Sophocles' *Antigone* Creon refuses to bury Antigone's brother Polynices for reasons of state security. Euripides' Jason, in *Medea,* has rejected his wife Medea and will marry a princess for economic and political reasons. In these dramas, once the woman is outside or cast out of the conventional order of things, she takes on male characteristics such as love of honor, and yet uses traditionally "feminine" means—seduction and deceit—to overcome the man. Once the man is overcome, he often says that he has been "made a woman." If the woman is still alive at this point, she tries to become a "good woman" again, but her "manly ways" stick to her.

In stark contrast to the remarkable women portrayed in Greek drama, the actual situation of Athenian women at this time was quite different. In terms of legal process, Athenian women could not vote, buy or sell property, or appear in court. A woman brought to her marriage a dowry, which her husband controlled but did not own. Marriages were arranged, typically between teenage girls and men perhaps fifteen years older, and women were always legally dependent upon men—father, husband, brother.

Married women were confined to the home, and were not supposed to appear in public without an escort. Girls typically were denied the education that boys had in favor of domestic skills, because of course they could not exercise their knowledge as citizens but only as homemakers. Women supervised the work within the household and the slaves who did the work. Women did the spinning and weaving and were probably involved in activities such as vase-making and the manufacture of jewelry.

Perhaps the "freest" women in Athens were the *hetaerae,* prostitutes who had access to the male world of Greek culture by being "hostesses" at men's symposia. They sometimes attained fame and influence in this way, as for example Aspasia, the companion of Pericles. In general, women were not "persons," as the state viewed them, and they never directly participated in politics or philosophy.

In religion, however, women held important priesthoods in Athens. When the Athenian assembly commanded all priests to curse the exiled politician Alcibiades, one priestess said that she was a praying priest, not a cursing priest. This is a hint, but no more, that through religious activities a woman could indirectly practice politics.

Athenian women were more severely restricted than women in perhaps any other period of Western civilization. That this repression should have existed precisely during the "Golden Age" of Athens and its most democratic period is an irony that has been highlighted by feminist scholars, who remind us that when we speak of "golden ages" and "renaissances" in Western history, we must always go on to ask, "For whom?" The restrictions on women which have existed historically (and still exist), and the current myths and ideologies surrounding the nature of women, are in part an inheritance from the Greeks.

SAPPHO

To conclude this chapter there are selections from the poems by Sappho. Sappho was not an Athenian woman, nor did she live in the period of the Golden Age. She was a woman who lived a century after Homer (seventh century BCE.) on the island of Lesbos in the Aegean off the coast of modern-day Turkey.

Little is reliably known of Sappho's life, and little of her poetry has survived, but her reputation as one of the greatest poets of all time remains secure. In antiquity she was celebrated as "the tenth Muse;" and she became an iconic, if somewhat enigmatic, figure in later European tradition. Today she is recognized not only for the quality of her art, but for her success in establishing the predominant themes of her poetry—the personal, emotional concerns of women—as being of equal significance to the public concerns of men and their heroic exploits celebrated in the epic poetry of Homer and others.

She seems to have married and refers to a daughter, Kleis, in at least one of her poems. The story that she committed suicide by throwing herself off a cliff out of unrequited love for a man name Phaon was probably an invention of later comic poets (it was also taken up by the Roman poet Ovid in his *Heroides*). Speculation about the nature of her

Sappho listens intently in the lower left foreground of this painting to the famed poet and musician, Alcaeus, who performs on a lyre at the right. This setting of an intimate open-air audience of women is typical of the sort in which Sappho's own poems were recited. Resting in front of Sappho is a laurel wreath that will presumably be awarded to Alcaeus for his talents and will consequently grant him immortality. Pictures of Sappho in classical, imaginary scenes like this one were immensely popular among the wealthy middle classes in nineteenth-century Europe at a time when new fragments of her poems were being discovered in archaeological digs.

Figure II-3 Lawrence Alma-Tadema. *Sappho and Alcaeus (Opus CCXXIII).* 1881. Oil on panel, 26 × 480" (66 × 122 cm). The Walters Art Museum, Baltimore. Courtesy of the Walters Art Museum.

relationships with the women and girls in her poems has abounded. One popular theory, now out of fashion, is that Sappho presided over a kind of finishing school for young women. The fact that the word "lesbian" comes from the name of Sappho's home island tells us more about later tradition (the word first appears with the meaning "female homosexual" in Roman times) than about Sappho's own sexuality or her own culture. Pamela Gordon puts it very well:

> An obvious problem with naming Sappho a "lesbian" is that the ancient Greeks seem generally not to have thought about desire in terms of sexual orientation. A seventh-century Greek might assume that erotic desire takes many shapes, but a Greek is unlikely to have thought in terms of fixed categories that can be neatly translated into modern terms such as "lesbian," "bisexual," or "heterosexual."

[Introduction to *Sappho, Poems and Fragments.* Translated by Stanley Lombardo Indianapolis: Hackett, 2004, xix.]

In the absence of any clear external evidence about Sappho's social and sexual relationships, it is best to let her poetry speak for itself.

At first glance it is difficult to see what Homer and Sappho might have in common as sources for our understanding of Greek culture. Indeed, the contrast between the two is significant and instructive. Homer, a male poet, has left us with two monumental epics. The *Iliad,* a continuous, tightly constructed poetic narrative nearly 16,000 lines long, is largely concerned with the values of a heroic, warrior society. His poetry was composed for public performance at festivals and in royal courts. Sappho, on the other hand, a female poet, composed brief lyric poems largely concerned with her own emotional life and that of her friends, poetry composed for private performance, probably recited or sung to the accompaniment of a lyre within an intimate circle of women.

But despite the differences in their chosen poetic genres, Sappho must have been exposed to Homer's poetry, which by then was well on its way to the preeminent status it achieved in Greek culture. In fact, there are clear indications in Sappho's surviving poetry that she might have been inviting her audience to compare her to Homer. In a gently satirical way, Sappho seems to be saying that love or passion for another person is just as noble, just as important, as heroic deeds in war.

Some time during the third century BCE editors at the Library of Alexandria arranged Sappho's poems into six books according to meter and genre. One complete poem and approximately two hundred fragments survive. Some were preserved by later Greek authors who quoted them for various reasons; others were discovered written on papyrus (these are mostly badly mutilated) and even on pottery shards. The selections presented here include most of the more famous pieces and several of the more fragmentary poems that are not as well known.

Keeping in mind the suggestion that Sappho might be setting the praise of love in opposition to the praise of war, let us look at some of Sappho's poems. In poem 1, Sappho is addressing Aphrodite, goddess of love. Note how in several places Sappho uses the language of battle to invoke the goddess's help in winning the love of another woman: "My heart in its lovesick raving"; "raving" and "rage" is battlefield language; ". . . release me from my agony . . .": heroes in war aren't the only ones who suffer. "Fight for me, fight at my side Goddess": here the language of battle is used to invoke Aphrodite's help.

Poems 4 and 24 include direct references to the *Iliad*. In poem 4 Sappho speaks of Helen and how her love for Paris was so strong that she left a good husband and her children. Such a love reminds Sappho of her lost love, Anactoria, whom she would much prefer to see than the machines of war. In poem 24 the theme again is love and this time it is the love between Hector and Andromache, two victims of the Trojan War. Could the wedding "march," poem 42, have been written for their marriage?

Poem 14 has the phrase "I love delicacy." We could go on to point out how Sappho's language affirms her love of beauty, luxury, sensuality.

One of the great delights of this poetry is that it speaks to the individual as it also tempts one to finish some of the fragments, for example:

> *It is Spring*
> *And I see* the earth embroidered with
>   flowers. (poem 29)
> Or
> The moon rose full,
> And when the women stood in place
> Around the altar
> *They prayed for those loved and lost.*
> (poem 70)

QUESTIONS FOR REFLECTION AND DISCUSSION

1. What were the origins of Greek drama? Describe how drama evolved into comedy and tragedy and define what those terms mean.

2. According to Aristotle, how does tragic drama produce in the audience the emotions of pity and fear? Can you think of any modern plays or films that exemplify his characterization of tragedy and its emotional effect?

3. What are the main themes of Greek tragedy? How are they illustrated in Sophocles' Oedipus plays? Do you find these themes in any Shakespearean tragedies you are familiar with such as *Hamlet*, *Macbeth*, and *King Lear*?

4. Define what is meant by Apollonian and Dionysian.

5. Who are the three great playwrights?

6. Explain what is meant by the paradox between the roles of women as seen in Greek drama and the actual roles of women in Greek society?

7. What are the two different laws to which Antigone and Creon appeal? Is there a case to be made for both views, or not?

8. What are the main themes of Sappho's poetry. In what ways are they a response and an alternative to the Homeric warrior ethos?

SUGGESTIONS FOR FURTHER READING

Original Works:

The Plays of Aeschylus, Sophocles, and Euripides. The Complete Greek Tragedies. Edited by D. Grene and R. Lattimore. Chicago: University of Chicago Press, 1962.

Secondary Works:

Fantham, E. et al. *Women in the Classical World.* New York: Oxford University Press, 1994.

Homer. *Iliad.* Translated by Stanley Lombardo. Indianapolis: Hackett Publishing Co., 1997

Kitto, Humphrey D. *Greek Tragedy: A Literary Study.* 3rd rev. ed. New York: Routledge Chapman & Hall, 1966.

Nietzsche, Friedrich Wilhelm, *The Birth of Tragedy: and The Genealogy of Morals*. Translated by Francis Golffing. New York : Anchor Books, 1956.

Nussbaum, Martha. *The Fragility of Goodness: Luck and Ethics in Greek Tragedy and Philosophy*. Cambridge: Cambridge University Press, 1986.

Sappho: Poems and Fragments. Translated by Stanley Lombardo. Indianapolis: Hackett Publishing Co., 2004.

Sparkes, Brian A. *Greek Civilization, An Introduction.* Oxford, England: Blackwell Publishers, 1998.

SAPPHO

1

Shimmering,

    iridescent,

        deathless Aphrodite,

child of Zeus, weaver of wiles,

              I beg you,

do not crush my spirit with anguish, Lady,
but come to me now,

          if ever before

you heard my voice in the distance
and leaving your father's golden house
drove your chariot pulled by sparrows
swift and beautiful
over the black earth, their wings a blur
as they streaked down from heaven

           across the bright sky—

and then you were with me, a smile
playing about your immortal lips
as you asked,

      what is it this time?
      why are you calling again?

And asked what my heart in its lovesick
   raving
most wanted to happen:

           "Whom now
should I persuade to love you?
Who is wronging you, Sappho?
If she runs now, she'll be chasing soon.
If she spurns your gifts, soon she'll be
   giving.
If she doesn't love you now, she will soon,
          willing or not."

Come to me again now, release me
from my agony, fulfill all
that my heart desires, and fight for me,

      fight at my side,
  Goddess.

2

Truly, I wish I were dead.
She was weeping when she left me,

and said many things to me, and said this:

Reprinted from *Sappho: Poems and Fragments*, translated by Stanley Lombardo, (2001), Hackett Publishing Company, Inc.

"We've been through so much together,
Sappho. I don't want to leave you."

And I answered her:
"Farewell. Go, and remember me.
You know how we cared for you.

And if you should not, I want
to remind you
        of our moments of grace

the many garlands of violets,
roses and crocuses
        you put on my head,
the many necklaces
woven of flowers
        on my soft skin

all the myrrh
expensive
you anointed   royal

and on soft coverlets
tender
quenched your desire

nor ever any
shrine
from which we held back

nor grove   dance
                noise

3

        from Sardis
often turning your mind here

we thought you were like a goddess
        everyone looked at you
she loved the way you moved in the
        dance

now among the women of Lydia

as at sunset the rose-fingered moon
        outshines all stars, spreading
    her light
over the salt sea, the flowering fields,

and the glimmering dew falls, roses
        bloom amid delicate starflowers
chervil and sweet clover

she walks back and forth, remembering
        her beloved Atthis,

the tender soul consumed with grief
to go there   this
mind   much
talks   in the middle

It is not easy for us to equal
goddesses in beauty

                Aphrodite
        poured nectar from
a golden

                Persuasion

        the Geraesteum
        dear ones

            nothing

4

Some say an army on horseback,
some say on foot, and some say ships
are the most beautiful things
    on this black earth,
                but I say
it is whatever you love.

It's easy to show this. Just look
at Helen, beautiful herself
beyond everything human,
    and she left
her perfect husband and went
        sailing off to Troy,

without a thought for her child
or her dear parents, led astray
    lightly

reminding me of Anactoria,
           who is gone
and whose lovely walk
    and bright
        shimmering face
I would rather see
    than all the chariots
and armed men in Lydia

    but it cannot be
humans

        pray to share

        unexpectedly

5

The black sword of night in my eyes

6

down from the mountain top
and out of Crete,

come to me here
in your sacred precinct, to your grove
of apple trees,

and your altars
smoking with incense,

where cold water flows babbling
through the branches,

the whole place
shadowed with roses,

sleep adrift down

from silvery leaves

an enchantment

horses grazing in a meadow

abloom with spring flowers
where the breezes blow sweetly,

here, Cypris,
delicately in golden cups

pour nectar
mixed for our festivities.

7

When you are dead you will lie

forever unremembered
and no one will miss you, for you have not

touched the roses
of the Pierian Muses. Invisible even

in the house of Hades
you will wander among the dim dead,

a flitting thing.

8

I have a beautiful child, graceful
as golden flowers, my precious Kleis,
whom I would not trade for all of Lydia
or lovely Lesbos

9

Like the sweet apple reddening on the
topmost branch
the topmost apple on the tip of the branch,
and the pickers forgot it;
well, no, they didn't forget—they just
couldn't reach it.

Like the hyacinth in the hills the shepherds
trample, and on the ground the purple
blooms

10

Eros has shaken my mind,
wind sweeping down the mountain on oaks

11

The beautiful is so only as far as seen,
But the good is beautiful of itself.

12

Hesperos, you bring all that the bright
dawn scattered,
the lamb, the kid, the child to its mother.

fairest of stars

13

Black dream
you come when sleep comes,
sweet god, truly dreadful agony

14

bitten
with all your names

wins for your mouth

lovely gifts children

song-lover, lyre-shell
old age already   all my skin
my hair turned white from black

knees do not bear

like fawns

but what could I do?
                    impossible to become
        rose-armed Dawn
                    carrying to the ends of the
earth
yet seized
                    immortal bedmate
            thinks
                        might give
but I love delicacy, and love has won for
    me
the sunlight's beauty, the light of the sun

15

The moon has set,
And the Pleiades.
Midnight.
            Time goes by.
I sleep alone.

17

heart
        completely
    I can
may it be mine
to shine on me
            your face
close whistling

20

Look at him, just like a god,
that man sitting across from you,
whoever he is,
            listening to your
            close, sweet voice,
your irresistible laughter
                    And O yes,
it sets my heart racing—
            one glance at you
and I can't get any words out,
            my voice cracks,
a thin flame runs under my skin,
my eyes go blind,
            my ears ring,
a cold sweat pours down my body,
I tremble all over,

                    turn paler than grass.
Look at me
            just a shade from dead

But I must bear it, since a poor

24

From Cyprus
A herald came
Idaeus   swift messenger:

"From the rest of Asia   undying fame
Hector and his cohorts lead her dancing-
    eyed
from sacred Thebes and out of Plakos,
delicate Andromache, in ships over the salt
sea, with many golden bracelets and
    clothing
shining purple, necklaces, jewels of many
    colors,
countless silver cups and ivory."
He spoke, and Hector's old father rose
    nimbly,
and the word spread throughout the broad
    city
to his dear ones, and the Trojan women
    yoked mules
to their gliding chariots and went out in
    crowds
together with the slender-ankled girls,
Priam's daughters in a separate proces-
    sion,
and the bachelors hitched up horses to
    their chariots,
young heroes in their might
        charioteers

                        like gods
                        holy throng
                        to Ilion

    and there rose
flute's melody sweet with the lyre
the rattle of castanets and shrill the
    maidens
sang the holy song and it reached bright
    heaven
eerie sound

and everywhere in the streets
mixing bowls and cups
myrrh and cassia and frankincense
   blended
and the older women with their alleluias
and all the men changing the paean
calling on Apollo his lyre his bright bow
praised Hector and Andromache, praised
   them as gods

29
earth embroidered with flowers

34
night

maidens
all night long
might sing of your love
      and the violet-breasted bride's

42
Raise high the roofbeam, carpenters,
   Here comes the bride
Raise it up high,
   Here comes the bride
Like Ares comes the groom,
   Here comes the bride
Taller far than a tall man,
   Here comes the bride

70
The moon rose full,
and when the women stood in place
around the altar

CHAPTER THREE

GREEK PHILOSOPHY: PLATO

The eminent mathematician and philosopher Alfred North Whitehead once said, "The safest characterization of the European philosophical tradition is that it consists of a series of footnotes to Plato." While perhaps an exaggeration, this statement contains a large grain of truth. There is scarcely a single figure in the history of Western civilization since Plato who does not owe something to his philosophy in some way or another. More than any other early figure, Plato sets the standards, methods, and vocabulary of philosophical debate in the Western tradition, which in turn influences the entire range of intellectual disciplines, including not only philosophy, but also science, politics, literature, and the arts. However, Plato did not create in an intellectual vacuum; no one ever does. An obvious influence on his thought was his famous teacher Socrates. Socrates' philosophical views and pedagogical methods greatly influenced those of Plato, as we shall see. Less obvious, but no less important, is the influence of a variety of intellectuals whom we broadly classify as the Pre-Socratics. These thinkers created the philosophical background and context in which both Socrates and Plato operated. Therefore, let us start with a brief discussion of the Pre-Socratics who were most influential on both Socrates and Plato.

THE PRE-SOCRATICS

The term "Pre-Socratics" is potentially misleading, in at least two ways. First, it suggests that the Pre-Socratics were not as important as later thinkers such as Socrates and Plato. While perhaps true to an extent, the classification actually has more to do with our relative ignorance of them compared to Socrates, Plato, and later philosophers. Whereas Plato's writings (which are also our main source for Socrates) are numerous and largely extant, the Pre-Socratics—despite the fact that they wrote quite a bit—have left us with little more than scattered fragments, many of them second-hand through later thinkers such as Aristotle and Diogenes Laertius. To think of the matter in concrete terms, Plato's writings fill several large books, but everything we have left of the Pre-Socratics could be printed in a single volume.

Second, the term "Pre-Socratics" is potentially misleading because, although it does in part refer to thinkers who lived and philosophized before Socrates, many of these schools of thought continued well into and past the time of Socrates. Thus, the Pre-Socratics represent not only potential influences on Socrates and Plato, but also competing schools of thought against which both Socrates and Plato vigorously argued.

It is neither possible nor necessary to examine each and every Pre-Socratic thinker. Instead, we shall consider the handful who are directly relevant to our understanding of Socrates and Plato and the texts of the *Apology* and the *Republic*. For our purposes here, we shall divide them into the following three pedagogically useful if perhaps simplistic categories: the Cosmologists, the Mathematicians, and the Sophists.

Cosmologists The word "cosmology" means "the study of the universe" (roughly translated; from the Greek "kosmos," meaning "well-ordered," and by derivation, "the universe," which the Greeks apparently saw as a good, well-ordered thing; and from the Greek "logos," which literally means

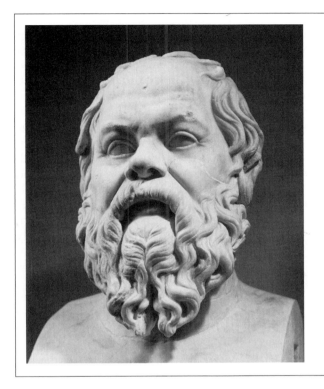

Most portraits of Socrates, like this one, depict him as a pudgy, bald man with a pug nose and fleshy lips. This comical image of the philosopher comes to us through written records, primarily from his pupils like Plato. This likeness may serve to emphasize the ugliness of the body because, according to Socrates, one should focus not on the body but instead on the inner self through the attainment of knowledge, truth, and moral perfection.

Figure II-4 Socrates, Roman copy after the Greek original. Late fourth century BCE. Marble, 21½″ (54.8 cm). Albani Collection, Museo Capitolino, Rome. Courtesy of Gianni Dagli Orti/Corbis.

"something said" or "word," but which comes to be associated with thinking, knowledge, study, etc.). The Cosmologists studied and tried to explain the basic structure and function of the universe. Thus, they represent some of the earliest known Western natural scientists. Important Cosmologists include the three Milesians—that is, persons from the city of Miletus in Ionia. Thales, probably born about 625 BCE, posited "All is water," that is, that the fundamental building block of physical universe was water or something like it. Anaximander, probably born about 610 BCE, posited "All is indefinite," that is, that the fundamental stuff of the universe must be something non-specific if it could be "built" into all sorts of specific things. Anaximenes, probably a younger contemporary of Anaximander, posited "All is air." Other important Cosmologists not from Miletus include Anaxagoras, who posited "All is Mind," and Heraclitus, who posited "All is fire" and "All is flux," and is known for such deep thoughts as "Everything changes but change itself" and "You cannot step into the same river twice."

If this all sounds rather odd, keep in mind that it is not unlike what modern theoretical physicists do. They too are engaged in discussions of the fundamental nature and constituents of the universe. For example, Newton could be characterized as having said "All is atom;" that is, that the atom is the basic building block of the material reality. Contemporary physicists then discovered that the atom could be broken into even smaller constituents. Physicists also discuss the basic forces of the universe, such as gravity and electro-magnetism, and are interested in discovering whether or not these forces really are the most basic, or whether they might be reducible to some other single, unified force ("Unified Field Theory"). As odd as the Pre-Socratics' theories might sound, they were simply engaged in asking the same questions that scientists today ask, albeit in a more sophisticated fashion. Thus, the Pre-Socratics represent the beginnings of modern scientific inquiry, and their emphasis on reason and natural inquiry provide a stark contrast to the mythological manner in which early poets such as Homer and Sappho attempted to understand the world.

Mathematicians The next category of important Pre-Socratics is the "Mathematicians," and it includes the Pythagoreans and the Parmenideans. They too engaged in cosmology, but did so in a manner so different as to warrant their own category. In particular, they took a mathematical view of and approach to cosmological issues, which in turn resulted in very different views on the nature of the universe than those of the Cosmologists.

The Pythagoreans were followers of Pythagoras, who was born around 570 BCE. They were quite literally mathematicians; specifically, they were geometricians—discovering for example the Pythagorean Theorem—which at that time was the most advanced of the mathematical sciences. They were also interested in harmonics, the mathematical characterization of musical tones. They discovered that there were regular, orderly mathematical ratios behind various harmonic intervals, and generalized this discovery to an all-encompassing theory of the cosmos which they summarized with the statement "All is number." We can understand this statement to mean that the universe is a well-ordered place ("kosmos") that can be understood and characterized in mathematical terms. This is not unlike the modern physicist's view on mathematics and its relation to science. The modern physicist also sees the natural universe as a largely

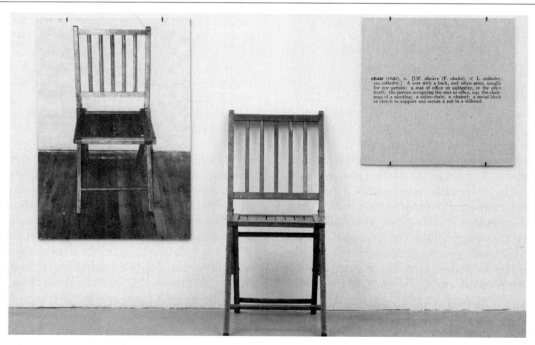

The American Conceptual artist Joseph Kosuth symbolically illustrates Plato's Theory of Forms in this installation. Art is transformed in this work into a concrete representation of an abstract idea. Three chairs are represented in this work: an actual chair, a photograph of a chair, and a dictionary definition of a chair. While Plato did not actually believe that concrete objects have Forms, these objects can give meaning to the abstract notion of the Forms.

Figure II-5 Joseph Kosuth. *One and Three Chairs.* 1965. Wooden folding chair, photographic copy of a chair, and photographic enlargement of a dictionary definition of a chair; chair, 32⅜ × 14⅞ × 20⅞" (82.2 × 37.8 × 53 cm); photo panel, 36 × 24⅛" (91.4 × 61.3 cm); text panel 24 × 24⅛" (61.3 × 62.2 cm). Larry Aldrich Foundation Fund (383.1970.a-c). The Museum of Modern Art, New York. Courtesy of The Museum of Modern Art/Scala/Art Resource, NY.

quantifiable place, and believes that at least part of the job of science is to actually go about quantifying it—just think of the amount of algebra, trigonometry, and calculus required to do physics. Some Pythagorean sects were also religious in nature, believing in reincarnation and the immortality of the soul. Both the Pythagoreans' mathematical and their religious beliefs may have influenced some of Plato's most important philosophical doctrines, such as the Theory of Forms and the Theory of Recollection, which we will examine later in this chapter.

Though less involved in actually doing hard mathematics, the Parmenideans also had a mathematical view of and approach to cosmology. The Parmenideans included Parmenides, probably born about 515 BCE, and his disciple Zeno. The Parmenideans believed that "All is One," that is, that the universe, though it appears to consist of a plurality of discrete objects which can move, change, come into or go out of existence and so forth, is in reality a single, perfect, unchanging, unmoving entity.

The Parmenideans used a variety of mathematical and logical arguments to show that this was supposedly the case. The most famous of these are "Zeno's Paradoxes," one of which is the argument that "proves" that an arrow shot from a bow can never reach its target: before it can travel the whole distance, it must travel halfway there; but before it can reach that halfway point, it must travel halfway to there; but before it can reach that point, it must travel halfway to there; and so on, *ad infinitum,* until it becomes apparent that the arrow can never leave the bow at all; therefore, motion is an illusion. Similar arguments are advanced to "prove" that change and plurality are also illusions; therefore reality is a single, unchanging, unmoving "Oneness." Though the invalidity of these arguments may seem obvious to us, it is only because we have more advanced systems of logic and mathematics than they did. Despite this, the Parmenideans remain important, if only because they were so influential on Plato, as we shall see.

SOPHISTS

Finally among the relevant Pre-Socratics, we come to the Sophists. A basic understanding of the Sophists will prove valuable to our study of Socrates and Plato, since the Sophists were the single most important philosophical rivals to Socrates and Plato. Indeed, much of the negative association of the word "sophist" to the contemporary ear—connoting for us as it does the notion of a charlatan, a fast-talker, someone who sounds smart but really isn't, and so forth—is the result of Socrates and Plato arguing so vigorously against them and "winning," in the view of most of the history of philosophy. However, in their own time, they were considered a respectable school of philosophy, as evidenced by the original meaning of the term "sophist," meaning "wise person." There are three primary characteristics of the Sophists: humanism, relativism, and rhetoric.

Humanism is the general philosophical orientation that sees human beings as having a special status in the universe. According to this view, human beings are the most important beings, and all human activities should be pursued for the benefit and betterment of humankind. This stands in stark contrast with some other points of view that hold some sort of divine or transcendent reality, such as gods or an afterlife, as ultimately more important than humans and the realm of human affairs, and hold that all human activities should be carried out with this divinity or transcendence in mind. The Sophists were strongly humanistic; as the Sophist Protagoras—born about 490 BCE—put it, "Man is the measure of all things." Regarding objects of divine status, they were largely agnostic—that is, they believed it was not possible to have knowledge of such things—and so believed that it was impractical to concern oneself about anything but human affairs. As a result, they were less interested in pursuing such abstract topics as religion or cosmology, and more interested in worldly concerns such as politics.

The second primary characteristic of the Sophists is *relativism.* Relativism is the view which rejects the notion of objectivity: there is no such thing as objective truth, at least, not so far as humans can know. Rather, "It's all relative." The so-called "truth" is simply a human construct, and can in a very real sense be whatever it is that we want it to be, whatever we decide and agree that it is. In the realm of ethics and politics, the relativistic Sophists would say that since there are no gods—at least, none that we can know anything about—to tell us how to live our lives, we are free to live them as we see fit, and to create whatever societies, governments, and laws we want.

The third primary characteristic of the Sophists is *rhetoric*, the art of persuasion. The relativistic Sophists claimed that there are no objectively right or wrong points of view, only those that we do or do not find compelling. Those that we do find compelling are simply those with the strongest—that is, most persuasive—arguments behind them. The tool for creating persuasive arguments is rhetoric. The Sophists were well known and widely sought after as teachers of rhetoric—an activity for which they were well-compensated—especially by those with ambitions in the public sphere, in which rhetoric played a key role.

Keep these three characteristics—humanism, relativism, and rhetoric—of the Sophists in mind, as they provide an interesting framework for comparison and contrast with Socrates, to whom we now turn.

SOCRATES AND THE *APOLOGY*

We have no texts written by Socrates himself. As far as we know, he never produced any. Everything we know about him is through other authors. In this respect, he is often compared to figures such as Jesus and the Buddha, and similar questions are asked of all three: "Who was he? What did he really say, do, and believe? Can we ever really know anything about him for certain, or are we limited to mere speculation? Did he even really exist?"

Though others also wrote about Socrates, our main source is undoubtedly Plato, who wrote dozens of dialogues—that is, philosophical essays written in conversation form—in which Socrates plays a key part. Contemporary philosophers, classicists, and historians debate how accurately Plato's dialogues represent the historical Socrates. There are a variety of opinions on the matter, but a standard view is that the earlier of Plato's dialogues—including the *Apology*—probably represent the historical Socrates and his views, whereas the later of Plato's dialogues—including the *Republic*—simply use Socrates as a mouthpiece for Plato's own developing ideas. The reliability of Plato as a source is certainly an open question that the reader should keep in mind while studying the *Apology* and the *Republic*, but for the moment we shall concentrate

on those details we can assert with a reasonable degree of certainty.

Socrates was a Greek of Athenian citizenship, probably born about 469 BCE. According to Platonic dialogues such as the *Apology* and the *Symposium*, Socrates began his philosophical career as a cosmologist, but soon became disillusioned with the field and abandoned it for more humanistic concerns, something he shared with the Sophists. However, he was hardly an arm-chair intellectual. He fought in the Peloponnesian War, quite bravely and fiercely if Plato's account through the character of Alcibiades in the *Symposium* can be believed. Alcibiades also recounts Socrates' endurance in harsh weather and marching conditions, as well as his ability to out-drink anyone without ever actually becoming drunk, a feat which Socrates also demonstrates during the course of the *Symposium*. Socrates may also have been epileptic: twice during the course of the *Symposium*, he is portrayed as standing unresponsively for long periods of time, staring off into space. He may have been contemplating deep philosophical truths, or he may simply have been experiencing mild seizures. Socrates is also portrayed as living a fairly Spartan life, avoiding physical luxuries. He was married and had three children, but he did not have a formal profession in his later life. Instead, he relied primarily on the support of his friends and followers, allowing him to concentrate on living a good life and pursuing knowledge and wisdom.

In about 399 BCE, Socrates was brought up on charges by the Athenian government, found guilty, and sentenced to death by drinking hemlock. The *Apology* is Plato's account of Socrates' trial, focusing on his defense. In this day, the word "apology" usually means "an admission of guilt" or "claiming to be sorry about something," but the original meaning of the Greek word *apologia* is "a speech made as a defense against legal charges." Thus, a more up-to-date (if loose) translation for the title of the work might be *The Defense of Socrates*. In the context of this defense, we learn a bit about Socrates' philosophical views and methods.

There were several charges brought against Socrates. Some of them were religious in nature, though they seem to lack coherent formulation: on the one hand, he is accused of worshipping gods other than those sanctioned by the state; on the other hand, he is accused of atheism. The contradiction between these claims is quickly pointed out by Socrates, but the root of these charges seems to be that Socrates' accusers believe him to be engaged in cosmology: that he "busies himself studying things in the sky and below the earth," and that by doing so he is either attempting to introduce new gods, or attempting to disprove the existence of the old gods. This is not unlike the manner in which some modern religious groups have claimed that science—especially Darwinian evolutionary theory—poses a threat to religion.

Socrates responds to the charges not only by pointing out the aforementioned contradiction, but also by simply denying that he was engaged in cosmology, which in fact he was not at that point in his life. Socrates asserts that no one can truthfully testify to having heard him discuss such matters, and explains that his accusers may be confusing him with his caricature in Aristophanes' satirical play *The Clouds,* in which Socrates is portrayed and intensely ridiculed as a cosmologist and a Sophist.

Given that Athens at that time was a fairly tolerant place religiously, it is likely that Socrates' accusers were not all that seriously concerned about Socrates' religious views, as long as he didn't cause trouble. Of course, it was the perceived "causing of trouble" that was the problem: the more serious and potentially accurate charges against Socrates are moral and political in nature. In particular, Socrates was charged with "corrupting the youth," primarily by "making the weaker argument the stronger"—that is, by in engaging in Sophistic rhetoric—and teaching the young men of the state how to do the same—that is, by acting as a teacher of Sophistry. This supposedly corrupted the youth by causing them to turn away from traditional values and beliefs, and to question the authority of the state, which in turn would supposedly result in serious social and political instability.

Once again, it is possible that Socrates' accusers were confusing him with his caricature in Aristophanes' popular play; however, Socrates admits that he himself is also at least partially to blame, even if unintentionally. In order to address these charges, Socrates relates how his friend Chaerephon once visited the Oracle at Delphi and asked the Pythian priestess if there was anyone wiser than Socrates, to which the oracle replied that no one was

wiser. Socrates found this answer very confusing, since he did not think of himself as wise. So, he decided to prove the Oracle wrong by finding someone wiser than he. In order to accomplish this, Socrates sought out those people reputed to be wise, such as politicians, craftsmen, and poets, but after speaking with them, it became apparent that none of them actually were. The method that Socrates used to demonstrate their ignorance is the famous "Socratic Method."

This phrase is an often used and abused one. It is often used to refer to pedagogical techniques in question-and-answer format: rather than just telling them the answer, the teacher questions the student until the student discovers the answer for himself or herself. However, Socrates' methods were usually more specific than this. A concise definition of the Socratic Method is difficult, primarily because it differs depending on which Platonic dialogue one reads. However, in the *Apology,* it is safe to say that the Socratic Method involves at least the following: Socrates begins by asking his interlocutor to take a position on something; for example, getting his prosecutor (Meletus) to state one of the charges against Socrates, for example, that he worships gods other than those sanctioned by the state. Then Socrates asks a series of additional questions, until the interlocutor says something that contradicts his initial position, for example, that Socrates is an atheist. Socrates then points out the contradiction, for example, he cannot both worship gods other than those sanctioned by the state and be an atheist at the same time. In this way, Socrates supposedly refutes his interlocutor's position. Socrates saw this as a service: he was helping to rid his interlocutor of ignorance, thus freeing him to the possibility of attaining real knowledge. Unfortunately, his interlocutor usually didn't see it that way, but only felt that he had been made to appear the fool, and in public too, more often than not.

Socrates' use of this method also implicitly refutes the charges that he is engaged in "making the weaker argument the stronger," that is, that he is engaged in Sophistic rhetoric. Socrates stands strongly against the Sophists in some important regards, especially their use of rhetoric to obfuscate the objective truth, a notion which Socrates, unlike the Sophists, embraced. Socrates never uses his method to strengthen a position, but only to refute inconsistent ones. Socrates repeatedly claims that he has no wisdom himself to impart, but is merely engaged in showing others their ignorance, for their benefit.

As one might guess, publicly pointing out to people that they do not know what they are talking about created some serious animosity towards Socrates. Many of these supposedly wise people were important Athenian public men, and humiliating them in public is primarily what got Socrates into trouble. Unfortunately, insult was added to injury: many of the Athenian youths who observed Socrates took to imitating him, going around interrogating and demonstrating the ignorance of the supposedly wise. Thus, Socrates was blamed for "corrupting the youth."

So in one sense, Socrates admits, these charges were not entirely baseless. However, they were the result of the accusers misunderstanding the true nature and purpose of Socrates' activities, which he believed were ultimately for the benefit of those questioned. Socrates likens Athens to a noble horse that has grown dull and complacent in its old age, and himself to a gadfly that stings the horse, rousing it back to full consciousness: irritating, to be sure, but ultimately for the best.

However, the jury is not convinced, and Socrates is found guilty. The prosecution asks for the death penalty, and Socrates is allowed to offer an alternative, lesser punishment. Socrates suggests that since he is so beneficial to Athens, he ought not to be punished; rather, he suggests, he should be rewarded with free meals at the Prytaneum, the town hall in which Olympic victors and other local heroes were honored! A sophisticated listener might interpret Socrates as suggesting that he represents a new kind of hero, one that represents reason, wisdom, and moral virtue, rather than the perhaps outdated military virtues of the Homeric heroes. However, one gets the distinct impression that most of the jury was not so sophisticated, and could only have seen Socrates' suggested "punishment" as unmitigated arrogance.

Anticipating this, Socrates raises the question of whether he should be sentenced to exile, or to live quietly, ceasing to question his fellow Athenians; these were probably the counter-punishments that the jury expected him to offer, and might even have accepted. However, Socrates could accept nei-

ther: he has lived his life in good faith in the best way he knows how. If freed, he would continue to do his best to improve Athens' citizens by questioning them. Finally, he suggests a reasonable fine, as much as he honestly believes he could scrape together. Plato and Socrates' other friends and pupils even offered to pay the fine.

The jury deliberates a second time, and decides on the penalty of death. Socrates is given one last chance to speak. This is when it would be usual for the defendant to beg for his life, perhaps parading his weeping wife and children in front of the jury, but Socrates will have none of it. Instead, he goes willingly to his death—a scene recounted in Plato's *Phaedo*—but not without a few parting thoughts. From these, combined with other comments throughout the *Apology,* we get a clear sense of some of Socrates" ethical views.

Socrates believes that there are moral laws and truths that can and sometimes will take precedence over the laws of the state, and that the good life sometimes requires that we pursue these ideals even when it requires civil disobedience. Right and wrong are not decided by political authority, nor relativistic rhetoric, but are open to each one of us through the power of reason. If we conclude that the right thing to do is something different than what the Powers That Be demand, we should respectfully but firmly stick to principle.

At the same time, Socrates believes that we have duties not only to pursue our own good, but also the good of society as a whole. Socrates' civil disobedience is motivated not by mere self-interest, but by a concern for the greater good, a good of which Socrates believes those in power had lost sight. Socrates develops more arguments on this topic in Plato's *Crito,* in which we see an early version of what comes to be known as Social Contract Theory, a theory which in part posits that the purpose of the government is to serve the good of the people rather than merely promote the interests of the rulers, and that the government's authority is legitimized by the will of the people, not by hereditary aristocracy, military power, or other traditional justifications. A modernized form of Social Contract Theory greatly influenced the writing of the American Documents and the establishment of the United States of America.

Raphael demonstrates the opposing sources of knowledge for the philosophers Plato and Aristotle in this detail of his large-scale fresco produced during the High Renaissance in Rome (Plate 28). Plato, standing on the left, points to the sky, suggesting that his knowledge derives from the celestial realm, whereas Aristotle, at the right, levels his palm toward the earth, the terrestrial realm, the source of his knowledge.

Figure II-6 Raphael, School of Athens, detail of fresco depicting Plato (left) and Aristotle (right) in the Stanza della Segnatura, Stanze di Raffaello, Vatican, Rome. ca. 1510–11. Courtesy of Scala/Art Resource, NY.

Indeed, death may not be an evil at all. Socrates is firmly agnostic about the nature of death, and says that it is at least as likely a blessing as an evil. For all we know, death may be nothing at all, like a long, dreamless sleep, and there is certainly nothing to fear from that. On the other hand, perhaps it is simply the relocation of the soul to another place; if so, Socrates will continue to test and examine those he finds there, hoping to relieve himself of his ignorance and discover the knowledge and wisdom he has always pursued. As he also famously said, "Philosophy is practice for dying."

On an important side note, it is an open question whether or not we should take Socrates' claim to ignorance seriously. Socrates uses a great deal of verbal irony; note for example the backhanded compliments he gives his accusers in the *Apology*. In particular, Socrates routinely claims not to know anything; but in context, readers often suspect that he is feigning this ignorance, perhaps as part of his use of the Socratic Method, allowing his "student" to reach the correct conclusions himself. This feigned ignorance is sometimes referred to as "Socratic Irony."

However, despite Socrates' routine claims of ignorance, he does at one point admit that if he has any wisdom at all, it is simply in knowing that he does not know anything. This is at least slightly wiser than those who foolishly and arrogantly believe they know that which they do not. Perhaps this special kind of humble ignorance, this "Socratic Ignorance" as it is sometimes called, is the wisdom of which the Oracle spoke when it claimed that no one was wiser than Socrates.

PLATO AND THE *REPUBLIC*

Plato was born about 428 BCE in Athens. As a young man, he tried his hand at both poetry and politics, but became disillusioned with both, as evidenced by the many criticisms of poets and politicians that appear in his dialogues. He was a "student" of Socrates; that is, one of the young people who followed Socrates around and observed his philosophical discussions with the supposedly wise. He was a prolific author, writing dozens of dialogues, most of which describe fictional philosophical conversations in which Socrates is featured as the main character. Plato was about thirty years

Socrates also clearly believes that seeking knowledge and wisdom, and helping others to do the same, is key to the good life. In a sense, Socrates is showing us that the good life involves, at the very least, the search for the good life. As he famously said, "The unexamined life is not worth living." Constantly striving to better himself and live well is the good life for Socrates, so much so that he would rather die than abandon it. Death cannot be worse than living a wicked life.

old when Socrates was tried and executed. As mentioned in the text of the *Apology*, Plato was present at the trial and it had a profound effect on him, especially in contributing to his disdain for Athenian democracy. Shortly thereafter, he traveled and studied in southern Italy and Sicily, likely making contact with—and being influenced by—other philosophical schools, especially the Pythagoreans. In about 387 BCE, he returned to Athens and established his own school, the Academy, which lived on for nine hundred years after his death in about 347 BCE. The Academy produced a number of important thinkers, the most famous being Aristotle.

The *Republic* is widely considered Plato's masterpiece. While it is debatable whether it portrays a definitive picture of Plato's views, it certainly is one of the clearer explications of a variety of Plato's theories, from the practical areas of ethics and politics to the theoretical areas of metaphysics (involving theories on the nature of being or reality) and epistemology (the philosophical study of knowledge), especially those theories which heavily influenced later thinkers such as Aristotle, Augustine, Aquinas, and even modern thinkers such as Nietzsche and Freud. The *Republic* is presented as one very long, and often one-sided, fictional philosophical conversation between Socrates and a variety of interlocutors. The central questions concern the nature of justice: What is justice, exactly? Why be just? Is justice beneficial for the just individual, to society as a whole, or only to those in power? Socrates' primary opponent is Thrasymachus, who initially posits a sort of "might makes right" position: justice is simply "the advantage of the stronger." Justice is nothing more than a social and legal principle that those in power enforce in order to make the rest of the society obey and serve those in power. Justice is not beneficial to those who actually observe it ("the weaker," political subjects), but only to those for whom it is observed ("the stronger," the rulers). Therefore, it is actually better to be unjust than just.

This "immoralist" position is greatly disturbing to Socrates (that is, the character of Socrates in the *Republic*, as portrayed by its author, Plato), and he spends the bulk of the dialogue attempting to refute it. In particular, he hopes to establish that justice is always to the benefit of the just person; that is, that the benefits of morality always outweigh the apparent benefits of immorality. However, in order

to establish this, he believes it is important to come to a clear prior understanding about the nature of justice. In order to do this, Socrates embarks on a philosophical quest to answer the question: "What is justice?"; that is, to define "justice."

Socrates admits that justice as it appears in a person's moral character is difficult to identify, much less understand, and suggests that they might gain a clearer picture of justice if they first look at how it operates on a larger scale; namely, that of the polis, the Greek city-state. If they can first identify justice within a society of people, then perhaps they will be able to identify it within an individual person by analogy. The conversational road to the just polis is a long and convoluted one, including a few preliminary and provisional versions of the city-state, but the end result is a tripartite polis; that is, one with "three parts," three social classes, each with a particular function, and justice within the city-state turns out to be each of the three classes performing its function well, both individually and in relation to the whole society.

The lowest class consists of the *producers*: farmers, artisans, merchants, and other types of trade people. It is their role to provide for the basic needs of the society: food, clothing, shelter, and the like. The middle class is that of the *auxiliaries*, the military class. It is their role to protect the city from dangers both within and without. The upper class is the *guardians*, whose job is to rule the polis. In order for this society to be a just one, it is necessary that it have certain virtues: temperance, courage, and wisdom.

The first virtue necessary for a just society is that of *temperance*. A common misunderstanding of the *Republic* is to identify temperance only with the lowest class, the producers; but according to Plato, it should be present in all three classes. Another common misunderstanding of temperance is to treat it as mere moderation or self-restraint; in reality, this is only one connotation of the Greek term that Plato uses (*sophrosune*) that we typically translate as "temperance." True, *sophrosune* does partially involve moderation and self-restraint: everyone in Plato's ideal society would learn to live in moderation, having and enjoying only those things really necessary for the health and stability of the polis as a whole; and luxuries and the accumulation of personal wealth would not be permitted, since such self-interested pursuits tend to distract from contributing to the good of the whole. For example, the guardians must rule on behalf of the polis instead of their personal benefit, the auxiliaries must not be distracted from protecting the city, and the producers must not be encouraged to amass personal wealth at the expense of the whole economy. However, sophrosune also involves a kind of deference, an understanding one's place in society and keeping to it. In Plato's ideal society, each class would do its own job and not try to do the job of another class: producers wouldn't try to rule, rulers wouldn't try to produce, etc.

The second virtue necessary for the just society is that of *courage*. Courage, as Plato seems to use the term here, primarily involves doing the right thing even in the face of fear or temptation. Certainly, every citizen requires courage to some extent, but it is primarily a virtue of the auxiliaries, who must have the courage to fight for the good of the whole polis, even at the threat of personal injury or loss of life.

The third virtue necessary for a just society is that of *wisdom*. Plato explicates wisdom primarily in term of knowledge of the good, which is especially important for proper rule of a society; thus, wisdom is primarily a virtue of the guardians. The exact nature of wisdom, this knowledge of "the Good," requires fuller explication, to which Plato returns in later sections of the *Republic* in which he discusses the Theory of Forms and the Theory of Recollection, which we will examine later.

The polis that has these three cardinal virtues, and has them in their appropriate places, is said to be a just society. Justice, as Plato explains it, is each class of a society functioning properly, both in itself and in relation to the other classes, and thus contributing to the whole society. Therefore, in Plato's view justice is a kind of social health and harmony. The character of Socrates admits on more than one occasion during the course of the conversation that such a society is probably just an ideal rather than a practical possibility. However, he has a variety of interesting ideas about how such a polis would be put into practice if it were feasible to do so.

Most importantly, it would require a certain kind of upbringing and education. Private property would be abolished so that no one would be distracted by wealth or luxuries. People would live communally, without privately established repro-ductive relationships such as marriages. Children would be raised in common, and since no one would know whether or not any particular child was his or hers, they would treat all the children as well as their own. As the children grow and develop, careful attention would be paid to their abilities and potentials so that they could be sorted into the appropriate social classes. In order to get them to embrace these social distinctions, their education and upbringing would include what Socrates calls a "noble lie," a myth about how the gods create people. According to this myth, people are born with different metals in their souls: bronze, silver, or gold. The kind of metal determines the person's abilities, and therefore social class: bronze for producers, silver for auxiliaries, and gold for guardians. Once they are sorted into their respective classes, they will be given the appropriate sort of vocational training and education necessary to develop fully the skills and character appropriate to their role in society.

Having fully described the nature of the just polis, Socrates claims that we can now discover the nature of the just person by analogy. Just as the polis is tripartite, so too is the human "soul." The Greek word we translate as "soul" is *psukhe,* meaning "mind" or possibility even "character," which has more psychological than religious connotations; we get the English word "psyche" from it, and "psychology" would literally mean something like "study of the soul."

The lowest part of the soul, analogous to the producers of the polis, is the "appetitive" part: that is, the part containing our emotions and desires (that is, "appetites"). This part is concerned with the pursuit of pleasure, which contrary to popular opinion Plato does not think of as necessarily bad: some of the appetites are natural and important, such as those associated with the important biological processes such as nutrition and reproduction. Its virtue is temperance, both in the sense of moderation in the pursuit of food, sex, material gains, etc. and in the sense of deference, in that it should consent to be ruled by the better parts of the soul, that is, the rational and spirited parts.

The middle part of the soul, analogous to the auxiliaries of the polis, is the "spirited" part (not "spirit" like ghosts and poltergeists, but as in "school spirit"). This part is concerned with the pursuit of honor and avoidance of shame, two key moral concepts for the Greeks; thus, the spirited part is like a moral conscience. Its primary virtue is courage, the strength to do the right thing, specifically, to enforce the rule of reason upon the sometimes impetuous and distracting appetites.

The highest part of the soul, analogous to the guardians of the polis, is the "rational" part. This part is concerned with the pursuit of the Good, a concept which Plato develops at length in other sections of the *Republic*. Its primary virtue is wisdom, that is, knowledge of the Good.

Finally, then, we can see what justice is in the individual by analogy to justice in the polis: justice in the individual is a kind of psychological and moral health and harmony, involving each part of the soul achieving its respective virtue, fulfilling its respective function, and serving in its proper place. More specifically, it involves the rational part ruling over the whole, especially by keeping the appetitive part in its place: that is, letting reason rather than emotion rule. In this it is helped by the spirited part, which through its desire to achieve honor and avoid shame acts as a kind of moral enforcer to help reason rule the emotions. Furthermore, just as was the case in the polis, this can be accomplished only with proper education and the pursuit of a materially simple life. Compare this to the sort of life Socrates says he has led in the *Apology*.

In addition to his ethical and political views, the *Republic* provides Plato the opportunity to put forward the most famous of this theories, the Theory of Forms (sometimes translated as the Theory of "Ideas," though this translation tends to be avoided for its subjective, psychological connotations). Many of Plato's dialogues focus on a central "What is X?" question; for example, the *Republic's* "What is Justice?", the *Euthyphro's* "What is piety?", the *Meno's* "What is virtue?", etc. In some of these cases, Plato provides an explanation of the term in question by positing a corresponding Form.

A Platonic Form represents the perfect, eternal, unchanging, transcendent essence of the item in question; universal concept under which all of its specific instantiations (that is, concrete embodiments) fall; an ideal standard by which all particular examples are judged; and an objective entity that can serve as a defining exemplar of the concept under consideration. For example, in order to

answer the question "What is the Good?" and provide some definition or standard by which we can identify and evaluate the goodness of all particular good things (good actions, good people, good laws, good governments, etc.), Plato posits the Form of the Good, a perfect model of Goodness, which gives all particular good things their goodness, and serves as a standard for judging whether or not any particular thing is good.

This all might sound rather odd. However, Plato is simply working from a conceptual framework common to mathematics, both at his time (recall the Pythagoreans and Parmenideans, both very influential on Plato in this regard), and much more recently (for example, Alfred North Whitehead). Take for example the concept of a triangle. What is a triangle? A triangle is defined as a closed three-sided polygon whose interior angles total 180 degrees. Draw a triangle on a piece of paper. Is what you've drawn an actual triangle? Not really: unless you happen to be some kind of geometric savant, the angles probably don't equal exactly 180 degrees and the line segments which make up the sides are probably not perfectly straight.

What if you programmed a computer to draw a triangle with perfectly straight sides and perfect interior angles? Would that be an actual triangle? Still, the answer is no: line segments have no width, but the lines printed by the computer would have some width. In fact, absolutely any visible representation of a triangle must use mere representations of line segments (that is, ones with width) rather than actual line segments (that is, ones without width), or else we wouldn't be able to see it.

Also, any particular triangle fails to capture the essence of all triangles for another reason: it would just be one example of the infinite number of possible triangles. After all, there are triangles with all sorts of different shapes and sizes. Therefore, any particular triangle can at best only represent a very small part of what a triangle is. A perfect triangle (one which exactly meets the definition of a triangle and could be used as a standard or exemplar by which to judge the accuracy of any particular, concrete example of a triangle) cannot exist as a concrete, empirical object. A perfect triangle exists in concept only, as a standard by which we judge empirical approximations of triangles as more or less accurate, but never perfect.

Does that mean that triangles do not exist? Of course not. Certainly, there are such things as triangles. We can define them, list their properties, sort them into various classes (for example: equilateral, acute, obtuse), and so on. Do triangles "exist" the way concrete, physical, empirical objects (like tables or chairs) exist? Of course not. They are abstract, rather than concrete, objects: they exist as concepts.

However, they are not just any old subjective concept which any particular person happens to have. They have an objective, independent status; for example, triangles have interior angles equaling 180 degree whether or not any particular person believes or knows so. In fact, it is not too far-fetched to say that even if there were no people whatsoever, it would still be true that the interior angles of a triangle equal 180 degrees. (At least, this is what most contemporary mathematicians believe: they call it "mathematical realism," though philosophers simply call it "Platonism.") Thus, Plato's Forms are no more primitive or mystical than contemporary mathematical concepts.

Plato then generalizes the mathematical approach he inherited from the Mathematicians to other areas of inquiry, especially ethics. For example, Plato believes that there are Forms for a variety of basic ethical concepts, such as the Form of the Good, which he investigates in the *Republic*. Goodness itself, the very essence of Goodness, is not and could not ever be a concrete, empirical object. Goodness is not something you can hold in your hand or put under a microscope. Rather, Goodness is a concept, a standard by which we are able to recognize and evaluate particular good things: good people, actions, laws, governments, and so forth. Moreover, Plato argues that since Goodness is not something we can come to know empirically, but is something of which we nonetheless have a concept, there must be a Form of Goodness, a Form of which we have knowledge in some non-empirical way.

Here we can see how Plato is influenced by Heraclitus as well as the Mathematicians. Plato takes seriously Heraclitus' claim that the world around us is constantly in flux. The empirical world and everything in it is chaotic, imperfect, and constantly changing. If that were all there were to reality, it would be impossible for us to have any sort of knowledge: any object about which we might attempt to form some opinion would change the very next second (according to Heraclitus, it wouldn't even be the same object anymore). However, clearly we do have knowledge; therefore, there must be some underlying stability and order to reality which transcends the changing world of appearances. Plato then borrows from the Pythagoreans and Parmenideans in positing a transcendent orderly, mathematical reality; his version of it is the Forms, the metaphysical reality behind the world of appearance that makes knowledge possible.

Unfortunately, Plato is often misunderstood (and improperly taught) as though he believes that there are Forms for everything: chairs, people, cows, trees, you name it. This is, at best, highly debatable. He certainly uses examples of these sorts of things, but it is likely that he is using them metaphorically. Obviously, such a debate lies outside of the scope of this chapter; however, the interested reader may wish to look at the first few pages of the *Parmenides*, in which Plato makes it clear that there are Forms for basic mathematical-logical, ethical, and aesthetic concepts, but that it is doubtful whether there are Forms for natural objects such as humans, fire, water, and the like.

A natural next question is: Exactly how can one come to know the Forms if they exist in some abstract, transcendent realm? In order to answer this, Plato posits the Theory of Recollection. The Theory of Recollection is explicated in a number of Platonic dialogues, and in a number of different ways. In the *Phaedo*, Socrates claims that the soul is immortal and continually reincarnated. In between incarnations, it lives among the Forms, "seeing" them directly, and thus having direct knowledge of them. However, when the soul is born into its next body, the process is very traumatic, and the soul (apparently suffering from a kind of post-traumatic stress disorder) forgets what it once knew of the Forms. However, it can regain that forgotten knowledge by living a philosophical life, and thus recollect or remember what it once knew. In other words, there is no true learning, only the uncovering of the innate knowledge buried within us.

There are various opinions about what exactly Plato meant by all of this. Some contemporary scholars argue that Plato believed in reincarnation and the immortality of the soul quite literally. If true, this would be a clear Pythagorean influence on Plato's beliefs. Others argue that we ought to take a more interpretive view, for which knowledge of the context of the *Phaedo* is important. The *Phaedo* recounts Socrates' last conversation with his friends before his execution. From this, we might infer that he is simply trying to make them feel better by "proving" the immortality of the soul. It is also interesting to note that his friends do not seem to buy it, a fact which Plato does not attempt to hide. Thus, we might more reasonably see this as a metaphor or an analogy rather than a literal account of the process of Recollection of the Forms. After all, like Jesus, Plato often uses "myths" (in the sense of metaphors, parables, analogies) to explain his views: consider for example the three myths (the cave, the sun, and the divided line) Plato uses in the *Republic*.

In other dialogues, Socrates gives a more literal and less otherworldly account of the Theory of Recollection. For example, in the *Meno*, Socrates uses a hypothetic-deductive version of the Socratic Method to help an uneducated slave boy unearth his innate knowledge of mathematics. This demonstrates a more plausible account of the Theory of Recollection: that there are certain basic concepts (that is, "Forms" in Plato's terminology) built right into human thinking which can be made explicit by way of the right sort of deductive scheme.

Despite the best Platonic apologetics, Plato's theories still have a way of sounding strange to the modern ear. Perhaps when all is said and done, they really are strange. However, it cannot be denied that they are influential, and that any minimally respectable understanding of the history of Western thought requires at least a basic knowledge of Plato. The thoughtful reader will keep Plato in the back of his or her mind when reading other thinkers: Plato's most famous student, Aristotle; Christian theologians such as Augustine and Aquinas; early modern scientists such as Galileo and Descartes; later scientists such as Freud; and even Plato's most ardent opponent, Nietzsche. Plato features throughout Western civilization whether implicitly or explicitly; indeed, Alfred North Whitehead was not exaggerating greatly when he claimed, "The safest characterization of the European philosophical tradition is that it consists of a series of footnotes to Plato."

QUESTIONS FOR REFLECTION AND DISCUSSION

1. Recall your readings in Chapter Two on ancient Greek tragedy. Compare and contrast *Antigone* and the *Apology*. Does the *Apology* meet the standards of tragedy? Compare and contrast Antigone (the character) and Socrates. Does Socrates meet the standards of a tragic hero?

2. Describe Plato's republic (that is, the ideal form of society described in the *Republic*). In your opinion, is it a good or bad form of society? Is it communist? totalitarian?

3. What does the *Republic* have to say about women? Are they treated the same as men or different from them? What sort of social roles could they fulfill?

4. What criticisms of democracy can you find in the *Apology* and the *Republic?* Do they apply to twenty-first century American democracy?

5. Describe the Myth of the Cave in the *Republic*. How is this myth an analogy for Plato's Theory of Forms and Theory of Recollection?

SUGGESTIONS FOR FURTHER READING

Original Works
Plato: Complete Works. Edited by John Cooper, Indianapolis and Cambridge: Hackett, 1997.

Secondary Works
Jones, W.T. *A History of Western Philosophy* [volume one]: *The Classical Mind* (2nd edition). Fort Worth: Harcourt Brace Jovanovich, 1980.

Irwin, Terence. *A History of Western Philosophy* [volume one]: *Classical Thought.* Oxford: Oxford UP, 1989.

Vlastos, Gregory (Ed.). *The Philosophy of Socrates.* Notre Dame: Notre Dame UP, 1971.

Pappas, Nickolas. *Plato and the Republic.* London: Routledge, 1995.

CHAPTER FOUR

GREEK PHILOSOPHY: ARISTOTLE

The influence of Plato's most famous student, Aristotle, on the history of Western thought has been enormous. He was a thorough and systematic scholar who collected and organized many of the ideas and observations of those who had lived before him. He was a powerfully original and creative thinker who created formal logic and whose interpretations of everything from biological organisms to tragic drama bequeathed a lasting intellectual legacy to the cultures of the West. His many writings show that he investigated just about everything: they range over logic, biology, physics, metaphysics, psychology, ethics, politics, rhetoric, and drama.

A measure of Aristotle's influence can be seen in the fact that when the whole body of his writings became available in Europe beginning in the twelfth century, thinkers came to be so impressed by the universal range and intellectual thoroughness of his writings that they often uncritically took his work as a final authority on all sorts of issues. His writings set the bounds of philosophical and scientific knowledge and dominated the curriculum in universities during the late Middle Ages and the Renaissance. This was particularly fateful in the area of natural science, in which Aristotle was a major source of geocentric astronomy and of ideas in physics such as the belief that heavy objects fall faster than light objects. Aristotle's authority meant that the pioneers of the Scientific Revolution in the sixteenth and seventeenth centuries, such as Galileo, had to oppose and discredit the authority of Aristotle in order to establish the foundations of modern science.

ARISTOTLE'S LIFE

Aristotle was born in 384 BCE in Stagira, a small town in the north of Greece. His father, Nicomachus, was physician to Amyntas II, king of Macedon and grandfather of Alexander the Great. In 367 Aristotle came to Athens to study in Plato's Academy, where he remained until Plato's death in 347. During those twenty years Athens, reviving after its defeat by Sparta in 404, was "booming" again as a cultural and commercial center. Plato's nephew Speusippus, with whom Aristotle was not on good terms, became head of the Academy when Plato died, and Aristotle and his friend Xenocrates left Athens. They settled in Assos, on the coast of Asia Minor near Troy, where Aristotle started a branch of the Academy. He also became an advisor and friend to the local ruler, Hermias, and married his niece Pythias. Moving to Mitylene on the island of Lesbos in 344, Aristotle carried on biological studies and engaged in philosophical reflection and discussion with a man named Theophrastus, who was later Aristotle's best-known follower.

In 342 BCE Philip, king of Macedon, invited Aristotle to live in Pella and tutor his son, Alexander, who was at that time thirteen. Aristotle spent six years in Macedon, the first three of them (ca. 342–339) educating the future king. When Alexander succeeded to the throne in 335, Aristotle returned to Athens and founded his own school, the *Lyceum*. The members of the school became known as the "Peripatetics" (Greek *peripatetikoi*, "walking about"), from their custom of walking back and forth while carrying on their discussions. More than the Academy, the Lyceum seems to have

141

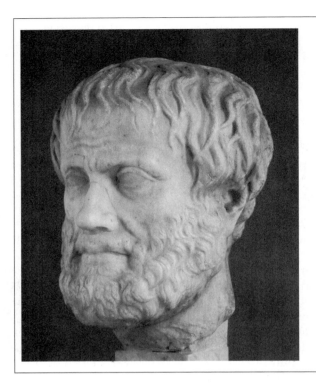

Aristotle is described by ancient sources as an aged, balding man with a broad skull, short beard and small, piercing eyes. This sense of specificity, observation, and individuality in this bust are some of the chief hallmarks of Greek Classical art, which parallel the tenets of Aristotle's own philosophy.

Figure II-7 *Aristotle,* Roman copy after the Greek original of the fourth century BCE. Marble, height 12″ (30.5 cm). Kunsthistorisches Museum, Vienna, Austria. Courtesy of Erich Lessing/Art Resource, NY.

had the character not only of an educational institution but also of a learned society in which mature scholars carried on research and dialogue. Here Aristotle lectured on many topics, presenting ideas he had developed over the years in which he parted company with Plato's views. When Alexander the Great died in 323, the negative reaction in Athens to Macedonian rule included a charge of impiety against Aristotle as former tutor of Alexander and old friend of Alexander's governor of Athens, Antipater. Aristotle fled the city, reportedly saying that he would not let the Athenians "sin twice against philosophy" by condemning him as they had condemned Socrates. He went to live on his mother's estate in Chalcis. Before his death not long afterwards in 322, Aristotle directed that he be buried next to his wife and that his adult slaves be freed.

Like Plato, Aristotle sought to unite the Pre-Socratics' interest in understanding nature with the Sophists' and Socrates' preoccupation with understanding human beings, their values and their institutions. Unlike Plato, Aristotle was absorbed in scientific investigation, observing, analyzing, classifying, and interpreting animal species, physical phenomena such as motion, and the heavens.

ARISTOTLE'S METHOD

A passage from the *Nicomachean Ethics* nicely illustrates one aspect of Aristotle's method:

> As in the other cases we must set out the appearances, and first of all go through the puzzles. In this way we must prove the common beliefs about these ways of being affected— ideally, all the common beliefs, but if not all, then most of them, and the most important. For if the objections are solved, and the common beliefs are left, it will be an adequate proof.

[Translated by Terence Irwin. Indianapolis: Hackett, 1985, 1145b1]

In reading Aristotle's writings we can see him proceeding as he says he does here: collecting the current knowledge, giving its rationale, examining the problems raised, and making a judgment.

Also basic to Aristotle's whole philosophy is the view that all things by their very nature carry on activity directed toward an end or goal. The goal of each class of things in nature is one proper to the kind of thing they are. This is called a *teleological* (from the Greek *telos,* end or goal) account of natural activity. Aristotle's teleology informs every area of his intellectual activity, from science and metaphysics to ethics and politics (as we shall see).

ARISTOTLE AND PLATO

Plato taught at his Academy, presumably giving lectures while his students took notes. None of Plato's lectures survive; only the many dialogues he wrote for "popular" reading. In striking contrast, his pupil Aristotle, who also taught for many years at the Lyceum, wrote a number of dialogues of which only a few fragments survive. What were preserved of Aristotle's were his lectures on the many topics he taught at his school. This makes it difficult to compare Plato and Aristotle fairly, either as philosophers or as writers. Plato has always been a favorite with readers—who would not rather read his appealing and beautifully written philosophical "plays" than Aristotle's dry lecture notes? What evidence we have suggests that Aristotle's dialogues were not lacking in literary grace and style.

Further complicating the problem of comparison is that for the author/lecturer, presenting philosophy in literary form for the reading public and teaching it in the classroom may well serve two quite different purposes. In dialogues—imagined philosophical conversations—the author can "play with ideas," try out different arguments, allow a variety of voices to be heard. In Plato's dialogues that is typically what is going on. By contrast, in his lectures Plato, no less than Aristotle, may have been concerned instead to present ideas and arguments in a very systematic and organized fashion, summarizing the knowledge available on the subject up to that point, covering every possible issue, and developing definite conclusions. When we read Plato's dialogues and Aristotle's lectures we should keep all this in mind.

But when due consideration has been given to the different types of philosophical writing that have survived from Plato and Aristotle, we must go on to acknowledge important differences not only in method but in the content of their thought.

For Plato the highest form of knowledge is pure contemplation of the Forms in themselves, supreme among which is the all-embracing Form of the Good, freed from sense experience and the world of becoming. This is the highest activity of the soul, available only to those who have devoted themselves intellectually and morally to the love of wisdom and spurned the attractions of worldly existence such as fame, power, and money. Later followers and many interpreters of Plato have seen a religious and even mystical quality to his thought, centering in the inner pilgrimage of the soul to liberation from the body and the world of becoming and reunion with true Being.

By contrast, Aristotle was more "worldly" in his thinking, dedicated to describing as accurately and systematically as possible the whole range of nature and human activities. He revised Plato's Theory of Forms, arguing that universals do not exist independently but only as instantiated; that is, in concrete, particular, empirically-observable things. In their observations of human beings, while Plato tended to speak of the soul as the essential person encased for a time in a physical body, Aristotle thought in terms of an "ensouled body," always viewing human characteristics and behavior, like those of other natural beings, as rooted in and shaped by our biological existence. There is a "down-to-earth" quality to Aristotle's interests and methods that also often makes his observations seem more practical and more in contact with the experience of the ordinary individual and ordinary social life. By the same token, Plato's "exalted" view can result in more radical ideas, as we have seen in the *Republic,* while Aristotle's can seem middle-of-the-road or conservative.

The French scholar, Jacqueline de Romilly, sums up the differences between Plato and Aristotle in this way:

> In Plato and Aristotle we thus have the maturation and supreme achievement of two different forms of philosophy, one oriented toward inner meditation and exalting the care of the soul, the other oriented toward a reasoned and descriptive ordering of things in the world. The complementarity is all the more striking when we

recall that one of these men was the other's student.

[Romilly, Jacqueline de. *A Short History of Greek Literature.* Translated by Lillian Doherty. Chicago: University of Chicago Press, 1985, 165]

The contrast is dramatically symbolized by the Renaissance painter, Raphael, in his famous *School of Athens*, where he portrays Plato pointing up toward the heavens and Aristotle gesturing down toward the earth.

ETHICS AND POLITICS

We should note that Aristotle has no simple answers to the questions, "how should a human being live" and "how should the state be organized." At the very beginning of his argument he makes the assertion that the realm of theory is different from the realm of action. This assertion has wide-ranging implications. As a result of it, in ethics he tends to bypass theoretical questions such as the abstract nature of goodness, and focuses instead on the good action, while in politics he has relatively little to say about the best state. In both cases, he organizes the field at hand, summarizes prevailing ideas and practices on each issue, subjects them to discerning criticism, and tries to work out what he considers to be the most reasonable and balanced solution.

Because of Aristotle's method, we are confronted in his ethical and political writings with both his own genius and his careful "data collection" from the Greek society of his day. Thus when we say that the *Nicomachean Ethics* and the *Politics* are immensely rich and influential, we are not only praising Aristotle. We are also recognizing the fact that the Greeks had assembled a considerable body of practical and theoretical political knowledge. This body of knowledge contains much of the concept of "the civilized" as it has been understood in later ages of Western history. To illustrate this point it is sufficient to quote a few Greek political slogans, most of which were around many years before Aristotle: "law and order" (*eunomia*), "equality under law (*isonomia*), "equality" (*to ison*), "justice" (*dike*), "freedom" (*eleutheria*), "freedom of speech" (*isegoria*), and "accountability" (*euthynia*).

Within these collections of prevailing thought and practice, Aristotle stresses certain themes. First,

Three themes

applying his teleological method to the human level, Aristotle believes that both the individual and the state inherently pursue certain goals. Second, the state is a complex organism, the individual a part of this organism. The state and the individual each pursues its "good," but the individual's good can only be pursued within the context of the good of the state. A third theme is that rule is not simply a matter of the more powerful dominating others. What Aristotle calls "constitutional rule"—ruling the purpose of which is the benefit of those who are governed—is also a natural form of government.

THE *NICOMACHEAN ETHICS* AND VIRTUE

In the *Nicomachean Ethics* Aristotle argues that the activity of individual human beings is always directed toward goals that they believe are good. In analyzing the goods humans seek, he finds that happiness is the only thing that people desire for its own sake and not as a means to something else. Clearly we pursue different sorts of goods that we believe will make us happy—sensual pleasure, fame, wealth, and power are typical. But the question is, what activity will actually produce the happiness that is the fullest natural expression of the kind of being a human is? In his discussion Aristotle has set aside "the absolutely good" as irrelevant in the context of action in the real world, and has defined the good in terms of the way that an ordinary person is to live. He defines the supreme good of happiness as a kind of action: activity of the soul in accord with perfect virtue. By making this point, Aristotle separates himself from the ethics and politics of Plato. For Plato, one could not behave virtuously until one knew what virtue was. Aristotle boldly declares that one must be inclined to behave virtuously before one can even begin to study what virtue is.

The concept of "virtue" involved here is not that of our current usage. For us, "virtue" has a connotation of refraining from doing certain things. But the word "virtue" has a wider connotation, preserved in our word "virtuoso" to describe a person who exhibits remarkable skill or excellence in, for example, performing music. In its ancient usage among the Greeks and the Romans, "virtue" means primarily courage, and it is displayed by winning. This is indicated by its etymology: "virtue" comes from the Latin *virtus*, from *vir*, meaning "man." The Greek word for virtue, *arete*, does not have this etymological link to a word meaning "man." However, it does seem to be linguistically related to the word for "best" (*aristos*), and the element of overcoming or excelling is usually present in the sense of the word. Thus virtue can also be thought of as *excellence*, which is achieved only by the disposition and the courage to excel. To say that moderation is a virtue is possible, but when the Greeks speak simply of "virtue," they have courage or excelling in mind. Thus when Socrates said "virtue is knowledge," he intended to startle his listeners with an unfamiliar definition.

Virtue and Psychology Aristotle analyzes virtue by analyzing the human mind or soul, since virtue can only be a quality of rational beings, and rationality is a property of the human soul rather than the body. At the same time, for Aristotle, unlike Plato, soul and body are inseparable and related to each other as form to matter. Thus Aristotle can talk about aspects of the soul that sound rather corporeal. The human soul, he says, contains both rational and irrational elements. The irrational aspect is divided into two parts. The first (a) is purely irrational and in fact shared with all living things: the "vegetative element" or "nutritive faculty," that which causes nutrition and growth. But (b) the other irrational aspect of the human soul is connected with the rational: the desires or appetites, which can be made to obey or resist the rational element, as when a person exercises self-control with regard to food, drink, or sex. The rational element in the soul is the source of all thinking; it is unique to and definitive of humans, whom Aristotle defines as "rational animals." As such the rational mind is by nature intended to be the governing part of the soul in human beings.

Aristotle's analysis of the human mind or soul:

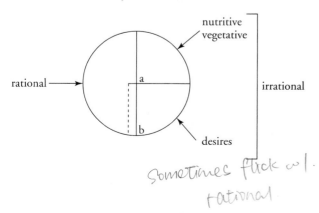

Two Kinds of Virtue Corresponding to the rational and the irrational-but-governable-by-reason elements in the soul are two kinds of virtue or excellence: intellectual and moral. The *moral virtues* are fostered in human beings by the cultivation from an early age of good habits that enable the reason to control and moderate the desires and passions. The person of good character, who excels in the practice of temperance, prudence, courage, and justice, is the one in whom these habits of self-control have become firmly established. The *intellectual virtues* are the purely rational pursuit of the various branches of knowledge, and are inculcated by teaching. Since humans are defined among species by their rationality, their most distinctive virtue is intellectual virtue or the committed and disciplined inquiry into truth. However, Aristotle gives a great deal of attention to the importance of the practical or moral virtues. Both forms of virtue are settled states of character developed only by training. The true happiness, which is the goal most fully appropriate to human nature, consists of those activities that express the highest moral and intellectual excellence. To put it in modern terms, happiness is "being all you can be" as a human being: realizing as fully and creatively as possible one's distinctively human potentialities in noble behavior and in the arts and sciences. But Aristotle insists that it never "just happens"; it requires early training and education.

Aristotle makes it clear in both the *Nicomachean Ethics* and the *Politics* that ethics and politics, the study of the good life for the individual and the good life for the state, are inseparable. That is because individual human life with all its needs and possibilities is impossible except in the context of human society and government, and the quality of the state depends upon the quality of its citizens. Aristotle begins his *Ethics* by pointing out that politics is the most all-embracing study because the city-state encompasses the lives of individuals and all other human activities. And he concludes his *Politics* with a discussion of how the polis should educate its young in order to develop virtue in its citizens.

THE *POLITICS*

In the *Politics* Aristotle declares that politics is not a theoretical but a pragmatic art; in our terms, politics is "the art of the possible." For Plato this means that the good man cannot be a politician. But Aristotle, who accepts that the world is imperfect, obviously thinks otherwise. Always thinking teleologically, Aristotle sees the question of the goal or aim of political rule as the most important question in politics. He argues strenuously that in the polis the goal of the ruler must be to benefit the ruled. This he refers to as "constitutional rule." The word translated "constitutional" in these passages is *politike,* which means "appropriate to the polis." Constitutional rule thus would be rule appropriate to the polis. Despite the importance of this word to Aristotle (who also used it to describe the "best" government, which no one on earth will ever achieve), he does not clearly define it. One assumes that Aristotle here is thinking of the good of the polis as the well-being and security of its citizens. But he also refers to the principle of "ruling and being ruled in turn" as inherent in constitutional rule.

Aristotle follows Greek tradition when he identifies society as a complex entity, composed of the family and the state. Each pursues its own good, and although the good of the state is higher than the good of the family, one cannot do away with the family without destroying the state. This line of reasoning is the most effective argument against totalitarianism and in favor of "private property," and is at the core of Aristotle's objections to Plato's *Republic,* which proposes a totalitarian state in which property is held in common.

Types of Governments   We first read of the three types of government—rule by one, rule by a few, and rule by the many—about a century before Aristotle. In the *Republic* Plato talks about a cycle in which the state degenerates from monarchy to oligarchy to democracy, and later writers such as Polybius, a third century BCE historian, developed a whole theory of the "natural cycles" through which governments pass from one of the three forms to the others until they come full circle. Aristotle does not approach the analysis of the three forms of government in this way. Instead, he delineates "true" forms of rule by one, by the few, and by the many, with the terms *monarchy, aristocracy,* and *constitutional* or "polity." He calls the "false" or degenerate forms *tyranny, oligarchy,* and *democracy.* In the true forms the rulers rule in the state's best interest; in

the degenerate forms the rulers rule in their own interest.

Aristotle examines all three types of government in relation to the age-old struggle between rich and poor, so there is definitely an important economic dimension to his analysis. When he discusses practical political activity, he refers only to democracy and oligarchy. Either the rich (normally the few) or the poor (normally the many) will be in control of a state, and the political art consists largely in accommodating the other class. Aristotle argues the merits of both oligarchy and democracy. As is usual with him, he wishes us to see that these two extremes both contain elements that the well-ordered state must have in the correct proportions.

When Aristotle asserts that the best political community is one in which the "middle people" are predominant, he reinforces a truism of Greek political thought. In their position as the mean between the rich and the poor, the people in the middle—those who neither wealthy nor desperately poor—are capable of being more rational. They are less tempted to arrogance and greed than the rich, and not servile or resentful like the poor. A polis composed only of the rich and the poor is the worst kind of state, made up only of "masters" and "slaves." At the same time, "the middle is best" is a principle that is operative throughout Aristotle's treatments of both ethics and politics. It is also related to the command, "nothing in excess," which is identified with Apollo's oracle at Delphi. In Roman times, the poet Horace would later come up with the famous phrase "the golden mean."

When Aristotle goes on to say that the state must either be ruled by the exceptional man or throw him out, he is again agreeing with conventional political practices. In Athens there was a procedure in which each citizen wrote the name of the person whom he considered to be the most dangerous to the state on a piece of pottery (*ostrakon*). If a person received a certain share of the votes, he had to go into exile for ten years. This was referred to as *ostracism.* Aristotle's comment that the exceptional person is either a "god or a beast" reflects the Greeks' view of the human world as being a middle ground between Hades and Olympus, between matter and form. There seems to be no modern political institution comparable to ostracism.

Much of Aristotle's argument in Book l of the *Politics* is directed against the view that the strong rule the weak by nature and that government is a conspiracy of the weak against the strong. Aristotle's famous remark, "Man is a political animal," is directed against this argument. That is, it is an assertion that government is innate in the species and not imposed by some special group on the rest of humankind.

The state as a natural entity   Aristotle's approach to politics seems to be influenced by his work in biology. He appears to be treating the state as another living organism when he says, "He who thus considers things in their first growth and origin, whether a state or anything else, will obtain the clearest view of them." This statement is also an example of a general tendency among the ancient Greeks to look to the primitive for information about the essential nature of society. For instance, Homer's *Iliad*, deliberately set in a more primitive era, is greatly concerned with politics. Aristotle considers the state—a governing structure for human society—to be natural to human beings, not a conventional arrangement artificially imposed on their "natural state," as in some influential forms of modern political thought. That is why he calls humans "political animals," and begins his analysis of the state by analyzing its natural development from the union of male and female through the kinship of families in a village to the community of villages that produces a state. But while we must begin with the earliest beginnings to understand the nature of the state, in the light of Aristotle's teleological method of explanation we must go on to say that since the state is the end toward which its earliest components are directed, the state is "prior to" the individual and the family—not chronologically, but in the sense of being the most complete reality.

The rights and duties of citizens   For all their privileges relative to women, Greek men operated under considerable restraints of their own. Citizen rights involved universal military training, and a man was subject to military service until the age of sixty. Military service was arduous, the citizen soldier making long marches and fighting in armor. If a citizen was chosen by lot to perform some official function he could easily become subject to fines or worse for improperly carrying out his office. It was not difficult to become involved in legal difficulties that led to the loss of citizen rights. The exile, and the Greek desiring to emigrate from a small town, would find it difficult to be made a citizen of another Greek state. Aristotle was such a one—as a native of Stagira he had no citizenship rights in Athens.

Apart from the stark contrast between the lives and roles of the sexes, one of the oddities of Greek political experience is that they discovered the value of "equality" as an organizing principle and yet retained "inequality" in so many respects. One reason for this is the Greek passion for elitism. In politics, athletics, literature, and even philosophy, the "contest" (*agon*) is important, and the Greeks had great respect for—and envy of—the best. Recall that the basic meaning of the Greek word for "virtue," *arête*, is "excellence," being the best in whatever one decides to do. "The stronger rule the weaker" is accepted as popular wisdom. We can tell by the effort Aristotle devotes to it that the idea that a ruler rules in the interest of the ruled and not in his own interest will not be easily accepted. In terms of politics, Aristotle argues that "true virtue"—temperance, courage, wisdom, and justice—requires leisure, money, and political experience, and no one but a citizen can possess them. And a citizen can possess these virtues only by making decisions in situations that involve danger; that is, only by exercising rule. Inferior and superior, ruled and ruling, are natural ideas for a Greek.

The role of women and slaves   Aristotle develops the distinction between despotic and constitutional rule by contrasting the rule of a man over his slaves and over his wife and children. As he develops this argument, he says things about slaves and women and children that offend our sensibilities. Did Aristotle say women were like slaves and children? Did he defend the institution of slavery? The answer is both yes and no.

The first thing to be noted is that Aristotle is describing current practice, not what he calls at one point "the world as we would like it to be." It was not unthinkable to advocate ending slavery and liberating women. Why Aristotle did not propose it may be at least partially explained by the general thrust of his argument. If he has a "radical proposal" in mind, it is to attack the two dominant modes of political organization of his time, oligarchy and democracy.

Let us take a deeper look at what Aristotle says about women and slaves. He asks whether slavery exists by nature or by law, and he finds that slavery exists by nature, although there is a kind of slavery that is by convention. (In other words, some people who are in fact slaves, say, in Athens, as a result of war and conquest, are not "natural slaves.") Slavery exists by nature because in nature there is an element that rules and one that is ruled, as for example the intellect rules the body. The slave, like the body, is a living tool. Yet Aristotle does not stop there. He distinguishes the slave from a tool: the slave possesses intelligence and uses tools. Then the concept "rule of slaves" is said to have two parts. Insofar as he is a tool, the slave is ruled despotically; insofar as he possesses intelligence, he is to be persuaded, taught. Aristotle does not pursue this line of reasoning further, because it does not interest him. His essential point is that slavery exists by nature and that rule of a slave is despotic. Further discussion is simply inserted to show that there are further complexities to the question.

Much more disturbing to us is Aristotle's assertion that the "artisan" is in a worse relationship to the possibility of virtue than a slave. An artisan is a person who possesses a skill, but who works with his hands. He takes orders from others and works for hire. Both the artisan and the slave perform jobs that do not involve virtue, since virtue is exercised by making choices. But the slave at least participates in his master's virtue, while the artisan is entirely cut off from virtue.

When we examine what Aristotle says about women, we see that Aristotle accepts the inferiority of women as a given, and that his interest is not in attacking or defending that inferiority, but in showing that rule of women is different in kind from rule of slaves. A woman is a free person and her husband's rule over her is "constitutional," not despotic. However, as "constitutional rule" in the political sphere involves ruling and being ruled in turn, Aristotle must explain why this is not true in the family. His explanation is curiously vague. A woman, he says, has the same intellectual capacities as a man, but these capacities are not "valid." His phrasing is ambiguous: it means both that a woman's intellect is not as constant and firm as a man's (a traditional view, and one which he gives as his own in the *Nicomachean Ethics*) and that a

woman's ability to make decisions does not possess "weight" in the political sphere, because she is denied the right to vote and to sell property. One explanation why Aristotle leaves this comment about women's inferiority so vague may be that it is, again, not a central question for him in this context. The essential point is that rule of women is "constitutional." The fact that "rule and be ruled in turn" is not allowed for women is a qualification which Aristotle grants and, briefly, tries to explain. In the discussion in the *Nicomachean Ethics* just mentioned, he also suggests that the male allows the female to rule in areas that are of primary concern to her—household management and the nurture of children—which suggests a kind of rule in turn.

In fact, if we assert that women in our culture "rule and are ruled in turn," then Aristotle's argument is strengthened, not weakened. His argument is that not all rule is despotic by nature. Even within the family, despotic power is exercised only in very limited areas. If we assert that in our culture rule of slaves no longer exists and women to some extent share power with men, then despotic rule all but disappears.

ARISTOTELIAN POLITICAL ISSUES IMPLICIT IN *ANTIGONE* AND THE *APOLOGY*

As we have seen, Aristotle can be seen as summing up the political wisdom of the Greeks. Indeed, the concepts we find in Aristotle can easily be applied to two works on which we have focused in illustrating Greek thought and art. In *Antigone*, for example, Creon has taken the end of the state to be security to the exclusion of the ultimate end of the state, which is living well. Antigone, on the other hand, is being constrained so that she cannot "act in accord with perfect virtue." Creon tries to rule both Antigone and Haemon "despotically, and not constitutionally." He denies both of them "equality of speech." At the end of the play Creon declares, "I have learned to live under the established laws." Aristotle would say that he has learned that rule in a city is not despotic but constitutional. And the chorus answers Creon with another political slogan, "at last you have learned good council (*euboulia*)."

In Greek tragedy, the chorus reflects what one might call a mass psychology. The chorus in Sophocles' *Antigone* is made up of old men who "worship power" (as Creon puts it), and they disapprove of Antigone's resistance to Creon because she flaunts the traditional reverence for power. On the other hand, once Creon has failed, they are quick to tell him that he was not wise. That is, they always back the winner. In Aristophanes' comedies the people are described as self-satisfied, quick to change their opinion, and basically interested in obtaining their little cup of soup.

In the *Apology* Socrates claims that his life as a philosopher has been one of encouraging his fellow citizens "to follow virtue." This is an activity that he intends to carry on even if it costs him his life. He recounts his actions at the trial of the generals (which we have related above) and declares that he risked his life to uphold law. On another occasion, he says, he refused to take part in an illegal arrest. The first act occurred under a democracy, the second under an oligarchy. But in both cases the ruling faction was acting without regard to law. It would appear that Socrates (at least as Plato presents him) acts by Aristotle's rule and not Plato's: he asserts his absolute right to act in accord with perfect virtue. At the same time, by having Socrates dare the jury to vote against him out of complacency and pride, Plato implies that the democracy put Socrates to death because it was a democracy of the worst sort, one that put its interests of the moment above the law.

Antigone and Socrates thus illustrate one of Aristotle's basic premises: despotic rule will not work with free citizens. *Antigone* depicts a free person in conflict with a monarch, the *Apology* a free person in conflict with a democracy. Both are depicted as destabilizing the state while behaving in accord with virtue. Both are powerless—the one a young woman, the other an old man. Both lose to the more powerful state. Yet both of them die of their own free will because they are convinced they are right, and by dying in this way treat their own personal pleasure and pain as if it were of relatively small importance. That they do lose illustrates that "the stronger rules the weaker." But the fact that the city cannot break their will and force them to yield illustrates that this is not the whole truth.

SOME THEMES IN ARISTOTLE'S *POLITICS*

In Book I, chaps. 1–7, of the *Politics* Aristotle introduces us to the foundation of his whole study of the polis: the city-state conceived as a natural human association, not an arbitrary convention as the Sophists and some modern political theorists have argued. Notice throughout your reading of the *Politics* Aristotle's method: (1) his teleological approach, which characterizes everything—in this case, the city-state—in terms of the natural end or aim of its activity; and (2) having done this, his then breaking things down into their constituent parts (which is the meaning of the term "analysis") in order to understand them. Aristotle argues that the city-state is the natural outcome of two kinds of natural human relationships that establish the household: husband/wife and master/slave. When he says that the polis is "prior" to the individual and the household, he does not mean prior in time but prior as the all-encompassing whole of which the individual and the household are parts. Aristotle also justifies slavery and defines two types of slaves, natural and legal. He argues that it is a natural "fact" that some human beings are so limited in their capacities as to be tools for others. These are not to be confused with "legal" slaves who are enslaved as a result of conquest and might be anyone from prince to peasant. Aristotle has difficulty maintaining the distinction between natural and legal slaves, but is sure of the legitimacy of legal slavery. In chapters 8–11 Aristotle discusses the acquisition and exchange of goods and recommends an economic policy that is surprisingly similar to Marxist economic philosophy. Aristotle speaks against trade, recommending that trade be kept at the level of barter. He opposes coinage and is against usury (the lending of money for interest).

In the last two chapters of Book I Aristotle returns to his concern for the household. Aristotle analyzes the different sorts of rule the (male) head of the household has over his wife, his children, and his slaves. How does he justify the natural superiority of free adult men on the basis of what he believes are differences among these "natural" groups in terms of the role reason plays? What do you make of his argument that virtue (excellence) in, say, a woman is not the same as in a man?

Book III addresses citizenship and the best constitution. Aristotle's definition of citizenship is so narrow that few would be able to participate (see Chapter Three). Based on his extensive knowledge of many different constitutions, Aristotle categorizes three basic types, which are subdivided into their "correct" and "deviated" forms: rule by one, rule by a few and rule by the many. The "correct" forms, respectively, are monarchy, aristocracy, and polity. The "incorrect" are tyranny, oligarchy, and democracy. (Do not confuse "deviated" with "deviant." Deviate means only to move away from a norm or ideal to greater or lesser degree.) You will come again to consider different forms of constitutions in the readings of Thomas Aquinas and Niccolo Machiavelli, and in the modern period in John Locke and Thomas Hobbes. You might consider here what Aristotle says in Book IV, 1289a8: ". . . some people think that there is only one democracy. . ." What does Aristotle say to this and how might we apply this to modern dialogue on best types of governments? A few lines later (1289a14) Aristotle offers a definition of a constitution. Note this.

Book IV sets out the task of the political theorist, which is to consider what is the best constitution. Clearly Aristotle establishes in chapter 1 that there is no one "best" constitution and enumerates four. In chapter 4, Aristotle offers concrete examples of the reasons for these differences as he cites names of towns and places. Aristotle is clear, however, in stating that whatever type of constitution or government, the rule of law must be sovereign.

In chapters 8–12, Aristotle describes what he calls "polity" as a mixture of democracy and oligarchy as the best type of constitution because it achieves one of Aristotle's basic principles, the mean. The mean is the position between two extremes and for Aristotle this is an important virtue. Even, he goes on to elaborate, in democracies and aristocracies: the "middle people," those who are neither rich nor poor, should be cultivated, as they will insure stability. In between this discussion of polity and the mean, Aristotle inserts a chapter, 10, on three forms of tyranny. You might consider whether Creon in Sophocles' play, *Antigone*, fits one of these descriptions and which one.

Except for a single chapter featuring plain-spoken opinions on the "Regulation of Marriage and Procreation" (Book VII, Chap 16), the remaining assigned readings deal with the subject of the correct education. In comparing his ideas with the current nationwide American policy known as "No Child Left Behind," Aristotle's policy can more accurately be described as "Educate Every Child According to His or Her Proper Place."

As is the case with many other issues, Aristotle's views on education and upbringing (Book VII, Chaps. 14, 15 & 17, Book VIII, Chaps. 1–3) contrast sharply with those of Plato. Whereas Plato suggested that in the ideal republic traditional marriages and family would be abolished and children would be raised in common, Aristotle maintains that traditional families and marriages are necessary, not only since they are natural, but also because the polis is simply a natural outgrowth of natural family associations. Furthermore, according to Aristotle proper education and upbringing are absolutely essential for the creation of good citizens, not merely so that they may achieve the good life for themselves, but also so that they may contribute to the creation and maintenance of a good polis.

In order to achieve *eudaimonia* (usually translated as "happiness" or "well-being" or perhaps even "the good life")—which he identifies in the *Nicomachean Ethics* as the human *telos*—human beings must develop and exercise a variety of *aretai* or virtues. According to Aristotle, the most important of these are the intellectual virtues: theoretical wisdom and practical wisdom. Aristotle claims that the happiest life is one of "theoretical contemplation"—by which he means the study and enjoyment of philosophy, science, mathematics, and the like—and obviously, a proper academic education is essential to such things. Furthermore, the good life requires the development and exercise of practical wisdom, by which Aristotle means moral and political understanding. Practical wisdom is necessary not only for living a morally proper life, but also for participation in government, an essential duty of the citizen. (It is interesting to note that the English word "idiot" derives from the Greek *idios*, a word used to refer to citizens who avoided serving in public affairs, and were thus seen as rather useless.) Such practical wisdom is developed through upbringing and education, as well as through real-world experience in the public sphere.

Although Aristotle defines humans as "the rational animal," he understands that we are not solely intellectual creatures. In addition to the intellectual virtues, we must also cultivate the moral virtues, such as temperance, courage, generosity, and the like. Our parents should start us on this path through a proper upbringing. When we are very young and incapable of understanding the complexities of moral philosophy, our parents should simply train us to behave properly by punishing bad behavior and rewarding good behavior; then as we mature, we should be given a moral education as well as an academic one. Ultimately, we become morally virtuous both by learning about morality and by practicing moral behavior, until such time as it becomes habituated into a strong and lasting moral character.

In addition to an intellectual and moral curriculum, Aristotle also believes that a good education will involve a variety of other components. Certain practical skills such as reading and writing should be taught, but not menial skills—such things are only proper for "mere" trades people, slaves, and women, not full-fledged (read "educated, well-off male") citizens. A complete education should also include *gymnastikos* (from which the English word "gymnastics" is derived)—that is, physical education—which not only promotes health, but also, Aristotle believes, helps promote courage. Clearly, a citizen who wished or was required to serve in the military would need to be physically fit. However, parents and educators ought to be careful not to emphasize physical education too much, since it might promote an overly aggressive demeanor. Finally, Aristotle advocates teaching *mousike* (from which the English word "music" is derived), which refers to the arts generally: not just music, but poetry and drama as well. The study of these arts served a dual purpose. First, the Greek poets and tragedians were often thought of as authorities on matters of morality and politics; thus, studying (for example) Homer and Sophocles would have been part of the typical Athenian's moral education. Second, Aristotle believes that such activities were proper ways for a citizen to spend his *otium*—that is, his leisure time. Note, however, that Aristotle's notion of leisure is much more sophisticated than that of mere "goofing-off;" it is rather the pursuit of supposedly more worthwhile pleasures, of which the arts are a good example. Indeed, Aristotle considered the luxury of *otium* as a primary difference between the life of a full citizen and a "mere" trades person or slave, who must engage in menial labor.

QUESTIONS FOR REFLECTION AND DISCUSSION

1. What are the main differences between Plato's and Aristotle's approaches to philosophy and the conclusions they draw? It has been said that in terms of the broad emphases or tendencies of their thinking, philosophers can be divided into "Platonists" and "Aristotelians." Which do you think you are? Why?

2. What does Aristotle mean by "virtue"? How does he relate it to his analysis of the human self or soul?

3. Explain why Aristotle says that the state is natural to human beings, using his account of how the state comes into existence. How is the teleological explanation essential to his argument? What would be the alternative to saying that the state is natural?

4. Briefly explain what constitutes the differences between the following sets of pairs: (a) the rule of the statesman and other kinds of rule; (b) master and slave; (c) natural and legal slavery; (d) men and women.

5. Aristotle's treatment of women and slaves raises questions because the history of the past century and a half has seen the abolition of slavery and the significant alteration of the situation of women. Since Aristotle clearly accepts slavery and women's unequal status as "natural," does this render invalid his statements about them or even about ethics and politics in general?

6. What are some of the main differences between the ideas about the state in Plato's *Republic* and Aristotle's *Politics?*

7. What constitutes the "best" form of government, according to Aristotle? Do economic conditions in a society have any bearing on this question? Are there any connections between his ideas on this and the modern state?

8. How would you characterize Aristotle's ideas on the best kind of education for a polis? How are they related to his analyses of gender and the role of the family?

SUGGESTIONS FOR FURTHER READING

Original Works

The Complete Works of Aristotle: The Revised Oxford Translation. 2 volumes. Edited by Jonathan Barnes. Princeton: Princeton University Press, 1984.

Aristotle. *Nicomachean Ethics*. Translated by W. D. Ross. London: Oxford, UP, 1972

Secondary Works

Barnes, Jonathan. *Aristotle* (Very Short Introductions series). Oxford: Oxford UP, 2000.

Bostock, David. *Aristotle's Ethics*. Oxford: Oxford UP, 2000.

Irwin, Terence. *A History of Western Philosophy* [volume one]: *The Classical Mind* (2nd, edition). Fort Worth: Harcourt Brace Jovanovich, 1980.

Kraut, Richard. *Aristotle: Political Philosophy* (Founders of Modern Political and Social Thought series). Oxford: Oxford UP, 2002

Mulgan, R.G. *Aristotle's Political Theory: An Introduction for Students of Political Theory*. New York: Oxford UP, 1987.

Zeller, Eduard. *Outlines of the History of Greek Philosophy*. New York: Dover Press, 1980.

Jones, W. T. *The Classical Mind* (2nd ed.). Forth Worth: Harcourt Brace Jovanovich College Publishers, 1980.

SECTION THREE

TIMELINE III
THE ROMAN WORLD

800–400 BCE Early Rome

753 BCE Legendary Founding of Rome

509 BCE Roman Republic is established

300–1 BCE Rise of Empire

270 BCE Rome rules all of Italy

264 BCE Punic Wars waged against Carthage until 146 BCE

202 BCE Scipio defeats Hannibal

70 BCE Birth of poet Virgil

49 BCE Julius Caesar crosses the Rubicon

44 BCE Assassination of Caesar

43 BCE Death of Cicero

27 BCE Augustus Caesar establishes empire

5 BCE Birth of Jesus

4 BCE Seneca is born in Cordoba, Spain

5 BCE–200 CE Birth of Christianity

30 CE Death of Jesus

46 CE Paul's missionary activity through 60 CE

64 CE Rome burns, Christians blamed

70 CE Destruction of Temple in Jerusalem, exile of Jews
Writing of New Testament Gospels begins

125 CE Construction of Roman Pantheon begins

Dates given are approximate

THE ROMAN WORLD

The death of Alexander the Great in 323 BCE left his vast empire disunited. Though his generals fought to keep the empire whole, by 300 BCE Alexander's territory had been partitioned into three separate kingdoms. The kingdom of Macedonia continued to dominate the Greek peninsula. In Egypt, the Ptolemies established themselves as kings in Alexandria and claimed territory that stretched from modern-day Lebanon to Morocco along the North African coast. The former Persian territories, ranging eastward from the Mediterranean to India, fell to the Seleucids. None of the three kingdoms was able to entirely dominate the Mediterranean. The next great imperial force came not from the Eastern Mediterranean but from the West: Rome would emerge as the undisputed power in the entire Mediterranean basin.

Indeed, at its height of power in the fourth century CE, Rome had conquered not just the Mediterranean region but also most of the inhabited world, stretching its Empire from modern-day Britain to Israel including all of what we consider to be modern Europe. Unlike either the Greeks or Macedonians under Alexander, the Romans granted citizenship to those they conquered. As a result, the Roman Empire was a much more integrated and therefore durable political entity, lasting well into the fifth century CE.

Today we admire the Romans not solely for their proficiency at empire building, but also for their administrative practices, legal codes, language, and engineering skills that brought uniformity and stability to the Empire. These quintessentially Roman skills deeply affected the course of Western civilization. London, Paris, Barcelona, and Vienna all began as Roman villages or encampments. When the founders of the United States looked for a political and legal model to emulate and apply to their fledgling nation, they looked not to the Greeks but to the Romans.

Rome also served as an important preserver and conduit of Greek culture, art, and philosophy. Without Rome, it is quite conceivable that Greek culture would have been lost to the West. Rome, however, did not simply broadcast Greek values to the West, but rather offered the Western world a merging of Greco-Roman values, adding distinctly Roman mores such as piety, patriotism, and gravitas to the Greek religious and cultural system. Yet the question remains: how did a small city-state on the south-central Italian peninsula come to dominate the inhabited world and leave an indelible stamp on the civilization of the West? For that we must look back to the city's humble origins in the eighth century BCE.

FOUNDATIONS OF ROME

According to legend, two brothers, Romulus and Remus, founded the city of Rome in the year 753 BCE. Indeed, the Romans traced their ancestry even further back, to Aeneas, a survivor of the Trojan War, who wandered the Mediterranean until he made his way to the Italian peninsula, a journey recounted in Virgil's epic the *Aeneid*. What we know about Roman history of this time comes from the Roman historian Livy (Titus Livius), who lived from 59–17 BCE.

The geography of Rome was very favorable for the city's growth. Rome was located on defensible hills next to the Tiber River, about fifteen miles from the coast. This made the city relatively safe from piratical raids. There was an island in the river close to the hills, which could easily be bridged by wooden bridges (later stone ones), and tolls could be levied on those who wished to cross the Tiber, which is wide and navigable from Tiber Island at Rome to the Mediterranean.

The Italian peninsula in 1000 BCE was inhabited by a number of tribes, including the Etruscans, Sabines, and Latins. There were also many Greek cities in the south. It was the Etruscans and the Greeks who seemed to have the most significant influence. The Romans said they learned the alphabet from the Greeks. The Etruscan influences on Rome, which occurred about the same time as Greek influences, were very important. This is understandable, as people of Etruscan origins made up a considerable portion of the Roman population by 600 BCE, maybe even one-third of the inhabitants. From the Etruscans the Romans seem to have learned the use of arms and armor and their methods of temple construction and decoration.

All of Rome's early traditions tell us that during the early period the city was ruled by a succession of kings. The first four kings of Rome had Latin names and the last three were Etruscan. Archaeologists at Rome have not uncovered any evidence of an Etruscan conquest of the city, so it seems more useful to think of the Etruscan element in the city as having become dominant by 600 BCE. As a consequence, one of the Luceres, from an Etruscan tribe who occupied one of the seven hills of Rome, became king and made favorable alliances with the flourishing Etruscan cities of the north, which were then at the zenith of their power and prosperity. During this period the Temple to Jupiter was built on the Capitoline Hill; the Forum area was drained by the first Roman sewer—the Cloaca Maxima; and the city became wealthier and more powerful than any of its sister Latin towns to the south.

THE ROMAN STATE, FAMILY, AND RELIGION

The Roman family was the basis of Roman society. Indeed, the Roman king was really just a Roman *pater familias* (father of the family) writ large. The Latin word *familia* is a noun that means more than our word *family:* it was multi-generational and in addition to the related members included slaves and other servants and the property and estate of the family. Families, not individuals, were the basic units of the *populus romanus* (Roman people). A clan (*gens*) was made up of a group of *familiae.*

Romans practiced ancestor worship. They believed that the spirits of the dead remained within the family and could give advice and bring prominence to the family if the proper rituals were observed. A perpetual fire was maintained in their honor in the home and small statues of the family members surrounded the fireplace and food was placed before it each day. There was an annual festival when family members would visit the graves of the deceased and make a procession through the streets holding aloft effigies of the prominent ancestors of the family.

The Romans also adopted elements of Greek religion, including the Olympian pantheon of gods which they gave Roman names (e.g., Zeus became Jupiter, Aphrodite became Venus, Athena became Minerva). Jupiter, the powerful and stern father, Juno (Hera to the Greeks), queen of the gods, and Minerva, the goddess of wisdom, were the three most important deities to the Romans. The three shared Rome's most revered temple on the Capitoline hill.

During the republic, the cult of Vesta grew to prominence. Vesta was the goddess of the hearth and the protector of the Roman family. In her shrine was housed an eternal flame symbolizing the power and endurance of the Roman state. The Vestal Virgins, six unmarried women, were sworn to chastity at the age of six and served in the shrine of Vesta for a term of thirty years. The Vestal Virgins were a high status position within Roman religious life. Not only was their role to ensure the continual burning of the flame, but their chastity represented the purity of the Roman family and thus the preservation of the republic itself.

An assembly of elders and leaders of Rome's leading families was responsible for electing the Roman kings. This assembly was called the *comitia curiata.* The assembly also voted on other important matters, such as war or peace. The *comitia curiata* eventually evolved into the Roman Senate, a deliberative body that, by the end of the early period of

Although produced by an Etruscan sculptor, this skillful bronze is more symbolically associated with the history and founding of Rome. According to Roman legend, twin infants named Romulus and Remus were abandoned along the Tiber River, suckled by a she-wolf, and then raised by a shepherd. In adulthood, the twins wished to found a city but could not agree on a location. Romulus killed Remus in the ensuing argument, then established a settlement that would become the city of Rome. The Etruscan sculptor here depicts a she-wolf with heavy teats, indicating that she has recently given birth. Castings of the suckling infants were added to the sculpture during the Renaissance, positioning the work as a symbol of the city's history.

Figure III-1 *She-Wolf.* ca. 500 BCE, twins added by Antonio Pollaiuolo in the fifteenth century. Bronze, height 33½″ (85.1 cm). Museo Capitolino, Rome. Courtesy of Scala/Art Resource, NY.

kingship, had become quite powerful in influencing the actions of the state.

The king, who held the *imperium* (sovereign power), was the general in times of war and also the head of the judicial system, as advised by the Senate; but very seldom was he a lawgiver. The king also presided over official sacrifices—sacrifices that Romans believed would bring favors from the gods.

THE EARLY REPUBLIC AND ROMAN CONQUEST OF THE ITALIAN PENINSULA

The monarchy came to an end in 509 BCE when, according to Livy, the son of the last Etruscan king, Tarquinius, raped the Roman matron Lucretia. She committed suicide, and the Roman Senate and people closed the gates of the city to Tarquinius and his family. Whatever the truth of this picturesque story, in about 500 Rome changed from a monarchy to a republic, and the word *rex* (king) was despised in Rome ever afterward. The *imperium* formerly held by the king was now under the control of two consuls elected annually. Their power was absolutely equal, but one could veto the acts of the other. A new assembly, the *comitia centuriata*, made up of all Roman citizens, elected the consuls each year. The *comitia centuriata* made laws which, to become binding, had to be confirmed by the Senate and the Senate—comprised of the patricians—was now more powerful than ever. The patricians were even more dominant than they had been during the era of the kings. In times of emergency, a consul could appoint a *dictator*. This appointment could not be vetoed by the other consul. A Roman dictator was a military ruler who briefly took over the government. His reign was to last no more than six months and his decisions could not be repealed. For the Romans, the word dictator simply meant "the one who dictates" or "gives orders." It did not have the negative connotation that it does today.

The next two and a half centuries the republic was almost continually at war, but by the end of the period Rome held control of the entire peninsula. First the Etruscans tried to retaliate for the expulsion of the Tarquins but were repulsed. In the ten year struggle that followed a leader arose from the patrician class, Marcus Furius Camillus (ca. 435–365 BCE). Camillus served as dictator several times, was a military tribune and held consular powers. At the conclusion of a war the Etruscan city of Veii was sacked, effectively ending Etruscan resistance (an incident that has sometimes been compared to the destruction of Troy). Shortly after, however, Rome came close to destruction when the Gauls from what is now Lombardy in Italy occupied Rome. They sacked and burned the Capitoline Hill but eventually accepted payment of gold to leave the city.

Camillus emerged as the leading figure in the Roman recovery of the next forty years. He supervised the building of the first stone wall (traditionally called the Servian Wall) around the seven hills of Rome. He also seems to have been responsible for the reform of the Roman army into the familiar Roman legions and maniples (military subdivision of some 60–100 men) that subsequently conquered Italy and Carthage. Camillus was thought of in his time as the "Second Founder of Rome."

In 354 BCE the Romans became interested in the rich lands of Campania, near the ancient Greek town of Naples. But the Samnites from central southern Italy were also interested. Rome allied with the neighboring Latin towns and together they defeated the Samnites in 341. There followed a quarrel with the Latins over the disposition of the conquered territory. A war between the two former allies ensued but was resolved when Rome made separate treaties

Etruscan and Roman Italy. Reprinted from *The Humanities in Western Culture*, Vol. I, Tenth Edition, by Robert C. Lamm, (1996), the McGraw-Hill Companies, Inc.

with each of the Latin cities. By 338 Rome controlled the Italian west coast as far as Naples and ruled a population in excess of one million.

Rome's expansion into Campania brought on a second war with the Samnites, one that lasted for more than thirty years, from 327 to 295 BCE. At first the Romans suffered serious reverses, and the Samnites picked up support from the Umbrians and some of the Etruscan cities in the north. But the anti-Roman allies were decisively defeated at the battle of Sentinum in 295, and almost all of the territory south of the Apennine Mountains passed under Roman control. The Romans separated all the cities under their control, binding them to Rome by a variety of treaties and controlling their foreign affairs. Otherwise the cities maintained their own governments, religions, and ways of life; but they had to supply manpower when Rome was at war.

The Greek city of Tarentum in the south had made a treaty with Rome whereby no Roman warships were to enter the Gulf of Tarentum without that city's permission. So when Rome's fleet came to the aid of Thurii while the Thurians were fighting Italian tribesmen, Tarentum declared war and invited the prince of Epirus, Pyrrhus, to its aid. Pyrrhus came with about twenty-five thousand men and a number of elephants. He won a couple of costly victories over the Romans, from which we get the phrase "a Pyrrhic victory," but he was finally defeated at Beneventum in 275 BCE and driven from Italy. After that, Rome took over the foreign affairs of all the Greek city-states in Italy and bound them to Rome by treaties. Thus by 264 Rome held all of Italy south of the Apennines.

POLITICAL AND SOCIAL UPHEAVAL

Roman society was divided between the *patricians* and the *plebeians*. The patricians were an aristocracy of mostly wealthy landowners from whose ranks were drawn the members of the Senate. Plebeians were the landless poor, who usually worked as clients for their noble patrician patrons. There were many slaves in Rome, as in all other ancient communities, but there was no racial basis for slavery.

During the wars of conquest, the plebeians of Rome had been struggling with their masters, the patricians, for political and economic equality. At the start of the Republic, the plebs got the right to appeal cases at law to the *comitia centuriata*, but this did not include such grievances as the lack of full franchise or enslavement for debt. The rich patricians did not grant the plebs allotments of state lands as these became available by the conquests, so from time to time the plebeians revolted, left the city en masse, and refused to work or serve in the army. They could not hope for fairness through the *comitia centuriata*; therefore they organized and eventually won the right to have their own council, the *comitia tributa*. The tribunes could veto any actions of the magistrates or the *comitia centuriata*. By 450 BCE the plebeians had forced the codification of the laws in the Twelve Tables, and five years later the Canuleian Law legalized intermarriage between plebs and patricians, thus permitting the gradual fusion of the two orders.

As the city of Rome grew larger, the consuls could not handle all the administration, and *quaestors* (treasurers), *aediles* (public-works administrators), and *praetors* (legal magistrates) became necessary—all elected by the *comitia centuriata*. Plebeians were excluded from all of these magistracies until about 400 BCE, but by 300 plebeians could hold all of the magistracies and even the priesthoods. The struggle between the orders really ended in 287 with the Hortensian Law, which provided that laws passed by the *comitia tributa* became binding on all Roman citizens with or without the approval of the Senate.

By 264 BCE, the Romans had completed their conquest of Italy and had integrated their patrician-plebeian society under the leadership—which was almost an oligarchy—of their office-holding families. *Mos* (custom) demanded that officeholders could be warriors, farmers, or politicians, while the equestrian class (a kind of lesser nobility) carried on the business and banking activities, which were still small, and the lower classes and slaves were the artisans and laborers. But the Romans had just begun to mint money, so small was their interest in commerce. Consequently they had no navy. This proved a considerable disadvantage when they were drawn into conflict with Carthage, a city-state on the north coast of Africa that with its powerful naval forces controlled the western Mediterranean.

THE PUNIC AND MACEDONIAN WARS (264–146 BCE)

The historian Polybius (ca. 205–125 BCE) is our main source of information about the conflicts between Carthage and Rome, called the Punic Wars. The city of Carthage, located on the North African coast near present-day Tunis, was founded by the ancient Phoenicians and was one of the greatest commercial powers in the Mediterranean. The island of Sicily was under the control of Carthage when, in 264 BCE, Messina, a city located on the northeastern tip, rebelled and called for help from the Romans. Rome came to their aid and thus began the First Punic War.

Roman forces were at first repelled by the Carthaginians. The Romans responded by building their first navy and defeated the Carthaginians in three major battles off the coast of Sicily between 260 BCE and 256 BCE. The war dragged on for many years, but finally in 241 BCE the Romans won a decisive naval victory off the west coast of Sicily, and Carthage sued for peace. Both sides seemed to have realized that this peace was only a truce, and Rome and Carthage set about improving their own strategic positions in anticipation of another war.

The most successful Carthaginian general in the First Punic War had been Hamilcar Barca. His son Hannibal grew up to be an enemy of Rome and was eager to avenge Carthage's defeat. The Second Punic War (218–202 BCE) began when Hannibal invaded northern Spain, which was considered to be Rome's sphere of influence, and made the difficult crossing of the Rhone and the Alpine passes with his elephants. He then descended into the Po Valley near Turin and proceeded to defeat the Romans in one battle after another. In 216 BCE Hannibal almost destroyed a Roman army of eighty thousand men at the battle of Cannae in southeastern Italy. Hannibal now attempted to persuade Roman allies to desert, but most remained faithful to Rome with the exception of Capua, Tarentum, and Syracuse in Sicily. Philip V, the king of Macedon, now joined Hannibal for what Philip thought would be the kill.

Despite these disasters, the Romans stood firm. They sent armies to follow Hannibal around, but the Roman generals were not to engage in battle. Other Roman armies besieged Capua and Syracuse and sacked both towns. Hannibal had no effective siege machinery, so although he marched to a point within sight of Rome, he never besieged the city. The Romans found a superb general in the person of Publius Cornelius Scipio. Scipio drove Hannibal's brother Hasdrubal out of Spain and conquered the peninsula. Hasdrubal took his army over the Alps in a vain attempt to join his brother. He and his invading army were destroyed on the banks of the Metaurus River in 207 BCE, thus ending Hannibal's last hope of obtaining reinforcements.

The Romans now chose Scipio (later immortalized by Cicero in *Scipio's Dream*) to lead an expeditionary force into North Africa. He landed in 204 BCE, and the Carthaginians sued for peace. An armistice was declared under which Hannibal and his troops were evacuated from Italy. Soon after Hannibal had returned to Carthage, the war was resumed. But Scipio defeated Hannibal and the Carthaginians at the battle of Zama in 202 BCE, and the long Second Punic War was at an end. Carthage was forced to give up Spain and West Africa and all but ten of its ships. It also had to agree that it would not carry on any wars outside of Africa or any in Africa without Rome's consent. Thus Carthage really ceased to be an autonomous state, and Rome by 200 BCE had become master of the western Mediterranean and the most powerful military state of the ancient world.

Almost immediately after the conclusion of the Second Punic War, Rome went to war with Philip V of Macedon. The conflict was not popular with a war-weary public; but the Senate wanted revenge for Philip's collaboration with Carthage in 215 BCE. Rome won the war by 197 BCE and established a kind of protectorate over the Greek city-states and leagues, promising to assist them if they were attacked. When King Antiochus III—the ruler of the sprawling Seleucid Empire, which controlled states all the way from Syria on the Mediterranean to India—invaded Greece in 191 BCE, the Romans swiftly came to the aid of their Greek allies and drove Antiochus's army from Greece and Asia Minor. Thus Rome became embroiled in the affairs of the Hellenistic monarchies of the eastern Mediterranean. They soon ended all resistance: dissolving the kingdom of Perseus of Macedon, and crushing the Greek leagues and city-states which had been under Corinthian leadership.

Fifty years after the end of the Second Punic Wars, Rome once again moved against Carthage. Though Carthage was no longer a military threat, Rome sought revenge against the city for the damage inflicted by Hannibal. In 146 BCE the Third Punic War began. Carthage fell after a six-month siege and every inhabitant of the city was either killed or enslaved. The city was destroyed and the surrounding territory made into a Roman province. Rome had become the master of the Mediterranean world, and not even the Seleucid Empire or the Ptolemaic kingdom of Egypt dared to oppose Rome.

THE COLLAPSE OF THE ROMAN REPUBLIC (146–30 BCE)

While these triumphs were being achieved abroad, back home Rome was experiencing severe growing pains. The central government now had to send governors to rule foreign provinces from Macedonia to Spain. During the Second Punic War, while Hannibal's army had lived off the countryside, the fields had lain fallow, the livestock had been slaughtered, and the farmers had flocked for protection into the walled cities, especially Rome. The Senate had allowed the wealthy to buy up huge tracts of land in excess of what Roman law allowed, while in the city there was a vast number of unemployed poor.

In 133 BCE, Rome was bequeathed Pergamum, a province in Asia Minor, and all its treasures. Tiberius Gracchus, a Roman tribune, decided that the time had come to relieve the suffering of the Roman urban poor. He proposed a bill that would have used the money from Pergamum to resettle the Roman poor on farms throughout Italy, on land now held illegally by wealthy Romans. The bill was passed, but not before Tiberius had used the *comitia tributa* to depose a fellow tribune who had vetoed the actions of the assembly. His action and the actions of the *comitia tributa* were unprecedented, and when Tiberius stood for re-election to the tribunate, gangs of ruffians hired by the wealthy murdered him. Thus began the struggle that we call the Roman Revolution, which was not ended until Octavian conquered the Roman world in 30 BCE. Ten years after Tiberius's death, his brother Gaius renewed attempts to help the urban poor, but in 122 BCE he met a similar fate. Although the Gracchi did not achieve their aims, they left a faction of their followers who made up a group of voters called the *populares*, the popular party, as opposed to the *optimates*, the party of wealth and of the office-holding families.

For some years after Gaius Gracchus's death, the *populares* had no leader, but in 107 BCE, Gaius Marius, a soldier who had conquered Numidia, achieved the consulship. Marius then proceeded to crush a very threatening invasion of the German tribes who had overrun parts of southern Gaul and the Po Valley. To muster enough troops to defeat these fierce northern invaders, who had previously annihilated three Roman armies, Marius obtained permission to enroll Roman citizens without any property qualifications into the legions, thus creating an army that was loyal to its commander but not necessarily to the state.

Marius's victory over the Germans made him a national hero. He served six consulships in a row, a violation of the unwritten Roman constitution, thus setting a dangerous precedent. In Rome, Marius's opponent was one of his former lieutenants, Sulla (138–78 BCE). When Sulla left the city to quell a revolt, Marius was elected to a seventh consulship. In Rome, many members of the *optimates* were killed or exiled by Marius. But Marius died shortly after assuming his seventh consulship in 86 BCE. Sulla returned to Rome in 83 BCE, and a year and a half of bloody civil war ensued between the partisans of Sulla and those of Marius. Many ancient cities were destroyed throughout the Italian peninsula until Sulla's forces emerged victorious. Sulla then proscribed more than four thousand of his enemies at Rome and confiscated their properties. Finally, as dictator, he tried to place the *optimates* firmly in control of Rome, after which he retired to private life, dying in 79 BCE.

Sulla's restoration of the wealthy to power did not long survive his own death, but many ambitious young Romans noted his example as a victorious general with a loyal army behind him. Among these, two rose rapidly to power during the next decade: Pompey (106–48 BCE) by his military victories in the civil wars in Spain, and Crassus (ca. 115–53 BCE) by his wealth. Both also shared the credit for suppressing the slave revolt in 71 BCE. This, the greatest slave revolt in Roman times, broke out in 73 BCE at a training school for gladiators at Capua, near Naples in Italy. Spartacus, a slave from Thrace, an area north of Greece, led the revolt, which attracted some seventy thousand slaves, farmers, and urban poor of the area. Spartacus and his slave army defeated nine Roman armies before they were destroyed by a large Roman army led by Crassus. Pompey, on his way back from victory in Spain with his army, fell upon a group of slaves who had escaped the victory of Crassus and then claimed a share of the victory over the slave revolt, much to Crassus's annoyance. However, because of these victories both Pompey and Crassus were chosen consuls for the year 70 BCE.

During the next decade, Pompey performed great services for the Roman state and was generally recognized as possessing more *auctoritas* (prestige) than any other contemporary Roman. In 67 BCE he received an extraordinary command over vast public wealth, armies, and navies; and in ninety days he cleared the Mediterranean and the Black Sea of piracy. Then he went east where he put an end to the Seleucid Empire, and reorganized the whole Near East into a group of Roman provinces and client states. He claimed to have conquered twelve million people, taken booty valued at 800 million sesterces (approximately 40 million dollars), and to have raised Rome's annual tribute from 200 million sesterces to 340 million sesterces. In 62 Pompey returned to Italy, quietly disbanded his troops, and entered Rome, expecting the Senate to confirm his eastern reorganization and to reward his veterans.

But Pompey's enemies in the Senate stalled action on these matters, and so Pompey, Crassus, and a bright young politician named Julius Caesar (100–44 BCE) formed an unofficial triumvirate to help Pompey and themselves. Caesar was promised the consulship for 59 BCE and, after that, governorship of Gaul, on the pattern of Pompey's recent commissions. Pompey wanted his acts in the east ratified, and he wanted his veterans rewarded; Crassus wanted special privileges for his equestrian bankers and tax collectors.

The First Triumvirate had its way, largely by threat of force, and from 58 to 50 BCE Caesar made his remarkable conquest of Gaul and his raids into Germany and the island of Britain. But while Caesar was away conquering Gaul, his supporters and those of Pompey in Rome began to drive the two leaders apart. When Pompey's wife Julia, Caesar's only daughter, died in 54 BCE, one of the chief links between triumvirs was broken, and in the next year another tie was broken when triumvir Crassus lost his life while fighting against the Parthians.

Pompey and Caesar were, by 50 BCE, the two most powerful leaders in the Roman world—Caesar with his well-trained veterans from the Gallic Wars, and Pompey with the fleet and armed forces of the Roman Senate. Compromises between the leaders and their adherents failed, and in January 49 BCE Caesar crossed the Rubicon into Italy, an illegal act that meant civil war. Pompey did not consider his forces well trained or reliable enough to face Caesar, so Pompey took his army and many of the senators to Greece, where he could train his forces and use the Roman navy. But the navy failed to prevent Caesar and his lieutenant Mark Antony from crossing to Greece, and in 48 BCE Caesar's army defeated Pompey's forces at the battle of Phrasalus. Pompey fled to Alexandria, Egypt, where he was murdered by order of the Egyptian King Ptolemy XIII (64–47 BCE).

Caesar now commenced to mop up what was left of his opponents. First he went to Alexandria,

where he avenged Pompey's murder by killing Ptolemy. After leaving Egypt in the spring of 47 BCE, Caesar put down a rebellion in northeast Asia Minor on the southern coast of the Black Sea. After the victory, Caesar wrote to a friend in Rome the famous laconic letter *"Veni, vidi, vici"*—"I came, I saw, I conquered."

The conqueror had now only one year of life left to organize the Roman government. From the time that he had crossed the Rubicon, Caesar had indicated that he did not intend to return to the old republican form of government. He believed that a new solution had to be found, but he did not survive his conquests long enough for us to know exactly what he planned. Caesar's power had rested in the dictatorship, which he held from 49 BCE until his death. After he defeated Pompey in 48 BCE he was given the dictatorship for one year; in 46 BCE he was made dictator for ten years; and after his victory in Spain in 45 BCE he was proclaimed dictator for life. In 48 BCE he had already been given the power of tribune in order to have veto power and had been awarded the proconsular power for life, so that he could legally command the Roman armies and navies by means of his legates.

Although Caesar was in Rome for only fifteen months after 49 BCE, he accomplished a number of important and lasting reforms: 1) He established the Julian calendar. 2) He ended imprisonment or outlawry for debt. 3) He suppressed all unlicensed organizations. 4) He sent colonists to rebuild Corinth and Carthage. 5) He began to extend full Roman citizenship to provincials outside of Italy. But his work of reorganization was cut short when he was assassinated in March of 44 by a group of conspirators, led by Marcus Brutus (ca. 85–42 BCE) and Caius Cassius (d. 42 BCE), who claimed that Caesar was about to make himself *rex* (king) and who proclaimed liberty and a return to the old Republic.

Contrary to the expectations of the conspirators, there was little enthusiasm for their deed or for a return to the old days. When Mark Antony made an impassioned speech over Caesar's body in the Roman forum, the populace burned down the Senate chamber, and the conspirators fled from Rome. Meanwhile, Caesar's will was made known. He left money and parks to all citizens, and the rest of his vast wealth he left to his grandnephew and adopted son, Caius Julius Caesar Octavianus (63 BCE–14 CE), who was nineteen years of age.

Octavian hastened back to Rome from Apollonia in Greece, where he had been studying oratory and military science, to claim his inheritance. But he found that Antony had already appropriated most of his legacy and ignored the claims of the rightful heirs. Octavian, who was a very able and bright young man, gathered support from the famous orator Cicero and the senatorial party and used the name of Caesar to raise an army of Caesar's veterans.

Octavian marched on Rome with his army and forced the Roman Senate and assembly to make him consul, despite the fact that he was below the legal age for such an office. The frightened Senate proclaimed Octavian, as well as Antony and a man named Lepidus, the triumvirs for the reestablishment of the Republic, the last thing in the world they intended to do. The triumvirs' first act was to proscribe many of their enemies, killing some, such as Cicero, and exiling others.

During the next few years Octavian assumed command of the western empire and Antony of the east. Lepidus was made pontifex maximus (a term which means something like "high priest"), but he was essentially powerless. Octavian and his generals quickly subdued all opposition in the west. However, Octavian was conciliatory in his attitude toward the conquered and initiated an age of peace and prosperity heretofore unknown. He became almost universally popular in his territories.

Antony's course in the east was far different. He became infatuated with Cleopatra, Queen of Egypt. He traveled with her to Alexandria, where they planned to establish a base for the conquest of the entire empire. Octavian, who had already decided that war between his forces and those of Antony was inevitable, declared that Antony was guilty of treason. Octavian persuaded the Senate to strip Antony of his triumviral powers and to declare war on Cleopatra. In the naval battle of Actium in Greece (31 BCE), Antony's and Cleopatra's navy was defeated and their land forces joined with Octavian against them. Both Antony and Cleopatra committed suicide in Alexandria in 30 BCE, and the whole Roman world, now including Egypt, lay at Octavian's feet.

AUGUSTUS (RULED 27 BCE–14 CE)

Having conquered the Roman Empire militarily, Octavian set about preserving it. He did this brilliantly by reestablishing the façade of the old Republic but actually making the government into a disguised autocracy. Avoiding the title "king" and using the precedents from Pompey's reign, Octavian was given both the tribunician and the proconsular powers, so he could rule both in Rome and, by legates, in the provinces. The consuls no longer commanded the armies and the navies, though these officials were still elected annually, but by the legates of Octavian. Octavian also was given the power of declaring peace or war and of recommending magistrates for the elective offices. In 27 BCE he took the name Augustus, which he would carry to his grave. Despite his vast power, Augustus continued the practice of prudent leadership, which he had begun in his conquest of the western territories, and when he died in 14 CE he was almost universally admired for having brought to the Roman world peace, order, and prosperity following several generations of civil war and disaster.

The reforms of Augustus touched almost every area of the state. The army was now a standing force with some twenty-five legions (125,000 to 150,000 men) stationed on the frontiers of the empire, especially on the Rhine and the Danube against the Germans, and on the Euphrates in Mesopotamia against the Parthians. The legates of Augustus, especially his stepson Tiberius, added many new provinces along the Rhine and the Danube frontiers. However, when the Romans suffered a severe defeat in the Teutoburg Forest in 9 CE, between the Rhine and the Elbe, Augustus advised the Romans to make the Rhine and the Danube their northern frontiers.

Augustus successfully revised the Roman coinage system, and he rebuilt much of Rome, claiming that he had found the city made of brick and had left it made of marble. When it came to changing the luxurious and often dissolute habits of many of the nobles—including members of the royal family—his laws were much less successful. He was forced to exile his own daughter Julia for adultery. Augustus had no sons. In order to secure the dynasty, he successively designated members of his family as his heir but each died—generally under suspicious circumstances—before he did. Finally, shortly before he died, Augustus settled the succession on his stepson Tiberius, the son of his second wife Livia (58 BCE–29 CE).

THE JEWS AND THE RISE OF CHRISTIANITY

In sixth century CE, during the reign of Augustus, Judea was made a Roman province. Two decades later, in about 29 CE, procurator Pontius Pilate ordered the execution of Jesus of Nazareth. Though a minor event at the time, the death of Jesus, and the reactions it provoked, would profoundly alter the course of Western history.

To understand the events that led up to Jesus' death we must first return to the previous century and review some of the events that took place then. In 67 BCE, Rome under the leadership of Pompey wrested control of Palestine from the Seleucids who controlled the area. Judea's short-lived period of independence under the Maccabees was at an end. The entire area of Palestine was now under Roman control. (The borders of Palestine at this time included Idumea in the south, Judea, Samaria, and Galilee. These boundaries fluctuated with each power struggle.) It was Rome's practice to appoint local rulers to administer their territories as long as these leaders could be trusted to remain loyal to Rome. In this instance they turned to the Herodians, Hellenized Jews who had curried the favor of each of the Roman generals in turn. This choice outraged the Jews. As Idumeans and converts the Herodians were not considered legitimate Jews. Following the death of the first Herodian leader Antipater, Augustus chose his son, Herod the Great, in 37 BCE and designated him "King of the Jews." Herod made a great pretense of being Jewish but the people were not fooled. His court was thoroughly Hellenized and full of plots and conspiracies. Herod levied heavy taxes on the people that were spent on many building projects including a magnificent palace and a new temple in Jerusalem, known as Herod's Temple. In the meantime the condition of the populace was one of misery. There had been a long period of crop failure and drought that further increased the suffering of the people. Unrest was rife, and following Herod's death in 4 BCE there were a series of revolts throughout the territory that lasted nearly ten years. This prompted the Romans to appoint procurators to administer the area.

The Jewish population at this time was divided about many key tenets of Jewish law as well as the proper response to Roman occupation. The Sadducees, composed of prominent families, were in charge of the Temple. They were religiously conservative, advocating a rigid adherence to Torah, but culturally they embraced Hellenism. This group favored cooperation and compromise with the Romans. The Pharisees took a more liberal view of Judaism, allowing for interpretation of Torah to accommodate to current times. They opposed intermingling with Rome and carried on their religious activities in synagogues. Despite their theological differences these two groups worked together in an administrative body, the Sanhedrin, that oversaw the Judean Jewish community. The Essenes were a group that withdrew from society and lived an ascetic lifestyle in the Dead Sea area of Judea where they awaited the coming of the Messiah. We know of them from the Dead Sea Scrolls that were only discovered in the mid-twentieth century. Finally, the Zealots were militant extremists who favored the violent overthrow of the Romans.

Many Jews held to the concept of the Messiah, which means, "anointed one" As far as scholarship can ascertain, this concept first arose in the eleventh century BCE with the establishment of the monarchy. It was a model of the warrior king who would come to restore the independence of the Jewish nation. The figures of Saul and David in the Hebrew Scriptures are models for the warrior king. Some considered the Maccabees messianic figures. According to the writings of the first-century Jewish historian Josephus, some of the bandit chiefs who led rebellions in the first century CE claimed the title of Messiah.

Of more recent origins was a messianic image that was apocalyptic in nature. It stems from the Book of Daniel that purports to tell the story of the figure of Daniel who served in the Babylonian court during the Exile, but in fact was probably written in the time of the Maccabees. It speaks of the "Son of Man" who would liberate the Jews in a final battle between good and evil. The early Christians appropriated both of these images, the messianic warrior-king and an apocalyptic savior,

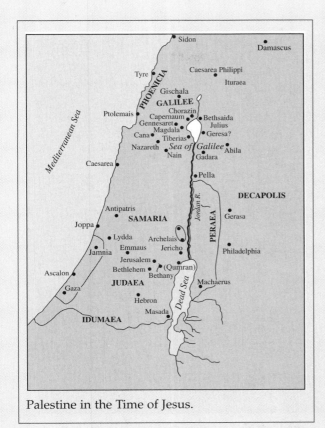

Palestine in the Time of Jesus.

labeled him the "anointed one" and spread the message that he had been resurrected by God. As interpreted influentially by the Apostle Paul the resurrected Jesus became the central hope for personal salvation and eternal life rather than his specific teachings. (The Book of Daniel envisions a general resurrection and judgment with the righteous eternally enjoying God's kingdom and the wicked eternally excluded. However, Jews have never held ideas of resurrection in the Christian understanding of the term.)

For the Romans, as for many Jews, Christianity simply represented a variation of Judaism. As the teachings of Jesus spread throughout the Mediterranean world, and as Christianity spread, thanks in large part to the work of Paul of Tarsus, Roman authorities came to see Christianity as a threat to the security of the Empire. As a result, beginning in about 64 CE Christians would increasingly become the victims of Roman persecution and violence. See Chapter Seven for more information on the life of Jesus, the spread of Christianity and the Christian Scriptures.

In 66 CE, led by the Zealots, Palestinian Jews erupted into open rebellion against their occupiers. Relations with the Romans during the period of the procurators, 6–66 CE, had always been turbulent. One reason was that the quality of men chosen by Rome to govern Palestine had been woefully inadequate. Some of them had been openly antagonistic toward the Jews. The incident that began the war was the refusal of the Jerusalem high priests to offer sacrifices to Rome and Caesar. Not all Jews were in favor of open rebellion, and over the course of the war that lasted four years there was considerable infighting that hindered the Jewish cause, although the idea that anyone could withstand a full onslaught by the Roman army was foolish. However, some compromise might have been reached had the differing parties been able to find common ground. In the end Titus, son of the newly elected emperor Vespasian, led his Roman legions into Jerusalem in 70 CE. The slaughter was horrific and the Jews who survived were sold into slavery. The final battle is memorialized on the Arch of Titus in Rome, on which the soldiers are depicted as returning with the spoils of Jerusalem including the seven-branched candlestick from the Temple. The Temple mount was totally destroyed and Jewish

combined them and applied them to Jesus, even though he did not fit either one.

It is within this context that Joshua ben Joseph (Jesus son of Joseph) lived and preached. Jesus grew up and began his teachings in Galilee, an important center of the militant Zealots. Some Jews saw Jesus as a political leader who would unite the disparate factions and rid Judea of the Romans. According to his followers, however, Jesus never embraced politics. His message was one of calling people to repentance and radical moral obedience to God in advance of the approaching Kingdom of God. In spite of that, Roman authorities clearly saw Jesus as a potential political troublemaker and a danger to Roman rule. Fearing unrest, procurator Pontius Pilate (ruled 26–36 CE) ordered Jesus arrested and crucified—the standard mode of execution within the Empire.

The death of Jesus did not put an end to matters, however. His followers claimed to have seen him in person after his crucifixion. Jesus' disciples

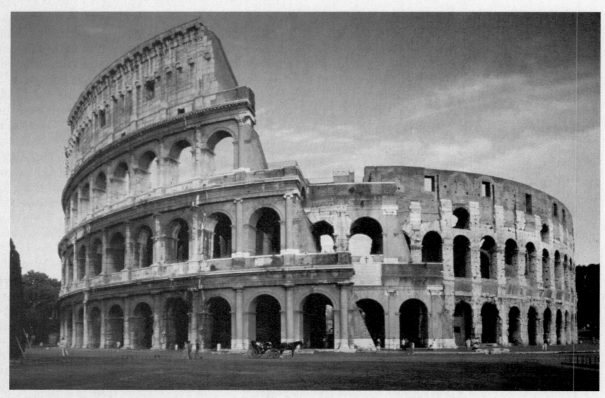

The construction of the Colosseum, known at the time as the Flavian Amphitheatre, was a literal and symbolic gift to the people of Rome from their new ruler, Vespasian. Departing from the tyrannical rule of Nero, Vespasian cultivated an image as one of the people and, in a wise political decision, built a grand public amphitheatre in the former private gardens of Nero's Golden House. The monumental structure showcased a variety of entertainment, from gladiatorial games to mock sea battles, and displayed an architecturally impressive design. The Colosseum featured a complex series of corridors for its 50,000 spectators as well as an elaborate system of passages below arena level for animals and their handlers. An awning system of ropes, pulleys, and canvas shaded the seating areas. Though now in disrepair, the amphitheater once displayed an ornate and decorative façade.

Figure III-2 Colosseum, Rome. 72–80 CE. Courtesy of John Heseltine/Corbis.

religious practice forbidden. Titus and his legions spent the next three years eliminating Jewish resistance in the region. The most famous holdout was in Herod's fort of Masada where the occupants committed suicide rather than be Roman captives (73 CE). Of the various divisions among the Jews, the Pharisees were the only group to survive. They became the foundation of Rabbinic Judaism.

The messianic hope did not die, however, with the destruction of Jerusalem. During the latter part of the reign of Hadrian (117–138 CE) a Jewish army under the leadership of a peasant warrior named Simon Bar Kochba came out of the Judean desert to assert its authority (132 CE). That such an event occurred is attested to by the Roman historian, Dio Cassius, and the Christian historian, Eusebius, but little was known prior to archaeological discoveries in the mid-twentieth century. The title "Bar Kochba" means "son of the star," and it seems clear that Jews viewed him as a messianic figure. The rebels withstood the Romans for three years before being defeated in a final siege southwest of Jerusalem. From this time forward until the founding of Israel in 1948, Jews lived in Diaspora, scattered in many nations throughout the world.

THE ROMAN EMPIRE FROM TIBERIUS TO DOMITIAN

When Tiberius came to power in 14 CE he did away with the assemblies *(comitias)* and controlled the selection of the magistrates elected to the Senate. He centralized power in the hands of the emperor. Tiberius was an experienced general and administrator, and the empire prospered under his rule. The decision to hold at the Rhine frontier was made by Tiberius. It was during the reign of Tiberius that Jesus of Nazareth was executed in Jerusalem. The family life of the emperor was marred by considerable tragedy and bitterness and in the middle of his reign, in 26 CE, he retired to the Isle of Capri, carrying on the business of the empire from his island retreat. He died at Misenum in 37 CE, having named Gaius Caligula (12–41 CE), the grandson of his step-sister, as his successor.

At first the new emperor was popular and showed promise of becoming an effective ruler. But following a serious illness his personality and behavior changed dramatically. He often acted erratically and perpetrated cruel, vicious, and outrageous acts, such as requesting the Senate to make his favorite horse a senator. After four years of misrule, Caligula was murdered by a conspiracy of the praetorian palace guard in 41 CE.

Caligula had been so hated that the praetorians murdered every member of his family residing in the palace on the Palatine except for his crippled uncle Claudius, whom they found hiding behind a curtain. The praetorians decided to proclaim Claudius emperor—for a price. Despite his limp and stutter Claudius (10 BCE–54 CE) proved that his disabilities by no means made him feebleminded. Following the example of the first Augustus, he made excellent appointments, personally took part in the successful invasion of Britain in 43 CE, and continued Augustus's policy of extending the Roman franchise to colonials. The empire grew in strength—especially Gaul; but Claudius left too much of the work of government to trusted freedmen and to a succession of dissolute wives.

Claudius's fourth wife, Agrippina, the mother of Nero, finally poisoned Claudius in 54 CE so that her son Nero could be proclaimed emperor. Shortly after his confirmation as emperor, Nero had his half-brother Britannicus poisoned.

Nero is famously known as the emperor "who fiddled while Rome burned"—an apocryphal story. During the fourteen years of Nero's reign (54–68 CE) the empire as a whole continued to prosper, but the emperor was mostly interested in his own pleasure and the arts, not in carefully ruling his empire. At first he was under the tutelage of Burrus, the praetorian praefect, and Stoic philosopher Seneca (4 BCE–65 CE) (see Chapter Six). Nero ruled the empire quite well while under the guidance of his two tutors, but when Burrus died in 62 CE and Seneca went into retirement, Nero decided to eliminate all restraints upon his activities. He killed his wife and his mother and he forced Seneca to commit suicide and to will Nero his vast fortune. Nero then spent most of his time traveling about the empire, competing in singing contests. Furthermore, he appointed his incompetent friends to important posts in the government. His extravagance and vanity made him so unpopular that he was accused of starting the great fire in Rome of 64 CE, which destroyed almost one-half of the city. To deflect suspicion from himself, Nero accused the Christians of Rome of setting the fire. He then tortured and killed many members of the new religion, thus initiating Rome's first persecution of the Christians. At last Rome's leading military men tired of Nero's follies, and insurrections broke out in Gaul, Spain, and Africa. The emperor took no effective measures against these revolts, and when the governor of Spain, Galba, and his troops approached Rome in 68 the praetorian guards deserted Nero, and the emperor fled from Rome and committed suicide, thus ending the Julio-Claudian dynasty.

There followed in quick succession three emperors, Galba, Otho, and Vitellius. Their successor was Vespasian, who despite humble origins had had a distinguished career. He had been one of the commanders during Claudius's invasion of Britain, and in 67 CE Nero had sent Vespasian to Judea to crush the rebellion of the Jews. Vespasian restored order following the chaos of Nero's reign and a year of civil war. He was a very diligent and just ruler who built a temple to peace

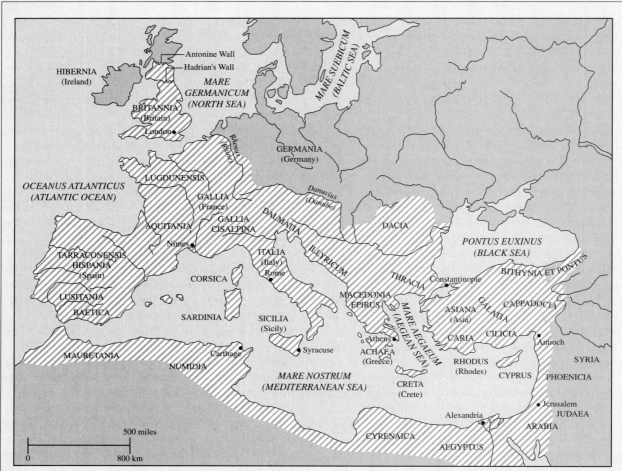

Roman Empire. Reprinted from *The Humanities in Western Culture*, Vol. I, Tenth Edition, by Robert C. Lamm, (1996), the McGraw-Hill Companies, Inc.

and the vast Colosseum in the heart of Rome. When Vespasian died in 79 CE, he left the city and the empire once again strong and prosperous.

Titus continued his father's policies during his brief two-year reign (79–81 CE). He inaugurated the Colosseum in a great ceremony. He proved himself such a just and benevolent emperor that his early death at the age of forty-one was almost universally mourned, except among the Jewish population of the empire. The great eruption of Vesuvius, which destroyed Pompeii and other towns in Campania, occurred in 79 CE during Titus's reign.

Titus's younger brother, Domitian (51–96 CE), became the next emperor, ruling from 81 to 96 CE.

At first he was well liked, but soon he began openly to show despotic tendencies. He took the title of censor for life because this enabled him to move citizens up and down the social class and thus control the senate. However, he added many buildings in Rome, including much of the vast palace complex on the Palatine Hill, called the Domus Augustana, and the race course in Rome, now known as the Piazza Navona. His legate Agricola also completed the conquest of Britain during Domitian's reign. His tyrannical acts garnered him many enemies and there were many plots against his life. Eventually one of the conspiracies was successful, and Domitian was murdered late in 96 CE.

THE ERA OF THE FIVE GOOD EMPERORS

The death of Domitian ushered in the period that Roman historians call the Era of the Five Good Emperors: Nerva (ruled 96–98 CE), Trajan (ruled 97–117 CE), Hadrian (ruled 117–138 CE), Antoninus Pius (ruled 138–161 CE), and Marcus Aurelius (ruled 161–180 CE). This was the period that the eighteenth-century historian Edward Gibbon called the happiest and most prosperous period the world had ever known. Certainly the Roman Empire enjoyed great security and prosperity during those years.

At the time of Domitian's murder, no provisions had been made for a successor. The Senate debated returning to the old republican form of government, but it finally decided to elect one of its members, the elderly and infirm Nerva. Nerva was a lawyer who twice had been consul, but he had no military experience and was suspect by the army. To improve his rapport with the legions he adopted Trajan, a general who was very popular with the armed forces and an excellent administrator. Nerva died after only a year and five months as emperor, during which time he tried to improve the condition of Roman society.

Trajan was a Roman citizen who had been born in Spain. He was serving as Nerva's legate in Upper Germany when he was named emperor. He decided that the time had come to expand Rome's frontiers, so he conquered Dacia (modern Romania), Arabia Petraea (in the general area of the Sinai peninsula), and much of Mesopotamia, thus expanding the Roman Empire to its greatest extent. He also built extensively in Rome and elsewhere. He treated the Senate almost as his partner in power, and he was a very careful administrator.

Before his death in 117 CE Trajan formally adopted Hadrian, another Roman from Spain. Except for the violent second Jewish Revolt of Bar Kochba, 132–135 CE, Hadrian's reign, which lasted twenty-one years, was free from foreign wars. Hadrian was one of the most literate and artistic of all the Roman emperors. He was the architect of the huge Temple of Venus and of the Pantheon in Rome; he also experimented with architectural forms at his extensive villa near Tivoli. A very conscientious administrator, Hadrian visited all of the Roman provinces at least once and Greece many times. He built frontier defenses along the Rhine and the Danube, and he protected the Britons from the Picts and the Scots by constructing Hadrian's Wall across Britain. Hadrian also began the codification of Roman law, perhaps Rome's greatest legacy. This would culminated in the *Codex Theodosianus* of the fifth century and Justinian's *Corpus Juris Civilis* of the sixth century

Hadrian chose as his successor a kindly middle-aged senator of wide experience, Antoninus Pius, who ruled from 138 to 161 CE. The imperial system of Hadrian, which Antoninus Pius continued, carried through Hadrian's imperial system and his was a peaceful reign. The emperor devoted himself to a revival of the Roman religion, but he was not a persecutor of other religions. The Stoic philosophy flourished during his reign, as did a number of Eastern mystery religions, such as the Magna Mater (Great Mother) of Asia Minor, the Isis cult of Egypt, and the Persian cult of Mithras, which became very popular with the Roman legions. The empire remained in a very stable and prosperous condition until the end of Antoninus Pius's reign.

Antoninus Pius adopted his son-in-law, Marcus Aurelius, as his heir. Unfortunately his reign (161–180 CE) was marked by war and calamity. A revolt of the governor of Syria had to be suppressed; then the Parthians had to be expelled from a raid on Rome's eastern provinces. Unfortunately, the Roman troops contracted some kind of plague from the Parthians, which they brought back with them to the West, where it caused great loss of life along the Rhine and Danube frontiers, in Gaul, in Rome, and throughout the rest of Italy. The weakening of the frontier from deaths because of the plague led to a series of invasions of the northern frontier by various Germanic tribes. Marcus Aurelius had to spend most of his later years, from 170 to 180 CE, in attempts, finally successful, to expel the invaders.

In his youth the best grammarians, rhetoricians, and philosophers had tutored Marcus Auerlius. He adopted the philosophy of Stoicism that he learned primarily through the writings of Epictetus. It was on the battlefield during a war against the German Marcomanni (or tribes) that he wrote down his thoughts about the meaning of life. In his book, *Meditations,* are found some of the most sublime expressions of Stoic philosophy. Marcus Auerlius affirms the idea of a divine reason that pervades all things. Whether the divine reason has planned for us a life as a slave or an emperor, we must play our role to the best of our ability, as in a cosmic play. If we do this, our soul will be at peace no matter what may happen to our bodies. Furthermore, we must be spiritually ready at any moment for whatever death the cosmic plan has in store for us.

One of Marcus Aurelius's policies in dealing with the barbarians, however, was full of dire consequences for the future. He allowed many Germans to take up permanent residence inside the Roman frontiers, on land that had virtually been denuded of population because of the plague and warfare. The Germans were considered to be military colonists, bound to the soil, but they were required to perform military service. Thus they learned Roman military techniques and tactics, and a considerable armed barbarian element was introduced into the Roman military establishment and inside the empire. This experiment seemed to work rather well during Marcus Aurelius's time, but during the third century the German and non-Roman citizen element in the army came to be a serious problem.

ART OF ANCIENT ROME

Innovation and assimilation may best describe Roman art and architecture. The Romans routinely employed artists and architects from lands thy occupied, so that "Roman" art incorporated designs and styles from other cultures and is therefore more broadly defined than that found around Rome itself. At its height, their empire stretched from Britain to Palestine and provided numerous traditions from which to draw. Most notably, Greek and Hellenistic sculpture was held in the highest esteem. Many Greek originals, now lost, are known only through their Roman copies. The majority of the copies, however, betray a blending of cultures, with newer elements and aesthetics added to the original form. Portraiture exhibited the likenesses of their sitters rather than the previously generic, more stylized renderings of earlier times. And Roman architects and engineers borrowed Greek style but developed new materials and discovered new structural principles that resulted in building feats previously unthinkable. Given the vastness of the empire and the length of its duration, no single Roman art could prevail, for the styles and functions often changed from ruler to ruler.

ARCHITECTURAL ACHIEVEMENTS

The earlier traditions blended with Roman innovation are seen in the empire's monuments, of which the Colosseum in Rome is an example. While featuring the Greek orders of columns, it incorporates distinctly Roman elements such as the classical arcade, or repetition of arches. Roman architects relied heavily on the arch and the vault as architectural elements, both of which allowed for larger and lighter structures and the spanning of greater spaces. Most significant, perhaps, is their use of new building materials. Romans developed a new form of cast concrete, which in contrast to quarried stone was less expensive and easier to transport. Nor did concrete require the same level of skilled workers as did stone structures. In addition, concrete was significantly lighter than stone, which facilitated building more massive structures.

One of the most impressive Roman architectural achievements is the *Pantheon* (exterior view, Plate 8), built 125–128 CE. It is constructed as a temple to the Olympian gods (its name means "all the gods"). The Pantheon's simple shape of a front porch connected to a domed rotunda, or circular building, conceals its many sophisticated elements. At first glance, the columned façade of the Pantheon, supporting a triangular pediment once decorated with sculpture, does not seem dissimilar from many Greek temples that preceded it. Once inside the enormous interior, however, Roman architectural innovations dominate.

The sheer size of the rotunda, measuring 143 feet in diameter and 143 feet in height, required feats of engineering previously unseen (interior view, Plate 9). In order to support the huge dome, the drum, or cylindrical wall, was built twenty feet thick. Not visible are the massive arches built within the drum, both lightening the walls and providing support for the dome. In addition, builders gradually altered the makeup of the concrete in the rotunda walls, so that the lower parts are made of heavier materials but, moving upwards, the concrete used is composed of progressively lighter materials. Engineers lightened the weight of the dome itself through the use of coffers, or square indentations, that decorate the interior while carving out unnecessary material. At the very top of the dome is a huge circular opening, or oculus, another daring engineering accomplishment. Measuring twenty-seven feet across, the oculus functions in practical as well as symbolic terms, letting in natural light while also showcasing the heavenly sphere inhabited by the gods that the temple honors.

Built during the reign of Hadrian (despite the exterior inscription, which honorifically attributes the building to Marcus Agrippa), the Pantheon has proven the most influential of Roman architectural achievements. Buildings throughout Europe and America pay tribute to the design, as seen for example in *Le Panthéon* in Paris and Thomas Jefferson's home of Monticello. None, though, replicates the spectacular scale and bold innovations of the original.

IMPERIAL SCULPTURE

Roman rulers unabashedly employed sculpture and architecture to promote imperial programs and draw attention to their own achievements. The handsome full-length imperial portrait, *Augustus of Primaporta* (Plate 10), early first century CE, is an example of full-on political propaganda, a Roman convention that began with Augustus. The sculpture not only advertises Augustus's military achievements, implicitly fostering his image as protector of the peace, but also celebrates his personage by situating him as a near-deity.

Octavian, grandnephew and heir of Julius Caesar, was granted the title *Augustus*, or "supreme ruler," in twenty-seven BCE. Augustus later earned the title *Pontifex Maximus*, or High Priest, which made him the empire's highest religious official and aided him in fulfilling his commission as supreme ruler. Elements of the *Primaporta* portrait suggest the adulation that surrounded, and was encouraged by, Augustus. Although Augustus is pictured in military attire, his feet are bare, representing him as a hero, or even a god. This suggestion of divinity is furthered by the presence of Cupid near his right leg. By including Cupid, the son of Venus, the sculptor made reference to the claim of Augustus's family to have descended from the goddess through her human son, Aeneas. While Augustus did not allow himself to be represented in public as a god, the iconography of the *Primaporta* seems a thinly veiled reference to divinity.

The decorations on Augustus's cuirass, or breastplate, celebrate his victory in 20 BCE over the Parthians as well as the peace that followed. A Parthian at the center refers to the specific battle, while Mother Earth below, holding a cornucopia of fruit, signifies the land of plenty and the peace now spread throughout the empire. The presence of Apollo and Diana, as well as the sun god Sol and moon goddess Luna, posit a heavenly endorsement of the Augustan peace while again implying the emperor's divine status.

The image of Augustus as a young, handsome, and perfectly athletic specimen not only propagated an image of a confident and powerful ruler but also reflected the incorporation of classical Greek sculptural elements. The *Augustus of Primaporta* departed from the *verism*, or candid realism, of Roman Republican portraiture. In a style that came to be known as Augustan classicism, Augustus's facial details are simplified and any sharp lines made smooth, much in the manner of Greek classicism. As in Greek art, here the perfect body of Augustus is intended to convey his heroism and magnificence as a benevolent ruler. The *Primaporta* is closely reminiscent of a Greek statue made by Polykleitos in the fifth century BCE, known as the *Doryphorous*, or Spearbearer. The figure of Augustus repeats the pose of the Spearbearer, weight resting on his right leg with his left drawn back, and head turned to the side. Despite the apparent influence, however, the Roman artist did make some subtle changes, as in the way that the Spearbearer seems to move through space while the Augustan statue is meant for a more static, head-on approach. As such, the *Primaporta* sculptor both drew on earlier aesthetics and modified certain elements to suit the emperor's needs.

The *Column of Trajan* (Plate 11) provides another excellent example of imperial propaganda. Dedicated in 113 CE, the column commemorates Trajan's military victory over the Dacians. In a continuous pictorial narrative of the Dacian campaign, carved reliefs spiral around the column from bottom to top. The innovative spiral form departs from the horizontal and vertical reliefs that decorated earlier historical monuments. The height of the frieze is three feet at the bottom of the column but nearly four feet at the top, so that the figures might be better seen from the ground. While the column is an impressive sculptural feat of 2500 individually carved figures, the artists clearly prioritized the propagandistic message over accurate details. The Roman legions are depicted as well organized, never losing a battle, while their barbarian enemies are pathetically haphazard and unsuccessful. Details of daily life abound, but never a reference to the death and destruction of war.

Simultaneously, the column extols the virtues of the emperor himself. Trajan's victories signify not only the success of the state but also the success of the individual emperor. Trajan's figure is the only one to incorporate classicizing elements. As in the *Augustus of Primaporta,* the sculptors may have intended the Greek-inspired body to convey the ruler's confidence and triumph as well as to imply his semi-divinity. The figure of Trajan dominates the narrative, physically outsizing all around him in the *hieratic,* or hierarchical, compositions. The column eventually came to serve as the tomb for the emperor's ashes, reinforcing the monument's role as a glorification of Trajan himself.

An equestrian statue of *Marcus Aurelius* (Plate 12), 161–80 CE, continues the propagandistic tradition of Roman imperial sculpture. Depicted as larger than life-size, the emperor's commanding presence conveys his military prowess and imperial beneficence. Although he wears the tunic and cloak of a military commander, he carries no armor or weaponry. Like earlier Roman emperors and Egyptian kings, Marcus Aurelius appears to conquer his foes without effort, simply by the will of the gods.

The sculptors of the equestrian statue incorporated a variety of elements from earlier Roman sculpture. The full beard and head of curly hair make reference to portraits of Hadrian, who popularized the look among Roman men. The emperor's body language also recalls earlier works. As in the *Augustus of Primaporta,* Marcus Aurelius raises his hand to the people in a gesture of benevolence. Even the convention of the equestrian portrait, where the emperor rides atop an enormous steed, seems to follow a lengthy tradition. Interestingly, however, the Marcus Aurelius portrait is the only bronze equestrian statue to have survived from antiquity. While all others were melted down for the re-use of their metal, this statue was saved because throughout the Middle Ages it was mistakenly believed to be a portrait of the first Christian emperor, Constantine.

MUSIC OF ANCIENT ROME

Just as the Romans borrowed heavily from Greek religion, philosophy, and art, to a large degree they simply took over Greek music "lock, stock, and barrel." Unlike the Greeks, however, the Romans enjoyed music entirely for its practical and entertainment value and not for its ability to educate and build character. Music did not play a significant role in Roman life until the period of the empire, beginning with the accession to power of Augustus in 31 BCE. For the next five hundred years music was very popular among all classes, especially the elaborate *pantomimes*, spectacles that combined drama, instrumental music, and dance and could involve anywhere from three hundred to three thousand performers in each category. In Rome there were almost daily religious processions to the accompaniment of music. Music was prominent in triumphal military parades. Sentimental and bawdy songs were sung in bars and brothels. Other sorts of music were cultivated by the wealthy patrician class, who would have music played with their meals and sometimes had their own household chorus and orchestra for their and their guests' entertainment. In intellectual and artistic circles poets like Horace, here following the Greek tradition, sometimes set their poetry to music.

The Romans took over Greek musical instruments—stringed instruments such as the lyre and the kithara, and wind instruments such as the aulos or flute, which Romans called the *tibia*. Flutes could have one, two, or three pipes, and the Romans also had multi-pipe syrinxes, often appearing in depictions of the god Pan. The Romans borrowed brass horns from the Etruscans, enjoying their loud and penetrating sounds, and developed a wide variety of horns of different shapes and sizes. As with the Etruscans, horns figured prominently in military music, as in triumphal marches for victorious generals. Percussion instruments, including drums and cymbals, were widely used. A favorite instrument, which the Romans inherited from the Hellenistic world, was the hydraulic or water organ. This big instrument produced big, deep sounds, and was popularly used in the pantomimes. The popularity of the water organ tells us something about Roman musical tastes, since it was admired at least as much as an impressive feat of engineering as for its musical qualities.

Unfortunately, as with the Greeks, we can only guess at and try to reconstruct what Roman music sounded like. There are extant examples of Roman "sheet music," but the meaning of the notations and how they represented the music performed is a matter of educated guesswork. Scholars have much information on the instruments, including artistic as well as verbal depictions and in a few cases an actual surviving instrument. But again, although music craftspeople and musicians have been able to recreate and perform with them, we have no idea exactly what sounds the Romans made with them.

CD SELECTIONS

The pieces recorded in the album *Somni Imperii: Roman Music*, were composed by David Marshall and are played on reconstructed instruments by the *Praecones Britanniae* group. As an expert on what is known of Roman music and instruments, Marshall has tried to create a variety of the kinds of music, both vocal and instrumental, that Romans would likely have sung, played, and listened to. The Praecones Britanniae musicians have striven to reproduce the sounds the Roman instruments might have made. The first selection, "Pompa Gladiatorum" ("Procession of the Gladiators"), on track #6, is the sort of processional song that would have been played as gladiators entered the arena. It features a large antelope horn, a double aulos, a tuba, and tympana. The other selection, "Copa," on track #7, is a poem by Virgil with musical accompaniment, read in the original Latin by Chris Grocock and in English translation by Valerie Marshall. The instruments include a tibia, a single aulos, tympana, cymbals, and a gong. The message of the poem is *Carpe diem* ("Seize the day"): enjoy yourself, for life is short.

CHAPTER FIVE
ROMAN LITERATURE AND VIRGIL

That someone else taught the Romans most aspects of their literary and artistic culture, they readily admitted themselves. Horace (65-8 BCE), one of the finest of their poets in the age of Augustus, the high tide of Roman achievement, commented:

> Captive Greece captured the fierce victor and introduced the arts to backwoods Latium . . . Late in time the Roman turned his wit to Greek books and found out what Sophocles, Thespis, and Aeschylus had of use to give. (*Epistles* 2.1.156–157, 161–63)

Horace meant that the Greek world, in his day completely under Roman domination, had overwhelmed its ruder masters; that Roman literature, art, architecture, and to a degree the very worship of the gods, were irreversibly Hellenized—made Greek. Another poet, one of Horace's contemporaries and personal friends, Virgil (70-19 BCE), acknowledges Greek supremacy in the plastic arts, in public speaking, and in science, but does not concede poetry to the Greeks. Some would ask that credit be given to the Etruscans, who schooled their latecomer Roman neighbors and introduced them to things Greek before the Greeks did. But whatever the argument for Etruscan influence, the clearest imprint on Roman culture is Greek.

Despite the fact that Greece and much of the Mediterranean area was subjugated under Rome, Greek artistic and intellectual life still remained vigorous in Greece and the great centers of Hellenistic civilization at Alexandria in Egypt, Antioch in Syria, Pergamum in Asia Minor, and Macedonia in Eastern Europe, where the patronage of wealthy monarchs attracted the talented. By the end of the fourth century BCE Roman diplomats, soldiers, and merchants knew all of these places. Wealthy Roman families would send their sons on the "grand tour" in the Greek east to learn Greek and study under Greek philosophers and teachers of rhetoric. If a wealthy Roman family could not afford to send a son abroad, they could at least hire or even buy a cultivated Greek as a household tutor. Literate Romans would be thoroughly schooled in Greek literature, but when did they develop a literature of their own?

EARLY ROMAN LITERATURE

The earliest literature that can be considered Roman that we know about appeared in the late third century BCE. It did not exhibit any great originality. Their very word for a poem, *carmen*, originally meant "incantation" or "ritual formula," and the earliest metrical form, known as Saturnian, seems crude in comparison with the Greek forms which replaced the older Roman verse style entirely. Romans were adapters rather than creators, and their adaptations were patriotic in message emphasizing the glory of Rome.

Romans produced tragedy and satire that showed intelligence and wit, but were basically adaptations of Greek plays. Best known among early Roman literary works that we can read today are comedies meant for outdoor performances at great religious festivals, just as was the case for all Greek drama. The Roman festivals seem to have been more boisterous and the audiences less sophisticated than the Greek, so that the playwrights had to "write down" to them. The first of these was Plautus, who was born in the middle of the third century BCE and lived into the second decade of the next. Although his life spanned two of the Punic wars, the most critical trial of Roman national survival, he mentions none of it, at least directly. He takes all the plots of his plays from a genre known as "New Comedy," the comedies of manners which developed in the fourth century and after in Greece when political tempers and despots made it no longer safe to indulge in the blunt political and social criticism of the Athenian Aristophanes.

We have only one complete Greek "new comedy," and bits of others. Plautus, it would seem, did not translate, but adapted, adding a good deal of vigor and bounce but also hammering his plots and jokes into an audience whose attention and comprehension he only half held. Yet it was from Plautus, not from Aristophanes, that the Medieval and Renaissance world learned of ancient comedy. Plautus's well-worn theme of mistaken identities, best seen in his *Brothers Menaechmus,* impressed Shakespeare enough to use it in his *Comedy of Errors.* Twenty plays survive to us and make us wonder what Plautus could have done if freed from the necessity of using Greek plots and Greek settings and if supplied with an audience worthy of his talent. Perhaps the best way for the modern theater fan to savor what Plautus was like on stage is not seeing a revival of one of his plays but indirectly through a musical, *A Funny Thing Happened on the Way to the Forum* (first produced in New York in 1962), where a hodgepodge of situations from Plautus can be served up well by a skillful director and a competent cast. Surely Plautus would have approved of Zero Mostel's immortal performance in the musical.

The life of the young Romanized African Terence (ca. 190–159 BCE) overlapped with the latter years of Plautus's career. Time has left us only six plays out of what was originally a much larger production. Terence lived in a time of increased sophistication and possessed a gentler, less bumptious dramatic manner than Plautus. Consequently a modern audience perhaps finds him less funny, but from the Renaissance through the nineteenth century he was widely appreciated. Terence was considered safe reading for the classroom because of his greater lucidity and less offensive stage morality (an absence of scatological language and immoral situations). He also exhibited greater

human sympathy for his plausible characters, yet all of these virtues didn't do much for him with his contemporaries, for he complains in a prologue that at an earlier performance of a play, a circus act outside the theater robbed him of his audience.

The only prose writer who survives from this period is the conservative politician Cato (234–149 BCE) known as "the Elder," to differentiate him from an even more reactionary descendant, "the Younger," an opponent of Julius Caesar's. Unfortunately for us, the Romans chose to preserve not his interesting and violent speeches in the Senate, with their ringing conclusion of "Carthage must be destroyed," or his curiously partisan historical writings, but a rough-hewn essay on agriculture and estate management. His hard-boiled advice to sell off slaves when they get too old to work has done nothing to endear him to posterity.

A work that survives from this period that is of considerable value is a portion of Polybius's *Histories.* Polybius (203–120 BCE) was a Greek resident of Rome and he wrote in Greek. He was acquainted with many of the high-ranking figures of his time, and accompanied the famous Scipio Aemilianus on diplomatic and military missions. What is notable about Polybius's history was not simply that he wrote to glorify Rome, but his writings demonstrate real research: the examination of documents, evidence of witnesses, and geographical accuracy.

ROMAN LITERATURE IN THE LATER REPUBLIC, 133–31 BCE

The accumulated wealth and arrogance of the Rome that substantially had completed its conquest of the Mediterranean by the middle of the second century BCE gave a great impetus to Roman cultural growth. There was a flourishing of written material. Oratory was highly praised, and while little survives from the first half of this period, it is notable that what did survive is a Latin textbook of oratory. From this we learn that there were two schools of rhetoric, the Atticist and Asianist. Characteristics of these two schools remind of us of the Greek characteristics of the Apollonian and Dionysian. Atticist oratory was noted for its passion and dramatic presentation. Asianist oratory was a more dignified and direct discourse.

Drama was most popular in the form of mime, with productions that would compare to early twentieth-century burlesque. Aristocrats wrote autobiographies generally to aggrandize themselves and blacken the reputations of their opponents. Histories continued to be written and were now in Latin. One author wrote a history of Rome from its beginnings to 91 BCE in seventy-five volumes!

Poetry, which had stumbled around ineffectually in Rome since the third century BCE, came to maturity in this period. Although it needs no apology for its quality, it must acknowledge its Greek roots. One of the surviving poets, Lucretius (ca. 94–55 BCE), writes in a genre utterly alien to our understanding, the "didactic" or "instructive" epic. His subject is the philosophy of the Athenian materialist Epicurus (341–270 BCE), a philosophy that had previously always been expounded in singularly unexciting Greek prose. In his epic, *On the Nature of the Universe,* Lucretius borrows an archaic style of epic from the Roman past and uses it in a colorful, imaginative, and passionate appeal to humanity to take up Epicureanism as an antidote to uncertainty and religious superstition. The fine, vigorous imagery and earnestness give Lucretius a permanent ranking among the world's poets, whatever the status of Epicurean philosophy may be. We will take up the discussion of Epicurean philosophy in the next chapter.

There was a group of aristocratic youth now referred to as the *Novi Poetae.* They wrote Greek lyric and elegiac poetry but mainly to each other, which is probably the reason none has survived. One poet from this time period who flourished in the fifties left a legacy that deserves our attention. Catullus (ca. 84–54 BCE) was known for his skillful expression of genuine passion. Among some efforts in "Alexandrian" epyllion ("little epic"), he has left us a strange and wild poem, the *Attis,* the account of a young aristocrat who, in a fit of madness induced by religious ecstasy, castrates himself and becomes the follower of the Asiatic goddess Cybele. The greater part of the poem is his lament at recovering his wits and seeing his irretrievable step into religious celibacy. The poem is unique in ancient literature. Most of Catullus's permanent fame derives from his short, passionate love lyrics to and about his mistress Lesbia, apparently a pseudonym for Clodia, the disreputable sister of an even more disreputable politician, Publius Clodius. He has also

left behind abusive, even pornographic, denunciations of people he disliked (Julius Caesar among them), and most significantly a gentle, wistful lament at the grave of his dead brother, a lament that has given posterity the famous phrase "hail and farewell."

Catullus's fame hardly endured through antiquity, and by the beginning of the Middle Ages he was all but forgotten. His collection of poems survived in one manuscript (compared to, say, 500 for Virgil), and he was rediscovered only in the Renaissance and has been commonly read only in the last two or three generations. The German composer Carl Orff in the twentieth century paid him a musical tribute in a choral and orchestral composition, *Catulli carmina, The Songs of Catullus,* a piece containing some vocal and instrumental fireworks that complement Catullus's passionate verse nicely.

Most of the sculpted portraits of the great figures of the first century BCE have to be identified from coins or by conjecture, but not that of Cicero (106–43 BCE). His portrait bust bears his name clearly in ancient lettering. Cicero was not a modest man. His name appeared everywhere, and we could take the opportunity to commend him here for his many achievements, had he not done so more than adequately himself in his varied writings. He was proudest of his role as an active politician, a role that eventually cost him his life in 43 BCE, a year after his equally literate rival Caesar was assassinated. We know him as the author of the only surviving body of Roman political or judicial oratory. In fact his achievements here made him such a textbook that other orators' speeches have vanished. He wrote a series of works on the technique of public speaking, which he had learned from the Greeks and perhaps improved on. His contributions to philosophy will be discussed in the next chapter.

The first surviving collection of personal letters, more than a thousand, comes from Cicero's hand, and most of them were written with no thought of publication. We have in them a racy, informal Latin written by a master of the language, who throws in Greek quotations, slang, gossip, and complaints about his tumultuous marriage, his disappointingly extravagant son, and lamentations for the death of his talented daughter. Their publication had an unfortunate effect, perhaps undeserved, on Cicero's reputation, for they revealed him off guard. They also had an unfortunate effect on literary figures and politicians of later generations, Romans and others, for they began to write with an eye to publishing or to posterity's publishing their letters, and these often became essays rather than revelations of a real personal life. This is an example of his gossipy tone:

> I am not speaking against that woman, but let us suppose that there is another woman, different from her, who gives herself freely to everybody—I mean everybody—who always has a lover to show off; let us suppose that in her garden, in her house, in her villa at Baiae, she gives complete freedom to the pleasures of all; that she goes so far as to maintain young men and to compensate with her largesse for the stinginess of their fathers; let us suppose that this woman is a widow and lives freely; that she is a hussy and lives brazenly; that she is a wealthy woman and lives extravagantly; that she is a slave to her appetites and lives like a whore. Should I consider a man an adulterer if he takes a little liberty when he meets her?"

Cicero, *Pro Caelio*, 16.

Cicero's finest literary moment probably was in a section of his great work, now largely lost, entitled the *Republic,* an imitation of Plato's work. Cicero's book, in fact, gave Plato's work the name by which we know it now, for Plato had called it, in Greek, the *Politeia.* In Cicero's book, more pragmatic in the Roman way than his Greek model, he despaired of the constitutional stability of the Roman Republic. As a means of national salvation he recommended retention of the institutions and titles of the old commonwealth with the addition of an extra-constitutional senior consultant, the *rector,* the "director" of the state. This was in fact to be the very way Augustus chose to represent himself, whatever the actuality was. Only the title was changed from *rector* to *princeps,* something like

"chief citizen," and Augustus thus indirectly complimented Cicero, a man in whose murder he had connived.

Among the other Roman prose authors preserved to us from the late Republic—and there are not many—only two deserve mention alongside of Cicero, though their writings belong to a different sphere. The most noteworthy of these is Gaius Julius Caesar himself. From 58 to 49 BCE as governor of the Roman province in southern Gaul (modern Provence in France), he had managed to pick fights with the native Gauls, the Germans across the Rhine, and even the Britons. The consequence was the addition of what is now France, Belgium, and Germany west of the Rhine to the Empire, a conquest controversial even by Roman standards. To justify himself Caesar sat in the evenings in his tent and wrote what are conventionally translated as *Commentaries,* though the Latin title more appropriately means *Notebooks.* In spite of this disarming name, which would imply informality, they are perhaps the subtlest and most successful propaganda ever put in writing. Their brisk, delusive directness gives the impression of a simple soldier telling us Gaul is divided into three parts and then setting forth his exploits, and so they were read by generations of school children from ancient Rome to the present. In fact, they attribute all the successes of the war to Caesar (who coyly refers to himself in the third person), blame any setbacks on incompetent subordinates, any aggressions on the enemy, and conceal completely the brutal conquest, and sometimes slaughter, of the Gauls and the ruin of Celtic civilization on the continent of Europe. His companion work, *Notebooks on the Civil War,* skillfully makes the case for his war with and defeat of the forces of the Roman Senate.

The prose writer, Sallust (80–35 BCE), unlike Caesar and Cicero, played no very significant role in the events of the time, but he did give us our first surviving formal Roman historiography, a genre in which the Greeks had excelled. Sallust has left us our first extant example of monographs, short historical accounts focused on a single event or character. One monograph, *The War with Jugurtha,* deals with the great warlord Gaius Marius, Caesar's father-in-law and mentor, and his success against a North African chieftain who had found corrupt and incompetent Roman generals easy to defeat. Sallust uses his essay as a platform for a denunciation of the moral degeneration he perceived in the aristocratic class at Rome that provided its politicians and generals. The other monograph, *The Conspiracy of Catiline*, recounts a failed attempt at a coup by a debt-ridden cabal of noblemen. Here Sallust offers us a corrective to Cicero's self-congratulatory version of the affair, wherein the great orator took more credit than he deserved for putting down the conspiracy and garnered more than his share of blame for violating the civil rights of the culprits in putting them to death unconstitutionally. Sallust left for posterity an earnest, terse style that would more than a century later be taken up by another and greater Roman historian, Tacitus.

Literature managed to function creatively during the tumultuous fifties BCE and even into the bloody civil wars of the next two decades, but resources were hardly available for the other arts. Thus we must wait until the consolidation of power under Augustus following his victory against Cleopatra and Mark Anthony at Actium in 31 BCE and his new beginning for Rome in 27 BCE, the year of what historians like to call Augustus's "great settlement."

THE AUGUSTAN AGE

The Emperor Augustus was determined to create a new order, one that would last forever, for his was the age to end all ages. He built massive buildings and much sculpture, and brought into his court circle a number of the leading writers of his day although not all of them. Some of them had even been on the other side in the Roman civil war, an

The legend of the Trojan War inspired not only the ancient Greeks, as seen in the epics of Homer, but the Romans as well. In their search for heroic origins, the Romans claimed themselves descendants of Aeneas, a Trojan warrior and son of Aphrodite. This sculpture, possibly a Roman copy of a first century original, depicts a scene from the battle at Troy. The priest Laocoön warned the Trojans not to accept the wooden horse, which was filled with Greeks. The gods who supported the Greeks in war then sent serpents to destroy Laocoön and his sons. Their twisting bodies and anguished faces portray a height of emotion that inspired later sculptors such as Michelangelo, after the sculpture was excavated in Rome in 1506.

Figure III-3 Hagesandros, Polydoros, and Athanadoros of Rhodes. *Laocoön and His Sons.* Second-first century BCE or a Roman copy of the first century CE original. Marble, height 8' (2.44 m). Musei Vaticani, Museo Pio Clementino, Rome. Courtesy of Dorling Kindersley Media Library.

example being the poet Horace. This son of a freed slave, once won over, gracefully complimented the emperor in many of his charming lyrics that have impressed readers with sufficient Latin to read them and challenged poets to translate or imitate them. He also wrote poetic epistles and satires, imitating a predecessor lost to us, Lucilius. Horace's *Satires* have had a productive history in English literature as have his theories of literary criticism set forth in an epistle. Other poets, such as the amorous Propertius (died ca. 2 BCE), nodded politely to the emperor and his official line, but then turned away and wooed their mistresses in verse. Augustus tended to be tolerant, provided the poets were discreet, as Propertius was. When they were not discreet, the result could be disastrous. The prolific Ovid (43 BCE–17 CE), who in his rambling epic *The Metamorphoses* transmitted to posterity more mythology than any other single figure in antiquity, was somehow indiscreet—we don't know how— and was packed off into lifelong exile in a cold and dangerous frontier fortress.

VIRGIL AND *THE AENEID*

Another kind of story—this of the founding of Rome—is told through the eloquence of the poet Virgil (70–19 BCE), the jewel in Augustus's crown of poets laureate. Virgil was a shy and talented son of a north Italian farming family who won the attention of one of Augustus's ministers by his short pastoral poems, called *Eclogues*. In these Augustus becomes "a young god" for having restored to the poet's family their farm that had been confiscated in order to be given to a veteran of the emperor's army as a retirement bonus. This sort of veterans' benefit program was, in fact, rapidly advancing the ruin of the small family farm in Italy, a process already under way for generations. The emperor tried to compensate by urging a "back to the farm" or at least "stay on the farm" movement (in spite of the fact that he had moved thousands off), and through his ministers he enlisted Virgil to write a sort of didactic epic poem on the joys and techniques of farming. As child of a farm family Virgil certainly knew about the latter

This early sculpture by Bernini recounts the story of Aeneas, a forefather of Rome, as told in Virgil's *Aeneid.* Aeneas, hero of Troy, rescues his father and son from the burning city. Aeneas' devotion to his family exemplifies filial love, while his father, who carries their household gods, demonstrates love of the gods. According to the Apostle Paul, these two kinds of love constituted *caritas*, or charity, a Christian virtue. Bernini's sculpture thus provides a union of pagan myth and Christian symbolism. Virgil's epic served to confirm the semi-divine status of the Roman lineage: Romulus, founder of Rome, was a descendant of Aeneas, who was in turn the son of Aphrodite, daughter of Zeus.

Figure III-4 Gian Lorenzo Bernini. *Aeneas, Anchises, and Ascanius Fleeing Troy.* 1619. Marble, 86⅝". Galleria Borghese, Rome. Courtesy of Alinari Archives/Corbis.

and at least professed to recognize the former. The result was a book called by a Greek title, *The Georgics* (literally, 'the farmer's life'). Whether *The Georgics* sent anyone scurrying back to the countryside we may doubt, but there is no doubt about the quality and enduring reputation of the work.

How did Virgil come to write the *Aeneid*? Augustus wanted a national epic extolling the glory of Rome that would rival the Homeric *Iliad* and *Odyssey*. Virgil took up the challenge and the result became the central work of all Roman literature: an account of Augustus's legendary ancestor, the Trojan prince Aeneas, who escapes from the burning city of Troy during the night of the Greek conquest.

Homer was the model for all subsequent epics, and Virgil intended that we should see the Homeric poems in his work. Virgil follows Homer in meter (dactylic hexameter) and in the use of similes (a comparison of two unlike things). Another common element is the involvement of the gods in the advancement of the plot. The role of the gods is, however, determined by the stated purpose of the poem, the glorification of Augustan Rome. Finally, Virgil's story reverses the tale. Where Homer begins with a war, the *Iliad,* and ends in a journey, the *Odyssey*, Virgil begins with a journey and ends in war.

The Plot   In Book 1 the role of the gods is made clear. Aeneas and his ships have set out across the Tyrrhenian Sea toward their destination Italy. Juno (Greek Hera) calls upon Aeolus, god of the winds, to raise a storm and sink Aeneas's ships. Venus, Aeneas's mother by the mortal, Anchises, appeals to Jupiter (Greek Zeus) to save them. He rescues Aeneas and his fleet, and in his words of comfort to Venus reveals the outcome of the entire story! From the very beginning of the poem then we know that Virgil will succeed in reaching Hesperia (Italy) and found a city from which will come the ancestors of the founders of Rome, Romulus and Remus, some four centuries hence. The rest of the poem tells the story of how this comes about and at what great cost in human suffering.

In a flashback in Book 2 we are returned to the story of the *Iliad* as Aeneas, guest of queen Dido of Carthage, rehearses the final hours of the destruction of Troy. Duped by the wooden horse and betrayed by Helen, the inhabitants of Troy are slaughtered and the city destroyed by the Greeks.

Aeneas manages to escape with his father Anchises and his son, Ascanius (Iülus), but loses his wife, Creüsa. He becomes the leader of a small band of survivors, and they build ships and set out on a journey to found a new city.

Book 3 narrates their journey prior to arriving at Carthage. They are frightened off from their first stop in Thrace by the discovery of the corpse of a Trojan warrior and the realization of the betrayal of former allies. When the second settlement, Crete, appears doomed, the gods in a dream reveal to Aeneas their final destination, Hesperia. The subsequent journey, reminiscent of Odysseus' voyage in the *Odyssey*, is fraught with dangers. They manage to escape the Cyclopes and safely pass Scylla and Charybdis, but after they find safe harbor at Drepanum in Sicily Father Anchises dies. Setting out again in their ships they are caught in the storm that opens the story.

The Trojans are tossed onto the shores of Libya near Carthage. Dido queen of Carthage welcomes them and invites them to settle there in her walled city. Dido, a Phoenician princess, fled her native city of Tyre with a group of followers when her brother murdered her husband. She had purchased the territory upon which she was building a great city with gold left to her by her husband. Once in Carthage Venus and Juno, two divine rivals, join in bringing Dido and Aeneas together. Venus through Cupid infects Dido with a passionate love for Aeneas. Juno contrives to bring them together in a cave where their love is consummated. Their motives differ. Juno wants to keep Aeneas from his dictated destination. Venus imagines a more temporary safety in Dido's love. Venus ponders whether Tyrians (Carthaginians) and Trojans can get along together.

In Book 4, the two lovers enjoy some months of happiness until Jupiter sends Mercury to remind Aeneas of his duty. Aeneas responds immediately by ordering his men to prepare the ships. His parting with Dido is more polite than tender. He emphasizes his duty, concluding, "It is not my own will—this quest for Italy."

Dido is devastated and endangered. Her public affair has weakened her authority among her people and left her more open to threat from the neighboring Moorish lord, Iarbus, who had wanted to marry her. More distant but still a danger is her brother. Finally, in giving in to her love for Aeneas she has broken her pledge of eternal fidelity to her dead husband, Sychaeus. To the crushing pain of rejection is added remorse for her faithlessness. What else can she do but die? As the ships move out to sea, Aeneas and his men see the flames from Dido's funeral pyre.

In Book 5, Aeneas lands in Sicily and there on the anniversary of his father's death he stages traditional funeral games. While these are going on the Trojan women, wearied by years of wandering and urged on by Juno's representative the goddess Iris, set fire to Aeneas's ships. A rainstorm sent by Jupiter saves most of the ships. Aeneas is magnanimous and allows a segment to stay behind, and he resumes his journey with a remnant of the Trojans.

Book 6 is the pivotal point in the epic where the journey ends and the struggle begins. Aeneas and his men beach the ships on the shore of Cumae in southern Italy, and Aeneas strikes out, as all heroes must, to visit the underworld before the quest can begin. He finds the golden bough, presents it to the Sibyl, and is led into Hades. Here he encounters the Homeric figures of the underworld and many dead friends. He sees Dido walking with her husband. When he attempts to speak to her she turns away and Aeneas cries. We are left to wonder why.

His last encounter is with his father, who begins with the lines:

> Now I will set forth the glory that awaits
> The Trojan race, the illustrious souls
> Of the Italian heirs to our names.
> I will teach you your destiny.

> lines 896–9

Anchises continues to foretell the future, concluding with "Your mission, Roman, is to rule the world." Aeneas responds with an enthusiasm for his task that he has never before expressed,

> When Anchises had led his son
> Through every detail and *enflamed his soul*
> with longing for the glory that was to come,
> He told him of the wars he next must wage,
> Of the Laurentine people and Latinus' town,
> And how to face or flee each waiting peril.

> lines 1058–63, italics added

At the opening of Book 7, the Trojans come to the mouth of the Tiber River and land their ships. Despite Anchises' prediction, it is their desire to settle peacefully. Aeneas sends ambassadors bearing gifts to appear before King Latinus, requesting ". . . a safe strip of shore, a little land for the gods of our country, and water and air that are common to all." The king of the Latium is a weak and indecisive figure who has recently been told in a dream that he should break the engagement of his daughter, Lavinia, to the native-born Turnus and instead give her to a stranger. He views the ambassadors as representatives of this stranger and is open to their appeals. He promises his daughter to Aeneas sight-unseen and sends back to him many gifts. His wife is outraged, as is the betrayed Turnus, a powerful prince who deeply loves Lavinia. Juno, having failed to stop Aeneas from reaching his destination, now promotes war against this gang of intruders. Turnus marshals an army and King Latinus retires to his palace. In the conclusion of Book 7, Virgil lists the major warriors on both sides of the conflict including the warrior maiden Camilla. And thus the battle begins.

Aeneas has been told in a dream to seek an alliance with the Arcadians. Thus much of the action in Book 8 is the story of this journey and the forging of an alliance. The king of the Arcadians, Evander, is too old to fight. He sends in his place his young son, Pallas, whom Aeneas pledges to keep safe. Meanwhile, Venus, in her concern to protect her son, has asked her husband the god Vulcan to forge a sword for Aeneas. He does so, and on the shield he portrays the future of Italy, now revealed for the third time in the text. But it is a future that Aeneas himself never quite grasps, a future that Aeneas does not understand:

> . . . Aeneas was moved
> To wonder and joy by the images of things
> *He could not fathom*, and he lifted to his
>   shoulder
> The destiny of his children's children.
>   (italics added)

The next three books depict battles as bloody and ferocious as anything in the *Iliad*. The lives of many high-born warriors from both sides are lost along with those of countless ordinary soldiers. By the end of Book 11 the two opposing forces meet together in an effort to make a truce. Turnus rages like an angry lion. Again Juno intervenes and the battle resumes. Aeneas is injured but mysteriously cured, probably at the instigation of Venus. Jupiter, perhaps a little wearily, calls upon Juno to end this slaughter. She must realize that Aeneas will win in the end. It has been predetermined. Juno complies but only after she has received something in return. It is agreed that the Trojans (Teucrians) shall be assimilated into the existing population. There will be no "new Troy." The blood of the Trojans will be blended with that of the native population and they will be known as Latins. Juno will be revered.

Turnus, despite his savagery in battle, can be considered a sympathetic figure. We can be repelled by his ferocity as a warrior, but in this he is no different from Homer's Achilles. (He is referred to as "A second Achilles" in Book 6.) Aeneas too can awaken a blood lust. Setting aside the intervention of Juno, isn't Turnus justified in his challenge? Are not Aeneas and his men invaders of his homeland? Latinus has gone back on his promise, and it is clear that there is affection between Turnus and his promised bride. The truce was broken not by Turnus, but by Juno's meddling. When Turnus and Aeneas face each other in the end, as we knew they would, Turnus admits defeat and begs for mercy. Why is it not granted? This brings us to the issue: how can we assess Aeneas?

Virgil intended that Aeneas would differ from the old heroic world of Achilles with its destructive and self-destructive pride. Nor would Aeneas model Odysseus's cunning talent for survival as a lonely and resourceful individual. Virgil's hero is more complicated. In the opening of the poem, Aeneas is described as "a man of faultless devotion." Throughout the epic he is repeatedly referred to as "pious Aeneas," obedient to his destiny, and faithful to his duties. Sacrifices are never forgotten. The frequent reference to Aeneas as "Father Aeneas" tells us that not only will he "father a race," but he must act like a father to his people and be their protector and defender. Sometimes we can recognize a characteristic sadness in Aeneas. Personal affections must give away to wider loyalties, love must be subordinate to patriotism, and survival is not for himself but for the gods, country, and family, the Roman hierarchy of duties.

These were the great Roman values also articulated by Cicero and Stoics like Seneca. The rewards will only come in the future when Aeneas and all his followers are dust.

Traditionally the *Aeneid* is seen as a panegyic, a great poem glorifying Augustus and his achievements. Virgil says that the epic announces the return of the Golden Age (an idea borrowed from the Greek Hesiod) in the reign of Augustus. For centuries most scholars have accepted its purpose as patriotic. Some have even seen it as representing the triumph of European civilization. Others have found it prophetically reflective of the victory of Christianity. There are those who explain the ending by saying that when Aeneas saw Turnus wearing the emblems of the slain Pallas, his fury became too great. But during the twentieth century and since, scholars have looked at the *Aeneid* for what it says about war. Viewed in this way it is not a poem in praise of war or the heroism of the *Iliad,* but an anti-war statement. W. R. Johnson, borrowing the title of a poem by the World War I poet Wilfred Owen, "Anthem for Doomed Youth," suggests:

> . . . Aeneas is angry with himself and with war itself and, though he doesn't know it, with Juno and even, or especially, with the Jupiter whom the Poem's poet himself had bitterly cried out against. This poem is crowded with victims, and among them are both Turnus and his despairing, reluctant killer.

[*Aeneid*. Translated by Stanley Lombardo with an Introduction by W.R. Johnson. Hackett Publishing Co., Indianapolis, 2005, xlv.]

Virgil grew ill soon after the poem was completed and asked that the epic be destroyed. Was it because it was unfinished, or could it have been that he was dissatisfied? We will never know but we can be grateful that his wishes were disobeyed.

Virgil is one Roman author who never suffered the least eclipse of popularity through the centuries. Ancient Rome made him a textbook for schools, as it had Cicero and Caesar. The Middle Ages revered Virgil at least in part for a misunderstanding. Medieval readers read one of his *Eclogues,* the fourth, as a prophecy of the coming of Christ, for there is mention there of the birth of a mysterious child who would bring an era of peace, the return of the Golden Age, to the earth. The poem was composed about thirty years before the birth of Jesus, and Christian readers leaped to the conclusion that this was a pagan testimony to the truth of Christianity. No great harm was done, and there was one splendid dividend. The poet who sums up best the thought world of the Middle Ages, Dante, learned to revere Virgil as both prophet and poet, and made him his guide through hell and part of purgatory in his *Divine Comedy*. The Italian epic pays abundant tribute to the great predecessor in its poetic style as well. Milton's *Paradise Lost* sounds a more distant echo of the *Aeneid*, for Milton lived in an age when Homer was accessible, and Milton knew the Greek poet well, but Virgil is nonetheless there.

A historian   Titus Livius or Livy (ca. 64 BCE–ca. 12 CE), another north Italian like Virgil, found a place in the imperial court circle. Like Horace, Livy had a bias in favor of the old Republic but managed to get along well with the emperor, even consulting with him on details of history. About a fourth of Livy's history survives, and even that is a considerable bulk of writing. What we have deals not with Augustus's own age or even the generations immediately preceding, but with the founding of Rome in the misty legends of the eighth century BCE and the more solidly historical realities of the great struggle with Carthage in the third century. Livy believes passionately in the moral fiber of the old Republic, which did not displease Augustus too much, for he in fact claimed to have restored it. A disregard for sober historical investigation may well underlie Livy's imaginative and colorful writing, but his vivid narrations and passionate attachment to his subject make him a literary classic.

Livy was not entirely forgotten in the Middle Ages, but generally readers preferred third-rate compilers, many of whom compiled out of Livy. Toward the close of the Middle Ages Dante mentions Livy as one "who does not err." A more balanced judgment came in the Renaissance from Machiavelli, in his *Discourses on the First Ten Books of Titus Livius*.

The high standards of the culture of the Augustan age have made it a byword for a period of excellence in literature and the arts. Cultural historians have used the term "Augustan" to describe the age of Louis XIV in France and of Queen Anne in England. The later Romans themselves were uneasily aware that they never quite attained to the level of the Augustan period again.

POST-AUGUSTAN

The reigns of Augustus's immediate successors, Tiberius, Caligula, and Claudius, were not propitious times for intellectuals. Under the gloomy Tiberius neither art nor literature particularly flourished, though they were by no means absent. Writing exhibits less energy, or at least no boldness, under Tiberius and his two successors. Our chief author is a freedman named Phaedrus (15 BCE–50 CE), who rewrote the fables of Aesop in verse form. These are stories whose morals teach caution, restraint, observance of due limits, and the wisdom of keeping a low profile, all useful survival skills in the reign of the suspicious Tiberius.

Although a revival of art and literature begins under the reign of Claudius, himself an educated but pedantic scholar, the real new era begins with the accession of Nero in 54 CE. However notorious this monarch may have been, he had the best possible education and fancied himself a poet and artist; in fact, his dying words at the time of his suicide in 68 CE were reported as, "What an artist is dying!" Nero's tastes ran to the spectacular and grandiose, in which there was nothing un-Roman, except for the degree to which he pushed his tendency. The art and architecture, even literature, of his age often bear the tag of "Neronian baroque."

Another figure of note during Nero's reign was Lucius Annaeus Seneca (4 BCE–65 CE), known in the ancient world as a statesman and advisor to the young Nero. The adult Nero accused him of treason and ordered him to commit suicide. He has been remembered best through the centuries as a Stoic philosopher. He will be discussed more fully in the next chapter.

Seneca's nephew Lucan (39–65 CE) also aroused Nero's jealousy and anger by composing an epic poem on the Roman Civil War. This war had resulted in Caesar's triumph and the establishment of the Empire, a move Lucan frankly equates with slavery in the later books of his poem. Forbidden to publish by the jealous Nero, he seems to have joined a futile conspiracy and he too was ordered to commit suicide.

Yet another suicide in this period was the courtier and intellectual Petronius (dead by 68 CE), a seemingly indolent esthete, but in fact a capable and energetic administrator when the occasion demanded. Nero appointed him "arbiter of tastes" and would accept nothing in court life not approved by Petronius—that is, until Petronius, too, fell under suspicion and was sent off to commit suicide, which he is reported to have done with wit and the best possible good taste. To us he is known as the author of a satirical novel, the first at Rome, called the *Satiricon*. Only a portion of this work survives and provides us with the marvelously funny "Trimalchio's Dinner Party," the account of a vulgar and lavish banquet put on by an uncouth ex-slave who has come into vast wealth. Our American novelist of the twenties, F. Scott Fitzgerald, alludes to Trimalchio in his *The Great Gatsby*, for the newly rich protagonist there puts on a lavish dinner party on his Long Island estate. One of the lost works of Roman literature posterity would benefit by having restored in full would surely be the remainder of the *Satiricon*.

From the reign of Vespasian comes the enormous compendium of the elder Pliny (23/24–79 CE), the *Natural History*, a generally unscientific accumulation of scientific lore, vastly admired in the Latin world until the rise of the disciplines of modern science. This same unsystematic curiosity of Pliny's led him to asphyxiate himself attempting to climb Mt. Vesuvius during its famous eruption of 79 CE, which buried Pompeii and Herculaneum. His nephew, the Younger Pliny (61–112 CE), has left us a vivid eyewitness description of this eruption in his carefully edited collection of correspondence. Alas, the Younger Pliny was aware that Cicero's *Letters* had brought their author not only great fame but posthumous ridicule by their revelation of the writer's personal foibles and weaknesses. Thus Pliny's letters are in fact essays cast in epistolary form. Good essays, but essays, not really letters. Only the tenth, the last book of his correspondence, is anything but essays, and this contains official dispatches from the province of Bithynia (northern Turkey, on the Black Sea), where Pliny served as a bewildered and vacillating governor in the early

years of the second century, consulting his emperor on all matters great and small—new water buckets for the fire brigades, for example. From this Asian outpost Pliny writes back (no. 97) about his investigation of a sect of "Christiani." He finds that they do nothing immoral but that they are illegal and that he has been reading anonymous accusations and torturing those who will not curse Christ. The humane emperor, Trajan, writes back (no. 98) that anonymous denunciations are not appropriate to his administration and that his governor is not to prosecute Christians unless they force themselves on his attention. From this the Middle Ages, in particular Dante, got the curious notion that Trajan was a Christian.

Titus's brother Domitian (51–96 CE, ruled 81-96) succeeded him, and contemporaries described him (once he was safely dead) as another Tiberius. While he was yet alive the safe course was flattery, however, and we find a good deal of it in the extensive epigram collection of Martial (40–104 CE). Martial was unusual in antiquity, for he seems to have actually made his living by writing, composing books of short, pointed poems called, from their Greek models, epigrams (a short, terse, and witty poem expressing a single thought or observation). Generally he runs to satire, savage and abusive, almost always witty, but he has a number of voices. He shows servility in addressing Domitian, tenderness in commending the soul of a dead slave child to the care of his parents in the underworld, humaneness in urging a school teacher to go easy on the children in the hot months of summer, and frank commercialism when he writes, for pay, labels for Saturnalia presents (the Roman equivalent of and in fact model for Christmas presents).

The one surviving Roman writer on education other than Cicero who survives to us is Quintilian (dead before 100 CE), whose book, the *Institutes of Oratory*, comes to us complete and was for long a standard text in Western culture. We should recognize that to a Roman, education meant training in rhetoric, the art of public speaking, the mainstay of Roman intellectual culture. No Roman writers from Cicero on can free themselves from the domination of rhetoric over their compositions, and it sometimes becomes a barrier for the modern reader, but in skillful hands it can add power and vigor to writing. As used by a historian it could and did sometimes make for colorful and impressive writing, as in the case of Livy and Sallust, and would with one other we will mention shortly, Tacitus. Certainly in dealing with Roman prose writing and even with poetry, we must be conscious of the pervasive role of rhetoric. Yet Quintilian's standards at least included knowledge of other disciplines, humane teaching methods, and the recognition of ethical standards in his ideal curriculum. In this he was true to Cicero's precepts.

The freedom of expression enjoyed under Trajan induced a Roman senator to undertake historical writing in which he criticized the earlier emperors quite freely. This author was Tacitus (ca. 76–115 CE), surely the most striking and certainly the most controversial of the Roman historians. He has left us two monographs modeled on his favorite, Sallust. One of these describes Germany in what is more an ethnographic or anthropological study than a historical one. The purpose, however, was to commend the unspoiled savages of the northern forests in comparison to the degenerate Romans of the south. Tacitus' biography of his father-in-law Agricola contains a detailed account of the Roman province of Britain, conquered by the emperor Claudius. As in the *Germany,* Tacitus loses no opportunity to dig at the worst aspects of his own national culture. He puts a speech in the mouth of a British rebel against Roman rule that purports to describe Roman occupation policy: "They make desolation; they call it peace." A short dialogue on oratory in the Ciceronian manner presents intellectuals of a few years previous discussing why the art of oratory had fallen on hard times in spite of the explosive growth of schools of rhetoric and of show-piece speeches. As always in Tacitus, there is apparent or latent the suggestion that there was once a better time, that of the free Republic.

Tacitus's two major works, the *Annals* (history "year-by-year") and the *Histories,* have not survived to us intact. A more substantial portion of the former has survived than of the latter. Originally they would have formed a continuous history from the death of Augustus down to the death of Domitian. Tacitus has attracted the most attention and stimulated the most criticism from modern revisionist historians for his portrayal of Tiberius. Tacitus begins his history with a statement that since he lies so far in time (it would be more than three-quarters of a century) from Tiberius he can write "without rancor or partisanship." He immediately begins of course to exhibit both, but his style, learned in the rhetorical schools and from Sallust, is put to a serious purpose, and he succeeds marvelously in producing a readable account that stresses gloom, hypocrisy, and suspicion in Tiberius, his court, and the senate. As for fairness, the jury is still out on that and no doubt always will be.

One of Hadrian's imperial secretaries, Suetonius (ca. 70–160 CE), who seems to have had access to the imperial archives, has left us biographies of "the twelve Caesars," beginning with Julius and continuing down to Domitian. The otherwise inaccessible archival data and the writer's taste for personal gossip have attracted readers rather more than has his sensitivity as a historiographer. The British novelist Robert Graves gave credit to Suetonius for providing the material for his sensationalized novels *I Claudius* and *Claudius the God,* though Graves depicts Claudius far more sympathetically than Suetonius or any other surviving Roman writer did.

The rhetorician Quintilian, whom we have mentioned above, once ran through the list of Roman writers useful in the education of a public speaker and conceded that virtually every genre of writing was learned from the Greeks, but at one point he boasted: "Satire is entirely ours." Whether the boast was justified may be debatable, but the Romans practiced satire enthusiastically. Under Hadrian it reached its pinnacle with Juvenal (active 100–127 CE), whose verse satires survive virtually complete and work over every aspect of Roman life that happened to annoy the author. Again as with Tacitus, fairness is a debatable issue with Juvenal, and it is from him that posterity has largely inherited the picture of ancient Rome as a sewer (the notion is Juvenal's) of every vice. Juvenal became a great favorite in seventeenth- and eighteenth-century Britain, where poetic satirists imitated him, and tags of his verse live on the lips of people today who never heard his name, as for example, "A sound mind in a sound body."

A remarkable Roman from North Africa named Apuleius wrote a bizarre and fascinating novel which Augustine of Hippo calls *The Golden Ass* but the manuscripts call *The Metamorphoses,* after Ovid's work. Unlike Petronius's work, we have this in its entirety. Like Pinocchio, whose story was suggested in part by this book, the protagonist, one Lucius, finds himself turned into a donkey, though for different reasons than the puppet—a curiosity about witchcraft rather than juvenile delinquency. He goes through a series of adventures, by turns comic, horrific, sexually explicit, and grim until the goddess Isis restores him to human form. This latter turn of events Apuleius describes in a passionately reverent tone quite unlike anything elsewhere in the novel, a passage that seems most at home among the great conversion accounts of religious literature.

The Christianization of the Empire brought new emphases in literature, but the Latin West and its inheritors never forgot ancient Rome, never ceased to use, comment on, and imitate its buildings and art, never stopped reading its books. For a thousand years the Greek world remained mute to Western Europe, though it lived on in the Byzantine East. Even the rediscovery of Greece in the Renaissance did not cause Western civilization to abandon the Rome that had been the carrier of classical culture for a millennium, and the Roman thread, inextricably entwined with the Greek, is also interwoven in our complicated fabric of civilization.

QUESTIONS FOR REFLECTION AND DISCUSSION

1. Discuss the early Roman literature and explain the Greek influences.

2. Tell about the life of Cicero and why he was an important figure in history.

3. List the Roman historians that are mentioned in the chapter and discuss their period and importance.

4. Why did Emperor Augustus want Virgil to write an epic story?

5. What was the message presented in the *Aeneid*? Is there more than one?

6. How do you view the personality of Aeneas? Cite quotations in your argument.

7. How do you view the personality of Dido? Cite quotations.

8. Describe briefly the Roman literary accomplishment in the post-Augustan era.

SUGGESTIONS FOR FURTHER READING

Original Works:

Suetonius. *The Twelve Caesars.* Translated by Robert Graves. Rev. Michael Grant. Harmondworth; New York: Penguin Classics, 1979.

Virgil. *The Aeneid.* Translated by Stanley Lombardo. Indianapolis, IN: Hackett Publishing, 2005.

Secondary Works:

Boardman J., J. Griffin and O. Murray. *The Oxford Illustrated History of the Roman World.* Cambridge: Oxford University Press, 2001.

Cornell, Tim. *The Beginnings of Rome: Italy and Rome from the Bronze Age to the Punic Wars.* London; New York: Routledge, 1995.

Davis, Sally and Gilbert Lawall, *Cicero's Somnium Scipionis*, White Plains, NY: Longman, 1988.

Gruen, Erich S. *Studies in Greek Culture and Roman Policy.* Leiden; New York: E. J. Brill, 1990.

Reading Vergil's Aeneid, An Interpretive Guide. Editor Christine Perkell. Norman, OK: University of Oklahoma Press, 1999.

Shelton, Jo-Ann. *A Sourcebook in Roman Social History.* New York: Oxford University Press, 1998.

Scullard, Howard Hayes. *From the Gracchi to Nero: A History of Rome from 133 B.C. to A.D. 68*, 5th ed. London; New York: Methuen, 1982.

Syme, Ronald, Sir. *The Roman Revolution.* London; New York: Oxford University Press, 1960.

Zanker, Paul. *The Power of Images in the Age of Augustus.* Translated by Alan Shapiro. Ann Arbor: University of Michigan Press, 1988.

CHAPTER SIX

ROMAN PHILOSOPHY: SENECA

The importance of the Roman philosophical heritage cannot be underestimated. Western philosophy and literature from the Middle Ages through the eighteenth century was almost entirely shaped by Roman philosophers and writers such as Cicero, Lucretius, Virgil, and Seneca, and Boethius. All educated Europeans during these centuries read Latin, not Greek. In order to speak of Roman philosophy we must begin by tracing the development of Greek philosophy following the deaths of Plato (347 BCE) and Aristotle (322 BCE). Alexander the Great created his empire in the years following Plato's death, thus inaugurating the Hellenistic Age that spread Greek civilization throughout the eastern Mediterranean world, the Middle East, and parts of India. The Hellenistic period is conventionally dated from the death of Alexander in 323 BCE to the creation of the Roman Empire by Augustus in 27 BCE. During this period Plato's Academy and Aristotle's Lyceum, and the philosophical traditions emanating from them, continued to flourish, but they were joined by new schools of thought.

The Hellenistic period produced philosophers who espoused new ideas, sometimes emerging out of and often at least influenced by earlier philosophies from the Pre-Socratics to Plato and Aristotle. Since we lack many of the original documents it is often difficult to tell just who influenced whom, but when a set of ideas, typically associated with a particular influential philosopher, became distinct in and of itself we can speak of it as a separate school of thought. *Skepticism* developed during this period, exemplified by Pyrrho of Elis (who had accompanied Alexander in the later years of his campaigns). Pyrrho was so dominant that his ideas gave us the term Pyrrhonism. Skepticism has a history going back to the earliest philosophers known to us and extending down to the present time. Around 260 BCE a philosopher named Arcesilaus was elected to be the director of Plato's Academy, inaugurating a kind of skeptical revolution in the Academy whose proponents believed, on the basis of their analysis of Socrates' arguments in some of Plato's dialogues, that Socrates was a skeptic. Thus the "Academics" came to be known as representatives of skepticism. There can be no one absolute definition of skepticism, but generally a skeptic is someone who doubts all assertions or conclusions regarding truth and knowledge, pointing out the counter-evidence and opposing arguments to any claim. Pyrrho and his followers stated that living one's life unattached to beliefs is the way to happiness or equanimity (*ataraxia*).

The two major new philosophical schools that emerged in the Hellenistic period were *Epicureanism* and *Stoicism*. The first was developed by the Athenian Epicurus (341–270 BCE). He was a materialist who adapted the atomism of his fifth-century predecessor Democritus, one of the Pre-Socratics. Epicurus established his own school in Athens in 306, which came to be known as the "Garden." Unlike the Academy and the Lyceum, which were primarily research centers, the Garden was a close-knit community of people drawn to Epicurean ideas and committed to the Epicurean way of life, including both men and women and even children. The second was started by Zeno of Citium (Cyprus), who established his school in Athens shortly after Epicurus, and was developed more fully by his immediate successors, Cleanthes and Chrysippus. It earned its name, Stoicism, from the fact that students and teachers discussed ideas as they walked the painted colonnaded porch called the *stoa poikile*, in Athens. Both of these philosophical schools will be discussed more fully below.

The older philosophical schools of Plato and Aristotle continued to be very influential and an ongoing source of new philosophical ideas and developments. The members of the Academy and developers of Plato's ideas generally were called Platonists, although as we have seen the Academics introduced a kind of skepticism not usually associated with Plato's thought. Aristotle likewise continued to exert an important influence. Those who were associated with his philosophical ideas and methods were often called the *Peripatetics*, because they "walked about" while discussing the problems of philosophy.

DEVELOPMENT OF ROMAN PHILOSOPHY

Roman philosophy was derivative from the Greeks just as were Roman literature, art, and religion, but the Romans characteristically put their own distinctive stamp on what they had appropriated. As late as the second century BCE the Romans viewed the various Greek philosophies, somewhat suspiciously, as novelties. When Carneades, a prominent Academic, visited Rome as an ambassador in 155 BCE and gave a popular series of public lectures, the Roman Senate voted to banish him from the city before he could corrupt its young men. However, by the last part of the second century leading Greek philosophers were spending time in Rome and teaching students who would go on to become eminent Romans.

What were the Romans seeking in philosophy, and why did they become interested when they did? In the second century BCE the Romans were emerging out of centuries marked by wars of conquest and expansion, and then in the following century they were plunged into a long period of civil war, with its internal chaos and bloodshed. Roman religion did not offer people a personal faith and a moral way of life. Its public rituals were chiefly dedicated to enlisting the favor of the gods in insuring the prosperity of the state. Thoughtful Romans searching for an understanding of the meaning of life and for moral guidance were more likely to turn instead to one of the Greek schools of philosophy, which were for their followers a whole way of life involving both thinking and conduct. There were also the needs of Roman education, at the very heart of which were rhetoric and grammar. The Greek schools of philosophy, and notably Stoicism, offered well-developed theories in those areas as well as practical instruction.

The Hellenistic school of thought that had the most influence on the Romans was Stoicism, and they developed it in distinctively Roman ways. Although Epicureanism had less impact, it appealed to some and offers a sharp contrast to Stoicism in its worldview and ethics. Let us now look at these two philosophies in more detail.

Epicureanism was developed by the Athenian materialist Epicurus (341–270 BCE). He wanted to eliminate the fear of death by denying any possibility of survival and possible punishment after death. The gods had no active role in human affairs, though he did not deny their existence. Like the other great Hellenistic school of thought, Stoicism, Epicureanism can be seen as a personal philosophy of life that helped individuals make sense out of life and gave them a moral code to live by amid the political and social insecurities of the Hellenistic world following the death of Alexander and the breakup of his empire. Few writings of Epicurus himself survive.

What were the main ideas of the Epicureans?

1. As atomists, they held that all reality, physical and mental, including the soul, consists of tiny, indivisible particles called "atoms" in constant motion that cluster together to form the many different entities in the world. When a living organism dies the atoms that comprise it disintegrate and re-form in other ways. At the human level, the soul atoms disintegrate with the death of the body, which is why humans need not fear death. As the great Roman Epicurean, Lucretius, put it: "Where I am, death is not; where death is, I am not." This atomistic worldview was revived centuries later as a scientific hypothesis describing the physical universe by some of the pioneering figures in the seventeenth century Scientific Revolution, notably Robert Boyle.

2. Epicureans believed in and promoted an egoistic hedonism. The highest good is the individual's (lasting) pleasure or happiness. In philosophical

discourse, "egoism" simply means related to the individual rather than the group, without necessarily connoting conceit or selfishness (egotism). "Hedonism"refers to moral theories which argue that pleasure or happiness is the essential or the highest good. The various forms of ethical hedonism interpreted this in terms of lasting rather than momentary pleasures, and argued that the pleasures of the mind were more enduring and ultimately more pleasurable than those of the body. This is very different from the popular usage of "hedonism" to refer to persons who indulge themselves in temporary and fleeting physical pleasures. Indeed, over the centuries the term "epicurean" itself came to be used of people who were devoted to luxurious living and sensual pleasures—a far cry from the teachings of Epicurus and his followers. In the nineteenth century the moral philosophy of John Stuart Mill and the Utilitarians continued the tradition of ethical hedonism, but they advocated a social rather than an egoistic hedonism, by which they meant an altruistic hedonism in which the highest good is the happiness of the greatest number of people in one's society.

3. With regard to the moral choices the individual should make to achieve happiness, the Epicureans took a "utilitarian" approach: the individual should choose what is most useful in producing personal happiness. The Epicureans argued that cultivating friendships and leading a quiet life of good conversation and study were the most conducive to lasting happiness: the Garden was the model of the good life for human beings. An Epicurean would thus be a person who lived his or her life with a community of like-minded friends in the private sphere, detaching himself or herself from public and political affairs, and calmly unafraid of death. It has to be noted here that the Epicurean ideal of withdrawal from public life ran directly counter to the Roman republican moral and political traditions of active citizenship and duty to country, which was one reason it was always less popular than Stoicism. However, the Epicurean good life required personal self-discipline, a point at which, as the Roman Stoic Seneca recognized, Epicureanism and Stoicism were similar despite their many differences.

Like Carneades and the Academics, Epicureanism was banned from Rome briefly in the second century BCE because it was too "un-Roman," but it had established itself firmly by the first century. Its most eloquent expositor was Lucretius (ca. 95–50 BCE) in his epic poem, *On the Nature of the Universe*. Some scholars consider this brilliant poem, which was discussed in the previous chapter, as rivaling Virgil's *Aeneid* in its scope and its genius, and in fact it is remembered more for its poetry than its philosophy.

Stoicism was founded by Zeno in Athens at the end of the fourth century BCE. His ideas, and those of his successors, would have the single greatest impact on Roman thought of any of the Greek schools of philosophy. It was the Greek Panaetius who introduced Stoic thought to Rome in the latter part of the second century BCE, and in the following centuries some of the greatest figures in Roman literature and public life would come to be associated with Stoicism, among them Cicero, Seneca, and the emperor Marcus Aurelius. Always named together with them is Epictetus, a Greek slave in Rome who won his freedom and founded a school in Nicopolis, Greece. Like Socrates, he is not known to have written anything, but a short book titled *The Enchiridion* ("handbook" or "manual"), a summary of his teaching as recorded by one of his followers, is one of the great classics of Stoic philosophy.

The three key precepts or ideas of Stoicism are 1) materialism: everything in the universe has some kind of bodily substance; 2) monism: everything is the manifestation of one ultimate reality; and 3) mutation: everything is perpetually changing.

Stoicism emphasized three branches of knowledge:

1. The first branch was Logic, emphasizing clear and accurate thinking, and the belief that all knowledge comes through the senses.

2. Physics, the second branch, focused on the investigation of natural phenomena as the way to study reality. Stoics called the source of all being "Mind-Fire," which has consciousness, purpose, and will. It was both creator and material of the universe and went by many names, among them God, Nature, Reason, and Providence. This view is a form of *pantheism*, in which God is to the universe as the human soul is to the body. Regarding the fate of humans upon death, there was a difference of opinion among Stoics as to whether death was an end or

merely a transition to another state. This ambivalence is evident in Seneca's writings.

3. Ethics, the third branch of knowledge, is what made Stoic philosophy most influential. Stoics, who greatly admired Socrates, saw the real business of philosophy as a guide for human conduct. It was this concern that attracted many Romans, who had long held such virtues as courage, duty, self-discipline, and fair dealing in the highest esteem.

The following five points describe the principles of Stoicism:

1. Human happiness is attained by "living according to Nature," or following the rational law of our being. That was how the Stoics defined virtue.

2. Control of the inner self is primary. The Stoics called this *apatheia*; it means that one is master of instead of slave to one's sensations and emotions. One seeks to achieve an inner detachment and tranquillity. The modern derivative "apathy" is misleading, since it is a negative term denoting indifference rather than a positive notion of inner equilibrium—although for the Stoics *apatheia* enabled a person to be "indifferent" in a healthy sense to being affected by the external circumstances of life.

3. Duty to others—family, friends, slaves, the state, the world (which the Stoics called *Cosmopolis,* the "universe city.")—is viewed as central, and these duties required compassion, justice, tolerance and active help. However, Stoicism was not revolutionary or transformative in its approach to social and political structures. For example, the Stoics advocated humane treatment of slaves as fellow human beings but did not advocate the abolition of slavery, and while they attributed full intelligence to women (there were female Stoic philosophers) they did not advocate the civil equality and independence of women.

4. Humans are seen as inherently social as well as reasoning creatures. It was this belief in human reasoning powers, combined with its monistic view of reality, which led Stoicism to develop one of the most important ideas in the Western world: natural law. Natural law refers to the idea of universal moral principles that are inherent in reason itself, and all human beings have a basic sense of these universal laws through their reason.

5. The Stoics accepted all events as a part of a universal network of cause and effect which they interpreted as the benevolent unfolding of the divine purpose. Humans have very limited power to change events, but they do have the power to change their attitudes and behavior.

Cicero (106–43 BCE)   Although often associated with Stoicism, Cicero was eclectic philosophically, borrowing from various schools of thought. He drew on aspects of Aristotle's cosmology and political thought. In his ethical teaching he was deeply indebted to Stoicism, and incorporated Plato's ideas of soul-body dualism and the immortality of the soul.

In popularizing Greek philosophical thought in a series of essays, generally cast in dialogue form, Cicero found himself compelled to invent a philosophical vocabulary for a language that did not possess one, and very well he did indeed, for much of it sticks with us yet. For instance, in ethical discourse, following Cicero we speak of "virtue," our derivative of the Latin *virtus*, whereas the Greek original *aretê* has no common, modern offspring. Of the four "philosophical virtues," three—"temperance," "justice," and "fortitude"—are close derivatives of the Latin Cicero used to translate now-obscure Greek terms. Only "wisdom" represents Anglo-Saxon in this catalogue of virtues, replacing Cicero's *sapientia*. Cicero added a great deal of grace and style to philosophical writing, although he contributed virtually nothing original except perhaps to practical political philosophy. Yet to a Medieval and early Renaissance world that had no access to, or not enough Greek to read, the works of Greek philosophy, he was the chief teacher. Cicero's essay *On Duties* remains an eminently readable ethical treatise, presenting as it does a Stoic moral ideal found congenial by many well into the nineteenth century.

As we saw in the previous chapter, one of Cicero's major works was his *Republic,* a long book based on Plato's *Republic* which actually gave us the (Latin) name by which we refer to Plato's great dialogue. While most of Cicero's *Republic* has been lost, the longest surviving portion is a narrative passage called "The Dream of Scipio." Here Cicero describes a vision of the universe a younger member of the great family of the Scipios had in a dream. The young man's grandfather Scipio Africanus (237–183 BCE), the conqueror of Carthage, guides his grandson through the cosmos, pointing out the workings of the Aristotelian geocentric universe, where, though the earth is the center, it is the least important spot in the universe. The center is in effect the bottom. By service to his country the younger Scipio can ascend to the divine realm after death. From the high point of heaven the grandfather explains how the grandson can merit a place there after death:

> But listen, Africanus, so that you will be all the more eager to protect your commonwealth. For all those who have preserved, aided, and improved their native country there is a sure, fixed place reserved in heaven where the blessed may enjoy eternity. Nothing, you see, is more acceptable to that chief god who rules all the universe than the assemblies and gatherings of people bound together by law—these we call "states." The guides [the "rectors"] and preservers of them go forth from here and return here. (*Dream of Scipio* 3.1)

Scipio's Dream is an example of Cicero's philosophical eclecticism. The description of the universe is Aristotelian, the portrayal of the soul and its destiny is taken almost verbatim from Plato's *Phaedrus*, and Africanus's message to his grandson is a Stoic ethics of duty.

Seneca   Seneca was born in Cordoba, Spain possibly in 4 BCE into a distinguished and educated family (he mentions that his mother studied philosophy!). His father was a teacher of rhetoric, and both his two brothers and his brother-in-law served in the government. Seneca learned the philosophy of Stoicism from his father and his tutors. Despite chronic physical problems—which may have been mitigated by a practiced Stoic discipline—he led an active political life. Educated in the law, he served in a number of governmental positions, as magistrate, senator, and tutor and adviser to the adoles-

cent Nero. But political appointments during the Julio-Claudian dynasty were uncertain and often dangerous. Those who survived often found it difficult to remain in favor with the reigning monarch. Seneca was exiled twice, in the reigns of Caligula and Claudius. After Nero came to power, Seneca and a military commander named Burrus were the real power behind the young Nero for several years. Then Seneca fell out of favor and voluntarily retired from public life. After a few years, however, Nero ordered Seneca's death by suicide because he believed him (probably rightly) to be implicated in a plot to assassinate him. The Roman historian Tacitus reports on the circumstances of his suicide. The assessment of Seneca's political career is that he was a talented and able administrator, but he was also very acquisitive. He was reputed to have accumulated an estate greater than that of the emperor, a fact that many have noted is contradictory to his writings recommending the simple life. At the same time, he was widely admired as a man of wisdom who in his personal life lived simply and austerely.

Seneca spent the periods of exile in writing, and his literary output was prodigious. He wrote plays, satires, and works on natural science, as well as letters that were written with an eye to publication. His essays make him the competitor with the sixteenth-century writer Montaigne for the title of father of the essay.

Seneca's large influence in Western civilization over many centuries rivaled that of Cicero. Early Christians saw in Seneca's writings a kindred spirit, and an anonymous writer in late antiquity created a correspondence between Seneca and the apostle Paul, which was accepted as authentic by the fourth-century Church Fathers Jerome and Augustine. Seneca provided European civilization with the only surviving Roman tragedies composed on the classical Athenian model. His tragedies do not seem to have been composed for actual stage performance, but they survived into the Middle Ages as the only model for tragic drama, since the Greek tragedies were inaccessible in the West for a thousand years. Seneca's plays continued to be widely read and admired during the Renaissance, and clearly influenced Shakespeare. The witches in *Macbeth* with their cauldron of repellent ingredients go back to Seneca's witch *Medea*, not to Euripides' tragic heroine of that name. A choral song in the same Senecan play predicts that some day sailors will cross the great ocean and discover a new land. Christopher Columbus's son Ferdinand noted in the margin of his copy of Seneca, "My father fulfilled this prophecy!" Queen Elizabeth I read and translated Seneca's works, and the Protestant Reformer John Calvin's first published book was a translation of Seneca's *De Clementia* (On Mercy).

Seneca's most widely read text today is *Epistulae Morales ad Lucilium* (Moral Letters to Lucilius). These are 124 letters of advice he wrote to his younger friend Lucilius, a man from Pompeii who was governor of Sicily at the time. Although these are letters to a friend, Seneca clearly wrote them with an eye to their eventual publication, and they have the form of short essays. We will highlight a few important themes from some of the letters in this text. We recommend that the reader pay careful attention to Seneca's rhetorical style. He is often in dialogue with the Epicureans. He first states their position and then refutes it.

In Letter V Seneca describes the life of the ideal Stoic, whose motto is "to live in conformity with nature"—that is, according to the reason that manifests itself in the workings of nature including human life. This involves following the mean between the extremes of extravagance and asceticism, not standing out externally but being inwardly free and disciplined, and limiting one's desires. Throughout the *Letters* Seneca draws attention to similarities between the Epicureans and the Stoics despite their differences. In Letter IX he discusses *apatheia* as a virtue recommended by both schools, observing that the ideal Stoic "feels his troubles but overcomes them," while the ideal Epicurean "does not even feel them." Seneca also praises friendship and community as a natural human desire and necessary to the good life, even though the wise person should cultivate self-sufficiency. Letter XVI is an important statement on the purpose of philosophy, which is to teach us how to live a good and happy life: "It moulds and builds the personality, orders one's life, regulates one's

This violent display of gladiatorial combat preserves for us a sense of how Romans understood human emotion in relation to their larger destiny. Baccibus, urged to fight the victor Astacius, hesitates with fear in his backward glance. In the end, however, he must put aside his emotion and give himself over to his fate. In his *Epistles,* Seneca writes of the beast fighters, or *bestiarii,* who were thrown to the animals as punishment and spectacle. Seneca relates how a German prisoner slated to be thrown into the ring chose instead to take his own life. Recognizing that the prisoner wished to free himself from servitude, Seneca praised him: "What a brave fellow! He surely deserved to be allowed to choose his fate! How bravely he would have wielded a sword." *Epistles,* LXX.20

Figure III-5 The Gladiator Mosaics. Late third-early fourth century CE. Colored stone mosaic. Galleria Borghese, Rome. Courtesy of Scala/Art Resource, NY.

conduct. . . . Without it no one can lead a life free of fear or worry." This is true whether the universe and our lives are governed by divine providence, fate, or chance.

Seeking the wisdom and inner tranquility that philosophy brings means dealing with aging and death, which are the theme of Letter XXVI. They are a natural process, and the wise person does not fear them: "Moving to one's end through nature's own gentle process of dissolution—is there a better way of leaving life than that?" The way to approach death wisely is to affirm one's inner freedom: "A person who has learned how to die has unlearned how to be a slave." In Letter XLI Seneca very interestingly discusses religion and God from a Stoic perspective: "God is near you, is with you, is inside you." God is the cosmic Reason that manifests itself as nature and in the human soul and is experienced as the element of the sacred or holy in human religious experience. Letter XC contains a fascinating account of human origins and early history, in which Seneca draws on traditional Greek and Roman accounts of an original "golden age" but interprets them in terms of the difference between the philosophical search for wisdom and the practical inventions needed for the emergence of human civilization.

Finally, part of the great value of reading the *Letters from a Stoic* is that Seneca not only shares insights into Stoic wisdom and its lessons for life, but also gives us a vivid picture of aspects of Roman life in his time. In Letter XVIII, for example, he describes the hustle and bustle of the Roman Feast of Saturnalia, in December, which Christianity replaced with Christmas in the fourth century. In other letters he talks about the games in the arena (such as the gladiatorial contests), warning of how susceptible each of us is to being swept along by crowds; the importance of exercising in moderation instead of being a body-building fanatic; architecture; plumbing; farming; sea travel; and medicine. In Letter LXXXVIII, Seneca gives us a picture of Roman education, and what he describes as "liberal studies" would become a source of the idea of the liberal arts and sciences. In that connection he mentions what literature a well-educated Roman read: Greek authors such as Homer, and Roman authors including Cicero, Virgil, and Ovid. He contrasts his own era, during the first hundred years

of the Empire, unfavorably with the old days of the Republic, invoking figures such as Scipio Africanus.

Very importantly, in Letter XLVII Seneca sharply criticizes the way in which Romans typically treat their slaves, arguing with his Stoic belief in our universal humanity that slave and free are fellow human beings who are both entitled to respect and kindness. Unlike Aristotle, who argued that there are "natural slaves," Seneca treats slavery as an accidental contingency of human life: the person who is now free might have been, and could still become, a slave; and the slave might well become a free person, as some (like the Stoic Epictetus) in fact did. Notice, however, that Seneca does not argue against slavery, an institution that was centuries old and considered essential to the functioning of Roman society, but simply for the humane treatment of slaves.

ROMAN PHILOSOPHY IN THE LATER ROMAN EMPIRE

The great Stoic emperor Marcus Aurelius (121–180 CE), one of the "Five Good Emperors" whose reigns spanned the second century, wrote one of the classics of Stoic philosophy, a book of what he called *Meditations* written not in Latin but in Greek, the language of philosophy enjoying a revival among Roman intellectuals at the time. These essays, composed during moments snatched in his tent as he led armies on campaigns to defend the overstretched frontiers of the empire, reveal a thoughtful, duty-obsessed Stoic, reverent and resigned, in keeping with the outlook of that school of thought. The Western world has read and been instructed by the *Meditations* down to the present day. It was very popular, for example, among the British during the Victorian Age in the nineteenth century, who saw themselves as creating a modern empire on the scale of the ancient Romans. The Victorian poet and cultural critic Matthew Arnold extolled Marcus Aurelius, seeing his view of life as very similar to that of Christianity.

Plotinus (205–250 CE) was a Greek, living in Alexandria, but clearly an influential figure in the Roman philosophical world. Plotinus was the father of Neoplatonism, the dominant form of Platonism in the third and fourth centuries. He and his student Porphyry, who were both pagans and opponents of Christianity, would be an important influence on Augustine, who became a Christian Neoplatonist. A fuller discussion of the main ideas of Neoplatonism appears in Chapter Eight.

The last influential philosopher of the Roman Empire was Boethius (ca. 480–ca. 524 CE), a Roman senator who lived during the period after the empire in the West was taken over by "barbarian" rulers who relied for administration on the Romans who continued in the civil service. Entering public life because of family tradition and out of a Roman and philosophical sense of civic duty, Boethius served as a high official of the greatest of the Ostrogothic kings, Theodoric, though his loyalties seem to have always been to the old Empire. Boethius was convicted of plotting with the Byzantine Roman emperor in the East to extend his power over the "barbarian" kingdom in the West, and for this he was sentenced to death by torture, a sentence that was carried out. Typically eclectic in his philosophical sources—including Platonism, Aristotelianism, and Stoicism—Boethius was a brilliant scholar who aspired to translate into Latin all the works of both Plato and Aristotle. While he did not achieve that goal, he did translate and write commentaries on all of Aristotle's books on logic, and wrote five more books of his own on logic. Boethius would become virtually the sole mediator of Aristotle's thought to medieval Europe for centuries, and in so doing laid the foundations for medieval Scholasticism. The Scholastics, of whom the greatest was Thomas Aquinas, used Boethius's works on Aristotelian logic to work out discrepancies and contradictions in the Bible and the Church Fathers.

While in prison Boethius wrote a book called *The Consolation of Philosophy* (ca. 524 CE), which like much Roman philosophical writing has a meditative and religious tone. In the book the despondent Boethius receives a supernatural visitor in his cell, Philosophy, represented as a woman clothed in white. By her arguments, interspersed and summed up with lyric poems, she turns him from despair to acceptance of his situation. The work resembles more closely Marcus Aurelius's *Meditations* and Augustine's *Confessions* than anything else in antiquity. Remarkably, though Boethius was almost certainly a Christian and even wrote a treatise on the Trinity, only a philosophical faith, not a revealed dogma, appears in his work. *The Consolation of Philosophy* has been throughout the centuries, from the Middle Ages down to the recent past, one of the most widely read and influential books of the Western tradition. After Boethius the Western philosophical tradition becomes thoroughly Christian, and philosophy subordinated to theology.

QUESTIONS FOR DISCUSSION AND REFLECTION

1. Explain the philosophy of skepticism and its origins.

2. Epicureanism and Stoicism became distinctively Roman philosophies. Explain the beliefs and practices of each.

3. Discuss the life and contributions of Cicero.

4. Discuss the political life of Seneca.

5. Select five of Seneca's Letters and explain the advice Seneca is giving.

6. Which of Seneca's Letters do you find most applicable to your life? Explain in detail.

SUGGESTIONS FOR FURTHER READING

Barnes, Jonathan and Miriam T. Griffin, editors *Philosophia togata. II: Plato and Aristotle at Rome.* Oxford: Clarendon Press; New York: Oxford University Press, 1997.

Davis, Sally and Gilbert Lawall. *Cicero's Somnium Scipionis,* White Plains, NY: Longman, 1988.

Everitt, Anthony. *Cicero, the Life and Times of Rome's Greatest Politician.* New York: Random House, 2001.

Gruen, Erich S. *Studies in Greek Culture and Roman Policy.* Leiden; New York: E. J. Brill, 1990.

Long, A.A. *Hellenistic Philosophy: Stoics, Epicureans, Sceptics,* 2nd ed. Berkeley, CA: University of California Press, 1986.

Seneca. *Letters from a Stoic.* Selected and translated by Robin Campbell. London: Penguin Classics, 1969, rpt. 1988.

Seneca. *Thyestes.* Duckworth Companions to Greek and Roman Tragedy. Translation and commentary by P. J. Davis. London: Duckworth, 2003.

The Cambridge Companion to Greek and Roman Philosophy. Edited by David Sedley. Cambridge: Cambridge University Press, 2003.

Plate 2 Black Obelisk of Shalmaneser III, from Nimrud (ancient Kalhu), northern Iraq, Neo-Assyrian 858–824 BCE, 197.85 × 45.08 cm. British Museum. Courtesy of Werner Forman/Corbis.

Plate 1 Stele of Hammurabi, detail of the upper section of the stele, from Susa (modern Shush, Iran). ca. 1792–1750 BCE Basalt, height of stele approx. 7' (2.13 m), height of relief 28" (71.1 cm). Musée du Louvre, Paris. Hervé Lewandowki. Courtesy of Réunion des Musées Nationaux/Art Resource, NY.

Plate 3 Moses Gives Water to the Tribes, detail of a wall painting from a house-synagogue, Dura-Europos, Syria. 244–45. Tempera on plaster. Courtesy of Art Resource, NY.

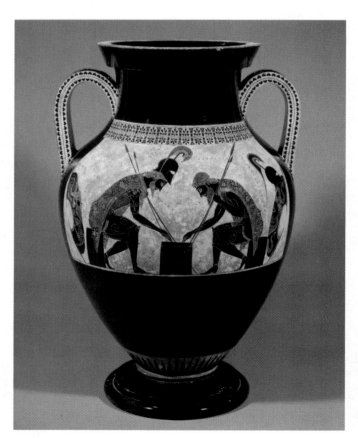

Plate 4 Exekias. *Achilles and Ajax Playing Draughts.* ca. 530 BCE. Black-figure decoration on an amphora. Ceramic, height of amphora 26⅜" (67 cm). Museo Gregoriano Etrusco, Vatican Museums, Vatican State. Courtesy of Scala/Art Resource, NY.

Plate 5 Iktinos and Kallikrates. Parthenon, Acropolis, Athens. 447–438 BCE. Marble. View from the northwest. Courtesy of Art Resource, NY.

Plate 6 Praxiteles. *Aphrodite of Knidos,* Roman copy after the Greek original marble of ca. 350–330 BCE. Marble, height 6'8" (2.03 m). Museo Pio Clementino, Vatican Museums, Vatican State. Courtesy of Nimatallah/Art Resource, NY.

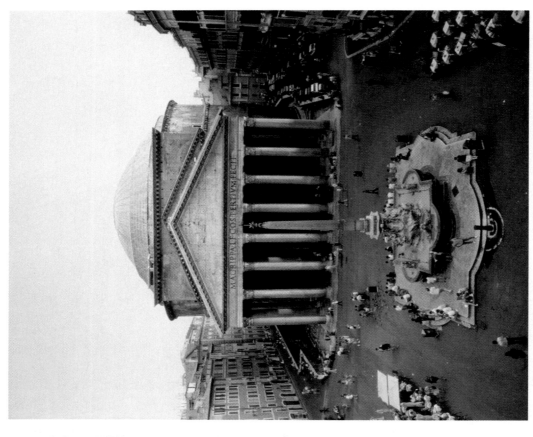

Plate 8 Pantheon, Rome. ca. 118–128 CE. Courtesy of Canali Photobank.

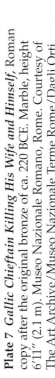

Plate 7 *Gallic Chieftain Killing His Wife and Himself,* Roman copy after the original bronze of ca. 220 BCE. Marble, height 6'11" (2.1 m). Museo Nazionale Romano, Rome. Courtesy of The Art Archive/Museo Nazionale Terme Rome/Dagli Orti.

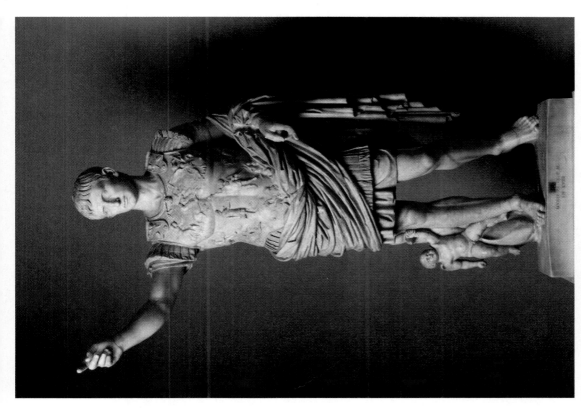

Plate 10 *Augustus of Primaporta.* Early first century CE (perhaps a copy of a bronze original of ca. 20 CE). Marble, originally painted, height 6′8″ (2.03 m). Musei Vaticani, Braccio Nuovo, Rome. Courtesy of Araldo de Luca/Corbis.

Plate 9 **Interior of the Pantheon.** 125–128 CE Brick, concrete, marble, veneer. Courtesy of Vanni Archive/Corbis.

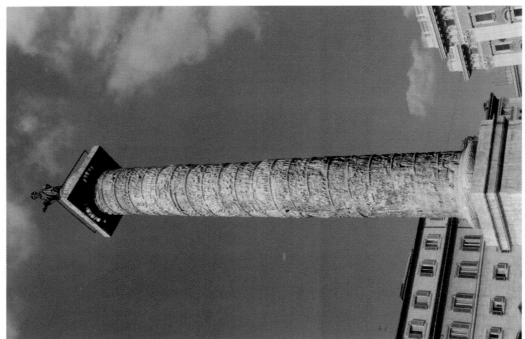

Plate 12 *Column of Trajan*. Rome. 106–113 CE. Marble, overall height with base 125′ (38m), column alone, 97′8″ (29.77m). Courtesy of Alinari Archives/Corbis.

Plate 11 *Marcus Aurelius*. 161–80 CE. Bronze, originally gilded. Height of statue 11′6″ (3.5m). Formerly in Piazza del Campidoglio, Rome. Courtesy of Alinari Archives/Corbis.

**Plate 13 Anthemius of Tralles
and Isidorus of Miletus. Church
of Hagia Sophia,** Istanbul, Turkey.
532–37. View from the southwest.
Courtesy of Francesco
Venturi/Corbis.

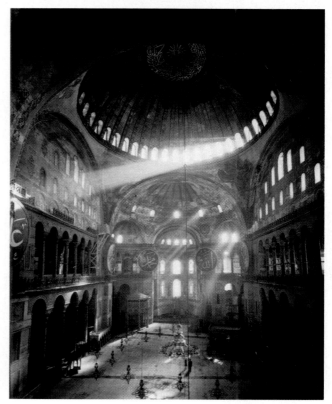

Plate 14 Church of Hagia Sophia.
(interior view). Courtesy of Art
Resource, NY.

Plate 15 Church of San Vitale, Ravenna, Italy. Begun ca. 520–47. Courtesy of Angelo Hornak/Corbis.

Plate 16 *Empress Theodora and Her Attendants*, mosaic on south wall of the apse, Church of San Vitale. ca. 547. 8'8" × 12' (2.64 × 3.65 m). Courtesy of Scala/Art Resource, NY.

SECTION FOUR

TIMELINE IV

THE MIDDLE AGES: PART I

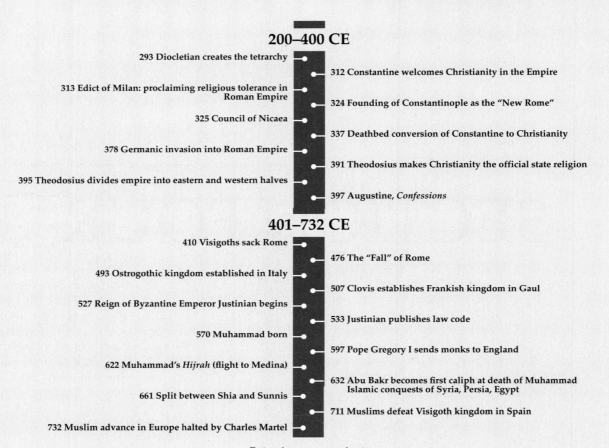

200–400 CE

293 Diocletian creates the tetrarchy

312 Constantine welcomes Christianity in the Empire

313 Edict of Milan: proclaiming religious tolerance in Roman Empire

324 Founding of Constantinople as the "New Rome"

325 Council of Nicaea

337 Deathbed conversion of Constantine to Christianity

378 Germanic invasion into Roman Empire

391 Theodosius makes Christianity the official state religion

395 Theodosius divides empire into eastern and western halves

397 Augustine, *Confessions*

401–732 CE

410 Visigoths sack Rome

476 The "Fall" of Rome

493 Ostrogothic kingdom established in Italy

507 Clovis establishes Frankish kingdom in Gaul

527 Reign of Byzantine Emperor Justinian begins

533 Justinian publishes law code

570 Muhammad born

597 Pope Gregory I sends monks to England

622 Muhammad's *Hijrah* (flight to Medina)

632 Abu Bakr becomes first caliph at death of Muhammad Islamic conquests of Syria, Persia, Egypt

661 Split between Shia and Sunnis

711 Muslims defeat Visigoth kingdom in Spain

732 Muslim advance in Europe halted by Charles Martel

Dates given are approximate

THE MIDDLE AGES: PART I

In his classic work from the eighteenth century, *The Decline and Fall of the Roman Empire*, British historian Edward Gibbon posited the theory that by 476 CE the Roman Empire had ceased to exist. According to the Gibbon thesis, the classical civilization that had survived and thrived since the ancient Greeks came to a crashing halt and brought about a "Dark Ages" that lasted a millennium. Gibbon's argument proved powerfully attractive to historians. Today scholars take a different view. Instead of seeing calamity and collapse, scholars recognize the period between 400 and 800 CE as one of remarkable vigor and achievement. In this section we will see that rather than speaking of a final "fall" taking place in 476, the Roman Empire actually experienced a complex and long-lasting set of transformations.

Central to those transformations was the dividing of the Roman Empire into eastern and western territories. Indeed, while a non-Roman general sat on the throne of the western Empire in 476, the eastern Roman Empire, called Byzantium, continued to thrive well into the fourteenth century. It was the eastern Empire that served as an important conduit to the West of ancient Greek values, science, philosophy, literature, and art.

The idea of the "fall" of the Roman Empire in 476 suggests another crucial transformation: the massive influx of Germanic tribes from present-day central and Eastern Europe into the West. Peoples such as the Angles and Saxons in Britain, the Gauls in France, and the Lombards in Italy all first make their appearance in the West during this time.

Christianity, a fledgling religion before this period, becomes the glue that binds the West together. In the Middle Ages, classical culture will be reinterpreted within a Christian worldview. Christianity will also spread to the new Germanic peoples in the West and provide a basis for assimilation into a common religious and cultural framework.

While Christianity becomes the dominant faith in the West during this period, it will not be the only one. Judaism continues to make important contributions to the Western world, and the rise of Islam will both contribute to and challenge the West in significant ways. Muslims will give the West its numbers (Arabic numerals), algebra, and chemistry symbols. Islamic achievements in art and architecture are remarkable, and will have important and lasting influences on European artistic developments. In short, it is during this period that the idea of the West—in its geographic, religious, and cultural expressions—begins to take shape. The period from 400 to 800 will lay the groundwork for the emergence of modern Western civilization.

A CENTURY OF DISORDER, 180–284

The age of the five good emperors gave way to a century of disorder and chaos. The reign of Marcus Aurelius's dissolute and pleasure-loving son Commodus (180–192) was disastrous. He appointed unqualified friends to important posts, and was violent and cruel to others. Finally a small band of conspirators assassinated him on 31 December, 192 CE.

After Commodus's death there was no emperor and no provision for a successor. The election of a new ruler reverted to the Senate, which chose one of its own, the soldier-senator Pertinax. But he was too strict with the praetorian guards, who murdered him after only three months in office. Then the soldiers auctioned off the office of emperor. A rich old senator, Didius Julianus, won, but he was not acceptable to the scandalized army commanders in the provinces. One of them, Septimius Severus (146–211 CE), the governor of Pannonia (roughly modern Austria), marched on Rome and, after a massive battle with another contender for the throne involving as many as three hundred thousand troops, seized power. The new emperor proscribed his enemies, killed all of the senators who had sided against him, and ousted members of the senatorial class from important administrative and military posts.

Septimius achieved his aim of founding a military state but his successes brought many problems, such as a debased coinage and high taxes. To his sons, Caracalla and Geta, Septimius on his deathbed stated his legacy: "Be harmonious with one another, keep the army happy with money, and don't bother with anything else." They followed his advice, but under their rule the army provided the empire with neither peace at home nor security from its enemies. Carcalla (ruled 211–217) quickly got rid of Geta and ruled as dictator. He treated his soldiers well, and in 217 he extended Roman citizenship to all provincials, but few mourned when he was murdered in 217.

This extinction of the family of the Severi ushered in the period that historians call the military anarchy, which lasted some fifty years, from 235 to 284. Twenty-five or more major emperors and a host of usurpers held power during this period, and the wonder is that the empire survived at all.

Starting with the reign of Decius (249–251), calamities of all kinds began to afflict the empire. Civil wars and constant invasions of the empire from the north and the east evidently convinced Decius that the gods were deserting Rome because the Christians, a growing element in the population, scorned the ancient Roman deities. Therefore, to punish the Christians and to gain revenue for his campaigns, Decius began a persecution of the Christians, especially prominent Christian leaders, which caused the death of the bishop of Rome, Pope Fabian, and Saint Cyprian, the eminent bishop of Carthage. However, after a reign of less than two years Decius was killed in a battle against the German Goths in 251.

Decius's successor was Trebonian Gallus. In Gallus's reign of two years, he witnessed even more disasters than had Decius, as the crisis of the empire grew more serious. He held off attacks in the north, but the Persians seized Syria and sacked the great city of Antioch. Furthermore, a plague swept over the empire. Gallus's soldiers lost faith in their leader and murdered him in 253.

The rule of Valerian and Gallienus, starting in 253, marks the low watermark of Roman fortunes in the third century. The empire almost dissolved at this time under a succession of disasters. Plague raged in large parts of the Roman world. Valerian himself lost his army and was captured by the Persians while he was advancing into Mesopotamia in 260. The Goths built ships, crossed the Black Sea, and fell upon the rich cities of Asia Minor. Other groups of Germans invaded Greece and sacked the ancient shrines of Olympia and Delphi. In the west, still other bands of barbarians, finding little resistance, swept across Gaul and Spain, sacking and pillaging, and even crossed over into the rich provinces of Rome in North Africa.

When Gallienus was murdered at Milan in 268, his empire was fragmented, his money was debased and almost worthless, and the Roman Empire showed every sign of dissolution. However, this proved to be the darkness before the dawn. His successor Claudius Gothicus in 268 won a great victory over the Goths at Naissus (Nish, in southeastern Yugoslavia, near the Danube). But soon thereafter he contracted the plague and died in 270.

The successor to Claudius Gothicus was Aurelian (270–275), one of the most important and successful Roman emperors of the third century. He was a stern soldier-emperor who had enormous energy. First he won successive victories over the Alemanii, the Vandals, and the Goths on the northern frontier, thus pacifying the area for many years. He also decided to abandon the province of Dacia, which lay to the east of the Danube, considering that the province was too exposed to barbarian attack. He moved those Romans and Dacians who wanted to remain in the empire south of the Danube. When he returned to Rome he ordered the wall that is now called the Aurelian Wall to be built around the city of Rome. He also began planning the reorganization of the coinage. Thus by 275, when Aurelian too fell by the hand of an assassin, this *Restitutor orbis* (restorer of the world), as Aurelian called himself on his coins, had militarily restored the Roman Empire, with the exception of

Like most Roman emperors, Constantine employed art as a forum for imperial propaganda. The most dramatic example is this colossal seated statue, which originally measured over 30 feet tall. At 8 feet 6 inches, the head alone measures much larger than a standing human and conveys a deep psychological intensity, particularly through its enormous, piercing eyes. Like the *Augustus of Primaporta* [Plate 10], the statue of Constantine exhibits perfect, stylized features in order to project an attitude of imperial power and dignity, disavowing any potential for human frailty. The Basilica sculpture served a practical purpose as well: in effect, the statue acted as a stand-in for Constantine in legal situations when the emperor's presence was required but he was absent from Rome.

Figure IV-1 *Constantine the Great,* from the Basilica of Maxentius and Constantine, Rome. 325–26 CE Marble, height of head 8′6″ (2.6 m). Palazzo dei Conservatori, Rome. Courtesy of Carmen Redondo/Corbis.

the province of Dacia, to the borders that it had enjoyed in the days of Marcus Aurelius.

From 275 to 284 Aurelian's successors maintained the empire as it had been reconstituted. However, they either chose not to or were not able to effect the needed reorganization of the whole Roman structure, its army, its administration, and its monetary system. This work was to be undertaken by Diocletian (284–305). His almost total reorganization of the Roman state into an eastern empire ushered in a new era in Roman history, which is now usually called by historians the Late Empire.

REORGANIZING THE EMPIRE

The Late Roman Empire was marked by fundamental transformations brought about under the emperors Diocletian (284–305), Constantine (306–337), and their successors. When people speak of the Roman Empire, they normally have in mind the united, dynamic, pagan empire that was in existence from 27 BCE to 284 CE. The Later Roman Empire, often called the Dominate (284–476), was far different. By 400, Christianity had been adopted as the official religion, and the Church was operating virtually as an arm of the government. The unity of the

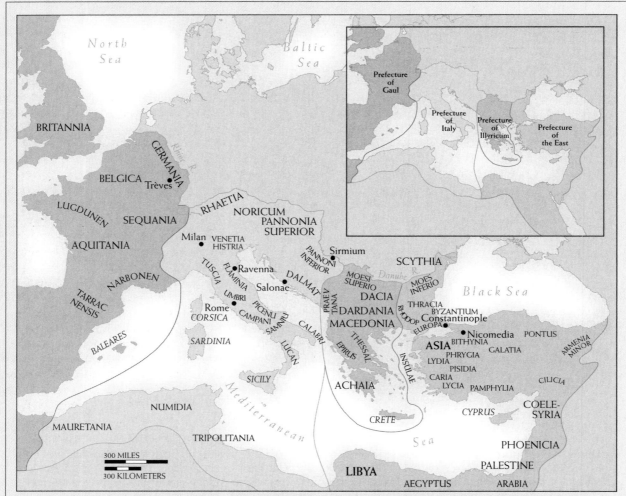

Divisions of the Roman Empire under Diocletian. Diocletian divided the sprawling empire into four prefectures for more effective government and defense. The inset map shows their boundaries and the large map gives some details of regions and provinces. The major division between East and West was along the line running from north to south between Pannonia and Moesia. Reprinted from *The Heritage of World Civilizations*, Seventh Edition, by Albert M. Craig et al. (2006), Prentice-Hall, Inc.

Roman Empire had been broken, and there were in fact two empires: the Eastern with its capital at Constantinople and the Western with its capital, for much of the time, at Ravenna in Italy. These two governments were supposed to co-operate, but in fact each acted largely independently, and the Eastern emperors were generally willing to sacrifice the West when it was in their interest to do so. In 284, Diocletian was made emperor by the army. His goal upon assuming the throne was to restore order and

stability to an empire that had been driven to the brink of collapse for much of the third century. His first attempt at reform was to strengthen the power of the emperor. Diocletian took the title of *Dominus* meaning "lord and master"—the same term that slaves used to refer to their masters. This brought to an end the centuries-long practice of Roman emperors assuming the title of *Principate* or "first citizen" of the Republic. The emperor's new power came at the expense of Rome's traditional ruling authorities, especially the Senate. While republican institutions continued to exist under Diocletian, they were stripped of any real authority and functioned largely as ceremonial bodies.

Perhaps Diocletian's most significant reform came with his reorganization of the Roman Empire. In order to guard against civil war and defend against invaders from the north and east, Diocletian carved up the vast territorial empire into four administrative districts—two in the west and two in the east. Historians call this regime a "tetrarchy" or rule by four. Although each of the four administrative units was to be ruled by its own emperor, Diocletian became a sort of "senior" emperor. The four new districts were further subdivided into smaller administrative units of twelve (called dioceses after Diocletian) and ruled by separate governors who reported to the four emperors.

One important result of this subdivision of the empire was that Rome was no longer the capital of the Roman Empire. Each of the four new administrative districts had its own capital chosen for its strategic military and commercial importance. Milan became the capital of the prefecture of Italy, which included not only present-day Italy but most of North Africa as well. Sirmium near the Danube River was chosen as the capital of the prefecture of Illyricum (present-day Greece and the Balkans). Trier became the capital of the prefecture of Gaul, which incorporated present-day France, England, and Spain. Finally, Nicomedia was the capital of the prefecture of the East, located in Asia Minor. The territory of the East included much of the present-day Middle East. Diocletian ruled the empire from Nicomedia and did not even visit the city of Rome until he had been emperor for twenty years.

Diocletian also undertook a significant reorganization of the military. His first task was to enlarge the army in order to defend the frontiers from invasion. This he did successfully but at a high price. By the end of his reign, Roman forces numbered about 450,000 soldiers. His method of enlarging the army was to allow Germanic tribes to settle in Roman territory in exchange for serving in the military and to fight the encroachment of other Germanic tribes. This process would continue under his successors, and by the end of the fourth century, Germans made up the bulk of the Roman army in the West. Ultimately this system of bringing Germans into the Roman army to keep other Germans out of the empire proved futile. As we will see below, barbarians were able to fight their way into the empire with dramatic consequences for both Rome and the West.

While enlarging the army, Diocletian sought to strip the army, particularly its commanders, of influence in Roman political affairs. To that end, the emperor broke the army into smaller units and relieved commanders of responsibility for supplying and paying their troops, which made it more difficult to use army backing in a bid for power. In the image of an oriental potentate, Diocletian clothed himself in purple, jeweled robes and crown, carried a scepter, and was constantly surrounded by courtiers. He instigated elaborate court procedures. His imperial council was called the sacred consortium. Persons seeking an audience were required to prostrate themselves before him. He declared himself to be the representative of Jupiter on earth and assumed the name of Jovius, designating his co-*augustus*, Maximian, the representative of Hercules. Thus, Diocletian became an emperor who demanded not only respect and obedience from his subjects but worship. To defy him would be as if to defy a god. All of this served his purpose of reviving commitment on the part of the people to the ancient Roman religion.

At this time, the end of the fourth century, Christianity had spread widely throughout the empire, but it cannot be said that it was the dominant religion. A substantial number of the populace continued to practice Roman rites and a variety of other religions. Christian beliefs prevented its followers from performing the traditional Roman sacrifices. Diocletian believed their obstinacy threatened the unity and thus the security of empire. Hence in 299 he reinstituted a persecution of Christians. Over the next several years many lost their lives, their property, their churches and their sacred books.

In 305 Diocletian suddenly and voluntarily retired, convincing his co-emperors to retire along with him. Though Diocletian's goal as emperor was to prevent further civil strife, upon his retirement war broke out among leading contenders to the throne. For the next ten years as many as six men claimed to be emperor somewhere in the empire. With the backing of the army, Constantine, son of Constantius, ruler in the West and a part of the tetrachy, emerged as the most likely successor. Constantine won control over the Western empire in 312 and emerged as sole emperor in 324.

Though Constantine (about whom much more will be said below) abandoned the "tetrarchy," he did maintain the administrative structure of the empire put in place by Diocletian. Constantine accelerated the eastward shift when in 324, for military and commercial reasons, he selected an old Greek city, Byzantium (present-day Istanbul), as the new capital of the empire. Constantine renamed the city Constantinople (literally "Constantine's City") and sought to make it into a "New Rome" by building a forum, arena, and hippodrome.

Constantine believed that the Christian god had helped him gain his victory in his battle for the empire. His loyalty and commitment to Christianity grew as he solidified his control over the empire. Through the Edict of Milan he had instituted a program of tolerance toward religion in general. Constantine recognized the authority of Christian bishops over those within the church; likewise he began to consider himself "bishop of those outside," the one appointed by God to govern all the people. Constantine, however, soon discovered that there was not unity among Christians.

Christian centers had grown up throughout the Empire and were modeled on the administrative structure of the provinces. Patriarchs ruled five districts: Alexandria, Antioch (Syria), Constantinople, Jerusalem, and Rome. These were divided in areas called Metropolitans and ruled by archbishops. Beneath them were smaller communities ruled by bishops. Superior status was granted to the pope or bishop of Rome because of the patrimony of Peter.

As Christianity grew and spread, differences had arisen among the leaders concerning the correct understanding of the gospel message. A major source of dispute was the understanding of the person and role of Jesus of Nazareth. The center of the Christian message was that Jesus was the Son of God, but just what did that mean? Was Jesus then a god? Another Christian belief was that Jesus died for the sins of humanity. Can a god die for human iniquity? And what of monotheism? Can Christianity still be considered monotheistic if God has a son who is equally God? These and similar arguments, referred to as christological issues, were seri-

ous and divisive and Constantine wanted them resolved. He wanted Christianity to serve not only as personal salvation to the individual, but also as a uniting factor in the Empire. In an effort to resolve the deep division over christology, he called the first ecumenical council in 325 in Nicaea. There were two dominant parties, the Arians and the Athanasians. The resolution reached at this council favored the Athanasian position and was the one that Constantine approved. It did not satisfy a large body of Christians, but eventually became official Christian doctrine. Centuries of continued controversy over doctrinal differences would become one of the reasons for the later separation of the Christian Church into the Western Catholic and the Eastern Orthodox Churches. A more detailed discussion of these differences and the parties that supported them are discussed in Chapter Eight.

In 337 Constantine contracted a fatal illness, and on his deathbed was baptized by Eusebius, Bishop of Nicomedia. (Postponement of baptism as long as possible was by no means uncommon in fourth-century Christianity.) With Constantine the Christian Church had finally achieved social freedom, political independence, and cultural respectability.

Constantine gave the power of the throne to his three sons to be shared equally. His hope was that they would re-establish the "tetrarchy." This was not to be. His sons plunged the empire into yet another round of brutal civil war. In addition to internal trouble, the Visagoths and Ostrogoths threatened the west and the Persians pounded the east. In the latter part of the century a soldier named Theodosius rose to power. He settled matters in the east with the Persians and then, turning to the west, led his armies to victory against a German usurper. He had again united the empire.

A permanent result of this power struggle was the splitting of the empire into two parts: the Western Empire now included all territory west of the Balkan peninsula, and the Eastern Empire was everything east of the Balkans. This territorial division became official in 395, when Theodosius (ruled 379–395) died, leaving his son Arcadius as emperor of the eastern half and his son Honorius of the western. Constantinople remained the capital city of the East and the city of Ravenna on Italy's northeastern coast was chosen as capital of the West. East and

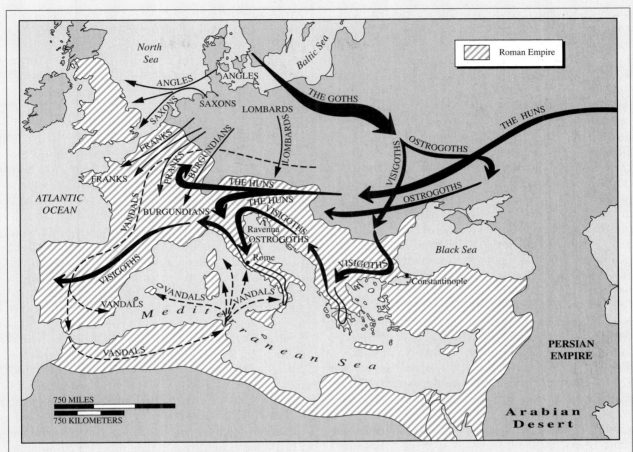

Barbarian Invasions. Reprinted from *The Western Heritage*, Combined Edition, Sixth Edition, by Donald Kagan, et al., (1998), Prentice-Hall, Inc.

West were intended to cooperate, but the permanent division launched the empire's halves on very different courses.

TRANSITIONS IN THE WESTERN EMPIRE

This was the state of affairs with the Roman Empire when the barbarian invasions began. What happened in the Western Roman Empire was merely part of a vast movement of peoples that affected all of the empires of the Eurasian continent. The Hsiung-nu invaded the Han Empire in China and succeeded in conquering its northern half; the Ephthalites seized portions of the Iranian plateau from the Sassanid emperors and of the Indus valley from the rulers of India; and the Huns moved west and south, towards Europe. The Germanic tribes, who had long lived along the Roman Empire's European frontier, were threatened by this move, and increased their pressure against the Romans.

The first tribe to gain entry was the Visigoths, who were admitted peacefully by the Romans in 376. They soon rebelled against imperial authority, however, and were deterred only by Eastern Roman diplomacy and bribes. The effort of defending itself against this threat subjected the Western Empire to intolerable strains, and, in order to defend Italy against invasion, the Western leaders eventually stripped their frontiers of troops. In 407, the Alans, Vandals, and Sueves crossed the Rhine unopposed. The Empire was thrown into turmoil, and other tribes soon joined the migrations into imperial territories.

To meet the threat of invaders from the east, the Romans pulled troops from other parts of the empire. By 410, the Roman army had all but abandoned defense of the British Isles in favor of meeting the invading Germanic forces in present-day central Europe. As a result, Britain was left vulnerable to attack, and, indeed, the Saxons from northern Germany invaded the island in the early part of the fifth century. Between 550 and 600 Britain was subjected to attack from groups of people whom scholars identify as "Anglo-Saxons." In the face of Germanic invasion, the indigenous Celts were increasingly confined to the northwest territory of the island. From this situation emerged the legend of King Arthur, a mythical Celtic knight who led his people to victory against marauding invaders.

The empire showed signs of collapse on its southern borders as well. In 430, in Roman North Africa, Augustine, Bishop of Hippo and a Father of the Latin Church, lay on his deathbed as the Vandals closed in upon his city. By 476, the last of the Roman emperors in the West was deposed, and barbarian leaders now controlled all the lands of the Western Empire.

It is somewhat misleading to call the invaders "barbarians," since at least some of the tribes had been neighbors of the Romans for centuries and had absorbed many Roman ways. Some had received a written language in the fourth century, and had accepted Christianity, although of a variety that the Roman Christians regarded as heretical. More importantly, the barbarians had absorbed Roman ideals to such a degree that they expended a great deal of effort to preserve the Roman administration, economy, and culture of those lands that they came to occupy. Under the Ostrogothic king Theodoric (took Ravenna 493), for instance, there was something of a Roman revival in Italy, and Roman scholars such as Boethius and Cassiodorus graced the barbarian king's court in the old imperial capital at Ravenna. In addition, it must be remembered that the number of barbarian invaders was actually very small compared to that of the Romans whom they were attempting to rule. As a consequence, they sought to legitimize their position in any way possible. By 500, the entire Western Empire was under the control of barbarian chieftains, but almost all of them had succeeded in obtaining authorization and delegated authority from Eastern emperors. Thus, in law the invaders were acting as agents of the Roman Emperor at Constantinople and had in theory succeeded in re-uniting the two halves of the empire.

THE ROLE OF CHRISTIANITY IN THE EMPIRE

The clashes between the pagan Roman Empire and the early church were marked by deficits on both sides: inflexibility, inability or even unwillingness to understand the opposition's point of view, and a paranoia which reached too quickly for simple answers. It may be that the early Apologists failed, because of either their excessive optimism about Roman justice and openness or their own inability to deal with Roman fears that Christianity was a subversive movement. The flaming polemics of some Christian writers and their zealous invitations to martyrdom may not have been among Christianity's finest hours, in that they only fed the frenzy of hostility. There can be no doubt, however, that the church's veneration of its martyrs, both men and women, was one of the most important aspects of its life and growth in the first three centuries of the Common Era. Martyrs were glorified as saints, stories about them grew into legends cherished by the Christian community, and their relics became objects of devotion.

Christianity itself, once it could claim a Roman emperor in its ranks, soon moved toward its own imperialism: the banning of other religions from its newly-won turf. Such banning took the form mainly of official neglect: no refurbishing of run-down shrines of traditional Roman religion, the removal of statuary from the provinces, the non-observances of formerly observed religious festivals. At times there were official bans against sacrifices and idolatry, and these bans could be ruthlessly enforced, but mainly in local areas. The only hiatus in Christianity's ascendancy was during the reign of Julian (ruled 360–363), who attempted to degrade Christianity and reestablish the traditional religions of the state. After him the pendulum swung back, and the road was open for the church to dominate religion in the empire once again. The Christian Roman Emperor Theodosius I declared

Christianity the state religion in 391 and banned public pagan rites.

The triumph of Christianity as the state religion of the Roman Empire had specifically fateful consequences for Jews, who of course stood in a unique relationship of rivalry with Christians. Relations between church and synagogue were not good in the fourth century, and in local areas there were occasionally anti-Jewish riots and synagogue burnings. Theodosius, in the Theodosian law code, actually improved the legal position of Jews somewhat, granting them freedom of worship, but under successive Roman governments toleration alternated with repression. The hostility between Jews and Christians certainly ran both ways, but it was the Christians who had the numbers and the power to impose their will. The characteristic Christian interpretation of Judaism is exemplified by the language used at the first ecumenical council of the church, at Nicaea in 325. The council changed the date of Easter, which had previously been observed at the same time as Passover, stating that "it appeared an unworthy thing that in the celebration of this most holy feast we should follow the practice of the Jews, who have impiously defiled their hands with enormous sin, and are, therefore, deservedly afflicted with blindness of soul. . . ."

Early Monasticism The discipline and strength of the Church would be greatly enhanced by the development of monasticism. The pagan world was familiar with the pattern of individuals withdrawing from the world to devote themselves to a life of contemplation and study. Such persons gained a reputation for being both holy and wise. The Christian message, with its focus on the individual, encouraged the monastic life. It also appealed to the poor who, denied education, believed that the life of an ascetic would grant them wisdom and holiness.

The earliest monastics were hermits, called anchorites. They were individuals who withdrew to the desert and lived in crude huts or caves, ate what food they could scavenge, and fought to overcome the demons of physical desires. Soon others gathered in the same vicinity. A loose community was formed in which they shared a common worship and adopted rules for this semi-communal structure. A fourth-century biography called the *Life of St Anthony* (thought to be largely fiction) did much to popularize the movement.

Monasticism first developed in the East and did not spread to the West until the fourth century. Eastern and Western monasticism evolved into somewhat different patterns. There were two types, eremites (hermits) and cenobites; both were popular in the East. Cenobite, or group orders, established themselves in Constantinople and other urban centers. Eastern monasticism played a much more active role in the Church. The patriarchs, the titular heads of the Eastern Church, were chosen from among monastic communities, as were all their fellow bishops. The great theologians of the Eastern Church were monks.

Monasteries in the West did not generally establish themselves in urban areas. Benedict of Nursia established the Benedictine Order in about 529 under the sponsorship of Pope Gregory the Great. He wrote a rule for monastic life, *The Rule of St. Benedict*, which served as a model document for many future monastic groups in the West. It was monks in both East and West who spread the message of Christianity. Within a few centuries, through the work of missionaries, the lands in both the East and the West of the empire had been brought under the influence of the Christian Church. The major and important difference, however, was that the language of the Church in the West was that of Latin, while the language of the Eastern Church was either Greek or the vernacular of the area. It was Eastern missionary monks who in the ninth century created the Russian language so as to establish the Christian religion in what became Russia.

The Church was especially important in the West during the long disordered period following the barbarian takeover. It was the pope who stood for both religious and secular power. The papacy maintained, insofar as was possible given the troubled times and scanty resources, imperial standards in administration, justice, and learning. Monasteries helped through their preservation of ancient documents and in education. Therefore, in some measure the Roman legacy continued.

THE BYZANTINE EMPIRE

Though the Western Roman Empire had fallen to the Germans, the Empire in the East enjoyed an economic revival during the fourth and fifth centuries. This recovery culminated with the emperor Justinian (527–565) and his empress, Theodora. Determined to restore imperial grandeur, the emperor patronized the arts and architecture. His reign saw the great codification of Roman law known as the *corpus iuris civilis* (The Body of Civil Law), which amounted to one of the most sophisticated legal codes ever created. Justinian also oversaw the construction of the great Church of the Holy Wisdom *(Hagia Sophia)* in Constantinople. Thanks to the influx of Hellenized easterners from Syria, Egypt, and elsewhere Constantinople also became the intellectual and cultural capital of the Empire. By the sixth century the city had at last become Constantine's "New Rome."

To meet the Persian threat, Justinian built up the army and navy. Aided by his great general Belisarius, the emperor beat back the Persians on his eastern frontier. He then embarked upon an attempt to regain direct control of the lands of the Western Empire. North Africa was recovered from the Vandals, the richest part of Spain from the Visigoths, Italy from the Ostrogoths, and the Roman fleet seized the islands of the western Mediterranean. At the time of Justinian's death, much had been accomplished to restore political unity to Roman lands.

And yet this enterprise was a failure. The Persians had grown stronger while Justinian had been involved in his Western venture and were soon to involve the Eastern Empire in a long and mutually exhausting war. The people of the Eastern Empire were wearied of the heavy taxes that had financed Justinian's campaigns, and were unwilling to exert themselves to maintain these conquests. They abandoned dreams of restoring Mediterranean unity, and their hard-won conquests slowly slipped from their control. The Eastern Roman Empire now followed its own path of development, yielding to the dominant Greek culture of the eastern Mediterranean, and evolving into what historians call the Byzantine Empire.

The Emperor's attempted reconquest also had significant, although unanticipated, consequences in the East. His long Western wars and ambitious building programs had impoverished the empire. Slavic and Avar tribesmen pressed upon it from the north, and a revived Persian Empire seized some of the richest and most productive of the Byzantines' Asiatic provinces. Taxation grew ruinous and all dissent, especially when expressed in departures from the official form of religion, was ruthlessly repressed. The nadir of Eastern Roman fortunes was reached in the year 619, when the Avars by land besieged Constantinople and a Persian fleet was stationed just across the Hellespont. Imminent destruction triggered a remarkable burst of energy; the army was re-organized, the imperial treasury replenished, and, in a series of three brilliant campaigns concluded in 630, the Emperor Heraclius (610–641) defeated the Persians and restored his Empire's frontiers. Soon after his victory, according to legend, the emperor was told that Arab nomads had raided some villages in Palestine. He had not been concerned by such a minor matter. It proved to be anything but minor.

THE RISE AND SPREAD OF ISLAM

Eight decades of war between the Byzantine and Persian Empires had brought about a number of changes. Blocked by the Persians from reaching markets in Syria and Egypt by the old overland route, Eastern merchants had taken to shipping their goods over the Indian Ocean and landing their goods at the southeastern tip of the Arabian Peninsula. Here ivory, gold, dyes, spices, and slaves from Africa were added to the silks and jades of China and the pepper, mace, and nutmeg of India, and the goods were carried on the caravan route that ran along the Red Sea coast of Arabia and through the holy city of Mecca.

It was in Mecca in the early part of the seventh century that the great monotheistic religion, Islam, was born. Although Arabs recognized the existence of a supreme deity, each tribe had its own god. In 612 a man in the city of Mecca, a member of the ruling Quraysh tribe named Muhammad, began to preach a new message, one that he claimed was actually an old message: "God is one." He also, like the prophets of Israel and Jesus of Nazareth, called for a radical return to social justice. Muhammad claimed that he had been instructed by God in a series of revelations to preach this message. These revelations would ultimately constitute the Holy Scriptures of Islam, called the Qur'an. While Muhammad gained some followers he was not welcomed by all and was forced to flee to the town of Medina, where he refined Islam into the faith that

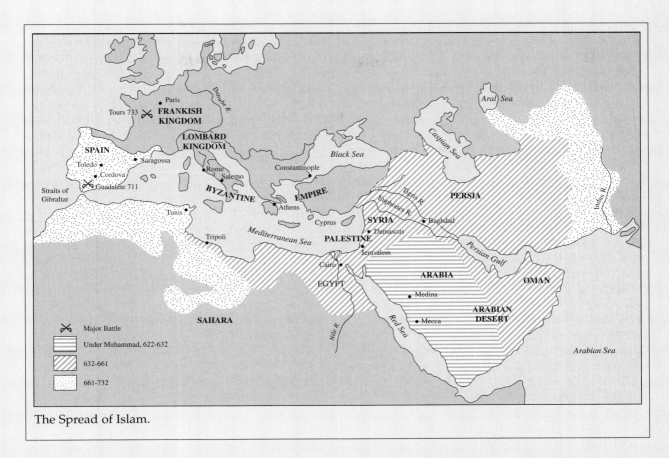

The Spread of Islam.

was eventually embraced by all the Arab world and whose adherents are called Muslims.

Following Muhammad's death, under the direction of the first four caliphs or "successors," the Arabs with breathtaking speed overran the Persian Empire, stripped the Byzantine Empire of some of its provinces and dominated northern Africa. During the eighth century Muslims established themselves in Sicily and much of Spain. Through conversion and conquest they spread the faith of Islam throughout the Mediterranean world. To the east, Islam's territory eventually extended into India and to the borders of China.

It has been asked how the Arabs were able to conquer such extensive, wealthy, and populous lands so quickly and establish so strong a hold that it is mostly unshaken to this day. Often Muslim Arabs were welcomed as liberators because they brought an end to oppressive governments and showed tolerance. The principles of the Qur'an

were a powerful attraction, and there were many who embraced Islam and joined forces with their former enemies to extend the faith to other lands.

Early in the history of Islam a split occurred over the manner in which the successors to Muhammad would be chosen. Within the space of twenty years this disagreement brought about civil war. The result was the basic division of Islam into *Sunni* and *Shia*.

THE CAROLINGIAN RENAISSANCE

Interestingly enough, Western Europe experienced a recovery during the eighth and ninth centuries. The Irish had embraced Christianity with fervor, and Irish missionaries carried their faith, learning, and art beyond the old borders of the Empire. The barbarian invasions had come to an end, and the Franks in France and the Angles and Saxons in England were able to bring a measure of political security to their lands. In 752, the Carolingian family seized royal power in France, and, for the next century an extraordinary series of individuals succeeded in bringing about what many historians have called "the Carolingian Renaissance."

The greatest figure of the time was King Charles the Great (771–814), best known by his French name Charlemagne. He brought unity to his realms, extended his territory in all directions and secured his frontiers, and provided his subjects a degree of peace and security that had been unknown for centuries in the West. He aspired to more than this, however, and brought about a cultural revival. The scholars assembled in his court emulated the Roman authors they had read when producing their new works of poetry, history, and biography. Carolingian script was introduced, a writing form that we continue to use to the present day. Artists and artisans created new and impressive works, all based upon the Roman and Byzantine models available to them. Perhaps the greatest enterprise, however, was to restore in the West the Roman Empire itself, at least as they conceived it to have been.

On Christmas Day in the year 800, the Pope in Rome crowned Charlemagne as the Holy Roman Emperor. The West had rejected the theoretical claim of the Byzantine emperor to be the heir to the Roman imperial power, and had claimed that distinction for itself. This was an action that angered the East and was an ongoing source of resentment. In the eyes of Charlemagne and his advisors, the Roman Empire meant imperial pomp, a high level of art and literature, internal peace and security, a professional bureaucracy, and a Church that worked in close cooperation with the State. All of this they had achieved as far as their means permitted. The Roman Empire also meant, however, the permanent concentration of political power in the hands of this Western emperor. This was harder to attain, since it was the custom of the Franks to divide the realm among the male heirs at the death of a monarch. Charlemagne was able to maintain the appearance of centralized authority while he lived, but civil wars broke out after his death, and the unity of the Carolingian realm had disappeared by the year 900.

ART OF THE EARLY MIDDLE AGES

Art and architecture of the Middle Ages primarily revolve around religion. Given the flourishing during this period of three major world religions—Christianity, Judaism, and Islam—it is not surprising that the arts shifted from a secular to a religious focus. This is not to say, however, that art and architecture existed solely to glorify God. On the contrary, much like the Roman emperors or the Egyptian kings, many rulers of the Middle Ages continued to use art and architecture to bring attention to themselves and their accomplishments, but under the guise of religion. Building monumental churches, for example, ostensibly celebrated God but simultaneously praised the pious governance of the rulers under whom they were built.

Along with newly-burgeoning religions, a variety of artistic media thrived during the Middle Ages. The glory of Byzantium is demonstrated in large part through its architecture. As part of a quest to reunite the Eastern and Western Empires, the emperor Justinian oversaw the construction of landmark churches in both Constantinople and Ravenna, Italy. The art of mosaic abounded during this period, embellishing houses of worship with images of Christ as well as of political rulers. Another aspect of religious art is found in the works surrounding centers of monastic living. Many convents and monasteries filled their churches with art and reliquaries as a way to attract Christian pilgrims on their journeys. Some monastic centers came to be known particularly for their elaborate manuscript illuminations. Manuscripts were not solely the territory of Christian art, however. Islamic manuscript illustrations, as well as other forms of art and architecture, spread throughout Europe with the rise of Islam.

BYZANTIUM AND THE ERA OF JUSTINIAN

The emperor Justinian (ruled 527–565), along with the empress Theodora, led Byzantium to the height of its political power and cultural achievement. Justinian expanded the Byzantine territories and sought to unite the Eastern and Western Empires. While Constantinople prospered as the capital of the Eastern Empire, Justinian also heavily invested in Ravenna, as the administrative capital of Byzantine Italy. In Constantinople, Justinian initiated a building and renovation campaign that served as a magnificent legacy. Following his conquest of Ravenna, churches there, too, paid tribute to the emperor.

A glorious example of Justinian's building campaign in Constantinople, and one of the few remaining structures from the era is the Church of Hagia Sophia (Holy Wisdom), 532–37 (exterior view, Plate 13). In keeping with Byzantine policy, Justinian was head of both church and state; accordingly, Hagia Sophia serves as a monument not only to Christianity but also to imperial power. While the church contained no explicit references to the emperor, his generous patronage and power were implied through the structure's monumentality and innovative design. Indeed, according to legend, Justinian himself found the finished church so breathtaking that he compared it to the First Temple in Jerusalem, saying, "Solomon, I have outdone you."

Justinian hired the scholar-architects Anthemius of Tralles and Isidorus of Miletus to design Hagia Sophia, and it was their study of geometry, physics, and vaulting that allowed for the church's impressive design. Hagia Sophia is a central plan church, meaning that instead of the long nave, or processional space, of earlier basilica designs, now the focus is drawn upward into loftier, domed central spaces. Hagia Sophia is primarily a square structure, with an enormous dome inscribed on top and smaller semi-domes, or conches, flanking the sides. In order to support a circular structure on a square base, the architects used four enormous piers and arches as well as *pendentives*, or triangular curving wall sections, for the corners. The pendentive became a common feature of Byzantine architecture and Hagia Sophia represents its earliest known use.

The dome of Hagia Sophia is its most remarkable feature. Unlike the dome of the Pantheon (Plate 8), a solid structure with a large opening at the top, Hagia Sophia's dome has a band of forty windows at its base, a feature that makes the dome appear to float and infuses the structure with sunlight (interior view, Plate 14). This daring design, which actually weakens the structural integrity of the dome, provides a soaring, illuminated space that symbolically draws the viewer's attention heavenward. So remarkable was the design for its era that rumors circulated of angels intervening to aid the builders. In fact, the vast structure was built in a mere five years.

Hagia Sophia remained a Christian church until 1453, when the Ottoman Turks conquered the city and converted the structure into a mosque. The four minarets, or towers for the call to prayer, flanking the exterior attest to this conversion, as do the large disks of Arabic writing seen on the interior. Hagia Sophia functioned as a mosque until 1935, when it was transformed into a museum.

Like Hagia Sophia, the Church of San Vitale in Ravenna, Italy, is a central plan structure that supports a dome on a geometric base (Plate 15). Rather than a square design, however, San Vitale is an octagonal configuration with complex interior spaces of arches, circular chapels, and a rectangular sanctuary. Semicircular *exedrae*, or niches, border the central domed space and frame the eight large piers that support the dome. While the circular dome is concealed on the exterior by an octagonal shell, its airy presence inside once again draws the viewer's attention forward to the liturgical space of the sanctuary as well as upward to the heavens.

Just as the architectural greatness of Hagia Sophia served as a reminder of Justinian's power, so, too, did San Vitale honor the emperor. Commis-sioned in 526 by the bishop of Ravenna, the church was not completed until after Justinian's conquest of the region. While Justinian and Theodora did not attend the church's dedication in 547, and may in fact have never seen the church, they appear in two large mosaic decorations. In the mosaic featuring Justinian, he wears a jeweled crown and purple cloak and carries a gold utensil of the Eucharist, symbolizing his dual position as head of both state and church, uniting secular and religious power. A mosaic on the opposite wall features the Empress Theodora (Plate 16). Although Theodora came from a lower social background, Justinian accorded her great power within his government and may have allowed her to act as co-ruler, suggested by her significant presence in the San Vitale mosaic. Surrounded by her attendants, Theodora is singled out by her golden halo and ornate costuming. As with the image of Justinian, Theodora functions as both empress and emissary of the church. At the bottom of her cloak, we see images of the Magi, the wise men who presented valuable gifts to Jesus upon his birth. Emulating their gestures, Theodora carries a jewel-studded chalice as an offering for Christ and the church.

Mosaics are an enduring hallmark of Byzantine art, appearing on floors and walls of domestic, civic, and religious buildings. The tiny fragments, or *tesserae*, that compose the mosaics varied from common stones in heavily trafficked floor mosaics to semi-precious stones and glass in more ornate wall decorations. A colorful mosaic from the Baptistry of San Giovanni in Florence (Plate 17) demonstrates the lavish detail possible in the medium when money was no object. The monumental scene of Hell is a graphic portrayal of damnation that may have inspired Dante's *Divine Comedy*. Satan presides over the chaos while devouring souls at random. Above this scene in the Baptistry is an equally sumptuous mosaic of Christ in Last Judgment, elevated toward the celestial realm.

MONASTIC ART

The late Middle Ages saw a tremendous increase in pilgrimage, where Christian faithful traveled long distances to visit holy sites. To more fully instruct these pilgrims in the Christian faith, many monasteries built large churches along pilgrimage routes and filled them with reliquaries (see Statue of

During the Middle Ages, crowds of pilgrims journeyed across Europe to visit major shrines and holy sites. Along the way, they stopped to venerate relics of local saints. Remains of bodies or items belonging to holy persons were housed in richly decorated containers called reliquaries. The jewel-encrusted reliquary of Saint Foy encases the skull of a child martyr. According to legend, the child burned to death in 303 for refusing to make sacrifices to pagan gods.

Figure IV-2 Reliquary statue of Saint Foy, for the Abbey Church of Conques, Midi-Pyrénées, France. Late ninth century with later additions. Silver gilt over a wood core, with enamel, gold with filigree, added gems and cameos. Height 33″ (85 cm). Church Treasury, Conques, France. Courtesy of Gemeinnutzige Stiftung Leonard von Matt.

St. Foy, Figure IV-2) and art depicting religious stories. It was believed that spectacular art and architecture would convey to the pilgrims the glory of heavenly paradise.

In France, however, the Cistercian monks and nuns of the eleventh and twelfth centuries largely turned away from the elaborate decoration of their churches and the previous focus on the arts, favoring a simpler, more ascetic life. The Abbey Church of Notre-Dame in Fontenay, attached to the monastery, is the oldest Cistercian structure in Burgundy. The interior view of its nave (Plate 18) makes evident the building's simplicity and lack of adornment. Rather than relying on ornate mosaics to engage the viewer, the church at Fontenay instead uses a wall of windows to let in a radiant light, drawing the viewer forward and providing a meditative atmosphere. By this time, church architects had moved away from the Byzantine central plan, favoring instead a large-scale cross shape with a long nave and short transept arms.

The architecture of this period is characterized as *Romanesque*, meaning "in the Roman manner," because of its use of arches and vaults as seen in Roman imperial buildings. Romanesque builders significantly adapted the arch and the vault from their original source, changes that are visible in the nave at Fontenay. Rather than round Roman arches, Fontenay displays a series of pointed arches; similarly, vaults are no longer rounded, but pointed, with exterior ribbing visible for support. The pointed arch and vault were more stable than their rounded predecessors, for they directed the structure's weight down to the floor instead of out to the sides. The adaptation of the pointed arch and vault allowed for the spanning of greater spaces and precluded the need for exterior buttressing. Additionally, the series of pointed arches and vaults along the nave, as seen at Fontenay, served a symbolic visual purpose, drawing the viewer's attention inward and upward.

Another art form long associated with monasteries is the illustrated book. Particularly in the eleventh and twelfth centuries, many monasteries and convents became known for their lavishly illustrated manuscripts. Monks and nuns were well regarded for their education and monastic libraries often housed *scriptoria*, where monks copied religious texts by hand and artisans added illustrations, also known as illuminations.

A painting from the opening page of the *Liber Scivias* by Hildegard of Bingen (Plate 19) tells us not only of the monastic manuscript tradition but also of women's roles during this era. Born into an aristocratic German family, Hildegard entered a convent at a young age and eventually rose to found and lead her own convent at Bingen. Hildegard was well-educated and wrote religious, medical, and scientific treatises. The *Liber Scivias* records what she believed were divine visions. The text describes "a fiery light, flashing intensely. . . And suddenly I could understand what such books as the psalter, the gospel and the other catholic volumes of the Old and New Testament actually set forth." The accompanying illustration shows Hildegard flanked by the architecture of the monastery and enveloped by the fiery light, recording her visions with the assistance of the monk Volmar. Hildegard's feet are raised above the earthly ground by a stool, indicating her divine inspiration.

The role of convents was crucial in the life of certain women of the Middle Ages. Since a dowry was required to join a convent, only upper-class women could afford to become nuns. For many women of this class, however, convents provided the only socially-acceptable alternative to marriage. Simultaneously, freed from a patriarchal system, convents allowed women to become educated, exercise leadership, and manage complex business affairs and land ownership. Nuns as well as monks illustrated the manuscripts produced in the scriptoria. While Hildegard was not a painter herself, she is believed to have designed the imagery that illustrates the *Scivias*.

ISLAMIC ART

The Middle Ages saw the rise of both Christian and Islamic art and architecture. Just as the two religions had common ancestry, so, too, did they share common art forms and characteristics. The pointed Romanesque arch, for example, may have originated in Islamic architecture of southern Europe. The tradition of manuscript illumination was not solely the province of Christian nuns and monks. Men and women of Muslim societies held a high level of literacy and books were produced on religious as well as secular subjects.

While some Islamic manuscripts contained illuminations of abstract, geometric patterning, as seen in much Islamic architectural decoration, others displayed figural illustrations of the texts. The degree of representation allowed in Islamic art, following the injunction against the making of idols, varied by location and period. A painted sixteenth-century illustration from a copy of a fourteenth-century text, *The Life of the Prophet*, shows the prophet Muhammad and his companions traveling to a fair (Plate 20). To prevent possible idolatry, the face of Muhammad is not shown, but covered by a white veil. Muhammad and his two associates, Abu Bakr and the young warrior Ali, travel by camel to a desert market in the hopes of gaining religious converts. Ali, the husband of Muhammad's daughter Fatima, and Abu Bakr, Muhammad's father-in-law, both became caliphs, successors of Muhammad who defended the faith with power from Allah.

MUSIC OF EARLY CHRISTIANITY

Music has been integral to Christian worship from the beginning down to the present day. While the musical forms have varied widely in different nations and cultures with communities of Christians, and have changed along with the general changes in music over the centuries, many churches still sing hymns the words of which go back to the earliest centuries of Christianity and the music of which comes from as early as the ninth century.

Jesus and his followers were Jews, who would have grown up singing the psalms from memory in the synagogue. The new communities of Christians, beginning in Jerusalem and spreading throughout the eastern Mediterranean world, would have continued the practice of singing the psalms when they went to the synagogue and also as part of their distinctively Christian worship when they met in one another's homes on the first day of the week (Sunday). There is evidence from the New Testament that the early Christian communities also sang other sorts of music. The gospels of Mark (14:26) and Matthew (26:30) tell of Jesus and his disciples singing a "hymn" at the Last Supper. Paul, in his Letter to the Colossian Christians (3:16), encouraged them to "sing psalms and hymns and spiritual songs." Many biblical scholars believe that there are passages, particularly in Paul's letters, that may be early hymns sung in worship, as for example Philippians 2:5-11. The earliest Christian liturgies (forms of worship) would have included reading and interpretation of texts from the Hebrew Bible, prayers, psalms, and other songs. Following the Jewish tradition, the singing would have been monophonic (melody only) and unaccompanied, and the psalms would have been sung either responsorially, with a solo leader and congregational response, or antiphonally, with the congregation in two parts singing alternating verses.

By the second century CE music was an integral part of the various liturgies emerging in the Christian churches. Probably the oldest hymn known to us, which is still sung in churches, is the Greek "Candlelighting hymn," *Phos Hilaron*, "O Gladsome Light," which the fourth-century Church Father Basil the Great quoted and already considered an old hymn. An important figure in the early development of the Western Christian musical tradition was Ambrose (340–397), Bishop of Milan, one of the most influential church leaders of the age and a major influence on Augustine's conversion. The tradition of what came to be called "Ambrosian chant" preceded him, but he decisively molded that tradition through his prolific composing of the words and sometimes the music to many hymns. Of the great number of hymns attributed to him, perhaps thirteen or fourteen survive. (Augustine quoted the texts of four of them in his essay *De Musica* [Of Music].) A well-known example, still sung throughout the Christian world to a variety of later tunes, is *Splendor paternae gloriae*, "O Splendor of God's glory bright." Ambrose created an antiphonal tradition in which the men would form one section and the women and children the other, giving greater vocal range and variety to the alternating parts. Ambrosian chant became a distinctive Christian musical tradition in Milan, that developed until the ninth century, and has been preserved and revived down to the present day.

Other notable hymn-writers of the Western church included Bishop Venantius Fortunatus and Pope Gregory the Great in the sixth century. The former wrote hymns still sung in churches, such as the Easter hymn "Hail thee, festival day." The latter is traditionally credited with standardizing and codifying the mode of singing that came to dominate Roman Catholic Christianity until the eleventh century, *plainsong* or *plainchant*, called (after Pope Gregory) *Gregorian chant*. It was communities of Western monks that developed plainsong into a fine art expressed in a variety of musical settings, with their chanting of the psalms and other parts of the liturgy several times throughout the day. Growing out of the tradition of Christian music that went back to earliest times, Gregorian chant was monophonic and unaccompanied, and designed to be a spiritual experience for those who chanted it. Another link to the earliest period of Christianity is the fact that although the Eucharistic liturgy of the Roman Catholic Church was in Latin for many centuries, an essential part of that liturgy remained in Greek, the main language of the early Christian communities: the *Kyrie eleison*, "Lord have mercy."

CD SELECTION

The two selections of early Christian music are both examples of Ambrosian Chant, from *Ambrosian Liturgical Chants* (Schola Hungarica, conducted by Janka Szendrei and Laszlo Dobszay, Hungaroton Records, 1998). Prior to the liturgical reforms under Pope Gregory the Great there was considerable liturgical and musical variation among churches in various areas of Europe, with a good deal of improvisation in the music. The church in Milan preserved and handed on one of the earliest of those musical and liturgical traditions, which traced its roots to Bishop Ambrose. The first selection, *Antiphonae cum Psalmis* (Antiphons with Psalms), on track #8 from the Christmas liturgy, is a good example of the continuation of the Jewish tradition of monophonic antiphonal singing of the psalms in Christian worship. The choir chants portions of Psalms 18, 2, 97, 46, and 71. Each psalm selection is preceded and followed by the soloist chanting a brief antiphon, also from the psalms. The second selection, on track #9, is the *Gloria* and the *Kyrie* from the Christmas mass. The *Gloria in excelsis Deo* ("Glory to God in the highest") is one of the oldest parts of the Christian liturgy in the West, as is the *Kyrie eleison*. The Ambrosian chants are much more freely structured than Gregorian chant, alternating between simplicity and elaborate variation.

MUSIC OF ISLAM AND THE MIDDLE EAST

The Middle East includes four distinct cultural groups: Arab (Saudi Arabia, Syria, Iraq, Lebanon, and Egypt), Persian (Iran), Turkish, and North African (Tunisia, Algeria, and Morocco). They share a common musical tradition, but expressed in a wide variety of forms. Historically the music of all the areas of the Middle East was profoundly influenced by the rise and dominance of the religion of Islam.

From its founding, Islam has been of a divided mind with regard to music. Music in Arabia was often associated with erotic dancing and with drinking, both of which were strongly opposed by Muhammad and his followers. Four different attitudes toward music, variously interpreting certain passages in the Qur'an and the sayings of the Prophet, have characterized Islam: 1) uncompromising purists who oppose any musical expression as sinful; 2) authorities who allow only the chanting of the Qur'an and the call to prayer and forbid all musical instruments; 3) many Muslims, among them scholars and musicians, who favor music, both religious and secular; and 4) the Sufis, for whom music and dancing are a means to achieve unity with God.

The first word of the first revelation to Muhammad is "Recite!" and *qur'an* means "recitation." There is a rich tradition of recitation of the Qur'an. From an early age Muslim children are taught to memorize and recite passages from the Qur'an. Muslims recite Qur'anic passages daily in their prayer and meditation, on various religious feasts and fasts both at home and in the mosque, and in our time on radio and TV. Muslims believe that the Qur'an is both informative and "performative," and do not distinguish between the two. Reciting the Qur'an aloud, whether speaking or chanting

the verses, internalizes what it teaches and is a realization of God's presence. The sound of the Arabic words has a powerful emotional as well as cognitive influence. There are, in some Muslim countries, festivals and contests that feature chanting of the Qur'an by people, both men and women, who commit themselves to the practice of this devotional art. Besides the Qur'an, the Call to Prayer or *adhan* is chanted five times daily from the minaret or tower of the mosque by a *muezzin*, someone designated to call the people to prayer. The call, which begins with *Allahu akbar*, "God is most great," draws Muslims out of their daily preoccupations to focus them on God. Significantly, in light of Islam's ambivalence about music, Muslims do not consider the chanting of the Qur'an or of the Call to Prayer "music."

Middle Eastern music goes back long before Islam. There was folk music, street entertainment, and music for the royal courts. In song and dance people celebrated love, the beauty of nature, the land they lived in, and the story of their tribe. Vocal music and poetry were inseparable in Arab and Persian cultures with their rich tradition of poetry. Music was part of both domestic and public life, from festive occasions like weddings to going into battle.

Classical Middle Eastern music is monophonic; it does not use harmony. It is sung or played by a soloist, who often improvises. A singer may be accompanied by a small chorus, but rather than harmonizing with the singer they repeat what the singer sang or engage in a musical dialogue with the singer. Musicians playing instruments might also accompany a singer, or play purely instrumental music. Among the main instruments are the kettledrum and tambourine, a double-reed, oboe-like instrument called a *shawm*, the flute, the bagpipe, and stringed instruments related to the violin and the guitar. Rhythm is very important and complex in Middle Eastern music, tapped out on the center or edge of the drum or tambourine. Unlike Western music, with its half-tone scales of 13 notes in an octave, Middle Eastern music uses a quarter-tone scale with 17, 19, or 24 notes in an octave. Because of its improvisational nature, the music is taught and learned orally rather than written down. An important authority for classical Middle Eastern music is the tenth-century Muslim philosopher Al-Farabi, whose book on music remains a valuable source for both the theory and practice of Middle Eastern music.

CD SELECTIONS

Both selections are examples of chanted Qur'anic recitation. They are taken from the CD accompanying *Approaching the Qur'an: The Early Revelations*, introduced and translated by Michael Sells (Ash-land, OR: White Cloud Press, 1999). A chapter of the book, "Hearing the Qur'an: The Call to Prayer and Six Suras," contains a discussion of Qur'anic recitation and of the chanting on the disc. Sells transliterates the sounds of the Arabic words, and explains the nature and varieties of recitation. The first selection we have chosen, track #10, is the Call to Prayer or *adhan*, chanted here by Mustafa Ozcan Gunesdogdu, a representative of the Turkish tradition of recitation who has received international recognition and prizes at Qur'an recitation festivals. The second selection, track #11, is *Surat al-Infitar*, Surah 82, recited by Muhammad Khalil al-Husari, for many years a master of Qur'anic recitation recognized throughout the international Muslim community. Sells translates the title, *al-Infitar*, as "The Tearing." In other translations it is entitled "The Cataclysm." It is one of the early Meccan revelations, powerful for both the poetic beauty of the language and the stark simplicity of its portrayal of the Last Judgment.

CHAPTER SEVEN

EARLY CHRISTIANITY

Jesus of Nazareth certainly was the major generative figure for the rise of Christianity. Yet no firsthand records have come down to us from his hand, and the reports about his life and teaching are secondary sources, written a generation or more after his death by his followers. What we call Christian scripture began with oral reports about Jesus' life. These were sayings and stories that were eventually put into written units and collections and used to compile the Gospels of Matthew, Mark, Luke, and John. (The word gospel comes from the Greek word *evangelion*, meaning "good news"). These texts, however, are neither biographies nor objective historical portraits of Jesus, but "witness literature": explicitly designed to express the author's own faith and likewise to elicit the readers' believing commitment. For instance, Luke 1:1-4 and John 20:30-31 indicate that the procedure for these writers was to select from various sources at their disposal that material which could best lead the reader to faith in Jesus.

Nevertheless these records are not historically worthless. Methodological distinctions can be made in these writings between religious witness on the one hand, and, on the other hand, information that the church could not have produced out of its own religious or theological imagination. For instance, passages that would have brought embarrassment, or even theological difficulties, to the later church may be considered for historical authenticity. Such information might include Jesus' origins in Galilee, especially Nazareth (see John 1:46 and 7:52), his baptism (see Matt. 1:14), his betrayal and denial by his closest followers, and his socializing with people of known disrepute. In short, information about Jesus written in the New Testament Gospels which

is not dependent on the church's theology after Easter is the starting point for reconstructing an acceptable "historical" portrait of the Nazarene.

JESUS' LIFE: A SKETCH

Jesus was born into the family of Joseph and Mary and grew up in the town of Nazareth. His father was a carpenter, and he himself practiced that trade (Mark 6:3). He had brothers and sisters (Mark 3:31, 6:3; Gal. 1:19), and John 7:5 indicates that during Jesus' lifetime his brothers attached no particular religious significance to him. His ministry generally took place in the cities of the regions of Galilee and Judea.

John the Baptist baptized Jesus in the Jordan River. This incident would never have been invented by the church since the church's understanding of baptism and of John's relation to Jesus made further explanation of Jesus' baptism necessary (see Matthew 3:14-15). The preaching of both Jesus and John was *eschatological*, that is, it announced the nearness of God's ruling activity. John's preaching, however, was also decidedly *apocalyptic* or visionary (Matt. 3:7-10; Luke 3:7-9). John was an ascetic who withdrew to the wilderness and practiced abstinence from certain food and drink. Jesus, on the other hand, was not an ascetic, did his work in the cities, and did not practice special dietary abstinence (see Matt. 11:18-19; Luke 7:33-34). That Jesus may originally have been a disciple of John the Baptist remains conjecture.

The portrait of Jesus as a teacher that emerges from our sources has four especially prominent features:

1. The first is the brief preface to many of his sayings, "Truly I say to you. . . ." Jesus asked people

This sarcophagus represents a convergence of Roman art and Early Christian art. The s-curve patterning denotes the work as a strigil sarcophagus, named after the curved body scrapers, or strigils, used by Roman athletes after strenuous exercise. Many strigil sarcophagi were embellished by lions' heads. Here, the sculptor has added a Christian element, the motif of the Good Shepherd, to an otherwise Roman object. Before Christianity became the official Roman religion in the fourth century CE, artists sought to assimilate images from other traditions and give them new meanings, a process known as syncretism. The Good Shepherd is the most important of these syncretic images, for in pagan art he was Hermes the Shepherd but early Jews and Christians understood him as the Good Shepherd of the Twenty-Third Psalm.

Figure IV-3 *The Good Shepherd, Strigil Sarcophagus with lion heads and claws.* Mid third century CE, Marble. Musée du Louvre, Paris. Courtesy of Réunion des Musées Nationaux/Art Resource, NY.

not to make their decisions on the basis of the traditions of the past, for then the responsibility for their decisions would not rest with them.

2. A second feature of Jesus' teaching style was the frequently asked question, "Which of you. . . ?" "Which of you, having a son or an ox that has fallen into a well, will not immediately pull him out on a sabbath day?" (Luke 14:5). Not only are people to quit hiding behind their traditions, they are to take hold of their lives and move toward responsible maturity.

3. Thirdly, Jesus taught in *parables* to illustrate the subject of the message and of his hearers' decision: the "kingdom," meaning the ruling activity of God. Jesus' message was that God's kingship was near, not remote, and that it could be seen in the everyday world. The parables illustrated God's active participation at work within the human situation, and they called his active listeners to a decision to live thoughtfully and responsibly from the resources presented to them by God's kingship.

4. A fourth and final feature of Jesus' teaching was his table fellowship with social and religious outcasts. The object of God's mercy and forgiveness is the sinner, and Jesus' association with sinners was an acted parable of God's drawing near to them in acceptance and love. When some objected that Jesus as a religious teacher was not properly distinguishing between the upright and the sinner, he replied, "Those who are well have no need of a physician, but those who are sick" (Mark 2:17).

Jesus said that God's rule was not to be limited to one cosmic place, such as "heaven," or to one religious institution or to one nation, but was limitless.

Hiding behind tradition to avoid present responsibility is nothing other than the attempt to control God (Mark 7:13), and "faith" is the decision to give up all attempts to control God. For Jesus God is not bound to tradition (Luke 18:9-14) or to legal codes (Matt. 5:21-6:48). The law of God represents God's claim on human beings, and should not be reversed into their claim on God. Moreover, since God's claim is total, there is no distinction between religious practice and everyday conduct (Mark 7:6-7).

A striking feature of the picture of Jesus in all four Gospels is the manner in which he interacts with women. While social convention placed restraints on public encounters between religiously observant men and women, there are several stories testifying to the fact that women found Jesus' work and teaching singularly liberating. He compliments women, notably those who are shunned by society, and for their faith (Matt. 15:28), publicly receives their gestures of care (Mark 14:3-9), extends healing to them (Mark 5:25-34), accepts socially rejected women (Luke 7:36-50), and dialogues publicly with foreign women (John 4). Women are among his closest friends, are with him during his death, aid in his burial, and discover the empty tomb. Small wonder that they were prominent among the body of believers that formed the first Christian community (Acts 1:14).

Even though Jesus refused to consider himself a political messiah (Mark 8:27-33, John 6:15), his teaching and activity awakened such hopes among his followers. He was taken captive in Jerusalem and executed on a Roman cross as a political agitator (Mark 15:26). But both the Jewish Sanhedrin, the ruling religious body dominated by the Sadducees, and the Roman government had a hand in his death, which can be dated around the year 30 CE. That God raised Jesus from death is the proclamation that gave rise to the Christian church.

This plaque is one of four scenes originally mounted on the sides of a square casket, each carved with episodes from Christ's Passion. *The Crucifixion of Christ* is the earliest known narrative portrayal of the crucifixion, showing more than one temporal scene in a single panel. Christ's death is combined with the later suicide of Judas, whose payment for betraying Jesus rests at his feet. Mary and John stand to the left of the cross, with Longinus to the right. In the branch of the tree, a bird feeds her chicks, symbolizing the life-giving power of Christ's death.

Figure IV-4 *The Crucifixion of Christ,* panel from a casket. Late Roman, ca. 420–430 CE. Ivory, 2.95 × 3.86" (7.5 × 9.8 cm). British Museum, London. Courtesy of HIP/Art Resource, NY.

GATHERING THE COMMUNITY

The stories of the discovery that Jesus' tomb was empty have one thing in common: they all say that that discovery by itself did not create faith in a risen Jesus. The circumstances of Jesus' burial are historically unclear, whether it was done by friends, as reported by all four Gospels, or by his enemies, as reported in a speech in Acts 13:29. That the empty tomb stories are later pieces of the tradition is clear, but they all report that the discovery was neither anticipated nor made by Jesus' inner circle of disciples, but by women related to them, while the leading male members of that circle were either in hiding or scattered, some returning to homes in Galilee.

But the discovery of an empty tomb itself was not the factor that created the disciples' reversal in mood and their determination to go public at the expense of their lives. What exactly brought this reversal about is historically difficult to reconstruct. But it is a fixed element in the early Christian tradition that it was Simon, whom Jesus had called "Peter," who experienced an appearance of the risen Jesus (1 Cor. 15:5, Mark 16:7, Luke 24:34; cf. Luke 22:31-32). It is natural that he would gather others within Jesus' circle to relate his experience, an experience that was then repeated within this circle (1 Cor. 15:5-7; John 20 & 21; Matt. 28:16-17). Others outside this circle and hostile to it, notably Paul of Tarsus and Jesus' brother James, also experienced Jesus as risen (1 Cor.15:3-8; cf. John 7:5). History cannot make judgments about the nature of these experiences, other than to report that the people in question say that they "saw" Jesus (cf. 1 Cor. 9:1) and that from the moment of that experience their lives were changed.

It was Peter's decision to return to Jerusalem that led to the founding of the earliest Christian community there. The second part of Luke's two-volume work, the Acts of the Apostles, counts 120 people, both men and women, who formed this initial group from which the church began (Acts 1:14-15). At first they continued their allegiance to the Temple and to the traditions of Judaism. Some Greek-speaking Jews (called "Hellenists") had already been interested in Jesus' teaching (John 12:20), and they immediately joined the new community of faith. This Greek-speaking component, along with strong prophetic activity, enabled a rapid expansion in Jerusalem and beyond, and soon attention had to be given to problems of organization (Acts 2-6). By the year 40 Christianity had spread throughout Palestine, and a strong community arose in the city of Antioch in Syria, where its members were first called "Christians." There in Antioch a mixed community of Jews and *Gentiles* (non-Jews) developed which had had no personal contact with Jesus of Nazareth or his teachings, but knew him only as the crucified and risen one of Christian preaching.

THE APOSTLE PAUL,

Paul's year of birth is unknown, but it may be placed in the first decade of the Common Era. Not much is known of Paul's origins because in his letters he says so little about himself. The Book of Acts gives us some information, namely that he was a "young man" present at the stoning of Stephen, which took place in the first half of the thirties (7:58). But scholars are always quick to point out that with regard to information about Paul the Book of Acts remains a secondary source, written a generation after Paul's death and designed to speak to problems in the church long after Paul's departure from the scene.

For instance, by the time Luke wrote Acts, Paul had become one of the great heroes of the church's past, whereas in each of Paul's letters we can readily see that during his lifetime he was fighting for his very standing in the church. Moreover, the sources Luke used (cf. Luke 1:1-4) in composing the Book of Acts depict Paul somewhat differently than Paul thought of himself. For example, Paul admitted that he was unskilled in speaking (2 Cor. 11:6), but throughout Acts 13–28 he is portrayed as a most eloquent and persuasive orator. Information in Acts, therefore, must be investigated in the light of Paul's letters in evaluating its presentation of Paul and his ministry. Once again, historical conclusions must be based on firsthand data available to us; where it is not available, we will have to work in terms of the highest probabilities.

That Tarsus in Cilicia (southeastern Asia Minor) was Paul's birthplace is mentioned only in Acts, which also mentions a popular characterization of it as "no mean city" (21:39). At that time Tarsus was a famous center of learning that had won interest and acclaim from several prominent literary personages. Cicero had resided there, as had the emperor Augustus' teacher Athenodorus, and Stoic philosophy was a strong component of its intellectual atmosphere. It is clear from Paul's writings that he is at home in an urban Hellenistic setting, but also that his training is decidedly in Jewish rather than that of Greek philosophy. Where there are elements of contemporary popular philosophy (for example see Romans 1-2), they appear in Jewish dress. Hellenistic Judaism made use of Greek philosophical concepts in its dialogue with Hellenism, and these were at times worked out quite thoroughly, as in the case of the influential Jewish philosopher Philo of Alexandria, an older contemporary of Paul. By contrast, Greek concepts and values are relatively lacking in Paul. At any rate, that Tarsus is Paul's place of birth need not be questioned.

Acts also reports that besides the Roman-Greek name of Paul, the apostle also carried the Jewish name of Saul. Paul nowhere used the latter name for himself. However, it was not unusual for

Jews to carry two names. Whenever such practice was the case, there was normally an attempt to make both names sound somewhat alike, and some Semitic names could easily be retouched (for example, Simon/Simeon). That Saul became "Paul" at his baptism is a conjecture no longer strongly advocated.

Paul himself reports that his family belonged to the tribe of Benjamin and that he belonged to the party of the Pharisees (Phil. 3:5). Acts 22:28 tells us that Paul was the son of Pharisees (23:6); this reference, if accurate, may indicate a family tradition. Paul's occupation, again according to Acts, is that of a "tent-maker," a trade common in and around Tarsus. The fact that he learned to do manual labor says nothing about his social position. This was a common thing for Jewish students of Torah, and here Judaism differed from Greek culture in its high estimation of the value of manual labor.

Acts mentions that Paul held Roman citizenship; indeed that he inherited it (22:28), while Paul himself is silent on this subject. Such information is

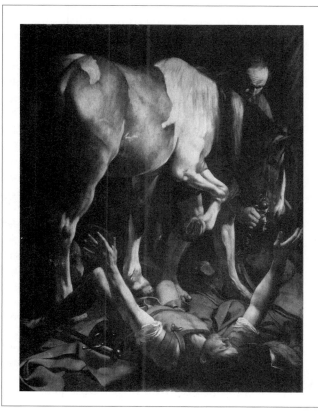

Caravaggio's painting depicts Paul's life-changing conversion to Christianity according to Acts 9. On the road to Damascus, where he planned to arrest Christians, Paul was struck to the ground, blinded by a light from heaven, and admonished by God. Caravaggio pictures the climactic moment when Paul lies prostrate on the ground. The painter's use of theatrical lighting and dramatic angles, where both Paul and the viewer are visually overwhelmed by the horse, underscores the powerful event.

Figure IV-5 Caravaggio, *The Conversion of St. Paul*. 1600–01. Oil on canvas, 7'6½ × 5'10" (230 × 178 cm). Cerasi Chapel, Santa Maria del Popolo, Rome. Courtesy Scala/Art Resource, NY.

useful to Luke and his apologetic purpose of show-ing that Christianity was not a politically or reli-giously subversive threat to Rome. Acts also reports (22:3, 26:4) that Paul received his theological educa-tion in Jerusalem from the famous rabbi Gamaliel, which accords with Luke's purpose in depicting Christianity's roots firmly in Judaism. But Paul, even when asserting his thorough grounding in Judaism, omits any reference to Gamaliel, and makes the statement that he was unknown by sight to Chris-tians in Judea (1:22).

Paul himself mentions that before his conver-sion he was an active persecutor of Christianity, describing that activity as "violent" with the intent to destroy the church (Gal. 1:13). He connects this activity with his devotion to Judaism and his zeal for "the traditions of the fathers" (1:14), which indi-cates that those Christians he persecuted were Jew-ish Christians who had already broken with some of those traditions.

Paul gives no details whatsoever concerning his conversion. The famous scene on the Damas-cus road, referred to three times in Acts (9:3-6, 22:6-11, 26:12-18), is legendary. When Paul does speak about his conversion, it seems more an "about-face" than a "conversion" which turned him from one religion to another. The new movement that he embraced was not in his eyes a new religion, but the fulfillment of the old one to which he was devoted, Judaism. Nor was his experience the con-version of a penitent sinner. He simply came to be convinced, in the midst of his persecutorial activ-ity, that the crucified Jesus was not under God's curse, but under God's blessing. He insists that he needed no reeducation (Gal. 1:12,15), for the doc-trines of God, creation, salvation, sin, and God's justice and mercy were already known to him. His experience of Jesus as risen also meant to him that he had been called to be a Christian missionary pri-marily among Gentiles.

What did Paul know about Jesus, and what is the connection between the two? It is most likely that during Jesus' ministry the two never met, and further conjecture depends only upon Paul's letters, which do not address this question. Yet it may be the case that Paul knew more about Jesus than the letters themselves convey. It is clear, however, that it was not because of Jesus' life and teaching that Paul became part of the Christian movement. Like some others in the Jewish community, he initially viewed Jesus as a "law-breaker," one who disre-spected Torah, and therefore could not be the Mes-siah. More than that, Jesus of Nazareth had been crucified, and Paul was among those who applied Deuteronomy 21:23 to Jesus: that "everyone who hangs on a tree" is under God's curse (Gal. 3:13). Therefore Paul engaged in attempts to destroy Christianity, since its adherents were clearly law-breakers and apostates themselves.

In the midst of his persecuting activities, as he dealt with Jewish-Christians and heard their expla-nations of their new faith, Paul himself came to the belief that the crucified Jesus was not under God's curse but under God's blessing. It was the devel-opment of this tenet that made Paul the most for-mative and influential thinker of the earliest Christian generation. His new belief meant that he had to reexamine his ideas on the place of Torah as well as the place of the crucified Jesus in the Chris-tian message.

Even though Paul knew some of the sayings and teachings of Jesus (see 1 Cor. 7:10; 9:14; 11:23-25; 1 Thes. 4:15-17), Jesus as teacher was not the dom-inant center of his theology, nor was Jesus the mir-acle-worker or Jesus the apocalyptic prophet. Paul told the Corinthian Christian community, "I decided to know nothing among you except Jesus Christ and him crucified" (1 Cor. 2:2), and made the complaint that others had come into Corinth after him and presented "another Jesus" than the one he had proclaimed (2 Cor. 11:4). For Paul, the Christian message had one theme: Jesus Christ crucified. All Christian sacred practices, all Christian living, all speaking of Jesus and the traditions about him—all these had for Paul one basic theme and surrounded one central event: the event of Jesus' cross.

Why was this so crucial for Paul? His answer was that at Jesus' cross all human claims before God, all human striving and achievement, were brought to nothing. It was the Messiah who was crucified. The highest form of human achievement and stature gave up all claims before God and died the death of a slave, so that the life he received beyond the cross was given to him by God's power alone. With the event of the cross of Jesus at the cen-ter of Christian preaching, human achievement must give way to a new self-understanding, namely one of receptiveness. Paul would then ask: "What do you have that you did not receive? If then you received it, why do you boast as if it were not a gift?" (1 Cor. 4:7)

Paul as Missionary It was only after many years of missionary activity that Paul met with the apostles in Jerusalem, visiting there on the occasion of the so-called "Apostolic Council," an event dated about 48 CE. According to Paul himself he had carried on mission work for at least fourteen years without any official contact with the recognized leadership of the church, commonly referred to as "the Twelve," in Jerusalem. Paul had taken to heart the admonitions that the message was given "to the Jew first, and also to the Greek" (Romans 1:16) but his had developed into a ministry to the Gentiles. Now it was important to meet with the leadership in Palestine in order to insure unity throughout the Christian mission, especially outside Palestine. Contrary to Paul's own understanding of the results of this meeting, unity was not the result after all, even though in the long run Paul's opinions prevailed.

At the council the differences became more acute, and it was Paul who pressed the Twelve to some decisions about the extent of Christian observance of Torah. According to Gal. 2:1-3 Paul understood the Council to have agreed not to require of his converts in the Gentile world circumcision and the dietary regulations. However, it seems that the decision was not as clear-cut as Paul had understood, as the letter to the Galatians indicates. He knew nothing of the so-called "Apostolic Decree" (Acts 15:23-29), and he was surprised by the incident at Antioch when representatives from Jerusalem objected to unrestricted table fellowship with Gentile believers (Gal. 2:11-21).

Paul's part of the agreement, which he assiduously promoted throughout his churches in Asia Minor and Europe, was that his mission churches provide monetary support to the mother church in Jerusalem (Gal. 2:10, 1 Cor. 16:1-3, Romans 15:26). And while the theology of freedom from Torah took effect very slowly, it finally prevailed, although not throughout the entire church until well after Paul's death.

As a missionary Paul was an organizational genius of the first rank. He used major cities of the empire—Ephesus, Thessalonica, Philippi, Corinth, and Rome itself—as bases of operations for his mission plans in the surrounding territories, and set up systems for future work in such areas without his having to be on the scene. He kept in touch with his congregations by means of letters, and his letters provide us with clues that the expansion of the church was not accomplished without conflict from both within and without. His letters also indicate that Paul encouraged both male and female leadership in the church. Women were his co-workers not only in name (cf. Romans 16) but also in fact: there were, for example, Phoebe in Cenchreae (16:1-2), Chloe in Corinth (1 Cor. 1:11), Euodia and Syntyche in Philippi (Philippians 4:2-3), and Priscilla (Acts 18 and Romans 16:3). Paul allowed women to preach in Christian services, provided they observe proper local dress codes (cf. 1 Cor. 11:5). In his churches his statement had its practical application in the ministry of the church: "There is neither Jew nor Greek, neither slave nor free, not male and female; you are all one in Christ Jesus" (Gal. 3:28).

The facts surrounding Paul's death are uncertain. Later church tradition has it that he was executed in Rome, most likely around 60 CE during the persecution of Christians under the Emperor Nero. The earliest testimony to his martyrdom—and also, in the same persecution, the martyrdom of Peter—is given in the First Letter of Clement, Bishop of Rome, written in Rome around 95. No details are given, but Clement's words suggest that Paul's missionary efforts may have reached all the way to Spain, as he himself had planned (Romans 15:24-25, 28).

JEWS AND JEWISH-CHRISTIANS

In the early 40s an event occurred that put serious strains on the Jewish and Jewish-Christian relationship in Jerusalem. Herod Agrippa I, the grandson of Herod the Great and king of Judea, in a peace-making gesture to the Romans for recent offenses on both sides, moved to legislate the practice of Judaism in Judea as the province's sole official religion, hence declaring any "Christian" reforms illegal. He also ordered the execution of James the son of Zebedee, one of Jesus' original disciples and a leader of the Jewish-Christians (cf. Acts 12:2-3). When Agrippa died in 44 CE, the Jewish-Christian leadership was able to pacify the situation by demonstrating through regular Torah observance their identity with Judaism, in spite of their commitment to Jesus' messiahship.

Jews in general were willing to give the Christian message a fair hearing in their synagogues and Jewish Christianity in Jerusalem did not understand itself as a new religion. Within the Jewish community it was not so much the Christian belief in Jesus as Messiah as its deliberate liberalization of the constraints of Torah that brought about hostility from mainstream Jews. Even within the Christian community there was heavy debate about how quickly this freedom from Torah should be pressed (cf. Galatians 2:1-21 and Acts 15:1-29).

As far as the fate of the original Jewish-Christian community in Jerusalem is concerned, there is almost total obscurity following the Apostolic Council in 48 CE. Primary sources for historical conclusions are non-existent. The fourth-century church historian Eusebius relates the precarious position of this community at the beginning of the Jewish-Roman War (66-70), a position that placed the Jewish-Christians at variance with both sides and caused them to depart *en masse* for the city of Pella, a Hellenistic city in the country east of the Jordan. It is difficult historically to verify Eusebius' report. Nevertheless, any major influence of Jewish Christianity in Jerusalem ended with the war, the destruction of the city, and the resultant exodus of the Jewish-Christian community. Later Christian authors mention centers of Jewish Christianity outside Palestine that continued into at least the fifth century, and two special groups are mentioned by name, the Nazarenes and the Ebionites.

ROME VS. CHRISTIANITY

As early as the late 40s Christianity had already arrived in Rome. The Roman historian Suetonius, writing around 120, mentions that Jews were expelled from Rome in the year 49 by edict of the Emperor Claudius because of disturbances "instigated by Chrestus" (*Lives of the Caesars*: "Claudius" 25:4). Acts 18 indicates that Jewish Christians were also caught in this expulsion order, which might suggest their initial commitment, even outside Palestine, to live within the framework of Judaism. Judaism had gained the status of a legally recognized religion in the Roman Empire. With the loss of its Jewish framework, Christianity had no status, and thus was exposed to investigation and persecution as a possibly subversive force in Roman society. Therefore the author of the Book of Acts took great pains

to show that Christianity posed no threat to governmental authorities, depicting Christian missionaries' appearances before kings and governors, some of whom are "almost persuaded" to join the new movement themselves (cf. Acts 26:24-32). This picture in Acts is not in accord with the hostility which existed between the government and the churches as reported by John of Patmos, evidently a leader in the Ephesian church in the mid-90s (cf. his writing, the Book of Revelation).

What made the Emperor Nero choose Christians as the scapegoats for the disastrous fire that destroyed entire districts of Rome in 64 CE has not been historically determined. Nero's decision was probably based on political considerations, an attempt to solidify support from various segments of the populace that had grown uneasy about his reign. This new religion was an easy target, especially since it seemed at variance both with officially recognized Judaism, particularly among its orthodox adherents, and with Roman religious practices as well.

Even though this Neronian persecution seems to have been an isolated incident at the time—never to be repeated even in Rome—later writings, both Christian and non-Christian, recall it vividly. Christian authors remembered it as a vicious event in which 977 Christians lost their lives. Roman historians, such as Suetonius and Tacitus, referred to it with little sympathy for Christianity, which they called an "atheistic superstition," an illegal and "evil religion," and Suetonius counted the persecution in Rome among Nero's better acts. At the turn of the century the emperor Trajan (98-117) appointed special commissioners to investigate the new religion, and one of them, Pliny, wrote of stubborn Christians in Asia Minor who, when brought to trial, rigidly maintained their faith in this "superstition," even upon pain of death (see Pliny the Younger, *Epistles* 10:96-97).

Nevertheless such sources indicate that Christians at least had the opportunity to defend themselves in court, with the right to cross-examination and counter-suit, which placed their accusers at risk similar to what they faced. General toleration of the new movement was the case throughout the empire, even though there were instances of local, often severe, persecution, as various New Testament writings indicate. The author of 1 Peter, written for

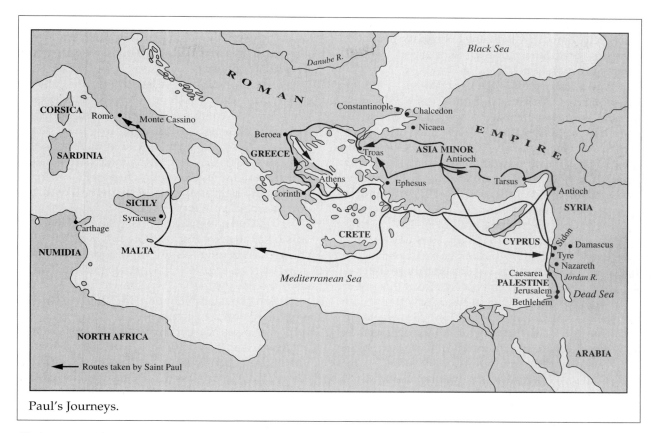

Paul's Journeys.

Christians in those territories of Pliny's investigatory activities, is the first Christian writing to refer to persecution of Christians as *Christians* (4:14-16). The writer of the Letter to the Hebrews knows that Christians have suffered public abuse and the plundering of their property (10:32-34). The Book of Revelation continuously speaks of many Christians who died at the hands of local governmental authorities, and mentions one of the martyrs by name, Antipas in Pergamum (Rev. 2:13). But there remains no evidence for widespread imperial hostility against Christianity other than localized episodes, and the general rule was one of tolerance.

THE EARLIEST TEXTS

The earliest Christian writings to become scripture are the letters of Paul. It was through letters that Paul kept in touch with the many mission churches that he founded and his letters reveal facts about his own life (mentioned above), facts about the situation of the congregations and some of their participants, and most importantly, Paul's understanding of the gospel message: Jesus died on the cross for our sins and salvation comes by virtue of God's grace through faith alone.

A study of the letters by scholars has determined that only seven of the letters are authentically Pauline. These are Romans, I & II Corinthians, Galatians, I Thessalonians, Philemon, and Philippians. II Corinthians and Philippians are actually viewed as composites or parts of letters. There is some debate about three others, II Thessalonians, Colossians, and Ephesians. These are considered by many scholars as "deutero-Pauline" or written "in the mind of Paul" following his death. I &II Timothy and Titus are referred to as the Pastorals and are dated in the early part of the second century. They reveal growing restrictions placed on women in church practice. Many factors determine authenticity. Some of these are: comparison of language use, textual survival, doctrinal differences, and contemporary references.

We have chosen to speak at some length about First Corinthians because in this letter, Paul discusses a number of important things: church organization, the articulation of the faith, the Eucharistic tradition, marriage, the primacy of *agape* (Christian love), and the resurrection hope.

Paul's First Letter to the Corinthians   Find the Greek city of Corinth on the map of Paul's missionary journeys, page 235. Then find Ephesus, on the coast of Asia Minor, which may have been where Paul was when he wrote the letter. Corinth was a major maritime and commercial city at that time, with a population of about 600,000. It also boasted a famous temple to Aphrodite, the goddess of love. Paul probably founded the Christian community in Corinth, perhaps around 50-52. Acts 18:1-18 offers an account of his first visit there, and the reference to Gallio (brother of Seneca), the proconsul of that region, helps to pinpoint those dates—assuming the Acts account is accurate at this point.

Paul may have written his first letter to the Christians in Corinth about 55. He wrote in response to two disturbing situations reported to him by a delegation from the church: (1) factions in the church, and (2) immorality, mainly of a sexual sort. Paul sent his co-worker Timothy to Corinth to follow up on the letter, and later made more than one visit there himself. The letter that appears in the New Testament as "Second Corinthians" reflects ongoing problems in the church, and may be made up of two or three different letters rather than being one continuous letter.

A central theme of First Corinthians is that the wisdom of God as manifested in the crucified Jesus is "foolishness" to the usual human ways of thinking, Jewish and pagan alike (1:18-31), but empowerment and salvation to all those who receive the gospel. Paul's distinctive focus on Jesus' death as God's supreme self-disclosure is often called his "theology of the cross."

Notice as you read how Paul sometimes distinguishes between advice he is offering "from the Lord" and his own advice (for example, 7:10, 12). When Paul advises the unmarried not to marry (chap. 7), his advice is based on the early Christian belief that Jesus would soon return in glory and the present order of things would no longer exist—not on the idea that celibacy is spiritually superior to marriage, as the church later came to believe. Paul's advice on woman, man, and marriage in chapter 11

has troubled many because among other things he seems to justify the subordination of women by saying that males are made in the image of God but females in the image of males (11:7-9), which contradicts Gen. 1:27. There is a profound tension throughout Paul's letters between his vision of Christianity as completely standing earthly arrangements on their head and calling for a new equality—as when he says that in Christ there is neither Jew nor Greek, slave nor free, male nor female—and statements like these in chapter 11 where he accepts the patriarchalism of his Jewish tradition and the social conventions of his day.

First Corinthians contains the earliest written version of an early Eucharistic liturgy of the young church, containing a tradition of what Jesus commanded his disciples at the last supper (11:23-25). It also contains the earliest written account of the resurrection of Jesus in chapter 15. Notice that Paul regards his own vision of Jesus as another resurrection appearance, even though it must have been at least eighteen months after Jesus' death. Throughout he simply uses the Greek word for "appeared," giving no details such as the gospels provide in what are later, much-elaborated stories about the tomb being empty. Paul also speculates on the nature of the resurrection life, saying that God will give everyone a "spiritual body"—a new corporeal existence—to replace the physical body that dies and disintegrates.

Paul introduces what was to become a very influential image of the church, the "body of Christ," in chapter 12, and you should look closely at what he does with the image. Also read closely the famous chapter 13, on the supremacy of love. "Love" here is *agape,* a little-used Greek word for love that the early Christians made central to their understanding of the nature of God and how humans should live. Unlike romantic love or friendship, *agape* unconditionally wills good for others, no matter who they are. Do you ever wonder about Paul's talk about speaking in tongues in this chapter? Tongue-speaking, *glossolalia,* in the early church was probably what it is in some other religious traditions and is today among Pentecostal and charismatic Christian groups: persons in a highly emotional state making ecstatic utterances in sounds that are mainly unintelligible. It was regarded, along with "prophesying" and certain other ecstatic activities, as a manifestation of the presence of God.

Paul himself was clearly a charismatic, ecstatic, even mystical figure. As you read through the First Letter to the Corinthians, notice how he abruptly switches back and forth from one set of topics and metaphorical expressions to another, sometimes saying obscure things that express what are for him visionary truths—as for example that Christians will "judge angels" (6:3). As a study-help we recommend that you make an outline of the topics discussed in the book.

The Gospels The four gospels, Matthew, Mark, Luke, and John, as we mentioned in the Introduction, are considered "witness literature" written primarily for the purpose of attracting converts. The name-titles they now carry were applied to them in the early second century as marks of approval for their apostolic content. Literary analysis supports the conclusion that Matthew and Luke used Mark, along with other sources (see Luke 1:1-4), to complete their works. John, on the other hand, while working in the same manner, proceeded with his own unique sources and his own structural framework.

The first three Gospels are called the *Synoptic Gospels* because of their "similar view" (Greek *synopsis*) of the sequence of Jesus' journey to Jerusalem, his teachings, and fate. Research has shown the interdependence of these writings, with a general consensus concerning the historical priority of Mark. In addition to the use of Mark's Gospel, Matthew and Luke also used a document now referred to as "Q," a collection of teachings attributed to Jesus, which is not extant but recoverable only by isolating material held in common by Matthew and Luke and not present in Mark (cf. Matt. 3:7-10 and Luke 3:7-9). In addition to the use of Mark and Q, Matthew drew upon a range of sources (M) known only to him in order to include additional material unique to his Gospel (for example, Matt. 1:18-2:23), and Luke did the same (L)(for example, Luke 1:5-2:52).

The Gospel According to Mark Mark is the earliest of the gospels and the shortest. Scholars

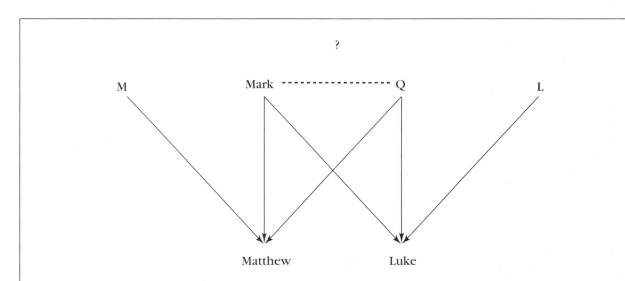

Figure IV-6 Diagram of Synoptic Gospels
This diagram illustrates the relationship between the three synoptic gospels: (a) Mark and Q originated prior to Matthew and Luke; (b) Matthew and Luke used both Mark and Q in the composition of their Gospels; (c) Matthew and Luke relied on additional sources (M and L respectively) to bring other material unique to their respective compositions. Whether Mark knew of the Q source or drew upon its contents is questionable and probably unlikely.

date its composition between 64–75 CE because of its emphasis on the cost of discipleship (8:34-38; 9:35; 10:29-31 & 35-45) and the detailed attention given to Jesus' suffering and death—about a fourth of the gospel. It was most probably written during or shortly after the Neronian persecution of the Christians in Rome, 64-68. As mentioned above, the authors of Matthew and Luke use Mark as a primary source, and it is believed that their intent, each for separate reasons, was to supplant Mark's gospel.

An old tradition is that the author of Mark was the missionary companion of Peter. However, modern historians are reluctant to support this theory, preferring to leave the question of authorship open. The perspective of the gospel is clearly more Gentile than Jewish, closer to Paul's theology, than are the gospels of Matthew or Luke. The way in which the story is told reveals unfamiliarity with the area of Palestine. Jesus is seen as the "Son of God" in the sense of a divine being, which contrasts with the Jewish understanding of a Messiah (Greek: *Christos*) who is a human leader. Also evident in the gospel is a shift in emphasis from the Jewish idea of obedience to God's will to the newer concept of redemption by God's grace through the savior Jesus the Christ.

Another distinguishing characteristic of this gospel is the negative way in which the disciples are portrayed. They are always not understanding, uncomprehending, and "their hearts are hardened." (See among others 4:13; 6:45; 8:14ff). Most scholars interpret this as a reflection of the growing conflict between Jewish-Christians and Gentile-Christians, a conflict in which Paul was engaged and which was deeply divisive.

You will note in your reading that Jesus is constantly instructing people not to tell what he has done following a healing or exorcism, but of course they do. This theme is referred to as the "Messianic Secret." One cannot be absolutely certain as to the reason the author set up his story this way, but two explanations are helpful. The first explanation is that it is a further polemic against Jewish-Christians who do not accept Jesus as he is understood within Gentile-Christian circles. A second explanation, perhaps not incompatible with the first, is that the author intended his gospel as an apologetic because Jesus was not immediately recognized as the unique representative of God.

The following is a sectional outline of the text that you will find useful in your study:

Chapter 1: 14: The proclamation by John the Baptist is much after the manner of the reception of eastern potentates. The author takes care of Jesus' baptism and temptation in a few short verses. It is clear that his concern is not a "life of Jesus" or even a description of the man; it is rather the proclamation of Jesus as Son of God and what that means to the world.

1:14–7:37: This section of the gospel tells the story of Jesus' ministry in Galilee. It may at first appear as though it is a continuous narrative, but if you read carefully you will realize that it is many individual stories strung together "like pearls on a string" often with no real connection between them. The fate of John the Baptist is told in 6:14-29. As we are told in 1:14, Jesus' ministry does not begin until after John is arrested. Also in 1:14 we are told that Jesus is quoted as appealing to his hearers that they should "believe in the gospel." Jesus would not have used the term "gospel" since "gospel," the good news about Jesus, is a post-resurrection word. Note that there are two "feeding stories" in this section that are symbolic of the Eucharist.

Chapters 8 and 9 tell of Jesus' ministry beyond Galilee. The transfiguration story, 9:2, is believed to be a displaced resurrection story. Chapter 10 is the story of Jesus' journey to Jerusalem, and chapters 11 and 12 relate reactions to Jesus in Jerusalem and the controversy that surrounds him.

Chapter 13 is referred to as the "little apocalypse." An apocalypse has the meaning of revealing what is hidden, and is generally presented as a prophetic revelation. The Book of Daniel in the Hebrew Scriptures and the Book of Revelation in the Christian scriptures are other examples of apocalyptic literature. This collection of sayings attributed to Jesus probably reflects more accurately the beliefs of the early church. Note that the secrets are given only to the four senior disciples, Peter, James, John and Andrew. Bound up with these stories is an anticipation of the second coming. At this time the Christian community expected Jesus' return in glory and the end of the world to come in their lifetime. The later gospels, Luke and Matthew, reflect the second Christian generation trying in different ways to come to grips with the delay of the *parousia* (second coming). While continuing to look forward fervently to Jesus' return in glory, they began to develop explanations for the delay—for example, allowing time to spread the Christian message more widely.

Chapters 14, 15, and 16 tell the Easter stories of the trial, judgment, passion, and resurrection of Jesus. Another criticism of Jewish-Christians can be read in the lines that tell us that the centurion (a Roman!) recognizes Jesus as the Son of God. The gospel ends (16:1-8) without a resurrection appearance, unless one considers the story in chapter 9. Later Christians added an additional eleven verses (9-20) that offer resurrection appearances to Mary Magdalene and the eleven disciples, but scholars have long dismissed these as not part of the original text.

The Gospel of John   The Gospel of John was the last of the four canonical gospels to be written, probably around 90–100. Although the author is traditionally identified as John "the beloved disciple" of Jesus, like the Synoptic authors he is an anonymous writer who almost certainly belongs to the second Christian generation, not to the generation of the apostles. The author was a member of what scholars call the "Johannine Circle," perhaps centered in Ephesus, members of which produced both the Fourth Gospel and the three Letters of John among the New Testament writings.

Every attentive reader of the four gospels, whether ancient or modern, recognizes that when we turn from the Synoptic Gospels to the Gospel of John we enter a very different world. The language is strikingly different, the way Jesus' story is told deviates in important respects from the story in the Synoptics, and the author's theological interpretation of the meaning and implications of who Jesus is advances well beyond anything in Mark, Matthew, and Luke. Indeed, John presents a Jesus whose person, activity, and way of teaching stand in marked contrast to the Jesus of the Synoptics.

Whether John's witness to Jesus was a "true" or a "false" gospel was disputed among Christians from the time it first circulated. Its critics point out how in many ways it departs from the Synoptic Gospels. For example, they portray Jesus' ministry as lasting about a year; in John's Gospel it is three years. Mark, Matthew, and Luke portray Jesus' cleansing of the Jerusalem Temple as his last public act before his arrest, while John places it at the

beginning of his ministry and interprets it quite differently. John's account of Jesus' last days also disagrees with those of the Synoptic authors. In the Synoptics, for example, the Last Supper is a Passover meal. In John's Gospel the Last Supper takes place before Passover, while Jesus the new "sacrificial Lamb" is crucified on Passover itself.

Whereas Mark, Matthew, and Luke portray Jesus as teaching primarily in parables and brief sayings, John often has Jesus teach in long discourses in which parable has been transformed into allegory. For example, Luke has Jesus tell a very brief story about a shepherd who loses a sheep and hunts for it until he finds it. By contrast, John constructs a long allegory about Jesus himself as the shepherd:

> . . . I am the door of the sheep. All who came before me are thieves and robbers; but the sheep did not heed them. I am the door; if anyone enters by me, he will be saved, and will go in and out and find pasture. The thief comes only to kill and destroy. . . . I am the good shepherd. The good shepherd lays down his life for the sheep. (John 10:7-11)

These long and heavily allegorical speeches of Jesus in John's Gospel have led many scholars to think of the Fourth Gospel as a kind of extended meditation on the person, the life, and the teaching of Jesus by someone who knows the basic story narrated by the Synoptic authors but chooses, on the basis of a distinctive and very well-developed theological perspective, to tell the story from this particular theological standpoint. The great third-century theologian Origen of Alexandria, defending John's Gospel, wrote: "although he does not always tell the truth literally, he always tells the truth spiritually," (Commentary on John 10.4-6).

At the deepest theological level the most striking difference between John and the Synoptics is that whereas Mark, Matthew, and Luke interpret Jesus as a human being who stood in a unique relationship to God, John interprets Jesus as God himself in human form, as in the "cosmic" prologue, imitating the opening of the Book of Genesis, with which the gospel opens: "In the beginning was the Word (Greek: logos), and the Word was with God, and the Word was God." (John 1:1). The fact that down through the centuries Christians have interpreted the Synoptic titles used of Jesus—"Son of Man," "Christ" (Messiah), and "Son of God"—as referring to Jesus' divine status is because Christians have interpreted the first three gospels through the lens of John's theology. At the time of the Synoptic authors, and within the Jewish context out of which Christianity arose, those titles referred, not to God incarnate in a human being but to a man gifted with the power of the holy spirit and designated by God to rule in God's kingdom.

Thus an early Christian writing that began as a dubious and debated candidate for status as an authoritative text became the gospel through which what became the dominant tradition in Christianity interpreted the other three. Indeed, John's Gospel, together with the letters of Paul, became a main foundation of Christian doctrine.

The Book of Revelation   We will close this chapter with some comments about the final book in the Christian New Testament, The Book of Revelation. These comments follow the perspective of the majority of Christian scholars. First we should note that there is a long history of apocalyptic literature from both Jewish and pagan sources that precedes this book. Apocalyptic literature is a literature that tells of the "last things" and it is always concerned with a current situation.

The author identifies himself as John of Patmos. (Patmos is an island off the coast of Asia Minor used by the Romans as a penal colony.) Some early Christians associated this John with the author of the Gospel, but this conclusion does not stand up to critical analysis. There are significant textual differences. Revelation does not demonstrate a full command of the Greek language and contains many Semitisms, indicating that the writer is an Aramaic speaker. The Gospel of John talks about the Church as a continuous faith moving into the future, while Revelation announces the end of existing time. The author writes as if he is looking back at the twelve disciples, but is not one of them (Rev. 21:14).

The Book of Revelation is specifically addressed to the churches in Asia Minor and is concerned to bolster the faith of the Christians of those churches in light of renewed persecution by the Emperor Domitian (ca. 90s). Using the number seven in a cyclical pattern John presents and reinforces his message of the coming of the end time. Within the Vision (Rev 4:1-22:19) which constitutes the majority of the text, one must search for the historical connections; for example, compare 17:1-19:10 to what you know about the Roman Empire of the time. Seven visions of the End are revealed in 19:11-21:14. These suggest a belief that history marches forward according to God's will. The world is redeemed and populated by the good and the evil perishes.

Through the centuries, as the world has continued long beyond the time when early Christians believed it would end, some Christians have interpreted the first-century symbolism and prophecy of the Book of Revelation as applying to their own quite different times and places, and on that basis have believed that the End-Time was at hand. This happened, for example, in medieval Europe with the approach of the millennium year 1000. In 1844 an American named William Miller led his followers to a hilltop to await the end of the world, based upon his reading of the "signs of the times" in Revelation. Martin Luther put the Book of Revelation at the bottom of the list of New Testament writings as an authority for Christians. He was skeptical of it because of its obscurity. "A revelation," he wrote, "should be revealing" (Roland Bainton, *Here I Stand: A Life of Martin Luther,* New York: New American Library, 1952, 261).

Other Christians since the church's early days have believed that the specific contents of the visions in the Book of Revelation are too cryptic and puzzling to be used as predictors of when God will bring the present world order to an end. They have preferred to interpret it much more generally and allegorically as a portrayal of the ultimate triumph of Christ and his followers. Yet some Christians continue to take the book out of its historical context and apply it to world events that are taking place in our time and which they believe herald the catastrophes and upheavals that will usher in the Last Days.

QUESTIONS FOR STUDY AND DISCUSSION

1. What criteria do New Testament scholars use in reconstructing the historical Jesus from evidence available? Why do the gospel stories present a problem for the historian?

2. What were the main features of Jesus' teaching? What is their relationship to the beliefs and practices of the Judaism that was his heritage?

3. What role did Paul of Tarsus play in the growth of the early church? What was his interpretation of the meaning and significance of Jesus?

4. How did the earliest Christians understand themselves in relation to Judaism? What problems arose regarding Christianity's relationship to Judaism?

5. Why were Christians periodically persecuted by Roman officials? Why weren't Jews also persecuted? Do you think the Christian unwillingness to compromise and glorification of martyrdom was necessary or desirable? Can you think of some other religious or political movements that have considered martyrdom for the cause important? P 234

6. Describe what makes the Gospel of John different from the Synoptic Gospels. P 234

7. Explain how the first three gospels are related. You may use a diagram.

8. Explain the probable authorship of the Book of Revelation. Also explain how this scripture has been understood and misunderstood over the centuries.

SUGGESTIONS FOR FURTHER READING

Bornkamm, Günther. *Jesus of Nazareth*. New York: Harper & Row, 1960.

Brown, Raymond. *An Introduction to the New Testament*. New York: Doubleday, 1997.

Carmody, Denise L. *Christian Feminist Theology*. Cambridge, MA: Blackwell. 1995.

Chilton, Bruce. *Rabbi Jesus*. New York: Random House, 2000.

Frend, W. H. C. *The Rise of Christianity*. Philadelphia: Fortress, 1984.

Hennecke, E. & Schneemelcher, W. *The New Testament Apocrypha*. 2 vols, rev. ed. Philadelphia: Westminster, 1991–92.

Koester, Helmut. *Ancient Christian Gospels: Their History and Development*. Philadelphia: Trinity, 1990.

Kloppenberg, J. S. *The Formation of Q*. Philadelphia: Fortress, 1987.

Meeks, Wayne. *The Origins of Christian Morality*. New Haven: Yale, 1993.

Murphy-O'Connor, Jerome. *Paul: A Critical Life*. Oxford: Clarendon, 1996.

Pagels, Elaine. *The Gnostic Paul*. Harrisburg, PA: Trinity Press International, 1975.

Schüssler Fiorenza, Elisabeth. *In Memory of Her: A Feminist Theological Reconstruction of Christian Origins*. New York: Crossroad, 1983.

Selections from the *CHRISTIAN SCRIPTURES*

The first English translation of the Bible from Hebrew and Greek texts was made by William Tyndale in the sixteenth century, who was burned at the stake for his efforts. However, his death was not in vain. Within the same century five other English translations appeared, all reliant on Tyndale's martyred efforts. Soon it became apparent that an official version was required, and this was authorized by King James I of England, Scotland and Wales, successor to Queen Elizabeth I. The King James version of the Bible appeared in 1611. It is noted for its eloquence of language, and even today holds its sway for those who admire "the music of its cadences and the felicities of its rhythm." The King James Bible has had a deep and pervasive influence on the English language and English-speaking cultures, from phrases in our common speech to the themes and language of great works of literature.

However, from a scholarly point of view the King James version has serious defects. Its translators did not have access to the oldest and most reliable Greek and Hebrew texts, and discoveries in the eighteenth and nineteenth centuries dated even the best of those. A committee to revise the King James version was formulated in the mid-nineteenth century and produced the English Revised Version of the Bible in 1881–1885. An American Standard Version was copyrighted—to protect the text from unauthorized changes—in 1901. The copyright was acquired by the International Council of Religious Education in 1928, and from the Council the ownership passed to the United States and Canadian churches affiliated with this organization. In 1937 they authorized a new revision which would "embody the best results of modern scholarship." The Revised Standard Version of the New Testament was published in 1946, followed in 1952 by the publication of the Revised Standard Version of both the Old Testament (Christian terminology for the Hebrew Scriptures) and the New Testament. The "RSV" has met with wide acceptance by Protestant, Catholic, and Orthodox Christians, and the version from which our New Testament readings are taken was published with the official approval of authoritative bodies of those three Christian groups.

In 1959 the committee reaffirmed this translation, and made some corrections in response to suggestions from readers. To quote from the introduction to this version, "The Revised Standard Version is not a new translation in the language of today. It is not a paraphrase which aims at striking idioms. It is a revision which seeks to preserve all that is best in the English Bible as it has been known and used through the years. . . . We have resisted the temptation to use phrases that are merely current usage, and have sought to put the message of the Bible in simple, enduring words. . . ." Students who are interested in learning more about the process of producing the Revised Standard Version of the Bible can consult two pamphlets, *An Introduction to the Revised Standard Version of the Old Testament* and *An Introduction to the Revised Standard Version of the New Testament*, written by members of the Committee.

THE GOSPEL ACCORDING TO MARK

1 The beginning of the gospel of Jesus Christ, the Son of God.
  [2] As it is written in Isaiah the prophet,

  "Behold, I send my messenger before thy face,
  who shall prepare thy way;

  [3] the voice of one crying in the wilderness:
  Prepare the way of the Lord,
  make his paths straight—"

  [4] John the baptizer appeared in the wilderness, preaching a baptism of repentance for the forgiveness

---

"The Gospel According to Mark," and "First Letter of Paul to the Corinthians," reprinted from *The Common Bible,* (1973), the Division of Christian Education of the National Council of Churches in the USA.

of sins. 5And there went out to him all the country of Judea, and all the people of Jerusalem; and they were baptized by him in the river Jordan, confessing their sins. 6Now John was clothed with camel's hair, and had a leather girdle around his waist, and ate locusts and wild honey. 7And he preached, saying, "After me comes he who is mightier than I, the thong of whose sandals I am not worthy to stoop down and untie. 8I have baptized you with water; but he will baptize you with the Holy Spirit."

9In those days Jesus came from Nazareth of Galilee and was baptized by John in the Jordan. 10And when he came up out of the water, immediately he saw the heavens opened and the Spirit descending upon him like a dove; 11and a voice came from heaven, "Thou art my beloved Son; with thee I am well pleased."

12The Spirit immediately drove him out into the wilderness. 13And he was in the wilderness forty days, tempted by Satan; and he was with the wild beasts; and the angels ministered to him.

14Now after John was arrested, Jesus came into Galilee, preaching the gospel of God, 15and saying, "The time is fulfilled, and the kingdom of God is at hand; repent, and believe in the gospel."

16And passing along by the Sea of Galilee, he saw Simon and Andrew the brother of Simon casting a net in the sea; for they were fishermen. 17And Jesus said to them, "Follow me and I will make you become fishers of men." 18And immediately they left their nets and followed him. 19And going on a little farther, he saw James the son of Zeb'edee and John his brother, who were in their boat mending the nets. 20And immediately he called them; and they left their father Zeb'edee in the boat with the hired servants, and followed him.

21And they went into Caper'na-um; and immediately on the sabbath he entered the synagogue and taught. 22And they were astonished at his teaching, for he taught them as one who had authority, and not as the scribes. 23And immediately there was in their synagogue a man with an unclean spirit; 24and he cried out, "What have you to do with us, Jesus of Nazareth? Have you come to destroy us? I know who you are, the Holy One of God." 25But Jesus rebuked him, saying, "Be silent, and come out of him!" 26And the unclean spirit, convulsing him and crying with a loud voice, came out of him. 27And they were all amazed, so that they questioned

among themselves, saying, "What is this? A new teaching! With authority he commands even the unclean spirits, and they obey him." 28And at once his fame spread everywhere throughout all the surrounding region of Galilee.

29And immediately he left the synagogue, and entered the house of Simon and Andrew, with James and John. 30Now Simon's mother-in-law lay sick with a fever, and immediately they told him of her. 31And he came and took her by the hand and lifted her up, and the fever left her; and she served them.

32That evening, at sundown, they brought to him all who were sick or possessed with demons. 33And the whole city was gathered together about the door. 34And he healed many who were sick with various diseases, and cast out many demons; and he would not permit the demons to speak, because they knew him.

35And in the morning, a great while before day, he rose and went out to a lonely place, and there he prayed. 36And Simon and those who were with him pursued him, 37and they found him and said to him, "Every one is searching for you." 38And he said to them, "Let us go on to the next towns, that I may preach there also; for that is why I came out." 39And he went throughout all Galilee, preaching in their synagogues and casting out demons.

40And a leper came to him beseeching him, and kneeling said to him, "If you will, you can make me clean." 41Moved with pity, he stretched out his hand and touched him, and said to him, "I will; be clean." 42And immediately the leprosy left him, and he was made clean. 43And he sternly charged him, and sent him away at once, 44and said to him, "See that you say nothing to any one; but go, show yourself to the priest, and offer for your cleansing what Moses commanded, for a proof to the people." 45But he went out and began to talk freely about it, and to spread the news, so that Jesus could no longer openly enter a town, but was out in the country; and people came to him from every quarter.

2 And when he returned to Caper'na-um after some days, it was reported that he was at home. 2And many were gathered together, so that there was no longer room for them, not even about the door; and he was preaching the word to them. 3And they came, bringing to him a paralytic carried by four men. 4And when they could not get near him

because of the crowd, they removed the roof above him; and when they had made an opening, they let down the pallet on which the paralytic lay. ⁵And when Jesus saw their faith, he said to the paralytic, "My son, your sins are forgiven." ⁶Now some of the scribes were sitting there, questioning in their hearts, ⁷"Why does this man speak thus? It is blasphemy! Who can forgive sins but God alone?" ⁸And immediately Jesus, perceiving in his spirit that they thus questioned within themselves, said to them, "Why do you question thus in your hearts? ⁹Which is easier, to say to the paralytic, 'Your sins are forgiven,' or to say, 'Rise, take up your pallet and walk'? ¹⁰But that you may know that the Son of man has authority on earth to forgive sins"—he said to the paralytic—¹¹"I say to you, rise, take up your pallet and go home." ¹²And he rose, and immediately took up the pallet and went out before them all; so that they were all amazed and glorified God, saying, "We never saw anything like this!"

¹³He went out again beside the sea; and all the crowd gathered about him, and he taught them. ¹⁴And as he passed on, he saw Levi the son of Alphaeus sitting at the tax office, and he said to him, "Follow me." And he rose and followed him.

¹⁵And as he sat at table in his house, many tax collectors and sinners were sitting with Jesus and his disciples; for there were many who followed him. ¹⁶And the scribes of the Pharisees, when they saw that he was eating with sinners and tax collectors, said to his disciples, "Why does he eat with tax collectors and sinners?" ¹⁷And when Jesus heard it, he said to them, "Those who are well have no need of a physician, but those who are sick; I came not to call the righteous, but sinners."

¹⁸Now John's disciples and the Pharisees were fasting; and people came and said to him, "Why do John's disciples and the disciples of the Pharisees fast, but your disciples do not fast?" ¹⁹And Jesus said to them, "Can the wedding guests fast while the bridegroom is with them? As long as they have the bridegroom with them, they cannot fast. ²⁰The days will come, when the bridegroom is taken away from them, and then they will fast in that day. ²¹No one sews a piece of unshrunk cloth on an old garment; if he does, the patch tears away from it, the new from the old, and a worse tear is made. ²²And no one puts new wine into old wineskins; if he does,

the wine will burst the skins, and the wine is lost, and so are the skins; but new wine is for fresh skins."

²³One sabbath he was going through the grainfields; and as they made their way his disciples began to pluck heads of grain. ²⁴And the Pharisees said to him, "Look, why are they doing what is not lawful on the sabbath?" ²⁵And he said to them, "Have you never read what David did, when he was in need and was hungry, he and those who were with him: ²⁶how he entered the house of God, when Abi'athar was high priest, and ate the bread of the Presence, which it is not lawful for any but the priests to eat, and also gave it to those who were with him?" ²⁷And he said to them, "The sabbath was made for man, not man for the sabbath; ²⁸so the Son of man is lord even of the sabbath."

3 Again he entered the synagogue, and a man was there who had a withered hand. ²And they watched him, to see whether he would heal him on the sabbath, so that they might accuse him. ³And he said to the man who had the withered hand, "Come here." ⁴And he said to them, "Is it lawful on the sabbath to do good or to do harm, to save life or to kill?" But they were silent. ⁵And he looked around at them with anger, grieved at their hardness of heart, and said to the man, "Stretch out your hand." He stretched it out, and his hand was restored. ⁶The Pharisees went out, and immediately held counsel with the Hero'di-ans against him, how to destroy him.

⁷Jesus withdrew with his disciples to the sea, and a great multitude from Galilee followed; also from Judea ⁸and Jerusalem and Idume'a and from beyond the Jordan and from about Tyre and Sidon a great multitude, hearing all that he did, came to him. ⁹And he told his disciples to have a boat ready for him because of the crowd, lest they should crush him; ¹⁰for he had healed many, so that all who had diseases pressed upon him to touch him. ¹¹And whenever the unclean spirits beheld him, they fell down before him and cried out, "You are the Son of God." ¹²And he strictly ordered them not to make him known.

¹³And he went up on the mountain, and called to him those whom he desired; and they came to him. ¹⁴And he appointed twelve, to be with him, and to be sent out to preach ¹⁵and have authority to cast out demons: ¹⁶Simon whom he surnamed

Peter; [17]James the son of Zeb'edee and John the brother of James, whom he surnamed Boaner'ges, that is, sons of thunder; [18]Andrew, and Philip, and Bartholomew, and Matthew, and Thomas, and James the son of Alphaeus, and Thaddaeus, and Simon the Cananaean, [19]and Judas Iscariot, who betrayed him.

Then he went home; [20]and the crowd came together again, so that they could not even eat. [21]And when his family heard it, they went out to seize him, for people were saying, "He is beside himself." [22]And the scribes who came down from Jerusalem said, "He is possessed by Be-el'zebul, and by the prince of demons he casts out the demons." [23]And he called them to him, and said to them in parables, "How can Satan cast out Satan? [24]If a kingdom is divided against itself, that kingdom cannot stand. [25]And if a house is divided against itself, that house will not be able to stand. [26]And if Satan has risen up against himself and is divided, he cannot stand, but is coming to an end.

[27]But no one can enter a strong man's house and plunder his goods, unless he first binds the strong man; then indeed he may plunder his house.

[28]"Truly, I say to you, all sins will be forgiven the sons of men, and whatever blasphemies they utter; [29]but whoever blasphemes against the Holy Spirit never has forgiveness, but is guilty of an eternal sin"——[30]for they had said, "He has an unclean spirit."

[31]And his mother and his brothers came; and standing outside they sent to him and called him. [32]And a crowd was sitting about him; and they said to him, "Your mother and your brothers are outside, asking for you." [33]And he replied, "Who are my mother and my brothers?" [34]And looking around on those who sat about him, he said, "Here are my mother and my brothers! [35]Whoever does the will of God is my brother, and sister, and mother."

4 Again he began to teach beside the sea. And a very large crowd gathered about him, so that he got into a boat and sat in it on the sea; and the whole crowd was beside the sea on the land. [2]And he taught them many things in parables, and in his teaching he said to them: [3]"Listen! A sower went out to sow. [4]And as he sowed, some seed fell along the path, and the birds came and devoured it. [5]Other seed fell on rocky ground, where it had not much soil, and immediately it sprang up, since it

had no depth of soil; [6]and when the sun rose it was scorched, and since it had no root it withered away. [7]Other seed fell among thorns and the thorns grew up and choked it, and it yielded no grain. [8]And other seeds fell into good soil and brought forth grain, growing up and increasing and yielding thirtyfold and sixtyfold and a hundredfold." [9]And he said, "He who has ears to hear, let him hear."

[10]And when he was alone, those who were about him with the twelve asked him concerning the parables. [11]And he said to them, "To you has been given the secret of the kingdom of God, but for those outside everything is in parables; [12]so that they may indeed see but not perceive, and may indeed hear but not understand; lest they should turn again, and be forgiven." [13]And he said to them, "Do you not understand this parable? How then will you understand all the parables? [14]The sower sows the word. [15]And these are the ones along the path, where the word is sown; when they hear, Satan immediately comes and takes away the word which is sown in them. [16]And these in like manner are the ones sown upon rocky ground, who, when they hear the word, immediately receive it with joy; [17]and they have no root in themselves, but endure for a while; then, when tribulation or persecution arises on account of the word, immediately they fall away. [18]And others are the ones sown among thorns; they are those who hear the word, [19]but the cares of the world, and the delight in riches, and the desire for other things, enter in and choke the word, and it proves unfruitful. [20]But those that were sown upon the good soil are the ones who hear the word and accept it and bear fruit, thirtyfold and sixtyfold and a hundredfold."

[21]And he said to them, "Is a lamp brought in to be put under a bushel, or under a bed, and not on a stand? [22]For there is nothing hid, except to be made manifest; nor is anything secret, except to come to light. [23]If any man has ears to hear, let him hear." [24]And he said to them, "Take heed what you hear; the measure you give will be the measure you get, and still more will be given you. [25]For to him who has will more be given; and from him who has not, even what he has will be taken away."

[26]And he said, "The kingdom of God is as if a man should scatter seed upon the ground, [27]and should sleep and rise night and day, and the seed should sprout and grow, he knows not how. [28]The

earth produces of itself, first the blade, then the ear, then the full grain in the ear. [29]But when the grain is ripe, at once he puts in the sickle, because the harvest has come."

[30]And he said, "With what can we compare the kingdom of God, or what parable shall we use for it? [31]It is like a grain of mustard seed, which, when sown upon the ground, is the smallest of all the seeds on earth; [32]yet when it is sown it grows up and becomes the greatest of all shrubs, and puts forth large branches, so that the birds of the air can make nests in its shade."

[33]With many such parables he spoke the word to them, as they were able to hear it; [34]he did not speak to them without a parable, but privately to his own disciples he explained everything.

[35]On that day, when evening had come, he said to them, "Let us go across to the other side." [36]And leaving the crowd, they took him with them in the boat, just as he was. And other boats were with him. [37]And a great storm of wind arose, and the waves beat into the boat, so that the boat was already filling. [38]But he was in the stern, asleep on the cushion; and they woke him and said to him, "Teacher, do you not care if we perish?" [39]And he awoke and rebuked the wind, and said to the sea, "Peace! Be still!" And the wind ceased, and there was a great calm. [40]He said to them, "Why are you afraid? Have you no faith?" [41]And they were filled with awe, and said to one another, "Who then is this, that even wind and sea obey him?"

5 They came to the other side of the sea, to the country of the Ger'asenes. [2]And when he had come out of the boat, there met him out of the tombs a man with an unclean spirit, [3]who lived among the tombs; and no one could bind him any more, even with a chain; [4]for he had often been bound with fetters and chains, but the chains he wrenched apart, and the fetters he broke in pieces; and no one had the strength to subdue him. [5]Night and day among the tombs and on the mountains he was always crying out, and bruising himself with stones. [6]And when he saw Jesus from afar, he ran and worshiped him; [7]and crying out with a loud voice, he said, "What have you to do with me, Jesus, Son of the Most High God? I adjure you by God, do not torment me." [8]For he had said to him, "Come out of the man, you unclean spirit!" [9]And Jesus asked him, "What is your name?" He

replied, "My name is Legion; for we are many." [10]And he begged him eagerly not to send them out of the country. [11]Now a great herd of swine was feeding there on the hillside; [12]and they begged him, "Send us to the swine, let us enter them." [13]So he gave them leave. And the unclean spirits came out, and entered the swine; and the herd, numbering about two thousand, rushed down the steep bank into the sea, and were drowned in the sea.

[14]The herdsmen fled, and told it in the city and in the country. And people came to see what it was that had happened. [15]And they came to Jesus, and saw the demoniac sitting there, clothed and in his right mind, the man who had had the legion; and they were afraid. [16]And those who had seen it told what had happened to the demoniac and to the swine. [17]And they began to beg Jesus to depart from their neighborhood. [18]And as he was getting into the boat, the man who had been possessed with demons begged him that he might be with him. [19]But he refused, and said to him, "Go home to your friends, and tell them how much the Lord has done for you, and how he has had mercy on you." [20]And he went away and began to proclaim in the Decap'olis how much Jesus had done for him; and all men marveled.

[21]And when Jesus had crossed again in the boat to the other side, a great crowd gathered about him, and he was beside the sea. [22]Then came one of the rulers of the synagogue, Ja'irus by name; and seeing him, he fell at his feet, [23]and besought him, saying, "My little daughter is at the point of death. Come and lay your hands on her, so that she may be made well, and live." [24]And he went with him.

And a great crowd followed him and thronged about him. [25]And there was a woman who had had a flow of blood for twelve years, [26]and who had suffered much under many physicians, and had spent all that she had, and was no better but rather grew worse. [27]She had heard the reports about Jesus, and came up behind him in the crowd and touched his garment. [28]For she said, "If I touch even his garments, I shall be made well." [29]And immediately the hemorrhage ceased; and she felt in her body that she was healed of her disease. [30]And Jesus, perceiving in himself that power had gone forth from him, immediately turned about in the crowd, and said, "Who touched my garments?" [31]And his disciples said to him, "You see the crowd pressing around you, and yet you say, 'Who touched me?'" [32]And he looked around to see who had done it. [33]But the woman, knowing what had been done to her, came in fear and trembling and fell down before him, and told him the whole truth. [34]And he said to her, "Daughter, your faith has made you well; go in peace, and be healed of your disease."

[35]While he was still speaking, there came from the ruler's house some who said, "Your daughter is dead. Why trouble the Teacher any further?" [36]But ignoring what they said, Jesus said to the ruler of the synagogue, "Do not fear, only believe." [37]And he allowed no one to follow him except Peter and James and John the brother of James. [38]When they came to the house of the ruler of the synagogue, he saw a tumult, and people weeping and wailing loudly. [39]And when he had entered, he said to them, "Why do you make a tumult and weep? The child is not dead but sleeping." [40]And they laughed at him. But he put them all outside, and took the child's father and mother and those who were with him, and went in where the child was. [41]Taking her by the hand he said to her, "Tal'itha cu'mi"; which means, "Little girl, I say to you, arise." [42]And immediately the girl got up and walked (she was twelve years of age), and they were immediately overcome with amazement. [43]And he strictly charged them that no one should know this, and told them to give her something to eat.

6 He went away from there and came to his own country; and his disciples followed him. [2]And on the sabbath he began to teach in the synagogue; and many who heard him were astonished, saying, "Where did this man get all this? What is the wisdom given to him? What mighty works are wrought by his hands! [3]Is not this the carpenter, the son of Mary and brother of James and Joses and Judas and Simon, and are not his sisters here with us?" And they took offense at him. [4]And Jesus said to them, "A prophet is not without honor, except in his own country, and among his own kin, and in his own house." [5]And he could do no mighty work there, except that he laid his hands upon a few sick people and healed them. [6]And he marveled because of their unbelief.

And he went about among the villages teaching.

[7]And he called to him the twelve, and began to send them out two by two, and gave them authority over the unclean spirits. [8]He charged them to take nothing for their journey except a staff; no bread, no bag, no money in their belts; [9]but to wear sandals and not put on two tunics. [10]And he said to them, "Where you enter a house, stay there until you leave the place. [11]And if any place will not receive you and they refuse to hear you, when you leave, shake off the dust that is on your feet for a testimony against them." [12]So they went out and preached that men should repent. [13]And they cast out many demons, and anointed with oil many that were sick and healed them.

[14]King Herod heard of it; for Jesus' name had become known. Some said, "John the baptizer has been raised from the dead; that is why these powers are at work in him." [15]But others said, "It is Eli'jah." And others said, "It is a prophet, like one of the prophets of old." [16]But when Herod heard of it he said, "John, whom I beheaded, has been raised." [17]For Herod had sent and seized John, and bound him in prison for the sake of Hero'di-as, his brother Philip's wife; because he had married her. [18]For John said to Herod, "It is not lawful for you to have your brother's wife." [19]And Hero'di-as had a grudge against him, and wanted to kill him. But she could not, [20]For Herod feared John, knowing that he was a righteous and holy man, and kept him safe. When he heard him, he was much perplexed; and yet he heard him gladly. [21]But an opportunity came when Herod on his birthday gave a banquet for his courtiers and officers and the leading men of Galilee. [22]For when Hero'di-as' daughter came in and danced, she pleased Herod and his guests; and the king said to the girl, "Ask me for whatever you wish, and I will grant it." [23]And he vowed to her, "Whatever you ask me, I will give you, even half of my kingdom." [24]And she went out, and said to her mother, "What shall I ask?" And she said, "The head of John the baptizer." [25]And she came in immediately with haste to the king, and asked, saying, "I want you to give me at once the head of John the Baptist on a platter." [26]And the king was exceedingly sorry; but because of his oaths and his guests he did not want to break his word to her. [27]And immediately the king sent a soldier of the guard and gave orders to bring his head. He went and beheaded him in the prison, [28]and brought his head on a platter, and gave it to the girl; and the girl gave it to her mother. [29]When his

disciples heard of it, they came and took his body, and laid it in a tomb.

[30]The apostles returned to Jesus, and told him all that they had done and taught. [31]And he said to them, "Come away by yourselves to a lonely place, and rest a while." For many were coming and going, and they had no leisure even to eat. [32]And they went away in the boat to a lonely place by themselves. [33]Now many saw them going, and knew them, and they ran there on foot from all the towns, and got there ahead of them. [34]As he went ashore he saw a great throng, and he had compassion on them, because they were like sheep without a shepherd; and he began to teach them many things. [35]And when it grew late, his disciples came to him and said, "This is a lonely place, and the hour is now late; [36]send them away, to go into the country and villages round about and buy themselves something to eat." [37]But he answered them, "You give them something to eat." And they said to him, "Shall we go and buy two hundred denarii worth of bread, and give it to them to eat?" [38]And he said to them, "How many loaves have you? Go and see." And when they had found out, they said, "Five, and two fish." [39]Then he commanded them all to sit down by companies upon the green grass. [40]So they sat down in groups, by hundreds and by fifties. [41]And taking the five loaves and the two fish he looked up to heaven, and blessed, and broke the loaves, and gave them to the disciples to set before the people; and he divided the two fish among them all. [42]And they all ate and were satisfied. [43]And they took up twelve baskets full of broken pieces and of the fish. [44]And those who ate the loaves were five thousand men.

[45]Immediately he made his disciples get into the boat and go before him to the other side, to Beth-sa′ida, while he dismissed the crowd. [46]And after he had taken leave of them, he went up on the mountain to pray. [47]And when evening came, the boat was out on the sea, and he was alone on the land. [48]And he saw that they were making headway painfully, for the wind was against them. And about the fourth watch of the night he came to them, walking on the sea. He meant to pass by them, [49]but when they saw him walking on the sea they thought it was a ghost, and cried out; [50]for they all saw him, and were terrified. But immediately he spoke to them and said, "Take heart, it is I; have no fear." [51]And he got into the boat with them and the wind ceased. And they were utterly astounded, [52]for they did not understand about the loaves, but their hearts were hardened.

[53]And when they had crossed over, they came to land at Gennes′aret, and moored to the shore. [54]And when they got out of the boat, immediately the people recognized him, [55]and ran about the whole neighborhood and began to bring sick people on their pallets to any place where they heard he was. [56]And wherever he came, in villages, cities, or country, they laid the sick in the market places, and besought him that they might touch even the fringe of his garment; and as many as touched it were made well.

7 Now when the Pharisees gathered together to him, with some of the scribes, who had come from Jerusalem, [2]they saw that some of his disciples ate with hands defiled, that is, unwashed. [3](For the Pharisees, and all the Jews, do not eat unless they wash their hands, observing the tradition of the elders; [4]and when they come from the market place, they do not eat unless they purify themselves; and there are many other traditions which they observe, the washing of cups and pots and vessels of bronze.) [5]And the Pharisees and the scribes asked him, "Why do your disciples not live according to the tradition of the elders, but eat with hands defiled?" [6]And he said to them, "Well did Isaiah prophesy of you hypocrites, as it is written,

'This people honors me with their lips,
   but their heart is far from me;
[7]in vain do they worship me,
   teaching as doctrines the precepts of men.'

[8]You leave the commandment of God, and hold fast the tradition of men."

[9]And he said to them, "You have a fine way of rejecting the commandment of God, in order to keep your tradition! [10]For Moses said, 'Honor your father and your mother'; and, 'He who speaks evil of father or mother, let him surely die'; [11]but you say, 'If a man tells his father or his mother, What you would have gained from me is Corban' (that is, given to God)—[12]then you no longer permit him to do anything for his father or mother, [13]thus making void

the word of God through your tradition which you hand on. And many such things you do."

¹⁴And he called the people to him again, and said to them, "Hear me, all of you, and understand: ¹⁵there is nothing outside a man which by going into him can defile him; but the things which come out of a man are what defile him." ¹⁷And when he had entered the house, and left the people, his disciples asked him about the parable. ¹⁸And he said to them, "Then are you also without understanding? Do you not see that whatever goes into a man from outside cannot defile him, ¹⁹since it enters, not his heart but his stomach, and so passes on?" (Thus he declared all foods clean.) ²⁰And he said, "What comes out of a man is what defiles a man. ²¹For from within, out of the heart of man, come evil thoughts, fornication, theft, murder, adultery, ²²coveting, wickedness, deceit, licentiousness, envy, slander, pride, foolishness. ²³All these evil things come from within, and they defile a man."

²⁴And from there he arose and went away to the region of Tyre and Sidon. And he entered a house, and would not have any one know it; yet he could not be hid. ²⁵But immediately a woman, whose little daughter was possessed by an unclean spirit, heard of him, and came and fell down at his feet. ²⁶Now the woman was a Greek, a Syrophoeni′cian by birth. And she begged him to cast the demon out of her daughter. ²⁷And he said to her, "Let the children first be fed, for it is not right to take the children's bread and throw it to the dogs." ²⁸But she answered him, "Yes, Lord; yet even the dogs under the table eat the children's crumbs." ²⁹And he said to her, "For this saying you may go your way; the demon has left your daughter." ³⁰And she went home, and found the child lying in bed, and the demon gone.

³¹Then he returned from the region of Tyre, and went through Sidon to the Sea of Galilee, through the region of the Decap′olis. ³²And they brought to him a man who was deaf and had an impediment in his speech; and they besought him to lay his hand upon him. ³³And taking him aside from the multitude privately, he put his fingers into his ears, and he spat and touched his tongue; ³⁴and looking up to heaven, he sighed, and said to him, "Eph′phatha," that is, "Be opened." ³⁵And his ears were opened, his tongue was released, and he spoke plainly. ³⁶And he charged them to tell no one; but the more he charged them, the more zealously they proclaimed it. ³⁷And they were astonished beyond measure, saying, "He has done all things well; he even makes the deaf hear and the dumb speak."

8 In those days, when again a great crowd had gathered, and they had nothing to eat, he called his disciples to him, and said to them, ²"I have compassion on the crowd, because they have been with me now three days, and have nothing to eat; ³and if I send them away hungry to their homes, they will faint on the way; and some of them have come a long way." ⁴And his disciples answered him, "How can one feed these men with bread here in the desert?" ⁵And he asked them, "How many loaves have you?" They said, "Seven." ⁶And he commanded the crowd to sit down on the ground; and he took the seven loaves, and having given thanks he broke them and gave them to his disciples to set before the people; and they set them before the crowd. ⁷And they had a few small fish; and having blessed them, he commanded that these also should be set before them. ⁸And they ate, and were satisfied; and they took up the broken pieces left over, seven baskets full. ⁹And there were about four thousand people. ¹⁰And he sent them away; and immediately he got into the boat with his disciples, and went to the district of Dalmanu′tha.

¹¹The Pharisees came and began to argue with him, seeking from him a sign from heaven, to test him. ¹²And he sighed deeply in his spirit, and said, "Why does this generation seek a sign? Truly, I say to you, no sign shall be given to this generation." ¹³And he left them, and getting into the boat again he departed to the other side.

¹⁴Now they had forgotten to bring bread; and they had only one loaf with them in the boat. ¹⁵And he cautioned them, saying, "Take heed, beware of the leaven of the Pharisees and the leaven of Herod." ¹⁶And they discussed it with one another, saying, "We have no bread." ¹⁷And being aware of it, Jesus said to them, "Why do you discuss the fact that you have no bread? Do you not yet perceive or understand? Are your hearts hardened? ¹⁸Having eyes do you not see, and having ears do you not hear? And do you not remember? ¹⁹When I broke the five loaves for the five thousand, how many baskets full of broken pieces did you take up?"

They said to him, "Twelve." [20]"And the seven for the four thousand, how many baskets full of broken pieces did you take up?" And they said to him, "Seven." [21]And he said to them, "Do you not yet understand?"

[22]And they came to Beth-sa'ida. And some people brought to him a blind man, and begged him to touch him. [23]And he took the blind man by the hand, and led him out of the village; and when he had spit on his eyes and laid his hands upon him, he asked him, "Do you see anything?" [24]And he looked up and said, "I see men; but they look like trees, walking." [25]Then again he laid his hands upon his eyes; and he looked intently and was restored, and saw everything clearly. [26]And he sent him away to his home, saying, "Do not even enter the village."

[27]And Jesus went on with his disciples, to the villages of Caesare'a Philippi; and on the way he asked his disciples, "Who do men say that I am?" [28]And they told him, "John the Baptist; and others say, Eli'jah; and others one of the prophets." [29]And he asked them, "But who do you say that I am?" Peter answered him, "You are the Christ." [30]And he charged them to tell no one about him.

[31]And he began to teach them that the Son of man must suffer many things, and be rejected by the elders and the chief priests and the scribes, and be killed, and after three days rise again. [32]And he said this plainly. And Peter took him, and began to rebuke him. [33]But turning and seeing his disciples, he rebuked Peter, and said, "Get behind me, Satan! For you are not on the side of God, but of men."

[34]And he called to him the multitude with his disciples, and said to them, "If any man would come after me, let him deny himself and take up his cross and follow me. [35]For whoever would save his life will lose it; and whoever loses his life for my sake and the gospel's will save it. [36]For what does it profit a man, to gain the whole world and forfeit his life? [37]For what can a man give in return for his life? [38]For whoever is ashamed of me and of my words in this adulterous and sinful generation, of him will the Son of man also be ashamed, when he comes in the glory of his Father with the holy angels."

9 And he said to them, "Truly, I say to you, there are some standing here who will not taste death before they see that the kingdom of God has come with power."

[2]And after six days Jesus took with him Peter and James and John, and led them up a high mountain apart by themselves; and he was transfigured before them, [3]and his garments became glistening, intensely white, as no fuller on earth could bleach them. [4]And there appeared to them Eli'jah with Moses; and they were talking to Jesus. [5]And Peter said to Jesus, "Master, it is well that we are here; let us make three booths, one for you and one for Moses and one for Eli'jah." [6]For he did not know what to say, for they were exceedingly afraid. [7]And a cloud overshadowed them, and a voice came out of the cloud, "This is my beloved Son; listen to him." [8]And suddenly looking around they no longer saw any one with them but Jesus only.

[9]And as they were coming down the mountain, he charged them to tell no one what they had seen, until the Son of man should have risen from the dead. [10]So they kept the matter to themselves, questioning what the rising from the dead meant. [11]And they asked him, "Why do the scribes say that first Elijah must come?" [12]And he said to them, "Eli'jah does come first to restore all things; and how is it written of the Son of man, that he should suffer many things and be treated with contempt? [13]But I tell you that Eli'jah has come, and they did to him whatever they pleased, as it is written of him."

[14]And when they came to the disciples, they saw a great crowd about them, and scribes arguing with them. [15]And immediately all the crowd, when they saw him, were greatly amazed, and ran up to him and greeted him. [16]And he asked them, "What are you discussing with them?" [17]And one of the crowd answered him, "Teacher, I brought my son to you, for he has a dumb spirit; [18]and wherever it seizes him, it dashes him down; and he foams and grinds his teeth and becomes rigid; and I asked your disciples to cast it out, and they were not able." [19]And he answered them, "O faithless generation, how long am I to be with you? How long am I to bear with you? Bring him to me." [20]And they brought the boy to him; and when the spirit saw him, immediately it convulsed the boy, and he fell on the ground and rolled about, foaming at the mouth. [21]And Jesus asked his father, "How long has he had this?" And he said, "From childhood. [22]And it has often cast him into the fire and into the water, to destroy him; but if you can do anything, have pity on us and help us." [23]And Jesus said to him, "If you can! All things are

possible to him who believes." 24Immediately the father of the child cried out and said, "I believe; help my unbelief!" 25And when Jesus saw that a crowd came running together, he rebuked the unclean spirit, saying to it, "You dumb and deaf spirit, I command you, come out of him, and never enter him again." 26And after crying out and convulsing him terribly, it came out, and the boy was like a corpse; so that most of them said, "He is dead." 27But Jesus took him by the hand and lifted him up, and he arose. 28And when he had entered the house, his disciples asked him privately, "Why could we not cast it out?" 29And he said to them, "This kind cannot be driven out by anything but prayer."

30They went on from there and passed through Galilee. And he would not have any one know it 31for he was teaching his disciples, saying to them, "The Son of man will be delivered into the hands of men, and they will kill him; and when he is killed, after three days he will rise." 32But they did not understand the saying, and they were afraid to ask him.

33And they came to Caper'na-um; and when he was in the house he asked them, "What were you discussing on the way?" 34But they were silent; for on the way they had discussed with one another who was the greatest. 35And he sat down and called the twelve; and he said to them, "If any one would be first, he must be last of all and servant of all." 36And he took a child, and put him in the midst of them; and taking him in his arms, he said to them, 37"Whoever receives one such child in my name receives me; and whoever receives me, receives not me but him who sent me."

38John said to him, "Teacher, we saw a man casting out demons in your name, and we forbade him, because he was not following us." 39But Jesus said, "Do not forbid him; for no one who does a mighty work in my name will be able soon after to speak evil of me. 40For he that is not against us is for us. 41For truly, I say to you, whoever gives you a cup of water to drink because you bear the name of Christ, will by no means lose his reward.

42"Whoever causes one of these little ones who believe in me to sin, it would be better for him if a great millstone were hung round his neck and he were thrown into the sea. 43And if your hand causes you to sin, cut it off; it is better for you to enter life maimed than with two hands to go to

hell, to the unquenchable fire. 45And if your foot causes you to sin, cut it off; it is better for you to enter life lame than with two feet to be thrown into hell. 47And if your eye causes you to sin, pluck it out; it is better for you to enter the kingdom of God with one eye than with two eyes to be thrown into hell, 48where their worm does not die, and the fire is not quenched. 49For every one will be salted with fire. 50Salt is good; but if the salt has lost its saltness, how will you season it? Have salt in yourselves, and be at peace with one another."

10 And he left there and went to the region of Judea and beyond the Jordan, and crowds gathered to him again; and again, as his custom was, he taught them.

2And Pharisees came up and in order to test him asked, "Is it lawful for a man to divorce his wife?" 3He answered them, "What did Moses command you?" 4They said, "Moses allowed a man to write a certificate of divorce, and to put her away." 5But Jesus said to them, "For your hardness of heart he wrote you this commandment. 6But from the beginning of creation, 'God made them male and female.' 7For this reason a man shall leave his father and mother and be joined to his wife, 8and the two shall become one flesh.' So they are no longer two but one flesh. 9What therefore God has joined together, let not man put asunder."

10And in the house the disciples asked him again about this matter. 11And he said to them, "Whoever divorces his wife and marries another, commits adultery against her; 12and if she divorces her husband and marries another, she commits adultery."

13And they were bringing children to him, that he might touch them; and the disciples rebuked them. 14But when Jesus saw it he was indignant, and said to them, "Let the children come to me, do not hinder them; for to such belongs the kingdom of God. 15Truly, I say to you, whoever does not receive the kingdom of God like a child shall not enter it." 16And he took them in his arms and blessed them, laying his hands upon them.

17And as he was setting out on his journey, a man ran up and knelt before him, and asked him, "Good Teacher, what must I do to inherit eternal life?" 18and Jesus said to him, "Why do you call me good? No one is good but God alone. 19You know the commandments: 'Do not kill, Do not commit adultery, Do not steal, Do not bear false witness, Do not defraud, Honor your father and mother.'" [20]And he said to him, "Teacher, all these I have observed from my youth." [21]And Jesus looking upon him loved him, and said to him, "You lack one thing; go, sell what you have, and give to the poor, and you will have treasure in heaven; and come, follow me." [22]At that saying his countenance fell, and he went away sorrowful; for he had great possessions.

[23]And Jesus looked around and said to his disciples, "How hard it will be for those who have riches to enter the kingdom of God!" [24]And the disciples were amazed at his words. But Jesus said to them again, "Children, how hard it is to enter the kingdom of God! [25]It is easier for a camel to go through the eye of a needle than for a rich man to enter the kingdom of God." [26]And they were exceedingly astonished, and said to him, "Then who can be saved?" [27]Jesus looked at them and said, "With men it is impossible, but not with God; for all things are possible with God." [28]Peter began to say to him, "Lo, we have left everything and followed you." [29]Jesus said, "Truly, I say to you, there is no one who has left house or brothers or sisters or mother or father or children or lands, for my sake and for the gospel, [30]who will not receive a hundredfold now in this time, houses and brothers and sisters and mothers and children and lands, with persecutions, and in the age to come eternal life. [31]But many that are first will be last, and the last first."

[32]And they were on the road, going up to Jerusalem, and Jesus was walking ahead of them; and they were amazed, and those who followed were afraid. And taking the twelve again, he began to tell them what was to happen to him, [33]saying, "Behold, we are going up to Jerusalem; and the Son of man will be delivered to the chief priests and the scribes, and they will condemn him to death, and deliver him to the Gentiles; [34]and they will mock him, and spit upon him, and scourge him, and kill him; and after three days he will rise."

[35]And James and John, the sons of Zeb'edee, came forward to him, and said to him, "Teacher, we want you to do for us whatever we ask of you." [36]And he said to them, "What do you want me to do for you?" [37]And they said to him, "Grant us to sit, one at your right hand and one at your left, in your glory." [38]But Jesus said to them, "You do not know what you are asking. Are you able to drink the cup that I drink, or to be baptized with the baptism with which I am baptized?" [39]And they said to him, "We are able." And Jesus said to them, "The cup that I drink you will drink; and with the baptism with which I am baptized, you will be baptized; [40]but to sit at my right hand or at my left is not mine to grant, but it is for those for whom it has been prepared." [41]And when the ten heard it, they began to be indignant at James and John. [42]And Jesus called them to him and said to them, "You know that those who are supposed to rule over the Gentiles lord it over them, and their great men exercise authority over them. [43]But it shall not be so among you; but whoever would be great among you must be your servant, [44]and whoever would be first among you must be slave of all. [45]For the Son of man also came not to be served but to serve, and to give his life as a ransom for many."

[46]And they came to Jericho; and as he was leaving Jericho with his disciples and a great multitude, Bartimae'us, a blind beggar, the son of Timae'us, was sitting by the roadside. [47]And when he heard that it was Jesus of Nazareth, he began to cry out and say, "Jesus, Son of David, have mercy on me!" [48]And many rebuked him, telling him to be silent; but he cried out all the more, "Son of David, have mercy on me!" [49]And Jesus stopped and said, "Call him." And they called the blind man, saying to him, "Take heart; rise, he is calling you." [50]And throwing off his mantle he sprang up and came to Jesus. [51]And Jesus said to him, "What do you want me to do for you?" And the blind man said to him, "Master, let me receive my sight." [52]And Jesus said to him, "Go your way; your faith has made you well." And immediately he received his sight and followed him on the way.

11 And when they drew near to Jerusalem, to Beth'phage and Bethany, at the Mount of Olives, he sent two of his disciples, [2]and said to them, "Go into the village opposite you, and immediately as you enter it you will find a colt tied, on which no one has ever sat; untie it and bring it: [3]If any one says to you, 'Why are you doing this?' say, 'The Lord has need of it and will send it back here immediately.'" [4]And they went away, and found a colt tied at the door out in the open street; and they untied it. [5]and those who stood there said to them, "What are you doing, unty-

ing the colt?" 6And they told them what Jesus had said; and they let them go. 7And they brought the colt to Jesus, and threw their garments on it; and he sat upon it. 8And many spread their garments on the road, and others spread leafy branches which they had cut from the fields. 9And those who went before and those who followed cried out, "Hosanna! Blessed is he who comes in the name of the Lord! 10Blessed is the kingdom of our father David that is coming! Hosanna in the highest!"

11And he entered Jerusalem, and went into the temple; and when he had looked round at everything, as it was already late, he went out to Bethany with the twelve.

12On the following day, when they came from Bethany, he was hungry. 13And seeing in the distance a fig tree in leaf, he went to see if he could find anything on it. When he came to it, he found nothing but leaves, for it was not the season for figs. 14And he said to it, "May no one ever eat fruit from you again." And his disciples heard it.

15And they came to Jerusalem. And he entered the temple and began to drive out those who sold and those who bought in the temple, and he overturned the tables of the money-changers and the seats of those who sold pigeons; 16and he would not allow any one to carry anything through the temple. 17And he taught, and said to them, "Is it not written, 'My house shall be called a house of prayer for all the nations'? But you have made it a den of robbers." 18And the chief priests and the scribes heard it and sought a way to destroy him; for they feared him, because all the multitude was astonished at his teaching. 19And when evening came they went out of the city.

20As they passed by in the morning, they saw the fig tree withered away to its roots. 21And Peter remembered and said to him, "Master, look! The fig tree which you cursed has withered." 22And Jesus answered them, "Have faith in God. 23Truly, I say to you, whoever says to this mountain, 'Be taken up and cast into the sea,' and does not doubt in his heart, but believes that what he says will come to pass, it will be done for him. 24Therefore I tell you, whatever you ask in prayer, believe that you have received it, and it will be yours. 25And whenever you stand praying, forgive, if you have anything against any one; so that your Father also who is in heaven may forgive you your trespasses."

27And they came again to Jerusalem. And as he was walking in the temple, the chief priests and the scribes and the elders came to him, 28and they said to him, "By what authority are you doing these things, or who gave you this authority to do them?" 29Jesus said to them, "I will ask you a question; answer me, and I will tell you by what authority I do these things. 30Was the baptism of John from heaven or from men? Answer me." 31And they argued with one another, "If we say, 'From heaven,' he will say, 'Why then did you not believe him?' 32But shall we say, 'From men'?"—they were afraid of the people, for all held that John was a real prophet. 33So they answered Jesus, "We do not know." And Jesus said to them, "Neither will I tell you by what authority I do these things."

12 And he began to speak to them in parables. "A man planted a vineyard, and set a hedge around it, and dug a pit for the wine press, and built a tower, and let it out to tenants, and went into another country. 2When the time came, he sent a servant to the tenants, to get from them some of the fruit of the vineyard. 3And they took him and beat him, and sent him away empty-handed. 4Again he sent to them another servant, and they wounded him in the head, and treated him shamefully. 5And he sent another, and him they killed; and so with many others, some they beat and some they killed. 6He had still one other, a beloved son; finally he sent him to them, saying, 'They will respect my son.' 7But those tenants said to one another, 'This is the heir; come, let us kill him, and the inheritance will be ours.' 8And they took him and killed him, and cast him out of the vineyard. 9What will the owner of the vineyard do? He will come and destroy the tenants, and give the vineyard to others. 10Have you not read this scripture:

'The very stone which the builders rejected
has become the head of the corner;
11this was the Lord's doing,
and it is marvelous in our eyes'?"

12And they tried to arrest him, but feared the multitude, for they perceived that he had told the parable against them; so they left him and went away.

13and they sent to him some of the Pharisees and some of the Hero'di-ans, to entrap him in his talk. 14And they came and said to him, "Teacher, we know that you are true, and care for no man; for you do not regard the position of men, but truly teach the way of God. Is it lawful to pay taxes to Caesar, or not? [15]Should we pay them, or should we not?" But knowing their hypocrisy, he said to them, "Why put me to the test? Bring me a coin, and let me look at it." [16]And they brought one. And he said to them, "Whose likeness and inscription is this?" They said to him, "Caesar's." [17]Jesus said to them, "Render to Caesar the things that are Caesar's, and to God the things that are God's." And they were amazed at him.

[18]And Sad'ducees came to him, who say that there is no resurrection; and they asked him a question, saying, [19]"Teacher, Moses wrote for us that if a man's brother dies and leaves a wife, but leaves no child, the man must take the wife, and raise up children for his brother. [20]There were seven brothers; the first took a wife, and when he died left no children; [21]and the second took her, and died, leaving no children; and the third likewise; [22]and the seven left no children. Last of all the woman also died. [23]In the resurrection whose wife will she be? For the seven had her as wife."

[24]Jesus said to them, "Is not this why you are wrong, that you know neither the scriptures nor the power of God? [25]For when they rise from the dead, they neither marry nor are given in marriage, but are like angels in heaven. [26]And as for the dead being raised, have you not read in the book of Moses, in the passage about the bush, how God said to him, 'I am the God of Abraham, and the God of Isaac, and the God of Jacob'? [27]He is not God of the dead, but of the living; you are quite wrong."

[28]And one of the scribes came up and heard them disputing with one another, and seeing that he answered them well, asked him, "Which commandment is the first of all?" [29]Jesus answered, "The first is, 'Hear, O Israel: The Lord our God, the Lord is one; [30]and you shall love the Lord your God with all your heart, and with all your soul, and with all your mind, and with all your strength.' [31]The second is this, 'You shall love your neighbor as yourself.' There is no other commandment greater than these." [32]And the scribe said to him, "You are right, Teacher; you have truly said that he is one, and there is no other but he; [33]and to love him with all the heart, and with all the understanding, and with all the strength, and to love one's neighbor as oneself, is much more than all whole burnt offer-

ings and sacrifices." [34]And when Jesus saw that he answered wisely, he said to him, "You are not far from the kingdom of God." And after that no one dared to ask him any question.

[35]And as Jesus taught in the temple, he said, "How can the scribes say that the Christ is the son of David? [36]David himself, inspired by the Holy Spirit, declared,

'The Lord said to my Lord,
Sit at my right hand,
till I put thy enemies under thy feet.'

[37]David himself calls him Lord; so how is he his son?" And the great throng heard him gladly.

[38]And in his teaching he said, "Beware of the scribes, who like to go about in long robes, and to have salutations in the market places [39]and the best seats in the synagogues and the places of honor at feasts, [40]who devour widows' houses and for a pretense make long prayers. They will receive the greater condemnation."

[41]And he sat down opposite the treasury, and watched the multitude putting money into the treasury. Many rich people put in large sums. [42]And a poor widow came, and put in two copper coins, which make a penny. [43]And he called his disciples to him, and said to them, "Truly, I say to you, this poor widow has put in more than all those who are contributing to the treasury. "For they all contributed out of their abundance; but she out of her poverty has put in everything she had, her whole living."

13 And as he came out of the temple, one of his disciples said to him, "Look, Teacher, what wonderful stones and what wonderful buildings!" [2]And Jesus said to him, "Do you see these great buildings? There will not be left here one stone upon another, that will not be thrown down."

[3]And as he sat on the Mount of Olives opposite the temple, Peter and James and John and Andrew asked him privately, [4]"Tell us, when will this be, and what will be the sign when these things are all to be accomplished?" [5]And Jesus began to say to them, "Take heed that no one leads you astray. [6]Many will come in my name, saying, 'I am he!' and they will lead many astray. [7]And when you hear of wars and rumors of wars, do not be alarmed; this must take place, but the end is not yet. [8]For nation will rise against nation, and kingdom against kingdom; there

will be earthquakes in various places, there will be famines; this is but the beginning of the birth-pangs.

9"But take heed to yourselves; for they will deliver you up to councils; and you will be beaten in synagogues; and you will stand before governors and kings for my sake, to bear testimony before them. 10And the gospel must first be preached to all nations. 11And when they bring you to trial and deliver you up, do not be anxious beforehand what you are to say; but say whatever is given you in that hour, for it is not you who speak, but the Holy Spirit. 12And brother will deliver up brother to death, and the father his child, and children will rise against parents and have them put to death; 13and you will be hated by all for my name's sake. But he who endures to the end will be saved.

14"But when you see the desolating sacrilege set up where it ought not to be (let the reader understand), then let those who are in Judea flee to the mountains; 15let him who is on the housetop not go down, nor enter his house, to take anything away; 16and let him who is in the field not turn back to take his mantle. 17And alas for those who are with child and for those who give suck in those days! 18Pray that it may not happen in winter. 19For in those days there will be such tribulation as has not been from the beginning of the creation which God created until now, and never will be. 20And if the Lord had not shortened the days, no human being would be saved; but for the sake of the elect, whom he chose, he shortened the days. 21And then if any one says to you, 'Look, here is the Christ!' or 'Look, there he is!' do not believe it. 22False Christs and false prophets will arise and show signs and wonders, to lead astray, if possible, the elect. 23But take heed; I have told you all things beforehand.

24"But in those days, after that tribulation, the sun will be darkened, and the moon will not give its light, 25and the stars will be falling from heaven, and the powers in the heavens will be shaken. 26And then they will see the Son of man coming in clouds with great power and glory. 27And then he will send out the angels, and gather his elect from the four winds, from the ends of the earth to the ends of heaven.

28"From the fig tree learn its lesson: as soon as its branch becomes tender and puts forth its leaves, you know that summer is near. 29So also, when you see these things taking place, you know that he is near, at the very gates. 30Truly, I say to you, this gen-

eration will not pass away before all these things take place. 31Heaven and earth will pass away, but my words will not pass away.

32"But of that day or that hour no one knows, not even the angels in heaven, nor the Son, but only the Father. 33Take heed, watch; for you do not know when the time will come. 34It is like a man going on a journey, when he leaves home and puts his servants in charge, each with his work, and commands the doorkeeper to be on the watch. 35Watch therefore—for you do not know when the master of the house will come, in the evening, or at midnight, or at cockcrow, or in the morning— 36lest he come suddenly and find you asleep. 37And what I say to you I say to all: Watch."

14 It was now two days before the Passover and the feast of Unleavened Bread. And the chief priests and the scribes were seeking how to arrest him by stealth, and kill him; 2for they said, "Not during the feast, lest there be a tumult of the people."

3And while he was at Bethany in the house of Simon the leper, as he sat at table, a woman came with an alabaster flask of ointment of pure nard, very costly, and she broke the flask and poured it over his head. 4But there were some who said to themselves indignantly, "Why was the ointment thus wasted? 5For this ointment might have been sold for more than three hundred denarii, and given to the poor." And they reproached her. 6But Jesus said, "Let her alone; why do you trouble her? She has done a beautiful thing to me. 7For you always have the poor with you, and whenever you will, you can do good to them; but you will not always have me. 8She has done what she could; she has anointed my body beforehand for burying. 9And truly, I say to you, wherever the gospel is preached in the whole world, what she has done will be told in memory of her."

10Then Judas Iscariot, who was one of the twelve, went to the chief priests in order to betray him to them. 11And when they heard it they were glad, and promised to give him money. And he sought an opportunity to betray him.

12And on the first day of Unleavened Bread, when they sacrificed the passover lamb, his disciples said to him, "Where will you have us go and prepare for you to eat the passover?" 13And he sent two of his disciples, and said to them, "Go into the city, and a man carrying a jar of water will meet you; follow him, [14]and wherever he enters, say to the householder, 'The Teacher says, Where is my guest room, where I am to eat the passover with my disciples?' [15]And he will show you a large upper room furnished and ready; there prepare for us." [16]And the disciples set out and went to the city, and found it as he had told them; and they prepared the passover.

[17]And when it was evening he came with the twelve. [18]And as they were at table eating, Jesus said, "Truly, I say to you, one of you will betray me, one who is eating with me." [19]They began to be sorrowful, and to say to him one after another, "Is it I?" [20]He said to them, "It is one of the twelve, one who is dipping bread into the dish with me. [21]For the Son of man goes as it is written of him, but woe to that man by whom the Son of man is betrayed! It would have been better for that man if he had not been born."

[22]And as they were eating, he took bread, and blessed, and broke it, and gave it to them, and said, "Take; this is my body." [23]And he took a cup, and when he had given thanks he gave it to them, and they all drank of it. [24]And he said to them, "This is my blood of the covenant, which is poured out for many. [25]Truly, I say to you, I shall not drink again of the fruit of the vine until that day when I drink it new in the kingdom of God."

[26]And when they had sung a hymn, they went out to the Mount of Olives. [27]And Jesus said to them, "You will all fall away; for it is written, 'I will strike the shepherd, and the sheep will be scattered.' [28]But after I am raised up, I will go before you to Galilee." [29]Peter said to him, "Even though they all fall away, I will not." [30]And Jesus said to him, "Truly, I say to you, this very night, before the cock crows twice, you will deny me three times." [31]But he said vehemently, "If I must die with you, I will not deny you." And they all said the same.

[32]And they went to a place which was called Gethsem'ane; and he said to his disciples, "Sit here, while I pray." [33]And he took with him Peter and James and John, and began to be greatly distressed and troubled. [34]And he said to them, "My soul is very sorrowful, even to death; remain here, and watch." [35]And going a little farther, he fell on the ground and prayed that, if it were possible, the hour might pass from him. [36]And he said, "Abba, Father, all things are possible to thee; remove this cup from me; yet not what I will, but what thou wilt." [37]And he came and found them sleeping, and he said to Peter, "Simon, are you asleep? Could you not watch one hour? [38]Watch and pray that you may not enter into temptation; the spirit indeed is willing, but the flesh is weak." [39]And again he went away and prayed, saying the same words. [40]And again he came and found them sleeping, for their eyes were very heavy; and they did not know what to answer him. [41]And he came the third time, and said to them, "Are you still sleeping and taking your rest? It is enough; the hour has come; the Son of man is betrayed into the hands of sinners. [42]Rise, let us be going; see, my betrayer is at hand."

[43]And immediately, while he was still speaking, Judas came, one of the twelve, and with him a crowd with swords and clubs, from the chief priests and the scribes and the elders. [44]Now the betrayer had given them a sign, saying, "The one I shall kiss is the man; seize him and lead him away under guard." [45]And when he came, he went up to him at once, and said, "Master!" And he kissed him. [46]And they laid hands on him and seized him. [47]But one of those who stood by drew his sword, and struck the slave of the high priest and cut off his ear. [48]And Jesus said to them, "Have you come out as against a robber, with swords and clubs to capture me? [49]Day after day I was with you in the temple teaching, and you did not seize me. But let the scriptures be fulfilled." [50]And they all forsook him, and fled.

[51]And a young man followed him, with nothing but a linen cloth about his body; and they seized him, [52]but he left the linen cloth and ran away naked.

[53]And they led Jesus to the high priest; and all the chief priests and the elders and the scribes were assembled. [54]And Peter had followed him at a distance, right into the courtyard of the high priest; and he was sitting with the guards, and warming himself at the fire. [55]Now the chief priests and the whole council sought testimony against Jesus to put him to death; but they found none. [56]For many bore false witness against him, and their witness did not agree. [57]And some stood up and bore false witness against him, saying, [58]"We heard him say, 'I will destroy this temple that is made with hands, and in three days I will build another, not made with hands.'" [59]Yet not even so did their testimony agree. [60]And the high priest stood up in the midst, and

asked Jesus, "Have you no answer to make? What is it that these men testify against you?" [61]But he was silent and made no answer. Again the high priest asked him, "Are you the Christ, the Son of the Blessed?" [62]And Jesus said, "I am; and you will see the Son of man seated at the right hand of Power, and coming with the clouds of heaven." [63]And the high priest tore his garments, and said, "Why do we still need witnesses? [64]You have heard his blasphemy. What is your decision?" And they all condemned him as deserving death. [65]And some began to spit on him, and to cover his face, and to strike him, saying to him, "Prophesy!" And the guards received him with blows.

[66]And as Peter was below in the courtyard, one of the maids of the high priest came; [67]and seeing Peter warming himself, she looked at him, and said, "You also were with the Nazarene, Jesus." [68]But he denied it, saying, "I neither know nor understand what you mean." And he went out into the gateway. [69]And the maid saw him, and began again to say to the bystanders, "This man is one of them." [70]But again he denied it. And after a little while again the bystanders said to Peter, "Certainly you are one of them; for you are a Galilean." [71]But he began to invoke a curse on himself and to swear, "I do not know this man of whom you speak." [72]And immediately the cock crowed a second time. And Peter remembered how Jesus had said to him, "Before the cock crows twice, you will deny me three times." And he broke down and wept.

15 And as soon as it was morning the chief priests, with the elders and scribes, and the whole council held a consultation; and they bound Jesus and led him away and delivered him to Pilate. [2]And Pilate asked him, "Are you the King of the Jews?" And he answered him, "You have said so." [3]And the chief priests accused him of many things. [4]And Pilate again asked him, "Have you no answer to make? See how many charges they bring against you." [5]But Jesus made no further answer, so that Pilate wondered.

[6]Now at the feast he used to release for them one prisoner for whom they asked. [7]And among the rebels in prison, who had committed murder in the insurrection, there was a man called Barab'bas. [8]And the crowd came up and began to ask Pilate to do as he was wont to do for them. [9]And he answered them, "Do you want me to release for you the King of the Jews?" [10]For he perceived that it was out of envy that the chief priests had delivered him up. [11]But the chief priests stirred up the crowd to have him release for them Barab'bas instead. [12]And Pilate again said to them, "Then what shall I do with the man whom you call the King of the Jews?" [13]And they cried out again, "Crucify him." [14]And Pilate said to them, "Why, what evil has he done?" But they shouted all the more, "Crucify him." [15]So Pilate, wishing to satisfy the crowd, released for them Barab'bas; and having scourged Jesus, he delivered him to be crucified.

[16]And the soldiers led him away inside the palace (that is, the praetorium); and they called together the whole battalion. [17]And they clothed him in a purple cloak, and plaiting a crown of thorns they put it on him. [18]And they began to salute him, "Hail, King of the Jews!" [19]And they struck his head with a reed, and spat upon him, and they knelt down in homage to him. [20]And when they had mocked him, they stripped him of the purple cloak, and put his own clothes on him. And they led him out to crucify him.

[21]And they compelled a passer-by, Simon of Cyre'ne, who was coming in from the country, the father of Alexander and Rufus, to carry his cross. [22]And they brought him to the place called Gol'gotha (which means the place of a skull). [23]And they offered him wine mingled with myrrh; but he did not take it. [24]And they crucified him, and divided his garments among them, casting lots for them, to decide what each should take. [25]And it was the third hour, when they crucified him. [26]And the inscription of the charge against him read, "The King of the Jews." [27]And with him they crucified two robbers, one on his right and one on his left. [29]And those who passed by derided him, wagging their heads, and saying, "Aha! You who would destroy the temple and build it in three days, [30]save yourself, and come down from the cross!" [31]So also the chief priests mocked him to one another with the scribes, saying, "He saved others; he cannot save himself. [32]Let the Christ, the King of Israel, come down now from the cross, that we may see and believe." Those who were crucified with him also reviled him.

[33]And when the sixth hour had come, there was darkness over the whole land until the ninth hour. [34]And at the ninth hour Jesus cried with a loud voice,

"E'lo-i, E'lo-i, la'ma sabachtha'ni?" which means, "My God, my God, why hast thou forsaken me?" [35]And some of the bystanders hearing it said, "Behold, he is calling Eli'jah." [36]And one ran and, filling a sponge full of vinegar, put it on a reed and gave it to him to drink, saying, "Wait, let us see whether Eli'jah will come to take him down." [37]And Jesus uttered a loud cry, and breathed his last. [38]And the curtain of the temple was torn in two, from top to bottom. [39]And when the centurion, who stood facing him, saw that he thus breathed his last, he said, "Truly this man was the Son of God!"

[40]There were also women looking on from afar, among whom were Mary Mag'dalene, and Mary the mother of James the younger and of Joses, and Salo'me, [41]who, when he was in Galilee, followed him, and ministered to him; and also many other women who came up with him to Jerusalem.

[42]And when evening had come, since it was the day of Preparation, that is, the day before the sabbath, [43]Joseph of Arimathe'a, a respected member of the council, who was also himself looking for the kingdom of God, took courage and went to Pilate, and asked for the body of Jesus. [44]And Pilate wondered if he were already dead; and summoning the centurion, he asked him whether he was already dead. [45]And when he learned from the centurion that he was dead, he granted the body to Joseph. [46]And he bought a linen shroud, and taking him down, wrapped him in the linen shroud, and laid him in a tomb which had been hewn out of the rock; and he rolled a stone against the door of the tomb. [47]Mary Mag'dalene and Mary the mother of Joseph saw where he was laid.

16 And when the sabbath was past, Mary Mag'dalene, and Mary the mother of James, and Salo'me, bought spices, so that they might go and anoint him. [2]And very early on the first day of the week they went to the tomb when the sun had risen. [3]And they were saying to one another, "Who will roll away the stone for us from the door of the tomb?" [4]And looking up, they saw that the stone was rolled back—it was very large. [5]And entering the tomb, they saw a young man sitting on the right side, dressed in a white robe; and they

were amazed. [6]And he said to them, "Do not be amazed; you seek Jesus of Nazareth, who was crucified. He has risen, he is not here; see the place where they laid him. [7]But go, tell his disciples and Peter that he is going before you to Galilee; there you will see him, as he told you." [8]And they went out and fled from the tomb; for trembling and astonishment had come upon them; and they said nothing to any one, for they were afraid.

Note: Many scholars believe that verses 9–20 were later additions and that the original text ends with verse 8.

[9]Now when he rose early on the first day of the week, he appeared first to Mary Magdalene, from whom he had cast out seven demons. [10]She went out and told those who had been with him, as they mourned and wept. [11]But when they heard that he was alive and had been seen by her, they would not believe it.

[12]After this he appeared in another form to two of them, as they were walking into the country. [13]And they went back and told the rest, but they did not believe them.

[14]Afterward he appeared to the eleven themselves as they sat at table; and he upbraided them for their unbelief and hardness of heart, because they had not believed those who saw him after he had risen. [15]And he said to them, "Go into all the world and preach the gospel to the whole creation. [16]He who believes and is baptized will be saved; but he who does not believe will be condemned. [17]And these signs will accompany those who believe: in my name they will cast out demons; they will speak in new tongues; [18]they will pick up serpents, and if they drink any deadly thing, it will not hurt them; they will lay their hands on the sick, and they will recover."

[19]So then the Lord Jesus, after he had spoken to them, was taken up into heaven, and sat down at the right hand of God. [20]And they went forth and preached everywhere, while the Lord worked with them and confirmed the message by the signs that attended it. Amen.

THE FIRST LETTER OF PAUL TO THE CORINTHIANS

1 Paul, called by the will of God to be an apostle of Christ Jesus, and our brother Sos'thenes,

²To the church of God which is at Corinth, to those sanctified in Christ Jesus, called to be saints together with all those who in every place call on the name of our Lord Jesus Christ, both their Lord and ours:

³Grace to you and peace from God our Father and the Lord Jesus Christ.

⁴I give thanks to God always for you because of the grace of God which was given you in Christ Jesus, ⁵that in every way you were enriched in him with all speech and all knowledge—⁶even as the testimony to Christ was confirmed among you—⁷so that you are not lacking in any spiritual gift, as you wait for the revealing of our Lord Jesus Christ; ⁸who will sustain you to the end, guiltless in the day of our Lord Jesus Christ. ⁹God is faithful, by whom you were called into the fellowship of his Son, Jesus Christ our Lord.

¹⁰I appeal to you, brethren, by the name of our Lord Jesus Christ, that all of you agree and that there be no dissensions among you, but that you be united in the same mind and the same judgment. ¹¹For it has been reported to me by Chlo'e's people that there is quarreling among you, my brethren. ¹²What I mean is that each one of you says, "I belong to Paul," or "I belong to Apol'los," or "I belong to Cephas," or "I belong to Christ." ¹³Is Christ divided? Was Paul crucified for you? Or were you baptized in the name of Paul? ¹⁴I am thankful that I baptized none of you except Crispus and Ga'ius; ¹⁵lest any one should say that you were baptized in my name. ¹⁶(I did baptize also the household of Steph'anas. Beyond that, I do not know whether I baptized any one else.) ¹⁷For Christ did not send me to baptize but to preach the gospel, and not with eloquent wisdom, lest the cross of Christ be emptied of its power.

¹⁸For the word of the cross is folly to those who are perishing, but to us who are being saved it is the power of God. ¹⁹For it is written,

"I will destroy the wisdom of the
     wise,
and the cleverness of the clever I will thwart."

²⁰Where is the wise man? Where is the scribe? Where is the debater of this age? Has not God made foolish the wisdom of the world? ²¹For since, in the wisdom of God, the world did not know God through wisdom, it pleased God through the folly of what we preach to save those who believe. ²²For Jews demand signs and Greeks seek wisdom, ²³But we preach Christ crucified, a stumbling block to Jews and folly to Gentiles, ²⁴but to those who are called, both Jews and Greeks, Christ the power of God and the wisdom of God. ²⁵For the foolishness of God is wiser than men, and the weakness of God is stronger than men.

²⁶For consider your call, brethren; not many of you were wise according to worldly standards, not many were powerful, not many were of noble birth; ²⁷but God chose what is foolish in the world to shame the wise, God chose what is weak in the world to shame the strong, ²⁸God chose what is low and despised in the world, even things that are not, to bring to nothing things that are, ²⁹so that no human being might boast in the presence of God. ³⁰He is the source of your life in Christ Jesus, whom God made our wisdom, our righteousness and sanctification and redemption; ³¹therefore, as it is written, "Let him who boasts, boast of the Lord."

2 When I came to you, brethren, I did not come proclaiming to you the testimony of God in lofty words or wisdom. ²For I decided to know nothing among you except Jesus Christ and him crucified. ³And I was with you in weakness and in much fear and trembling; ⁴and my speech and my message were not in plausible words of wisdom, but in demonstration of the Spirit and of power, ⁵that your faith might not rest in the wisdom of men but in the power of God.

⁶Yet among the mature we do impart wisdom, although it is not a wisdom of this age or of the rulers of this age, who are doomed to pass away. ⁷But we impart a secret and hidden wisdom of God, which God decreed before the ages for our glorification. ⁸None of the rulers of this age understood this; for if they had, they would not have crucified the Lord of glory. ⁹But, as it is written,

"What no eye has seen, nor ear
   heard,
nor the heart of man conceived,
what God has prepared for those who
   love him,"

[10]God has revealed to us through the Spirit. For the Spirit searches everything, even the depths of God. [11]For what person knows a man's thoughts except the spirit of the man which is in him? So also no one comprehends the thoughts of God except the Spirit of God. [12]Now we have received not the spirit of the world, but the Spirit which is from God, that we might understand the gifts bestowed on us by God. [13]And we impart this in words not taught by human wisdom but taught by the Spirit, interpreting spiritual truths to those who possess the Spirit.

[14]The unspiritual man does not receive the gifts of the Spirit of God, for they are folly to him, and he is not able to understand them because they are spiritually discerned. [15]The spiritual man judges all things, but is himself to be judged by no one. [16]"For who has known the mind of the Lord so as to instruct him?" But we have the mind of Christ.

3 But I, brethren, could not address you as spiritual men, but as men of the flesh, as babes in Christ. [2]I fed you with milk, not solid food; for you were not ready for it; and even yet you are not ready, [3]for you are still of the flesh. For while there is jealousy and strife among you, are you not of the flesh, and behaving like ordinary men? [4]For when one says, "I belong to Paul," and another, "I belong to Apol'los," are you not merely men?

[5]What then is Apol'los? What is Paul? Servants through whom you believed, as the Lord assigned to each. [6]I planted, Apol'los watered, but God gave the growth. [7]So neither he who plants nor he who waters is anything, but only God who gives the growth. [8]He who plants and he who waters are equal, and each shall receive his wages according to his labor. [9]For we are God's fellow workers; you are God's field, God's building.

[10]According to the grace of God given to me, like a skilled master builder I laid a foundation, and another man is building upon it. Let each man take care how he builds upon it. [11]For no other foundation can any one lay than that which is laid, which is Jesus Christ. [12]Now if any one builds on the foundation with gold, silver, precious stones, wood, hay, straw—[13]each man's work will become manifest; for the Day will disclose it, because it will be revealed with fire, and the fire will test what sort of work each one has done. [14]If the work which any man has built on the foundation survives, he will receive a reward. [15]If any man's work is burned up, he will suffer loss, though he himself will be saved, but only as through fire.

[16]Do you not know that you are God's temple and that God's Spirit dwells in you? [17]If any one destroys God's temple, God will destroy him. For God's temple is holy, and that temple you are.

[18]Let no one deceive himself. If any one among you thinks that he is wise in this age, let him become a fool that he may become wise. [19]For the wisdom of this world is folly with God. For it is written, "He catches the wise in their craftiness," [20]and again, "The Lord knows that the thoughts of the wise are futile." [21]So let no one boast of men. For all things are yours, [22]whether Paul or Apol'los or Cephas or the world or life or death or the present or the future, all are yours; [23]and you are Christ's; and Christ is God's.

4 This is how one should regard us, as servants of Christ and stewards of the mysteries of God. [2]Moreover it is required of stewards that they be found trustworthy. [3]But with me it is a very small thing that I should be judged by you or by any human court. I do not even judge myself. [4]I am not aware of anything against myself, but I am not thereby acquitted. It is the Lord who judges me. [5]Therefore do not pronounce judgment before the time, before the Lord comes, who will bring to light the things now hidden in darkness and will disclose the purposes of the heart. Then every man will receive his commendation from God.

[6]I have applied all this to myself and Apol'los for your benefit, brethren, that you may learn by us not to go beyond what is written, that none of you may be puffed up in favor of one against another. [7]For who sees anything different in you? What have you that you did not receive? If then you received it, why do you boast as if it were not a gift?

[8]Already you are filled! Already you have become rich! Without us you have become kings!

And would that you did reign, so that we might share the rule with you! [9]For I think that God has exhibited us apostles as last of all, like men sentenced to death; because we have become a spectacle to the world, to angels and to men. [10]We are fools for Christ's sake, but you are wise in Christ. We are weak, but you are strong. You are held in honor, but we in disrepute. [11]To the present hour we hunger and thirst, we are ill-clad and buffeted and homeless, [12]and we labor, working with our own hands. When reviled, we bless; when persecuted, we endure; [13]when slandered, we try to conciliate; we have become, and are now, as the refuse of the world, the offscouring of all things.

[14]I do not write this to make you ashamed, but to admonish you as my beloved children. [15]For though you have countless guides in Christ, you do not have many fathers. For I became your father in Christ Jesus through the gospel. [16]I urge you, then, be imitators of me. [17]Therefore I sent to you Timothy, my beloved and faithful child in the Lord, to remind you of my ways in Christ, as I teach them everywhere in every church. [18]Some are arrogant, as though I were not coming to you. [19]But I will come to you soon, if the Lord wills, and I will find out not the talk of these arrogant people but their power. [20]For the kingdom of God does not consist in talk but in power. [21]What do you wish? Shall I come to you with a rod, or with love in a spirit of gentleness?

5 It is actually reported that there is immorality among you, and of a kind that is not found even among pagans; for a man is living with his father's wife. [2]And you are arrogant! Ought you not rather to mourn? Let him who has done this be removed from among you.

[3]For though absent in body I am present in spirit, and as if present, I have already pronounced judgment [4]in the name of the Lord Jesus on the man who has done such a thing. When you are assembled, and my spirit is present, with the power of our Lord Jesus, [5]you are to deliver this man to Satan for the destruction of the flesh, that his spirit may be saved in the day of the Lord Jesus.

[6]Your boasting is not good. Do you not know that a little leaven leavens the whole lump? [7]Cleanse out the old leaven that you may be a new lump, as you really are unleavened. For Christ, our paschal lamb, has been sacrificed. [8]Let us, therefore, celebrate the festival, not with the old leaven, the leaven of malice and evil, but with the unleavened bread of sincerity and truth.

[9]I wrote to you in my letter not to associate with immoral men; [10]not at all meaning the immoral of this world, or the greedy and robbers, or idolaters, since then you would need to go out of the world. [11]But rather I wrote to you not to associate with any one who bears the name of brother if he is guilty of immorality or greed, or is an idolater, reviler, drunkard, or robber—not even to eat with such a one. [12]For what have I to do with judging outsiders? Is it not those inside the church whom you are to judge? [13]God judges those outside. "Drive out the wicked person from among you."

6 When one of you has a grievance against a brother, does he dare go to law before the unrighteous instead of the saints? [2]Do you not know that the saints will judge the world? And if the world is to be judged by you, are you incompetent to try trivial cases? [3]Do you not know that we are to judge angels? How much more, matters pertaining to this life! [4]If then you have such cases, why do you lay them before those who are least esteemed by the church? [5]I say this to your shame. Can it be that there is no man among you wise enough to decide between members of the brotherhood, [6]but brother goes to law against brother, and that before unbelievers?

[7]To have lawsuits at all with one another is defeat for you. Why not rather suffer wrong? Why not rather be defrauded? [8]But you yourselves wrong and defraud, and that even your own brethren.

[9]Do you not know that the unrighteous will not inherit the kingdom of God? Do not be deceived; neither the immoral, nor idolaters, nor adulterers, nor sexual perverts, nor thieves, [10]nor the greedy, nor drunkards, nor revilers, nor robbers will inherit the kingdom of God. [11]And such were some of you. But you were washed, you were sanctified, you were justified in the name of the Lord Jesus Christ and in the Spirit of our God.

[12]"All things are lawful for me," but not all things are helpful. "All things are lawful for me," but I will not be enslaved by anything. [13]"Food is meant for the stomach and the stomach for

food"—and God will destroy both one and the other. The body is not meant for immorality, but for the Lord, and the Lord for the body. [14]And God raised the Lord and will also raise us up by his power. [15]Do you not know that your bodies are members of Christ? Shall I therefore take the members of Christ and make them members of a prostitute? Never! [16]Do you not know that he who joins himself to a prostitute becomes one body with her? For, as it is written, "The two shall become one flesh." [17]But he who is united to the Lord becomes one spirit with him. [18]Shun immorality. Every other sin which a man commits is outside the body; but the immoral man sins against his own body. [19]Do you not know that your body is a temple of the Holy Spirit within you, which you have from God? You are not your own; [20]you were bought with a price. So glorify God in your body.

7 Now concerning the matters about which you wrote. It is well for a man not to touch a woman. [2]But because of the temptation to immorality, each man should have his own wife and each woman her own husband. [3]The husband should give to his wife her conjugal rights, and likewise the wife to her husband. [4]For the wife does not rule over her own body, but the husband does; likewise the husband does not rule over his own body, but the wife does. [5]Do not refuse one another except perhaps by agreement for a season, that you may devote yourselves to prayer; but then come together again, lest Satan tempt you through lack of self-control. [6]I say this by way of concession, not of command. [7]I wish that all were as I myself am. But each has his own special gift from God, one of one kind and one of another.

[8]To the unmarried and the widows I say that it is well for them to remain single as I do. [9]But if they cannot exercise self-control, they should marry. For it is better to marry than to be aflame with passion.

[10]To the married I give charge, not I but the Lord, that the wife should not separate from her husband [11](but if she does, let her remain single or else be reconciled to her husband)—and that the husband should not divorce his wife.

[12]To the rest I say, not the Lord, that if any brother has a wife who is an unbeliever, and she

consents to live with him, he should not divorce her. [13]If any woman has a husband who is an unbeliever, and he consents to live with her, she should not divorce him. [14]For the unbelieving husband is consecrated through his wife, and the unbelieving wife is consecrated through her husband. Otherwise, your children would be unclean, but as it is they are holy. [15]But if the unbelieving partner desires to separate, let it be so; in such a case the brother or sister is not bound. For God has called us to peace. [16]Wife, how do you know whether you will save your husband? Husband, how do you know whether you will save your wife?

[17]Only, let every one lead the life which the Lord has assigned to him, and in which God has called him. This is my rule in all the churches. [18]Was any one at the time of his call already circumcised? Let him not seek to remove the marks of circumcision. Was any one at the time of his call uncircumcised? Let him not seek circumcision. [19]For neither circumcision counts for anything nor uncircumcision, but keeping the commandments of God. [20]Every one should remain in the state in which he was called. [21]Were you a slave when called? Never mind. But if you can gain your freedom, avail yourself of the opportunity. [22]For he who was called in the Lord as a slave is a freedman of the Lord. Likewise he who was free when called is a slave of Christ. [23]You were bought with a price; do not become slaves of men. [24]So, brethren, in whatever state each was called, there let him remain with God.

[25]Now concerning the unmarried, I have no command of the Lord, but I give my opinion as one who by the Lord's mercy is trustworthy. [26]I think that in view of the present distress it is well for a person to remain as he is. [27]Are you bound to a wife? Do not seek to be free. Are you free from a wife? Do not seek marriage. [28]But if you marry, you do not sin, and if a girl marries she does not sin. Yet those who marry will have worldly troubles, and I would spare you that. [29]I mean, brethren, the appointed time has grown very short; from now on, let those who have wives live as though they had none, [30]and those who mourn as though they were not mourning, and those who rejoice as though they were not rejoicing, and those who buy as though they had no goods,

[31]and those who deal with the world as though they had no dealings with it. For the form of this world is passing away.

[32]I want you to be free from anxieties. The unmarried man is anxious about the affairs of the Lord, how to please the Lord; [33]but the married man is anxious about worldly affairs, how to please his wife, [34]and his interests are divided. And the unmarried woman or girl is anxious about the affairs of the Lord, how to be holy in body and spirit; but the married woman is anxious about worldly affairs, how to please her husband. [35]I say this for your own benefit, not to lay any restraint upon you, but to promote good order and to secure your undivided devotion to the Lord.

[36]If any one thinks that he is not behaving properly toward his betrothed, if his passions are strong, and it has to be, let him do as he wishes: let them marry—it is no sin. [37]But whoever is firmly established in his heart, being under no necessity but having his desire under control, and has determined this in his heart, to keep her as his betrothed, he will do well. [38]So that he who marries his betrothed does well; and he who refrains from marriage will do better.

[39]A wife is bound to her husband as long as he lives. If the husband dies, she is free to be married to whom she wishes, only in the Lord. [40]But in my judgment she is happier if she remains as she is. And I think that I have the Spirit of God.

8 Now concerning food offered to idols: we know that "all of us possess knowledge." "Knowledge" puffs up, but love builds up. [2]If any one imagines that he knows something, he does not yet know as he ought to know. [3]But if one loves God, one is known by him.

[4]Hence, as to the eating of food offered to idols, we know that "an idol has no real existence," and that "there is no God but one." [5]For although there may be so-called gods in heaven or on earth—as indeed there are many "gods" and many "lords" — [6]yet for us there is one God, the Father, from whom are all things and for whom we exist, and one Lord, Jesus Christ, through whom are all things and through whom we exist.

[7]However, not all possess this knowledge. But some, through being hitherto accustomed to idols, eat food as really offered to an idol; and their conscience, being weak, is defiled. [8]Food will not commend us to God. We are no worse off if we do not eat, and no better off if we do. [9]Only take care lest this liberty of yours somehow become a stumbling block to the weak. [10]For if any one sees you, a man of knowledge, at table in an idol's temple, might he not be encouraged, if his conscience is weak, to eat food offered to idols? [11]And so by your knowledge this weak man is destroyed, the brother for whom Christ died. [12]Thus, sinning against your brethren and wounding their conscience when it is weak, you sin against Christ. [13]Therefore, if food is a cause of my brother's falling, I will never eat meat, lest I cause my brother to fall.

9 Am I not free? Am I not an apostle? Have I not seen Jesus our Lord? Are not you my workmanship in the Lord? [2]If to others I am not an apostle, at least I am to you; for you are the seal of my apostleship in the Lord.

[3]This is my defense to those who would examine me. [4]Do we not have the right to our food and drink? [5]Do we not have the right to be accompanied by a wife, as the other apostles and the brothers of the Lord and Cephas? [6]Or is it only Barnabas and I who have no right to refrain from working for a living? [7]Who serves as a soldier at his own expense? Who plants a vineyard without eating any of its fruit? Who tends a flock without getting some of the milk?

[8]Do I say this on human authority? Does not the law say the same? [9]For it is written in the law of Moses, "You shall not muzzle an ox when it is treading out the grain." Is it for oxen that God is concerned? [10]Does he not speak entirely for our sake? It was written for our sake, because the plowman should plow in hope and the thresher thresh in hope of a share in the crop. [11]If we have sown spiritual good among you, is it too much if we reap your material benefits? [12]If others share this rightful claim upon you, do not we still more?

Nevertheless, we have not made use of this right, but we endure anything rather than put an obstacle in the way of the gospel of Christ. [13]Do you not know that those who are employed in the temple service get their food from the temple, and those who serve at the altar share in the sacrificial offerings? [14]In the same way, the Lord commanded that those who proclaim the gospel should get their living by the gospel.

15But I have made no use of any of these rights, nor am I writing this to secure any such provision. For I would rather die than have any one deprive me of my ground for boasting. 16For if I preach the gospel, that gives me no ground for boasting. For necessity is laid upon me. Woe to me if I do not preach the gospel! 17For if I do this of my own will, I have a reward; but if not of my own will, I am entrusted with a commission. 18What then is my reward? Just this: that in my preaching I may make the gospel free of charge, not making full use of my right in the gospel.

19For though I am free from all men, I have made myself a slave to all, that I might win the more. 20To the Jews I became as a Jew, in order to win Jews; to those under the law I became as one under the law—though not being myself under the law—that I might win those under the law. 21To those outside the law I became as one outside the law—not being without law toward God but under the law of Christ—that I might win those outside the law. 22To the weak I became weak, that I might win the weak. I have become all things to all men, that I might by all means save some. 23I do it all for the sake of the gospel, that I may share in its blessings.

24Do you not know that in a race all the runners compete, but only one receives the prize? So run that you may obtain it. 25Every athlete exercises self-control in all things. They do it to receive a perishable wreath, but we an imperishable. 26Well, I do not run aimlessly, I do not box as one beating the air; 27but I pommel my body and subdue it, lest after preaching to others I myself should be disqualified.

10 I want you to know, brethren, that our fathers were all under the cloud, and all passed through the sea, 2and all were baptized into Moses in the cloud and in the sea, 3and all ate the same supernatural food 4and all drank the same supernatural drink. For they drank from the supernatural Rock which followed them, and the Rock was Christ. 5Nevertheless with most of them God was not pleased; for they were overthrown in the wilderness.

6Now these things are warnings for us, not to desire evil as they did. 7Do not be idolaters as some of them were; as it is written, "The people sat down to eat and drink and rose up to dance."

8We must not indulge in immorality as some of them did, and twenty-three thousand fell in a single day. 9We must not put the Lord to the test, as some of them did and were destroyed by serpents; 10nor grumble, as some of them did and were destroyed by the Destroyer. 11Now these things happened to them as a warning, but they were written down for our instruction, upon whom the end of the ages has come. 12Therefore let any one who thinks that he stands take heed lest he fall. 13No temptation has overtaken you that is not common to man. God is faithful, and he will not let you be tempted beyond your strength, but with the temptation will also provide the way of escape, that you may be able to endure it.

14Therefore, my beloved, shun the worship of idols. 15I speak as to sensible men; judge for yourselves what I say. 16The cup of blessing which we bless, is it not a participation in the blood of Christ? The bread which we break, is it not a participation in the body of Christ? 17Because there is one bread, we who are many are one body, for we all partake of the one bread. 18Consider the people of Israel; are not those who eat the sacrifices partners in the altar? 19What do I imply then? That food offered to idols is anything, or that an idol is anything? 20No, I imply that what pagans sacrifice they offer to demons and not to God. I do not want you to be partners with demons. 21You cannot drink the cup of the Lord and the cup of demons. You cannot partake of the table of the Lord and the table of demons. 22Shall we provoke the Lord to jealousy? Are we stronger than he?

23"All things are lawful," but not all things are helpful. "All things are lawful," but not all things build up. 24Let no one seek his own good, but the good of his neighbor. 25Eat whatever is sold in the meat market without raising any question on the ground of conscience. 26For "the earth is the Lord's, and everything in it." 27If one of the unbelievers invites you to dinner and you are disposed to go, eat whatever is set before you without raising any question on the ground of conscience. 28(But if some one says to you, "This has been offered in sacrifice," then out of consideration for the man who informed you, and for conscience' sake—29I mean his conscience, not yours—do not eat it.) For why should my liberty be determined by another man's scruples? [30]If I partake with thankfulness, why am I denounced because of that for which I give thanks?

[31]So, whether you eat or drink, or whatever you do, do all to the glory of God. [32]Give no offense to Jews or to Greeks or to the church of God, [33]just as I try to please all men in everything I do, not seeking my own advantage, but that of many, that they may be saved. Be imitators of me, as I am of Christ.

11 [2]I commend you because you remember me in everything and maintain the traditions even as I have delivered them to you. [3]But I want you to understand that the head of every man is Christ, the head of a woman is her husband, and the head of Christ is God. [4]Any man who prays or prophesies with his head covered dishonors his head, [5]but any woman who prays or prophesies with her head unveiled dishonors her head—it is the same as if her head were shaven. [6]For if a woman will not veil herself, then she should cut off her hair; but if it is disgraceful for a woman to be shorn or shaven, let her wear a veil. [7]For a man ought not to cover his head, since he is the image and glory of God; but woman is the glory of man. [8](For man was not made from woman, but woman from man. [9]Neither was man created for woman, but woman for man.) [10]That is why a woman ought to have a veil on her head, because of the angels. [11](Nevertheless, in the Lord woman is not independent of man nor man of woman; [12]For as woman was made from man, so man is now born of woman. And all things are from God.) [13]Judge for yourselves; is it proper for a woman to pray to God with her head uncovered? [14]Does not nature itself teach you that for a man to wear long hair is degrading to him, [15]but if a woman has long hair, it is her pride? For her hair is given to her for a covering. [16]If any one is disposed to be contentious, we recognize no other practice, nor do the churches of God.

[17]But in the following instructions I do not commend you, because when you come together it is not for the better but for the worse. [18]For, in the first place, when you assemble as a church, I hear that there are divisions among you; and I partly believe it, [19]for there must be factions among you in order that those who are genuine among you may be recognized. [20]When you meet together, it is not the Lord's supper that you eat. [21]For in eating, each one goes ahead with his own meal, and one is hungry and another is drunk. [22]What! Do you not have houses to eat and drink in? Or do you despise the church of God and humiliate those who have nothing? What shall I say to you? Shall I commend you in this? No, I will not.

[23]For I received from the Lord what I also delivered to you, that the Lord Jesus on the night when he was betrayed took bread, [24]and when he had given thanks, he broke it, and said, "This is my body which is for you. Do this in remembrance of me." [25]In the same way also the cup, after supper, saying, "This cup is the new covenant in my blood. Do this, as often as you drink it, in remembrance of me." [26]For as often as you eat this bread and drink the cup, you proclaim the Lord's death until he comes.

[27]Whoever, therefore, eats the bread or drinks the cup of the Lord in an unworthy manner will be guilty of profaning the body and blood of the Lord. [28]Let a man examine himself, and so eat of the bread and drink of the cup. [29]For any one who eats and drinks without discerning the body eats and drinks judgment upon himself. [30]That is why many of you are weak and ill, and some have died. [31]But if we judged ourselves truly, we should not be judged. [32]But when we are judged by the Lord, we are chastened so that we may not be condemned along with the world.

[33]So then, my brethren, when you come together to eat, wait for one another—[34]if any one is hungry, let him eat at home—lest you come together to be condemned. About the other things I will give directions when I come.

12 Now concerning spiritual gifts, brethren, I do not want you to be uninformed. [2]You know that when you were heathen, you were led astray to dumb idols, however you may have been moved. [3]Therefore I want you to understand that no one speaking by the Spirit of God ever says "Jesus be cursed!" and no one can say "Jesus is Lord" except by the Holy Spirit.

[4]Now there are varieties of gifts, but the same Spirit; [5]and there are varieties of service, but the same Lord; [6]and there are varieties of working, but it is the same God who inspires them all in every one. [7]To each is given the manifestation of the Spirit for the common good. [8]To one is given through the Spirit the utterance of wisdom, and to another the utterance of knowledge according to the same Spirit,

9to another faith by the same Spirit, to another gifts of healing by the one Spirit, 10to another the working of miracles, to another prophecy, to another the ability to distinguish between spirits, to another various kinds of tongues, to another the interpretation of tongues. 11All these are inspired by one and the same Spirit, who apportions to each one individually as he wills.

12For just as the body is one and has many members, and all the members of the body, though many, are one body, so it is with Christ. 13For by one Spirit we were all baptized into one body—Jews or Greeks, slaves or free—and all were made to drink of one Spirit.

14For the body does not consist of one member but of many. 15If the foot should say, "Because I am not a hand, I do not belong to the body," that would not make it any less a part of the body. 16And if the ear should say, "Because I am not an eye, I do not belong to the body," that would not make it any less a part of the body. 17If the whole body were an eye, where would be the hearing? If the whole body were an ear, where would be the sense of smell? 18But as it is, God arranged the organs in the body, each one of them, as he chose. 19If all were a single organ, where would the body be? 20As it is, there are many parts, yet one body. 21The eye cannot say to the hand, "I have no need of you," nor again the head to the feet, "I have no need of you."22 On the contrary, the parts of the body which seem to be weaker are indispensable, 23and those parts of the body which we think less honorable we invest with the greater honor, and our unpresentable parts are treated with greater modesty, 24which our more presentable parts do not require. But God has so composed the body, giving the greater honor to the inferior part, 25that there may be no discord in the body, but that the members may have the same care for one another. 26If one member suffers, all suffer together; if one member is honored, all rejoice together.

27Now you are the body of Christ and individually members of it. 28And God has appointed in the church first apostles, second prophets, third teachers, then workers of miracles, then healers, helpers, administrators, speakers in various kinds of tongues. 29Are all apostles? Are all prophets? Are all teachers? Do all work miracles? 30Do all possess gifts of healing? Do all speak with

tongues? Do all interpret? 31But earnestly desire the higher gifts.

And I will show you a still more excellent way.

13 If I speak in the tongues of men and of angels, but have not love, I am a noisy gong or a clanging cymbal. 2And if I have prophetic powers, and understand all mysteries and all knowledge, and if I have all faith, so as to remove mountains, but have not love, I am nothing. 3If I give away all I have, and if I deliver my body to be burned, but have not love, I gain nothing.

4Love is patient and kind; love is not jealous or boastful; 5it is not arrogant or rude. Love does not insist on its own way; it is not irritable or resentful; 6it does not rejoice at wrong, but rejoices in the right. 7Love bears all things, believes all things, hopes all things, endures all things.

8Love never ends; as for prophecies, they will pass away; as for tongues, they will cease; as for knowledge, it will pass away. 9For our knowledge is imperfect and our prophecy is imperfect; 10but when the perfect comes, the imperfect will pass away. 11When I was a child, I spoke like a child, I thought like a child, I reasoned like a child; when I became a man, I gave up childish ways. 12For now we see in a mirror dimly, but then face to face. Now I know in part; then I shall understand fully, even as I have been fully understood. 13So faith, hope, love abide, these three; but the greatest of these is love.

14 Make love your aim, and earnestly desire the spiritual gifts, especially that you may prophesy. 2For one who speaks in a tongue speaks not to men but to God; for no one understands him, but he utters mysteries in the Spirit. 3On the other hand, he who prophesies speaks to men for their upbuilding and encouragement and consolation. 4He who speaks in a tongue edifies himself, but he who prophesies edifies the church. 5Now I want you all to speak in tongues, but even more to prophesy. He who prophesies is greater than he who speaks in tongues, unless some one interprets, so that the church may be edified.

6Now, brethren, if I come to you speaking in tongues, how shall I benefit you unless I bring you some revelation or knowledge or prophecy or teaching? 7If even lifeless instruments, such as the flute or the harp, do not give distinct notes, how will any one know what is played? 8And if the bugle gives an indistinct sound, who will get ready for battle? 9So with yourselves; if you in a tongue utter speech that is not intelligible, how will any one know what is said? For you will be speaking into the air. 10There are doubtless many different languages in the world, and none is without meaning; 11but if I do not know the meaning of the language, I shall be a foreigner to the speaker and the speaker a foreigner to me. 12So with yourselves; since you are eager for manifestations of the Spirit, strive to excel in building up the church.

13Therefore, he who speaks in a tongue should pray for the power to interpret. 14For if I pray in a tongue, my spirit prays but my mind is unfruitful. 15What am I to do? I will pray with the spirit and I will pray with the mind also; I will sing with the spirit and I will sing with the mind also. 16Otherwise, if you bless with the spirit, how can any one in the position of an outsider say the "Amen" to your thanksgiving when he does not know what you are saying? 17For you may give thanks well enough, but the other man is not edified. 18I thank God that I speak in tongues more than you all; 19nevertheless, in church I would rather speak five words with my mind, in order to instruct others, than ten thousand words in a tongue.

20Brethren, do not be children in your thinking; be babes in evil, but in thinking be mature. 21In the law it is written, "By men of strange tongues and by the lips of foreigners will I speak to this people, and even then they will not listen to me, says the Lord." 22Thus, tongues are a sign not for believers but for unbelievers, while prophecy is not for unbelievers but for believers. 23If, therefore, the whole church assembles and all speak in tongues, and outsiders or unbelievers enter, will they not say that you are mad? 24But if all prophesy, and an unbeliever or outsider enters, he is convicted by all, he is called to account by all, 25the secrets of his heart are disclosed; and so, falling on his face, he will worship God and declare that God is really among you.

26What then, brethren? When you come together, each one has a hymn, a lesson, a revelation, a tongue, or an interpretation. Let all things be done for edification. 27If any speak in a tongue, let there be only two or at most three, and each in turn; and let one interpret. 28But if there is no one to interpret, let each of them keep silence in church and speak to himself and to God. 29Let two or three prophets speak, and let the others weigh what is said. 30If a revelation is made to another sitting by, let the first be silent. 31For you can all prophesy one by one, so that all may learn and all be encouraged; 32and the spirits of prophets are subject to prophets. 33For God is not a God of confusion but of peace.

As in all the churches of the saints, 34the women should keep silence in the churches. For they are not permitted to speak, but should be subordinate, as even the law says. 35If there is anything they desire to know, let them ask their husbands at home. For it is shameful for a woman to speak in church. 36What! Did the word of God originate with you, or are you the only ones it has reached?

37If any one thinks that he is a prophet, or spiritual, he should acknowledge that what I am writing to you is a command of the Lord. 38If any one does not recognize this, he is not recognized. 39So, my brethren, earnestly desire to prophesy, and do not forbid speaking in tongues; 40but all things should be done decently and in order.

15 Now I would remind you, brethren, in what terms I preached to you the gospel, which you received, in which you stand, 2by which you are saved, if you hold it fast—unless you believed in vain.

3For I delivered to you as of first importance what I also received, that Christ died for our sins in accordance with the scriptures, 4that he was buried, that he was raised on the third day in accordance with the scriptures, 5and that he appeared to Cephas, then to the twelve. 6Then he appeared to more than five hundred brethren at one time, most of whom are still alive, though some have fallen asleep. 7Then he appeared to James, then to all the apostles. 8Last of all, as to one untimely born, he appeared also to me. 9For I am the least of the apostles, unfit to be called an apostle, because I persecuted the church of God. 10But by the grace of God I am what I am, and his grace toward me was not in vain. On the contrary, I worked harder than any of them, though it was not I, but the grace of God which is with me. 11Whether then it was I or they, so we preach and so you believed.

[12]Now if Christ is preached as raised from the dead, how can some of you say that there is no resurrection of the dead? [13]But if there is no resurrection of the dead, then Christ has not been raised;[14] if Christ has not been raised, then our preaching is in vain and your faith is in vain. [15]We are even found to be misrepresenting God, because we testified of God that he raised Christ, whom he did not raise if it is true that the dead are not raised. [16]For if the dead are not raised, then Christ has not been raised. [17]If Christ has not been raised, your faith is futile and you are still in your sins. [18]Then those also who have fallen asleep in Christ have perished. [19]If for this life only we have hoped in Christ, we are of all men most to be pitied.

[20]But in fact Christ has been raised from the dead, the first fruits of those who have fallen asleep. [21]For as by a man came death, by a man has come also the resurrection of the dead. [22]For as in Adam all die, so also in Christ shall all be made alive. [23]But each in his own order: Christ the first fruits, then at his coming those who belong to Christ. [24]Then comes the end, when he delivers the kingdom to God the Father after destroying every rule and every authority and power. [25]For he must reign until he has put all his enemies under his feet. [26]The last enemy to be destroyed is death. [27]"For God has put all things in subjection under his feet." But when it says, "All things are put in subjection under him," it is plain that he is excepted who put all things under him. [28]When all things are subjected to him, then the Son himself will also be subjected to him who put all things under him, that God may be everything to every one.

[29]Otherwise, what do people mean by being baptized on behalf of the dead? If the dead are not raised at all, why are people baptized on their behalf? [30]Why am I in peril every hour? [31]I protest, brethren, by my pride in you which I have in Christ Jesus our Lord, I die every day! [32]What do I gain if, humanly speaking, I fought with beasts at Ephesus? If the dead are not raised, "Let us eat and drink, for tomorrow we die." [33]Do not be deceived: "Bad company ruins good morals." [34]Come to your right mind, and sin no more. For some have no knowledge of God. I say this to your shame.

[35]But some one will ask, "How are the dead raised? With what kind of body do they come?" [36]You foolish man! What you sow does not come to life unless it dies. [37]And what you sow is not the body which is to be, but a bare kernel, perhaps of wheat or of some other grain. [38]But God gives it a body as he has chosen, and to each kind of seed its own body. [39]For not all flesh is alike, but there is one kind for men, another for animals, another for birds, and another for fish. [40]There are celestial bodies and there are terrestrial bodies; but the glory of the celestial is one, and the glory of the terrestrial is another. [41]There is one glory of the sun, and another glory of the moon, and another glory of the stars; for star differs from star in glory.

[42]So is it with the resurrection of the dead. What is sown is perishable, what is raised is imperishable. It is sown in dishonor, it is raised in glory. [43]It is sown in weakness, it is raised in power. [44]It is sown a physical body, it is raised a spiritual body. If there is a physical body, there is also a spiritual body. [45]Thus it is written, "The first man Adam became a living being"; the last Adam became a life-giving spirit. [46]But it is not the spiritual which is first but the physical, and then the spiritual. [47]The first man was from the earth, a man of dust; the second man is from heaven. [48]As was the man of dust, so are those who are of the dust; and as is the man of heaven, so are those who are of heaven. [49]Just as we have borne the image of the man of dust, we shall also bear the image of the man of heaven. [50]I tell you this, brethren: flesh and blood cannot inherit the kingdom of God, nor does the perishable inherit the imperishable.

[51]Lo! I tell you a mystery. We shall not all sleep, but we shall all be changed, [52]In a moment, in the twinkling of an eye, at the last trumpet. [53]For the trumpet will sound, and the dead will be raised imperishable, and we shall be changed. For this perishable nature must put on the imperishable, and this mortal nature must put on immortality. [54]When the perishable puts on the imperishable, and the mortal puts on immortality, then shall come to pass the saying that is written:

"Death is swallowed up in victory."
[55]"O death, where is thy victory?
O death, where is thy sting?"

[56]The sting of death is sin, and the power of sin is the law. [57]But thanks be to God, who gives us the victory through our Lord Jesus Christ.

⁵⁸Therefore, my beloved brethren, be steadfast, immovable, always abounding in the work of the Lord, knowing that in the Lord your labor is not in vain.

16 Now concerning the contribution for the saints: as I directed the churches of Galatia, so you also are to do. ²On the first day of every week, each of you is to put something aside and store it up, as he may prosper, so that contributions need not be made when I come. ³And when I arrive, I will send those whom you accredit by letter to carry your gift to Jerusalem. ⁴If it seems advisable that I should go also, they will accompany me.

⁵I will visit you after passing through Macedo'nia, for I intend to pass through Macedo'nia, ⁶and perhaps I will stay with you or even spend the winter, so that you may speed me on my journey, wherever I go. ⁷For I do not want to see you now just in passing; I hope to spend some time with you, if the Lord permits. ⁸But I will stay in Ephesus until Pentecost, ⁹for a wide door for effective work has opened to me, and there are many adversaries.

¹⁰When Timothy comes, see that you put him at ease among you, for he is doing the work of the Lord, as I am. ¹¹So let no one despise him. Speed him on his way in peace, that he may return to me; for I am expecting him with the brethren.

¹²As for our brother Apol'los, I strongly urged him to visit you with the other brethren, but it was not at all his will to come now. He will come when he has opportunity.

¹³Be watchful, stand firm in your faith, be courageous, be strong. ¹⁴Let all that you do be done in love.

¹⁵Now, brethren, you know that the household of Steph'anas were the first converts in Acha'ia, and they have devoted themselves to the service of the saints; ¹⁶I urge you to be subject to such men and to every fellow worker and laborer. ¹⁷I rejoice at the coming of Steph'anas and Fortuna'tus and Acha'icus, because they have made up for your absence; ¹⁸for they refreshed my spirit as well as yours. Give recognition to such men.

¹⁹The churches of Asia send greetings. Aquila and Prisca, together with the church in their house, send you hearty greetings in the Lord. ²⁰All the brethren send greetings. Greet one another with a holy kiss.

²¹I, Paul, write this greeting with my own hand. ²²If any one has no love for the Lord, let him be accursed. Our Lord, come! ²³The grace of the Lord Jesus be with you. ²⁴My love be with you all in Christ Jesus. Amen.

CHAPTER EIGHT

FROM MOVEMENT TO INSTITUTION: AUGUSTINE

At the turn of the century the emperor Trajan (98–117) appointed special commissioners to investigate the new religion, and one of them, Pliny, wrote of stubborn Christians in Asia Minor who, when brought to trial, rigidly maintained their faith in this "superstition," even upon pain of death (see Pliny the Younger, *Epistles* 10:96–97).

This quote tells of renewed persecution of Christians at the end of the first century CE. Christians enjoyed some acceptance in the Empire as long as there was a connection between Christians and Jews. Rome had already faced the issue of monotheism in its dealings with Judaism and had made concessions. But by the end of the first century Christianity and Judaism had split. Rome saw Christian monotheism as diluted by its Christology—its allegiance to Jesus of Nazareth. It did not understand its practices, especially with regard to the Eucharist, and was angered by the refusal of Christians to pay homage to the emperor. In other words, in a religiously pluralistic society, Christianity was without officially recognized standing.

What was required was that Christians define their faith. They needed to reassure the Roman authorities that they were not a threat. In order to do this they needed to codify their beliefs and practices, and establish structure and leadership. Internally there was another issue: to protect the faith from heretical interpretations.

THE CANON

In the middle of the second century a Christian named Marcion (died ca. 160) from Asia Minor showed up in Rome and established a community that was known as Marcionites. Marcion proposed that the God of Jesus was wholly a God of love, incompatible with the God of the Old Testament, as Christians refer to the Tanakh, which often describes God as a warrior, leading peoples into war, and inflicting judgment by the sword. Marcion declared a set of sacred writings authoritative for Christians that omitted entirely the Old Testament, and included only Paul's letters and the Gospel of Luke as the scriptural canon of Christianity. He distinguished between a god of the world and the god of Jesus who is the god of spirit and love. He preached a doctrine of separation between spirit and matter and denied a physical resurrection. These beliefs were associated with Gnosticism, an interpretation seen by many Christians as a heresy. The rest of the church came to reject Marcion's "canon," and eventually excommunicated him as a heretic. However, Marcion's attempt to establish a canon prompted the wider church to develop a list of sacred writings, a Christian canon.

There was already a body of literature circulating that served as witness to the Christian faith, and from this a selection was made of two primary genres: gospels and letters. A compilation was made in 180 and is referred to as the Muratorian Canon, named after its discoverer and first editor. The first canon appears to have included the four gospels, the letters of Paul, Peter, Jude, and James, and the Hebrew Scriptures as the Old Testament. Discussion of the content continued over the next century and a half until the present list of twenty-seven separate writings was composed by Bishop Athanasius of Alexandria in 367 and approved by the Council of Hippo in 393. The canon has never been considered closed, which is the reason for the lower case "c." Catholic, Orthodox, and Protestant Churches agree on the selection of Christian scriptures, but differ on some of the Old Testament writings.

THE APOLOGISTS

Christians who interpret the Christian faith to non-Christians are called apologists, from the Greek *apologia*, a speaking in defense; compare Socrates' *Apology*. The Book of Acts is viewed as an apology. For example, Paul is seen as defending Christianity to local populaces (14:8-18), philosophers (17:22-34), local merchants (19:1-41), governors (24-25), and even territorial kings (26:1-32). In its depiction of the crucifixion, blame is placed entirely on the Jews, exonerating Roman involvement. Paul's letters themselves show that the apostle was at home in the forms and methods of popular philosophical debate, especially those forms and methods represented by the Stoic and Cynic philosophical schools.

In the second century Christianity consciously developed its capacity to debate with the prevailing philosophical schools of thought. The church's interest in such debate was not only to decrease imperial suspicion against it, but also because of its high regard for Greco-Roman culture, which served so well as a vehicle for its own expression of the gospel. Christianity therefore took seriously the objections of the major philosophical schools—Stoic, Platonic, Peripatetic (Aristotelian), and Epicurean, with an ear toward the Cynics and Skeptics. Christian authors developed argumentation within various philosophical frameworks and borrowed from them as need arose in their debates. A recurrent theme throughout the teaching of those second-century theologians called Apologists, was that Christians should treat the emperor and the government with honor and respect, live as upright citizens, and make the contributions expected of socially responsible people. Nevertheless, because of Christian refusal to perform acts of worship bestowing divine honor on the emperor, the official attitude toward Christians remained that of suspicion and hostility. The precedent set by Trajan continued, if not programmatically throughout the empire, at least in various localities.

In 165 Polycarp, the bishop of Smyrna, after refusing to curse Christ, was burned alive, and in 177 a pogrom against Christians occurred in the city of Lyons. Appeals by various Christian apologists, some directly to the emperor, fell on deaf ears. By the end of the second century the Emperor Commodus (ruled 180–192) upheld legislation forbidding the practice of Christianity, subjecting those who engaged in the faith to the death penalty. His father, the Stoic philosopher Marcus Aurelius (121–180), had written that it was noble to be willing to face death at all times, but not "out of simple obstinacy, like the Christians" (*Meditations* 11:3).

One of the Apologists was a Samarian-born student of philosophy known as *Justin Martyr* (100–165). His account of his conversion is an important record of a young man's encounter with various philosophical schools. Justin left behind two documents, *Apology* and *Dialogue with the Jew Trypho*. Both are considered apologetics since in his dialogue with the Jew he continues his defense of the Christian faith. The *Apology* is especially interesting because it contains a description of baptism as practiced in the mid-second century.

Justin studied with Stoic, Peripatetic, Pythagorean, and Platonist teachers. Justin conceived of philosophy's goal as achieving the knowledge of God, and since true knowledge of God could come only from its source, namely God, the concept of revelation became dominant in his thought. He determined that it was the ancient prophets of the Hebrew Scriptures who, inspired by God, provided such revealed knowledge, and that they addressed the same philosophical questions as the Greeks, especially the questions of first principles or origins as well as the goal of life. In addition, the fulfillment of their prophecies in Jesus constituted proof for Justin that the prophets' teachings were unassailable. He was martyred around 165 for his Christian beliefs.

Tertullian (ca. 160–220) is one of the great figures of the early church: apologist, theologian, and finally heretic! He was a Carthaginian lawyer who converted to Christianity about 195. His famous defense of Christianity, the "Apologeticum," addressed to Roman state authorities, dealt with the absurdities of the accusations made against Christians. Tertullian argued that their citizenship should not be called into question because of their refusal to offer divine honors to the emperor. He argued forcefully that Christians were good citizens who happened to be monotheists, and who therefore could not participate in idolatry.

Tertullian argued against the Gnostic heresy by denying the validity of individualistic interpretations of Scripture, saying that the Bible is God's gift to the entire church, not just to a privileged few who claimed special inspiration. But Tertullian was not especially hard on pagans. He believed that paganism was natural religion. People were fulfilling an innate religious need in pagan practices. Christianity had come to give meaning to pagan worship. As Paul had written, "Do you not know that your body is a temple of the Holy Spirit within you, which you have from God?"(1 Cor. 6.19) God did not dwell in man-made shrines but in humans.

Tertullian was the first Christian theologian to write in Latin. The Latin theological vocabulary he developed—such as the term "Trinity" (Latin *Trinitas*), which was instrumental in shaping the Trinitarian and Christological debates and the resulting credal formulations of the fourth century—resulted in Latin becoming the sacred language of the West. The Churches of the east, however, continued to use Greek. Complications that naturally arise when the participants speak in different languages were to further complicate many of the issues on which West and East differed.

But Tertullian the shaper of Christian orthodoxy is not the whole story. Conversion to Christianity had always meant to him a transformed moral life that did not bend to the practices of the surrounding society. Tertullian came to believe that the Montanists (see below) embodied the living Spirit of God and the strict moral life of earliest Christianity in his day. He became a Montanist Christian in 207 (although he never left the Church) and remained one for the rest of his life, turning from defender to severe critic of Catholic Christianity for its worldly compromises and institutionalizing of the activity of the divine Spirit.

We know nothing of the spread of Christianity in Egypt until the second century. Much of the earliest material was declared heretical and destroyed. But one figure emerges in the latter half of the second century who had an important influence on the early church. *Origen,* ca. 185–254, was born in Alexandria and reared as a Christian in a largely pagan society. When his teacher, the Bishop of Alexandria, had to flee to escape persecution, Origen at the age of eighteen replaced him as head of his school. Origen was a prolific writer and he soon established himself as a

major scholar, biblical exegete, and theological and spiritual writer. Origen's homilies are among the oldest extant examples of Christian preaching. He produced commentaries on every book of the Bible, using allegorical method as a means of debate with the Platonists of Alexandria. Origen's major work was his *Hexapla,* a six-column version of the Bible printed in various Hebrew and Greek versions, which exhibited his interest and ability in biblical criticism.

Origen wrote the first book of "systematic theology," *On First Principles,* which was intended as a response to the heretical Gnostic groups. In it he speculated that God's original creation was spiritual and not material, strongly affirmed both divine love and human freedom, and denied an everlasting hell in favor of everlasting possibilities of both sin and redemption even for Satan. Ironically, the church would later condemn some of his more speculative work as being "too Gnostic." Nevertheless, the breadth of Origen's work, at times reaching genius proportions, contributed mightily to the church's developing theology.

HERETICAL MOVEMENTS

Another second-century figure who addressed heretical movements was *Irenaeus* (ca. 130–200), Bishop of Lyons in what is now France. For many centuries it was only through his writings that we had knowledge of these groups. Since he was an opponent we must be careful about taking Irenaeus's account at face value as correct or fair. In the mid-twentieth century a discovery in the Egyptian desert uncovered original documents of the Gnostic groups. We can now say with more authority what these groups believed. Irenaeus, viewing himself as a faithful biblical theologian, countered Gnostic interpretations of Christianity by demanding scriptural documentation. He opposed speculative thinking, arguing that Gnostics and Montanists were disjoined from apostolic tradition. Irenaeus's arguments rested on the objective presence of the Spirit in scripture and episcopacy, which contrasted with the subjective claims of Spirit-possession in the teaching of his opponents.

Montanism Montanism was an apocalyptic movement in the latter half of the second century, whose adherents claimed a special possession of the Spirit of God. Its founder was Montanus, who claimed to be the Paraclete, or the Spirit of Truth, promised in the Gospel of John (see John 16:7-13). The disciples of Montanus were charismatics who engaged in speaking in tongues and were convinced that they were living in a time immediately before the end of the world. They met persecution and execution willingly, convinced that such persecution was proof that the end of all things was at hand. Two of the most prominent prophet-leaders of the Montanist movement were women. Prisca preached the imminent return of Jesus and described a vision in which she saw him in female form. Maximilla assumed the leadership of the Montanist group upon the death of Montanus. Through the centuries other movements claiming direct revelation and inspiration have appeared within Christianity, some led by women.

Gnosticism   In 1945 a discovery in Nag Hammadi in Egypt (south of Alexandria bordering on the Nile) opened a door to a completely different interpretation of the early Jesus movement. Some Arab peasants unearthed a six-foot earthenware jar that contained thirteen codices (52 texts) written in Coptic, an ancient Egyptian language written in Greek letters, which purported to be the "secret teachings" of Jesus. From these twentieth-century discoveries scholars have been able to determine some of the specific beliefs of the Gnostics.

The two principal builders of Gnostic theology were Valentinus (d. ca. 165) and Basilides (d. ca. 161). Based on the Platonic distinction between the world of forms and the world of phenomena, Gnosticism (from the Greek word *gnosis,* meaning "knowledge") can be summarized as follows:

> The world is evil, bound for decay and ultimate destruction. It is under the control of spiritual powers hostile to God, and was created by an evil deity (called the "Demiurge") locked in eternal conflict with God. The only escape for humanity had to be provided by the good deity, an escape that could be accomplished only by the sending of a redeemer from outside the evil world into it to give people *gnosis*—knowledge of the means of escape into the world of God.

The goal of the Gnostic believer, then, was to achieve this gnosis and thereby to escape from this material existence in which the evil deity had imprisoned his or her soul. As Christians, the Gnostics saw in Jesus the other-worldly redeemer, but as Gnostics they denied his humanity. Jesus could not have participated in the evil creation: he only *appeared* to be human, but was not really so. This is called a *docetic* interpretation of Jesus (from the Greek *dokeo* "to seem"). In Gnostic worship believers participated in the divine redeemer's descent and ascent into the world of human beings by means of ritual observances in which they partook of the "food of immortality," by which the soul was equipped for its heavenly journey.

Women were prominent in the Gnostic as well as in the Montanist movements. There is some evidence that female Gnostic Christians in North Africa were permitted to serve as priests, leading worship and baptizing. The writings of these two groups described God in strikingly female images. We found this feminine imaging in the Hebrew Scriptures as well.

Summary of Gnostic beliefs:

Gnostics did not accept the bodily resurrection. They instead preached a symbolic interpretation of the resurrection.

Gnostics denied the virgin birth and again offered an interpretation of a spiritual birth through the "holy virginal spirit."

Gnostics spoke of God in both masculine and feminine terms, as Father and Mother.

Gnostics interpreted the Kingdom of God as a state of self-discovery; the kingdom is within each person.

Gnostics did not consider Jesus as a physical being as significant; rather it was the message that he brought. It was possible to become like him: "Whoever drinks from my mouth will become as I am, and I myself will become that person, and things that are hidden will be revealed to him." (Gospel of Thomas, 108)

The scholars who study these manuscripts speculate that there could be a relationship with Eastern religions such as Buddhism and Zoroastrianism. It is traditionally believed that the apostle Thomas traveled to India and with the rapid spread of Christianity it is not hard to imagine that some of the missionaries traveled to areas where they came into contact with Eastern philosophies.

It should be noted that the theme of a "secret teaching" of Jesus has roots in the canonical Christian writings. The Gospel of Mark indicates that Jesus taught certain things in public and others in private, to his disciples alone: "To you is given to know the mystery of the kingdom of God, but to those outside all things are in parables, so that seeing, they may not perceive, and hearing, they may not understand." Mark, 4:11-12. Paul, too, in second Corinthians 6-13, declares that he hides teachings concerning sacred wisdom and mysteries from the majority of his hearers, entrusting them only to those he calls "initiated," or "spiritual."

Both Gnosticism and Montanism drew upon various strands and facets of pre-Christian religiosity, including the mystery religions of the Mediterranean world. Little in them was unique and most was eclectic and syncretistic. Their challenge to the Christian church at large was a serious one and the response would become the orthodox doctrine of the Church Catholic.

CREEDS

The Doctrine of the Trinity: Another organizing principle for Christian "orthodoxy" (from the Greek *orthodoxia,* "correct opinion") was the codification of belief in the form of creeds (from the Latin *credo* = "I believe"). Compared to Judaism and Islam, Christianity is a creedal religion. This means that the followers have to affirm specific statements that provide the definition of Christian faith. Sometimes in the modern world, individuals calling on the "freedom which comes through Christ" formulate a more or less religious individualism and refer to themselves as Christians. From the standpoint of Christian orthodoxy, however, this will not pass. All who call themselves Christians must accept the creeds. What are creeds? They are statements that primarily define the person and nature of Jesus interpreted as the Christ and his relationship with God the Father and the Holy Spirit, and also affirm other central articles of faith.

The creeds that now define orthodox Christianity emerged very slowly and only through intense, heated, and protracted wrangling over differences that finally came to threaten the unity and peace of the church universal. Already before Con-

stantine's designation of Christianity as the preferred religion of the Empire, radical differences over the Incarnation were the source of conflict in the wider church. Constantine wanted to put an end to this. With this intent he convened the first *ecumenical council* (ecumenical = the whole or universal church) in Nicaea, in what is now Turkey, in 325. Two hundred and twenty bishops were in attendance, representing sees (the official jurisdiction of a bishop) from all over the Empire. It was their job to decide between the positions of Athanasiaus, Bishop of Alexandria and Arius, a priest with charismatic appeal from Alexandria. A third position was suggested, but pleased neither side.

Positions on the Doctrine of the Trinity   Arians believed that Jesus was the first and highest of all created beings but fundamentally *different* from the being of God. (Greek *anomoios* = unlike)

Athanasians believed that God became incarnate in the man Jesus so Jesus was of *the very being, of God.* (Greek *homoousios* = same being)

A third group tried to interject a compromise position when it suggested that Jesus was a "similar" being. (*homoiousios* = similar)

This is known as the Trinitarian debate and is resolved in the words of the Nicene Creed, below, which is recognized by Roman Catholics, Eastern Orthodox, Lutherans, Anglicans, and other Christian denominations.

The Nicene Creed

I believe in one God the Father Almighty, maker of heaven and earth, and of all things visible and invisible.

And in one Lord Jesus Christ, the only-begotten Son of God, begotten of his Father before all worlds, God of God, Light of Light, very God of very God; *begotten, not made, being of one substance (homoousios) with the Father by whom all things were made* (italics added); who for us men and for our salvation came down from heaven, and was incarnate by the Holy Ghost of the Virgin Mary, and was made man and was crucified also for us under Pontius Pilate. He suffered and was buried, and the third day he rose again according to the Scriptures and ascended into heaven, and sitteth on the right hand of the Father; and he shall come again, with glory, to judge both the quick and the dead, whose kingdom shall have no end.

And I believe in the Holy Ghost, the Lord, and Giver of life, who proceedeth from the Father and the Son, who with the Father and Son together is worshiped and glorified, who spake by the prophets. And I believe in the one holy Catholic and Apostolic church; I acknowledge one baptism for the remission of sins, and I look for the resurrection of the dead, and the life of the world to come. Amen.

The attendants at the Council of Nicea agreed with Athanasius (with the Athanasian definition). Despite this, Athanasians and Arians would continue their conflict over the next several decades. Athanasius was thrice removed from his see, Arius was excommunicated and reinstated. The Emperor Theodosius I, in 381, called the second ecumenical council that met in Constantinople. The result of this meeting was a reaffirmation of the Nicene Creed, the Athanasian position.

Man and God: Christology   A further issue was to resolve how the human and divine exist within the person of Jesus. Two ecumenical councils, in Ephesus in 431 and in Chalcedon in 451, responded to the "christological" issue (*Christos* = messiah, *logos* = knowledge). One side, represented by the Antiochene school of biblical scholars, tended sharply to distinguish between the divine and the human in the person of Jesus, assigning certain activities to his divinity and others to his humanity. They were accused by opponents of thinking of Jesus simply as a Spirit-inspired human being like the prophets.

The other side, led by a group of theologians and church leaders centered in Alexandria, emphasized the unity of the divine and the human in Jesus and rejected trying to divide up his activities. The Antiochenes accused them of denying Jesus' full humanity, swallowing it up in his divinity. The Council of Ephesus in 431, the third ecumenical council, laid the groundwork for a "formulary of peace" that in 433 became the basis for the decision at the fourth council, the Council of Chalcedon, in

451. The bishops at Chalcedon both reaffirmed Nicaea and Constantinople and declared that in his person Christ consists of "two natures [human and divine], without confusion, without change, without division, without separation." As with the Arian controversy in the fourth century, the christological disputes of the fifth century were endless, heated, and deeply immersed in politics and in profound differences between the eastern and the western parts of the church. Even after Chalcedon the christological conflict raged on for some time, but Chalcedon became the definition of the orthodox Christian view of the person of Christ down through the centuries.

LEADERSHIP

The first leaders of the church were the apostles, who themselves or their disciples were also missionaries. Soon we read in the scriptures of presbyters, deacons, and elders. A leadership structure was beginning to evolve. The first instructions on leadership roles appear in the letters of *Bishop Ignatius* of Antioch, written in the first two decades of the second century, indicate an advance in the definition of ministerial order. A hierarchical gradation is now carefully articulated, in which a bishop presides over presbyters, (priests), and deacons. Ignatius justified this structure doctrinally by means of interweaving ideas about the nature of the church and its sacraments, God, and salvation itself. The bishop represents God in the community, and all worship practices, especially the Eucharist, must be done only with the bishop's authorization. The monarchical episcopate (rule by bishops) has begun.

There are indications in the New Testament that women could initially fill leadership roles (Acts 17:4). Paul frequently mentions women serving in this capacity in his letters (Phil. 4:2-3; Rom. 16.1 &12, and I Cor. 19). However, as the church develops as an institution there is a gradual limiting of the role of women in leadership positions. There are noncanonical writings attesting to an active role of women in the early church. Pliny writes of two deaconesses, Perpetua and Felicitas, who were martyred. *The Acts of Paul and Thecla* tells the story of a young woman who refuses the dictates of her family and social convention to leave home and become a follower of Paul's. While of dubious historical accuracy it is evidence that the gospel was a liberating message for women. Eventually, however, mainstream Christianity increasingly reserved offices in the church solely for males. Where leadership positions remained open were in certain early Christian movements that would eventually be declared heretical, such as the Montanists and the Gnostics.

THE CHURCH FATHERS

Authority in the developing church fell to a series of leaders who attained the distinction of Church Fathers. These were the theologians whose interpretations of the Bible and Christianity shaped the doctrine and practice of the church during the period from about 100–600. They were called the "fathers" of the church, and their authority was second only to that of scripture. Among the fathers were bishops, priests (presbyters), and monks; some wrote in Latin, some in Greek. Many were declared saints and doctors (teachers) of the church. The study of these individuals and their work is called Patristics. In the West during the Middle Ages the scholastic movement came to define the proper method of interpreting the Fathers and reconciling theology and philosophy. The Western church continued to look to the Fathers as authorities, but it came to see the papacy as a "living," ongoing source of authoritative teaching. The Eastern Church has much more clearly continued to remain with the Fathers as the permanent, unchanging authority for the Church.

In the Western Church Augustine of Hippo was early recognized as the most important of the Fathers followed by Jerome and Ambrose. In the Eastern Church, however, he was quite controversial for some of his doctrinal positions (original sin, grace, and predestination). Today he is respected as a theologian and one of the Fathers.

AUGUSTINE SETS THE COURSE FOR THE WEST

Augustine's influence is so massive that it stretches into the centuries far beyond him. Summaries of the early church end with him; the history of the medieval church begins with him; the Reformation was imbued with his theology; and some items in modern Christian thought, such as the church's role in shaping social justice (for example, the limits of justifiable warfare) stem directly from him. For some of the Renaissance humanists of the fifteenth and sixteenth centuries who revived interest in Plato's philosophy after a long period in which Aristotle's thought dominated through Aquinas, Augustine the Christian Platonist was a kind of "patron saint."

Early Life   Aurelius Augustinus (354–430) was born in Tagaste, in the North African Roman province of Numidia (Tagaste is now Souk-Ahras in Algeria), and lived his life entirely during the early period of the legalization and hegemony of Christianity in the Roman Empire. His mother Monica was a fervent Christian, and she played a large role in his life until her death in 387. His father Patricius was a pagan until shortly before his death in 371. Although instructed in Christianity by his mother, Augustine was not a practicing Christian when a teenager and young man. Indeed, he was for some years highly critical of the naively literalistic biblical interpretation of the North African Christians he knew.

A brilliant student, Augustine was trained in Carthage to be a rhetorician. After finishing his studies he opened a grammar school in Tagaste (373–374) and then taught rhetoric at Carthage until 383. Some time around 371 Augustine took a mistress. They were together for some fifteen years and had a son, Adeodatus, born in 372, with whom Augustine became quite close in the years before his son's untimely death as a teenager.

In 373 Augustine became a member of the *Manichaean* religion, and remained an adherent for nine years. A popular faith of the day founded by a third-century Persian prophet named Mani, the Manichaeans attracted Augustine because they seemed to offer a rational account of the problem of evil, which bothered him a good deal. According to Manichaeism, there are two ultimate realities or principles: one the source of light and goodness, the other the ruler of darkness and evil. The mixture of good and evil in human beings and in the world is the playing out of the conflict between these two cosmic ultimates. Somewhat like the Gnostics, Manichaean dualism also expressed itself in the identification of the good with the realm of spirit and the evil with the realm of matter. But both are part and parcel of the created order and grounded in ultimate reality. The Manichaeans

Illustrating a scene from the *Confessions*, this fresco depicts Augustine's conversion at the moment when he hears a voice in the garden directing him to "take up the book and read." Augustine sits in the center foreground reading a passage from Paul's Epistles about refraining from sexual sins, while his intellectual friend, Alypius, offers him his hand and two others cautiously observe in the background.

Figure IV-7 Benozzo Gozzoli, *Saint Augustine Reading the Epistles of Saint Paul*. 1464–65. Fresco in an apsidal chapel in Sant'Agostino, San Gimignano, Italy. 86.61 × 90.55" (220 × 230 cm). Courtesy of Scala/Art Resource, NY.

incorporated Jesus into their mythology, and the Christian elements they adopted made it popular with people from a Christian context.

Maturity Augustine's disillusionment with Manichaeism coincided with his moving to Rome in 383. In 384 he got a job as city instructor in rhetoric in Milan. His two years in Milan were to be decisive in bringing about his conversion to Christianity. Augustine attended some of the sermons of Ambrose (ca. 340–397), Bishop of Milan. Ambrose helped him overcome his old problem with the Bible by introducing him to *allegorical interpretation*. With allegorical biblical interpretation persons, events, and portrayals of God that on a literal level seemed primitive or even immoral could be seen as symbols and parables of higher spiritual meanings. (Allegorical interpretation came to dominate Christian exegesis of the Bible until the Reformation.)

Milan was also a center for the study of *Neoplatonic* philosophy, the "New Platonism" of the philosopher-mystic Plotinus (205–270) and his successor Porphyry (232–305). The "Books of the Pla-

tonists," as Augustine called them, had a profound influence on him. Together with allegorical interpretation of the Bible, Neoplatonism enabled him to take Christianity seriously and brought about his intellectual conversion. From one point of view, in fact, Augustine can be seen as a Christian Neoplatonist who came to believe that Christianity was the "true philosophy." His early writings, which he produced during the years immediately following his conversion, are almost straight Neoplatonic philosophy in Christian form.

Neoplatonism taught Augustine two things: the reality of the non-material, and the unreality of evil. Basic to his problem with God was his inability to think of anything real as not being physical or material. Through Neoplatonism he became convinced that thought and the ideas it thinks, which are certainly real, are not material. From there he could move on to think of non-material realities as in fact the most real, and of God, the ultimate reality, as pure Spirit, infinite and eternal.

Neoplatonism also enabled Augustine to deal with the problem of evil in a way he finally found intellectually and morally satisfying. In Neoplatonic thought all things flow from the indefinable ultimate, the One or the Good, to form a great hierarchy of being, and everything is good simply by virtue of being, although good in a lesser sense than the perfect Good. Evil is a lack or privation of being rather than a positive reality. Augustine put this together with the affirmation of Genesis 1 that God pronounced the universe he had created "very good," and developed a Christian theodicy. In sharp contrast to his former Manichean views, there is only one ultimate reality, God, who is perfect goodness and the creator of everything that exists both physical and spiritual. Everything created, simply by virtue of having been brought into and sustained in existence by God, is good. Evil is a deficiency or distortion in things that are in themselves good but not perfectly good; it is not anything ultimate in itself. For Augustine it was the first humans' disobedience in the Garden of Eden—their misuse of the great good of freedom bestowed only on humans and angels—that introduced all the evil into the world.

By 386 Augustine had become intellectually converted to Christianity. His mind was converted, but not yet his will. What he continued to struggle with was his resistance to Christianity's moral demands, focused on his continuing need for sexual pleasure. Having reached the breaking point in his long personal struggle, Augustine had a conversion experience in the garden next to his house in the summer of 386. After moving to a country retreat for several months, he and his son Adeodatus were baptized the day before Easter in 387. Following his mother's death later that year, Augustine returned to North Africa and lived a monastic life of study and writing in a community in his hometown. In 391 he was ordained priest and in 396 was consecrated Bishop of Hippo Regius (now Bône), a city on the Mediterranean coast.

Bishop of Hippo   The rest of Augustine's years were filled with the activities of his diocese, the writing of many books, and vigorous debate against various heresies. Shortly after becoming Bishop of Hippo, he wrote a book called *Confessions*, recounting his life up to the time of his baptism and the death of his mother. Augustine also wrote an important work *On the Trinity* that became a major study of Christian doctrine, and numerous biblical commentaries. Some eight hundred of his sermons on biblical texts have been preserved, and about two hundred of his letters—these in addition to about 100 books and essays. That so many of Augustine's writings have been preserved attests to the stature he achieved even in his own time.

As bishop Augustine was called upon to combat three heresies threatening the church: Manichaeism, Donatism, and Pelagianism. Against the Manichaeans, who solved the problem of evil by positing evil's existence as a part of the creation, Augustine, as we have seen, argued that God's creation was wholly good and that evil is a distortion of what is good. Against the *Donatists,* rigorous ascetics who argued that Christians must remain pure and unwavering in their faith and that priests who even momentarily lapse invalidate their ministries as well as the sacramental rites at which they officiate, Augustine argued that the church, like all of humanity, included both the strong and the weak, the good and the bad, and that the efficacy of the sacraments depended on Christ, not on the faith of those who administer them. Then there was the pious British (or Irish) lay monk Pelagius who held that the human being had to initiate the encounter with God, and that the human being was capable of living the holy life with God's grace needed only as an enabler for various daily acts of piety. Augustine saw *Pelagianism* as a perversion of the Christian gospel and detraction from the historical moment of the work of Christ.

SUMMARY OF AUGUSTINE'S THEOLOGICAL POSITIONS:

1. *Creation, fall, sin, and redemption.* Augustine's Neoplatonic interpretation of evil as parasitic on good—as a deficiency or distortion of that which is in itself good—was very influential. But so was his interpretation of the human fall and original sin. He interpreted the second creation story in Genesis in this way: God creates Adam and Eve as "finitely perfect," living in an earthly paradise. There is no sin, no natural evil, no death. But God also creates them with the great good of free will, which they misuse to turn against God and in upon themselves. Since humans are the crown of God's creation, their rebellious sin introduces distortion into the order of

nature as well. God's punishment brings into existence death, disease, hardships, and natural disasters. All human beings are descended from Adam and Eve and are therefore born into original sin from which we cannot escape on our own. It is the sex act by which original sin is transmitted from one generation to the next. From the standpoint of God's justice, the whole human race is a condemned mass, and deserves only eternal punishment. But God is Love, and through the divine love manifested supremely in Christ God elects (chooses) some for salvation. We meet again the issue of theodicy (God's justice). Some out of this condemned mass will enjoy eternal fellowship with him. Through faith the chosen enter into relationship with God. The rest are left to their just deserts. This interpretation of the cosmic drama of creation, fall, sin, and redemption has had a lot of influence in Western Christian art and music as well as theology.

2. *Augustine's dualism.* Augustine never quite overcame his Manichaeism, a dualistic religion in which matter is associated with evil. Although he says all the right things about how the whole of creation, as the work of God, is good, for Augustine the created order is so permeated and distorted by human sin that he continually downgrades it. Physical life with all its desires, including food and drink, sex, music and art, even the beauty of the world, drags the soul down and separates it from God. Augustine's ascetical attitude toward the world is an important expression of what became the monastic ideal in the church: In order to devote oneself entirely to God, one must renounce sex, marriage and family, property of one's own, and the other pleasures of life and live a life of austere simplicity and complete devotion in the company of other like-minded persons—of the same sex, of course. When his dualism is applied to a number of pairings the results are a proliferation of superiority/inferiority dualisms with negative results: Latin vs. Teuton, clergy vs. laity, Kingdom of Heaven vs. earthly kingdom; spirit (male) vs. flesh (female).

4. *Redemption or Grace.* Augustine came to have extreme ideas on predestination and free will. God's electing grace is prevenient (anticipatory), irresistible, and all-sufficient: the elect can claim no role in bringing about their salvation; it is a free gift. Since Adam's and Eve's fall no one has free will in

the sense of the ability to cooperate with God through our own efforts in bringing about our salvation. The medieval Catholic Church took a more moderate view on both issues, but Luther and Calvin revived these ideas in their awful splendor.

The City of God   In 410 the barbarian general Alaric and his troops sacked Rome. Many were the voices who blamed the fall of Rome on Christianity's ascendancy and its abolishing of the gods of Rome. It was Augustine's victory over the Donatists that prompted him to write out his position on the relationship between the church and the world, between the city of God and the earthly city. Over a span of thirteen years (413–426) he completed his path-breaking work, *The City of God,* not only a comprehensive philosophy of history but in germ a blueprint for the development of the medieval papacy. In it Augustine argued that within history, which began with God's creation and will end with the day of God's judgment, exist two cities, the city of God (in Latin *civitas Dei*), created out of love, and the earthly city (*civitas terrena*), created out of human desire and love of self. Because of human pride the state is necessary to restrain the evils that occur in society as a result of this fallen human condition. Secular government and its powers remain under God's rule: they exist to preserve order in society, endangered by human self-love and greed. Because of the pervasiveness of evil in a fallen creation, the Christian Church is itself a mixture of the "wheat and the tares," not yet the perfect manifestation of the city of God. But God has commissioned the church as his representative in the world, and therefore it has a right to wield secular power and to direct it in the interests of the heavenly city. Both cities, the heavenly and the earthly, remain under the rule of God, and the church exists to remind humanity of that. In short, Augustine was looking "for a city that had foundations whose builder and maker is God."

Confessions   Augustine's *Confessions,* which he wrote in 397–398, represents a new type of literature in the Western world. Skillfully constructed and written in very good late-classical Latin prose, this book is the foundation of all later Christian confessional literature and became the prototype of Western autobiography. You may not see much similarity between Augustine's *Confessions* and the latest movie-star autobiography, but the very important tradition in the Western world of telling one's own life story has its roots in and was shaped by this book.

Have you ever thought how you would go about writing your own life story? How old should you be? How should you organize it? At what point should you end it? Would you see your life in terms of some principle of interpretation tying it all together? At the age of fifty, would you interpret yourself at seventeen the same way you did when you were seventeen? These are difficult questions to keep in mind as you read Augustine. Augustine ends the portion of the book telling of his past (Books 1–9) with the death of his mother in 387, ten years before he wrote the *Confessions* as the busy Bishop of Hippo. Peter Brown, perhaps Augustine's best biographer, suggests that his interpretation of the meaning of his conversion in 397–398 was certainly different from what it had been in 386.

The word "confession" in the title has a twofold meaning for Augustine. It meant both a profession of faith (such as we find in some famous Christian statements of belief like the *Nicene Creed*) and a confession of sin. The book has a threefold structure that reflects Augustine's understanding of time, a famous discussion of which appears in Book 11. Books 1–9 are about the past—his life up through his conversion and the death of his mother. Book 10 is about the present, and reveals the state of Augustine's soul at the time he wrote the *Confessions*. Books 11–13 deal with the future in the light of the past, as Augustine contemplates the divine purpose for the whole of creation by meditating on the first chapter of *Genesis*. By moving from consideration of his own creation, fall, and redemption to the creation, fall, and redemption of the whole universe, Augustine clearly sees in the story of his own (and indeed of every human's) life the cosmic drama in miniature. He told his story in the hope that it would set an example and be an encouragement to other Christians and would-be Christians.

Augustine typifies the fact that because of Rome's far-flung empire and its cosmopolitan understanding of citizenship, notable Romans came from all over the empire and not just from Italy. Recall that Paul, from the Near East, and Seneca, from Spain, were Roman citizens. By the time Augustine was born his North African province of Numidia had been Roman for about five hundred years. (There are many Roman ruins in North Africa today, all the way from Morocco in the west to Egypt in the east.) Augustine grew up in a thoroughly Roman environment, as modified by the conditions of North Africa. The literalistic and mainly non-intellectual North African Christianity to which he was exposed as a child and youth put him off. In school Augustine never liked or really mastered Greek, and read the Greek philosophers— as for example the Neoplatonists Plotinus and Porphyry—in Latin translation. It was the great Latin orator and essayist, Cicero, whose book *Hortensius* inspired Augustine with a love of philosophy. Augustine was trained in Carthage as a rhetorician, which meant someone who taught not only the art of public speaking but also grammar and literature.

One theme to note in your reading of the *Confessions* is Augustine's relationship with his mother, the most prominent and enduring of his human relationships. Monica was a fervent Christian throughout her life, while Augustine's father Patricius was a pagan until shortly before his death. Long-suffering, Monica pursued her wayward son everywhere, managing his marital prospects along the way, until to her great joy they were reunited in Christian faith; and it is appropriate that Augustine ends the story of his past with his mother's death and his tribute to her.

The other woman in Augustine's life was his unnamed lover of fifteen years, who is forced (presumably by Monica) to leave him because a "proper" marriage has been arranged for him with a young girl. The lover returns to North Africa, vowing lifelong celibacy, and Augustine praises and envies her for her ability to make a commitment that he cannot make. She leaves with him their son, Adeodatus, who is baptized together with his father and dies very prematurely at age seventeen. As you will discover in your reading, Augustine's experience of sex played an important role in his struggle over Christianity—as indeed it did in his later theology of the relationship between original sin and procreation.

Important themes appear in Book 5 and include Augustine's membership in the Manichaean religion, which was truly a "world religion" during the period of the Roman Empire, and why he became disillusioned; and what Bishop Ambrose of Milan's allegorical interpretation of the Bible was and what obstacle it overcame in Augustine's return to Christianity. In Book 6 Augustine tells how he comes to prefer the Catholic to the Manichaean teaching, and what he continues to struggle with even as he is coming intellectually to accept Christianity. In this book he also introduces us to his two close friends, Alypius and Nebridius, who play an important role in his life and whose own lives take interesting directions.

Book 7 contains the important account by Augustine of how it was his reading of "the books of the Platonists"—writings of the Neoplatonic philosophers such as Plotinus and Porphyry—that enabled him to resolve two long-time obstacles to his acceptance of Christianity: the problem of evil, and the claim that God is spiritual (non-material; bodiless). Beginning with faith in the Christian revelation as given in Bible and church teaching, Augustine believed that one could thereby use one's reason more correctly and become a better and truer philosopher.

The "climax" of Augustine's story comes in Book 8, which contains his account of his full conversion to Christianity. He describes the conflict of wills within him as he struggles to overcome his continued resistance. In his theological writings Augustine was to go on to characterize will, desire, or choice as the primary factor in human behavior, and said that the kind of life humans live is determined by the kinds of things they truly love. Augustine attributes his conversion entirely to divine grace, another theme he was to generalize in his later theological writings with his doctrine of the all-sufficiency of God's grace and God's predestination of who would be saved and who lost.

In Book 9 Augustine recounts how he, Adeodatus, and his friends formed a small community of study and meditation at a country house in Cassiciacum for a few months, before returning to Milan to be baptized. Book 9 concludes with the beginning of the journey back to North Africa, his mother's death, his grief, and his reverent telling of the story of her life and character. Augustine's relationship with his mother, and his praise of her submissive "example" to other women who were being beaten by their husbands, are a good point at which to raise the question of his views on marriage and celibacy and on women. Augustine's views on marriage would become those of the medieval Catholic Church: that marriage is an honorable and even sacramental relationship, but that celibacy for the sake of service to God is a spiritually higher calling. While he recognized among his friends those who were married and Christians, he believed that given his sexual past and proclivities the only way he personally could give himself wholeheartedly to God in Christ was through celibacy. In his comments on woman and man in his theological writings, Augustine struggled to reconcile two irreconcilables: On the one hand, Platonism and the first chapter of Genesis affirmed the equality of all souls; on the other hand, Genesis 2–4 and Paul's First Letter to the Corinthians (chap. 11:3-12) clearly affirmed the subordination of women to men. Augustine came to the view that women are intellectually equal but physically inferior, created to be man's helpmate, subject to their husband's rule, and a symbol of the flesh and desire. Like some of the other Church Fathers and the emerging monastic movement, Augustine said that women could achieve spiritual equality through the monastic life, which for them meant becoming "spiritually male."

Rhetorician, bishop, teacher, philosopher, eminent theologian, and creative thinker, Augustine's thought has had a profound influence on the church subsequent to him, and his writings retain a remarkable vitality even into the present age.

QUESTIONS FOR STUDY AND DISCUSSION

1. List the Apologists and explain what they were attempting to do.

2. What is the purpose of the canon? What were some of the issues surrounding the issue of what belonged in the canon?

3. What were the two "heretical" groups discussed in the chapter? Explain their positions.

4. What are the creeds and what is their significance for Christian belief?

5. Who are the Church Fathers and why are they important?

6. How did Augustine's own life and personal struggles influence his interpretation of Christianity? Be specific. What does it mean to say, as interpreters of Augustine do, that in the *Confes-*

sions he used his own life to symbolize the human condition as understood by Christianity?

7. What attracted Augustine to Manichaeism and kept him a member for nine years? What caused his disillusionment?

8. What is the problem of evil? How does Augustine resolve it in terms of Christian theology, and how does Neoplatonism enable him to do it? Compare and contrast his theodicy (attempt to reconcile the justice of God with the world's evil) with that of Job.

9. How does Augustine portray the women in his life in the *Confessions?* How does he interpret the status and role of women generally, and specifically the role of women in the church?

10. How did Neoplatonism influence Augustine? Greek and Roman philosophy played an important role for some leading Christian theologians in the early centuries and throughout the Middle Ages, and the main movements in modern philosophy have also had an impact on theology. What do you think should be the relationship between claims to revelation and the claims of reason—between, say, the Bible and philosophy?

SUGGESTIONS FOR FURTHER READING

Augustine of Hippo. *The City of God.* Translated by Marcus Dods. New York: Modern Library, 1950.

Brown, Peter. *Augustine of Hippo.* London: Oxford University Press, 1967.

Brown, Peter. *The Making of Late Antiquity.* Cambridge: Harvard University Press, 1978.

Brox, Norbert. *A Concise History of the Early Church.* New York: Continuum, 1995.

Gaarder, Jostein. *That Same Flower: Floria Aemilia's Letter to Saint Augustine.* Translated by Anne Born. New York: Farrar, Straus, Giroux, 1998.

Grant, Michael. *Constantine the Great: the Man and His Times.* New York: Macmillan (Collier books), 1990.

Pagels, Elaine. *The Gnostic Gospels.* New York: Random House, 1988.

Pelikan, Jaroslav. *The Christian Tradition: A History of the Development of Doctrine.* Vol 1, *The Emergence of the Catholic Tradition (100–600).* Chicago: University of Chicago Press, 1971.

Robinson, James M., editor. *The Nag Hammadi Library.* New York: Harper, 1977.

Rubenstein, Richard E. *When Jesus Became God.* New York: Harcourt & Co. 1999.

Schatz, Klaus. *Papal Primacy: From Its Origins to the Present.* Translated by John A. Otto and Linda M. Maloney. Collegeville, MN: Liturgical Press, 1996.

Williams, Daniel H. *Ambrose of Milan and the End of the Nicene-Arian Conflicts.* Oxford: Clarendon Press, 1995.

CHAPTER NINE

THE RISE OF ISLAM

Islam arose out of the dry and inhospitable region of Arabia in the early seventh century amd is now the second largest religion in the world. Its founder, Muhammad, claimed that it is both the first and last religion and has existed with God since the beginning of time. God first spoke to the Hebrews and then to the Christians, but they eventually corrupted the revelation. Islam acknowledges several of the prophets of the Hebrew Scriptures and accepts Jesus as a prophet, but denies that he died on the cross. God then delivered both the original and final words to Muhammad, declaring him to be God's last prophet.

The population of Arabia at this time was composed mostly of nomadic tribes (Bedouin) who made a poor living herding sheep and competing with each other over scant pastureland. Oases dotted the country, where a small sedentary population did some farming. The land, however, was ruled by nomads who were skilled warriors. All were bound to absolute loyalty first to their families (clans) and then to the tribe. An affront or attack against a member of a clan must be avenged. Rival caravans were often attacked for their booty (the basis of their economy) but there were strict prohibitions against harming members of the other tribe because vengeance would be required. On the other hand intra-tribal loyalties were equally binding. Bedouin ethics demanded the care of all its members, especially widows, orphans, the elderly, and the sick.

It was a subsistence existence until during the sixth century when a new technology in the design of the camel saddle was developed which allowed camels to carry amazingly heavy loads. Merchants soon discovered that transportation by camel was much more economical than by donkeys and carts. New trade routes were developed that did not require roads. Prosperity came to many of the Bedouins and trade centers grew across the country and were in the control of the merchants. The largest and most cosmopolitan was Mecca, which was controlled by the Quraysh tribe, of which Muhammad's clan was a member.

Trade centers were protected zones. Tribal disputes were forbidden so people were able to engage in business and social intercourse without fear of violence. They were also religious centers, and Mecca was the major center in the land. Here was the ancient shrine known as the *Kaba*, which tradition said was built by Abraham and his son Ishmael. Abraham had sent Ishmael and his mother, Hagar, into the desert at the bidding of his wife Sarah (Gen. 21:1-21). It is through Ishmael that Muslims claim descent from Abraham. The Kaba is a large black cube with a stone, possibly a meteorite, embedded in its side. Legend says that it once contained 360 stone idols that Muhammad smashed upon the Meccan acceptance of Islam. A pre-Islamic religious ritual, *umrah*, was to circle the Kaba seven times and kiss the stone.

Each Arabian tribe had its own god, but all tribes recognized one supreme god whom they called Allah, which simply means "god." Every year during the month of Ramadan, the tribes made a pilgrimage, a *hajj*, to a holy site. Mecca was a popular destination. There pilgrims performed the umrah, then traveled to the valley of al-Marah where they prayed and held vigil through the night. Other ceremonies were practiced including shaving

The Kaba, or Ka'bah (Arabic, meaning cube) is the building in the center of the great mosque at Mecca, the holiest site in Islam. Also called the house of Allah, the Kaba is believed to stand directly beneath an equivalent Kaba in heaven and is the point toward which Muslims turn in their daily prayers. It is also the destination of the annual hajj, or pilgrimage. The Kaba is covered with a huge cloth, or kiswa, and is entered only at the time of the hajj. According to Islamic tradition, the Kaba was originally built by Adam, rebuilt by Abraham and his son, and later cleansed of pagan idols by Muhammad.

Figure IV-8 Kaba, Mecca, Saudi Arabia. Approx. 35′ (10.5 m) × 40′ (12 m) × 50′ (15 m). Courtesy of Photo Researchers, Inc.

of the head, and animal sacrifice took place on the final day. These rituals were included in the practice of Islam.

A hajj was also an occasion for poetry contests. The Arabic language is particularly suited to poetry; poets were highly esteemed and poems helped to build strong bonds for the tribes. In the contests the winning poems were embroidered on black silk and hung in the Kaba. In Islam the recitation of the Qur'an replaced that of poetry.

THE MESSENGER

Muhammad (570–632) was a native of Mecca. Orphaned by the age of six, he was put under the care of his uncle. It is essential in Arab society to have a family affiliation, someone who acts as both a protector and an avenger should a wrong be done to anyone in the community. Muhammad spent his early years as part of the tribal commu-

nity with its internal moral code of mutual care and compassion. By the time he was twenty he was traveling with caravans to locations in Syria. Muhammad was known for his honesty and hard work. He came to the attention of Khadija, a wealthy widow owner of caravans. She hired him to run her business and before long they were married. Khadija was some fifteen years older than Muhammad but it is clear that their marriage was a love match. They had at least six children together but only one, Fatima, survived her father.

Muhammad was a thoughtful and introspective man, and deeply religious. He did not like what he saw in the society around him, the greed and corruption that had come with the recent prosperity. The divide between rich and poor had become greater. The weak and sick were allowed to suffer and injustice was done with impunity. This went against the tribal ethic that called for social justice.

It was Muhammad's habit to retreat periodically (especially during Ramadan) to the desert for meditation and prayer. In 610 Muhammad received the first of what he came to believe were messages from Allah delivered by the angel Gabriel (the same angel who announced the forthcoming birth of Jesus). At first Muhammad found these experiences frightening and physically painful. He thought he might be possessed by spirits (jinns). His eighth-century biographer, Ibn Ishaq, tells of the terror Muhammad expressed, reporting that he went to Khadija and asked her to "cover him." Surah 96 of the Qur'an, the first of many revelations to Muhammad, suggests an auditory experience: Muhammad is told to "Recite in the name of your lord who created . . ." Surah 53 tells of a vision: "His own heart did not deny his vision. How then can you question what he sees?"

Khadija, a religious person and perhaps associated with a monotheistic Arabic sect called Hanifism, was convinced that these were messages from God. She called in her cousin, Waraqua bin Naufal, a Christian who lived in the household. Waraqa is reported to have said:

> Surely, by Him in whose hand is Waraqa's soul, thou art the prophet of this people. There hath come unto thee the greatest Namus [angel of Gabriel] who came unto Moses. Like the Hebrew prophets, Thou wilt be called a liar, and they will use thee despitefully and cast thee out and fight against thee.

[The Life of Muhammad, translated from the eight century biography by Ibn Ishaq A. Guillaume, London: Oxford University Press, 1955]

Muhammad continued to receive messages intermittently until his death twenty-two years later. These messages are what constitute the surahs of the Qur'an, which will be discussed more thoroughly below.

Muhammad began preaching his message to the Meccans in 612. He reminded the people of their tribal loyalties and the ethical rules that bound the community to each other in egalitarian unity. He was described as a "warner"or nadhir in Surah 74:1: "You [Muhammad] that are wrapped up in your cloak, arise and give warning." Muhammad must remind his people that they had to answer for their actions before God. This was surely shocking to a community that had no belief in an afterlife.

Muhammad attracted followers, including many women, but to the tribal leaders who had grown rich on trade, his message was not welcome. He preached that allegiance to the family tribe must be transferred to the ummah, the tribe of God. God asks their submission (islam), but not a passive submission. They must engage rather in a striving (jihad) to actively realize God's will in the world. Humans are meant to be God's representatives on earth, entrusted with responsibility for the creation, and they are rewarded or punished on the basis of how they carry out that responsibility. This was the obligation of the tribe writ large: social justice in an egalitarian society. God's ummah would be the vehicle for realization of the divine will in society and an example to the rest of the world. Muhammad's words were not only disagreeable, they were insulting. The leaders in Mecca ostracized Muhammad's clan even to the extent of refusing to sell them food.

HIJRAH

In 620 representatives from the town of Yathrib, an agricultural center 250 miles north of Mecca, asked Muhammad to come to their community and act as mediator in some tribal disputes. Muhammad saw this as an opportunity to finally establish a truly Islamic community. In 622 he and his followers, estimated at some seventy families, departed Mecca, slipping away in small groups at night so as not to incite attack. This journey became known as the Hijrah and marks the first year of the Muslim calendar.

Muhammad built the first mosque in Yathrib and settled his family on its boundaries. He established the rituals that would become those of Islam, and Yathrib was renamed as al-Medina (the City), the first truly Muslim city. A significant portion of the population of Yathrib was Jewish. Muhammad was excited about this as he was desirous of learning more about the Jewish religion. He had been exposed to both Jews and Christians in his travels. He anticipated, if not an alignment, at least mutual acceptance between his followers and the Jews. Unfortunately, the Jews rejected Muhammad as a prophet and even conspired with the Meccans against the Muslims. This antagonism between early Muslims and the Jewish tribes of Medina did not, however, result in anti-Jewish feeling towards Jews by the religion of Islam. Islam, certainly in the early centuries and well into modern times, was tolerant towards Judaism, generally allowing Jews full expression of their religion within Muslim-ruled territory providing they pay a tax.

MUHAMMAD AND HIS WIVES

Many in the West have drawn negative conclusions about the fact that Muhammad had several wives, eleven to be exact. In order to understand this, we must be reminded that polygamy was the cultural norm in the tribal culture in Arabia. Indeed, most tribal cultures, including those that founded the Jewish religion, were polygamous. Also it was an indicator of power for a leader to have many wives. Muhammad was married to Khadija and faithful to her until her death in 617. He then entered into marriages with several women, many of whom were widows. However, it seems clear by evidence and tradition that these were contractual arrangements for the protection of the women or to solidify tribal bonds. Muhammad appeared to enjoy the company of his wives and women in general. He consulted with them and sometimes took their advice and sometimes admonished them for their quarreling. Muhammad was especially fond of his last wife, Aisha, who was much younger than he. She was the daughter of Abu Bakr, who would become Muhammad's first successor, and would become involved in the conflicts over Muhammad's successor.

WARFARE

Despite some success in Medina, the community was not large enough to support the growing Muslim population and those who were native to the land. One of the ways in which Arab tribes survived was through *gahzu*, raids against rival tribes. Muhammad led his Muslims against various caravans of the Quraysh tribe, his tribe. The Quraysh retaliated but Muhammad's inferior force defeated the Meccan superior force at the battle at the Well of Badr in 624. Enraged, the Quraysh now desired not merely to defeat the Muslims but to annihilate them. They delivered a severe blow to the Muslims, killing a number of its leading members. The struggle went on until Muhammad took a bold step.

With 1000 volunteers he led a hajj to Mecca in March of 628. Dressed in pilgrim robes and without arms they succeeded in reaching the protected zone surrounding Mecca despite an attempt by the Quraysh to attack them before they reached this boundary.

Muhammad's daring impressed several Bedouin tribes, who joined the ummah. The Quraysh agreed to a treaty but they renounced it in 630 and resumed hostilities. Muhammad, now with an enlarged force, captured Mecca, but was merciful and took no reprisals. Impressed by Muhammad's compassion, the Meccans capitulated and accepted Islam. In the remaining two years of his life, Muhammad put an end to warfare in Arabia and organized Arabian tribal culture into one "super-tribe," the ummah, the tribe of God.

THE RASHIDUN OR THE RIGHTLY-GUIDED CALIPHS

Muhammad had made no provision for his successor. There were those who felt that a successor should be chosen from the family of Muhammad. Others desired that successors be chosen by leaders of the ummah. Abu Bakr, father of Aisha, his last wife, and a close friend of Muhammad, was selected the first caliph (successor) by the elders of the community. Bakr's term (632–34) was short but effective. Following Muhammad's death some tribes had rebelled against the ummah. False prophets arose claiming Muhammad's inheritance. Bakr swiftly put down the revolts and passed on a unified ummah at his death.

Bakr's successor was Umar ibn al-Khattab 634–44), who was a son-in-law of Muhammad. His selection was disputed by those who favored the family lineage. Umar was a skilled general, and it was he who launched the Muslim conquests of foreign territories. Now that all of Arabia was united in God's ummah, they could not steal from each other. Thus they were eager to cross borders in search of booty that was not forbidden. Many times before they had attempted conquest of their neighbors, but the major empires of Byzantium and Persian were too strong. These empires were now at their weakest point, and the outlying areas were poorly ruled and defended. Over the course of the next decade Muslims moved into Egypt, Syria, and Iraq and captured the city of Jerusalem. Muslim soldiers were not allowed to occupy the cities they captured, but instead built fortresses in strategic locations from which they ruled the territory. Some Muslims disagreed with this policy. They wanted to own land, build estates, and colonize the area. Some of the conquered converted to Islam, but this was not encouraged. Islam was tolerant to Jews and Christians, only requiring of them a special tax issued on non-Muslims. Muslims saw their success as favor from God, but they did not consider themselves at this time to be a proselytizing religion.

Caliph Umar was assassinated by a Persian prisoner. He had left directions that his successor be appointed by a council of the elders. The third caliph was Uthman ibn Affan (644–56), a member of the Quraysh tribe but not related to Muhammad's family. The opposing group—those who demanded leadership through the family—supported Ali ibn Abi Talib, a cousin of Muhammad's. They were called *Alids*, supporters of Ali. Uthman was a pious man, but he was faced with the problem of administering an ummah which had grown very large and difficult to manage. He adopted some of the administrative structures of the conquered territories and appointed members of his family to important posts. He provoked the anger of disaffected soldiers and was assassinated by one. Perhaps his most lasting legacy is the Uthman recension of the Qur'an, which will be discussed in more detail in the section on the Qur'an.

Those responsible for Uthman's death proclaimed Ali caliph (656–61). Ali was married to Fatima, daughter of Khadija and Muhammad. Two groups opposed Ali: one led by Muhammad's widow Aisha, the other by Uthman's nephew, Muawiyyah, whom Uthman had appointed governor of Syria. Ali defeated Aisha's troops in the "Battle of the Camel," so named because the battle carried on around a camel upon which Aisha was seated. The confrontation between Muawiyyah and Ali was another story. The governor's troops placed the Qur'an on the tips of their swords and called for arbitration. "Let God decide." Arbitration ended in Ali's deposition.

The more conservative of Ali's supporters could not accept Ali's abdication. They were a group that split from the Alids called *Kharajites*. They felt that both leaders had acted in bad faith, Uthman for showing favoritism to his family, and Ali for agreeing to arbitration and not avenging the death of Umar, a relation. For the Kharajites there was no compromise: a Muslim guilty of such a serious sin could not remain a Muslim. Ali was assassinated by a member of the Kharajites. Every religion experiences breakaway groups which are frequently purists. "Fundamentalist" groups have been a part of the history of Islam since these early beginnings. Descendants of the Kharajites are known today as the Ibadi and live mostly in Oman in East Africa.

THE UMAYYADS

Caliph Muawiyyah moved the capital from Medina to Damascus in 661. The caliphate was not yet a monarchy—something Arab tribalism violently opposed—but the trappings of imperialism were beginning to appear. It was during the reign of Muawiyyah's son, Yazid I, that the confrontation occurred that split Islam into the two major divisions that exist today, *Sunni* and *Shia*. Ali, the fourth caliph, had two sons, Hasan and Husayn. Muawiyyah had persuaded the first son, Hasan, to reject all claims to leadership following his father's death and retire quietly to Medina. However, with the accession of Yazid I, the Shia in Kufa put forward Ali's second son, Husayn. Husayn set out with a small band of followers and his family for Kufa to lay claim to his inheritance. They were met on the plain of Karbala (in modern-day Iraq) by Yazid I's troops and slaughtered. A revolt of the Shia was quickly put down. Overwhelmed by the brutality and injustice in society the Shia adopted a policy of withdrawal. The Sunni, on the other hand, while condemning the sins of the leaders, were more optimistic about reform. The remembrance of Husayn's death is celebrated by Shia Muslims as one of their holiest days.

A decade of civil war followed the death of Hasayn. Finally, an Umayyid cousin (Abd al-Malik) was able to restore the Umayyad dynasty in 691. Malik desired to restore the unity of the ummah. He put down the rebellious tribes and suppressed the Shia and the Kharajites. During Malik's rule the Dome of the Rock was completed in Jerusalem. This monument is a splendid example of Islamic religious art. Human imagery was forbidden in Islam. Instead verses from the Qur'an written in elegant calligraphy decorate the walls and ceilings on public and private buildings. It was during the rule of

The Dome of the Rock is the third holiest site in Islam after Mecca and Medina. The sanctuary's octagonal design, though influenced in plan by Byzantine and early Christian architecture, supports a unique and opulent decoration that includes intricate mosaics, hundreds of feet of Arabic inscriptions, and a golden dome that dominates the Jerusalem skyline. The Dome of the Rock stands on the Temple Mount and encloses a rock outcropping sacred to both Muslims and Jews. Muslims identify it as the site from which Muhammad ascended to heaven, while Jews recognize it as the place where Abraham prepared to sacrifice his son Isaac.

Figure IV-9 Dome of the Rock, Jerusalem. Begun 692. Courtesy of Richard T. Nowitz/Corbis.

Malik's son, al-Walid I, that Islam established a kingdom in Spain that survived for 700 years. When the Muslim army moved into the region of southern France, it was defeated by Charles Martel at Tours in 732. This was the extent of Muslim incursions into Europe.

Islam had become an empire, but Umayyad control was weakening. There was an economic downturn, and a war with Constantinople proved a disaster. Non-Muslims (*dhimmis*) had been encouraged to convert and many did, but as Muslims they no longer had to pay a non-Muslim tax. This was another financial blow. Some of the lead-

ers during the decades 720–750 were devout, but others were not. The empire was being ruled much like a military dictatorship and this was offensive to many Muslims. Various groups became restive.

THE ABBASIDS

A group called the Abbasid arose that had two distinct advantages. They claimed as their leader a direct descendant of Muhammad's family. Through this and their pledge to renew the ummah they won the support of the Shia. They defeated the last Umayyad caliph in Iraq in 750. Once in power, however, they threw off their mantle of religiosity and established a caliphate along the lines of the former Byzantine and Persian absolute monarchs. They slaughtered all the Umayyads they could find, and also Shia leaders who they thought might be dangerous. The capital was moved once more, this time to Baghdad, a city that lent itself to the style of a great oriental kingdom. The next century of Abbasid rule produced an intellectual and artistic flourishing that has never again been surpassed in the history of Islam. Abassid rulers established what was called the House of Wisdom. They engaged both Arab and non-Arab scholars, including Jews and Christians, and produced translations of Greek works that would have been lost to us if the Muslims had not preserved them. They appropriated Persian and Byzantine bureaucracy and culture. They made contributions to literature, philosophy, mathematics, medicine, art, and architecture. They completed the "Arabization" of the culture that had begun with the Umayyids. Ironically this "golden era" of accomplishment was a low point for Islamic religious practice. The religion of the empire was indeed Islamic, and the Caliph was styled the "Shadow of God on Earth." But this was not in any way a model of the egalitarian community that Muhammad had established some three centuries earlier.

CONCLUDING OUR HISTORY

The goal of this historical section has been to narrate the origin and establishment of Islam into the Middle Ages. The Abbasid glory was followed by a decline that left it weakened and vulnerable. The Abbasids had created an army from Turkish slaves who eventually took control but left the caliphs in place as puppets. The empire was now divided into regions ruled over by *amirs* (chieftans) who acquired the name of the Seljuq Turks. It was the Turks that the Crusaders faced when they entered Jerusalem in 1099, and it was a Turk named Saladin who recaptured Jerulasem in 1187. Islam received a devastating blow in 1258 when the Mongol tribes swept across the steppes and destroyed Baghdad and its wonderful center of learning. Mongols followed the regional ruling system of the Turks and eventually accepted Islam and assimilated into its population. Meanwhile Western Europe had revived and the Spanish, newly united, expelled the last of the Muslim conquerors in 1492.

RELIGIOUS DEVELOPMENTS

We have rehearsed for you the early decades that followed the death of Muhammad and the resulting struggles over the leadership and rules for the ummah. Muhammad had preached the principle of *tawhid* or perfect balance between the sacred and the secular, a unity of the whole of human life. But the first few decades had produced nothing but chaos and conflict. We have reported on the dispute over leadership. Others struggled over theological issues. What should be the relationship between faith and politics? What of sin and forgiveness? The Kharajites had viewed Ali's compromise with Muwayyid as an unforgivable sin. Are there sins that can be forgiven and those that cannot? Did humans have free will or did God determine the universe? In other words what were the beliefs of Islam, and more importantly, what behavior manifested Muslim belief? This struggle is reminiscent of a similar struggle in Christianity in its formative centuries. (see Chapter Eight)

Islam never developed a clergy with special schools for training religious leaders, such as Christian priests and Jewish rabbis. Instead there is a long tradition of scholars called *ulamas* who became authorities on the religious matters. The ulama served as the guardians of tradition and were often advisers to governments. Ulama were also legal scholars (*mujtahids*), developing and interpreting the law. The more famous ones had their names attached to schools (*madhhab*).

The ulama set down the rules for establishing the *Sharia*, which is the legal code that rules Muslims to this day. Law is rooted first in divine revelation, the Qur'an, as it was given to Muhammad and which is the embodiment of God's will. Second, it is based in Muslim practice, *Sunna*. Once the ulama began searching for legal commands they found that only a small part of the Qur'an deals with law, so they knew they must look to Muslim practice or *Sunna*. They had to ask, What would Muhammad have done in this situation? In order to determine this, beginning in the eighth century ulama began collecting statements from witnesses. The written collection of these reports is called the *Hadith*, and considerable care was taken in checking the authenticity of these reports. The most famous of these collections are by Al-Bukhari and al-Shafii, produced in the late eighth century.

Two other criteria were used: analogy and consensus of the community. Some ulama took a more liberal attitude towards analogy, accounting for a certain amount of independent reasoning (*ijtihad*). *Ijtihad* has been a controversial issue throughout the subsequent centuries. Consensus was permitted because Muslims believed that God would not allow error to slip in, but some ulama dislike the idea of consensus as it might allow human interpretation to intrude. In the fourteenth century there was a move to close *ijtihad* permanently, but a crack in the door has always remained open.

Sharia Law provided the blueprint for Muslim society, a comprehensive code of life covering not only prayer and almsgiving but also family, criminal, commercial, and international law. This legalistic approach has always appealed to the Sunni.

Imam is another word for a leader in Islam, but unlike the term ulama, which is an indicator of scholarly background, imam can be used as a designation for a prayer leader or elder of a mosque. In Shia Islam, however, it is applied specifically to a descendant of Muhammad's family. It can also be used to refer to the head of an Islamic state and a leader in a holy war.

ISLAMIC PHILOSOPHY

The rapid spread of Islam led to its encounter with Greek philosophy during the intellectual and artistic flowering of the eighth and ninth centuries, which produced a tradition of Islamic philosophy. Islamic scholars laid the foundations by translating many Greek philosophical texts, including the works of Plato and Aristotle, into Arabic. These Arabic translations played a key role in transmitting Greek learning to Christian Europe in the twelfth and thirteenth centuries.

Greek philosophy challenged Islamic theologians and scholars to work out the relationship between revelation and reason, faith and logic, in Islam. Initially they were concerned to define and defend Islam against the older and more developed religions such as Judaism and Christianity; they needed "an argument to refute heretics," using philosophical arguments to explain Muslim doctrines and to reconcile apparent contradictions in the Qur'an and other authoritative texts. Those who used philosophy to provide greater understanding of Islam were known as *falasifa*. One of the earliest

groups to make use of philosophy were the more "liberal" *Mu'tazili*, who tried to resolve philosophically issues such as the relationship between divine omnipotence and free will; and the more "conservative" *Ash'arites*, who strictly limited the role of reason and denied that revelation needed to be justified by reason.

Islamic philosophy developed and flourished during the centuries of the "Golden Age" under the Abbasid dynasty. With increasing boldness Islamic philosophers built on and developed further the ideas of Plato, Aristotle, and the Neoplatonists: the most influential were Al-Farabi (ca. 870–950), Ibn-Sina (980–1037), known in the West by his Latin name Avicenna, and Ibn-Rushd or Averroes (1126–1198). These philosophers "pushed the envelope" philosophically, with Averroes arguing that philosophy must be completely independent of theology and reaching conclusions that were considered heretical by orthodox Islam. A major opponent of the philosophers was al-Ghazali (1058–1111), who began as an Ash'arite and for many years taught Islamic law in Baghdad. He wrote an influential book rejecting Greek philosophical ideas that had been taken up by Islamic philosophers, while affirming the importance of logic. Later in life al-Ghazali underwent a spiritual crisis, becoming thoroughly disillusioned with theology and philosophy and adopting the life of a Sufi mystic.

In the final analysis the great Islamic philosophers proved to be without lasting influence in Islam. Their influence was much greater on Jewish thinkers like Moses Maimonides and Christian thinkers like Thomas Aquinas. Perhaps because of its identification of revelation with the text of the Qur'an, which seemed to address every issue, and its strong emphasis on the unity of all things in the one God, Islam became much more suspicious of all efforts to reason about the world and human life independently of divine revelation. By contrast, the medieval Christian tradition absorbed first Platonic and then Aristotelian thought and became increasingly "rationalistic," as we will see in the Scholastic tradition. Revelation and reason came to be seen as two different and to some degree autonomous sources which the one God had provided humans to come to know about God and the world around them, and Thomas Aquinas's achievement was to show how these two sources of knowledge harmonized. For example, he influentially formulated the theory of natural law as the moral law of God that can be known by every human being simply by virtue of being a rational creature, apart from direct divine revelation. Islam, by contrast, never accepted the idea of natural law, instead deriving all its understanding of ethics from the Qur'an and the other authoritative texts.

THE FIVE POINTS OF MUSLIM BELIEF

To identify oneself as a Muslim one need only to proclaim: "There is no God but Allah, and Muhammad is his Prophet." This declaration of faith is called the *shahadah*, and is pronounced daily by faithful Muslims. Beyond this belief in the unity of God, Muslims accept angels as divinely appointed agents of God's activity and helpers in many other tasks. They believe in prophecy and sacred books that have been revealed to prophets in the past, and above all acceptance of Muhammad and the Qur'an as the final "seal" of prophecy in human history. Muslims believe in the Last Day (day of judgment), when all the dead will be raised and humankind will gather at the judgment seat of God, the righteous to be saved into the eternal bliss of paradise and the wicked cast into a fiery hell. Finally, Islam affirms the divine decree and predestination.

This last belief concerns the profound mystery of the relationship between God's all-powerful governing of all things and human freedom to submit or not to submit. A similar tension exists in Judaism and Christianity. The Qur'an affirms but does not explain the reality of both God's omnipotence and human freedom. Our original, God-created nature (*fitra*) is good, and as in Judaism, in Islam humans are always free to turn back to God. The human task is to recover this original *fitra*, having fallen away from it. It is a process not so much of *con*version as of *re*version. But unlike in Christianity, God's grace and human choice are sufficient for human salvation; no mediator is needed. You might want to compare this with what you learned in studying Augustine's struggle over the existence of evil and human freedom.

The primary authoritative document in Islam (compares to the Tanakh and the Christian Scriptures) is the Qur'an. Muslim tradition believes these words are not the product of human involvement but direct auditory inspiration (*wahy*). As the messages were received Muhammad dictated them to amanuenses who copied them down. At Muhammad's death there existed a complete manuscript of the Qur'an. Hence when Abu Bakr assumed leadership following Muhammad's death he was in possession of a text of the Qur'an. Knowledge of the Qur'an, however, had been passed along orally by reciters, and a decade or so later in the Caliphate of Uthman (644–656) it was discovered that the Qur'an was being recited in different dialectal forms. The Caliph called in all existing copies and substituted for those one that had been written out in pure Quraysh dialect. This is referred to as the "Uthman recension" and is the standard for Qur'ans of today. Human hands were involved in the verse numbering, arrangement, and naming of the 114 surahs, but Muslims believe that the words are those received by Muhammad from Allah. It is customary today for Muslims all over the world to learn the Qur'an in Arabic, whether they fully understand the language or not. Many people simply appreciate the great beauty of the poetry of the Qur'an which emerges through its recitation. Surahs are arranged by order of length, from the longest to the shortest. The earliest Surahs are the shortest and thus are at the end of the Qur'an. They tend to be purely visionary or spiritual, whereas the longer Surahs also contain detailed descriptions of ethics and laws for the new Muslim society and narratives about biblical figures such as Abraham, Moses, and Jesus.

Most Muslims do not accept the idea that the Qur'an can be translated, and refer to translations in other languages as "interpretations." By contrast, scholars of the religion consider the Hebrew Scriptures and the Christian Scriptures to be inspired by God, but nevertheless originating with humans and hence open to discussion and interpretation. Such a view is not possible in reference to the Qur'an.

MUSLIM PRACTICE

Islam is a religion of *praxis,* which means good works are essential in being a good Muslim. This compares with Judaism, more than with Christianity, in which it is the acceptance of doctrines, centrally a belief in Jesus as the incarnation of God, that defines a believer. There are five duties or "pillars" of Islam that define Muslim practice. They are as follows:

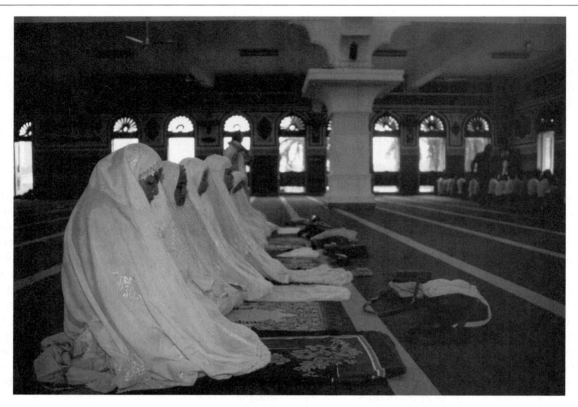

In the days of the Prophet Muhammad, women prayed in the same space as men. Over time, however, a body of Islamic law emerged that separated men and women. In many mosques, women have separate spaces in balconies and behind glass partitions or lace curtains, so that men and women will not be distracted from their prayers by the presence of the opposite sex.

Figure IV-10 Muslim Indonesian Women Praying During a Sholat Service in the El-Azhar Mosque in Jakarta, Indonesia. ca. 1995. Courtesy of Sergio Dorantes/Corbis.

(1) **Witness (*Shahada*)** is embodied in saying daily, "I bear witness that there is no god but Allah; I bear witness that Muhammad is the messenger of God." This is in fact how one becomes a Muslim, by saying the *Shahada* with complete sincerity.

(2) **Worship (*Salat*)** is the most frequently performed of Islam's devotional duties, a unique and visible daily activity of Muslims throughout the world. *Salat* is required five times daily and on certain other occasions. The worshipper must face in the direction of Mecca, and goes through a precisely observed rhythm of spoken prayers and bodily postures. *Salat* is performed both individually and communally. All Muslims must know the *Salat* and be able to lead it if called upon. In this connection it is worth mentioning that Islam is a "lay" religion; there are no clergy in the Christian sense. The leader of *Salat* is called an *imam*. Ritual purification is required before *Salat*. The Muslim house of worship is a *mosque*, from the Arabic *masjid* that means a place of prostration, referring to *Salat*. The mosque is essentially a sacred space where corporate worship is held on Fridays. In every mosque there is a niche in a wall that shows the direction of Mecca. The call to prayer is performed by a *muezzin*, who typically does so from the top of a *minaret*, which means "lighthouse."

(3) Almsgiving (*Zakat*) is an obligatory religious tax, paid at the end of the year. The tax is used for a variety of charitable purposes in the Muslim ummah or community, and is an expression of the oneness of the ummah and our human role as representatives or stewards of God in the world.

(4) Fasting (*Sawm*) refers to the month of *Ramadan* in the Muslim calendar, which lasts 29–30 days. Since the Muslim calendar is a lunar rather than a solar calendar, in any given year Ramadan may take place in winter or spring. During Ramadan, between dawn and dark every day Muslims are to abstain from food, drink, medicine, smoking, and sex. It is a time of spiritual self-examination, with special prayer services in the evenings. Ramadan is somewhat parallel to the period in Judaism between Rosh Hashana and Yom Kippur. Ramadan is a serious but not a sad time, and the evenings are joyful occasions, times of caring and sharing.

(5) Pilgrimage (*Hajj*) to Mecca once in a lifetime is obligatory for the individual Muslim only if personal, financial, and family circumstances permit. A special period of the year is set aside for the Hajj, and hundreds of thousands of Muslims go to Mecca. It is for them an unforgettable experience of the universal, international reality of Islam. Elaborate rituals surround the Hajj, including prescribed clothing, purification, circumambulating the Kaba in the Great Mosque, a journey into the desert with ritual stops at various points, and the Great Feast or Feast of Fast-breaking at the end. Making the pilgrimage can be a life-changing experience, and confers special status on the pilgrim back home.

Sometimes people speak of *jihad*, exertion or struggle, as the "sixth pillar" of Islam. The deepest meaning of *jihad* is the spiritual struggle of each individual truly to submit to God in his or her faith and life. This is the "greater *jihad*." Derivatively, early in the history of Islam it was extended to refer to armed conflict against the enemies of Islam, what people typically refer to as "holy war." This is the "lesser *jihad*." During the early years Muhammad and his followers believed that this enlarged meaning was forced upon them. Conversion to Islam is not supposed to be through conquest but through sincere belief that it is true.

MYSTICAL ISLAM

Retreat into the inner self has long been a response to a troubling and dangerous world. So it is in Islam. As was mentioned above, many of the Shia withdrew from active society and some became mystics. They did not resist the secular power because they privately had their own religious leader, their imam, who maintained the line of descent from Muhammad. At a certain historical point, however, the imam ceased to appear. The leaders explained that it was too dangerous for the actual imam to appear in society. Therefore, the imams continued to exist in a state of occultation, which means to be hidden from view. One group of Shia believed that the occultation of the imam occurred following the death of the sixth iman; hence they were called "seveners." The seveners took a more politically active part in the world. In the eleventh century they took the name *Ismaili* and captured and founded Tunisia. Another group of Shia anticipated the return of the twelfth imam as the *Mahdi*, divinely-guided ruler. They also practiced a mystical interpretation of scripture, believing that its words had secret meanings.

Sufis were a mystical sect that originated in the seventh century and were an arm of the Sunni. They meditated and chanted sacred words to induce trance, the goal of which was to reach the state in which Muhammad received divine messages. History contains the name of one woman mystic, Rabiah (d. 801). Her message was that of a God of Love and perhaps that is the reason she is remembered. The following quote comes from *Rabia the Mystic and Her Fellow-Saints in Islam*, by Margaret Smith.

> O my Lord, if I worship Thee from fear of Hell, burn me in hell, and if I worship Thee in hope of Paradise, exclude me thence, but if I worship Thee for Thine own sake, then withhold not from me Thy Eternal Beauty.

Sufism was sometimes persecuted by other Muslims, but a leader appeared in the fourteenth century who popularized Sufism and whose popularity has continued to the present day. Rumi was a student of law, theology, Arabian and Persian literature. In his mystical practice he sought the dissolution of the self in order to be one with God. He initiated the group known as the whirling dervishes. They spin in one direction, repeating the word "Allah" until they are in a trance. In the twenty-first century Rumi is well known for his love poetry—not sexual, but metaphysical love.

SURAHS

On the CD that accompanies this volume you can listen to a chanted recitation of Surah 82, one of the early, shorter revelations to Muhammad at Mecca. Listen to it for the sound of the Arabic Language and the "music" of the chanted version. The CD selection is entitled "The Tearing," from Michael Sells' translation of the early Surahs in *Approaching the Qur'an*. Its awe-full theme is the end of the world and the final judgment on humanity:

> When the sky is rent asunder; when the stars scatter and the oceans merge together; when the graves are hurled about: each soul shall know what it has done and what it has failed to do.
>
> Oh man! What evil has enticed you from your gracious Lord who created you, and gave you due proportions and an upright form? In whatever shape He willed He could have moulded you.
>
> Yet you deny the Last Judgement. Surely there are guardians watching over you, noble recorders who know of all your actions.
>
> The righteous will sure dwell in bliss. But the wicked shall burn in hell upon the Judgement-day: nor shall they ever escape from it.
>
> Would that you knew what the Day of Judgement is! Oh, would that you knew what the Day of Judgement is! It is the day when every soul will stand alone and God will reign supreme.

By contrast, the Surahs discussed below are longer revelations from the later period when Muhammad and his followers were in Medina: "The Cow," "Women," "The Table Spread," "The Thunder," "Abraham," "The Prophets," and "Time" or "Man."

The Qur'an came out of a society and a language—Arabic—in which poetry was highly prized and poets greatly honored. For Muslims the miracle of the Qur'an, and strong evidence of its authenticity as coming from God, is the fact that Muhammad was illiterate and yet spoke the words of the Qur'an in language of incomparable poetic beauty—a kind of Arabic equivalent of Shakespeare. The sheer beauty and eloquence of the language of the Qur'an was one important reason Arabs were attracted to the new religion.

In what follows we wish to highlight some Surahs, but in no way can we mention all the important themes contained in them. Each Surah opens with the invocation, "In the name of Allah, the Beneficent, the Merciful." This is called the *basmala* and is used daily by Muslims in speech and writing and as a table grace.

"The Cow" is sometimes called "the Qur'an in miniature," because it contains all the main features of the message of Islam. It was revealed at Medina, after the Hijrah, when the main elements of Islam had been established. A good exercise is to review the beliefs and practices above and locate passages that support these. A central theme is the unity of God (*tawhid*) that, as it is repeated through the book, is directed against the Christian doctrine of God as a Trinity. It is also aimed at Arab polytheism, which like Greek and Roman polytheism spoke of gods and goddesses as having many children. For Muslims the absolute unity of God has both cosmic and social implications. As God is one, so God's creation the universe is one, which can be seen as an important foundation for science; and among human beings God desires that we affirm and work actively for the unity of humankind.

In "The Cow" you will recognize stories from the Hebrew Scriptures as well as the Christian Scriptures about Adam and Eve, Abraham, Isaac, Moses, Jesus and other important biblical figures. They differ, however, in detail from the biblical version. Muslims consider their version of these stories as the correct one. See, for example, the story of Adam and Eve, verses 31*ff*, and compare this story of Adam and Eve with that in the second creation story in Genesis 2-4. Notice that there is no serpent in the Qur'an's version; the tempter is directly identified as Satan (*Iblis*). Eve does not succumb first and then persuade Adam. For Muslims the "fall" of the first humans does not result in original sin, which is a Christian interpretation of the biblical version of the story. There is no doctrine of original sin in Islam, although Muslims are serious about sin. Islam, by the way, honors Adam as the first Messenger or Prophet of God.

The brief introduction that precedes "Women" explains that the central concern of this Surah is for the welfare of widows and orphans left uncared for as a result of violence in Islam's formative years. It is thus viewed as presenting certain women's rights. It is true that a large portion of the Surah does deal with "women's rights," but the Surah also returns to and reiterates themes that are repeated throughout the book. We suggest that you make a list of the rules and regulations that apply to women. In recent decades Muslim women have been working throughout the world for the empowerment of women in Muslim cultures. They point to the fact that the Arabic word for "humankind" is gender-inclusive. And they argue that the Qur'an, the supreme authority for Islam, is much more gender-equal than the later traditions of Muslim law regarding women. The argument has interesting similarities to those of Jewish and Christian feminists, who appeal to the biblical literature interpreted as containing a message of human liberation that should be the standard rather than later laws and customs. In practice, different Muslim societies vary widely in their laws and practices regarding women, from the extreme seclusion demanded of women in the former Taliban government in Afghanistan to the high degree of emancipation in a country such as Turkey.

Much of "The Table Spread" is directed towards the errors of Christianity and Judaism. Some verses are probably the source of Muslim anti-Judaism today, such as verse 82. The major error of Christianity is that it claims divinity for Jesus. Note that intermingled with major criticisms of Judaism and Christianity are admonitions as to personal behavior. Verse 90 prohibits strong drink, games of chance, belief in idols or divination. All are works of the devil. Dietary rules are also mentioned.

"Thunder" evokes the mightiness of God and is not unlike the section in *Job* where God appears out of a whirlwind and responds to Job's challenge with the words, "Where were you when I laid the earth's foundations?" (Job: 38:4). "Who is wise enough to give an account of the heavens?" (38:37). Clearly the God of Islam is seen by Muslims as the same God of Judaism and Christianity. Another theme in this Surah is that salvation is by individual choice. But is it? What do you make of these two verses: "He could have guided all mankind?" verse 31; "He whom he sendeth astray," verse 33?

"Abraham" is named after the Hebrew patriarch who offers a prayer for his son Ishmael by his concubine, Hagar. Ishmael, traditionally the father of the Arab peoples, occupies a special place in the Qu'ran. Review the story in Genesis. Descriptions of "heaven" and "hell" are repeated and the Surah closes with the declaration that God is One.

"Prophets" recalls all the "messengers" (referred to as "Reminders" as well) beginning with the angels that have been sent to humankind to instruct them in belief and behavior. Note in this Surah as in others the different pronouns that are used for Allah: "us", "we," "he," as well as the noun, "Lord." Your final Surah, "Time" or "Man," is a description of paradise, the destination for those whom "Allah willeth," verse 30.

QUESTIONS FOR STUDY AND REFLECTION

1. Describe the Arabian culture at the time of Muhammad.

2. What was the "Golden Age" of Islam and how did the Western world benefit from this?

3. List the five basic beliefs of Islam. Compare those beliefs with the beliefs as you understand them of Judaism and Christianity.

4. What is meant by the statement "Islam is a religion of *praxis*"? Define specifically what is meant by praxis.

5. Explain the reason for the split between the Sunni and Shia.

6. List the Surahs you have been assigned to read and comment in a paragraph on what you find interesting in each.

SUGGESTIONS FOR FURTHER READING

Armstrong, Karen. *Islam: A Short History*. London: Orion Publishing Group, 2002. A recent history of Islam for the non-specialist.

Abbott, Nabia. *Aishah The Beloved of Mohammed*. London: Saqi Books, 1985, rpt. 1998. (First printed in 1942) This is the story of Muhammed's second favorite wife, Aishah, written by a Turkish Muslim woman and Islamic scholar.

Bulliet, Richard. *The Camel and the Wheel*. Cambridge, MA: Harvard University Press, 1975. This is a book about the camel as a pack animal.

Esposito, John L. *Islam: The Straight Path*, 3rd ed. rev. New York & Oxford: Oxford University Press, 1998.

Denny, Frederick M. *Islam and the Muslim Community*. New York: HarperSanFrancisco, 1987.

Goldschmidt, Arthur, Jr. *A Concise History of the Middle East*. Boulder, CO: Westview Press, Inc., 1991.

Hourani, Albert. *A History of the Arab Peoples*. Cambridge, MA: Belknap Press, 1991.

The Glorious Qur'an. Translated by Mohammed Marmaduke Pickthall. Elmhurst, NY: Tahrike Tarsile *Qur'an*, Inc., 2000. This translation is recommended by followers of Islam.

Interpretation of the Meanings of the Noble Qur'an in the English Language. Muhammad Taqui-ud-Din Al-Hilali and Muhammad Muhsin Kahn. Riyadh, Saudi Arabia, Darussalam Publishers. This is the 15th edition of the official Arabian interpretation of the Qur'an. It also contains a summarized version of At-Tabari, Al-Qurtubi, and Ibn Kathir with comments from Sahih Al-Bukhari (Ulamas and collectors of the Hadith), 1996.

Leaman, Oliver. *An Introduction to Classical Islamic Philosophy*. Cambridge: Cambridge University Press, 2002.

Reston, James, Jr. *Warriors of God*. New York: Anchor Books, 2001. This is a gripping story of the Third Crusade led by Richard the Lionheart of England and the remarkable Saladin for Islam.

Smith, Jane I. *Islam in America*. The Contemporary American Religion Series. New York: Columbian University Press, 1999.

SECTION FIVE

TIMELINE V

THE MIDDLE AGES: PART II

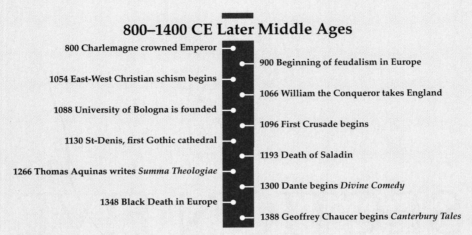

800–1400 CE Later Middle Ages

800 Charlemagne crowned Emperor

        900 Beginning of feudalism in Europe

1054 East-West Christian schism begins

        1066 William the Conqueror takes England

1088 University of Bologna is founded

        1096 First Crusade begins

1130 St-Denis, first Gothic cathedral

        1193 Death of Saladin

1266 Thomas Aquinas writes *Summa Theologiae*

        1300 Dante begins *Divine Comedy*

1348 Black Death in Europe

        1388 Geoffrey Chaucer begins *Canterbury Tales*

Dates given are approximate

THE MIDDLE AGES: PART II

The previous historical section provided an introduction to the thousand-year period known as the Middle Ages. Territorially the Roman Empire reached its zenith in the third century, but soon was divided into the "Eastern Empire" and the "Western Empire." Christianity triumphed as the religion of the Empire but developed uniquely Western and Eastern interpretations. In the West, monastic communities help to preserve Greco-Roman and Judeo-Christian culture during a "dark age." In the seventh century a new religion, Islam, arose in the Arabian Peninsula and quickly spread into Christian territories. A leader from Frankish territory (Charlemagne) briefly revived the Roman Empire in the West, but when this collapsed the West was fragmented and with no leadership. In the meantime the Eastern or Byzantine Empire was increasingly threatened by the growth of Islam. However, in the thirteenth century there was an intellectual and artistic flowering which has come to signify what we imagine as the Middle Ages: Gothic cathedrals, universities, courtly love, and the music of the troubadours. Although the waning of the Middle Ages was a time of troubles—plague, war, famine, and corruption in the Church—the foundations had been laid for the period of renewal, the Renaissance and the Reformation.

FRAGMENTATION OF EUROPE
AND THE RISE OF FEUDALISM, 850–1050

By the end of Carolingian rule in the ninth century, what had once been Charlemagne's vast empire had been carved up by his grandsons into three separate kingdoms—modern-day France, modern-day Germany, and the territory of Italy. Charlemagne's heirs fought bitterly among themselves in attempts to reclaim the territorial integrity of their grandfather's empire, but none were successful. The collapse of a centralized authority left the empire fragmented into a number of smaller "kingdoms" headed by powerful lords who were often at war with each other. A further threat to peace and security came from the Arabs in southern Europe, the Magyars in central Europe, and the Vikings in northern Europe. There was no single power strong enough to ward off these threats. By the ninth century, law and order had broken down in much of Europe and violence had become the norm. Out of this chaotic and unstable milieu emerged a new social order—feudalism—that provided a certain stability for the next three hundred years.

Feudalism consisted of a complex hierarchy of relationships governed by loyalty and reciprocal obligations. Medieval society consisted of three separate classes: nobles, clergy, and peasants. Each had its own function. Ninety-five percent of the population were peasants, with the duty to farm the land and provide the food for everyone. In exchange they received protection from the nobles and spiritual guidance from the clergy. Although patterns of life varied widely, most of the peasants lived in small villages, surrounded by large fields that they worked co-operatively. Peasants were not expected to engage in warfare, but their life was hard, their diet poor, their protection from disease primitive at best, and their life span short.

About two percent of the population belonged to the nobility or aristocracy. The noble and his family typically lived in a fortified house near the village. The peasants in the village paid him a portion of their crops, worked lands set aside for his use, and performed a number of incidental services. The noble had many rights, such as a monopoly on hunting in the surrounding forest, and a certain degree of control over the villagers' actions. In exchange, the noble maintained a group of fighting men to defend the villagers and their lands, enforced law and order within the village, and took general responsibility for the villagers' material welfare. In addition, each noble was bound by an oath to a still stronger noble to provide him military and other services. In exchange he could call upon the more powerful noble for aid should he need it. In this fashion, local needs were served and the major limitations of a highly decentralized political and military system were overcome.

The remaining two or three percent of the population was composed of the clergy, whose function was to provide for the spiritual needs of the population. There were two classes of clergy, the secular and the regular. The secular clergy worked directly with the people. Each village typically had its own church, in which the local priest provided those religious services that the people of the time believed were essential to their salvation, offered moral leadership, and could exercise some check upon the power and authority of the local noble. The priest was under the direction of a bishop who oversaw all parishes in a larger area, perhaps the size of a county. Above the bishop was an archbishop who had authority over a still larger area. Archbishops answered to the pope who as head bishop and "vicar of Christ" was responsible for the whole church. Communication during this time was limited. Roads, where they existed, were poor, narrow, and rutted, and travelers were easy prey to robbers. It fell to the priest, to the extent of his abilities, to provide a cultural link to the wider world. In return, the villagers paid a portion of their crop to the priest, as well as performing various other services for him.

On the edges of the feudal community, the other branch of the Church was the regular clergy, consisting of monks and nuns who had withdrawn from the secular world, embraced vows of poverty, chastity, and obedience, and entered a community to live a religious life in accordance with an established rule, *regula*, of conduct. Their function was to pray, and the people of the times believed that such prayers were necessary to the survival of society and the salvation of its members. It was a char-acteristic of Western monasticism that these communities were usually self-supporting. The monks and nuns lived simply, worked hard, and contributed substantially to society. Western monasteries and convents provided the only hospitals, orphanages, and schools that were available for centuries. They also were responsible for the preservation of learning from the past. Many monasteries had large scriptoriums where monks labored long hours to copy the manuscripts of the past. The regular clergy were the ideal of the times, and the people rewarded them by endowing their communities with lands that the monks then improved by their enlightened labor. In this fashion the Church came to control almost a quarter of the land of Europe, and over time many monasteries became wealthy and powerful.

THE BEGINNING OF THE HIGH MIDDLE AGES

By the eleventh century, some of the most powerful feudal nobles emerged as monarchs over large kingdoms. Through ambition, ability, wealth, military prowess, and politically advantageous marriages, these members of the feudal nobility extended their sovereignty over larger territories, forged their men-at-arms into armies, and reduced the power and independence of their rivals. Most notably, France and England emerged as sovereign states with strong monarchies as their leaders successfully consolidated power and territory. French and English kings began to make laws and impose some measure of administrative control over their kingdoms. After the eleventh century, rulers could raise and command armies, mint money, impose taxes, summon advisors, and appoint officials to represent their will. This process of centralization laid the foundation for the emergence of the modern European national states. The modern state is an organized territory, with laws and institutions designed to unite a large population. With unity comes stability, protection of peoples' rights and property, and an atmosphere conducive to artistic, intellectual, cultural, and economic activity. While national states of this sort will not exist in the West for several centuries, in the High Middle Ages we do begin to see signs of the emergence of modern Europe.

The two nations leading this process were France and England. French kings had little real power during the early medieval period, controlling only the lands around Paris (known as the Île-de-France). The great majority of French territory, including Normandy, Brittany, and Aquitaine, was held by the English or, like Burgundy, were independent duchies. The reign of King Philip II Augustus (ruled 1180–1223) was an important turning point in the growth of French monarchical authority. Philip waged war against England and succeeded in winning control over Normandy, Aquitaine, and other key territories. To administer justice and collect taxes, Philip appointed new royal officials, thus beginning the French royal bureaucracy in the thirteenth century. Philip's successor, Philip IV (ruled 1285–1314), later created the Estates General and the first French parliament. The Estates General was designed to be a meeting of representatives of all three classes of feudal society in France (clergy, nobles, and commoners). The Estates General was not a sitting institution but rather was called only when the French monarch wanted to consult with, and receive advice from, representatives of the nation. The Estates General was not a parliament in the modern-day sense of the term and in practice had little real power. However, the creation of the Estates General captures the desire of the French crown to govern, at least symbolically, with the advice and consent of the nation. By the end of the thirteenth century France was the largest, wealthiest, and best-governed monarchical state in Europe.

England too emerged as a stronger monarchical state during the late medieval period. Earlier, during the ninth and tenth centuries and under the threat of Viking invasion, the seven kingdoms of Anglo-Saxon England united under one king. This made it easier for subsequent kings to further the process of administrative and bureaucratic centralization.

On October 14, 1066, Duke William of Normandy defeated his Anglo-Saxon rival Harold and claimed the English throne. Taking the name

Thomas Becket, chancellor of England and archbishop of Canterbury, was a trusted friend of King Henry II. After they quarreled over the rights of the church, however, the King's knights killed Becket at the altar of Canterbury Cathedral in 1170. Becket was named a saint within three years and proclaimed a hero for defending the church against a tyrant. This manuscript illustration is perhaps the oldest representation of the archbishop's murder.

Figure V-1 The Martyrdom of Saint Thomas Becket, miniature from a Latin psalter from England. ca. 1220. Illuminated manuscript panel, 5.9 × 8" (15 × 21.5 cm). British Library, London. Courtesy of Snark/Art Resource, NY.

William the Conqueror, he was crowned king of England and then set about combining Anglo-Saxon and Norman institutions to create a new England. William made all knights swear an oath of loyalty to him as the sole ruler of England. One of William's successors, Henry II (ruled 1154–1189), continued to expand monarchical authority by extending the jurisdiction of royal courts of law at the expense of local courts. One important result of this expansion of royal authority was the establishment of a *common law*, or law that was common throughout the realm that replaced local and traditional laws. It is common law today that makes up the British "constitution."

Many of England's nobles grew to resent the imposition of monarchical authority and rebelled during the reign of King John (ruled 1199–1216). In 1215 King John was forced to sign the *Magna Carta*, the "great Charter of Liberties." The King agreed not to impose new taxes on the people without permission of a "great council" that represented local barons and lords. One of John's successors, King Edward I (ruled 127–1307), summoned barons, lords, bishops and other representatives from England's cities in the hope of achieving an agreement on going to war with France. Out of this tradition of consultation with leading subjects came the origins of England's parliament and constitutional government.

A more decentralized and therefore weaker form of monarchical rule developed in the central part of Europe (mainly the territory encompassing what are now Germany and Italy). In the tenth century the kings of Saxony established control over Germany and revived Charlemagne's idea of a Christian or "holy" Roman Empire as successor to the old pagan Roman Empire.

The Holy Roman emperors saw themselves as the protectors of the papacy and of all of Christendom. This also meant that the emperor was thoroughly enmeshed in the world of Italian politics. The Holy Roman Empire encompassed three hundred semi-autonomous states ranging from several large territories to a whole host of smaller states and principalities. The emperor could not exert his influence, levy taxes, or raise armies on the entire territory, unlike the kings of France and England. This meant that the Holy Roman emperors remained relatively weak and incapable of maintaining a centralized monarchical state. Nevertheless, the Holy Roman Empire became a powerful symbolic ideal of European *political* unity, as the Roman Catholic Church and the papacy symbolized European *religious* unity.

MEDIEVAL ECONOMICS

The economy of the early Middle Ages was based in the feudal arrangement—an interdependent relationship of nobles, clergy, and peasants in a self-contained community—and had grown and expanded to cover most of the territory of Europe. During this period the peasants of Europe had made a series of advances in agricultural technology. The use of the wheeled plow, capable of utilizing much more of the soil's fertility and of tilling the heavy bottomlands of northern Europe, was a great improvement over Roman methods. The horse collar and iron horseshoes made possible the use of the horse, a far faster and more efficient draft animal than the traditional ox, for plowing. The use of leguminous crops, such as peas and beans, in regular systems of crop rotation brought more land into production, increased yields, and improved soil fertility. All of these innovations increased agricultural productivity and resulted in surpluses.

The restoration of order and political stability helped create urban centers throughout the west. Areas that had begun as Roman villages, such as Bordeaux in southwestern France and Cologne in western Germany, experienced a revival as merchants and traders gathered to settle at commercially advantageous locations. Artisans and service personnel eventually joined them and thus towns began to reappear. Manufacturing—aided by newly developed water- and wind-driven machinery—concentrated in these town, creating markets both for raw materials for processing and for consumer goods. The advantages of specialization soon became obvious. An example is Flanders (now in Belgium). They raised excellent sheep and wove fine woolen cloth, but produced insufficient grain and wine to serve the population, so it was necessary to "import" these items from different regions.

This is how internal trade within Europe of bulk goods for manufacturing and consumer needs began. Essential to this new development were innovations in transport technology such as improved roads, and a great increase in the num-

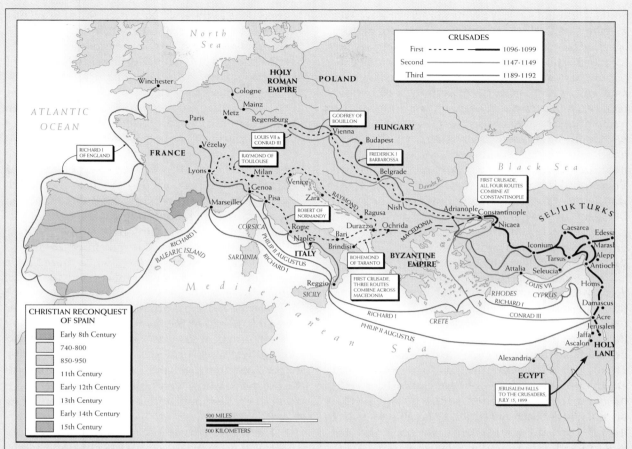

The Early Crusades. Routes and several leaders of the Crusades during the first century of the movement are shown. The names on this map do not exhaust the list of great nobles who went on the First Crusade. The even showier array of monarchs of the Second and Third Crusades were, on balance, ineffective in achieving their goals. Reprinted from *The Heritage of World Civilizations,* Seventh Edition by Albert M. Craig et al. (2006), Prentice-Hall, Inc.

bers of merchants. This new economic order brought about sweeping social and economic changes during the course of the eleventh and twelfth centuries. What we are witnessing over this period is a gradual shift from small independent and self-sufficient communities to an interdependency covering the territory of Western Europe. This is an early form of capitalism.

The movement to urban centers altered the previously rural character of medieval European society forever. Within the towns, often the dominant institutions were the guilds. Every town had its civil offi-

cers, generally functioning with the approval of the local noble, but the guilds wielded considerable power since often the civil officials were members of the guilds. Guilds were societies formed around a skill or profession. There were merchant guilds, artisan guilds, and guilds for the professions. A main concern of the guilds was to assure that the standards of that particular skill or profession were upheld. They served to guarantee product or service quality, but also functioned to limit participation. To become a member of a guild was a long and arduous process. The candidate, nearly always male, was apprenticed while a young teenager by his family for a fee. He served as an apprentice for several years, from seven to as many as twelve years, living under the roof and under the control of the master. Once he passed his "qualifications" he was a journeyman and could finally earn his own money. He would only become a master if his work was judged adequate by a jury of his peers.

Guilds tended to cluster in the same neighborhood or even on the same street, and ran their businesses co-operatively rather than competitively. They united in setting prices, establishing trade standards, maintaining an apprenticeship system to train new masters, and generally acted for the common good of the members of the guild. Often guilds undertook to provide municipal services, defense, hospitals, and the like.

The relations between the merchants, traders, and artisans on the one hand, and on the other hand the nobles, who were after all owners of the land, were often strained. Urban dwellers desired freedom from restrictions of the feudal system, while the nobility clung tenaciously to their feudal rights. This clash between new social groups and entrenched social and economic authority would fundamentally change the nature of feudal relations. Urban dwellers needed to be able to collect their own taxes, maintain their own courts, travel at their own discretion, and regulate their own affairs if this nascent form of economic activity was to survive. The nobles generally came to recognize that the towns that had grown up on lands they controlled could be a source of great profit and were usually willing, for a price, to grant such towns charters of liberties that guaranteed them the freedoms they required.

The Church, which was also a major landholder and owned some of the land on which these urban centers grew, was less compliant. Churchmen viewed the activities of the towns with suspicion, since the pursuit of profit as a way of life conflicted with the traditional ideals of Christian life. Also, Christian doctrine forbade the loaning of money at interest. Often it was Jews who served as bankers, but there were Christians who became powerful through banking. The Medici in Florence are particular examples. To avoid condemnation from the Church these Christian bankers were very generous in their contributions, and Western culture owes

a great deal to the "penance money" of Christian bankers. Moreover, the Church in the West had evolved in response to a rural environment and was poorly equipped to deal with the urban setting of the new towns. As a consequence, merchants, traders, and artisans were often driven to seize their liberties by force from ecclesiastical overlords. In the late eleventh and early twelfth centuries, a wave of urban rebellions accomplished this aim.

The peasantry was also affected by the new economic climate of Europe. With new markets for agricultural produce, industrious peasants could, and did, make a profit. Some used this money to free themselves of feudal obligations and labor services by agreeing with their lord that they and their heirs would pay an annual rent in place of performing these onerous duties. Since there was a gradual inflation throughout this period, the actual value of such rents decreased, to the advantage of the peasant and the detriment of the nobles. Other peasants moved to the towns to swell the ranks of the new urban areas, and yet others were lured to underdeveloped locales, to open up new lands. Labor became scarce, and for the first time in centuries, the peasants were able to exercise some control over where and under what conditions they would work.

The net result was that many nobles no longer controlled enough labor to till their personal lands, and were forced to lease them to those of their peasants who were able to rent them. The character of the nobility changed; they became a landlord class with little actual contact with their tenants. These tenants, in the meantime, continued to enjoy the prosperity of expanding markets. Not all peasants were equally successful, however, and the richer bought the land rights of the poorer. Thus a well-to-do class of yeoman farmers was created on the one hand, and a form of rural proletariat on the other. Nevertheless, agriculture expanded in both extent and intensity. By the year 1300, more land was under cultivation in Europe than ever before, or, indeed, ever since.

THE CHURCH

During the ninth and tenth centuries—concurrent with the growth of feudalism—religious life in Europe was on the decline. Because of the lack of strong, stable political states, many parish churches had been abandoned or destroyed. Those that did survive were often regarded as the personal property of powerful local noble families. Most popes during this time were incompetent or corrupt, the sons or tools of powerful Roman families who sought to control the papacy in order to enrich themselves and gain effective control over the city of Rome. As a consequence, popes during this period lacked the moral and spiritual rigor to effectively lead the church. Pope John XII, deposed in 963, was killed by a jealous husband who found his wife in bed with the pope.

The first efforts at reforming the church came from within the monastic movement. The Benedictine monastery at Cluny (in the French region of Burgundy) led the way. The monastery was founded in 910, and unlike existing monasteries, Cluny was placed under the direct authority of the Pope. The hope was to keep Cluny free of local and secular entanglements. This idea soon spread throughout Europe, and Cluny monks were sent out to help start other monasteries. By the eleventh century, the Cluny model became the focal point of a reform effort with sixty-seven Cluniac monasteries spread throughout the West. Cluniac monks became famous for their high ethical standards as well as their devotion to piety and prayer. From their monastic centers, Cluniac monks began to lobby the church for reform, focusing their demands on celibacy (in the tenth century, the vast majority of priests were married), personal poverty, and attacking the practice of simony (the buying and selling of church offices).

Even though Cluny was under the direct authority of the popes, the reforms offered by the Clunaics were not embraced wholeheartedly by the papacy. The eleventh century was one of the "lowest points" in the history of the papacy and popes were simply not receptive to reform. At one time there were actually three Roman nobles who claimed the title of pope. That situation was put to rest in 1046 when the Holy Roman Emperor, Henry III, invaded Rome, deposed the three claimants and installed a German reformer as pope. Leo IX (ruled 1049-1054) moved quickly to institute the Cluniac reform agenda, promulgating decrees that prohibited simony and clerical marriages.

The church's primary concern, however, was to free itself from the degree of secular control to which it had been subjected during the feudal period. This inevitably drew the papacy into a political struggle with the Holy Roman Emperors of Germany. For many years German kings had been in the habit of appointing bishops and abbots to their positions. Inevitably, men were chosen for high church positions not for their spirituality and piety, but rather for their loyalty to the monarchy and interest in secular affairs. As a result, churches were secularized, and Germanic law claimed that churches belonged to the state, not to the papacy in Rome. By the eleventh century, church leaders realized the need to reclaim the right to appoint its leading officials. Pope Gregory VII (1073–1085) chose to fight the practice of lay investiture (the practice of secular rulers appointing church officials), and the ensuing conflict has become known as the "Investiture Controversy."

The "Investiture Controversy" was one of the great conflicts between church and state in the medieval period. Pope Gregory claimed that as God's representative on earth, his authority reigned absolute over all of Christendom. This position brought him into conflict with the Holy Roman Emperor, King Henry IV (ruled 1056–1106). Both men agreed that it was the job of earthly rulers to lead their subjects to heaven. Where they profoundly disagreed was on the question of who was to be the supreme ruler of Christian society: emperor or pope. The controversy over lay investiture came to a head when Henry refused to relinquish his right to appoint church officials. Pope Gregory responded by excommunicating a number of bishops appointed by the emperor and several of the emperor's ministers, and threatened to excommunicate Henry himself. The emperor responded by calling for the pope's resignation, which prompted Gregory to excommunicate the emperor. Pope Gregory went farther, however, claiming that since Henry IV was no longer a faithful son of the church, he was no longer King of Germany or Holy Roman Emperor. The pope called on Henry's subjects to rebel against his rule. Heeding the pope's call—for political more than religious reasons—the Saxon nobility rose up in civil war against Henry IV. Realizing he had been outmaneuvered, in 1077 Henry made a humiliating public admission of wrongdoing and was absolved of his excommunication.

The controversy was formally resolved at the Concordat of Worms in 1122. The solution was an uneasy compromise of sorts. The emperor acknowledged the right of the pope to invest bishops and other church officials with spiritual authority, and the pope recognized the right of the emperor to give fiefs (heritable lands) to the bishops once they were invested. The long-term consequences were more far-reaching than the compromise reached at Worms might suggest. The resolution to the "Investiture Controversy" helped to create a lasting conceptual distinction between religion and politics in Western Europe, and to identify the church with religious authority and the state with political authority. After 1122 it was increasingly difficult to see a secular ruler as head of the church. Also, because of the outcome, the pope began to solidify his authority over all of Christendom in the Western world. Indeed, by the twelfth century, the papacy had reached the height of its power and historians speak of the period immediately following the controversy as a time of the "papal monarchy." The papacy had grown as strong as any secular ruler, with an administrative system, ability to collect taxes, and law courts to match.

ISLAM AND THE CRUSADES (1096–1292)

Christianity had rejected Islam from its beginning, denying its claimed to be the inheritor of Judaism and Christianity. It considered Islam a heretical religion and its believers infidels. The presence of Muslim kingdoms in Spain and Portugal both alarmed and outraged the Western Christian world. Christian forces continuously over five centuries tried to drive the Muslims from Spain. They gradually reduced the Muslim territory but did not succeed in finally driving out all Muslims (along with all Jews) from Granada, until 1492.

When the Seljuk Turks conquered Jerusalem in 1077, Christian Europe launched a series of crusades to recapture the "Holy Land" from the "infidel" Muslim Turks who ruled it. What made the Crusades possible at this time was the expanding power of the papacy, increased economic dynamism, and political consolidation. The immediate causes of the Crusades lay 1) in the east where religious strife between divisions in Islam destabilized the Islamic state, and 2) in relations between the Roman and Orthodox Churches.

By the 900s, the Islamic world had splintered, pitting Sunni and Shia Muslims against each other. In 1050 the Sunni Muslim Seljuk Turks captured Baghdad from the Shia. This represented a direct threat to the Byzantine Empire and in 1071 the emperor, Romanus IV, raised an army and attacked the Turks. The two forces met at Manzikert (present-day eastern Turkey) where Romanus' forces were decimated and the emperor himself taken prisoner. The humiliating rout represented the end of Byzantine domination of the region.

Following the defeat at Manzikert, the imperial court in Constantinople appealed to Pope Urban II (1088-99) and to Western kings for assistance. The plea was heeded, but not because Urban had any desire to rescue the Orthodox Church or to retake lands for the eastern emperor. Indeed, by 1054 a deep schism had developed between the Catholic and Byzantine churches. The pope demanded that the patriarch of Constantinople acknowledge the primacy of the papacy in Rome. When the leader of the Orthodox Church refused, dual excommunications followed. The pope saw the crisis as an excellent opportunity to provide papal leadership in the cause of liberating the Holy Land from the infidel. At the Council of Clermont in southern France in 1095, Urban II challenged Christians to take up their weapons and join in a holy war to recover Jerusalem.

> Oh, race of Franks, race from across the mountains, race beloved and chosen by God.... Let hatred depart from among you, let your quarrels end, let wars cease, and let all dissensions and controversies slumber. Enter upon the road of the Holy Sepulcher; wrest that land from the wicked race, and subject it yourselves.

[From *A Source Book for Medieval History*, (New York: Scribners, 1905), 513–17]

The assembled crowd responded with one voice: God wills it. Thousands of knights took the cross, the symbol of the crusaders, and pledged themselves as warriors dedicated to fight for Christ. The First Crusade (1096–1099) had begun.

There are many reasons why knights would leave their homes and undertake the long and perilous journey to the Holy Land. Some hoped for plunder and others for adventure. Chief among the reasons knights took up the cross was that, put simply, knights were born to fight. Much of the literature of the High Middle Ages glorified war and warriors, and knights saw the Crusades as an opportunity for glory and honor. Further, throughout the period, bishops and priests had sought to limit and control warfare in an effort to protect certain groups within the population. The movement, called the Truce of God and the Peace of God, led knights to pledge not to attack peasants, merchants, or churchmen and not to engage in any fighting of any kind on Christian holy days. The Crusades freed the knights from this obligation and also offered them a most tempting target: the infidel Muslims.

The First Crusade ended in success for Christian Europe. Though the crusader army was beset by infighting and poor leadership, one force did manage to seize Jerusalem in 1099. Other cities in the Holy Land were also captured by the crusaders, so that by 1100 a string of crusader states stretched from Antioch in the north to the Dead Sea in the south. The victories, however, were short-lived. The Second Crusade (1147–1149) was a disaster for the West. In 1144 a new Seljuk chief, Zengi, recaptured the crusader state of Edessa, in what is now Turkey. From there, several other crusader strongholds fell to the Muslims. This led to a call in the West for a new crusade. The crusade came to an end when, after four days of unsuccessfully attempting to seize the city of Damascus, the crusaders gave up and went home.

The era of the crusades produced one of the greatest Muslim figures of the Middle Ages, Saladin (Salah-al-Din) (1138–1193), Sultan of Egypt and Syria. In 1187 Saladin recaptured Jerusalem from Christian Crusader forces. A brilliant military leader, Saladin was renowned for his courage and magnanimity. He avoided slaughter and favored negotiation whenever possible. Saladin became a legend not only to the Islamic world but also to Christian Europe, and in Dante's *Inferno*, the great

early-fourteenth-century Catholic-Christian poem about a journey through hell, Saladin dwells in a not-unpleasant Limbo after death together with the other virtuous non-Christians such as Homer, Plato, and Virgil.

In response, German and English kings led a crusader force to the Holy Land in an effort to once again occupy Jerusalem. This third expedition ended in defeat and humiliation. Frederick I of Germany (ruled 1152-90) died along the way and Richard the Lionheart, the English king (ruled 1189–99), was captured and the English had to pay a huge ransom for his release.

The Fourth Crusade (1202–04) had disastrous consequences for relations between the West and Byzantium. In 1204 Crusaders, encouraged by the pope, stormed Constantinople, sacked the city, destroyed its important and renowned library and stole thousands of relics (which were eventually sold off in Europe). While the stated goal of the Crusades was to unite all of Christendom, the attack by one faction of Christians upon another led to a permanent enmity between the two churches. The sacking of Constantinople also led to the ultimate dissolution of the Byzantine Empire. In the fifteenth century, Constantinople was attacked by Turks. The West refused to come to the city's aid. Constantinople fell and the Byzantine Empire ceased to exist.

The series of eight Crusades lasting nearly two hundred years finally came to an end in 1292 with Jerusalem and the other major cities in Muslim hands. Three powerful Muslim empires arose following the Crusades: The Ottoman (Turkish) Empire in the West, the Safavids in Iran (formerly Persia), and the Moghuls in India. It was the Ottomans who most influenced Western history. They conquered what was left of the Byzantine Empire, including Greece and the other Balkan areas of southeastern Europe. The Ottoman Empire reached its height in the sixteenth century and then declined, finally collapsing in the late nineteenth and early twentieth centuries. That was the period when the great powers of Europe were vigorously extending their colonial empires all over the world. Britain and France gained control of the predominantly Muslim countries of the Middle East, and carved them up to their liking.

Historians consider the Crusades to ultimately have been a failure in retaking the Holy Land from the Muslims. It nonetheless remains a pivotal period in Western civilization. It gave Christian Europe a better understanding of Islam, and led to increased trade with the eastern world. But it also left a legacy of bitterness between the two faiths and between European and Islamic civilization. The Crusades, perhaps more than any other single factor, forged Europe into a militant, expansionist Christian civilization whose zeal for mission and conquest would manifest itself in the Renaissance voyages of discovery that led to the modern creation of European colonial empires.

JEWS IN THE MIDDLE AGES

During the First Crusade, one group from the West (named the Peasant's Crusade by historians) took a route through the Rhineland of Germany on their way to free the Holy Land from the infidels. This route was purposely chosen. Many Jews had settled in the major cities of the Rhineland. The Peasant's Crusade saw the German Jews as yet another group of infidels that needed to be forcibly converted to Christianity or killed. Jews in cities such as Metz, Worms, Mainz, and Cologne either converted, paid for their lives, or were massacred.

Throughout the Middle Ages Jews faced special forms of discrimination and persecution. According to Church decrees Jews could not hold public office, nor take excessive interest on loans. Church doctrine also placed severe restrictions on the Jews' daily movements. Jews were forbidden to appear in public on Christian holidays, and it was further ruled that every Jew must wear a yellow patch and a horned cap. These decrees were made in spite of the attempts by a delegation of Jews from Provence in southern France to ensure against such pronouncements. Certainly these measures mirrored prior and prevailing attitudes towards the Jews. The very early Church councils of Elvira in 312 and of Nicaea in 325 had also issued edicts discriminating against Jews. But the decrees from the Fourth Lateran Council in 1215 formally approved punitive and exclusionary measures that incited *pogroms*, organized massacres of helpless people, directed at Jews.

The doctrinal fuel for anti-Semitism in the Middle Ages was found in religion. Jews do not believe that Jesus is the Christ (Messiah) or son of God, while Christians do. Consequently, Jews and Christians have the Hebrew Scriptures (which Christians call the Old Testament) in common, but they do not share the Christian New Testament. In the early centuries of the Common Era this theological difference became the justification for injustices toward Jews by Christians. Because of this difference, Christian interpretation of the Bible perpetuated a negative bias toward Jews.

During the Middle Ages Jews lived mainly in Babylonia (Iraq), North Africa, Spain, France, Germany, and Italy. It is estimated that in the twelfth century, Spain and the Arabic countries were home to approximately fourteen million Jews, while the next largest group, around 100,000, lived in Germany. Jews in the countries of the world dominated by Islam—which included much of Spain between the eighth and thirteenth centuries—flourished for the most part in an atmosphere of greater tolerance than they experienced in Christian Europe. Although conquering Muslims welcomed converts to Islam, they respected the Jewish and Christian religions because, according to the Qur'an, each shared a belief in the supremacy of one God whose message was interpreted for believers through holy scriptures. Later ages designated those Jews who lived in Germany as the *Ashkenazi*, while those who lived in Spain and the Muslim countries were called the *Sephardi*.

In Islamic Spain, Jews and Christians belonged to specially protected groups who, however, were forced to pay special taxes. After the Arabic conquest in 711, most Jews moved to towns where they engaged in crafts or became merchants. They were distinguished from their Muslim counterparts mainly in that most Jewish men could read Hebrew, while most Muslims could not read at all. A few Jews were very successful politically and financially, some rising to important positions and becoming patrons of science and literature. Their support enabled the flourishing of Jewish poetry, grammar, philosophy, science, and medicine in the tenth to the thirteenth centuries. The wealth of their contributions in these areas is partly demonstrated by the large numbers of Hebrew manuscripts surviving from this time. In Spain of the twelfth and thirteenth centuries, the intellectual activity of both Muslim and Jewish scholars gave rise to works of literature, science, philosophy, and medicine, and to translations of Aristotle, that greatly influenced the Christian world. In addition, Jewish and Syrian traders established routes that brought luxury items to the Western world.

Although Jews lived in Spain in relative peace, they were not entirely free from persecution even there. Before the Muslim conquest in 711, Jews had been persecuted by Christian leaders. After the conquest, Christians began to assert themselves especially in the north where they formed states. The Christians in northern Spain, who at various times were allied with the French and the English, began a movement called the *Reconquista* ("reconquest") that was intended to reclaim Spain for Christianity.

Eventually the *Reconquista* did achieve its goal. By the mid-thirteenth century the only remaining Muslim territory was Granada, and it had to pay tribute to Christian Spain. With the increasing success of the *Reconquista*, a number of Muslims and Jews converted to Christianity and were called *Mudéjares* and *Conversos* respectively. But assaults on Jews also increased. These culminated after the troubled years of the Black Death (1347–1350): in 1391 when Jews were massacred in Valencia and other cities, in 1478–1492 when the Spanish Inquisition condemned and burned Jews, and in 1492 when Jews were expelled from the country.

How Jews lived elsewhere in Western Europe also reflects anti-Semitism. Jews were said to have come to England via Rouen in France with William the Conqueror, who ruled England from 1066 to 1087. Although they were granted certain economic privileges under King Henry I, who ruled England from 1100 to 1135, persecution began in 1144. In 1290 England became the first European country to expel Jews, who numbered 16,000. Jews were not readmitted until 1655.

In France, Sephardic Jews from Spain thrived and contributed to intellectual life in Provence until the fourteenth century, when they suffered persecution. Northeastern France was the area chosen by Ashkenazi Jews from Germany, who were able to conduct biblical studies, but who became victims of attacks in the eleventh century. During the First Crusade (1096-1099), Jews were murdered or forced to convert to Christianity in both areas. In the thirteenth century Jews suffered pogroms in Brittany, Anjou, and Poitou in France. In 1240 Jews were expelled from Brittany, in 1289 they were expelled from Gascony and Anjou, and by 1294 Jews in most

of France were required to live in restricted quarters or ghettos. In 1395 they were ordered to leave France, and by 1501 only a few Jews were left in the entire country.

In Germany, Jews lived in relative peace during the tenth and much of the eleventh centuries. They were allowed rights to trade and to govern themselves in Speyer in 1074 and in Worms in 1090. Regional expulsions, however, began as early as 1012 in Mainz. By the sixteenth century many Jews had fled to Poland. Only Worms and Frankfurt-am-Main were left in Germany as important Jewish centers. Those who remained were subjected to much prejudice, and we find the depiction of Jews as allies of Satan in many medieval plays.

A small Jewish community had existed in the territory that is now Italy since the second century BCE. From the late thirteenth century on, when Ashkenazi Jews fled to Italy, Italian Christians sheltered persecuted Jews. After 1391 and 1492 Sephardic Jews also came to Italy, while North African Jews arrived in the late sixteenth century. Problems arose among these culturally and linguistically different Jews, resulting in the primacy of the Italian language among them and a high degree of assimilation. They were able to write literature and philosophy as well as to hold positions as university professors. But in spite of the relative peace Jews experienced in Italy, restrictions were continually placed on them. In 1267 Jews were forbidden to study and practice medicine at the medieval university in Salerno, although they were among those who had translated Greek and Arabic medical treatises for use by this medical center. They were restricted to ghettos in parts of Italy in 1555, and during his papacy (1566–1571) Pope Pius V expelled Jews from all Papal States except Rome and Ancona.

CREATIVITY AND VITALITY IN THE HIGH MIDDLE AGES

The twelfth and thirteenth centuries gave rise to a remarkable blossoming of literary, artistic, and intellectual vitality. There was a rapid spread of schools and universities throughout the West during this period. The main centers of education in the twelfth century were cathedral schools located in the major urban areas of Europe. Initially, the goal of such schools was to train and educate priests. By 1100, however, the curriculum at cathedral schools was vastly expanded to meet the growing need for educated secular elites such as lawyers, administrators, and notaries to staff the growing bureaucratic needs of governments. Thus, in addition to basic literacy, cathedral schools also began teaching Latin grammar and composition based on the study of classical authors such as Cicero and Virgil. In 1050 only about one percent of the West was literate. By 1340, about forty percent of Florentines could read and a century later roughly half of the English population was literate.

The Western university began as a cathedral school but eventually grew to offer advanced studies outside the general purview of most cathedral schools. The first university, the University of Bologna, became a renowned center for the teaching of Roman law, attracting students from all over the West. The great majority of students at Bologna were bureaucrats who served kings and princes throughout Europe. While secular subjects made up a large portion of university curricula, theological concerns also played a central role in the intellectual life of the Middle Ages. By the eleventh century, the effort to apply reason or logic to basic church doctrine had a significant impact on the study of theology. It is important to note that it was due largely to Muslim and Jewish scholars that Greek scientific and philosophical works survived and became accessible to scholars in the Middle Ages.

Medieval universities offered a method of teaching and learning called *scholasticism*. Scholastics taught that there was a basic compatibility between 1) knowledge of the world and the universe that humans could attain through their ability to reason about and experience the world and 2) knowledge of the universe and human nature and destiny that came from divine revelation. That is, there was a harmony between faith and reason. The task of the scholastic was to demonstrate this harmony between Christian teachings and classical Greek learning, especially philosophy. The most famous attempt to reconcile Aristotelian philosophy and the doctrines of Christianity was that of Saint Thomas Aquinas. See Chapter Ten for more on scholasticism and the life and works of Aquinas.

Perhaps the best symbols of the thirteenth-century achievement were the soaring Gothic cathedrals that sprang up all over Western Europe. Most were dedicated to the Virgin Mary, who was referred to as Our Lady, Queen of Heaven. The Cathedrals were the product of the zeal and commitment of all classes of society, each contributing in its own measure and fashion. In addition to the Gothic cathedral's religious and aesthetic importance, it was also the center of economic transactions. Pilgrims would journey to view and touch the relics (body parts or possessions) of saints that were preserved in cathedrals in the hope of improving their own lives. At the same time, markets in which craftspeople could sell their wares were held in front of the cathedral's steps. Some historians have seen in the dynamic harmony of Gothic architecture at its height the epitome of the medieval accomplishment, a unity achieved without the imposition of uniformity, through the harmonious integration of disparate elements. Whether or not this characterization is justified, the condition was merely temporary. In a very few years, medieval society once again entered an era of conflict and change.

THE FOURTEENTH CENTURY: THE END OF THE HIGH MIDDLE AGES

The fourteenth century has sometimes been called the "calamitous century," and there is much to justify such a characterization. Western Europe was afflicted by a series of natural and human-made disasters that strained the fabric of society to such a degree that an inevitable and irreversible process of change and adaptation began. In this process, the institutions of medieval society were displaced or modified, and the foundations of modern Europe began to emerge.

A simple enumeration of the misfortunes of the period is sufficient to suggest the degree of hardship suffered by the people of the time. In 1305, in the face of increasing turmoil in Rome, the papacy moved to the town of Avignon on the border of France, where the troops of the French king could provide the papal administration the security it had lacked in Rome. Originally conceived as a temporary measure, this state of affairs, sometimes called "the Babylonian Captivity of the Church," lasted until 1378. The period was not a happy one for the Church. It was forced to adopt grasping financial practices to secure sufficient funds to maintain two capitals, it felt the lack of the prestige that its identification with Rome had always provided, and it was conceived by many as being a puppet of the French monarchs. It was in poor condition to provide spiritual leadership or comfort in the face of the adversities to come.

The climate of Europe was deteriorating at the same time that its population was growing dramatically. This became evident in the years 1315–1317, when a series of long winters and cold, wet summers led to poor harvests. The consequence was the first general famine in centuries, a famine in which perhaps ten percent of the population perished.

In 1337, the long-standing friction between England and France led to open conflict. Once having led their people into war, the monarchs of England and France seemed incapable of getting them out and it came to be called the Hundred Years War. Hostilities dragged on intermittently until 1453, devastating the North of France and often spilling beyond French borders to involve the other states of Western Europe. The fourteenth century was thus one of continuous war in which the peasants suffered, the nobility was decimated, and the economy was yet further disrupted.

For much of the medieval period, the low population density and relative isolation of Europe had protected the region from the great plagues that swept across most of the other civilizations of the Old World. This relative immunity ended in 1346 with the coming of the Black Death: a pandemic of bubonic and pneumonic plague. Although accurate estimates are not possible, it seems likely that between twenty-five and thirty-five percent of the European population perished during the next five years. Traditional attitudes and institutions were unable to cope with the enormity of the disaster. The Church, for instance, had long preached that the sacraments were essential for salvation. Once the plague struck, the numbers of dead were so great and the numbers of clergy so diminished that it was simply not possible to administer the sacraments to all those requiring them. Among the results of the trauma of the times were that many sought a more direct communion with God through mysticism and still others turned against the insti-

tutional Church to swell a new tide of popular religious dissent.

In 1378, Pope Gregory XI died while in Rome, and the local populace forced the cardinals who had followed him to elect an Italian pope who would return the papal capital to Rome. A number of the cardinals left the city shortly afterward, declared the election null and void, and proceeded to elect a French pope who immediately returned to Avignon. There were now two popes, each excommunicating the other and declaring himself to be the supreme authority in ecclesiastical affairs. This was more than a political problem, since no one who put his faith in an excommunicate, false pope could hope for salvation, and no one could determine which was the true pope. This sorry situation persisted until 1415, causing the faithful great suffering and the Church serious damage.

The economic dislocations of the century had severe social repercussions, most particularly for the lower and middle classes. The devastation of the wars and the mortality of the famines and plagues fell most heavily on the peasants, who finally rose in open rebellion against a social and economic system that was ever more clearly aimed at their subjection and exploitation. The peasants of northern France rebelled in 1369 and those of southern England in 1381. Throughout the remainder of the medieval period, peasant uprisings were common throughout Western Europe. These peasant rebels were poorly armed, ill-led, and had no clear goals. As a consequence, their movements accomplished little, but by the fifteenth century there was little talk of an integrated and harmonious society.

Merchants and artisans also suffered. Markets were stagnating or even contracting, and a general economic recession occurred. This led to a period of fierce competition, a state of affairs for which the guilds, designed to promote co-operation and stability, were ill-adapted. As a consequence, the guilds began to decay, and urban dwellers began, like the peasantry, to split into a group of successful merchants and tradesmen on the one hand, and an exploited collection of wage-workers and lesser artisans on the other.

GOTHIC ART

Art of the high and later Middle Ages is generally termed Gothic art. During the twelfth century, a distinctive new style of architecture appeared in France, characterized by soaring interiors and huge expanses of stained glass. While the style originated in France, it quickly spread to others parts of the European continent and lasted for several centuries. The Italian historian Giorgio Vasari coined the name "Gothic" during the sixteenth century. Vasari meant the term as one of derision, attributing the style to the Goths, or Germanic northerners, who had destroyed the classical Roman Empire. Italy proved surprisingly resistant to the Gothic architectural style, but variations of the aesthetic flourished in France, England, and Germany.

The period from 1150 to 1400 is recognized as the great age of cathedral building. The towering, magnificent structures arose as towns throughout Europe gained prominence in politics, commerce, and the arts. Unlike their predecessors, the rural monasteries, cathedrals occupied urban settings and dominated their surroundings. Their grandeur testified to the power of the church and to bountiful religious patronage. Since the Gothic style endured for several centuries, it is not surprising to find an evolution of sorts within the style, from the Romanesque-inspired arches and vaults of early Gothic to the flying buttresses and stained glass of high Gothic, ending with the glass-filled walls of the later Gothic style known as Rayonnant.

While architectural monuments are the most recognizable form of Gothic art, other art forms developed as well. Manuscript illumination prospered in France and England, though in France its production moved away from the monastic scriptoria of earlier times to urban centers overseen by both university and royal officials. Italy witnessed the burgeoning of painting on wood panels, primarily in the form of countless altarpieces commissioned for cathedrals, parish churches, and private chapels. The central subject of such altarpieces was most often the Virgin and Child; donors who paid for the altarpieces also received prominent placement within the panels.

EARLY GOTHIC

The Abbey Church of Saint-Denis in France, begun in the 1130s, is considered to be Europe's first Gothic structure. Although it was connected to a Benedictine monastery, unlike most Gothic cathedrals that stood independently, the church of Saint-Denis paved the way for the blossoming Gothic style through its prototypical use of space, color, and light. Its overseer, Abbot Suger, traveled widely and brought to its design a love of international art and architecture, importing foreign aesthetic elements as well as skilled craftsmen from other regions.

The plan of Saint-Denis incorporates many architectural elements previously seen in Romanesque buildings, such as ribbed groin vaults, round piers, and pointed arches. What set Saint-Denis apart from its predecessors, however, was the integration of these elements into a whole that emphasized an open, continuous, flowing space rather than a segmenting of separate areas within the church. The view of the ambulatory choir (Plate 21) illustrates this interconnectedness of space: the piers and vaults do not physically separate the ambulatory, or walkway around the sanctuary, from the radiating chapels, but rather lead the viewer forward into these spaces.

The abundance of windows and light seen here further unifies the space and draws the viewer along. Like medieval mystics, Abbot Suger believed that color and light could illuminate the soul. Accordingly, the design of Saint-Denis uses stained-glass windows in place of masonry walls as a way to bring churchgoers closer to God.

The Abbey Church at Saint-Denis initiated a new era of experimentation in church architecture. Subsequent buildings capitalized on Saint-Denis's system of interior vaulting and exterior buttressing to create increasingly tall spaces. Stained glass came to dominate Gothic construction, letting in more and more light and color. Such rich decoration in church architecture is the legacy of Abbot Suger and Saint-Denis.

HIGH GOTHIC

During its development, the Gothic style became increasingly ornate in sculptural decoration, with stone statues covering the exterior and intricate stained-glass window designs filling ever-larger wall surfaces. One church that bridges the transition from early to high Gothic is the Cathedral of Notre-Dame in Paris (Plate 22), begun in 1163. Although Notre-Dame was begun in the twelfth century, many of its parts were not completed until the thirteenth century, perhaps explaining the mix of early and high Gothic elements. Notre-Dame carries on the innovations begun at Saint-Denis, such as the lofty, unified interior space and the increasing use of light and color, but adds high Gothic elements such as flying buttresses and exterior sculpture and even makes reference to the Rayonnant style of later Gothic architecture through its two large rose windows. The tall spire is a nineteenth-century addition, but adds to the soaring quality of the cathedral.

While the architects of Notre-Dame sought to enclose a large, towering interior, they continued to use the thick masonry walls and vaults of the Romanesque era. As such, they needed to provide buttressing, or exterior support, for the heavy roof vaults. Notre-Dame illustrates the first use of a new Gothic architectural element, the flying buttress. Built along the exterior of the building, these repeated arches transferred the weight of the walls and roof to the ground through the detached piers. The "flying," or soaring, quality of the buttresses furthered the Gothic idea of architectural lightness, or symbolic spiritual elevation.

The portals, or large entrance doors, of Notre-Dame are decorated with figural sculpture, a common characteristic of high Gothic cathedrals. Often, tall column statues of saints and apostles flank the doorways, while the tympanum, or semi-circular space above the doorway, may showcase momentous biblical scenes such as the Ascension of Christ or the Last Judgment. At Notre-Dame, two of the tympana are dedicated to the Virgin Mary (Our Lady, or *Notre Dame* in French).

In the early thirteenth century, new builders attempted to modernize Notre-Dame, replacing some smaller, Romanesque windows with large rose windows of stained glass. In these round windows, thin stone bars, or tracery, create an elaborate pattern of wheel spokes, physically supporting the fragile structure through intricate, rose-like designs. By replacing large sections of masonry wall with stained glass and tracery, the rose windows of Notre-Dame make reference to a later Gothic style where light and color are found in even greater abundance.

In addition to its centuries of use as a Christian church, Notre-Dame has seen its share of historical occurrences. In the late eighteenth-century, French Revolutionaries temporarily transformed Notre-Dame from a church into a secular Temple of Reason. Following its return to sacred use, Napoleon crowned himself emperor at Notre-Dame in 1804. In August 1944, French citizens celebrated the liberation of Paris from the Nazis at Notre-Dame. Even today, Notre-Dame endures as a symbol of Paris, a tourist attraction rivaling the Eiffel Tower.

RAYONNANT

By the mid-thirteenth century, a new style in Gothic architecture came into fashion. Known primarily for its vast expanses of stained glass and daring engineering, the style is termed Rayonnant because of the "radiating" sections of tracery and the "radiant" infusion of color and light. Other hallmarks include fine painted and sculptural details. The Rayonnant style is sometimes referred to as Court Style because of its association with the royal court in Paris.

One of the earliest, and perhaps best-known, structures of the Rayonnant style is the Sainte-Chapelle in Paris, begun in 1243. Originally part of

King Louis IX's palace, it was constructed to house the king's collection of relics from Christ's Passion, which supposedly included the crown of thorns and a nail from the Crucifixion, among other items. This giant reliquary was intended not only to celebrate the life of Christ but also to proclaim the piety of the king.

The upper chapel of the Sainte-Chapelle (Plate 23) epitomizes the Rayonnant style: more than three-quarters of the structure is composed of stained glass, a higher glass to stone ratio than found in any other Gothic building. The walls give way almost entirely to stained glass, with only slender columns of stone in between for support. Painted statues of the Twelve Apostles adorn the thin columns so that any appearance of functionality is masked by decoration. The stained-glass windows contain a variety of narrative scenes, from the Nativity and Passion of Christ to the Last Judgment. Although it is a much smaller space than seen in the massive Gothic cathedrals, the Sainte-Chapelle provides a scaled-down but similar experience of high-ceilinged, symbolically soaring space with a profusion of color and light.

GOTHIC PAINTING

Just as the many Gothic cathedrals were dedicated to Notre-Dame, so did the majority of Gothic paintings pay tribute to her. Particularly in Italy, where schools of painting flourished in Siena and Florence, altarpieces depicted biblical scenes of the Virgin and Child as well as apocryphal scenes from the Life of the Virgin. Depicted in a blue cloak to indicate her divinity, Mary often is rendered as the Queen of Heaven.

One of the most influential painters of the Gothic period was Giotto di Bondone. The dubious tale of Giotto's "discovery" is that another painter, Cimabue, found the talented shepherd boy and nurtured his artistic gifts. Vasari, the sixteenth-century historian, relayed this account and credited Giotto with changing the direction of art by learning to draw accurately from life.

Giotto's painting, *Virgin and Child Enthroned*, ca. 1310 (Plate 24), illustrates Vasari's assertion by combining earlier Byzantine characteristics with a new aesthetic. Giotto showed the influence of his predecessors by continuing such elements as the profile views of stylized facial types, the profusion of gold halos, the flat gold background, and the symmetrical composition. Giotto's representation of the Virgin, however, set a new precedent. While earlier paintings used a hierarchy of scale to emphasize Mary's importance, Giotto's Virgin takes on a new monumentality, physically overpowering those around her. What best demonstrates Vasari's assertion is the way that Giotto used light and shadow to define Mary's physical form. By observing from life the plays of light on a human form, Giotto was able to convey the impression of three-dimensional figures occupying real space.

MUSIC OF THE MIDDLE AGES

Medieval Europe was dominated by Roman Catholic Christianity, and the Church's teachings, institutions, values, and practices thoroughly permeated society and culture. So it should come as no surprise to learn that the earliest medieval music of which we have any record was music of and for the Church, and that the Middle Ages produced a rich and varied tradition of religious or sacred music. The Europe of the eleventh through the fourteenth centuries, however, also saw the flowering of a secular musical heritage articulated by popular entertainers, troubadours, and composers of sacred music who began writing secular music as well. The invention of a standardized system of written musical notation during the eleventh century made possible the stabilizing and preserving of musical forms that led to the whole development of modern music in the West.

The oldest recorded musical tradition in medieval Europe is Gregorian chant, to which you were introduced in the section on early Christian music. Although according to tradition Pope Gregory the Great standardized both the music and the liturgy of the Western Church at the end of the sixth century, the plainchant or plainsong we call "Gregorian" did not achieve a universal and stable form until the reign of Charlemagne in the late eighth to early ninth centuries. This monophonic music for soloist or chorus, sung *a capella* (unaccompanied) in Latin by male or female voices, *was* the music of the Western Church until the eleventh century. About 3,000 different plainsong melodies are preserved to the present day, and include musical settings of various parts of the liturgy of the Mass, such as the *Kyrie eleison* and the *Gloria*, and also of the Psalms.

For a long time the various melodies of Gregorian chant were transmitted orally. In the eighth century a written system of notation developed, which used symbols for musical pitches called *neumes*. Dissatisfied with the lack of precision of neumes, a monk named Guido d'Arezzo (ca. 990-1050) invented the five-line musical staff with four spaces in between on which neumes or notes symbolized precise pitches, an innovation that made possible modern music. Guido also started the practice of naming the musical tones by syllables (do, re, mi, fa, etc.), which simplified the teaching of music.

Gregorian chant underwent creative changes that likewise laid the foundation for further musical developments. One was the *trope,* an addition to or interpolation in an authorized musical text, such as the prescribed parts of the mass. These additions "broke the monotony," allowing the composer to introduce interesting variations. Some tropes became elaborated into *sequences*, which were separate compositions rather than simply elaborations of the set form. By expressing greater compositional freedom and creativity, tropes and sequences paved the way for the modern Western tradition of individuality and independence in musical creation.

These imaginative elaborations of Gregorian chant also led to the emergence, beginning in the tenth century, of *polyphony* ("many sounds"), in which two or more melodies were sung or played together. Eventually the main melody was always given to the tenor voice and referred to as the *cantus firmus* ("fixed song"). Perhaps the greatest polyphonic composer of the Middle Ages was Guillaume de Machaut (ca. 1300–77), who wrote both secular and sacred music including a polyphonic setting of the Mass. Polyphony laid the foundation for modern *homophonic* ("like sounds") music, consisting of melody and harmony.

Secular music, and increasingly also sacred music after the development of polyphony, was not only vocal but also instrumental. Among the main instruments in medieval Europe were stringed instruments including the harp, the lute, and the *rebec* (a precursor of the violin); wind instruments such as the trumpet, the flute, and the recorder; percussion instruments like drums and bells; and the organ. There were songs that were entirely instrumental, including music for dancing.

Medieval secular music included popular entertainers such as goliards and jongleurs, and troubadours and trouveres. The goliards wrote and sang bawdy poems about love, drinking, and springtime, among them a group of poems called *Carmina Burana* which were famously given a twentieth-century musical setting by the German composer Carl Orff. The repertoire of the wandering *jongleurs* (French for "tumblers" or "jugglers") included *chansons de geste*, including *The Song of Roland*, and, as their name suggests, performing circus-like routines.

The troubadours of Provence in southern France and their northern counterparts, the trouveres, composed and sang the finest lyric poems and songs of the Middle Ages—and in abundance: something like 6,000 of their poems and 1,800 of their melodies survive. The troubadors, both men and women, were educated members of the nobility who exemplified the age of chivalry and the tradition of courtly love, marked by the mutual devotion to each other of a knight and a lady and the elaborate etiquette surrounding it. The troubadours' main theme was romantic love, and their poems were all written to be sung. The earliest known troubadour was Duke William IX of Aquitaine, a Crusader, adventurer and lover, poet, and performer. One of the most influential sponsors of the troubadours was Queen Eleanor of Aquitaine (1122–1204), at her court in Poitiers. Perhaps the greatest of the many female troubadours was Beatriz, Countess of Dia in southern France in the twelfth century.

CD SELECTIONS

The selections of medieval music are in roughly chronological order, beginning with two examples of plainsong for the Church's liturgy. Track #12 is the *Kyrie* from a traditional Gregorian chant setting of the mass for Easter, *Hodie Christus Resurrexit* (Today Christ is Risen), sung by the Schola Hungarica conducted by Laszlo Dobszy. Choir and soloist alternate singing the ancient words, still in the original Greek: *Kyrie eleison, Christe eleison, Kyrie eleison*—"Lord have mercy, Christ have mercy, Lord have mercy." In the section on Renaissance music we will have occasion to listen to the *Kyries* from two later musical settings of the mass, one from the fifteenth and one from the sixteenth century, to show the dramatic changes that took place in sacred music over a few hundred years.

The other example of plainsong, track #13, was written by one of the most remarkable women of the Middle Ages, Hildegard of Bingen (1098–1179). The abbess of a Benedictine monastery on the Rhine River near Bingen, Germany, she was a mystic and visionary, artist, scientist, playwright, poet, composer, and adviser to kings and popes. Hildegard had vivid spiritual visions, which she portrayed in her art and music. She wrote three books of theology, two books on natural history and medicine, and the first of what came to be known as "morality plays." As a composer Hildegard was uniquely creative, writing both the words and the music to her songs and displaying an individual and musically sophisticated style that makes her plainsongs not simply "more Gregorian chant." The selection from Hildegard is *Ave, generosa* ("Hail, girl of noble birth"), a hymn expressing her devotion to the Virgin Mary. It is sung by members of a Benedictine monastery of women in Germany, in an album of her music entitled *Hildegard von Bingen*. The words (in Latin of course) are an example of the erotic imagery that was often used and spiritualized in monastic devotion to the Virgin and to Christ, from Hildegard to St. Teresa of Avila and beyond. Here is an English translation presenting the poetry in "prose form":

> Hail, girl of a noble house, shimmering and unpolluted, you pupil in the

eye of chastity, you essence of sanctity, which was pleasing to God. For the Heavenly potion was poured into you, in that the Heavenly word received a raiment of flesh in you. You are the lily that dazzles, whom God knew before all others. O most beautiful and delectable one; how greatly God delighted in you! In the clasp of his fire He implanted in you so that His son might be suckled by you. Thus your womb held joy, when the harmony of all Heaven chimed out from you, because, Virgin, you carried Christ whence your chastity blazed in God. Your flesh has known delight, like the grassland touched by dew and immersed in its freshness; so it was with you, o mother of all joy. Now let the sunrise of joy be over all Ecclesia [the Church] and let it resound in music for the sweetest Virgin, Mary compelling all praise, mother of God. Amen.

The other two selections of medieval music represent secular music traditions. Both are taken from *A Golden Treasury of Mediaeval Music* (Amon Ra), performed by Sine Nomine, a Canadian musical group dedicated to performing medieval music on medieval instruments. Track #14 is a *saltorello*, from around the end of the fourteenth century. *Saltorelli* were a form of Italian dance, and the selection provides an example of medieval instrumental music, here featuring the recorder, the lute, and the *vieille*, a stringed instrument played with a bow. The other selection, track #15, is from the courtly musical tradition of the troubadours and trouveres. *Je ne vis oncques la pareille* ("I have never seen the equal"), written by Gilles de Binchois (ca. 1400–60), is a typical song of a knight to his lady. Here, as in much medieval secular music, a religious reference is included quite naturally: "I have never seen the equal of you, my gracious lady, for your beauty is, upon my soul, far above all others. Seeing you, I marvel, and say that this is Our Lady. Your great sweetness revives my spirit and stimulates my eye; my heart, of which I may speak without rebuke, prepares me to serve you." A performance of this song is actually recorded. In 1454 Philip the Good of Burgundy staged a grand spectacle, the "Feast of the Pheasant," to raise support for a crusade to recapture Constantinople from the Turks. A boy dressed in splendid clothes sang this song as part of the festivities. On the recording the singer is accompanied by a lute and a harp.

CHAPTER TEN

INTELLECTUAL MOVEMENTS
OF THE MIDDLE AGES: THOMAS AQUINAS

UNIVERSITIES IN THE MIDDLE AGES

The first universities in Europe appeared in Italy, France, England, and Spain in the eleventh and twelfth centuries. Throughout the early Middle Ages education, like the preservation of learning itself, was centered in monasteries, and the monastery school provided both elementary and advanced schooling. But by the eleventh century the growing complexity of medieval society and institutions was requiring more specialized and sophisticated professional education, beginning with the clergy. Bishops founded cathedral schools to train clergy, not only in theology and preaching but also in church administration and canon law. Other professions, notably law and medicine, likewise began developing special centers for professional learning. Amidst a growing demand for well-educated members of the professions, and for teachers to teach them, some cathedral schools and professional centers developed into universities.

The first university to be chartered in medieval Europe was the University of Bologna in Italy, which had been a school for the study of law since the tenth century, in 1088. The University of Oxford (England) followed in 1117, and the University of Paris in 1150. Paris specialized in the study of theology, and Thomas Aquinas would be one of its most illustrious students and faculty members. Among the other early universities were Cambridge (England), Padua and Salerno (Italy), and Salamanca and Seville (Spain). Padua and Salerno specialized in the study of medicine.

There were three types of universities according to the way they were chartered: 1) Students would organize themselves into a school and hire and pay the salaries of the teachers, as at Bologna. Both of the other two types of universities were begun by groups of teachers, who would organize themselves into a school and recruit students. Of these 2) some were mainly supported by the king or the state, as were Oxford and Cambridge, while 3) others were sponsored and financed by the Church, as at Paris. The first teacher-founded universities were organized as guilds; in fact the word *universitas* means "guild," and was often applied to any sort of group or corporation recognized as part of the medieval system of urban guilds. The special name for a university was *studium generale* (general studies), which indicated that the purpose of this guild was intellectual training rather than training in a craft. But like other guilds, the university had its "masters" (teachers) and its "apprentices" (students).

The basic university program of study was the liberal arts curriculum, which usually took six years and led to a bachelor's degree. The seven liberal arts included the *trivium*, which consisted of grammar, rhetoric, and logic—all of which were treated in far more detail and depth in the Middle Ages than they are now. Grammar, for example, not only meant the study of the structure of language but also the art of interpreting literature. Upon completing the *trivium*, the student would move on to the *quadrivium*, which consisted of arithmetic, music, astronomy, and geometry. Music appears in the quadrivium because music theory included study of the mathematics of music. All instruction was in Latin, the language of the Church, which functioned as the "international language" of Europe.

Once a student had attained the bachelor's degree, he could pursue what we would call graduate education in theology, law, or medicine, culminating in a master's or a doctor's degree. (The Latin word *doctor* means "teacher.") The program of graduate study could take up to twelve additional years; typically a student of theology could not achieve the doctorate until he was thirty-five. The "masters" and "doctors" were those who were admitted to the guild of university teachers.

Virtually all students were men. Women were barred from university education because university students typically had to belong to one of the lower orders of clergy in order to be admitted. There is evidence that women were allowed to study medicine at the renowned university in Salerno, until they were banned along with Jews in the thirteenth century. In their early years the medieval universities did not have "campuses." Classes met wherever there was available space, such as churches and homes, although in time the universities would buy or rent rooms in which to conduct classes. The *universitas* was understood as a group of people who had incorporated, not as a place.

By the thirteenth century, close to fifty percent of the highest positions in the Church (abbots, bishops and archbishops) were held by men with graduate degrees, certified as masters. And of course some of the greatest philosophers and theologians of the High Middle Ages, such as Thomas Aquinas, were university masters and doctors.

SCHOLASTICISM
The intellectual approach to knowledge or method of inquiry that came to dominate the schools and then the universities is called *scholasticism*. The word comes from the Greek and Latin words for "school," as do "scholar" and "scholarship," and the scholastics were called the "schoolmen." Scholasticism flourished in European thought from 1000 to 1600, although it reached its peak in the thirteenth century. In its broadest sense, scholasticism was the application of reason to revelation: the effort to think clearly and systematically about the

teachings of Christianity believed to have been revealed to humanity by God, as found in the Bible and interpreted by Church doctrine. The scholastic method was governed by the assumptions of faith, and faith in turn was supported by rational arguments. This presumed unity or harmony between faith and reason was essential to scholasticism, and it reached its most comprehensive expression in the thought of Thomas Aquinas in the thirteenth century. When that harmony came to be seriously called into question, either from the side of faith (as in late medieval thought and the Protestant Reformation) or from the side of reason (as in the Scientific Revolution of the seventeenth century), scholasticism declined.

In this broad sense, scholasticism characterized medieval thinking from as early as Augustine in the fifth century, a thinker who was probably the single greatest influence on medieval Christian thought. But in the eleventh century scholasticism began to develop the approach to reasoning with which it became distinctively identified: what the scholastics called *dialectic*. Dialectic has meant a variety of things in the history of Western philosophy, beginning with Socrates' approach to truth by discussion of ideas. For the scholastics dialectic was a method of investigation and discussion that used the rules of logical reasoning that went back to Aristotle, whose books on logic were the only of his writings available to medieval Europeans until the twelfth century.

Scholastic dialectic replaced the older monastic emphasis on reading and meditating on the Bible and the Church Fathers with formal methods of critical investigation, discussion, and debate. Scholars and students would carefully study an authoritative theological text, which might be from the Bible or the Church Fathers (above all Augustine). Following this reading, they would read commentaries on the primary text, such as the decisions of ecumenical Church councils, papal letters, and other theological interpretations. Questions would be posed and apparent contradictions noted. Arguments pro and con were presented and then an attempt made to resolve the question or questions posed. This method of discussion became standard in the university classroom, in public scholarly debate, and in philosophical and theological writings.

NOMINALISTS AND REALISTS

One of the issues that the scholastics debated intensely was the problem of *universals.* Universals are general concepts, such as "humans," "justice," "goodness," and "number." Think back to your readings on Plato and Aristotle and their thinking on universals. Plato argued that universals, or Forms as he called them, have independent existence. They are the most "real" realities, existing eternally and without change. The particular things that make up the physical universe are what they are only by "participating" imperfectly in or being shadow-representations of the Forms. Aristotle believed in the reality of universals or Forms, but unlike Plato he argued that they do not exist separately apart from the particular things that embody them. Both Plato and Aristotle were realists: that is, they argued for the real existence of universals. The opposing position that arose in the Middle Ages was that of the *nominalists,* who denied the existence of universals, saying that what is real only is the individual thing itself. What we call "universals" are nothing but names (*nomina*).

Universals became a matter for inquiry through the books that provided the basis for dialectic: besides Aristotle's books on logic, the commentaries on Aristotle's logic by the second-century Neoplatonic philosopher Porphyry and the sixth-century philosopher Boethius. In his *Isagoge,* commenting on Aristotle, Porphyry raised the question whether those general concepts called universals, on which all human knowledge depends, exist separately from objects or in them. Boethius contributed another question in his commentary on Aristotle, where he asks whether universals are things in their own right or simply names. These issues, as filtered through Porphyry and Boethius, became popular as a problem in scholastic dialectic.

The early realists in the scholastic debates were influenced by Platonic thought. They argued that universals reflect common natures in creatures and ideas in the mind of God. Their earliest opponents claimed that things can exist only individually, not universally; universals were only words. This issue definitely had theological consequences. Critics of the Platonic realists argued that if universals are the realities of which particulars are only shadowy representations, then God does not know and love human beings as individuals but

only as "humanity." Critics of the extreme nominalists argued that if universal concepts are only names, then a deep skepticism pervades human knowledge that extends to the knowledge of God. One of the greatest of the early scholastics, Peter Abelard (1079–1147), at the University of Paris, contributed what he considered a mediating position to the debate by arguing that concepts are essential for making sense out of things and important for grasping the organization of ideas, but he still argued that the real exists only in individual things.

ANSELM AND THE ONTOLOGICAL ARGUMENT

Although scholasticism became associated with universities, it was perhaps first successfully practiced by Anselm (ca. 1033–1109), who at the end of his life became the Archbishop of Canterbury in England. Anselm himself was taught at the Benedictine abbey of Bec in Normandy by Lanfranc and later became the abbey's teacher and finally its abbot. Anselm, who was deeply influenced by Augustine and a realist, believed that the universe reveals God's truths. That being the case, he argued, reasoned argument can contribute to faith without resorting to the authoritative writings of the Church for proof, which was the traditional method of argumentation. His former teacher Lanfranc suggested that he follow traditional modes of argumentation by simply appealing to authoritative authors, but Anselm replied that all he wrote could be supported by authorities, and his writings were briefer this way. Thus his phrase *Fides quaerens intellectum* ("faith seeking understanding") emphasized the ability to arrive at truth through reasonable conclusions.

Using this method, Anselm developed an argument for the existence of God called the *ontological argument.* He began with a brief definition of God that would encapsulate all the characteristics or predicates ascribed to God as supreme and supremely perfect reality; that is, a definition with which he thought everyone could agree. God, Anselm said, is a being "than which nothing greater [i.e., more perfect] can be conceived." Everyone grants that we can conceive of such a being as an idea in our minds—even the "fool" in the ancient psalm who "says in his heart, 'There is no God.'"

But that of course still leaves open the question whether such a being also exists outside our minds, in reality. Anselm then proceeded to argue that to exist in reality as well as in the mind is greater or more perfect than to exist only as an idea in the mind, because to possess more real being is to be more perfect. (Horses, for example, are more perfect than unicorns, which are only fictional creatures.) If that is the case, then if I agree that God is that than which nothing more perfect can be conceived but deny that God exists in reality, I have contradicted myself. Therefore the perfect being exists in reality as well as in the mind, and we know this simply by carefully thinking through what the very idea of God entails. The ontological argument was later rejected by Thomas Aquinas, but six centuries after Anselm, René Descartes, the "father of modern philosophy," revived it, as he reports in his *Discourse on Method* and *Meditations on First Philosophy.*

THE MUSLIM AND JEWISH LEGACY

Beginning in the twelfth century the dialectical tools of scholastic thought were greatly expanded by the introduction into Europe, through Muslim and Jewish translators and philosophers, of the rest of Aristotle's surviving books, which covered just about the whole range of human knowledge. With the rapid influx of Aristotle's works, together with commentaries on them and original works by leading Muslim and Jewish philosophers, reason as a way of understanding reality threatened to become no longer a servant of faith and revelation but a rival. Christian Scholastics like Thomas Aquinas read and were influenced by the great Muslim philosophers such as Avicenna and Averroes and by the preeminent Jewish philosopher Moses Maimonides (1135–1204), who wrestled with the relationship between revelation and reason in the context of different religious traditions using Aristotelian ideas and offered new insights into major theological issues such as reconciling divine omnipotence and human freedom. Maimonides, who grew up in Muslim Spain and later became physician in the court of Saladin in Egypt, was the greatest Jewish scholar of the Middle Ages—mathematician, astronomer, philosopher, author of a commentary on the Mishnah and codifier of Jewish law. Influenced by Aristotle and Neoplatonism, al-Farabi and Avicenna, Maimonides' *Guide of the Perplexed* is one of the great writings of the Middle Ages dedicated to harmonizing theology and philosophy. He believed that philosophy, properly understood, supports rather than destroys faith, and adopted arguments for the existence of God and the nature of the soul from the Muslim philosophers. However, in the final analysis philosophy must be subordinate to theology, and where philosophical demonstration is not possible or inconclusive, we must rely solely on divine revelation as contained in the Hebrew Bible.

By contrast, the last and perhaps the most influential of the Muslim philosophers, Ibn Rushd or Averroes (1126–1198), boldly reasoned that at the top level of knowledge there was philosophy, followed by theology, religion, and faith. Faith made knowledge accessible to lower intellects, while the supremely rational mind dwelled in philosophy. This conclusion was unacceptable both to Islamic and to Christian thought, for which theology was considered to be higher than philosophy and faith as essential to human knowledge. Averroes' influence was considerable in Europe, and there were "Averroists" at the University of Paris who, on the basis of Aristotle and Averroes, were asserting religiously heretical opinions in the name of reason. That was the challenge Thomas Aquinas accepted.

THOMAS AQUINAS

Thomas Aquinas (1225–1274) is almost certainly the most influential of the medieval scholastics, and one of the important figures in the history of both philosophy and theology. Since the late nineteenth century he has been the "official" philosopher of the Roman Catholic Church, and his influence had been considerable for centuries before that. The approaches to philosophy and theology that look to Thomas's methods and ideas as their model are called *Thomism.* His achievement is to have harmonized and synthesized Aristotelian philosophy and Christian theology into what has seemed to many the highest realization of the scholastic belief in the unity between revelation and reason. Although by now the comparison has become a kind of cliché, Aquinas' masterful unification of what he believed was the best in secular and sacred knowledge under the aegis of the latter has often been likened to the remarkable architecture of the Gothic cathedrals, which also attained their finest expression in the

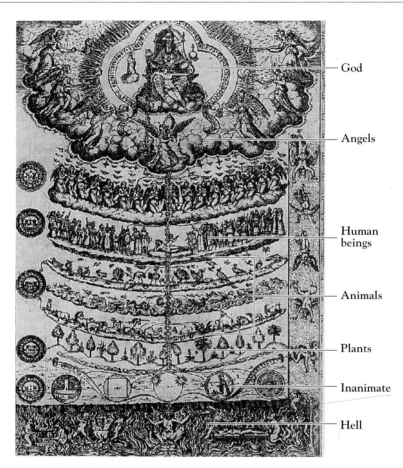

God

Angels

Human beings

Animals

Plants

Inanimate

Hell

In the medieval Christian worldview, all of reality was a hierarchy called the "great chain of being," with God at the top and created beings arranged in descending order: angels, human beings (represented here only by males), the various orders of air, sea and land animals, and plants. Below the hierarchy is hell—that part of reality that lies completely outside the realm of God's creative love. Thomas Aquinas's thought is thoroughly hierarchical, categorizing things in terms of "natural" superiority and inferiority. This portrayal of the "great chain of being" dates from 1579. Thinking of the universe in this way persisted until the nineteenth century, although it was progressively undermined by scientific development.

Figure V-2 The Great Chain of Being. 1579. From *Rhetorica Christiana* by Didacus Valades.

thirteenth century: a soaring symmetry made up of opposing forces in perfect equilibrium.

Born into a noble family, Aquinas was the youngest of the nine children of Landolfo d'Aquino (Lord of Roccasecca and Montesangiovanni and an official for the Holy Roman Emperor, Federick II) and his second wife Teodora of Chieti. At the age of five or six Thomas was presented to the old Benedictine abbey of Monte Cassino in hopes that he

might eventually become an abbot. However, he was strongly drawn to the Dominicans, a new order of mendicant or begging friars, whom he joined at the age of sixteen despite intense opposition from his parents, who could not bear the thought of his belonging to a begging order.

Aquinas eventually won the struggle and began studying as a Dominican at the University of Paris in 1245 under Albertus Magnus, whom he later followed to Cologne. He became Albert's junior bachelor teaching assistant in 1250–1252 and lectured briefly to students. Since he himself was such an outstanding student, Aquinas was allowed to become a full master of theology after studying again in Paris in the spring of 1256, even though he was under the required age of 35, and against some opposition from those who opposed the mendicants. From 1256 to 1259 Aquinas lectured on the Bible, held scholastic disputations, preached, and wrote. From 1259 to 1268, he was working in his own region of Italy. But Aquinas was ordered to return to Paris to defuse the anti-mendicant sentiment there, which he did. In 1272 he again returned to Italy, this time to his home priory in Naples. On December 6, 1273, Aquinas suffered a breakdown that culminated in his death en route to the Second Council of Lyons on March 7, 1274. He was canon-

ized as a saint on July 18, 1323, and declared a doctor or learned master of the church in 1567.

In the context of the nominalist-realist debate, Aquinas was a realist after the manner of Aristotle, arguing for the existence of common natures and ideas as universals. For example, in commenting on what happens when an object is perceived, Aquinas reasoned that the object impresses actual likenesses (*phantasmata*) onto the sense organs, which in turn abstract universal forms from these likenesses that are relayed further to the reasoning faculty.

Central to all Aquinas's writings and his method of inquiry was the relationship between faith and reason. He argued that to study the liberal arts and theology deeply, it was important to have mastered Aristotelian philosophy and logical method. The seeker of knowledge should push the

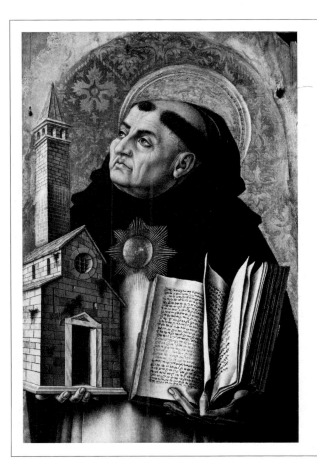

Crivelli painted thirteen panels in 1476 as the high altarpiece for San Domenico in Ascoli Piceno, east central Italy. The Madonna and Child occupied central placement and were surrounded by images of saints. Here, Saint Thomas Aquinas is shown with a book and a model of the church. The entire grouping, or polyptych, has been known as The Demidoff Altarpiece since it resided in the collection of Prince Anatole de Demidoff in the nineteenth-century.

Figure V-3 Carlo Crivelli, *St. Thomas Aquinas,* panel from *The Demidoff Altarpiece.* 1476. Egg tempera on wood panel. National Gallery Collection, London. Courtesy of National Gallery Collection; by kind permission of the Trustees of the National Gallery, Lond/Corbis.

capacities of reason as far as possible, not prematurely relying on faith and religious authority as a substitute for rational inquiry. At the same time, the knowledge we have of reality and ourselves through our senses and reasoning power is incomplete and insufficient. Through the divine gift of faith we give our willing assent to truths communicated to us directly by God: truths about the ultimate meaning and purpose of things and about who we are and what we should do which are essential for the true fulfillment of our destiny as humans. Aquinas, like his scholastic predecessors, believed that all truth is from God, who is Truth itself, and therefore all truth is one. The truth God gives us in revelation goes beyond but cannot contradict the truth we know through reason rightly applied. Using philosophical methods developed by Aristotle, Aquinas confidently worked out a theological and philosophical system in which he tried to harmonize knowledge.

Aquinas rejected Anselm's ontological argument. He argued that although it is indeed God's very nature to exist, it is not something we can establish simply by correctly understanding the idea of God. We can only demonstrate God's existence indirectly, arguing from features of the world we all experience. The first three of Aquinas' five proofs or "Five Ways" are forms of what is called the *cosmological argument* for God's existence, since they argue from aspects of nature or the cosmos to God. Building on things we all experience such as cause and effect, change, and the dependence of one thing on another for its existence, Aquinas tried to show that the universe is not self-explanatory and is therefore either ultimately unintelligible or dependent upon something other than itself—namely, God. These proofs of the divine existence are purely philosophical. Aquinas believed that anyone capable of understanding the argument—whether Christian, Jew, Muslim, pagan, or agnostic—would come to the same conclusion. But Aquinas the theologian went on to say that what we can know of God through philosophical reasoning alone (God's existence and some of his attributes) is a long way from all that we know of God through his own revelation, as for example his trinitarian nature and his love for us. The five proofs appear in Aquinas' most comprehensive book, the *Summa Theologiae*, a massive work that fills three volumes.

A DISCUSSION OF SOME OF THE WRITINGS OF THOMAS AQUINAS

Thomas's essay, *On Kingship,* is an important and influential medieval treatise on politics and is representative of the general approach taken to the study of government in the Middle Ages. The essay reflects Aristotle's strong influence on Thomas. But, unlike Aristotle, he argues that monarchy or kingship is the best of the three types of government. He invokes analogies in nature and in God to political rule by one ruler. Like other medieval thinkers who wrote about politics, Thomas characterized kingship as an elective office and the king's powers as limited. This is in contrast to the "new" view of the character and task of the ruler in Machiavelli's *The Prince,* as we will see later.

Aquinas's largest work, the *Summa Theologiae* or "Summary of Theology," is a scholastic treatise with a formal structure derived from the scholastic debate structure: a question (*quaestio*) is posed, followed by a series of objections, a statement of—and argument for—the author's answer to the question, and finally a reply to each objection. In this format Aquinas asks and answers the question "Does God Exist" (*Summa*, Part I, Qu. 2). Other subjects of Thomas's scrutiny are God's love, our knowledge of God, the nature of the soul, and how humans acquire knowledge. On the question of the creation of woman, Aquinas accepts and simply repeats Aristotle's biology of reproduction and arguments for female inferiority, adding to them further arguments for the subordination of women taken from the Bible. Look carefully at these arguments, because the belief in the inherent or "natural" inferiority of women—both in body and in mind—has been a dominant theme in Western religion, philosophy, institutions, laws, and mores. Many of our authors in Western Civilization have expressed this belief in a variety of ways well into the twentieth century.

Part II of the *Summa Theologiae* includes discussion of the attainment of happiness in this life which both builds on and goes beyond Aristotle. Thomas adds the three "theological virtues"—faith, hope, and charity—to the four "classical" or "Greek" virtues—justice, prudence, temperance, and courage. These virtues from Plato, Aristotle, and the Stoics were endorsed and passed on in the Middle Ages, with the argument that the theological virtues are made possible only by divine grace. Part II continues with a brief discussion of original sin.

Four Types of Law According to Thomas Aquinas

The very influential portion of the *Summa Theologiae* called the "treatise on law" defines law as "an ordinance of reason for the common good, made by him who has care of the community, and promulgated." Thomas then classifies law under four types.

1. *Eternal law* is the plan of everything in the mind of God, by which he governs the universe. This includes both the laws of nature in our sense of the term, such as gravity, and also the moral laws that are to govern human life.

2. *Natural law* is what human beings can know of the eternal moral law through their God-given reason. Natural law here refers to universal moral laws that everyone can know, not to laws of nature such as science discovers and explains. In other words, all human beings know basic principles of right and wrong simply by being "rational animals" living in the world. Here Aquinas draws on an old tradition in moral philosophy that has its roots in Plato and Aristotle, but was given its influential form by the Stoic philosophers, and through Aquinas and other medieval thinkers became important in the Western world as a way of thinking about ethics and politics. In the seventeenth and eighteenth centuries, for example, influential political philosophers such as John Locke and Jean-Jacques Rousseau argued for the "natural rights" of human beings—rights people have independently of governments and their laws. This way of thinking is embodied in the U.S. Declaration of Independence in the statement that "We hold these truths to be self-evident: that all men are created equal."

3. *Human law.* These are all the actual laws by which different human societies live. Human laws are expressions, albeit imperfect ones, of the natural law. Accordingly, although there are many differences among different societies, as anthropologists point out, there are also many similarities, and the differences reflect both our limited grasp of natural law and matters of custom rather than morality proper. So, for example, every society believes that murder is wrong and has laws regulating sexual conduct, although societies may differ in the ways they understand and apply those laws.

4. *Divine law.* But as we have seen, it is essential to Aquinas' whole outlook that unaided human reason is not enough. As another expression of the eternal law, God has given us divine law, the moral rules contained in the Bible and therefore directly from God. In part, divine law restates and clarifies natural law, as in some of the Ten Commandments. But divine law also gives us moral rules for leading us to our ultimate goal of union with God that we could not know through our own efforts and knowledge of natural law: as for example that we must love even our enemies.

The readings in Part II of the *Summa* include a miscellany of topics. The discussions of "unbelievers" (non-Christians) are important because they exemplify standard medieval attitudes on these issues. For medieval Christians like Aquinas, the religious unity of Europe was viewed as essential. Jews and other non-Christians, people of heretical or incorrect beliefs, and apostates (people who had renounced the church)—all were problems to a society that defined itself as Christian, and church and state responded with measures varying from second-class citizenship to inquisitions, expulsions, and wars. The remaining selections are on various moral issues: war, sedition, justice, murder, suicide, theft, private property, fraud usury (charging interest), political obedience, lying drunkenness, virginity, and "lecher" (including fornication, adultery, masturbation, bestiality, and homosexuality). In each case Aquinas uses two kinds of arguments: (1) arguments from natural law, known to everyone through reason, and (2) arguments from the Bible and church doctrine, known by acceptance through faith of divine revelation. Of particular interest to us looking at these thirteenth-century discussions from the beginning of the twenty-first century are such important continuing issues as war (Aquinas, building on Augustine, is one of the great exponents of what is called the "just war" theory) and sexuality, an area in which many of our moral views have changed but in which the thinking of many (for example, on homosexuality) still reflects ideas of the sort expressed by Thomas Aquinas.

NEW MONASTIC ORDERS

In Thomas Aquinas two revolutions of thirteenth-century Europe found expression: spiritual renewal as embodied in the Franciscan and Dominican orders, and the appearance of new texts of Aristotle that were turning the universities upside down. Aquinas' achievement was to combine a deep and intense Christian spirituality with rigorous philosophical and theological reasoning. As a devout Dominican monk Aquinas wrote hymns that are still sung and liturgies that are still used, and at the end of his life he had a vision that caused him to regard everything he had written as "straw." Since he effected a harmonious synthesis of Christian theology with the secular knowledge, Aquinas was controversial in his own day and for some time afterwards. Nevertheless, eventually he became for Catholic Christianity the model of how to think in both a Christian and rational manner about the nature of reality. In 1278 his fellow Dominicans began to ensure that his writings would be treated with proper respect, actions that allowed Aquinas to make a lasting impact on Western thought.

Although scholastics dominated the academic picture in the late Middle Ages, there were other scholars who furthered different and also important schools of thought. For example, in the twelfth century the school of Chartres in France emphasized Platonic readings of nature, its unity, and its laws. The great scholar Bernard of Chartres taught there from 1114 to 1124, and Chartrian thought was expounded by those who had not studied there, such as the scholar and poet Alan of Lille (1115–1203). Its impact was also to be felt, as twentieth-century literary scholar Winthrop Wetherbee reveals, in courtly literature.

Another medieval direction in theology was mysticism, which scholars such as Bernard of Clairvaux (1091–1153), Hugh of St. Victor (1097–1226), and Johannes Eckhart (1260–1327) wrote upon, emphasizing the role of faith in theology and the mystical union of God and humanity. Typical of Christian mysticism was characterizing God through what he is not, a method which was called the *via negativa* (the negative way). As a theological school, mysticism did not belong solely to the Christians; Jewish biblical commentary, as represented by *Kabbalah*, could also be called mystical. Finally, mysticism was not only written about, it was also actively put into practice. For example, Francis of Assisi (1182–1225) founded the Franciscan order on mystical principles, and mystical movements emerged that often included women who wrote passionately of Christ as their spiritual lover, such as did Catherine of Siena (1347–1380).

Although matters of theology dominated the intellectual scene at the time, attention was also paid to natural science, which involved the study of astrology, alchemy, and magic. In contrast, the philosophers Roger Bacon (1212–1294) and Robert Grosseteste (ca. 1175–1253) contributed to modern science through their insistence on quantitative measurements. But generally less empirical methods dominated. Thus, the practice and study of medicine were based on principles that we would not associate with scientific analysis. Medieval scholars considered the individual to be a "microcosm" or "little universe" that mirrored the entire universe or "macrocosm." Both the human being and the universe were composed of four elements: earth, water, fire, and air. When these four elements were held in balance, either in the individual or the universe, then microcosm or macrocosm was in a state of good health. Medical practice attempted to cure ills mainly by re-establishing the balance of these four elements.

QUESTIONS FOR STUDY AND DISCUSSION

1. How did the European universities originate, and where were some of the first universities located How was the curriculum organized?

2. What is scholasticism? Explain the scholastic method.

3. Who was Anselm and why is he remembered?

4. What are Aquinas' arguments that kingship is the best form of government? In what ways is his essay *On Kingship* based on the philosophy of Aristotle? What does Aquinas say are the duties and purposes of a ruler? Why does a ruler have to be virtuous in order to be a good ruler? Do you think these standards are appropriate for leaders of nations today? Why or why not?

5. What are Aquinas's "five Ways" or five proofs for God's existence? What is the basic assumption running through all of them?

6. What is the relationship between faith and reason, according to Aquinas? What is the basis of their harmony?

7. What is Aquinas's analysis of the nature and status of women, and on what does he base it? Does the actual situation of women in the Middle Ages reflect this view—whether wholly or partly? Be specific in you answer. Do you see continuing vestiges of Aquinas's views in the modern world?

8. How does Aquinas define law? What are the four types of law, and what are the relationships among them?

9. What are the conditions under which Thomas argues that a war may be morally just?

SUGGESTIONS FOR FURTHER READING

Copleston, F. C. *Aquinas*. Harmondsworth, England: Penguin Books, 1965.

Gilson, Etienne. *The Christian Philosophy of St. Thomas Aquinas*. Translated by L. K. Shook. New York: Random House, 1956.

Kreeft, Peter. *A Summa of the Summa: The Essential Philosophical Passages of St. Thomas Aquinas'* Summa Theologica. (Edited and Explained for Beginners). San Francisco: Ignatius Press, 1990.

Leff, Gordon. *Medieval Thought: From Saint Augustine to Ockham*. Harmondsworth, England: Penguin Books, 1958.

McInerny, Ralph. *St. Thomas Aquinas*. Notre Dame: Notre Dame University Press, 1982.

Pieper, Josef. *St. Thomas Aquinas*. Translated by D. MacLaren. New York: Sheed & Ward, 1948.

CHAPTER ELEVEN

MEDIEVAL NARRATIVE ART: GEOFFREY CHAUCER

Medieval artists, authors, and artisans probably had two characteristics in common: a more immediate sense of who their audience was than their modern counterparts, and the assumption that the immediate present belonged within a larger historical context. The artists and artisans involved in the building of the cathedrals lived with or near the townspeople for whom they were creating their art. People who hand-copied manuscripts (the way publishing was done) made them for scholars living in monasteries as well as for those who came to the *scriptoria* to buy or borrow books. Authors wrote their works for audiences to whom they might well present them face-to-face. Since books were very expensive and only a small percentage of people were literate, written works were usually read aloud to a group of listeners, who might interrupt the story with comments.

In their painting, stained glass, sculpture, music, and literature, however, medieval artists saw things in terms of the "big picture." They typically placed the present within the wider historical—indeed, cosmic—context provided by the Bible, with its narratives covering everything from the creation of the universe and human beings to the coming of Christ to the future end of the world and coming of the kingdom of God. That biblical "grand narrative" was of course interpreted for the peoples of Europe by the Roman Catholic Church in its teachings, and all medieval artists assumed and worked within this Christian religious worldview. This manifested itself in a variety of ways in the main forms of medieval narrative art (literature): drama, chronicles, epic poems, and courtly literature.

1. In the late Middle Ages *drama* was supported by the Church and by secular organizations including craft guilds in England, fraternities in France, and municipal authorities in Germany. Originally, drama seems to have become a part of medieval life around the tenth century, when parts of the liturgical service were dramatized in churches. Classical Roman drama by Seneca and other writers was known to medieval scholars, but not understood as plays meant to be performed. By the time drama was supported by secular sources, it was no longer performed in Latin, and it was produced outside the churches in the market squares or on the village greens. Although most of what survives from this period is religious in orientation, sometimes its spiritual orientation is worldly in expression. For example, the fifteenth-century Middle English *Second Shepherds' Play* tells the story of the birth of Christ, while vividly depicting the harsh lot of peasants, complete with what we presume were lower-class speech patterns.

In the thirteenth century religious plays called mysteries, miracles, and moralities emerged. Sometimes a number of plays evolved into cycles that treated large spans of biblical history. The Corpus Christi (Body of Christ) plays may have grown out of church controversy over how to interpret the bodily presence of Christ in the eucharistic bread and wine. The Fourth Lateran Council in 1215 resolved the issue by defining the doctrine of *transubstantiation:* when consecrated by a priest, the substance of the bread and wine actually becomes the body and blood of Christ. Probably to popularize this decree, the Feast of Corpus Christi was first instituted in 1264 and formally adopted in

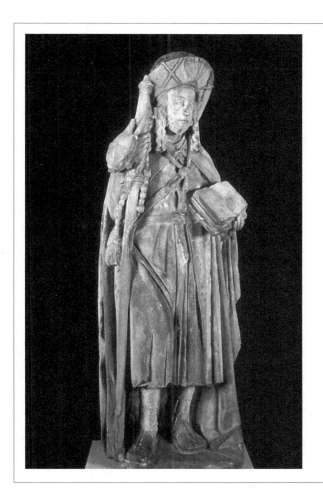

St. James is often depicted in art as a pilgrim. According to legend, the apostle James traveled on a mission to Spain and was later buried there following his execution by Herod Agrippa in Jerusalem. Santiago (Spanish, meaning St. James) de Compostela, the supposed site of James' burial, became a great center of Christian pilgrimage. In this sculpture, James bears all the attributes of a pilgrim: a broad-brimmed hat and cloak, a walking stick, a water gourd, and a shell. The scallop shell on his hat is the symbol of Santiago de Compostela and St. James, and can represent pilgrimage in general.

Figure V-4 St. James the Elder as a Pilgrim. Unknown artist, French or Netherlandish. Late-fifteen century. Limestone, height 40½". Courtesy of the Spencer Museum at University of Kansas.

1311, and the Corpus Christi plays formed part of that celebration.

2. In medieval *chronicles* that became popular in the twelfth century, events of human history were presented through religious lenses that made them highly predictable. They often began with the story of creation as recorded in Genesis and proceeded to condense biblical history. They then focused on actual medieval kingdoms and many times ended with some reference to the apocalyptic prophecies of the last book of the Bible, Revelation. Although there was clear interest in actual medieval kingdoms in these histories, the sense that all was proceeding as it should and would culminate as prophesied, dominates. There appeared to be little sense of openness about the future.

3. *Epic poems*, called in French *chansons de geste* or "songs of [great] deeds," were very popular in the high and late Middle Ages, between about 1100–1400. Written to be performed, they were recited to the accompaniment of music at social gatherings and celebrations. The *chansons de geste* extolled the heroic deeds of Christian kings and knights battling various forces of evil in defense of Christianity, feudal society, chivalric honor, and noble ladies.

The greatest of the French epic poems, and the first great narrative poem in the French language, is *The Song of Roland (La Chanson de Roland)*. Roland stands in the tradition of epic heroes such as Achilles, Odysseus, and Aeneas, embodying an ideal of humanity in its medieval European-Christian form. The poem was probably written at the end of the eleventh century or very early in the twelfth century, following the First Crusade (1095–99). The First Crusade had culminated in a great victory for the invading Christian forces against the Muslims in Palestine and Syria, including the conquest of Jerusalem. The author takes a historical incident and transforms it into a stirring tale of Christian knights who, despite treachery by one of their own and slaughter by Muslim forces, are ultimately avenged and triumph.

The historical incident was the ambush and slaughter of the rearguard of King Charlemagne's Frankish army by Basque forces in the Roncesvalles Pass of the Pyrenees Mountains in 778 during his military campaign in Spain. Roland, "Lord of the Breton Marches," was killed in the ambush. Charlemagne was unable to avenge the defeat, because the Basque warriors dispersed into the general population. The disaster at Roncesvalles caused him to rethink his Spanish strategy defensively, taking and holding a few key areas as buffers between his empire and the Muslim kingdoms of Spain that flourished in the south.

The author of *The Song of Roland* transformed the historical event considerably. By the beginning of the twelfth century Charlemagne was a medieval legend: the great Christian king who had first unified European Christendom into a Christian version of the Roman Empire that would become the Holy Roman Empire. In the epic the Basques have become Muslims, whom the poet calls Saracens or pagans and to whom he attributes very un-Muslim beliefs such as polytheism and the worship of Muhammad. Roland has become one of the chief nobles of the Frankish empire and nephew to Charlemagne, a brave and even impetuous warrior. His forces are outnumbered five to one, but he refuses to call for reinforcements, and after valiant fighting they are killed to the last man. Roland dies finally blowing his horn to call back the main force and bursting his temples with the effort. The battles are grand and spectacular, and include divine intervention. Charlemagne gets his revenge, defeating the Saracens and taking the city of Saragossa, where they destroy Jewish and Muslim religious places and objects and force the conversion to Christianity of everyone in the city except Queen Bramimonde, who voluntarily converts. Thus has the story of Charlemagne's defeat at Roncesvalles

become a great medieval epic of the triumph of Christianity, which is "right," against Islam, which is "wrong," and a call to Christian knights to defeat and destroy "paganism" wherever it threatens.

4. Medieval epics belong to the wider category of *courtly literature*. The sense of set-in-the-world predictability takes a different form. Medieval drama's messages and biblical framework were simple and accessible to both the literate and the illiterate. Courtly literature, by contrast, was more secular and intended for a literate audience. Those who could read and write belonged to the clergy, the royal court, the nobility, and the emerging educated middle class (people like Chaucer himself)—the "upper orders" of medieval society. As we might expect, the messages in courtly literature are correspondingly subtler and more sophisticated. Even the courtly writers' use of popular stories (like folk tales, beast fables, and the bawdy stories known as *fabliaux*) was complex once they became part of their literary works. We can see this in the twelfth-century Old French *Romance of Reynard* (a beast epic) and some of the tales found in the fourteenth-century *Decameron* by Giovanni Boccaccio and Geoffrey Chaucer's *Canterbury Tales*, to be discussed in detail below. Further, the polished language and settings of courtly literature often underscored a text's subtlety and multiple meanings.

One of the most refined forms of courtly literature was the *romance*, which, in effect, was a novel that was very frequently written in verse. Two of the most famous characters of courtly romances belong to two probably imaginary English courts: the court of King Arthur and the court of King Mark. Both courts are found in Celtic literature, and may be Celtic in origin. Originally, the Celts were Gallic tribes who between 1200 BCE and 500 CE dominated most of western Europe. By the late Middle Ages their influence in western Europe was most strongly felt in France, Britain, and Ireland. Celtic literature includes the Irish sagas of Cuchulain and Conchubar in the eighth through the tenth centuries, the Welsh *Mabinogion* of the eleventh century, and some tales of King Arthur's Camelot. One of the most popular was *Tristan and Isolde,* which is known today largely through the nineteenth-century German composer Richard Wagner's opera of the same name. It is the story of Isolde, given as a bride to King Mark to bring peace between two warring kingdoms. However, she falls in love with Tristan, the king's nephew, and the lovers come to a tragic end. These Celtic tales, along with tales derived from ancient Greek and Roman stories, often became the material for medieval romances.

Another important form of secular literature is the courtly *lyric*. Courtly lyrics, short love poems usually addressed to some idealized lady, were sung by troubadours of Provence in southern France and their counterparts in northern France *(trouvères)* and Germany *(Minnesänger)*. Some were written by women *(trobarite)* as well. In Italy, this form of lyric poetry was framed in philosophical material taken from the great debates of the scholastics and formed the new approach to poetry called the *dolce stil nuovo,* the "sweet new style."

Dante Alighieri (1265–1321). No presentation of medieval narrative art would be complete without consideration of Dante Alighieri, universally acknowledged as one of the supreme writers of the Western world. Dante, an Italian of the latter thirteenth and the early fourteenth centuries, creatively synthesized philosophical and theological learning and mystical vision in the long poem that is his masterpiece of the imagination, the *Divine Comedy.* So rapidly did it establish itself in European literature that by 1400 twelve commentaries on it had appeared. Geoffrey Chaucer read Dante and mentioned him in his *Canterbury Tales,* and his influence on Western literature and imagery has continued down to the present day.

Dante was born in Florence to a family that belonged to the minor nobility but lived in modest economic circumstances. He may have been educated at the monastery schools at the churches of Santa Croce and Santa Maria Novella, run respectively by the new Franciscan and Dominican religious orders, where he would have begun to learn Scholastic philosophy and theology and also the Catholic mystical tradition. Dante was profoundly influenced by Thomas Aquinas, and through him Aristotle. He diligently studied the classical Roman poets, above all the epic poet Virgil, who became an important influence on his poetry. Early in his career Dante began writing poems in the vernacular language of his native Tuscany, rather than in Latin, Europe's common language of religion and learning, and in so doing shaped the future development of the Italian language. Other writers of the

high and late medieval period were likewise innovators of and influences on vernacular literature in other languages, notably including the author of *The Song of Roland* (French) and Geoffrey Chaucer (English).

According to his own account, as a boy of nine Dante saw a girl of about the same age, Bice Portinari, whose grace and beauty awakened in him a lifelong emotional attachment and dedication to love, divine and human, as the key to the meaning of things. He later called her "Beatrice," which means "the bringer of blessings." They encountered each other only a few more times. Each married someone else, and Beatrice was dead by the age of twenty-five. Dante himself entered into an arranged marriage, shortly after his father's death in 1283, to a noblewoman named Gemma Donati. They had several children, of whom two sons and a daughter can be identified.

Yet Dante remained faithful to the memory of Beatrice, transfiguring her and his love for her into Christian-Platonic ideals of divine beauty and love, and devoting his poetry to immortalizing her. She becomes an embodiment of divine love and beauty, and in the *Divine Comedy* Dante's guide at the summit of the mountain of purgatory and into paradise, the ultimate goal of human longing, a realm flooded with the light and love of God.

Although a voracious reader of philosophy and literature and a very active writer, Dante was also passionate about political issues both local and international, and thoroughly involved in the turbulent and sometimes dangerous Florentine politics of his day. In 1289 he fought as a cavalryman for Florence at the Battle of Campaldino. In 1295 he became a member of the guild of physicians and pharmacists of Florence, which allowed him to hold political office. Dante did hold important elective and appointed offices, and in 1300 became one of the six "priors" of Florence, the supreme magistrates of the city, who served two-month terms. However, as was often the case, Florence was riven by factions, and in 1300 Dante was on the losing side in a bitter and violent dispute and was permanently exiled from the city-state, forbidden to return on pain of death.

Dante spent the rest of his life as a wanderer, living in various cities in the north of Italy. Meanwhile he was becoming famous as a writer, and things became less difficult as the years went by as he was welcomed and enjoyed patronage wherever he went—except in Florence, despite his repeated efforts over the years to have his banishment lifted. Dante, together with his children and perhaps also his wife Gemma, spent his last years in Ravenna. He died in Ravenna in 1321, where he is buried. In the centuries following his death his native city of Florence tried in many ways to make amends for exiling its most famous son. The visitor today can visit the heroic statue of him next to the Church of Santa Croce, walk down the Via Dante Alighieri, visit the "Dante House," and read verses from the *Divine Comedy* inscribed on walls throughout the city.

Both before and during his exile Dante read virtually all the learning and literature available to him in Latin or Latin translation—from Plato, Aristotle, Virgil, Cicero, and Ovid through Augustine, Boethius, and the Church Fathers to the Islamic philosopher Ibn Rushd (Averroës), the medieval mystics, and Thomas Aquinas, who died when Dante was a child.

Out of his political experiences and wide-ranging reading the exiled Dante also became absorbed in issues of political philosophy. Like Machiavelli two centuries later, Dante looked for guidance to history and especially to the Roman Empire. He denounced all the existing parties or factions, whether pro-pope or pro-emperor. Probably between 1310 and 1313 he wrote a treatise in Latin called *De Monarchia* ("Of Kingship"). In it he set forth his political theory, but he also presented a practical guide to restoring peace and unity in Europe. Dante rejected the Church's official teaching that made the popes supreme authority in temporal as well as spiritual matters, with the Holy Roman emperors subordinate to them. His alternative model was to see pope and emperor as two equal powers, one spiritual and one temporal, the authority of each coming directly from God. The Church, led by the pope, directs humanity to salvation by divine grace and revelation; the state, ruled by the emperor, directs humanity to temporal peace and happiness by philosophical wisdom and education. What is strikingly original in Dante's recommendations is that he envisions a Holy Roman Emperor, located in Rome, as ruler, not just of Europe, but of a "universal community of the human race." In a time when the only global unity

imagined was the religious unity of the Catholic Church under the pope, Dante's idea of a "world government" presided over by a universal temporal monarch was daring and flirted with heresy. Some years after his death representatives of the papacy sought out copies of the book for burning, and when the Church's *Index of Forbidden Books* was created in the sixteenth century, *De Monarchia* was one of the first to be put on it. Interestingly, some of Dante's ideas about the equality of temporal and spiritual power and his criticisms of the papacy anticipate those of Martin Luther.

Dante's life, his learning, and his passions all came together in a grand vision in the *Divine Comedy*. It is a strikingly "visual" epic poem; a literary synthesis of philosophy, theology, and mysticism; and a portrayal of the medieval Christian universe. Dante began work on it sometime around 1307 and completed it shortly before his death in 1321. He named it simply *Commedia*—"Comedy." The adjective *Divina*, "divine," was added in the sixteenth century as a reverential tribute to the by-then legendary author. Dante had published the first two parts several years before his death, and they were already well-known and enormously admired during his lifetime.

Dante divided the *Commedia* into three parts: *Inferno* (Hell), *Purgatorio* (Purgatory), and *Paradiso* (Heaven). The story is Dante's imagined journey through the three destinations of souls, representing every person in his or her quest for salvation. The poet Virgil, sent by Beatrice and representing reason or understanding, is Dante's guide through the nine circles of the damned in Hell and up to the summit of the Mount of Purgatory, where souls ultimately destined for Heaven undergo further punishment for their sins. For the final ascent to God and salvation Beatrice, representing divine revelation and grace, takes over and guides Dante to Heaven, where he is enfolded by the light and love of God and beholds the happiness of the saved.

One of the remarkable features of the *Divine Comedy* is that Dante draws on his considerable knowledge of Greek and Roman history and mythology, the history of Christianity, and the events of his own time and the recent past, to fill hell, purgatory, and heaven with an extraordinary number of people both real and legendary. Particularly striking is his boldness in deciding to locate some of his Italian contemporaries in hell or purgatory. Here we can see Dante's political experiences and partisan passions, as well as his moral and religious judgments, clearly at work. The human tapestry in the *Commedia* is a wonderfully rich weave of a "cast of thousands" and many references to historical and mythological events.

Why would Dante have called his great work a "comedy"? For most people today, "comedy" means a story that makes people laugh. But historically, comedy was considered the opposite of tragedy. Comedy might begin with serious troubles and even lack much humor; the defining characteristic was that the story had a happy ending. In tragedy, by contrast, the story might begin happily but it always ended unhappily. So despite the fact that the *Divine Comedy* begins with the unrelieved and often "fiendish" torments of the damned and the punishments of those in purgatory, it concludes with heaven, that state of eternal happiness which is God's goal for humanity.

GEOFFREY CHAUCER

The best-known English literary figure of the Middle Ages is Geoffrey Chaucer (ca. 1340–1400) author of *The Canterbury Tales.* We do not know exactly where and when Chaucer was born, but he was almost certainly born in the early 1340s. His father and grandfather were both prosperous wine merchants and held positions in the customs service. Thus Chaucer grew up as a member of the burgeoning late- medieval urban middle class.

Probably when he was in his early teens Chaucer served as a page in the Yorkshire estate of Elizabeth de Burgh, Countess of Ulster and wife of Prince Lionel. During the long reign of King Edward III, he was a soldier in the Hundred Years War between England and France, and was taken prisoner and ransomed. After his release Chaucer was back in service as a messenger carrying letters to and from England. Nothing is known about him for the years between 1360 and 1366. In 1367 Chaucer received a royal annuity and is first recorded as being a member of the royal household.

Probably in 1366, Chaucer's father died and he married Philippa Paon, connected by marriage to the royal family, who also received an annual salary for service to the queen. They probably had two sons, Thomas and Lewis, and two daughters, Elizabeth and Agnes. It is likely that Philippa Chaucer died in 1387.

Geoffrey Chaucer spent his own career in public service. After military service in France and diplomatic missions to Italy and elsewhere, in 1374 he was made Controller of Customs and Subsidy of Wools, Skins, and Hides for the port of London. Between 1376 and 1381 he was again on diplomatic missions for the government. In 1382 Chaucer was appointed Controller of Customs on wines and other merchandise, but he left the customs service completely in 1386. The same year he served briefly as a member of Parliament, but was defeated for re-election. In 1389 Chaucer was appointed to the important office of Clerk of the King's Works. For two years he was in charge of buildings and repairs in the Tower of London, Westminster Palace, eight other royal residences, and various parks and other buildings. He managed large numbers of workmen and large sums of money, and had to travel constantly.

During the last part of his life Chaucer retired from public life, although he continued to receive gifts and pensions from the royal court. At the end of 1399 he took a long lease on a house in the garden of Westminster Abbey, but he died on October 25, 1400, after living in it for less than a year.

Somehow in the course of this busy life Chaucer managed to write not only *The Canterbury Tales* but also a number of other poems. Noteworthy among them are *Troilus and Criseyde* (Chaucer's version of medieval Europe's favorite subject, the Trojan War), *The Book of the Duchess, The Parliament of Fowls,* and *The Legend of Good Women.* Chaucer also wrote an English translation of one of the most discussed French verse narratives of the Middle Ages, *The Romance of the Rose.*

Chaucer's writing displays an extraordinary mastery of verse forms, an impressive knowledge of important literary works, and a deep and abiding interest in revealing people in various settings and stations of life. He also looked behind stereotypes and let us imagine what characters thought. This is particularly interesting, because often enough he portrayed women in detail as well. This in and of itself was noteworthy in an age when attitudes toward women were frequently divided between exaltation of the Virgin Mary and damnation because of Eve. In the latter view, women were particularly disposed to evil. Now let us turn to Chaucer's most

The printing industry in England was born in the fifteenth century with the advent of the printing press. Books such as Chaucer's *Canterbury Tales* enjoyed a wide audience because of such technical innovations. Illustrations, however, were still drawn by hand and sometimes added many years later to the mass-produced texts. Chaucer's bawdy tales, told by pilgrims on their journey to Canterbury, provided the inspiration for many artists and book illustrators. This drawing, from a book by John Lydgate, shows the pilgrims beginning their return trip home.

Figure V-5 Lucas Horenbout, Pilgrims Leaving Canterbury, from the *Siege of Thebes* by John Lydgate. Book of verses ca. 1455–62; illumination ca. 1520–30. Ink and pigments on vellum, (395 × 280 mm). British Library, London. Courtesy of Art Resource, NY.

famous poem, written for the most part probably between 1388 and 1400.

The Canterbury Tales is unquestionably one of the great works of English literature, written in the Middle English of the fourteenth century. Many editons have the Middle English and a modern English rendering on facing pages, so you can see what the language looked like in Chaucer's time. The general Prologue introduces you to the whole story and all the characters. A group of pilgrims are journeying to the shrine of Thomas Becket, the Archbishop of Canterbury who was murdered by agents of King Henry II before the cathedral's high altar in 1170 and subsequently declared a saint. Pilgrimage, typically to churches containing relics of saints but sometimes to holy places as far away as Palestine, was a very

important religious activity throughout the Middle Ages, encouraged by the church as one important way to gain merit with God. By the time of Chaucer, pilgrimage had often become a social as much as a religious activity, for the middle and upper classes at least, a kind of vacation often marked more by revelry than by penance and fasting.

The General Prologue introduces us to the situation and the whole colorful cast of characters, beginning with its famous opening lines, here in the original and in a modern English rendering:

> Whan that Aprill with his shoures soote
> The droghte of March hath perced to the
>   roote,
> and bathed every veyne in swich licour
> Of which vertu engendred is the flour;

Whan Zephirus eek with his sweete breeth
Inspired hath in every holt and heeth
The tendre croppes, and the yonge sonne
Hath in the Ram his halfe cours yronne,
And smale foweles maken melodye,
That slepen al the nyght with open yë
(So priketh hem Nature in hir corages),
Thanne longen folk to goon on pilgrimages
And palmeres for to seken straunge
    strondes,
To ferne halwes, couthe in sondry londes;
And specially from every shires ende
Of Engelond, to Caunterbury they wende,
The holy blisful martir for to seke
That hem hath holpen, whan that they
    were seeke. (ll. 1–18)

(When April with his sweet showers has
pierced the drought of March to the root,
and bathed every vein in such moisture
as has power to bring forth the flower;
when, also, Zephyrus with his sweet breath
has breathed spirit into the tender new
    shoots
in every wood and meadow, and the young
    sun
has run half his course in the sign of the
    Ram,
and small birds sing melodies and
sleep with their eyes open all the night
(So Nature pricks them in their hearts):
then people long to go on pilgrimages,
and palmers long to seek strange shores
and far-off shrines known in various lands,
and, especially, from the ends of every shire
in England they come to Canterbury,
to seek the holy, blissful martyr
who helped them when they were sick.)

[*The Canterbury Tales by Geoffrey Chaucer*, edited by Kent Hieatt and Constance Hieatt, selected, with translations, a critical introduction, and notes by the editors, New York: Bantam Books, 1964. All modern-English quotations from *The Canterbury Tales* in this chapter are from this edition.]

Note here that already Chaucer is combining the language of earthly love—with birds and flowers signaling the coming of spring—with the desire to go on a pilgrimage. Some pilgrims go for religious reasons, but as the opening lines also imply, love is in the air.

In Chaucer's story the narrator meets up with twenty-nine pilgrims at the Tabard Inn in Southwark, just south of the Thames in London. The innkeeper proposes that on the trip from London to Canterbury and back (the two cities were about sixty miles apart) each pilgrim tell two stories on the way to Canterbury and two on the way back. It will not only pass the time but be a contest. The innkeeper and Host, Harry Bailly, will ride along and judge which are the best stories, with the winner getting a free meal when they get back to the inn. That, at any rate, was the plan as Chaucer presented it in the Prologue, and he also introduced the reader to all the pilgrims. But *The Canterbury Tales* as we have it is unfinished. We have twenty-three tales, one by each of twenty-three of the pilgrims, and twenty of the tales have prologues. Even some of the tales we have are unfinished. Chaucer wrote the tales mainly in the last part of his life (from about 1386–1400), but some of the stories come from earlier.

The Wife of Bath   "The Wife of Bath" has both a prologue and the tale itself. Chaucer apparently spent more time working on "The Wife of Bath" than on all the other tales combined. In creating his portrait of the shrewd, lusty widow Chaucer was influenced by earlier medieval sources, most directly by the Old Woman's speech in Jean de Meun's *The Romance of the Rose*.

Chaucer introduces us to the Wife of Bath in the general Prologue. He tells us what she looks like, how she is dressed, and what her trade is—an excellent weaver of fine cloth. We find out that her name is Dame Alison or Alice, and that she has been on a number of pilgrimages including three to Jerusalem (which was in those days an exceptionally long, arduous, and hazardous journey from Europe). *The Canterbury Tales* is earthy and explicit in its depiction of late-medieval life, and Dame Alison is one of its earthiest characters—no prudery here!

We have selected to discuss "The Wife of Bath's Prologue and Tale" not only because she is one of Chaucer's best characters, but also because her Prologue and Tale are a remarkably good window on gender roles and relations in the late Middle Ages, a kind of condensed summary particularly of images of women which brings together standard sources on the subject from the Bible to classical Greek and Roman literature. Recent feminist literary scholarship has caused us to look at "The Wife of Bath" with fresh eyes: to ask new questions of the story and to see in it a subtlety that was often not fully appreciated before. As you read "The Wife of Bath's Prologue," ask yourself, "Is Chaucer here simply presenting and confirming traditional attitudes toward women, or is he also slyly challenging or at least questioning them?" Dame Alison is clearly one of his strongest characters—formidable both as a physical presence and as a very shrewd and perceptive person—and Chaucer puts into her mouth some very telling arguments about why women behave the way they do and the injustices they endure from men. Are Alison's complaints in some sense justified? What have historically been the only sorts of ways open to the large majority of women to exercise any power—to "rule"—in a world run by men?

At the beginning of her Prologue the Wife of Bath announces her theme: "the woe that is in marriage." First married at the age of twelve (which was common in an age when the average life expectancy was 35–40 years), she has had five husbands. Note Alison's extensive references to the Bible on the subject of marriage—above all Paul's First Letter to the Corinthians. She deals with a familiar medieval issue: whether virginity or marriage is a higher state of life spiritually and more pleasing to God. Notice also her references to Seneca, who was a highly regarded classical author during the Middle Ages. Alison catalogues the stereotypical attitudes toward and images of women, and tells of how she cleverly turned the traditional view that women are less rational than men against her fourth husband. The focus of the Prologue is Alison's romance with and marriage to her fifth husband, Jankin the clerk (a clerk or cleric was someone who had been a university student, which normally required that he be ordained in one of the lower orders of clergy). Jankin, whom Alison genuinely loves, reads to her from a book he reads daily containing writings against women by famous Greek, Roman, and Christian authors. The consequences of her anger and violence against the book and Jankin, and his retaliation, are their reconciliation and his letting her "rule."

The Wife of Bath's Tale (following the Prologue) is a retelling of an old fairy tale that existed in many versions and with different morals, set in the time of King Arthur. The Arthurian legends were among the most widely told and written stories in the Middle Ages. The theme of the tale is a generalization of the theme of Alison's own married life: that women want to rule. This is the task that is given to the knight in order to save his life, having been condemned to death for the rape of a young maiden: to learn what it is that women want. He is given the answer by an ugly, old, poor hag who then asks that he marry her. Horrified, the knight enumerates those repellent qualities: ugliness, old age, and poverty. The hag's response to each accusation is both clever and moving, containing a moral and Christian message within the framework of medieval society.

The Pardoner   Like the Wife of Bath, the Pardoner has both a Prologue and a Tale to tell. In the medieval Catholic Church, a pardoner was a member of the clergy who was authorized by the church to sell pardons, also called indulgences, which were certificates that forgave sins by remitting some of the time that a person would have to spend in purgatory for sins he or she had committed in this life. The selling of indulgences lent itself to abuse and corruption, and by the time of Chaucer it had become a money-making scheme for the church and a profitable business for unscrupulous pardoners like the one we meet in *The Canterbury Tales*. Little over a hundred years later, it would be the selling of indulgences that prompted Martin Luther's protest and the beginnings of the Protestant Reformation.

As with the Wife of Bath, in the General Prologue Chaucer presents a vivid portrait of the Pardoner, both as to physical appearance and to character, and prepares the reader for his prologue and tale. He is described as having thin, stringy, carefully arranged yellow hair, staring eyes, and a thin goat-like voice. Many readers and scholarly interpreters of *The Canterbury Tales* have been fascinated by what seems to be the sexual ambiguity of the Pardoner. In addition to his thin, high voice and carefully arranged hair, the narrator describes him as beardless, and speculates that perhaps he is a "gelding or a mare"—equine terms to suggest a man who is either a eunuch (the traditional term for a male who lacks the normal function of the testes through disease, castration, or congenital defect) or "feminine." Yet later, in his Prologue, the Pardoner describes how he likes to "have a jolly wench in every town," which seems to undercut the implication of either sexual incapacity or homosexuality—but perhaps he asserts his "normality" precisely for that reason.

But it is Chaucer's description of the Pardoner's character that really prepares us for what is to come. In an age devoted to veneration of relics—the bones and clothing of saints—as holy and powerful objects, he carries a bag full of phony relics which, with "false flattery and tricks," he sells, along with the indulgences, to gullible folk seeking salvation and miraculous divine help with their hard lives. Very importantly, Chaucer tells us that in the service of worship the Pardoner preaches, reads the lessons, and sings "beautifully," and of course he is singing (not a religious song) when we first meet him. The Pardoner has a "smooth" tongue, and it is precisely his rhetorical ability that makes him so successful at fooling and exploiting people.

By the time we have read the Pardoner's Prologue we know that he is a despicable person, thoroughly corrupt and self-serving, cynically manipulating the church's doctrine and moral teaching to line his own pockets. So skillful is he at preaching that he can completely "sucker" his listeners into taking what he says seriously as Christian teaching and persuade them to buy his indulgences or false relics. But here is what makes Chaucer's Pardoner so interesting: in his Prologue he tells his fellow pilgrims exactly what he is and does, and then in his Tale shows them that he can still make them believe what he says. Like any good preacher, he has a biblical text on which he will "preach," the famous statement by the author of the First Letter of Timothy in the New Testament that "the love of money is the root of all evil" (I Tim. 6:10)—in the Latin Vulgate Bible of the Middle Ages, *Radix malorum est cupiditas*. But before he begins the "sermon"—the Tale—he tells his audience exactly and fully what he is: one who lives his life in complete contradiction to the warning in First Timothy. He uses his ecclesiastical authority to preach what the church believes to be true but he considers falsehoods, to take advantage of his hearers' belief in the church as the vehicle of their salvation, precisely in order to make money off their gullibility. The Pardoner asserts frankly:

> my intention is to win money,
> not at all to cast out sins.
> I don't care, when they are buried,
> If their souls go a-blackberrying! (lines 75–78)

The Pardoner preaches against avarice and solemnly warns his listeners against it, but practices it avidly himself. That is his sole motive for doing what he does. His fellow pilgrims, knowing of the office he holds, request that he tell a tale that will teach them "moral thing[s]" (l. 8). The Pardoner concludes his Prologue saying that he will grant their request.

> For although I am myself a very vicious man,
> yet I can tell you a moral tale,
> which I am accustomed to preach for profit. (lines 131–133)

The Pardoner's Tale is his "sermon," and the story it tells belongs to a literary category called the "exemplary narrative." He tells of three young men who are complete libertines, spending their time drinking, gambling, visiting prostitutes, and blaspheming. They exemplify three sins against which the Pardoner persuasively preaches, drawing on Scripture and classical authors (including Seneca): gluttony, gambling, and swearing false oaths.

After expounding on the three sins, the Pardoner tells the tale of the three young carousers, who commit all three sins and come to a bad end. In a tavern one morning they learn of the death of an old companion from a plague that has killed a thousand people. In their outrage the three swear a solemn oath to each other to kill Death, pledging "to live and die each for the other." They go out and meet an old man who, under threat, tells them where to find Death: under a nearby oak tree. What they find when they get there is a large quantity of gold coins. That of course shifts their desires immediately from killing Death to greed for the gold. Agreeing that the gold should be removed under cover of night, they draw lots to decide which one of them will go into town and bring back bread and wine to see them through the rest of the day. Once the youngest one has left for town the other two plot to kill him when he returns. Meanwhile, however, he has purchased poison to kill them. The story ends with all three dead, each of them a victim of his greed. As the old man had said, they did indeed find Death under the oak tree.

The Pardoner ends his sermon with a stern admonition to his fellow pilgrims about remaining in sin, above all gluttony, and urges them to purchase his pardons and relics. He invites the Host, Harry Bailly, as "the most enveloped in sin," to be the first to step forward. The Host is furious over what a complete scoundrel and "con" the Pardoner is, and becomes menacing. But everyone else is laughing, and the good Knight invites the Host and the Pardoner to reconcile and join in the laughter.

As a representative of Christianity and the church, the Pardoner stands in sharp contrast to some of the other Canterbury pilgrims—most notably the Parson and the Knight. As we might expect, and as is the case in any time and place, the late-medieval church had its share of both saints and reprobates and all shades in between, and Chaucer's portraits of the pilgrims vividly capture that range of piety and worldliness. The Pardoner interests us both as a character in his own right and as a caricatural embodiment of the corruption to which a common practice of the medieval church was all too prone: the selling of pardons or indulgences. In the early sixteenth century this was the specific issue that touched off the revolt led by Martin Luther that would forever change the face of Western Christianity.

QUESTIONS FOR STUDY AND REFLECTION

1. In what ways is *The Song of Roland* related to the Crusades? Why do you think it is considered an epic?

2. What is the journey that Dante the pilgrim takes in *The Divine Comedy*? Why? Who are his guides? Why does he call his great work a "comedy"?

3. Write a character sketch of Dame Alison and of her husband Jankin. What beliefs, attitudes, customs, and institutions (social, religious, educational, etc.) of late-medieval society are presented in the story?

4. What attitudes toward and images of women does Chaucer present in "The Wife of Bath's Pro-

logue and Tale"? How can our present perspectives on and knowledge of women's history and lives enrich our understanding of both of these portrayals of women?

5. The Wife's tale begins with the knight violating the will of a young maiden. In what ways is the knight's own will violated by the old woman at the end of the story?

6. Given the Pardoner's self-presentation, why do you think the narrator, in the General Prologue, calls him "gentle," and later refers to him as "a noble ecclesiastic"?

7. The Pardoner is completely honest with his fellow pilgrims about his real motives for doing the things he does. Then, in his Tale—which is a sermon with a dramatic story as illustration—he shows them how good he is at making people believe him when he tells them things he doesn't believe himself. What are we to make of this character?

SUGGESTIONS FOR FURTHER READING

Benson, Larry D., editor. *The Riverside Chaucer*. Boston: Houghton Mifflin, 1987.

Boitani, Piero and Jill Mann, editors. *The Cambridge Companion to Chaucer*. Cambridge: Cambridge University Press, 2003.

Claster, Jill. *The Medieval Experience (300-1400)*. New York & London: NYU Press, 1982.

Coulton, George. *Chaucer and His England*. Senate, 1998 rpt. (London: Methuen, 1908).

Gardner, John. *Life and Times of Chaucer*. New York: Alfred A. Knopf, 1977.

Howard, Donald R. *Chaucer: His Life, His Works, His World*. New York: E. P. Dutton. 1987.

Lerer, Seth, *Chaucer and His Readers*. Princeton, 1993.

F. N. Robinson. Introduction to *The Works of Geoffrey Chaucer*, 2nd edition, Cambridge, MA: The Riverside Press, 1957.

Sturges, Robert. *Chaucer's Pardoner and Gender Theory: Bodies of Discourse*. New York: St. Martin's Press, 2000.

Plate 18 Nave, Abbey Church of Notre-Dame, Fontenay, Burgundy, France. 1139–47. Courtesy of Anthony Scibilia/Art Resource, NY.

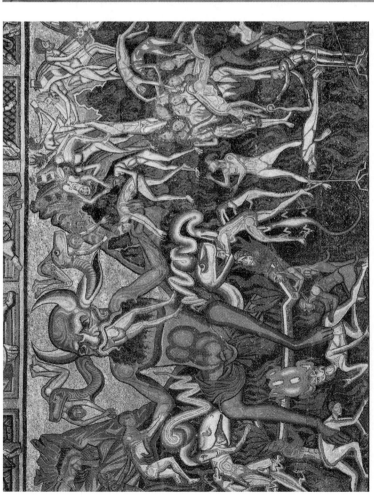

Plate 17 Coppo di Marcovaldo, *Hell,* detail of mosaic in the dome, Baptistry of San Giovanni, Florence, Italy. Late thirteenth century. Courtesy of Erich Lessing/Art Resource, NY.

Plate 20 *Mohammed, Abu Bakr and Ali travel to the Ukaz Fair,* from a copy of the fourteenth-century *Siyar-I Nabi (Life of the Prophet)* of al-Zarir, Istanbul, Turkey. 1594–95. Ink, color and gold on paper, 10⅝ x 15″ (27 x 38 cm). New York Public Library. Courtesy of The New York Public Library/Art Resource, NY.

Plate 19 Facsimile frontispiece with Hildegard and Volmer, *Liber Scivias.* 1165–75. Original manuscript lost during World War II. Courtesy of Wiesbaden Hessische Landesbibliothek.

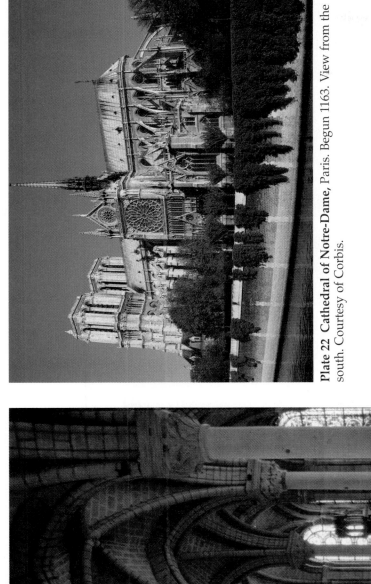

Plate 22 Cathedral of Notre-Dame, Paris. Begun 1163. View from the south. Courtesy of Corbis.

Plate 21 Ambulatory choir, Abbey Church of Saint-Denis, Saint-Denis, France. 1140–44. Courtesy of Anthony Scibilia / Art Resource, NY.

Plate 24 Virgin and Child Enthroned, for the high altar of the Church of the Ognissanti (All Saints). ca. 1305–10. Tempera and gold on wood panel, 10'8″ × 6'8¼″ (3.53 × 2.05 m). Galleria degli Uffizi, Florence. Courtesy of Scala/Art Resource, NY.

Plate 23 Upper chapel, Sainte-Chapelle, Paris. 1243–48. Courtesy of Erich Lessing/Art Resource, NY.

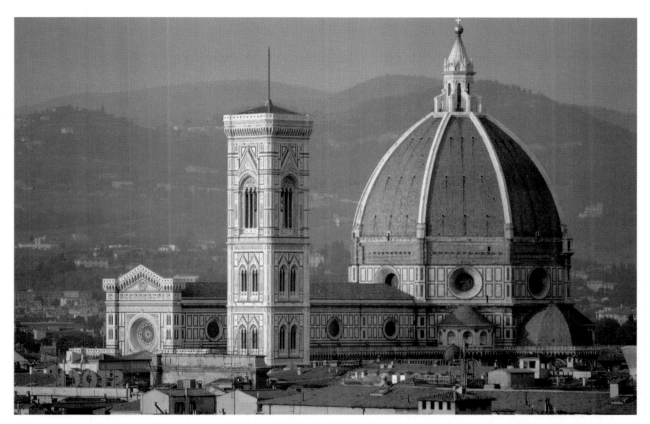

Plate 25 Arnolfo di Cambio, Francesco Talenti, Andrea Orcagna, and others. Florence Cathedral, Florence, Italy. Begun 1296; campanile by Giotto di Bondone, Andrea Pisano, and Francesco Talenti, ca. 1334–50; redesigned 1357 and 1366; drum and dome by Filippo Brunelleschi, 1417–36; lantern completed, 1471. Courtesy of Jonathan Blair/Corbis.

Plate 26 Attributed to Michelozzo di Bartolomeo. Palazzo Medici-Riccardi, Florence. Begun 1446. Courtesy of Scala/Art Resource, NY.

Plate 27 Attributed to Luciano Laurana. *View of an Ideal City.* ca. 1470. Oil on panel. 23⅝ × 78½″ (59.7 × 200.7 cm). Galleria Nazionale della Marche, Palazzo Ducale, Urbino. Courtesy of Scala/Art Resource, NY.

Plate 28 Raphael. School of Athens, fresco in a lunette in the Stanza della Segnatura, Stanze di Raffaello, Vatican, Rome. ca. 1510–11. 19 × 27′ (5.79 × 8.24 m). Courtesy of Scala/Art Resource, NY.

Plate 29 Michelangelo. *David.* 1501–4. Marble, height 17' (5.18 m). Galleria dell'Accademia, Florence. Courtesy of Tony Gentile/Reuters/Corbis.

Plate 30 Jan van Eyck. *Portrait of Giovanni Arnolfini and His Wife, Giovanna Cenami.* 1434. Oil on wood panel, 33 × 22½" (83.8 × 57.2 cm). The National Gallery, London. Courtesy of National Gallery Collection; by kind permission of the Trustees of the National Gallery, London/Corbis.

Plate 31 Pieter Bruegel the Elder. *Return of the Hunters.* 1565. Oil on wood panel, 3'10½" × 5' 3½" (1.18 × 1.61 m). Kunsthistorisches Museum, Vienna. Courtesy of Erich Lessing/Art Resource, NY.

Plate 32 Albrecht Dürer. *Four Apostles.* 1526. Oil on wood panel, each panel 7'½" × 2'6" (2.15 × 0.76 m). Alte Pinakothek, Munich. Courtesy of Scala/Art Resource, NY.

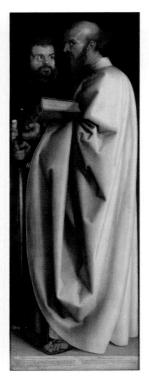

SECTION SIX

TIMELINE VI

RENAISSANCE AND REFORMATION

1400–1500 CE The Renaissance

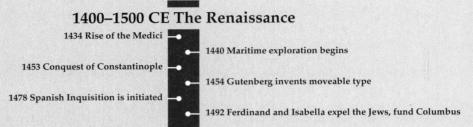

1434 Rise of the Medici

1440 Maritime exploration begins

1453 Conquest of Constantinople

1454 Gutenberg invents moveable type

1478 Spanish Inquisition is initiated

1492 Ferdinand and Isabella expel the Jews, fund Columbus

1500–1650 CE High Renaissance and Reformation

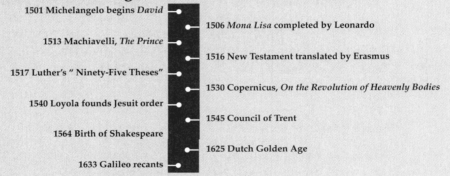

1501 Michelangelo begins *David*

1506 *Mona Lisa* completed by Leonardo

1513 Machiavelli, *The Prince*

1516 New Testament translated by Erasmus

1517 Luther's " Ninety-Five Theses"

1530 Copernicus, *On the Revolution of Heavenly Bodies*

1540 Loyola founds Jesuit order

1545 Council of Trent

1564 Birth of Shakespeare

1625 Dutch Golden Age

1633 Galileo recants

Dates given are approximate

RENAISSANCE AND REFORMATION

The previous historical section ended with a discussion of the "calamitous" fourteenth century—an era that brought drought, arctic winters, economic depression, war, rebellion, and plague to the European continent. Neither the church nor the state was equipped to deal effectively with these multifaceted problems. Yet from these desperate times emerged one of the most vibrant and important periods in the history of the West: the Renaissance and Reformation. In the fifteenth and sixteenth centuries, Renaissance thinkers—beginning first in Italy and then spreading to the capitals of Europe—looked back to the culture of the Greco-Roman period in an effort to recover the classical past. The Renaissance ushered in artistic, intellectual, and religious changes that included what we call the Reformation. Just as Renaissance thinkers looked to the past in order to reform and renew the present, so the Protestant reformers sought to rekindle the spirit of the early Church, viewed as a golden age in Christendom. This enthusiasm for the classical age became the vehicle for changes in the West that would shape the next five hundred years.

During the period of the Renaissance and Reformation distinctly modern outlooks and institutions developed and spread throughout the Western world. In the realm of economics, proto-capitalist methods of exchange took root in the merchant-dominated republics and principalities of northern Italy. Capital accumulation in the hands of merchants helped to foster the emergence of a "middle class," a group that had had no official status in the hierarchical society of the Middle Ages, but in the Renaissance would generate much of the economic vitality of the period. The dominant trend in politics during the Renaissance and Reformation was toward centralized states. It was during this period that European states took on the national boundaries that still largely exist today. With the voyages of discovery and conquest of other parts of the world, Europeans began a process of global imperialism that would determine modern world history with dramatic and often tragic results. The Reformation dominated the religious life of the period, forever shattering the religious unity of Christendom. Finally, remarkable scientific and technological progress not only helped remake Western society but also fostered a revolution of the mind. Europeans began to develop distinctly secular attitudes. Faith came to be increasingly challenged by science, and a concern with life in this world replaced Europeans' emphasis on salvation and the after-life which had dominated medieval thinking. The growing secular outlook initiated by the Renaissance had enormous ramifications in the West, perhaps most keenly and tangibly demonstrated in the realm of the arts and literature. As the influential nineteenth-century Swiss historian Jacob Burckhardt noted, our modern world begins with the Renaissance and Reformation.

THE "RENAISSANCE"

What does the word mean, and what does it imply? For most, "Renaissance" perhaps suggests the artworks created by certain very famous Italian artists, especially Michelangelo and Leonardo da Vinci. It also brings to mind a few widely used phrases, including "Renaissance man" or "the world of the Renaissance." Such descriptions imply great beauty, outstanding achievement, the best that can be attained by creative talent and intellectual brilliance.

When the term "Renaissance" is applied to the fifteenth and sixteenth centuries—the period of Michelangelo and Leonardo da Vinci—it means an extraordinary level of effort and talent applied to the revival of something valuable which had been allowed to wither away or be destroyed outright. This lost and then reborn "something" has two major and related parts: 1) ancient Greek and Roman books; and 2) the values which intellectual leaders developed on the basis of their study of these "reborn" books. The scholars who began the movement, first in Italy and then throughout the north and west, believed that the medieval monks who had destroyed and neglected ancient Greek and Roman books had deprived Western culture of a unique source of wisdom. They were determined to seek out the fragments of these books still in existence, piece them together to form texts as nearly complete and correct as possible, and then uncover the meaning they would have had in Greek or Roman times.

The term "Renaissance," a French term meaning "rebirth," was given to this period by those engaged in such work, not by later historians. Renaissance Italians self-consciously saw themselves as engaged in a project of rescuing the arts and literature of the "golden age" of Greece and Rome from obscurity and reclaiming lost learning. To help draw a bright line between their own day and the historical period immediately preceding it, Renaissance thinkers coined the phrase "Middle Ages" to describe the thousand- year period that separated the ancient Roman Empire from their own times. Enthusiasts saw the Renaissance as an awakening from a long sleep, or returning home from lengthy exile. Whatever metaphor they employed, the message was clear: by reviving Greco-Roman culture, those engaged in the project of the Renaissance were rescuing Europe from a cultural darkness, creating a new era of light and vitality and fostering a revolution in learning and living.

RENAISSANCE HUMANISM

Renaissance scholars engaged in the project of reviving classical cultural forms were given the special name of "humanists." A humanist is someone who primarily studies and celebrates human culture in its many expressions, rather than God or nature. This did not imply that humanists were atheists, for many were members of the clergy or devout lay persons. Petrarch (Francesco Petrarca, 1304–1374) and Giovanni Boccaccio (1313–1375) were both priests and also among the most avid early humanists. Boccaccio, in particular, was passionately involved in the quest for ancient Greco-Roman texts and would burst into tears of mixed joy and grief upon finding one in particularly bad condition in the library of a monastery near Naples. Another outstanding humanist of the age was Marsilio Ficino (1433–1499), scholar, priest and Neo-platonist. He translated many of Plato's works and wrote commentaries. A protégé of the Medici family in Florence, he supervised a group of scholars as part of what was called the "Platonic Academy."

One of the clearest expositions of humanism is to be found in the work of Giovanni Pico della Mirandola (1463–1494). His *Oration on the Dignity of Man* is perhaps the quintessential humanist statement. Here we can see not only the Renaissance fascination with ancient literature and classical learning, but also the profoundly optimistic nature of Renaissance humanism. Pico's humanism was a philosophy suited to inspire the privileged, educated classes during the Renaissance. In the *Oration*, Pico suggests that man is an artist of supreme talents, able to fashion himself into anything he wishes to be. It sets an extremely high standard for all areas of human endeavor. Indeed, such notions as Pico's helped motivate extraordinary contributions in many aspects of creative and intellectual life. Two of these are worthy of special mention: Renaissance achievement in the visual arts and in the natural sciences.

THE ARTS AND SCIENCES IN THE RENAISSANCE

Italian artists themselves believed that the recovery of past literary and artistic practices was essential if society was to recover from the "barbarism" that had characterized the recent past. Renaissance artists drew extensively upon humanist study of the literature of antiquity to provide themselves with a whole new range of themes. No longer confined to religious subjects, artists introduced ancient mythology and history into their studios.

The importance of the study of the ancient world in Renaissance art can most readily be seen in the representation of ancient architectural ruins in

Renaissance painting and in Renaissance architecture itself. For example, Andrea Mantegna (1431–1506) copied directly from Roman remains in and around Padua when painting the fresco *St. James Led to Martyrdom* for the Eremitani Church in Padua (destroyed during World War II). When the architect Michelozzo (1396–1472) designed the Medici-Ricciardi Palace in Florence, he imitated the plan of ancient Roman houses, with an interior courtyard to provide light and air, contrasting with a heavy exterior on the ground floor to suggest that the Palace could protect its inhabitants.

In the realm of painting, Renaissance artists not only studied the art of the ancient world but also pursued rigorous studies of perspective and the natural forms of the body and landscapes. The art of the "high Renaissance" (the later and more mature period of Renaissance creativity), including the work of Leonardo Da Vinci (1452–1519), Michelangelo (1475–1564), and Raphael (1483–1520), perfectly capture the increased emphasis on human activity, the beauty of the human body, and the natural world as the human eye perceives it. The section on Renaissance art history goes into greater detail on the artistic vitality of the period.

The Renaissance ushered in an era of great scientific advancement, as more and more scientists and philosophers began to rely on observation and experimentation instead of received opinion in matters ranging from the movements of the stars to the circulation of blood through the bodies of living things. Historians label the scientific advances of the sixteenth and seventeenth centuries the "Scientific Revolution."

The ideal of the perfectibility of human knowledge, championed by Pico, was even more influential in the natural sciences than in the visual arts. Leonardo da Vinci seems to have been impelled by his work as a painter to investigate such scientific areas as optics, anatomy, botany, and hydraulics. The Polish astronomer Nicolaus Copernicus (1473–1543) strove to push human understanding of the workings of the heavens further than it had ever gone before when he hypothesized that the sun is the center around which the earth moves, rather than the earth being the center for the sun. Late in the Renaissance, Galileo Galilei (1564–1642) employed observation rather than logic alone in order to establish major laws of mechanics and open a new era in the study of astronomy.

The new scientists' work challenged and ultimately overturned theories that had been in currency since ancient times. These ancient theories, however, were often supported by religious authorities and put to work supporting Christian doctrine. Therefore, in the sixteenth and seventeenth centuries, scientific progress frequently collided with Christian beliefs. Ultimately, the scientists of the Renaissance offered an alternative way to view the cosmos: one that was mechanistic, orderly, predictable, and followed laws of nature as compared to the Christian cosmos which was hierarchical, closed, and centered on the earth as God's special creation. Greater detail will be paid to these events in Chapter Fourteen.

A NEW WORLDLINESS

In Renaissance humanism and the accompanying emphasis on human activity, human power and the human body as well as the workings of the physical world we can see the rise of a more secular outlook on life, a greater concern with the here-and-now world and less emphasis on spiritual matters. While the Middle Ages was characterized by otherworldly concerns, salvation, and eternal life, a growing number of the elite among scientists, artists, and philosophers, as well as the emerging middle class merchants, embraced more earthly concerns. Renaissance people often held strong and deep spiritual beliefs, but Renaissance society was becoming increasingly secular: attention was concentrated on the here and now, often on the acquisition of material things. Wealth made possible greater material pleasures, a more comfortable life, the leisure time to appreciate and patronize the arts. The new attitude indeed conflicted with the worldview of the Middle Ages, but in the Renaissance Church leaders did little to combat this new spirit. Renaissance popes beautified the city of Rome, patronized artists and writers, and expended enormous sums of money. Pope Julius II (ruled 1501–1513), called "the Renaissance Pope," hired Michelangelo to paint the ceiling of the Sistine Chapel in the newly constructed Saint Peter's basilica.

RENAISSANCE POLITICS

The major political trend across Europe during the Renaissance was a gradual turning away from European peoples' conception of themselves as a population loosely united, whether as tribal peoples converted and united under the papacy or under the Holy Roman Empire, or as "Christendom" at war with Muslim Arab "pagans." Instead Europeans began to think of themselves more and more as having particular national identities. With the exception of Italy, which remained a loose federation of city-states until the nineteenth century, and the Germanic states that formed the basis of the Holy Roman Empire, most major European countries during the Renaissance became increasingly nationalistic, drawing diverse political factions together under powerful monarchs.

In the fifteenth and sixteenth centuries Spain became a united and intensely Catholic nation. The marriage in 1479 of King Ferdinand II of Aragon with Queen Isabella of Castile had brought much of the Spanish peninsula under one government,

Renaissance Italy.

yet the two sovereigns were not content with the unprecedented administrative unity of the peninsula. They strove to make all of Spain Spanish in a uniform sense, and unvaryingly Catholic as well. In 1492, the fateful year of Columbus' voyage under their aegis, these monarchs oversaw the fall of Granada, the last Muslim stronghold in Europe, and banished all Jews who would not convert to Christianity. In 1480 they had set up a central royal court whose job it was to enforce religious uniformity in order to increase a sense of national unity and enhance their authority. Entirely distinct from the earlier-established papal inquisitions, this court became known as the Spanish Inquisition. Later, under Charles I (1516–1556), Spain enjoyed a "golden age" when its economy was greatly enriched by the wealth of the Americas.

England suffered greatly in the fifteenth century under the combined weight of the Hundred Years War, the Black Death, and civil war (the War of the Roses). Stability was ultimately achieved, however, by the Tudor monarchs, particularly Henry VII (ruled 1461–1483), Henry VIII (ruled 1509–1547), and then his daughter Elizabeth I (ruled 1558–1603). During her reign, the English Renaissance reached its apex, both in the flowering of artistic and intellectual enterprises and in overseas expansion. Tudor success lay largely in the alliance they forged between the crown and the emerging middle-class landowners. Commerce thrives on peace and stability, and the Tudors sought to provide that, in exchange for their loyalty and tax revenues, at all costs.

In the fifteenth century, France as well began the slow process of recovery from the Hundred Years War. Although victorious, France was left depopulated and weak. Yet by the end of the century, the nation would not only recover but significantly expand, doubling its territory and assuming close to its modern boundaries. Louis XI (ruled 1461–1483), called the "Spider King" by his people because of his treacherous and cruel character, was largely responsible for the nation's turnaround. He was able to accomplish this in two ways: first, through military conquest—seizing large tracts of Burgundy after the death of Charles the Bold in 1477—and then through inheritance and dynastic succession. Once firmly in control of the new borders, Louis XI sought to consolidate his authority over the nation. He maintained Europe's first standing army, and dispensed with the Estates General, a weak parliamentary body that would play almost no role in French political affairs until 1789. Louis XI also laid the groundwork for controlling the Church in France by controlling revenues and appointing bishops.

On the Italian peninsula, we do not see the move toward centralization that occurred in northern Europe. Instead, five powers dominated Italy: Venice, Milan, Florence, the Papal States, and the kingdom of Naples. Many of these were called republics but were actually governed by an oligarchy—usually alliances among wealthy merchant families. For example, by 1422 Venice had a population of 84,000 but 200 men held all the power. In Florence, merchants dominated key elements of the economic life of Europe, most notably the banking business. The profits from banking, from loans and investments, were reinvested in local Florentine businesses like the wool industry. Florence was officially a republic, but from 1434 to 1494 power rested with the great Medici banking family.

In the history of the Renaissance, Florence stands alone as a remarkable and singularly important city. Home of Petrarch, Boccaccio, Masaccio, Giotto, Pico, Botticelli, Leonardo, Donatello, and Michelangelo, Florence was rightly considered in the fourteenth and fifteenth centuries to be the "new Athens." Perhaps the most important writer and theorist during the Renaissance, Niccolo Machiavelli (1469–1527), also made his home in Florence. The subject of his book, *The Prince*, is political power, and how a ruler should, get, maintain, and keep it. While Machiavelli wrote his treatise for Lorenzo de Medici, Duke of Urbino and ruler of Florence, his advice captures and reflects the spirit of politics during the Renaissance. In an age of increased nationalism and centralization of authority, Renaissance monarchs needed to be tough, cynical, manipulative, and calculating. Rulers could not afford to look to Christian notions of morality while trying to reduce violence, put down uprisings from malcontent nobles, and establish domestic tranquility. Machiavelli's work would serve as a handbook for rulers in the sixteenth century and continue to influence politics throughout the modern period. See Chapter Twelve for more on Machiavelli.

NEW WORLD WEALTH AND THE SLAVE TRADE

Perhaps the most significant events of the Renaissance happened not in the humanists' studies, libraries, and studios, but aboard ships that left from European ports in pursuit of non-European sources of wealth. The story of Columbus's first voyage is too well-known to require rehearsal here. It should be recalled, however, that his understanding of navigational instruments, based on Renaissance scientific learning and new technologies, was an important factor keeping him on his course despite the doubts of his crew. Columbus's son reported that his father had studied astronomy, geometry, and mathematics in northern Italy in his youth, before becoming a sailor. His study of geographical theories led him to believe, with many other students of astronomy and geography in the late Middle Ages and early Renaissance, that the world was spherical.

The westerly variation on the compass as the ship *Santa Maria* sailed into uncharted western waters frightened many on board until Columbus explained that these variations were indicative of the presence of land. The sighting, in the early morning of October 12, 1492, of one of the Caribbean islands in what would come to be known as the "New World" was the first in a series of discoveries Columbus made on his first voyage ("discoveries," of course, only from a European viewpoint, since the Native American inhabitants already knew they were there).

By the spring of 1493, Columbus was back at the Spanish court to display the wealth found on such islands as Cuba and Haiti: gold, cotton, exotic birds and plants, and people. He had brought these people—who came to be described as Indians because it was mistakenly thought that Columbus had traveled around the world to the East Indies, in the Orient—to be baptized. This was the modest beginning of a long tradition of displacement of the peoples of the New World by their European conquerors, and the earliest transfer to the New World of the European idea, already used by the Spanish in their dealings with Jews and Muslims, that people with religious and cultural practices different from those of Christian Europe should be forced to convert and conform to European ways.

Columbus made several other voyages to the New World. On the second he took with him more than fifteen hundred men, in order to take permanent possession of and colonize the new lands, and a dozen missionaries to convert the natives to European Christian religious practices. During this voyage of 1493–94 there was considerable trouble between Native American inhabitants and colonizers, leading to violence. Such conflict between Spaniards and Native Americans led the Spaniards to believe that Native Americans, on their own home ground, made poor slaves. The Spaniards' desire for slave labor eventually brought about the institution of the Caribbean slave trade, in which Europeans bought or captured Africans and brought them to the Americas as slave laborers, to cultivate land or work in the gold mines. Before the European discovery of the New World, it had long been the practice among Mediterranean peoples, Christian and Muslim alike, to make slaves of conquered peoples. Columbus followed this practice in sending off to Spain, in June, 1495, five shiploads of Caribbean inhabitants to be sold into slavery.

On a third voyage, in 1498, Columbus at last discovered continental land, on the coast of South America, and gave his attention to the governance of a colony on San Domingo. The original Caribbean inhabitants were confined in restricted villages and forced to convert to Christianity. The colonists were quite successful in early attempts at mining gold. Nevertheless, Columbus, not satisfied with the apparent riches of the New World, continued until his death to seek a passageway through it to the Orient. Other explorers soon followed, with the same goal of learning how to reach the East by a western route.

The Italian Amerigo Vespucci (1454–1512) had in his youth been a clerk in the commercial offices of the Medici, the family that ruled his native Florence. He went to Spain, presumably as a Medici employee, at about the time of Columbus's first voyage and indeed seems to have been involved in arrangements for outfitting one of Columbus's voyages. He himself claimed to have made several trips to the New World in the final years of the fifteenth century. Certainly, his first name became associated with the new lands during the first decade of the sixteenth century because of the wide dissemination of two letters he wrote describing them, the first to the then-head of the Medici firm and the second, after the Florentines had expelled the Medici, to Piero Soderini (elected to the highest office in Florence in 1502), the man whom Niccolò Machiavelli served as a secretary for foreign affairs and ambassador. Printers throughout Europe realized there would be widespread interest in reading Vespucci's account and arranged to have the letters translated into several languages. The "Americas" were thus named for their first successful publicist.

The Italian Giovanni Caboto (ca. 1450–ca. 1499), like Columbus a native of the great seafaring city of Genoa, began to dream of a western trade route to the East at about the same time as his countryman. He moved to England (and changed his name to John Cabot) in order to get the support of British merchants for this commercial enterprise. The British hoped to follow the example of the Spanish in exploiting the wealth of the New World. Caboto organized several unsuccessful voyages prior to Columbus's and, in 1497, encouraged by news of Columbus's discovery to the south, arrived at North America, which he took to be Northern China.

The long-term consequences of European involvement in the Americas ought not to be overlooked. The civilizations of the "new world" had long and rich histories before the arrival of Europeans. Contact with Europeans would prove devastating for native American civilizations. Whole civilizations with long histories and a record of enormous social, architectural, and technological advancement were effectively destroyed. Columbus and those who followed in his wake brought European law, government, legal institutions, languages, trade, and religion. Europeans also brought microbes for which the gene-pool of Americans had no immunity, and epidemic disease resulted. Smallpox was perhaps the most devastating. It was introduced by Europeans and then spread to Native populations with devastating consequences. Mexico had a population of about 25 million people before the arrival of Columbus in the early sixteenth century. A hundred years later, by 1600, that population had declined to about 2 million. Smallpox swept through the Aztec capital of Tenochtitlan, making the city virtually defenseless. This helps us understand how a relatively small number of European invaders were able to conquer the great Aztec and Inca civilizations.

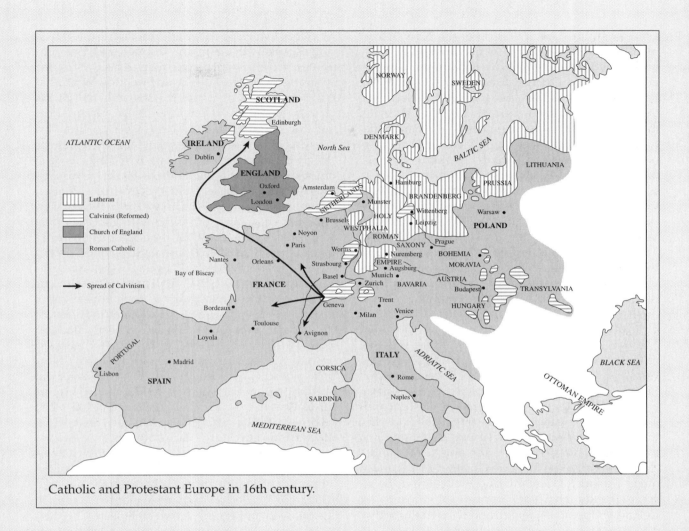

Catholic and Protestant Europe in 16th century.

SPREAD OF THE RENAISSANCE

By 1500, the Renaissance had spread from Italy to the rest of Europe. Aiding this process was the advent of printing. In the fifteenth century the desire to own and to read complete texts of classical works was widespread, but the number of copies was severely limited by the time and expense of hand-copying, collating, and checking manuscripts. The invention of printing with movable lead type changed things dramatically. Johann Gutenberg invented movable type in the 1450s, allowing printing to become a practical way to produce books. The first book produced by this new method was the Bible, called the Gutenberg Bible. By 1500, 1000 presses were operating in 265 towns. Printing allowed for the creation of standardized editions in law, theology, philosophy, and science. Multiple copies of texts allowed for the wide dissemination of rare texts as well.

Outside of Italy, humanists tended to be more interested in religious than in political reform. Most humanists did not consider the study of ancient cultures a conflict with their Christian faith. The Renaissance notion of renewal based on a deep understanding and imitation of the past remained at the center of the movement.

North of the Alps the most prominent humanist was Erasmus of Rotterdam (ca.1466–1536). Erasmus spent his life cultivating contacts with other scholars while publishing a variety of works that included new editions of the Church Fathers (theologians of the early church) and of the New

Testament. His Greek edition of the New Testament in 1516 was a major achievement that was immediately used by biblical scholars and preachers who would emerge during the Reformation. Erasmus also advocated the reform of society and the church. With biting satire he criticized both the monastic life and scholastic theology, that is, the traditional method of teaching theology that drew heavily on Aristotle in Latin translation. Erasmus believed that every layperson could understand and practice the Christian faith by following the teaching of Jesus. For Erasmus, church reform lay in Scripture. Thus we must see Erasmus and the humanistic impulse as providing an important ideological and methodological bridge between the Renaissance and the Reformation. In many ways, the Reformation was the natural result of the Renaissance and Renaissance humanism.

THE REFORMATION

The Reformation of the sixteenth century was the religious upheaval that led to the radical restructuring of the Christian Church in Europe. During the Middle Ages Catholic Christianity had established itself as the official religion of Western and Central Europe under the authority of the Pope. By the end of the sixteenth century that religious monopoly had been broken, and new "Protestant" churches were to be found in Great Britain, Scandinavia, Holland, Germany, and Switzerland. Even where the Roman Church remained dominant—in Ireland, France, Italy, Spain, and Eastern Europe—it too underwent significant changes.

The way for the Reformation was paved by the general desire for reform of the late medieval Roman Church. Prior to 1517, the year usually taken as the beginning of the Reformation, abuses in the church had long been criticized by advocates of reform. The papacy itself was blamed for allowing the clergy to amass wealth while neglecting their pastoral duties. Wealthy monasteries and chapters of clergy had inspired widespread anti-clerical feeling especially in Germany. Throngs of clergy populated the cities but few of them served as parish pastors. Most were supported by endowments that paid them to say private masses on behalf of the donor. In the meantime, the higher clergy were securing more than one endowed position for themselves and were hiring chaplains for a pittance to say their masses at one place while they lived at another. The vast system of fees and bribes associated with gaining ecclesiastical office extended resentment against the papacy even to the nobility. The church practice of selling indulgences, a total remission of penalties for sin (and thus ensuring swift entry into Heaven), also invited criticism from several quarters and would be one of the impetuses driving Martin Luther's revolt against the church.

The call for the reform of such abuses came from a variety of sources. Prominent individuals like John Hus (ca.1369–1415) in Czechoslovakia and John Wyclif (ca.1329–1384) in England led popular reform movements in their own countries. Councils of the church sought to shift ecclesiastical authority from the papacy to representative groups of clergy. The Council of Constance (1414–1418) claimed that its authority superseded that of the popes and called for reform councils to be held at regular intervals. During the fifteenth century, however, the papacy was able to regain its control of the church. Although the Fifth Lateran Council (1512–1517) called on the pope to reform the church, its call went unheeded. As we have seen, Christian humanists such as Erasmus also provided a significant critique of the church rooted in Scripture, and it seemed for a while that humanism and the conciliar movement would join forces. Neither humanism nor the conciliar movement, however, was able to effect permanent change. The impulse for lasting reform came from a different source. Martin Luther and the Protestant Reformation are the subject of Chapter Thirteen.

ART OF THE RENAISSANCE

The visual arts of the fifteenth and sixteenth centuries in Europe differed dramatically from art of the Middle Ages. Just as the Renaissance witnessed a renewed interest in classical learning and literature, so, too, did it usher in a perceived "rebirth" of classical art. Particularly in Italy, artists looked to the classical past for inspiration. In the late Middle Ages, Giotto sought accurately to depict the human figure, rendering it three-dimensionally in realistic space. Artists of the Renaissance followed his lead, viewing Greek and Roman art as a source of visual knowledge. Whereas Medieval artists greatly stylized the human figure, repeating stock poses and facial types, Renaissance artists aspired to depict a lifelike individuality in painting and sculpture.

Artistic patronage underwent similar changes during the Renaissance, which led to a diversification of subject matter as well. Economic growth enabled the rise of a prosperous middle class in various parts of Europe, particularly in Italy, France, and the Netherlands. This newly wealthy group widely supported the production of literature and art, replacing in part the role held previously, and exclusively, by the church. The role of the middle class as patrons of art coincided with the effects of the Protestant Reformation. Protestant zealots considered any religious art to be idolatrous and destroyed all they could. Even in more moderate religious climates, artists lost much of their patronage from the church. As a result, art of the fifteenth and sixteenth centuries includes fewer religious subjects than seen previously. Instead, middle-class patrons commissioned portraits, landscapes, and other secular subject matter.

RENAISSANCE ART IN ITALY

The Gothic architecture that originated in France never took hold in Italy the way it did in other parts of Europe. By the fifteenth century, Italian architects were reviving elements of classical architecture and adapting them for both sacred and secular building projects. From town houses to churches, Italian architecture displayed such classical characteristics as columns, pilasters (rectangular, decorative columns), round arches, and arcades.

The Florence Cathedral (Plate 25) combines a variety of styles because it was overseen by a succession of architects over the course of two centuries. Begun in 1296 by Arnolfo di Cambio, cathedral construction occurred intermittently under Giotto, Andrea Pisano, and Filippo Brunelleschi, among others, until its eventual completion in 1471. The cathedral exhibits elements of the classical revival, such as an oculus at the top of the dome, but also draws upon features of Gothic building, as seen in the ribbed vaulting.

By far the most significant feature of the cathedral is the dome, a feature that even today dominates the Florence skyline. Fourteenth-century architects had intended a dome but did not know how to engineer it until Brunelleschi offered a solution in 1407. Brunelleschi's design called for a double-shelled dome, where the inner and outer shells would be linked internally by a system of arches, providing an internal support structure and, in theory, eliminating the need for exterior buttressing. Perhaps Brunelleschi's greatest contribution was in solving the logistics of how to build such an enormous dome, which measures 138 feet in diameter; at the time, it was the tallest dome ever built. The design called for the dome to be built up layer by layer. To aid the construction workers, Brunelleschi invented a hoisting machine that could carry building materials up to the scaffolding.

Prior to his work on the cathedral, Brunelleschi studied the remains of ancient architecture in Rome, returning to Florence with ideas of how best to integrate the old with the new. Elements of the dome showcase this attempted unification. While the inner shell of the dome is rounded, as seen in the Pantheon, the outer shell exhibits Gothic traits such as pointed arches and ribbed vaults. The dome is surrounded by a series of oculi, or round windows, rather than pointed Gothic windows. Originally topped by a large oculus, the dome perhaps paid tribute to the Pantheon. Following Brunelleschi's death, a small structure called a lantern was built to cap the dome, covering the oculus but still admitting natural light.

Another Florentine building to exhibit elements of the classical revival was the Palazzo Medici-Riccardi, begun in 1446 (Plate 26). While the structure was large in scale, the word palazzo actually designates a town house rather than a palace. The Palazzo occupies an entire city block and is constructed around a central courtyard. Its lower story, flanking the courtyard, houses a continuous classical arcade and covered walkway, or loggia. The Palazzo's exterior, however, is remarkably unornamented. Perhaps because the city of Florence had sumptuary laws that forbid ostentatious displays of wealth, or perhaps in order to honor Christian ideals of poverty and charity, the Medici family dwelling is understated in its decoration. The main ornamentation of the façade is rustication, or rough stonework, which becomes progressively smoother in ascending stories. The greatest indication of the family's wealth and stature is in the sheer scale of the residence: each story is over twenty feet high.

A painting from the fifteenth century highlights the intentional revival of classical architecture in the Renaissance. *View of an Ideal City,* from ca.1470 (Plate 27), depicts an Italian city center empty of people but full of classically inspired buildings. Each building exhibits such architectural details as round arches, arcades, and classical columns and pilasters. The painting displays the one-point linear perspective that flourished in the Renaissance, where all elements appear to recede in space to a distant vanishing point. In a subtle form of visual propa-

ganda, the classical references and precise perspective were intended to convey the ideal of an orderly civic life, one overseen by a benevolent government in a cool and logical manner.

A similar use of imaginary classical architecture appears in Raphael's *School of Athens,* 1510–11 (Plate 28). One of four paintings commissioned to fill the walls of the Vatican Library, the *School of Athens* displays a classical setting with rounded barrel vaults, columns, pilasters, and classical sculpture. The library paintings illustrate four branches of knowledge: religion, poetry, law, and, as seen here, philosophy. Plato and Aristotle, the two central figures framed by an arch, debate their personal philosophies: Plato gestures up to the heavens as the source of his beliefs, while Aristotle motions instead to the ground, illustrating his dedication to gathering knowledge through observation. Surrounding the two philosophers, well-known ancient mathematicians, astronomers, scientists, and geographers listen to the debate and conduct deliberations of their own. The large, classical hall in which they are set likely was not intended to suggest an existing building but rather to provide an appropriately dignified setting for such momentous debate.

In addition to its many classical references, the *School of Athens* draws clear connections with Renaissance art. The semi-circular wall niches of the Vatican Library determined the shape of Raphael's compositions. To accommodate the format, Raphael painted the scene as if seen through a *trompe l'oeil* arch. The entire composition appears to recede in space through a Renaissance system of linear perspective. The barrel-vaulted interior, while not a real building, may have been inspired by the new design for St. Peter's Cathedral in Rome. Raphael included his own visage in the painting and made reference to other Renaissance artists as well: in the left foreground, a solitary figure sketches and leans on a block of marble. His features are those of Michelangelo, who was then at work on the Sistine Chapel ceiling and whose contorted pose is highly reminiscent of the figures seen there.

A few years before his work on the Sistine Chapel, Michelangelo sculpted a colossal statue of *David* (Plate 29) that pays definite homage to the sculpture of Greek and Roman antiquity. While the subject is a biblical figure rather than a god or emperor, its pose draws definite parallels to its predecessors. The nudity of *David* implies his heroic qualities, just as nudity in antiquity often served to suggest divinity. His muscularity embodies an athleticism idealized in earlier times. The contrapposto pose makes further reference to classical precedents, where the figure's weight is visibly shifted to one leg, in turn slanting the hips and shoulders.

Michelangelo's sculpture of *David* functioned not only as part of a classical revival but also as a form of political propaganda. The specific subject matter, of David preparing for his confrontation with Goliath, insinuates that the righteous will prevail, even over the mighty. As such, the sculpture emblematized the people of Florence, who twice rose up against the tyrannical Medicis. In spite of a posture at rest, the intensity of David's facial expression and the sling over his shoulder indicate his readiness for battle. In its original commission, *David* was to be placed atop the Florence Cathedral, where he would have gazed confidently over the city. When completed, however, the sculpture was installed in the public square next to the seat of the city government.

NORTHERN RENAISSANCE ART

While Italian Renaissance artists looked to classical precedents and continued to pursue religious subjects, given the Catholic majority of the country, artists of northern Europe sought other inspiration. Because of the Protestant leanings of the Netherlands, artists there no longer counted on church patronage but instead painted portraits, landscapes, and other secular subjects for private, middle-class patrons. Logically, much painting and sculpture decreased in scale, for the final destination of art often was not the church, but rather the smaller domestic interior.

An Early Renaissance painting by Netherlandish artist Jan van Eyck foreshadows the rise of portraiture and domestic scenes in the north. *Portrait of Giovanni Arnolfini and his Wife, Giovanna Cenami*, 1434 (Plate 30), is most frequently interpreted as a wedding portrait. In the fifteenth century, marriage was more often observed through signing a legal contract than holding a religious ceremony. Van Eyck's painting, then, may visually record the nuptials, with the two requisite witnesses (one of whom may be the artist himself) appearing in the mirror. Various elements of the painting make reference to married life: the nuptial bed; the fruits by the window, indicating fertility; and the dog, symbolizing fidelity. The divided composition of the painting designates the roles that the husband and wife will play. Standing on the open side of the room, near the window, the man will occupy the public sphere, while the woman, set within the domestic interior, will function solely as wife and mother.

The *Arnolfini* portrait is rich with associations, combining secular and religious references. Despite the legal nature of the ceremony, van Eyck emphasized the importance of religion within marriage. The convex mirror that reflects the room is surrounded by tiny images from the Passion of Christ. On one side of the mirror, a set of prayer beads hangs on the wall; on the other, an image of St. Margaret, protector of women in childbirth, adorns a chair. Other elements of the painting may hold dual symbolism: the single burning candle in the chandelier may suggest the presence of Christ, or may function as a nuptial taper; similarly, the fruit by the window can signify fertility as well as the Fall of Adam and Eve.

By the sixteenth century, landscape painting gained increasing popularity in the Netherlands. Pieter Brueghel the Elder, perhaps the greatest practitioner of the genre, depicted the many variations of nature. Brueghel was particularly known for his cycles of paintings, illustrating such themes as the four seasons or the five senses. *Return of the Hunters* (Plate 31), of 1565, is one of a six-part series of paintings, each segment corresponding to two months of the year. The panel seen here represents November and December, showing a cold winter scene with short daylight hours. Brueghel's painting also symbolizes a northern artistic interest in depicting scenes of everyday life, a genre that would flourish in the seventeenth century under artists like Johannes Vermeer. *Return of the Hunters* functions in part as a landscape painting and as a slice of daily life. The viewer looks down on the scene to see not only the hunters and their dogs but also the innkeeper at work, moving a table and roasting a pig, while below, tiny figures skate on a frozen pond.

Neighboring the Netherlands, Germany had a more politically fragmented situation and harbored both Catholic and Protestant strongholds. German Renaissance artists explored portraiture and landscape but continued to depict religious subject matter as well. Albrecht Dürer, a painter and printmaker from Nuremberg, greatly admired the writings of Martin Luther. In a painting of the *Four Apostles*, from 1526 (Plate 32), Dürer seems to have acknowledged his belief in Lutheranism. While Dürer included John, Peter, and Mark, Paul, the apostle whose teachings and writings were most admired by Protestants, arguably receives the most prominent placement on the right panel. Even more telling is Dürer's inscrip-

tion below the painting, warning the viewer not to be led astray by "false prophets" but to heed the New Testament.

Unlike Protestant extremists, Dürer did not view religious art as idolatrous, nor did Luther ever support its destruction. Dürer presented his painted panels as a gift to the Lutheran city of Nuremberg. Through this painting, Dürer likely intended to defy the zealots and demonstrate the possibility of a Protestant religious art.

MUSIC OF THE RENAISSANCE AND REFORMATION

The Renaissance era in the history of Western music lasted from around 1400 to 1600. This period saw major developments in music composition, new types of music, musical instruments, and the ability to make music available to a wider public. Composers and musicians traveled extensively throughout Europe, taught and learned from one another, and created genuinely international European musical styles. Patronage of composers and musicians was no longer limited to the Church and the royal courts, but widened to include members of the new class of wealthy merchants and bankers who came to dominate the cities of the Renaissance. During the Renaissance polyphonic music composed and performed for the Church continued to dominate, and the Reformation created new forms of sacred music, but lively and varied traditions of secular music became increasingly prominent, and all the leading composers of the era composed both sacred and secular music.

The dominant style of the early Renaissance in music (1400s) was that of the Flemish and French composers. The royal court of Burgundy drew composers and musicians from throughout Europe. The first major composer was Guillaume Du Fay (1397–1474), who wrote masses and motets based on traditional Gregorian chants and also musical settings of French poetry. He was followed by the finest composer of the early Renaissance, Josquin Des Prez (ca. 1450–1521). Des Prez traveled widely throughout Europe, writing music for patrons at various places in France and Italy. Like Du Fay, Des Prez mainly composed Latin masses and motets, but in a wide variety of styles, and also wrote a good deal of secular music, including arrangements of French popular music. During this period vocal music, commonly unaccompanied, remained supreme in both sacred and secular music, but composers were developing it with increasing complexity, creating choral works with four or more parts. They became interested, working within the framework of polyphony, in creating pleasing chords (especially thirds and sixths) to accompany the melody line, which marked the beginning of the harmonic music (homophony) with which we are familiar.

In 1501 a Venetian printer named Ottaviano Petrucci published the first important collection of polyphonic music, which led to music publishing throughout Europe. Before 1501 all music had to be copied by hand or learned by hearing. With the development of printed music many more people could own their own musical texts and also instruction books for learning music and dance. In time the ability to sing, play an instrument, and participate in popular dances became a standard expectation on the part of middle- and upper-class men and women, and an essential part especially of girls' education.

Instrumental music really began to come into its own about the same time. While purely instrumental music had long been played to accompany dancing, for the most part it was limited to serving as accompaniment to the human voice. With the printing of musical works and advances in musical technology in the sixteenth century this began to change, with the composition and performance of an increasing number of pieces written entirely for instrumentalists. This in turn led to the development of chamber and orchestral music as an independent musical genre. Among the leading instruments of the Renaissance period were the *viola da gamba* or *viol* (a precursor of the violin), the lute, the harpsichord, the organ, the recorder, the flute, the *shawm* (an early oboe) and the *krummhorn* (another double-reed instrument), the *sackbut* (an early version of the trombone), the *cornetto* (a small trumpet), and a variety of drums, bells, and cymbals. Instruments like the viol and the recorder were produced in sets or families of different sizes and musical ranges, and were performed together in consorts or ensembles. So, for example, there were soprano, alto, tenor, and bass recorders.

In the 1500s, building on the polyphonic tradition, European composers explored and expanded the distinctive musical traditions of the various cultures of the continent—the French *chanson*, the Italian and English madrigal, the German *Tenorlieder*, and the Spanish *villancico*. Italians and English now came to dominate among the leading composers of the Renaissance: among them were Andrea Gabrieli (ca. 1532–1585); Madalena Casulana (ca. 1540–ca. 1590), the first published woman composer; Thomas Tallis (ca. 1505–1585); William Byrd (1543–1623); Giovanni Pierluigi da Palestrina (ca. 1525–1594), the greatest composer of sacred music of the late Renaissance; and Claudio Monteverdi (1567–1643), who created some of the first operas.

The Reformation of the sixteenth century inspired a new, Protestant tradition of sacred music. Martin Luther himself was a hymn-writer who founded the Protestant tradition in sacred music, and congregational hymn-singing eventually became central to Protestant worship. Luther wrote all the words to his hymns, but often adapted the music from traditional and even popular tunes. The Lutheran tradition in Germany produced some of the greatest composers and church music of the seventeenth and early eighteenth centuries, notably Johann Sebastian Bach (1685–1750) and George Frederick Handel (1685–1759), and masterpieces like Bach's *Mass in B Minor* and Handel's *Messiah*. The Reformed, and specifically the Calvinist, churches were more austere in their approach to worship, simplifying the liturgy and incorporating only what could be based on the Bible. The only singing could be the chanting of the Psalms. Composers like Louis Bourgeois, an associate of Calvin, wrote simple tunes for psalm-singing, and others wrote metrical versions of the Psalms. These were the hymns of the Puritans in colonial New England.

In the modern period, however, churches in the Calvinist tradition have shared in and contributed to the larger Protestant tradition of hymn-singing.

Palestrina was the leading composer of the Roman Catholic Counter-Reformation. According to legend, it was hearing a work by Palestrina that persuaded the cardinals and bishops at the reforming Council of Trent (which met intermittently between 1545 and 1563) not to ban all polyphonic music in the Church. He spent his career as *maestro di cappella* (master of the chapel) for three churches in Rome, including St. Peter's. His most famous composition is the *Pope Marcellus Mass*, and his music is considered beautiful in its clarity and balance.

Claudio Monteverdi is a transitional figure between the Renaissance and the Baroque eras in music, and one of the most remarkable innovators in the history of Western music. He wrote sacred music, especially for St. Mark's Cathedral in Venice, but he also composed many madrigals, and was one of the first composers of opera. In 1607 he wrote his first opera, *Orfeo*, based on the ancient Greek legend of Orpheus.

CD SELECTIONS

The selections from the Renaissance period provide a sampling of some of the important developments in European music described above. We begin, on track #16, with the *Kyrie* from one of the finest masses composed by one of the preeminent Renaissance composers, Josquin Des Prez: the *Missa Pange Lingua*. It was recorded by the Spandauer Kantorei conducted by Martin Behrmann (SPJ Music). He was Luther's favorite composer, whom Luther described as "the master of notes, they have to do as he bids them." Des Prez was also the master of words, beautifully crafting a natural and intimate relationship between text and music. He wrote eighteen masses, a hundred motets, and some seventy madrigals and chansons. His masses are polyphonic, but with some homophonic aspects, using secular tunes as the *cantus firmus*.

Track #17 is a recording of Martin Luther's most famous hymn, *Ein Feste Burg ist unser Gott* ("A Mighty Fortress is our God"), by the Westfälische Kantorei conducted by Wilhelm Ehmann (Cantate-Musicaphon). Composed in 1528, it is widely regarded among Protestants as the "hymn of the

Reformation," and in our time it is also sung in Roman Catholic churches. The second stanza especially expresses Luther's Reformation theology. In translation, it reads: "With our own might we can do nothing, we would soon be lost; But for us fights the right man, whom God himself ordained. You ask who this might be? It is Jesus Christ, the Lord Sabaoth, and is no other God. He must hold the field of battle."

Appropriately following the "hymn of the Reformation," on track #18, is the *Kyrie* from the *Pope Marcellus Mass* by Giovanni Pierluigi da Palestrina, the "official" composer of the Catholic Counter-Reformation. The performance is by the Vienna Motettenchor conducted by Bernhard Klebel (Qualiton Imports). The *Pope Marcellus Mass* is often regarded as the perfect example of the Counter-Reformation style in polyphonic sacred music. You have now had the opportunity to hear three *Kyries* illustrating the elaboration of European church music from monophonic Gregorian chant to the polyphony of the early Renaissance (Des Prez) and the high Renaissance (Palestrina).

The final selection, on track #19, marks the transition from the Renaissance to the Baroque period of the seventeenth and the first half of the eighteenth centuries. It is a brief selection from what has been called the "first true opera," composed by Claudio Monteverdi, the revolutionary musical genius who more than anyone else brought about that transition. *Orfeo* was his first opera, which he composed in 1607 for the annual carnival in Mantua, Italy, and it remains his most popular. An opera is a drama set to music—as it was called in Monteverdi's Italy, a *dramma per musica*—and it was Monteverdi who first revealed its potentialities as a major form of musical and dramatic art. The selection is a soprano *recitative*, "Io no diro" ("I will not say"), sung by Marinella Pennicchi on a recording by Naxos. In opera a recitative is a passage which the singer "sings" using the rhythm of natural speech, with only slight melodic variation. *Orfeo* is one of many tellings of the ancient Greek myth of the singing god Orpheus and his mortal wife Eurydice. She dies, and he braves the journey down through the underworld to bring her back, on condition that when is bringing her up he must not look back at her. He forgets, and loses her forever.

CHAPTER 12

A NEW POLITICAL PHILOSOPHY: NICCOLÒ MACHIAVELLI

INTRODUCTION

For many Westerners the word "Renaissance" brings to mind Florence, a city in the north-central region of the country of Italy. At the time of the Renaissance, however, there was no "country of Italy" but a patchwork of small states with different sorts of governments. Florence was the capital of the state of Tuscany and, although dominated by its wealthy and powerful families, a republic.

The Romans settled Florence as the city of Florentia in the first century BCE, although there is evidence of prior occupation, probably Etruscans. It was built in a hilly valley on the banks of the Arno River, which flowed west to Pisa and the sea. The Romans laid out the town in traditional grid-like Roman style, enclosed within walls, constructed a temple, capitol, theatre, forum, arena, and baths, and provided it with an aqueduct to feed a deep well in the forum. There is no material evidence of their occupation except what exists in the names of some of the streets: Via delle Terme "street of the baths," and Via del Campidoglio, "street of the Capitol." Christianity arrived sometime in the third century, probably by ship from Pisa. Florence claims one martyr, a Greek named Miniato, a victim of the Decian persecutions. In the tenth century the bishop of Florence founded the monastery and church of San Miniato al Monte to honor this legendary saint. The monastery is built on a hilltop to the south of the city which commands a spectacular view of Florence and the surrounding valleys.

Florence developed into a prosperous—but quiet—commercial town. However, the barbarian invasions of the fifth century that caused the upheaval of the Western Roman Empire threw Florence into decline. The trade route that had previously been so profitable was abandoned because it was too dangerous. The population fell from 10,000 in the second century to less than 1,000 in the sixth century. Despite the decline in trade, Christianity had taken hold and new churches and monasteries were founded. It is generally accepted that it was during these dark times that the Church of Santa Reparata was built in gratitude for a battle won over the Lombards. Santa Reparata was located where the Church of Santa Maria del Fiore, the magnificent *Duomo* (cathedral), now stands.

When Charlemagne established the Holy Roman Empire, Florence came under the rule of a succession of margraves (German for "prince") who ruled Tuscany as feudal lords. In the eleventh century the ruling margrave died and his widow Matilda was made Countess of Tuscany. She moved to Florence, a city she favored, from her birthplace in Lucca, and came to be held in high esteem by the citizens. Even Dante sang her praises in his *Commedia*. At this time the local government was organized as a *comune* (commune) with elected consuls. Florence was again a flourishing commercial center, but the merchants and the aristocracy, because of their differing interests, were often at each others' throats. In an effort to better manage the quarreling, Florence chose to go outside the city to hire a *podestà* (chief magistrate). Today this would be something like a city manager. The reasoning was that a podestà selected from the local populace could easily be influenced by one side or the other in a dispute, or simply assert his own interests, whereas a podestà from the outside would be expected to be impartial. The term of the podestà was generally a year. He

Most of Florence's major structures and its bridges over the Arno River were crowded inside fortress-like walls, some of which are still standing. At the left is the Palazzo Vecchio (figure VI-8), which held the office of Machiavelli. Behind it, near the fortification, is the Church of Santa Croce, where Galileo is buried. "Pianta della Catena," or Map of the Chain, refers to a painted chain around the map's border that symbolizes the city's protection from foreign enemies.

Figure VI-1 View of Florence in 1470, called the Map of the Chain, detail of an eighteenth-century reproduction in tempera. Museo di Firenze com'era, Florence, Italy. Courtesy of Alinari/Art Resource, NY.

was housed handsomely in a palace that was also a prison (today's Bargello Museum).

It was Matilda who was responsible for bringing about a division in the populace of Florence that would rage for over a century. It was during her rule that the Investiture Controversy between Pope Gregory VII and the Emperor Henry VII took place. This controversy was over whether the emperor or the pope had the right to make clerical appointments. Henry had given his chaplain an archbishopric and encouraged disobedience to the pope among his German assembly. The pope held a powerful weapon in his authority to excommunicate the emperor, which had the result of releasing all his subjects from their allegiance to him. Matilda threw her support to the pope, and those who followed her were called *Guelphs*. The aristocracy supported the emperor, and they were named *Ghibellines*. The pope's weapons proved stronger than the emperor's, and Henry was forced to undergo a humiliating recantation in front of the castle of Canossa, Matilda's family home.

Henry's heirs resented the papal favoritism of Florence and they forced their own podestà on the City. This gave the Ghibellines temporary control, but much of the thirteenth century was a violent see-saw between the Guelphfs and the Ghibellines. When the power was with the emperor the Ghibellines were in ascendance, and when it was with the pope it was the Guelphs who dominated. However, sometimes the pope-emperor struggle took a back seat to disputes over local and regional matters.

Toward the end of the thirteenth century another division arose which began as a family quarrel. This was the struggle between the Whites and the Blacks. In many ways this polarization divided along the same lines as the Guelphs and Ghibellines. The Whites were led by an "upstart" Florentine, not from one of the ancient families but popular. The Blacks were led by a "grande" and were supported by the French, in the person of Charles of Valois, and by the pope. In 1301 the Whites held control of the city and most of the leading Blacks were in exile. When French soldiers approached the city gates, the Whites mistakenly understood them to be emissaries from the pope. When they opened the gates the French soldiers entered and proceeded to pillage, rape, and murder.

Dante Aligheri had been born in Florence in 1265. Dante's family were loyal Guelphs, and he doubtless was influenced by their accounts of the Guelph-Ghibelline struggle. Many of the main figures in the controversy appear prominently in Dante's *Divine Comedy*, especially in the first part, the *Inferno*. At the time of the defeat of the Whites, Dante, who was a White, was in Rome as their envoy to the pope. Dante was condemned *in absentia* and never returned to Florence.

Florence had its disasters in the fourteenth century, but they more often took the form of natural disasters, floods, fires, and plagues. The people were tired of fighting and when conflicts arose which required soldiers the local governments hired mercenaries led by *condottieri*, men generally of noble birth. However, this was expensive and often the mercenaries were more interested in their paychecks than in completing their assignments. The lines between old factions blurred and new ones along the lines of professions increased. A new picture of the medieval city began to emerge in the fifteenth century.

FLORENTINE GOVERNMENT

The government of Florence evolved over the centuries but was always dominated by the most influ-

ential citizens in some form of oligarchy. The one that was in place by the 1450s is described here.

The actual elected officials were representatives of the guilds. There were two categories of guilds, the *arti maggiori* (major guilds) and the *arti minori* (minority guilds). The *arti maggiori* were the guilds of judges, lawyers, wool, silk and leather merchants, bankers, doctors, and apothecaries. The *arti minori* were the working-class guilds: the butchers, bakers, blacksmiths, and carpenters. Artists were sometimes incorporated into the trade guilds, but eventually formed their own separate guilds. There were seven major and fourteen minor guilds.

Members of the ruling council, the *priori* or *signoria*, were chosen from candidates put forward by the guilds. Every two months each guild put forth names of candidates and these names were placed in a *borse* (a leather bag). Names were pulled out of the bag and those who were for one reason or another were not eligible were discarded. Six men were chosen from the *arti maggiori* and two from the *arti minori*. A ninth man was chosen who would be the *gonfaloniere*, a sort of presiding magistrate. They were required to live in the Palazzo dei Priori (now the Palazzo Vecchio or "old palace") for these months, but were provided for in great luxury. They made laws, sometimes consulting with heads of various elected councils. There were two permanent officials, a chancellor, who was a man of letters and promulgated decrees, and the podestà, whose role we have described above. During times of crisis the priori would call a *balìa*. The bell in the high tower of the palazzo would ring and the citizens from the four quarters of the city would gather carrying identifying banners. The crisis was presented and solutions proposed. A decision was based on the priori's being satisfied that a majority approved.

THE FAMILY MEDICI

The story of the Medici of Florence, who were powerful figures in Florence for over four centuries, begins with Giovani di Bicci di Medici (1360–1429). Giovani was a man of modest background who began work in a bank in Rome and "worked his way up," as the saying goes. He established a bank in Florence, and by the time of his death he had founded banks in six other cities in the Italian peninsula including Rome. He was a cautious and retiring man who advised his two sons to keep a

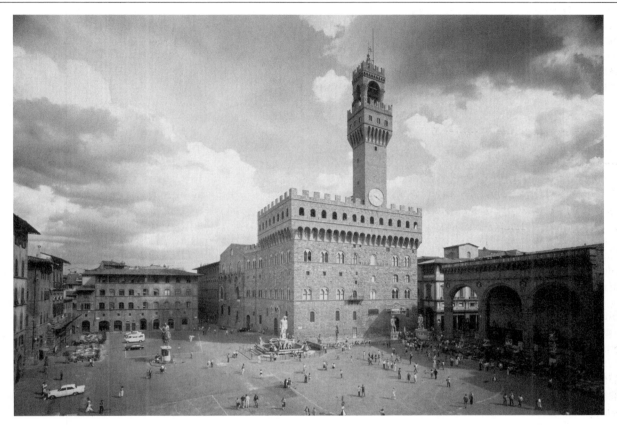

In the Italian city-states, government buildings competed with churches in both size and artistic magnificence. Arnolfo di Cambio's Palazzo dei Priori (Palace of the Priors), named after the principal governing body of Florence, physically dominates an entire section of the city. Its imposing, block-like structure, which incorporates several additions from the fifteenth and sixteenth centuries, rises above all surrounding buildings and supports the tallest tower in Florence. The palace's history includes housing government offices, along with an office for Machiavelli, and briefly accommodating the Medici family. Following the departure of the Medicis to the Palazzo Pitti across the river, the palace became known as the Palazzo Vecchio, or old palace. A copy of Michelangelo's *David* stands on the right near the entrance.

Figure VI-2 Arnolfo di Cambio. Palazzo Vecchio, Florence, Italy. 1299–1310. Courtesy of Scala/Art Resource, NY.

low profile and never dress or live ostentatiously. He did not seek office but served when asked, which was the duty of a good Florentine citizen. The social classes divided between the aristocracy and the *popolani* (common people), and Giovani considered himself a member of the popolani. He was known for his easy generosity, hospitality and artistic patronage, and yet he aroused the jealousy of his competitors. This enmity among the leading families of Florence—the Medici, the Pazzi, the Bardi, the Albizzi and others—in many ways defined the life and politics of Florence during the Renaissance.

Giovanni's son Cosimo succeeded him as manager of the business in 1429. Under his management the business grew to international status, with banks in Geneva, London, and Bruges. Cosimo followed his father's advice and never sought political office, but through his considerable influence he was the unofficial ruler of Florence. Resentment towards him was strong, however, and in 1434 the Albizzi gathered sufficient support to have him expelled from Florence. Cosimo did leave Florence for awhile, but when he returned his power was stronger than ever while that of his opponents diminished.

Giovanni had not received a formal education, but he saw to it that his sons were well-educated by the best scholars in Florence, many of whom were among the new humanists of the Renaissance. In an effort to achieve reconciliation between the Roman Catholic and the Orthodox Churches, which had been formally estranged since 1054, Cosimo hosted representatives from Western and Eastern Christendom in Florence. Known as the Council of Ferrara-Florence, it took place between 1438–39. While reconciliation was eventually achieved by the council representatives, it was later rejected in Constantinople. With the conquest of Constantinople by the Muslim Turks in 1453, the issue became buried by events.

Cosimo continued the patronage of the arts his father had started. The list of Renaissance artists he supported reads like a "who's who" of the early Renaissance—names like Donatello, Brunelleschi, Michelozzo (who built the Medici Palace on what is now via Cavour), Della Robbia, and Fra Filippo Lippi. He maintained good relations with the Church in part through his generosity.

The son who succeeded Cosimo in 1469 was not the chosen one. Piero, referred to as the Gouty, was a shy, reserved man, but he was highly capable. He too was sabotaged by his enemies but was saved through his own astuteness and the help of his son and successor, Lorenzo.

Lorenzo may best be described by the appellation given to him, *il magnifico*—the magnificent. Lorenzo the Magnificent (1449–1492) and his younger brother Giuliano were raised as princes and cut dashing figures on horseback as they rode about the streets of Florence. But they were also well-educated in humanist literature and art. Little more can be said of Giuliano (other than his having fathered an illegitimate child who would become Pope Clement VII), because in 1478 he was brutally murdered in the Florence cathedral by members and fellow conspirators of the Pazzi family. Lorenzo was wounded but escaped, and presided over the bloody retribution against the Pazzi.

Lorenzo was not primarily interested in business, and the Medici banks experienced financial difficulties under his management, in part because the papacy transferred its funds to a competitor. He was, however, know for his skill at diplomacy. He was able to maintain peace in the region through negotiation despite intense factionalism. Lorenzo continued and enhanced the Medici patronage of many artists and invited the young Michelangelo Buonarotti into his home, where he lived for nearly a decade. His greatest love was intellectual discourse, and for this purpose he surrounded himself with a group of humanists, the most famous of whom was Marsilio Ficino. Ficino translated all of Plato's works into Italian, and a group formed around him called the Neoplatonic Academy. Although its exact function and composition are not definitively known, it was definitely not a formal school.

It was the "splendor" of Florence that drew a dour and intense Dominican monk to the city in 1488. Girolamo Savonarola viewed the success of Florence as excess and sin. He was a millenarian, an apocalyptic preacher who called for an end to the sinful habits of the citizens. Savonarola was also highly suspicious of the "new learning," believing it to be heretical. The name of an event staged by Savonarola has come down through the centuries, and in recent decades was used as the title of a popular novel by Tom Wolfe, *The Bonfire of the Vanities* (1987). On Shrove Tuesday of 1497 Savonarola instructed the citizens of Florence to bring their jewels, books, and other items of fancy and indulgence to the Piazza Signoria, where they were burned in a great bonfire.

In the midst of the upheaval of Savonarola's "Reformation," Lorenzo became ill and died in his villa at Careggio in 1492. Lorenzo's successor, his son Piero, was vain, arrogant, and stupid. Within two years he was thrown out of the city. The city which had never stopped being ruled in the form of a republic now became a true republic. In 1498 Savonarola ran afoul of the pope, encouraged no doubt by the citizens of Florence who were tired of this obsessive ascetic. Along with two companions from the Dominican order, he was burned in the Piazza della Signoria, where today a plaque in the cobblestones commemorates the event.

NICCOLÒ MACHIAVELLI

This is the background into which Niccolò Machiavelli was born in 1469 in the city of Florence. He was the son of a lawyer who owned a small amount of property. He entered public life in 1494, when the ruling Medici family was driven out of Florence. From 1498 to 1512 he served as second chancellor and secretary to the Republic, with functions relating to war and the management of Florentine territory. He frequently served as ambassador both to the courts of major powers (such as those of Louis XII of France and of the German Emperor Maximilian) and to smaller principalities of Tuscany (such as Siena and Imola). Machiavelli's time as ambassador to Cesare Borgia, Duke of Valentinois, in 1502, made a particularly strong impression on him.

Machiavelli's career in public service virtually came to an end when the republican government of Florence fell in 1512. The Medici family had regrouped in the person of Lorenzo, last child of Lorenzo the Magnificent, with strong support from the Medici pope, Leo X. The new Medici government arrested Machiavelli on suspicion of his involvement in a conspiracy (he denied it), tortured, imprisoned, and then exiled him from Florence and specifically prohibited him from setting foot in the Palazzo dei Priari, where he had served the republican government. He spent the remainder of his life living on a farm outside Florence. With the exception of a brief period of the revival of the republic (1527–30), the Medicis would retain control of Florence for the next two and a half centuries. Another Cosimo di Medici from another family branch was awarded the title Grand Duke in 1537, and the Duchy of Tuscany lasted until well into the eighteenth century.

It was out of his exile that Niccolò Machiavelli wrote *The Prince* and *Discourses on the First Ten Books of Titus Livius*. Indeed, it was exile that gave him the time to distill his experiences in government service and write the works for which he is primarily remembered. He wrote the *Prince* within the first two years of exile (completed in 1515). He spent a much longer time writing his commentary on the *History of Rome* by the Roman historian Livy (Titus Livius). He also wrote a treatise on warfare, a history of Florence modeled on Livy, and several plays including *Mandragola*, considered one of the best comedies of the Italian Renaissance. From 1519 on,

he was to some extent called upon as a consultant by the Medici government and was also sent on minor missions. He died in Florence in 1527.

The new circumstances created in European politics by the emergence of large, centralized nation-states provide the context that shapes the often shocking recommendations set forth in *The Prince*. In *The Prince*, one can see quite clearly how Machiavelli's experiences as a diplomat are reflected as a concern with how the smaller states can resist being taken over by larger centralized ones. Chapter three is devoted to an analysis of the failure of one of the major new powers of the day, France, to hold on to the territory of Milan, in northern Italy, after capturing it in 1494. Machiavelli's argument constitutes a warning to all the squabbling princes of Italy, for he shows that King Louis XII of France lost Milan by making mistakes, not through any lack of military power or because the Italians successfully campaigned against him. The clear message is that if France (or Spain) ever has a king who understands political conduct as Machiavelli does, he will be able to take over all of Italy. In other words, as Machiavelli sees it, the only way for a small state to maintain some degree of autonomy in the face of far superior resources is to have a government that follows the political rules set forth in *The Prince*.

That Machiavelli himself preferred republican government, that is, government carried out by leaders the people have chosen, is proved both by his career as a diplomat and eventually secretary of state in such a government and by his argumentation in the *Discourses on Titus Livius*. Nonetheless, when the republican government of Florence which he served fell as a result of the departure from Italy of its French allies, leaving it at the mercy of Spain, the other super-power of the day, Machiavelli was forced to withdraw from political life and was left to meditate on how singularly ill-equipped the kind of government he preferred was to deal with the political circumstances of Renaissance Europe. *The Prince* is concerned with the survival of an autonomous state whose back, so to speak, may at any moment be pushed against the wall by a super-power. Moreover, Machiavelli understands that the small states of the Italian peninsula will ultimately never be able to maintain themselves against foreign invaders until all of Italy is united under a single government, making Italy, too, a nation-state. He closes *The Prince* with an appeal to Lorenzo de Medici, Duke of Urbino (1492–1519), to enlist his cousin, Pope Leo X (1475–1521), and an army made up of native Italians rather than mercenaries, in a campaign to drive Spanish, French, and German invaders permanently from Italian soil.

The new nation-state of the Renaissance requires, in Machiavelli's view, a new form of political philosophy. Medieval political writings had argued from certain fixed principles, such as the subjection of secular to ecclesiastical power or the legitimacy of the Holy Roman Empire. The new political thought of Machiavelli and some other Renaissance statesmen, by contrast, was based on the attempt to free the study of politics from all preconceived notions and to found it, like a science, on the observation of contemporary and historical reality. Thus Machiavelli is impatient with all the truisms of political thought and argues that it is "better to go after the real truth of the matter than to repeat what people have imagined." Political proverbs and slogans are of no help because they cannot take present circumstances into account.

Machiavelli's view of how to establish and maintain an autonomous state is based on a pessimistic view of human nature. In concluding the main body of his argument, at the end of chapter twenty-three of *The Prince*, he observes that "men will always turn out badly for you unless they are forced to be good." Thus, his political thought stands apart from any ethical principles; he is not striving to find ways to increase the happiness of citizens, give them greater individual liberties, or cultivate their talents. His only goal is to keep them free from enslavement by foreigners. The modesty of his goal contrasts markedly with the ambition of many later political philosophers. It may also remind Machiavelli's readers how bleak life could seem for a Florentine who was, in fact, the contemporary of that great symbol of Renaissance triumph, Michelangelo.

If Machiavelli's view of human nature seems gloomy and cynical, it is no more so than his attitude toward the Church of his day. As he points out in detail in chapter eleven, the role of the Church in political life changed dramatically during the Renaissance. This was especially true after the elec-

tion to the papacy of the Spaniard Rodrigo Borgia (also in the fateful year of 1492). Borgia, who took the name Alexander VI, was clearly more devoted to advancing the interest of his children, especially Lucrezia and Cesare, than to serving the Church. As Machiavelli remarks, however, "he showed, more than any other pope that ever was, how much can be done in that office with money and arms." He raised enormous sums of money by declaring that certain kinds of documents, or indulgences, sold in 1500 could be of enormous benefit to Christians in the afterlife, and set a standard of commercialism in religious matters that brought the papacy to its highest level of military power and greatest achievements in patronage of the arts. Such ecclesiastical commercialism, however, was shortly to threaten the Church's spiritual authority even while increasing the resources available to extend its secular power.

With the advent of the Reformation, and especially with the Church's vigorous reaction to it, the Renaissance begins to draw to a close. The Counter-Reformation, in areas which remained largely Roman Catholic, brought with it an intellectual conservatism that put a stop to much of the creative ferment of the Renaissance, especially in humanism and the sciences. By this time, the last vestiges of the medieval world, often represented as a unified entity, had long since disappeared, fragmented into the many and often conflicting worlds of the Renaissance. The Old World and the New, the world of science and that of faith, the world of the worker and that of the employer, the public world of middle-class men and the private world of middle-class women: all these made the world of the mid-sixteenth century a more dynamic place than that of the early Renaissance humanists. The very changeability of the conditions of life became one of the defining characteristics of the Renaissance. It is also that characteristic that makes it most evident how much life in the early twenty-first century shares with the Renaissance. For this and other reasons, some scholars have recently begun to drop the term "Renaissance" in favor of a new term: "the early modern period." Whatever one chooses to call it, this period of transition has left on the Western world a long series of marks, some for good, others for ill, but all of them indelible.

THE PRINCE

Niccolò Machiavelli is the first modern political theorist and one of the pioneers of modern political thought and practical strategy. He was a Renaissance humanist, steeped in and deeply influenced by the ancient classics especially of the Roman world. In *The Prince* and his other important work on political theory, *Discourses on the First Ten Books of Titus Livius*, he bases his political ideas to a great extent on Greek and Roman histories. There is no better account of Machiavelli's reverence for the classics than a scene from a letter he wrote in 1513 to his friend Francesco Vettori, during the period when Machiavelli had been exiled from Florence by the Medicis and was living at his home in the country. After describing the way he spends his day, Machiavelli writes:

> When evening comes, I go back home, and go to my study. On the threshold I take off my work clothes, covered in mud and filth, and put on the clothes an ambassador would wear. Decently dressed, I enter the ancient courts of rulers who have long since died. There I am warmly welcomed, and I feed on the only food I find nourishing, and was born to savor. I am not ashamed to talk to them, and to ask them to explain their actions. And they, out of kindness, answer me. Four hours go by without my feeling any anxiety. I forget every worry. I am no longer afraid of poverty, or frightened of death. I live entirely through them.

Machiavelli goes on in the letter to say that he has been writing *The Prince*, and what he has learned from the actions of "rulers who have long since died" provides the historical foundations and arguments of the book.

Machiavelli's influence has given us the words "Machiavellian" and "Machiavellianism," both of which have negative connotations. A typical "dictionary definition" characterizes "Machiavellian" as "suggestive of or marked by the principles of expediency, deceit, and cunning imputed to Machiavelli." "Machiavellianism" is defined as "the polit-ical doctrine of Machiavelli, which denies the relevance of morality in political affairs and holds that craft and deceit are justified in pursuing and retaining power." As you read *The Prince*, an important question for you to ponder will be whether or not you think these definitions are fair to Machiavelli himself.

The meanings of "Machiavellian" and "Machiavellianism" are based entirely on *The Prince*. In addition to the question whether or not they are a fair summary of the views of that book, there is the fact that Machiavelli wrote other books—notably *Discourse on the First Ten Books of Titus Livius*, which sets forth his political philosophy much more fully and comprehensively. In the *Discourse* Machiavelli argues, using as his model the ancient Roman republic as described by the Roman historian Livy (Titus Livius), that republics are the best and most enduring form of government: "The people are wiser and more trustworthy than princes." Ironically in view of Machiavelli's reputation in our time, in his own time his enthusiasm for representative popular government was unusual. His view went *against* the main Western tradition in political theory, which was deeply suspicious of popular rule. (In different ways, both Plato and Thomas Aquinas reflect this mainstream tradition.) It was for *this* reason, as much as for *The Prince*, that Machiavelli was for a long time unpopular. The "republican" Machiavelli came into his own with the growth of modern political thought and democratic institutions beginning in the seventeenth century. The United States' "Founding Fathers" who created the Constitution knew well the history of political thought, ancient and modern, and knew of Machiavelli as an important exponent of republican government

But in all his political writings Machiavelli represents a new departure in Western political thought. You have now read Plato, Aristotle, and Thomas Aquinas on politics, and it will be important for you to compare and contrast Machiavelli's approach with what you have seen in theirs. In different ways both Plato in the *Republic* and Aristotle in the *Politics* were preoccupied with the cultivation of *virtue* or human excellence as a supreme goal of politics. Aquinas, as an Aristotelian, follows this tradition.

Perhaps the most illuminating contrast is between Machiavelli's *The Prince* and an essay by

Thomas Aquinas entitled *On Kingship* which was discussed in Chapter Ten. Thomas's essay reflects the dominant approach to governing and the state in medieval thought, and that is the immediate background against which Machiavelli sets his own ideas. Both *On Kingship* and *The Prince* are about rulers and ruling, but there the resemblance ends. Thomas says that the best ruler is a virtuous person, one who is wise and just, and that the duties of a ruler are to promote peace, unity, and virtue among the people he rules. Like other medieval political thinkers, Thomas also believed that the ruler's power and authority ultimately derive from the community he or she rules, and that there are strict limitations on the ruler's power set by God, morality, and the community. When we look at Machiavelli's picture of the "best" ruler in chaps 15–19 of *The Prince*, we see something radically different.

In *The Prince*, power is the fundamental reality in political life: who has it, how to get it, and how to maintain it. Notice in *The Prince* the importance of playing off powerful forces (whether groups within a society or competing states) against one another—a version of the "balance of power" idea in modern international politics. Observe, too, that whereas Thomas focuses on moral principles in governing, Machiavelli is more concerned simply with the relation between means and ends: given a desired end (maintaining oneself in power, insuring the security of one's people), what are the surest and most efficient means to achieving it? Machiavelli also completely rejects discussing those ideal states that have been the dream of past political thinkers (such as Plato in his *Republic*), because "the gap between how people actually behave and how they ought to behave is so great that anyone who ignores everyday reality in order to live up to an ideal will soon discover he has been taught how to destroy himself, not how to preserve himself" (chapter fourteen). Interestingly, only three years after Machiavelli wrote *The Prince*, the Northern humanist Thomas More of England coined the term and wrote the influential book *Utopia* (1516) about an ideal society. *U-topia* is from the Greek and means "no place," existing only in human imagining and wishing. Machiavelli preferred to deal only with realities.

Completed in 1515, *The Prince* was not published until 1532, five years after Machiavelli's death.

Notice the dedication, to Lorenzo de Medici (Duke of Urbino), ruler of Florence from 1516–1519 and grandson of Lorenzo the Magnificent. The dedication pages are important, because there Machiavelli announces the method he is going to follow. Very important to keep in mind as you read *The Prince* is that it was written for a specific purpose; it was not intended as a general study of politics. The book is a practical manual for rulers, and its context is a fragmented Italy at the mercy of foreign powers. Among other things Machiavelli appears to have been an Italian nationalist, as is clear in the final chapter, "Exhortation to Seize Italy and Free Her from the Barbarians." Notice his call to his fellow Italians to revive the spirit of their Roman ancestors, and the contrasts he draws between the ancient Italians and his contemporaries. He seems to be calling for a strong, effective prince to lead the other city-states and principalities in driving out foreign invaders such as the French and the Spanish.

In *The Prince* Machiavelli appeals to history as a practical guide to the present. For many centuries it was taken for granted in Western thought and education that the study of history was essential for every generation in understanding who they were, what was going on in the world, and how they should live. The experience of the past was a guide to the present, teaching new generations about human nature, behavior, and morality. Studying history reminded people that human identity is never simply individual but profoundly social: the individual is part of a people, part of a continuum that spans past, present, and future generations. Machiavelli learned his love of history from his father, an editor of Livy's history. The widespread lack of interest in and knowledge of history in our day, among otherwise educated people, is from the point of view of previous generations a puzzle and an aberration.

In examining Machiavelli's chapters on the behavior of princes you need to attend carefully to his discussion of the *goals* of political rule and the best *means* to achieve them. Notice in particular his discussion of *limits* on the prince's actions, including limits on violence to achieve ends. In reading about Machiavelli's preoccupation with the ruler's *image*, consider how important "image" has become in contemporary U.S. politics.

When you have finished reading *The Prince*, return to the question with which we began: Is Machiavelli's reputation as a "Machiavellian" justified? Is he an *amoral cynic* or simply a *moral realist*? Is the advice in *The Prince* a recipe for ruthless, authoritarian government—as modern political leaders like Mussolini believed—or does it tell us something more generally applicable about getting and keeping political power? Do leaders of democratic nations like the U.S. ever behave in a "Machiavellian" fashion? If they do, what then is the crucial difference between a democratic and a fascist or totalitarian government? Majority rule? the rule of law? Constitutional checks and balances? a Bill of Rights?

PICO DELLA MIRANDOLA

Pico della Mirandola (1463–1494), the famous Italian humanist, settled at Florence in 1484 and died there when only 31 in 1494, having been poisoned, it is believed, by his secretary. He was a protégé of Lorenzo the Magnificent and Marsilio Ficino, who admired the young man's brilliant studies of Hebrew, Arabic, and the Cabala. Pico became renowned for his scholarship, his vast learning, his piety, and his library of the classics, which was one of the best in Italy at that time. (On his death bed, Lorenzo the Magnificent is reported to have said to Pico that one of the things he regretted about dying was that he would not be able to continue to help Pico complete his library.) He wrote, among others works, a Neo-platonic theological and philosophical treatise *De Ente et Uno* (On Being and the One), *Heptaplus*, a mystical account of the creation of the world, and *De Hominis Dignitatae* (*On the Dignity of Man*), which celebrates the uniqueness and possibility of humanity.

In 1486 Pico posted a list of nine hundred theses at Rome for debate. He proposed to discuss such subjects as logic, ethics, physics, mathematics, theology, and magic. He declared that he would defend his ideas about these subjects against any opponent. But his debate never took place, for Pope Innocent V had a commission investigate Pico's theories. When some of Pico's ideas seemed heretical to the commission, and to the Pope, the Holy See forced Pico to cancel the proposed debate.

Since Pico died so young, he was never able to carry out the great synthesis of Oriental, Greek, Roman, and Christian ideas which he proposed. But his *Oration on the Dignity of Man* shows his enthusiasm for the wonder of man and it has sometimes been called the "Declaration of Independence" of the humanism of the Italian Renaissance. Here is an eloquent passage that exemplifies the message of the *Oration*. Pico has God say to Adam: *imagine.*

> "We have given to thee, Adam, no fixed seat, no form of thy very own, no gift peculiarly thine, that thou mayest feel as thine own, have as thine own, possess as thine own the seat, the form, the gifts which thou thyself shalt desire. A limited nature in other creatures is confined within the laws written down by Us. In conformity with thy free judgment, in whose hands I have placed thee, *(you)* thou art confined by no bounds; and thou wilt fix limits of nature for thyself. I have placed thee at the center of the world, that from there thou mayest more conveniently look around and see whatsoever is in the world. Neither heavenly nor earthly, neither mortal nor immortal have We made thee. Thou, like a judge appointed for being honorable, art the molder and maker of thyself; thou mayest sculpt thyself into whatever shape thou dost prefer. Thou canst grow downward into the lower natures which are brutes. Thou canst again grow upward from they soul's reason into the higher natures which are divine."

Pico della Mirandola, *On the Dignity of Man*. Translated Charles Glenn Wallis. Hackett Publishers, 1998]

After Pico's death, Sir Thomas More wrote *The Life of John Picus, Earl of Mirandula*, which was an English translation of a biography written by Pico's nephew. From this work it is obvious that More greatly admired Pico's writings, perhaps almost as much as he did the works of his friend Erasmus; and thus through Thomas More we can connect the lives and writings of three of the greatest humanists of the Renaissance, More, Erasmus, and Pico.

QUESTIONS FOR STUDY AND REFLECTION

1. What does it mean to say that Florence was a republic? How was it governed in the fifteenth century?

2. Who were the Medicis, and how did they become politically powerful?

3. To whom was Machiavelli's *The Prince* addressed and what was his purpose in writing it? Why is the book not a complete statement of his political theory?

4. Briefly contrast his approach to government with the medieval approach as seen in Thomas Aquinas's *On Kingship*.

5. What does Machiavelli say in *The Prince* about what the role of the Catholic Church in the politics of his day is and what it should be? How does he characterize the Renaissance popes whom he talks about in *The Prince*?

6. Machiavelli says clearly at the beginning of *The Prince* that he is going to limit his discussion to monarchies. What were his views on republican or representative government?

7. Describe the characteristics of an effective ruler according to Machiavelli. Discuss the relevance of the characteristics he talks about to contemporary political leadership in the U.S.

8. In the final analysis, which term defines Machiavelli's approach in *The Prince*, amoral cynic or moral realist? Defend your answer.

9. What is the theme of Pico's *Oration on the Dignity of Man*? How does it exemplify the spirit of Renaissance humanism?

SUGGESTED READINGS

Allen, Michael J.B. and Valery Rees with Martin Davies, editors *Marsilio Ficino: His Theology, His Philosophy, His Legacy*. Boston, MA: Brill, 2002.

Black, Robert. "Machiavelli, Servant of the Florentine Republic," in *Machiavelli and Republicanism*, edited by G. Bock, Q. Skinner, and M. Viroli. Cambridge: Cambridge University Press, 1999.

Burckhardt, Jacob. *The Civilization of the Renaissance in Italy*, 2 volumes, 1860; Harper Torchbooks English ed. New York: Harper and Row, 1958.

Chabod, Federico. *Machiavelli and the Renaissance*. New York: Harper and Row, 1965.

Hibbert, Christopher. *The Rise and Fall of the House of Medici*. 1974; Harmondsworth: Penguin Books, 1979.

Jordan, Constance. *Renaissance Feminism*. Ithaca: Cornell University Press, 1990.

Kirkpatrick, Robin. *The European Renaissance 1400–1600*. London: Pearson Education, 2002.

Machiavelli, Niccolò. *Florentine Histories*. Translated by Laura F. Banfield and Harvey C. Mansfield, Jr. Princeton, NJ: Princeton University Press, 1988.

Pocock, J.G.A. *The Machiavellian Moment: Florentine Political Thought and the Atlantic Republican Tradition*. Princeton, NJ: Princeton University Press, 1975.

Ridolfi, Roberto. *The Life of Niccolò Machiavelli*. Translated by C. Grayson. Chicago: University of Chicago Press, 1963.

Skinner, Quentin. *Machiavelli*. Oxford: Oxford University Press, 1981.

A SPEECH BY
GIOVANNI PICO DELLA MIRANDOLA,
Prince of Concord

Most venerable fathers, I have read in the records of the Arabians that Abdul the Saracen, on being asked what thing on, so to speak, the world's stage, he viewed as most greatly worthy of wonder, answered that he viewed nothing more wonderful than man. And Mercury's, "a great wonder, Asclepius, is man!" agrees with that opinion.[1] On thinking over the reason for these sayings, I was not satisfied by the many assertions made by many men concerning the outstandingness of human nature: that man is the messenger between creatures, familiar with the upper and king of the lower; by the sharpsightedness of the senses, by the hunting-power of reason, and by the light of intelligence, the interpreter of nature; the part in between the standstill of eternity and the flow of time; and, as the Persians say, the bond tying the world together, nay, the nuptial bond; and, according to David, "a little lower than the angels."[2] These reasons are great, but not the chief ones, that is, they are not reasons for a lawful claim to the highest wonder as to a prerogative. Why should we not wonder more at the angels themselves and at the very blessed heavenly choirs?

Finally, it seemed to me that I understood why man is the animal that is most happy, and is therefore worthy of all wonder; and lastly, what the state is that is allotted to man in the succession of things, and that is capable of arousing envy not only in the brutes but also in the stars and even in minds beyond the world. It is wonderful and beyond belief. For this is the reason why man is rightly said and thought to be a great marvel and the animal really worthy of wonder. Now hear what it is, fathers; and with kindly ears and for the sake of your humanity, give me your close attention:

Now the highest Father, God the master-builder, had, by the laws of his secret wisdom, fabricated this house, this world which we see, a very superb temple of divinity. He had adorned the super-celestial region with minds. He had animated the celestial globes with eternal souls; he had filled with a diverse throng of animals the cast-off and residual parts of the lower world. But, with the work finished, the Artisan desired that there be someone to reckon up the reason of such a big work, to love its beauty, and to wonder at its greatness. Accordingly, now that all things had been completed, as Moses and Timaeus testify, He lastly considered creating man.[3] But there was nothing in the archetypes from which He could mold a new sprout, nor anything in His storehouses which He could bestow as a heritage upon a new son, nor was there an empty judiciary seat where this contemplator of the universe could sit. Everything was filled up; all things had been laid out in the highest,

---

[1]*Asclepius* I. 6 (*Hermetica,* ed. W. Scott, I, 294).
[2]Psalms 8:5.
[3]Plato, *Timaeus,* 41b ff.

Reprinted from *On the Dignity of Man,* translated by Charles Glenn Wallis, Indianapolis: Hackett Publishing Company, Inc., 1998.

the lowest, and the middle orders. But it did not belong to the paternal power to have failed in the final parturition, as though exhausted by child-bearing; it did not belong to wisdom, in a case of necessity, to have been tossed back and forth through want of a plan; it did not belong to the loving-kindness which was going to praise divine liberality in others to be forced to condemn itself. Finally, the best of workmen decided that that to which nothing of its very own could be given should be, in composite fashion, whatsoever had belonged individually to each and every thing. Therefore He took up man, a work of indeterminate form; and, placing him at the midpoint of the world, He spoke to him as follows:

"We have given to thee, Adam, no fixed seat, no form of thy very own, no gift peculiarly thine, that thou mayest feel as thine own, have as thine own, possess as thine own the seat, the form, the gifts which thou thyself shalt desire. A limited nature in other creatures is confined within the laws written down by Us. In conformity with thy free judgment, in whose hands I have placed thee, thou art confined by no bounds; and thou wilt fix limits of nature for thyself. I have placed thee at the center of the world, that from there thou mayest more conveniently look around and see whatsoever is in the world. Neither heavenly nor earthly, neither mortal nor immortal have We made thee. Thou, like a judge appointed for being honorable, art the molder and maker of thyself; thou mayest sculpt thyself into whatever shape thou dost prefer. Thou canst grow downward into the lower natures which are brutes. Thou canst again grow upward from thy soul's reason into the higher natures which are divine."

O great liberality of God the Father! O great and wonderful happiness of man! It is given him to have that which he chooses and to be that which he wills. As soon as brutes are born, they bring with them, "from their dam's bag," as Lucilius says, what they are going to possess.[4] Highest spirits have been, either from the beginning or soon after, that which they are going to be throughout everlasting eternity. At man's birth the Father placed in him every sort of seed and sprouts of every kind of life. The seeds that each man cultivates will grow and bear their fruit in him. If he cultivates vegetable seeds, he will become a plant. If the seeds of sensation, he will grow into brute. If rational, he will come out a heavenly animal. If intellectual, he will be an angel, and a son of God. And if he is not contented with the lot of any creature but takes himself up into the center of his own unity, then, made one spirit with God and settled in the solitary darkness of the Father, who is above all things, he will stand ahead of all things. Who does not wonder at this chameleon which we are? It was not unfittingly that Asclepius the Athenian said that man was symbolized by Prometheus in the secret rites, by reason of our nature sloughing its skin and transforming itself; hence metamorphoses were popular among the Jews and the Pythagoreans. For the more secret Hebrew theology at one time reshapes holy Enoch into an angel of divinity, whom they call *malach hashechina*, and at other times reshapes other men into other divinities.[5] According to the Pythagoreans, wicked men are deformed into brutes and, if you believe Empedocles, into plants too.[6] And copying them, Maumeth [Mohammed] often had it on his lips that he who draws back from divine law becomes a brute. And his saying so was reasonable: for it is not the rind which makes the plant, but a dull and non-sentient nature; not the hide which makes a beast of burden, but a brutal and sensual soul; not the spherical body which makes the heavens, but right reason; and not a separateness from the body but a spiritual intelligence which makes an angel. For example, if you see a man given over to his belly and crawling upon the ground, it is a bush not a man that you see. If you see anyone blinded by the illusions of his empty and Calypso-like imagination, seized by the desire of scratching, and delivered over to the senses, it is a brute not a man that you see. If you come upon a philosopher winnowing out all things by right reason, he is a heavenly not an earthly animal. If you come upon a pure contemplator, ignorant of the body, banished to the innermost places of the mind, he is not an earthly,

---

[4]Lucilius, *Satyrarum* VI (22), in Nonius Marcellus, *De compendiosadoctrina* II (Lindsay, I, 109).
[5]Book of Enoch 40:8
[6]Empedocles, fr. 117 (Diels).
[7]Genesis 6:12; Numbers 27:16 Mark 16:15.

not a heavenly animal; he more superbly is a divinity clothed with human flesh.

Who is there that does not wonder at man? And it is not unreasonable that in the Mosaic and Christian holy writ man is sometimes denoted by the name "all flesh" and at other times by that of "every creature"; and man fashions, fabricates, transforms himself into the shape of all flesh, into the character of every creature.[7] Accordingly, where Evantes the Persian tells of the Chaldaean theology, he writes that man is not any inborn image of himself, but many images coming in from the outside: hence that saying of the Chaldaeans: *enosh hu shinuy vekamah tevaoth baal chayim,* that is, man is an animal of diverse, multiform, and destructible nature.

But why all this? In order for us to understand that, after having been born in this state so that we may be what we will to be, since we are held in honor, we ought to take particular care that no one may say against us that we do not know that we are made similar to brutes and mindless beasts of burden.[8] But rather, as Asaph the prophet says: "Ye are all gods, and sons of the most high," unless by abusing the very indulgent liberality of the Father, we make the free choice, which he gave to us, harmful to ourselves instead of helpful toward salvation.[9] Let a certain holy ambition invade the mind, so that we may not be content with mean things but may aspire to the highest things and strive with all our forces to attain them: for if we will to, we can. Let us spurn earthly things; let us struggle toward the heavenly. Let us put in last place whatever is of the world; and let us fly beyond the chambers of the world to the chamber nearest the most lofty divinity. There, as the sacred mysteries reveal, the seraphim, cherubim, and thrones occupy the first places. Ignorant of how to yield to them and unable to endure the second places, let us compete with the angels in dignity and glory. When we have willed it, we shall be not at all below them.

But by what method? or by doing what? Let us see what they are doing, what life they are living. If we too live that life—for we can—we shall equal their lot.

---

[8]Psalms 48:21 (King James version, Psalms 49:20).
[9]Psalms 81:6 (Kings James, 82:6), cf. John 10:34.

CHAPTER 13

THE REFORMATION: MARTIN LUTHER

INTRODUCTION

Just as the Renaissance thinkers recaptured the classical past so, too, did the reform-minded humanists seek to recapture the spirit of the early Church. An important factor in the speedy dissemination of the Reformers message was the recent invention of the printing press and the subsequent rise in literacy within Europe. The initiator of the Reformation, Martin Luther, an Augustinian monk, lived in Saxony, one of many small German principalities within the Holy Roman Empire. There, he was protected by a supportive ruler and his message was not suppressed. The infant Reformation was able to survive its early years, too, because of the political situation in the Empire. Charles V, the newly-elected emperor, had a poor relationship with Pope Leo X, and he was distracted by a territorial tug-of-war with his rival Francis I of France. In addition, the Turks were threatening the eastern border of his empire. Charles simply did not have time to focus on the meddlesome monk.

LUTHER AND HIS MOVEMENT

Martin Luther (1483–1546) was born in Eisleben, located in Saxony, one of the small German states in the Holy Roman Empire that was under the rule of Elector Frederick the Wise. His father, who had elevated himself from peasant status to ownership of a copper mine, had great hopes for his son. Luther was sent to a monastery school and at the age of seventeen to the University of Erfurt. After earning both the Bachelor and Master of Arts degrees, he began to study law. However, all that changed when in the summer of 1505 he had some type of frightening experience in which he thought his life was threatened. He reveals in one of the many volumes of his autobiographical reminiscences *Table*

Talk, that at that moment he pledged his life to God. As a consequence he left the study of law and entered the Augustinian cloister in Erfurt. Despite the disapproval of his father, Luther stayed in the cloister, took his vows, was ordained a priest, and studied theology until he earned the doctorate in 1512. In that same year he assumed the post that he would hold until the end of his life—Professor of Biblical Theology at the University of Wittenberg in Saxony.

Luther was deeply troubled about the general corruption of the Church, but he had no intention of splitting the Church when he posted the *Ninety-five Theses* on the door of the Wittenberg Church in 1517. Despite the fact that the *Theses* were written in Latin for debate among scholars, Luther soon became widely known. The *Theses* questioned the practice of buying indulgences instead of doing penance for sin. Penance in the form of almsgiving, extra prayers, or making pilgrimages was the core of late medieval piety, but many found it burdensome and preferred to purchase a letter of pardon instead. The Roman Church was all too willing to oblige, since indulgences, authorized by the popes, had become a major source of income. The specific target of Luther's *Theses* was the indulgence authorized by Pope Leo X for rebuilding St. Peter's Basilica in Rome. Luther knew that priests like the Dominican, John Tetzel, were assuring people that the purchase of indulgences would guaranteed them forgiveness of their sins and would release the souls of their relatives from purgatory. "As soon as the coin in the coffer rings, the soul from purgatory springs!" To Luther, such a claim was a blatant deception of the faithful and a distortion of the word of God. "It is vain," he warned, "to trust in salvation by indulgence letters, even though the indulgence seller or

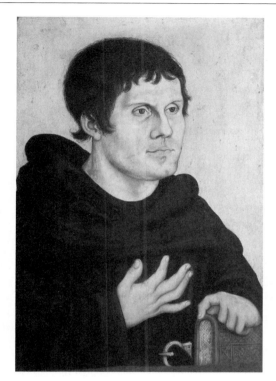

Lucas Cranach was both a versatile Renaissance painter and a publicist for the Reformation. While working as a court painter in Wittenberg, Cranach frequently illustrated Luther's pamphlets. The two developed a great friendship, with Cranach serving as witness to Luther's marriage and as godfather to his son. Cranach depicted the reformer more than fifty times in various guises, as seen in this painting from ca.1522.

Figure VI-3 Lucas Cranach the Elder. Martin Luther as a Monk. 1522–24. Oil on wood panel, 17⅕ × 11¾″ (43.6 × 29.8 cm). Germanisches Nationalmuseum, Nuremberg, Germany. Courtesy of Scala/Art Resource, New York.

the pope himself were to offer their souls as security" (*Thesis* 52).

People were naturally disturbed to hear that they were being cheated by the church, but Luther was not the first to criticize indulgences. Luther's message was especially attractive because of the alternative that he offered to the traditional ritual

of penance. He did not tell people to stop praying or to withhold alms; he even stressed that works of charity were far superior to buying indulgences. But no act of charity or penance, however well-motivated, could bring forgiveness of sin and salvation. These gifts of God came instead to people who felt genuine sorrow for their sin and trusted in God's mercy alone. The revolutionary theological insight called justification by faith had come to Luther as he prepared lectures on the Bible for his students at the University of Wittenberg. In the indulgence controversy he applied this discovery to daily religious life, and people received it as liberation from the deception of indulgences and from the strict demands of penance.

The most controversial edge to Luther's *Theses* was, however, their criticism of the papacy. Luther did not attack all papal authority and the *Theses* should not be seen as a rebellious protest against the church. The famous posting of the *Theses* on the door of the Castle Church in Wittenberg, an event now disputed by historians, was at most a public announcement of the debate for which they had been written. Nevertheless, Luther did question the extension of the pope's power to souls in purgatory and, with clever irony, criticized the motives of Pope Leo X. "Christians are to be taught that the pope would and should wish to give of his own money, even though he had to sell the basilica of St. Peter, to those from whom the hawkers of indulgences cajole money" (*Thesis* 51).

The thinly-veiled criticism of the papacy in Luther's *Theses* thus fell on ears that were tuned to hear his message. They spread rapidly throughout Germany, inspiring acceptance but provoking fear and opposition as well. After reading them on his deathbed, the dean of the cathedral chapter in Hamburg, Albert Krantz, exclaimed: "Brother, go back to your cell and say, 'God, have mercy on me.'" More ominously, Archbishop Albert of Mainz sent a copy to Rome with a note that the Wittenberg monk was spreading new teachings among the people.

The Debate   Almost immediately, an official investigation of Luther was launched in Rome. Luther published a defense of his *Theses* and insisted at first that he had no intention of undermining papal authority. But when he was repeatedly attacked on this issue, he argued that the power of the papacy

Luther's initial call for reform centered around a single practice: the sale of indulgences. These releases from the temporal punishments of sin through the payment of money were sold in order to raise funds for the church, such as for the building of Saint Peter's in Rome. Luther understood this exchange of money for absolution as a corrupt and heretical church practice. Here we see an example of a printed indulgence. The single line following the first paragraph reads: "Having [given] a full confession this form absolves [the recipient] in full."

Figure IV-4 Indulgence. 1515. Indulgence granted to Johannes Angelus Arcimboldus printed on parchment, 8.2 × 5.5" (20.9 × 13.9 cm). Bibliothèque Nationale et Universitaire de Strasbourg. Courtesy of the Granger Collection, New York.

was limited, especially since the Bishop of Rome had never ruled over the Eastern (Orthodox) churches. This specific assertion led to the confrontation between Luther and one of his sharpest opponents, John Eck, at Leipzig in 1519. At issue was the "divine right" of the papacy, that is, whether the words of Jesus to Peter, "You are Peter, and upon this rock I will build my church" (Matt. 16:18), made the successors of Peter, the bishops of Rome, supreme over the church. According to Eck, many theologians of the early church, the Church Fathers, supported this position; but Luther disagreed and appealed to scrip-

ture alone. This principle of *sola scriptura*, which became one of the slogans of the Reformation, did not mean that Luther discounted the Church Fathers or early church councils; but when agreement could not be reached on what they meant, the most direct meaning of scripture had to be the final judge. On these grounds, Luther concluded that the words of Jesus to Peter did not give to his successors, if indeed the bishops of Rome were Peter's successors, divine authority to rule the church.

Eck boasted of his triumph at Leipzig and professors from the universities who judged the debate agreed with him. In pamphlets written for the laity, supporters and opponents of Luther declared their own verdicts. Luther's case became a public cause. Nevertheless, Luther faced almost certain excommunication and even death if he were delivered to Rome and, like the Czech reformer John Hus a hundred years earlier, had to stand trial for heresy. At Leipzig, Eck had proclaimed Luther guilty by association with Hus after Luther had defended some of Hus' propositions. In late 1519 Luther's future looked bleak.

Luther was indeed excommunicated in January, 1521, after he refused to recant what he had written. Despite that he survived, and his supporters coalesced into a reforming movement. They owed their survival both to the political situation in Germany and to the quiet maneuvering of Luther's prince, Elector Frederick the Wise of Saxony. Germany was not a unified country but a federation of many independent cities and territories within the Holy Roman Empire. Both the emperor and the pope needed the political and financial support of local rulers like Elector Frederick. Consequently, when Luther was cited to Rome, Frederick used his political leverage to keep Luther in Germany and to gain for him a hearing before the new emperor, Charles V, and the "Diet" of the empire, the annual assembly of territorial rulers that in 1521 was held in the city of Worms.

At this historic meeting, Luther refused to disown his writings, which had been piled on a table in front of him. After requesting a day's adjournment, he delivered a brief but eloquent defense of his motivation (in Latin and German). It concluded with his famous appeal: "Unless I am convinced by the testimony of the scriptures or by clear reason (for I do not trust either in the pope or in councils alone, since it is well known that they have often erred and contradicted themselves), I am bound by the scriptures I have quoted and my conscience is captive to the word of God. I cannot and I will not retract anything, since it is neither safe nor right to go against conscience."

Luther's appeal was not an assertion of religious liberty in the modern sense. He did not intend to strike down the establishment of religion or to defend the civil liberties of non-believers. Nor did he approve of every individual interpretation of scripture regardless of how fanciful it might be. He appealed not to scripture alone but to scripture and clear reason, which meant an interpretation of scripture supported by the best evidence. He did, however, reject the enforcement of a certain interpretation of scripture by the church. That rejection was a significant step toward freedom of conscience and religious toleration, even though Luther's own conscience sought its certainty in the word of God.

Flight   Luther left Worms before he was declared an outlaw of the Empire, but he would have been seized had not Elector Frederick arranged for his kidnapping during his journey home to Saxony. For ten months Luther remained in hiding at the Wartburg Castle, disguised as Knight George and giving as his return address the "kingdom of the birds and the air." In the meantime, Elector Frederick was caught in a delicate political situation and Luther's supporters mulled over what to do. It was one thing to sympathize with an outspoken monk against exploitation by the papacy, but it was another, potentially dangerous, thing to support publicly a declared outlaw of the Empire. Nevertheless, Luther was immensely popular in Germany. The papal delegate to the Diet of Worms, Jerome Aleander, reported from Germany that nine-tenths of the people cried "Luther, Luther," and the rest shouted "Death to the Roman Pope." Over the next four years (1521–1525), some of those cries would turn hostile to Luther as events gradually sifted his sympathizers into different camps and a manifold Protestant movement was born.

Lutheran belief   The main elements of Luther's theology can be summarized with reference to three writings that are known as his Reformation Treatises of 1520.

In *Christian Liberty* Luther eloquently stated the doctrine of justification by faith. Justification by faith alone (*sola fide*), Luther's key "discovery," became the basic doctrine of the Reformation. He found the idea in the letters of Paul in the New Testament, particularly in Paul's Letter to the Romans, on which Luther lectured in 1515–1516 (see, for example, Romans 5:1–2). The Christian was made righteous or just only by faith in the promises of God and not by religious works. Charity was an essential part of the Christian life, but works of charity flowed from faith and did not merit favor with God.

In *Address to the Christian Nobility* Luther appealed to the lay rulers of German society to reform the church because the clergy had failed to do so. Luther asserted that the laity had just as much right to call councils and to interpret scripture as did the clergy, because all Christians were priests before God. This important Reformation concept came to be known as the "priesthood of all believers."

In *The Babylonian Captivity of the Church* Luther attacked the seven sacraments of the Roman Church. He argued that only penance, baptism, and the Lord's Supper were genuine sacraments. Luther also radically altered the meaning of the Lord's Supper. It was not a reenactment of the sacrifice of Jesus on the cross, but a visible and tangible form of God's promise of forgiveness. Luther stressed that Christ was truly present in the bread and wine, and insisted against long Catholic practice that both elements should be given to the laity and not just the bread. The reception of both elements became an early hallmark of Protestant worship.

Luther's writings were numerous. The following are particularly noteworthy:

In 1523 Luther wrote on the ordering of worship where he stressed the importance of preaching and reading of scripture. Luther also strongly encouraged literacy among the faithful for the purpose of reading the Bible. Luther debated with the humanist scholar Erasmus on the issue of free will versus determinism. In *On the Bondage of the Will vs The Freedom of the Will*, 1524–1525, they engaged in the old Augustinian/Pelagian argument over whether humans can participate in their salvation. The argument rests on a negative versus a more positive view of human nature.

Initially Luther held out the hope that the Jews would convert to his version of Christianity. When they didn't, at the end of his life he wrote *Against the Jews and their Lies* (1543). Here he said: "Let their synagogues be burnt, their houses razed, their prayer books seized, let them be reduced to the condition of agrarian servitude, and—as a final solution—let them be expelled from the country." As harsh as this sounds, it was no worse than the general attitude towards Jews at this time.

Major religious changes were eventually made in Wittenberg and in other cities and territories that became Lutheran. Wine was given to the laity along with the bread; much of the mass, such as the Words of Institution and the lessons from scripture, were spoken in German. Luther ended celibacy and encouraged marriage. The proper role for women was that of wife and mother, "for this is the purpose for which they exist." The highest role that a woman could attain was that of a pastor's wife. He emphasized work, and herein lie the origins of the "Protestant work ethic." "If a man will not work, neither shall he eat." Luther is critical of universities, viewing them as encouraging loose living. He condemns Aristotle as an "arrogant pagan rascal." He greatly reduces the number of religious feasts and festivals saying that they encourage drinking and sloth. Pilgrimages are both expensive and foolish. Luther dictates a rather austere way of life, but not as austere as Calvin will later.

THE PEASANTS' WAR

In 1525 an event took place which did not reflect well on Luther. The so-called Peasants War was a social revolution of the "Common Man," a sixteenth-century term that denoted tillers of the soil as well as urban laborers. The movement began in south Germany in 1524. Its cause was injustices that afflicted the peasants as their local custom was gradually eroded by Roman law. Their leaders articulated these grievances in the *Twelve Articles of the Peasants* (1525), a document that united various groups of dissidents in Germany. The articles listed legal and economic complaints such as the curtailment of hunting and fishing privileges and the loss of hereditary rights; but they also demanded the right of parish members to choose their own pastors and supported their grievances with citations from Scripture. Furthermore, they appealed to Luther and other theologians for support. Clearly, common people were associating Luther's Christian freedom with liberation from their own kind of bondage.

The leader of the peasants in Saxony was Thomas Müntzer, an early supporter of Luther. He had developed a revolutionary theology that predicted that the kingdom of God would be given to the common people and that a new order of equality and justice would prevail. In his response to the

Twelve Articles, Luther agreed that most of the peasants' demands were just, but he disagreed that they were specifically Christian and could be identified with Christian freedom. He also criticized the nobility for allowing the peasantry to suffer such injustice and proposed that both sides negotiate the grievances in peace. However, Luther supplemented his response to the peasants' *Articles* with a separate admonition to the princes to kill, if necessary, the "robbing and murdering hordes" of peasants. Luther's area of Saxony was not greatly affected, but the German princes brutally put down various rebellions and executed their leaders. Luther was blamed for the carnage and his reputation in Germany suffered a severe blow. More importantly, the defeat of the peasants throughout Germany and Austria meant that the Reformation would not become a social revolution.

OTHER LEADERS
OF THE PROTESTANT MOVEMENT

Ulrich Zwingli   One of the most influential of the early Protestant leaders was Ulrich Zwingli (1484–1531). Unlike Luther, he was trained as a humanist at the universities of Vienna and Basel. Zwingli also corresponded with Erasmus and, after the publication of Erasmus' Greek New Testament, Zwingli studied it intensively while serving as a priest in his native Switzerland. His public career as a reformer in Switzerland coincided with Luther's emergence in Germany. On his thirty-fifth birthday, January 1, 1519 (the same year as the Leipzig Debate), Zwingli preached his first sermon in Zurich directly from the Greek New Testament. Later he claimed that as early as 1516 he had taught the same message of justification by faith that Luther also discovered in the Bible. Beyond dispute is the power of his preaching and his assertion of Christian freedom against the rules of the late medieval church.

Zwingli defended this freedom against the requirements of the Lenten fast. The very week that Luther returned from the Wartburg to Wittenberg, Zwingli was present in Zurich as some friends consumed sausages on Ash Wednesday. Although Zwingli did not eat the meat, he defended the freedom to do so, and the reform movement in Zurich was underway. To change non-biblical practices such as compulsory fasting, Zwingli worked care-

fully to gain the support of the city council against the Bishop of Constance. The turning point came at the First Zurich Disputation in 1523. Against the bishop's delegate, Zwingli skillfully defended sixty-seven theses in favor of reform and convinced the council to mandate a reformation of the city. Finally, in 1525, Zwingli was able to replace the medieval mass with a simple rite of communion.

John Calvin   The origin of the Reformation in France is uncertain. It seems clear that church reforming activity was going on prior to Luther and sponsored by a member of the royal family. But in 1534 the French King became enraged over the distribution of flyers criticizing the Mass. This was called the Affair of the Placards. He took measures to suppress the movement and many fled including John Calvin, who left for Switzerland. Born in Noyon in 1509 (the same year that Luther began his theological lectures), Calvin spent his young adulthood in France, studying theology at the renowned College de Montaigu in Paris and law at Orleans and at Bourges. Simultaneously, however, Calvin also received a thorough humanist education in classical languages and philosophy, and his first publication (1532) was a commentary on a book by the Roman Stoic philosopher Seneca. During his studies Calvin also became acquainted with the circle of French humanist reformers, and probably just before the Affair of the Placards he underwent a "sudden conversion" (as he described it) to Protestantism that led to his complicity in the Affair.

Forced to flee France, Calvin went to Basel, where he completed the first edition (1536) of his *Institutes of the Christian Religion*, which became one of the most influential of all Protestant writings. In 1541 he was called to lead the reform of the church in Geneva.

Calvin's reforming career in Geneva was not easy. Living there, he said, was like being surrounded by unbelievable thorns. The shape of the Genevan church was established immediately through the adoption of Calvin's *Ecclesiastical Ordinances*. They provided for the four offices that became typical of Calvinist or Reformed churches: pastors, teachers, elders and deacons. The pastors and twelve of the elders formed the Consistory, the body that met weekly to supervise religious discipline and morals in the city. The strictness of the consistory and Calvin's popularity with the French refugees who poured into the city alienated some of the old Genevan families. In 1549 Calvin's opponents gained control of the city council and refused to concede to the Consistory the right of excommunication. Not until 1555 did Calvin consolidate his control of the Genevan church. Never, however, did either Calvin or the church rule Geneva. Church and state remained separate, although Calvin certainly intended for the city to approximate a community of saints.

Calvin's greatest influence was achieved through the foundation of an academy in Geneva for training leaders of church and state. Its curriculum, built around the study of classical languages, reflected Calvin's own humanist education. The clearest triumph of Calvinism was the Scottish Reformation led by John Knox, but its destiny in France proved to be tragic and disappointing. In 1559 Calvinist churches were able to hold a national synod in France, but the so-called wars of religion between Protestants (called Huguenots) and Catholics ended with the tragic Massacre of St. Bartholomew in 1572. Thousands of Protestants were killed; and, although the Edict of Nantes in 1598 allowed Huguenot churches to exist, French Protestants would remain a minority located mostly in the south of Calvin's native land.

The theology of Calvin that was imprinted on Calvinist churches shared with Luther's thought the basic Protestant doctrine of justification by faith, but it also possessed distinctive features. First, Calvin stressed the importance of discipline and self-denial for the life of the believer who was already justified by faith alone. More so than Luther, Calvin believed that Christians would be clearly recognizable by their conduct. Second, Calvin adhered to a strict doctrine of predestination that became more of a hallmark of his thought than he had intended. According to this doctrine, God had elected some to salvation while consigning others to eternal rejection. Although Luther had also held this view of predestination, he and his followers played down its importance and emphasized only God's merciful election.

THE LORD'S SUPPER CONTROVERSY

A serious division arose over the Lord's Supper in 1525 that would result in a permanent division among the reformers. Both Zwingli and Luther had criticized the sacrificial nature of the mass. They also rejected the official medieval explanation of how the bread and wine were changed into the body and blood of Christ. That explanation, known as transubstantiation and defined by the church in 1215, was rejected by Luther in 1520 in *The Babylonian Captivity of the Church*. For him, the key to the sacrament was not the elements but the Words of Institution that promised forgiveness and confirmed faith. Because, however, those same words said, "This [bread] is my body and this cup is the new covenant in my blood," he accepted the real presence of Christ's body and blood in the elements of bread and wine.

To Zwingli, however, the acceptance of a real presence sounded like transubstantiation and encouraged people to think that something magical happened in the sacrament. Zwingli argued that the Words of Institution should be understood figuratively. When he said, "This is my body," Jesus meant that the bread signified his body, not that the bread was his body. Accordingly, the purpose of the sacrament for Zwingli was to recall the death of Jesus and unite the congregation spiritually in this remembrance. His simple rite of communion as a meal shared in the congregation reflected this theology.

Calvin taught a spiritual presence of Christ in the Lord's Supper that was closer to Luther than the symbolic understanding of Zwingli but still different from Luther's concept of a real bodily presence of Christ. Calvin's view superseded that of Zwingli and became normative for the Reformed tradition of Protestantism, but it never became acceptable to most Lutherans. More than any other issue, the disagreement over the nature of Christ's presence in the Supper continued to divide Lutherans and Calvinists throughout the sixteenth century and beyond.

Underneath the polemic, however, was a fundamental difference of opinion about how the salvation gained by Jesus' death was transferred to believers. For Zwingli, it happened through faith when that death was remembered; for Luther, it happened through the promise of forgiveness whenever that word was heard and received in faith. As Protestant theologians, both believed faith was necessary, but Luther believed that faith always had to have a clear, external promise on which to rely, even in the sacrament. A conference held in

Marburg consisting of the leaders of the Protestant movement did not produce a reconciliation of the Lord's Supper controversy. The Protestant movement would remain divided between Lutheran and Reformed camps.

THE ANABAPTISTS

While the Lord's Supper controversy was raging, another division occurred in Switzerland and south Germany. The "Anabaptists" became the core of a persistent Radical Reformation that dissented from Protestants and Catholics alike. It is hard to find a common denominator for the Radical Reformation. The Swiss Brethren, who originated mainly in Zurich, required that the radical community separate itself from the world by breaking bread only with one another. They also prohibited members from taking the sword, swearing oaths, or serving as magistrates, and they banned from the fellowship any members who broke these rules. Many Anabaptists were indeed pacifists. In Moravia, Jacob Hutter (ca. 1500–1535) became the leader of a highly organized community that held its property in common. By the end of the sixteenth century these Hutterites numbered in the thousands.

On the whole, however, the Anabaptists remained a small minority; they never comprised much more than one percent of the population and, not counting the Hutterites, in most locales their congregations numbered fewer than a dozen adherents. But their historical significance far outweighed their numbers. Although their beliefs were not uniform, they upheld an ancient Christian idea: believers ought to be different from non-believers, they thought, and not pay allegiance to political authorities, worldly morals, or even to professional clergy. By maintaining their convictions in the face of persecution, they also symbolized the need for religious toleration, which the sixteenth century was not yet ready to grant. The Quakers or Society of Friends, a later movement founded in the seventeenth century in England, shared some of the ideas of the Radical Reformation, notably their pacifism, and later became very influential in movements for social reform.

In Holland and North Germany, many Anabaptists coalesced into a loose organization under the leadership of Menno Simons (1496–1561). As a Catholic priest, Menno was already sympathetic to the Anabaptists when the movement was severely shaken by the takeover of the German city of Münster by fanatical Anabaptists from Holland. In 1535 the so-called "Kingdom of Münster" was defeated by a combined force of Catholics and Protestants and most of the inhabitants were slaughtered. Horrified by these events, Menno quit the priesthood and became an apostle of non-violent Anabaptism. Most of his years were spent traveling throughout northern Germany shepherding the communities that came to bear his name.

THE SPREAD OF THE REFORMATION

The divisions in the Protestant movement did not halt its spread. In Germany, the cities and territories that adhered to Luther fought for legal recognition between 1525 and 1555. Emperor Charles V had tried to reconcile the antagonistic Protestant and Catholic parties at the Diet of Augsburg in 1530, but he failed. At that Diet, Philipp Melanchthon, Luther's "second in command" and successor, defined the beliefs and practice of the Lutheran cities and territories in the *Augsburg Confession*. Thereafter, the Lutherans formed a political alliance, called the Smalcald League, to defend themselves against the Emperor. Although Charles temporarily defeated the Lutherans in 1547, he was eventually forced to recognize the legal existence of all cities and territories that subscribed to the *Augsburg Confession*. This agreement, known as the Peace of Augsburg (1555), also awarded the right of determining the religion of each city and territory to its ruler, establishing the principle of *cuius regio, eius religio*: "whose region, his religion." Charles had been unable to preserve all of Germany for the Roman Church. One year later he abdicated his crown and retired to a monastery in Spain.

In Scandinavia the Lutheran churches were born amid the struggle of Sweden for independence from Denmark. The king who led that struggle, Gustav Vasa, seized church property and revenue from the Catholic bishops in order to relieve financial pressures. Meanwhile, Vasa encouraged the spread of Lutheran teachings in Sweden by appointing as the city pastor of Stockholm Olaus Petri, son of a Swedish blacksmith who had studied in Wittenberg. At the Diet of Västeras in 1527, Vasa had the approval of church appointments placed in the king's hands and gradually replaced Catholic bishops with Lutheran ones. In 1531 a new Swedish mass was adopted and Laurentius Petri, the brother of Olaus, was consecrated archbishop without papal approval. However, not until after Vasa's death in 1560 did Lutheranism become the religion of the people, and doctrinally the Swedish church did not become officially Lutheran until a church council in 1593 adopted the *Augsburg Confession*. The Reformation in Denmark followed a similar pattern.

The Reformation in England resulted in a unique form of Protestantism called Anglicanism. It combined elements of Lutheran and Calvinist theology with a modified Catholic liturgy and the apostolic succession of bishops, so that it is best described by the name that it later assumed in North America: a Protestant Episcopal Church. It took shape gradually over twenty-five years, from 1534–1559, and, similar to the Lutheran churches in Scandinavia, it was imposed on the country by the crown, starting with King Henry VIII (1509–1547).

COUNTER-REFORMATION

By 1560 Protestantism had taken over Scandinavia, most of Great Britain, at least half of Germany and Switzerland, and had made inroads into France, Holland, and Eastern Europe. It did not spread further because Catholic rulers resisted it and because the Catholic Church, especially in Italy and Spain, was able to renew itself. This combination of resistance and renewal is called the Catholic Counter-Reformation.

Reform impulses were present in the Church of Rome prior to the rise of Protestantism. Far and away the most significant form of Catholic spiritual renewal, however, was the Society of Jesus. The Jesuits were founded by the former Spanish soldier Ignatius Loyola (1491–1556). A strict religious discipline, embodied in the *Spiritual Exercises* of Ignatius, and a thorough education prepared Jesuits to debate with Protestants, to tutor the children of rulers, and to start Catholic schools and seminaries. Through these channels Jesuits were able to reclaim territory for Rome.

Along with the Jesuits, the Counter-Reformation was propelled by the Inquisition and by the Council of Trent (1545–1563). The Inquisition was a medieval system of church courts which had been instituted to suppress heresy in southern France and in Spain. There, the papal delegate Gian Pietro Caraffa, later Pope Paul IV, saw it in operation and persuaded Pope Paul III to found the Roman Inquisition in 1542. Caraffa supported its work in Italy and France, and in both countries Protestants were arrested and sometimes executed. When he became pope in 1555, Caraffa also had published the first general *Index* of prohibited books.

The Council of Trent reasserted Catholic doctrine and dictated important reforms. Meeting in three separate periods between 1545 and 1563, in Trent, Italy, the council gave shape to the modern Roman Catholic Church. It opposed Protestant positions on every important doctrine, reasserting that not just faith but also works were necessary to justification and that the mass was indeed a sacrifice. Its most effective decree was to insist that bishops reside in their dioceses and attend to the pastoral needs of their parishioners. Having seen how effective preaching had been to the spread of Protestantism, Trent now declared that preaching was the chief duty of Catholic bishops. The impact of Trent can best be seen in Germany where important territories like Bavaria and Cologne were saved for the Roman Church.

CONFESSIONS

In the second half of the sixteenth century, the renewed Roman Catholic Church took its place as one among several religious "confessions" in Reformation Europe. This term refers both to the official documents that defined the new religious bodies in Europe and to their territorial distribution. So, for example, Lutheranism was defined by adherence to the *Augsburg Confession* of 1530, to Luther's Catechisms, and to several other documents that were finally collected in the *Book of Concord* (1580). When princes and city councils in Germany, or kings in Scandinavia, adopted these documents as part of their new church constitutions, those territories became officially Lutheran. The decrees of the Council of Trent served the same purpose for the renewed Roman Catholic Church. For the Anglican Church the *Thirty-nine Articles* and the *Book of Common Prayer* functioned as confessional documents. The Calvinist or Reformed churches, which were the most scattered, adopted confessional statements in each country, for example, the *Heidelberg Confession* (1563) in Germany, the decrees of the Synod of

Dort (1619) in Holland, and the *Westminster Confession* (1647) in England. Even the Radical Reformation had its confessions. The Swiss Brethren, the descendants of the original Anabaptists, appealed to an early statement formulated in Schleitheim in 1527. In 1632, the Mennonites produced the *Confession of Dordrecht*, and became the best-known modern descendants of the Radical Reformation.

One way to understand the Reformation, therefore, is as a process of confessionalization. The medieval Roman Church was already in ferment when the Reformation began, and the new confessions that emerged from the upheaval of the sixteenth century represent the sediment that settled. That sediment, however, did not lie still in a stagnant pool. First, the different confessions continued to debate which was the true form of Christianity and which had the right interpretation of Scripture. Second, some territories changed their confession, especially in Germany, where a few Lutheran areas became Calvinist and vice versa. And finally, new religious movements appeared and grew strong, especially in England, where the internal Puritan protest against the Anglican establishment was overtaken by more radical voices from without. It is hard to tell when the Reformation ended.

IMPACT OF THE REFORMATION

The rise and spread of new confessions indicate that the main impact of the Reformation was to alter the religious map of Europe. In so doing, the Reformation also determined the shape of Christianity that accompanied the exploration and colonization of the New World. Where Spain, Portugal, and France conquered, Roman Catholicism also gained new territory. Where England established trading companies, the Anglican or the Calvinist Puritan churches were also established. Where the Dutch landed, that form of Calvinism was also implanted. Where the Scandinavians settled or, years later, immigrated, they carried their Lutheranism with them. Germans might take with them any one of three confessional allegiances; and the unwanted groups, like Mennonites on the continent or the separatist Pilgrims in England, fled to safer havens such as North America. European expansion meant also the expansion of a diverse Christianity.

The variety of new Protestant confessions and the controversies among them, however, could not disguise their basic agreement on a new view of God and human nature. Human beings were regarded as unable to lift themselves out of their sinful state, even with the aid of pious works. Instead, Protestants were to put aside all thoughts of impressing God, openly confess their sin, and trust in God's mercy alone. This personal relationship between God and the believer replaced the rituals of Catholicism as the focus of the Christian life. The Protestant Reformation abolished the medieval system of piety based on saints, pilgrimages, endowments to churches, rosaries, processions, private masses, and monasticism, and replaced it with a personal piety based on regular worship, religious instruction of children through catechisms, and devotions in the home. Although they differed in the significance that they gave to preaching and the sacraments, Protestants shared a fundamental shift in their religious orientation from doers and spectators to receivers, readers, and listeners.

In Reformation Europe religious pluralism and personal liberty became more widespread than before. This is not to say that the Reformation brought religious toleration and complete freedom in matters of faith, but it did pave the way for them to emerge after the Enlightenment. Neither Luther nor any other reformer thought that people could believe whatever they wished about God. Protestant cities and territories did attempt to enforce conformity to their confessions, whether Lutheran, Calvinist, or Anglican. Nor did the reformers believe reading the Bible by oneself was sufficient for salvation. They did make the Bible available in the languages of the people; the Reformation was the great age of vernacular translations. But Protestant theologians, taught by the humanists, also believed that the Bible should be studied and interpreted by pastors trained in Greek and Hebrew and schooled in theology. Their catechisms, more than the Bible itself, became the form through which new generations of Protestant laity learned the new faith.

Reformation Europe, however, was still Christian Europe, and that meant little tolerance for Judaism. The sixteenth century was not more anti-Jewish than the Middle Ages, but neither did the Reformation enhance relationships between Christians and Jews. Prior to the Reformation Jews had been expelled from ninety cities in Germany, and some reformers like Martin Luther hoped that the

Hogenberg's engraving depicts one of many scenes of iconoclastic violence from the summer of 1566 in the Netherlands. Motivated by the sermons of Calvinist preachers, mobs descended on hundreds of churches throughout the country, seeking to strip them of their idols. In Hogenberg's print, a group of iconoclasts pulls down images and smashes stained glass windows. The artist subtly suggests the shameful nature of the rioting: with candles and torches visible, the violence and subsequent looting occurs under the cloak of darkness.

Figure VI-5 Frans Hogenberg.
The Calvinist Iconoclastic Riot of August 20, 1566, from De Leone Belgico.1583. Copper engraving, approx. $10^7/_8 \times 7^3/_8''$ (27.6 × 18.6 cm). British Museum, London. Courtesy of Foto Marburg/Art Resource, NY.

evangelical message would make Christianity more appealing to the Jewish people. But that hope was soon disappointed, and Luther eventually set the Jews alongside "papists," Turks (Muslims), and sectarians as enemies of the Gospel. As a biblical scholar who treasured the Old Testament, Luther was especially upset by the opposition of medieval rabbis to Christian claims that Old Testament prophecies pointed to Jesus as the Messiah. We have spoken of Luther's anti-Jewish tract, *Against the Jews and Their Lies.* Unfortunately his attitude was shared by many of his contemporaries, but it was not the ancestor of twentieth-century National Socialist (Nazi) anti-Semitism. The Reformation was an intramural Christian affair that did not encourage the Christian culture of Europe to engage Judaism as its equal.

Although it is doubtful, as some have argued, that Calvinism promoted modern democracy, the Reformation did contribute to the rise of political liberties. In the cities of Switzerland and Germany, demands for Protestant worship were often accompanied by demands for greater representation in urban government. Although princes and kings did use conversion to Protestantism as an occasion to consolidate their power, theologians like Luther and Calvin distinguished carefully between church and state and reminded rulers that they were subject to God's law. Protestants were also quick to defend the right of resistance to tyrants, especially in cases of religious coercion. Lutherans and Calvinists maintained the right to resist with force Catholic emperors and kings; most Anabaptists did not approve violence, but they refused to be bullied by Protestants and Catholics alike. Insistence on civil liberties like religious rights was the Reformation's contribution to representative government in Western society.

The Reformation had a greater impact on social and economic life than it did on government. By taking wealth away from the church and redirecting it toward education and social welfare, Protestants advanced the rational administration of these services. The reformers insisted that providing schools and caring for the disadvantaged were just as much the duty of Christian citizens as supporting the church. In both Calvinist and Lutheran lands, excellent secondary schools and new universities were founded.

With a few prominent exceptions the Reformation probably affected little the lives of women inside and outside the family. In Protestant areas, the closing of cloisters and the freedom of clergy to marry increased the availability of men and women for marriage, although it did not guarantee that women could find partners or that they would fare better in marriages than they had in religious orders. In fact, female religious orders, which had provided many medieval women educational opportunity and a measure of independence they did not have in marriage, put up greater resistance to the Reformation than did the monasteries. The reformers praised and advocated marriage, and prominent male clerics married quickly; but the famous example of a former monk and nun establishing a Protestant parsonage—Martin Luther and Katherina von Bora—should not be seen as typical. Marital disputes were placed under civil jurisdiction in most Protestant areas, and divorce was legalized. This arrangement gave more legal rights and protection to women, but it is hard to argue that the quality of family life was enhanced.

Prominent women were visible during the Reformation as rulers, writers, patronesses, and co-reformers. The list includes Elizabeth I of England, Elisabeth of Calenberg in Germany, Marguerite of Navarre and her daughter, Jeanne d'Albret, Argula von Grumbach, and Catherine Zell in Strasbourg. To concentrate on these figures distorts the picture, however. Most women were relegated to home-making or, at the beginning of the sixteenth century, employed in a variety of gainful but equally invisible occupations. By the end of the century economic pressures had eliminated women from many jobs and confined them to the most menial labor. While this decline was not the fault of the Reformation, neither was it reversed by the religious upheaval.

Finally, the Reformation had a mixed influence on higher culture. It took advantage of the rise of printing to put thousands of pamphlets, broadsheets, and books into people's hands, thus stimulating the demand for printing and the desire to read. The Lutheran culture in Germany encouraged the best artists and sculptors of the northern Renaissance: Albrecht Dürer, Tilman Riemenschneider, Lucas Cranach the elder, and Matthias Grünewald. At the same time, early Protestants in England and on the continent were iconoclasts, destroying statues and pictures as "idols" of the old religion. Some leaders did not want such visual representations in their churches, although they were not completely hostile to the arts. They also differed with Luther on the place of music in worship. Others removed organs from their churches and refused to sing hymns, replacing them with chanted psalms. In contrast, the first Lutheran hymnal was published in 1524 and Luther himself wrote stirring hymns such as "A Mighty Fortress is our God." Later, the compositions of Heinrich Schütz, Paul Gerhardt, Johann Sebastian Bach, and George Frederick Handel would emerge from Lutheran Germany.

The sixteenth century was an age of enormous change and ferment. The Protestant and Catholic Reformations were major factors in that ferment but they were not the whole story. Judged by the scientific, political, and industrial revolutions—which came one, two, and three centuries later—the religious revolution called the Reformation was not yet modernity. It can better be described as the centerpiece of early modern Europe that formed a bridge to modernity. Viewed from within the history of Christianity, the Reformation was more distinctly modern owing to the rise of confessions and their expansion beyond Europe. In neither case, certainly, was it medieval. For Western society, the Reformation meant that modern times were just beginning.

SELECTIONS FROM
ADDRESS TO THE CHRISTIAN NOBILITY OF THE GERMAN NATION CONCERNING THE REFORM OF THE CHRISTIAN ESTATE

This reading is one of the three major Reformation documents that Luther wrote in 1520. His intent is to demolish the foundation on which the Catholic Church claims its authority. To continue the building or structural imagery, he speaks of this foundation as being comprised of three walls. His audience—the German nobility—is a sympathetic one, because they have resented the authority of the pope for a long time. The "young man of noble birth" to whom Luther refers in the opening Address is Emperor Charles V, whom we have mentioned above and in whom Luther hoped to find a sympathetic listener. He did not.

Luther uses the term "Romanists" throughout to refer to the pope and his supporters. The first "wall" is the papal claim that spiritual power, the power invested in the clergy by virtue of their office, is greater than temporal, or secular authority. Luther attacks this argument by means of liberal quotations from the Bible. He claims that all Christians through baptism are priests and spiritually equal, no matter what their work in the world is. Priests, monks, and popes are Christians assigned to perform certain functions in the church. There is nothing special or privileged about their vocation, they are simply "officeholders." This is what is meant by Luther's doctrine of the "priesthood of all believers." Luther extends his reasoning to repudiate the authorities. The "Evil One" is a reference to the Antichrist, which Luther may be identifying as Pope Leo X!

The second "wall" is the claim by the Roman Catholic Church that only the pope can interpret scripture. This right came to the popes through St. Peter, who was viewed as the head of the church. Again, Luther attacks this argument with quotations from the Bible, claiming that Christ's word to Peter, "I have prayed for thee that they faith fail not," was not meant to apply to the pope alone but to the entire body of believers. Western Christianity had retained Latin as the language of the church, which meant that only educated persons were able to read the scriptures. This contrasted with Eastern Orthodox Christianity, which translated the Bible into the vernacular. Luther's translation of the Bible into German during his months in hiding at Wartburg Castle made the Bible accessible to a much broader audience. However, the idea that the Bible was open to interpretation by anyone proved divisive, as the Reformers soon learned, when the movement began to fragment based on different interpretations by its leaders.

The third "wall" fell quickly on the heels of the first two. Scriptural authority contradicts the papal claim that the pope alone can convene a council. Hence, Luther removed the roadblock that had thwarted the reforming movements of the previous century.

In the remaining section Luther presents twenty-seven proposals for improving the state of Christendom. They are practical and direct: local matters should be handled locally; the pope should continue his attention to religious matters alone and exercise no authority over the emperor; pilgrimages are discouraged as expensive and foolish; the church should limit feast days, which only encourage drinking and sloth; and priests should be permitted to marry. He attacks the monastic orders, lays the foundation for what we refer to as the "Protestant work ethic," condemns luxuries such as rich food and fancy dress, criticizes the universities, and vilifies Aristotle. He states that the foundation of all education should be Holy Scripture and that even girls should know it! As you read and mentally list his suggestions, you can assemble a picture of what society looked and acted like in Luther's day. The zeal of the Reformers imposed many correctives on society. As you read, ask yourself whether these were always justified.

QUESTIONS FOR STUDY AND DISCUSSION

1. Trace the events that led to the Reformation. Describe its first leader.

2. What is the meaning of *sola fide* and *sola scriptura*?

3. What were some of the primary reasons for the divisions in the Protestant Movement?

4. Explain the purpose and role of religious confessions.

5. How would you assess the impact of the Reformation?

6. What was the Counter-Reformation?

7. What arguments did Luther put forward in the *Address to the Christian Nobility*?

8. Explain John Calvin, his background, and tell where his influence was strongest.

9. Who were the Anabaptists and how did they differ from the other Protestant groups?

SUGGESTIONS FOR FURTHER READING

Bainton, Roland. *The Reformation of the Sixteenth Century*. Revised edition Boston: Beacon, 1985.

Blickle, Peter. *The Revolution of 1525: The German Peasants' War from A New Perspective*. Translated by T. A. Brady, Jr. & H. C. Erik Midelfort. Baltimore: Johns Hopkins, 1981.

Cameron, Euan. *The European Reformation*. Oxford: Clarendon Press, 1991.

DeMolen, Richard L. (editor). *Leaders of the Reformation*. Selinsgrove: Susquehanna; London and Toronto: Associated Univ. Presses, 1984.

Hendrix, Scott H. *Luther and the Papacy: Stages in a Reformation Conflict*. Philadelphia: Fortress, 1981.

McGrath, Alister E. *Reformation Thought: An Introduction*. 2nd edition, Oxford: Blackwell, 1993.

Oberman, Heiko A. *Luther: Man Between God and the Devil*. New Haven & London: Yale University Press, 1989.

The Oxford Encyclopedia of the Reformation. Ed. Hans Hillerbrand. 4 volumes, New York: Oxford University Press, 1995.

Ozment, Steven. *Protestants: The Birth of a Revolution*. New York: Doubleday, 1991.

Pelikan, Jaroslav. *Reformation of Church and Dogma 1300–1700*. Chicago and London: Univ. of Chicago, 1984.

Wiesner, Merry. *Women and Gender in Early Modern Europe*. Cambridge: University Press, 1993.

Williams, George. *The Radical Reformation*. 3rd edition, Kirksville, MO: Sixteenth Century Journal Publishers, 1992.

MARTIN LUTHER
Selections from *Address to the Christian Nobility of the German Nation Concerning the Reform of the Christian Estate*

To His Most Illustrious, Most Mighty, and Imperial Majesty, and to the Christian Nobility of the German Nation, from Doctor Martin Luther.

Grace and power from God, Most Illustrious Majesty, and most gracious and dear lords.

It is not from sheer impertinence or rashness that I, one poor man, have taken it upon myself to address your worships. All the estates of Christendom, particularly in Germany, are now oppressed by distress and affliction, and this has stirred not only me but everybody else to cry out time and time again and to pray for help. It has even compelled me now at this time to cry aloud that God may inspire someone with his Spirit to lend a helping hand to this distressed and wretched nation. Often the councils have made some pretense at reformation, but their attempts have been cleverly frustrated by the guile of certain men, and things have gone from bad to worse. With God's help I intend to expose the wiles and wickedness of these men, so that they are shown up for what they are and may never again be so obstructive and destructive. God has given us a young man of noble birth as head of state,[6] and in him has awakened great hopes of good in many hearts. Presented with such an opportunity we ought to apply ourselves and use this time of grace profitably. . . .

. . . The Romanists have very cleverly built three walls around themselves. Hitherto they have protected themselves by these walls in such a way that no one has been able to reform them. As a result, the whole of Christendom has fallen abominably.

In the first place, when pressed by the temporal power they have made decrees and declared that the temporal power had no jurisdiction over them, but that, on the contrary, the spiritual power is above the temporal. In the second place, when the attempt is made to reprove them with the Scriptures, they raise the objection that only the pope may interpret the Scriptures. In the third place, if threatened with a council, their story is that no one may summon a council but the pope. . . .

. . . May God help us, and give us just one of those trumpets with which the walls of Jericho were overthrown[14] to blast down these walls of straw and paper in the same way and set free the Christian rods for the punishment of sin, [and] bring to light the craft and deceit of the devil, to the end that through punishment we may reform ourselves and once more attain God's favor.

Let us begin by attacking the first wall. It is pure invention that pope, bishop, priests, and monks are called the spiritual estate while princes, lords, artisans, and farmers are called the temporal estate. This is indeed a piece of deceit and hypocrisy. Yet no one need be intimidated by it, and for this reason: all Christians are truly of the spiritual estate, and there is no difference among them except that of office. Paul says in I Corinthians 12 [:12–13] that we are all one body, yet every member has its own work by which it serves the others. This is because we all have one baptism, one gospel, one faith, and are all Christians alike; for baptism, gospel, and faith alone make us spiritual and a Christian people.

Reprinted from *Luther's Works,* Vol. 44, James Atkinson, ed., (1966), Fortress Press.

The pope or bishop anoints, shaves heads,[15] ordains, consecrates, and prescribes garb different from that of the laity, but he can never make a man into a Christian or into a spiritual man by so doing. He might well make a man into a hypocrite or a humbug and blockhead, but never a Christian or a spiritual man. As far as that goes, we are all consecrated priests through baptism, as St. Peter says in I Peter 2 [:9], "You are a royal priesthood and a priestly realm." The Apocalypse says, "Thou hast made us to be priests and kings by thy blood" [Rev. 5:9–10]. The consecration by pope or bishop would never make a priest, and if we had no higher consecration than that which pope or bishop gives, no one could say mass or preach a sermon or give absolution.

Therefore, when a bishop consecrates it is nothing else than that in the place and stead of the whole community, all of whom have like power, he takes a person and charges him to exercise this power on behalf of the others. It is like ten brothers, all king's sons and equal heirs, choosing one of themselves to rule the inheritance in the interests of all. In one sense they are all kings and of equal power, and yet one of them is charged with the responsibility of ruling. To put it still more clearly: suppose a group of earnest Christian laymen were taken prisoner and set down in a desert without an episcopally ordained priest among them. And suppose they were to come to a common mind there and then in the desert and elect one of their number, whether he were married[17] or not, and charge him to baptize, say mass, pronounce absolution, and preach the gospel. Such a man would be as truly a priest as though he had been ordained by all the bishops and popes in the world. That is why in cases of necessity anyone can baptize and give absolution. This would be impossible if we were not all priests. Through canon law[18] the Romanists have almost destroyed and made unknown the wondrous grace and authority of baptism and justification. In times gone by Christians used to choose their bishops and priests in this way from among their own number, and they were confirmed in their office by the other bishops without all the fuss that goes on nowadays. St. Augustine,[19] Ambrose,[20] and Cyprian[21] each became [a bishop in this way].

Since those who exercise secular authority have been baptized with the same baptism, and have the same faith and the same gospel as the rest of us, we must admit that they are priests and bishops and we must regard their office as one which has a proper and useful place in the Christian community. For whoever comes out of the water of baptism can boast that he is already a consecrated priest, bishop, and pope, although of course it is not seemly that just anybody should exercise such office. Because we are all priests of equal standing, no one must push himself forward and take it upon himself, without our consent and election, to do that for which we all have equal authority. For no one dare take upon himself what is common to all without the authority and consent of the community. And should it happen that a person chosen for such office were deposed for abuse of trust, he would then be exactly what he was before. Therefore, a priest in Christendom is nothing else but an office-holder. As long as he holds office he takes precedence; where he is deposed, he is a peasant or a townsman like anybody else. Indeed, a priest is never a priest when he is deposed. But now the Romanists have invented *characteres indelebiles*[22] and say[23] that a deposed priest is nevertheless something different from a mere layman. They hold the illusion that a priest can never be anything other than a priest, or ever become a layman. All this is just contrived talk, and human regulation.

It follows from this argument that there is no true, basic difference between laymen and priests, princes and bishops, between religious and secular, except for the sake of office and work, but not for the sake of status. They are all of the spiritual estate, all are truly priests, bishops, and popes. But they do not all have the same work to do. Just as priests and monks do not have the same work. This is the teaching of St. Paul in Romans 12 [:4–5] and I Corinthians 12 [:12] and in I Peter 2 [:9], as I have said above, namely, that we are all one body of Christ the Head, and all members one of another. Christ does not have two different bodies, one temporal, the other spiritual. There is but one Head and one body.

Therefore, just as those who are now called "spiritual," that is, priests, bishops, or popes, are neither different from other Christians nor superior to them, except that they are charged with the administration of the word of God and the sacraments, which is their work and office, so it is with the temporal authorities. They bear the sword and rod in their hand to punish the wicked and protect the good. A cobbler, a smith, a peasant—each has the work and office of his trade, and yet they are all alike consecrated priests and bishops. Further, everyone must benefit and serve every other by means of his own work or office so that in this way many kinds of work may be done for the bodily and spiritual welfare of the community, just as all the members of the body serve one another [I Cor. 12:14–26].

Consider for a moment how Christian is the decree which says that the temporal power is not above the "spiritual estate" and has no right to punish it.[24] That is as much as to say that the hand shall not help the eye when it suffers pain. Is it not unnatural, not to mention un-Christian, that one member does not help another and prevent its destruction? In fact, the more honorable the member, the more the others ought to help. I say therefore that since the temporal power is ordained of God to punish the wicked and protect the good, it should be left free to perform its office in the whole body of Christendom without restriction and without respect to persons, whether it affects pope, bishops, priests, monks, nuns, or anyone else. If it were right to say that the temporal power is inferior to all the spiritual estates (preacher, confessor, or any spiritual office), and so prevent the temporal power from doing its proper work, then the tailors, cobblers, stonemasons, carpenters, cooks, innkeepers, farmers, and all the temporal craftsmen should be prevented from providing pope, bishops, priests, and monks with shoes, clothes, house, meat and drink, as well as from paying them any tribute. But if these laymen are allowed to do their proper work without restriction, what then are the Romanist scribes doing with their own laws, which exempt them from the jurisdiction of the temporal Christian authority? It is just so that they can be free to do evil and fulfill what St. Peter said, "False teachers will rise up among you who will deceive you, and with their false and fanciful talk, they will take advantage of you" [II Pet. 2:1–3]. . . .

. . . So, then, I think this first paper wall is overthrown. Inasmuch as the temporal power has become a member of the Christian body it is a spiritual estate, even though its work is physical.[25] Therefore, its work should extend without hindrance to all the members of the whole body to punish and use force whenever guilt deserves or

necessity demands, without regard to whether the culprit is pope, bishop, or priest. Let the Romanists hurl threats and bans about as they like. That is why guilty priests, when they are handed over to secular law, are first deprived of their priestly dignities.[26] This would not be right unless the secular sword previously had had authority over these priests by divine right. Moreover, it is intolerable that in canon law so much importance is attached to the freedom, life, and property of the clergy, as though the laity were not also as spiritual and as good Christians as they, or did not also belong to the church. Why are your life and limb, your property and honor, so cheap and mine not, inasmuch as we are all Christians and have the same baptism, the same faith, the same Spirit, and all the rest? If a priest is murdered, the whole country is placed under interdict.[27] Why not when a peasant is murdered? How does this great difference come about between two men who are both Christians? It comes from the laws and fabrications of men.

Moreover, it can be no good spirit which has invented such exceptions and granted sin such license and impunity. For if it is our duty to strive against the words and works of the devil and to drive him out in whatever way we can, as both Christ and his apostles command us, how have we gotten into such a state that we have to do nothing and say nothing when the pope or his cohorts undertake devilish words and works? . . .

. . . Where sin is, there is no longer any shielding from punishment. St. Gregory writes that we are indeed all equal, but guilt makes a man inferior to others.[29] Now we see how the Romanists treat Christendom. They take away its freedom without any proof from Scripture, at their own whim. But God, as well as the apostles, made them subject to the temporal sword. It is to be feared that this is a game of the Antichrist,[30] or at any rate that his forerunner has appeared.

The second wall is still more loosely built and less substantial. The Romanists want to be the only masters of Holy Scripture, although they never learn a thing from the Bible all their life long. They assume the sole authority for themselves, and, quite unashamed, they play about with words before our very eyes, trying to persuade us that the pope cannot err in matters of faith,[31] regardless of whether he is righteous or wicked. Yet they cannot point to a single letter.[32] This is why so many heretical and un-Christian, even unnatural, ordinances stand in the canon law. But there is no need to talk about these ordinances at present. Since these Romanists think the Holy Spirit never leaves them, no matter how ignorant and wicked they are, they become bold and decree only what they want. And if what they claim were true, why have Holy Scripture at all? Of what use is Scripture? Let us burn the Scripture and be satisfied with the unlearned gentlemen at Rome who possess the Holy Spirit! And yet the Holy Spirit can be possessed only by pious hearts. If I had not read the words with my own eyes, I would not have believed it possible for the devil to have made such stupid claims at Rome, and to have won supporters for them.

But so as not to fight them with mere words, we will quote the Scriptures. St. Paul says in I Corinthians 14 [:30], "If something better is revealed to anyone, though he is already sitting and listening to another in God's word, then the one who is speaking shall hold his peace and give place." What would be the point of this commandment if we were compelled to believe only the man who does the talking, or the man who is at the top? Even Christ said in John 6 [:45] that all Christians shall be taught by God. If it were to happen that the pope and his cohorts were wicked and not true Christians, were not taught by God and were without understanding, and at the same time some obscure person had a right understanding, why should the people not follow the obscure man? Has the pope not erred many times? Who would help Christendom when the pope erred if we did not have somebody we could trust more than him, somebody who had the Scriptures on his side?

Therefore, their claim that only the pope may interpret Scripture is an outrageous fancied fable. They cannot produce a single letter [of Scripture] to maintain that the interpretation of Scripture or the confirmation of its interpretation belongs to the pope alone. They themselves have usurped this power. And although they allege that this power was given to St. Peter when the keys were given him, it is clear enough that the keys were not given to Peter alone but to the whole community. Further, the keys were not ordained for doctrine or government, but only for the binding or loosing of sin.[34] Whatever else or whatever more they arrogate to themselves on the

basis of the keys is a mere fabrication. But Christ's words to Peter, "I have prayed for you that your faith fail not" [Luke 22:32], cannot be applied to the pope, since the majority of the popes have been without faith, as they must themselves confess. Besides, it is not only for Peter that Christ prayed, but also for all apostles and Christians, as he says in John 17 [:9, 20], "Father, I pray for those whom thou hast given me, and not for these only, but for all who believe on me through their word." Is that not clear enough?

Just think of it! The Romanists must admit that there are among us good Christians who have the true faith, spirit, understanding, word, and mind of Christ. Why, then, should we reject the word and understanding of good Christians and follow the pope, who has neither faith nor the Spirit? To follow the pope would be to deny the whole faith[35] as well as the Christian church. Again, if the article, "I believe in one holy Christian church," is correct, then the pope cannot be the only one who is right. Otherwise, we would have to confess,[36] "I believe in the pope at Rome." This would reduce the Christian church to one man, and be nothing else than a devilish and hellish error.

Besides, if we are all priests, as was said above, and all have one faith, one gospel, one sacrament,[37] why should we not also have the power to test and judge what is right or wrong in matters of faith? What becomes of Paul's words in I Corinthians 2 [:15], "A spiritual man judges all things, yet he is judged by no one"? And II Corinthians 4 [:13], "We all have one spirit of faith"? Why, then, should not we perceive what is consistent with faith and what is not, just as well as an unbelieving pope does? . . .

. . . The third wall falls of itself when the first two are down. When the pope acts contrary to the Scriptures, it is our duty to stand by the Scriptures, to reprove him and to constrain him, according to the word of Christ, Matthew 18 [:15–17], "If your brother sins against you, go and tell it to him, between you and him alone; if he does not listen to you, then take one or two others with you; if he does not listen to them, tell it to the church; if he does not listen to the church, consider him a heathen." Here every member is commanded to care for every other. How much more should we do this when the member that does evil is responsible for the government of the church, and by his evil-doing is the cause of much harm and offense to the rest! But if I am to accuse him before the church, I must naturally call the church together.

The Romanists have no basis in Scripture for their claim that the pope alone has the right to call or confirm a council.[38] This is just their own ruling, and it is only valid as long as it is not harmful to Christendom or contrary to the laws of God. Now when the pope deserves punishment, this ruling no longer obtains, for not to punish him by authority of a council is harmful to Christendom

Thus we read in Acts 15 that it was not St. Peter who called the Apostolic Council but the apostles and elders. If then that right had belonged to St. Peter alone, the council would not have been a Christian council, but a heretical *conciliabulum*.[39] Even the Council of Nicaea, the most famous of all councils, was neither called nor confirmed by the bishop of Rome, but by the emperor Constantine.[40] Many other emperors after him have done the same, and yet these councils were the most Christian of all.[41] But if the pope alone has the right to convene councils, then these councils would all have been heretical. Further, when I examine the councils the pope did summon, I find that they did nothing of special importance.

Therefore, when necessity demands it, and the pope is an offense to Christendom, the first man who is able should, as a true member of the whole body, do what he can to bring about a truly free council.[42] No one can do this so well as the temporal authorities, especially since they are also fellow-Christians, fellow-priests, fellow-members of the spiritual estate, fellow-lords over all things. Whenever it is necessary or profitable they ought to exercise the office and work which they have received from God over everyone. Would it not be unnatural if a fire broke out in a city and everybody were to stand by and let it burn on and on and consume everything that could burn because nobody had the authority of the mayor, or because, perhaps, the fire broke out in the mayor's house? In such a situation is it not the duty of every citizen to arouse and summon the rest? How much more should this be done in the spiritual city of Christ if a fire of offense breaks out, whether in the papal government, or anywhere else! The same argument holds if an enemy were to attack a city. The man who first roused the others deserves honor and gratitude. Why, then, should he not deserve honor who makes known the presence of the enemy from hell and rouses Christian people and calls them together?

But all their boasting about an authority which dare not be opposed amounts to nothing at all. Nobody in Christendom has authority to do injury or to forbid the resisting of injury. There is no authority in the church except to promote good. Therefore, if the pope were to use his authority to prevent the calling of a free council, thereby preventing the improvement of the church, we should have regard neither for him nor for his authority. And if he were to hurl his bans and thunderbolts, we should despise his conduct as that of a madman. On the contrary, we should excommunicate him and drive him out as best we could, relying completely upon God. This presumptuous authority of his is nothing. He does not even have such authority. He is quickly defeated by a single text of Scripture, where Paul says to the Corinthians, "God has given us authority not to ruin Christendom, but to build it up" [II Cor. 10:8]. Who wants to leap over the hurdle of this text? It is the power of the devil and of Antichrist which resists the things that serve to build up Christendom. Such power is not to be obeyed, but rather resisted with life, property, and with all our might and main.

Even though a miracle were to be done against the temporal authority on the pope's behalf, or if somebody were struck down by the plague—which they boast has sometimes happened—it should be considered as nothing but the work of the devil designed to destroy our faith in God. Christ foretold this in Matthew 24 [:24], "False Christs and false prophets shall come in my name, who shall perform signs and wonders in order to deceive even the elect." And Paul says in II Thessalonians 2 [:9] that Antichrist shall, through the power of Satan, be mighty in false wonders.

Let us, therefore, hold fast to this: no Christian authority can do anything against Christ. As St. Paul says, "We can do nothing against Christ, only for Christ" [II Cor. 13:8]. But if an authority does anything against Christ, then that authority is the power of Antichrist and of the devil, even if it were to deluge us with wonders and plagues. Wonders and plagues prove nothing, especially in these evil latter days. The whole of Scripture foretells such false wonders. This is why we must hold fast to the word of God with firm faith, and then the devil will soon drop his miracles!

With this I hope that all this wicked and lying terror with which the Romanists have long intimidated and dulled our conscience has been overcome, and that they, just like all of us, shall be made subject to the sword. They have no right to interpret Scripture merely by authority and without learning.[43] They have no authority to prevent a council, or even worse yet at their mere whim to pledge it, impose conditions on it, or deprive it of its freedom. When they do that they are truly in the fellowship of Antichrist and the devil. They have nothing at all of Christ except the name. . . .

. . . 4. It should be decreed that no temporal matter is to be referred to Rome, but that all such cases shall be left to the temporal authority, as the Romanists themselves prescribe in that canon law of theirs, which they do not observe. It should be the pope's duty to be the most learned in the Scriptures and the holiest (not in the name only but in fact) and to regulate matters which concern the faith and holy life of Christians. He should hold the primates and archbishops to this task, and help them in dealing with these matters and taking care of these responsibilities. This is what St. Paul teaches in I Corinthians 6 [:7], and he takes the Corinthians severely to task for their concern with worldly things. That such matters are dealt with in Rome causes unbearable grief in every land. It increases the costs, and, moreover, these judges do not know the usage, laws, and customs of these lands, so that they often do violence to the facts and base their decisions on their own laws and precedents. As a result the contesting parties often suffer injustice.

In addition, the horrible extortion practiced by the judges in the bishops' courts[115] must be forbidden in every diocese so that they no longer judge anything except matters of faith and morals, and leave matters of money and property, life and honor, to the temporal judges. The temporal authorities, therefore, should not permit sentences of excommunication and exile to be passed where faith and morality are not involved. Spiritual authorities should rule over matters which are spiritual; this is just a matter of common sense. But spiritual matters are not money or material things; they are faith and good works. . . .

. . . 9. The pope should have no authority over the emperor, except the right to anoint and crown him at the altar just as a bishop crowns a king.[126] We should never again yield to that devilish pride which requires the emperor to kiss the pope's feet, or sit at his feet, or, as they say, hold his stirrup or the bridle of his mule when he mounts to go riding. Still less should he do homage and swear faithful allegiance to the pope as the popes brazenly demand as though they had a right to it. The chapter *Solite*, which sets papal authority above imperial authority, is not worth a cent, and the same goes for all those who base their authority on it or pay any deference to it. For it does nothing else than force the holy words of God, and wrest them out of their true meaning to conform to their own fond imaginations, as I have shown in a Latin treatise.

This most extreme, arrogant, and wanton presumption of the pope has been devised by the devil, who under cover of this intends to usher in the Antichrist and raise the pope above God, as many are now doing and even have already done. It is not proper for the pope to exalt himself above the temporal authorities, except in spiritual offices such as preaching and giving absolution. In other matters the pope is subject to the crown, as Paul and Peter teach in Romans 13 [:1–7] and I Peter 2 [:13], and as I have explained above.

The pope is not a vicar of Christ in heaven, but only of Christ as he walked the earth. Christ in heaven, in the form of a ruler, needs no vicar, but sits on his throne and sees everything, does everything, knows everything, and has all power. But Christ needs a vicar in the form of a servant, the form in which he went about on earth, working, preaching, suffering, and dying. Now the Romanists turn all that upside down. They take the heavenly and kingly form from Christ and give it to the pope, and leave the form of a servant to perish completely. He might almost be the Counter-Christ, whom the Scriptures call Antichrist, for all his nature, work, and pretensions run counter to Christ and only blot out Christ's nature and destroy his work.

It is also ridiculous and childish for the pope, on the basis of such perverted and deluded reasoning, to claim in his decretal *Pastoralis*[132] that he is rightful heir to the empire in the event of a vacancy. Who has given him this right? Was it

Christ when he said, "The princes of the Gentiles are lords, but it shall not be so among you" [Luke 22:25–26]? Or did Peter bequeath it to him? It makes me angry that we have to read and learn such shameless, gross, and idiotic lies in the canon law, and must even hold them as Christian doctrine when they are devilish lies.

That impossible lie, the *Donation of Constantine*,[133] is the same sort of thing. It must have been some special plague from God that so many intelligent people have let themselves be talked into accepting such lies. They are so crude and clumsy that I should imagine any drunken peasant could lie more adroitly and skilfully. How can a man rule and at the same time preach, pray, study, and care for the poor? Yet these are the duties which most properly and peculiarly belong to the pope, and they were so earnestly imposed by Christ that he even forbade his disciples to take cloak or money with them [Matt. 10:9–10]. Christ commanded this because it is almost impossible for anybody to fulfill these duties if they have to look after one single household. Yet the pope would rule an empire and still remain pope. This is what those rogues have thought up who, under the cover of the pope's name, would like to be lords of the world and would gladly restore the Roman Empire to its former state through the pope and in the name of Christ.

10. The pope should restrain himself, take his fingers out of the pie, and claim no title to the kingdom of Naples and Sicily.[134] He has exactly as much right to that kingdom as I have, and yet he wants to be its overlord. It is property gotten by robbery and violence, like almost all his other possessions. The emperor, therefore, should not grant him this realm, and where it has been granted, he should no longer give his consent. Instead, he should draw the pope's attention to the Bible and the prayer book, that he preach and pray and leave the government of lands and people—especially those that no one has given to him—to the temporal lords. . . .

. . . 12. Pilgrimages to Rome should either be abolished or else no one should be allowed to make such a pilgrimage for reasons of curiosity or his own pious devotion, unless it is first acknowledged by his parish priest, his town authorities, or his overlord that he has a good and sufficient reason for doing so. I say this not because pilgrimages are bad,

but because they are ill-advised at this time.[139] At Rome men do not find a good example, but, on the contrary, pure scandal. The Romanists themselves devised the saying, "The nearer Rome, the worse Christians." After a pilgrimage to Rome men bring back with them contempt for God and his commandments. They say the first time a man goes to Rome he seeks a rascal; the second time he finds one; the third time he brings him back home with him.[140] Now, however, the Romanists have grown so clever that they can make three pilgrimages in one! The pilgrims have brought back such a pretty mess of experiences from Rome that it would be better never to have seen Rome or known anything about it.

Even if this were not the case there is still another and a better reason: simple people[141] are led into error and misunderstanding of the divine command. Such people think that going on a pilgrimage is a precious good work. This is not true. It is a very small good work—frequently it is evil and misleading, for God has not commanded it. But God has commanded that a man should care for his wife and children, perform the duties of a husband, and serve and help his neighbor. Today a man makes a pilgrimage to Rome and spends fifty, maybe a hundred, gulden, something nobody commanded him to do. He permits his wife and child, or his neighbor at any rate, to suffer want back home. And yet the silly fellow thinks he can gloss over such disobedience and contempt of the divine commandment with his self-assigned pilgrimage which is really nothing but impertinence or a delusion of the devil. The popes have encouraged this sort of thing with their false, feigned, foolish "golden years,"[142] by which the people are excited, torn away from God's commandments, and enticed to follow the popes' own erroneous undertakings. The popes have done the very thing they ought to have prevented. But it has brought in money and fortified their illegitimate authority. That is why it has to go on, even if it is contrary to God and the salvation of souls. . . .

. . . 14. We also see how the priesthood has fallen, and how many a poor priest is overburdened with wife and child, his conscience troubled. Yet no one does anything to help him, though he could easily be helped. Though pope and bishops may let things go on as they are, and allow what is heading for ruin to go to ruin, yet I will redeem my conscience and open my mouth freely, whether it vexes pope, bishop, or anybody else. And this is what I say: according to the institution of Christ and the apostles, every city should have a priest or bishop, as St. Paul clearly says in Titus 1 [:5]. And this priest should not be compelled to live without a wedded wife, but should be permitted to have one, as St. Paul writes in I Timothy 3 [:2, 4] and Titus 1 [:6–7] saying, "A bishop shall be a man who is blameless, and the husband of but one wife, whose children are obedient and well behaved," etc. According to St. Paul, and also St. Jerome,[150] a bishop and a priest are one and the same thing. But of bishops as they now are the Scriptures know nothing. Bishops have been appointed by ordinance of the Christian church, so that one of them may have authority over several priests.

So then, we clearly learn from the Apostle that it should be the custom for every town to choose from among the congregation a learned and pious citizen, entrust to him the office of the ministry, and support him at the expense of the congregation. He should be free to marry or not. He should have several priests or deacons, also free to marry or not as they choose, to help him minister to the congregation and the community with word and sacrament, as is still the practice in the Greek church. Because there was sometimes so much persecution and controversy with heretics after the apostolic age, there were many holy fathers who voluntarily abstained from matrimony that they might better devote themselves to study and be prepared at any moment for death or battle.

But the Roman See has interfered and out of its own wanton wickedness made a universal commandment forbidding priests to marry.[151] This was done at the bidding of the devil, as St. Paul declares in I Timothy 4 [:1, 3], "There shall come teachers who bring the devil's teaching and forbid marriage." Unfortunately so much misery has arisen from this that tongue could never tell it. Moreover, this caused the Greek church to separate,[152] and discord, sin, shame, and scandal were increased no end. But this always happens when the devil starts and carries on. What, then, shall we do about it?. . .

. . . I will advise neither for nor against marrying or remaining single. I leave that to common Christian order and to everyone's better judgment. I will not conceal my real opinion or withhold com-

fort from that pitiful band who with wives and children have fallen into disgrace and whose consciences are burdened because people call them priests' whores and their children priests' children. As the court-jester[153] I say this openly.

You will find many a pious priest against whom nobody has anything to say except that he is weak and has come to shame with a woman. From the bottom of their hearts both are of a mind to live together in lawful wedded love, if only they could do it with a clear conscience. But even though they both have to bear public shame, the two are certainly married in the sight of God. And I say that where they are so minded and live together, they should appeal anew to their conscience. Let the priest take and keep her as his lawful wedded wife, and live honestly with her as her husband, whether the pope likes it or not, whether it be against canon or human law. The salvation of your soul is more important than the observance of tyrannical, arbitrary, and wanton laws which are not necessary to salvation or commanded by God. You should do as the children of Israel did who stole from the Egyptians the wages they had earned;[154] or as a servant who steals from his wicked master the wages he has earned: steal from the pope your wedded wife and child! Let the man who has faith enough to venture this, boldly follow me. I shall not lead him astray. Though I do not have the authority of a pope, I do have the authority of a Christian to advise and help my neighbor against sins and temptations. And that not without cause or reason! . . .

. . . 15. Nor must I forget the poor monasteries. The evil spirit, who has now confused all the estates of life and made them unbearable through man-made laws, has taken possession of some abbots, abbesses and prelates. As a result they govern their brothers and sisters in such a way that they quickly go to hell and lead a wretched existence here and now, as do the devil's martyrs. That is to say, these superiors have reserved to themselves in confession, all, or at least some, of the mortal sins which are secret, so that no brother can absolve another on pain of excommunication and under the vow of obedience. Now nobody finds angels all the time in all places; but we do find flesh and blood which would rather undergo all excommunications and threats rather than confess secret sins to prelates and appointed confessors. Thus these people go to the sacrament with such consciences that they become irregulars[157] and even worse. O blind shepherds! O mad prelates! O ravenous wolves! . . .

. . . 16. It is also necessary to abolish all endowed masses for the dead,[158] or at least to reduce their number, since we plainly see that they have become nothing but a mockery. God is deeply angered by these, and their only purpose is money-grubbing, gluttony, and drunkenness. What pleasure can God take in wretched vigils[159] and masses which are so miserably rattled off, not read or prayed. And if they were prayed, it would not be for God's sake and out of love, but for the sake of money and of getting a job finished. Now it is impossible for a work which is not done out of unconstrained love to please or suffice God. So it is altogether Christian to abolish, or at least diminish, everything we see which is growing into an abuse and which angers God rather than reconciles him. I would rather—in fact, it would be more pleasing to God and much better—that a chapter, church, or monastery combine all its anniversary masses and vigils and on one day, with sincerity of heart, reverence, and faith, hold one true vigil and mass on behalf of all its benefactors, than hold thousands every year for each individual benefactor without reverence and faith. O dear Christians, God does not care for much praying but for true praying. In fact, he condemns long and repetitious prayers, and says in Matthew 6 [:7; 23:14] "They will only earn the more pun-ishment thereby." But greed, which cannot put its trust in God, brings such things to pass. Avarice is anxious lest it starve to death. . . .

. . . 18. All festivals should be abolished, and Sunday alone retained.[165] If it were desired, however, to retain the festivals of Our Lady and of the major saints, they should be transferred to Sunday, or observed only by a morning mass, after which all the rest of the day should be a working day. Here is the reason: since the feast days are abused by drinking, gambling, loafing, and all manner of sin, we anger God more on holy days than we do on other days. Things are so topsy-turvy that holy days are not holy, but working days are. Nor is any service rendered God and his saints by so many saints' days. On the contrary, they are dishonored; although some foolish prelates think that they have done a good work if each, following the prompt-

ings of his own blind devotion, celebrates a festival in honor of St. Otilie[166] or St. Barbara. But they would be doing something far better if they honored the saint by turning the saint's day into a working day.

Over and above the spiritual injury, the average man incurs two material disadvantages from this practice. First, he neglects his work and spends more money that he would otherwise spend. Second, he weakens his body and makes it less fit. We see this every day, yet nobody thinks of correcting the situation. In such cases we ought not to consider whether or not the pope has instituted the feasts, or whether we must have a dispensation or permission [to omit them]. Every town, council, or governing authority not only has the right, without the knowledge and consent of the pope or bishop, to abolish what is opposed to God and injurious to men's bodies and souls, but indeed is bound at the risk of the salvation of its souls to fight it even though popes and bishop, who ought to be the first to do so, do not consent.

Above all, we ought to abolish church anniversary celebrations[168] outright, since they have become nothing but taverns, fairs, and gambling places, and only increase the dishonoring of God and foster the soul's damnation. It does not help matters to boast that these festivals had a good beginning and are a good work. Did not God set aside his own law, which he had given from heaven, when it was perverted and abused? And does he not daily overturn what he has set up and destroy what he has made because of the same perversion and abuse? As it is written of him in Psalm 18 [:26], "You show yourself perverse with the perverted."

19. The grades or degrees within which marriage is forbidden, such as those affecting godparents or the third and fourth degree of kinship, should be changed. If the pope in Rome can grant dispensations and scandalously sell them for money,[170] then every priest may give the same dispensations without price and for the salvation of souls. Would to God that every priest were able to do and remit without payment all those things we have to pay for at Rome, such as indulgences, letters of indulgence, butter letters, mass letters, and all the rest of the *confessionalia* and skullduggery[171] at Rome and free us from that golden noose the canon law, by which the poor people are deceived and

cheated of their money! If the pope has the right to sell his noose of gold and his spiritual snares (I ought to say "law")[172] for money, then a priest certainly has more right to tear these nooses and snares apart, and for God's sake tread them underfoot. But if the priest does not have this right, neither has the pope the right to sell them at his disgraceful fair.

Furthermore, fasts should be left to individuals and every kind of food left optional, as the gospel makes them.[173] Even those gentlemen at Rome scoff at the fasts, and leave us commoners to eat the fat they would not deign to use to grease their shoes, and then afterward they sell us the liberty to eat butter and all sorts of other things. The holy Apostle says that we already have freedom in all these things through the gospel.[174] But they have bound us with their canon law and robbed us of our rights so that we have to buy them back again with money. In so doing they have made our consciences so timid and fearful that it is no longer easy to preach about liberty of this kind because the common people take offense at it and think that eating butter is a greater sin than lying, swearing, or even living unchastely. It is still a human work decreed by men. You may do with it what you will, yet nothing good will ever come of it. . . .

. . . 21. One of the greatest necessities is the abolition of all begging throughout Christendom. Nobody ought to go begging among Christians. It would even be a very simple matter to make a law to the effect that every city should look after its own poor, if only we had the courage and the intention to do so. No beggar from outside should be allowed into the city whether he might call himself pilgrim or mendicant monk. Every city should support its own poor, and if it was too small, the people in the surrounding villages should also be urged to contribute, since in any case they have to feed so many vagabonds and evil rogues who call themselves mendicants. In this way, too, it could be known who was really poor, and who was not.

There would have to be an overseer or warden who knows all the poor and informs the city council or the clergy what they needed. Or some other better arrangement might be made. As I see it, there is no other business in which so much skullduggery and deceit are practiced as in begging, and yet it could all be easily abolished. Moreover, this unrestricted universal begging is harmful to the com-

mon people. I have figured out that each of the five or six mendicant orders[190] visits the same place more than six or seven times every year. In addition to these there are the usual beggars, the "ambassador" beggars,[191] and the panhandlers.[192] This adds up to sixty times a year that a town is laid under tribute! This is over and above what the secular authorities demand in the way of taxes and assessments. All this the Romanist See steals in return for its wares and consumes for no purpose. To me it is one of God's greatest miracles that we can still go on existing and find the wherewithal to support ourselves!

To be sure, some think that if these proposals were adopted the poor would not be so well provided for, that fewer great stone houses and monasteries would be built, and fewer so well furnished. I can well believe all this. But none of it is necessary. He who has chosen poverty ought not to be rich. If he wants to be rich, let him put his hand to the plow and seek his fortune from the land. It is enough if the poor are decently cared for so that they do not die of hunger or cold. It is not fitting that one man should live in idleness on another's labor, or be rich and live comfortably at the cost of another's hardship, as it is according to the present perverted custom. St. Paul says, "Whoever will not work shall not eat" [II Thess. 3:10]. God has not decreed that any man shall live off another man's property, save only the clergy who preach and have a parish to care for, and these should, as St. Paul says in I Corinthians 9 [:14], on account of their spiritual labor. And also as Christ says to the apostles, "Every laborer is worthy of his wage" [Luke 10:7]. . . .

. . . 23. The brotherhoods,[194] and for that matter, indulgences, letters of indulgence, butter letters, mass letters, dispensations, and everything of that kind, should be snuffed out and brought to an end. There is nothing good about them. If the pope has the authority to grant you a dispensation to eat butter, to absent yourself from mass, and the like, then he ought also to be able to delegate this authority to the priests, from whom he had no right to take it in the first place. I am speaking especially of those brotherhoods in which indulgences, masses, and good works are apportioned. My dear friend, in your baptism you have entered into a brotherhood with Christ, with all the angels, with the saints, and with all Christians on earth. Hold fast to this and live up to its demands, and you have all the brotherhoods you want. Let the others glitter as they will. Compared with the true brotherhood in Christ those brotherhoods are like a penny compared with a gulden. But if there were a brotherhood which raised money to feed the poor or to help the needy, that would be a good idea. It would find its indulgences and its merits in heaven. But today nothing comes of these groups except gluttony and drunkenness. . . .

. . . 25. The universities, too, need a good, thorough reformation. I must say that, no matter whom it annoys. Everything the papacy has instituted and ordered serves only to increase sin and error. What else are the universities, unless they are utterly changed from what they have been hitherto, than what the book of Maccabees calls *gymnasia epheborum et graecae gloriae?*[210] What are they but places where loose living is practiced, where little is taught of the Holy Scriptures and Christian faith, and where only the blind, heathen teacher Aristotle rules[211] far more than Christ? In this regard my advice would be that Aristotle's *Physics, Metaphysics, Concerning the Soul,* and *Ethics,* which hitherto have been thought to be his best books, should be completely discarded along with all the rest of his books that boast about nature, although nothing can be learned from them either about nature or the Spirit. Moreover, nobody has yet understood him, and many souls have been burdened with fruitless labor and study, at the cost of much precious time. I dare say that any potter has more knowledge of nature than is written in these books. It grieves me to the quick that this damned, conceited, rascally heathen has deluded and made fools of so many of the best Christians with his misleading writings. God has sent him as a plague upon us on account of our sins.

Why this wretched fellow in his best book, *Concerning the Soul,* teaches that the soul dies with the body, although many have tried without success to save his reputation. As though we did not have the Holy Scriptures, in which we are fully instructed about all things, things about which Aristotle has not the faintest clue! And yet this dead heathen has conquered, obstructed, and almost succeeded in suppressing the books of the living God. When I think of this miserable business I can only believe that the devil has introduced this study.

For the same reasons his book on ethics is the worst of all books. It flatly opposes divine grace and all Christian virtues, and yet it is considered one of his best works. Away with such books! Keep them away from Christians. No one can accuse me of overstating the case, or of condemning what I do not understand. Dear friend, I know what I am talking about. I know my Aristotle as well as you or the likes of you. I have lectured on him and been lectured on him,[212] and I understand him better than St. Thomas or Duns Scotus[213] did. I can boast about this without pride and if necessary, I can prove it. It makes no difference to me that so many great minds have devoted their labor to him for so many centuries. Such objections do not disturb me as once they did, for it is plain as day that other errors have remained for even more centuries in the world and in the universities.

I would gladly agree to keeping Aristotle's books, *Logic, Rhetoric,* and *Poetics,* or at least keeping and using them in an abridged form, as useful in training young people to speak and to preach properly. But the commentaries and notes must be abolished, and as Cicero's *Rhetoric* is read without commentaries and notes, so Aristotle's *Logic* should be read as it is without all these commentaries. But today nobody learns how to speak or how to preach from it. The whole thing has become nothing but a matter for disputation and a weariness to the flesh.

In addition to all this there are, of course, the Latin, Greek, and Hebrew languages, as well as the mathematical disciplines and history. But all this I commend to the experts. In fact, reform would come of itself if only we gave ourselves seriously to it. Actually a great deal depends on it, for it is here in the universities that the Christian youth and our nobility, with whom the future of Christendom lies, will be educated and trained. Therefore, I believe that there is no work more worthy of pope or emperor than a thorough reform of the universities. And on the other hand, nothing could be more devilish or disastrous than unreformed universities.

I leave the medical men to reform their own faculties; I take the jurists and theologians as my own responsibility. The first thing I would say is that it would be a good thing if canon law were completely blotted out, from the first letter to the last, especially the decretals. More than enough is written in the Bible about how we should behave in all circumstances. The study of canon law only hinders the study of the Holy Scriptures. Moreover, the greater part smacks of nothing but greed and pride. Even if there were much in it that was good, it should still be destroyed, for the pope has the whole canon law imprisoned in the "chamber of his heart,"[215] so that henceforth any study of it is just a waste of time and a farce. These days canon law is not what is written in the books of law, but whatever the pope and his flatterers want. Your cause may be thoroughly established in canon law, but the pope always has his chamber of the heart in the matter, and all law, and with it the whole world, has to be guided by that. Now it is often a villain, and even the devil himself, who rules the *scrinium* —and they proudly boast that it is the Holy Spirit who rules it! Thus they deal with Christ's poor people. They impose many laws upon them but obey none themselves. They compel others to obey these laws, or buy their way out with money. . . .

. . . The number of books on theology must be reduced and only the best ones published. It is not many books that make men learned, nor even reading. But it is a good book frequently read, no matter how small it is, that makes a man learned in the Scriptures and godly. Indeed, the writings of all the holy fathers should be read only for a time so that through them we may be led into the Scriptures. As it is, however, we only read them these days to avoid going any further and getting into the Bible. We are like men who read the sign posts and never travel the road they indicate. Our dear fathers wanted to lead us to the Scriptures by their writings, but we use their works to get away from the Scriptures. Nevertheless, the Scripture alone is our vineyard in which we must all labor and toil.

Above all, the foremost reading for everybody, both in the universities and in the schools, should be Holy Scripture—and for the younger boys, the Gospels. And would to God that every town had a girls' school as well, where the girls would be taught the gospel for an hour every day either in German or in Latin. Schools indeed! Monasteries and nunneries began long ago with that end in view, and it was a praiseworthy and Christian purpose, as we learn from the story of St. Agnes and of other saints. Those were the days of holy virgins and martyrs when all was well with Christendom. But today these monasteries and nunneries have come to nothing but praying and singing. Is it not only right that

every Christian man know the entire holy gospel by the age of nine or ten? Does he not derive his name and his life from the gospel? A spinner or a seamstress teaches her daughter her craft in her early years. But today even the great, learned prelates and the very bishops do not know the gospel. . . .

. . . Moreover, even if the universities were diligent in Holy Scripture, we need not send everybody there as we do now, where their only concern is numbers and where everybody wants a doctor's degree. We should send only the most highly qualified students who have been well trained in the lower schools. A prince or city council ought to see to this, and permit only the well qualified to be sent. I would advise no one to send his child where the Holy Scriptures are not supreme. Every institution that does not unceasingly pursue the study of God's word becomes corrupt. Because of this we can see what kind of people they become in the universities and what they are like now. Nobody is to blame for this except the pope, the bishops, and the prelates, who are all charged with training young people. The universities only ought to turn out men who are experts in the Holy Scriptures, men who can become bishops and priests, and stand in the front line against heretics, the devil, and all the world. But where do you find that? I greatly fear that the universities, unless they teach the Holy Scriptures diligently and impress them on the young students, are wide gates to hell. . . .

. . . 27.[234] Enough has now been said about the failings of the clergy, though you may find more and will find more if you look in the right place. We shall now devote a section to the failings of the temporal estate.

In the first place, there is a great need for a general law and decree in the German nation against extravagant and costly dress, because of which so many nobles and rich men are impoverished.[235] God has certainly given us, as he has to other countries, enough wool, hair, flax, and everything else necessary for the seemly and honorable dress of every class. We do not need to waste fantastic sums for silk, velvet, golden ornaments, and foreign wares. I believe that even if the pope had not robbed us with his intolerable fleecing, we would still have more than enough of these domestic robbers, the silk and velvet merchants. We see that now everybody wants to be like everybody else, and pride and envy are thereby aroused and increased among us, as we deserve. All this misery and much more besides would be happily left behind if only our desire to be noticed would let us be thankful and satisfied with the good things God has already given us.

It is also necessary to restrict the spice traffic,[236] which is another of the great ships in which money is carried out of German lands. By the grace of God more things to eat and drink grow in our own land than in any other, and they are just as nourishing and good. Perhaps my proposals seem foolish, impractical, and give the impression that I want to ruin the greatest of all trades, that of commerce. But I am doing my best, and if there is no improvement in these matters, then let him who will try his hand at improving them. I do not see that many good customs have ever come to a land through commerce, and in ancient times God made his people Israel dwell away from the sea on this account, and did not let them engage in much commerce.

But the greatest misfortune of the German nation is certainly the *zynskauf*.[237] If that did not exist many a man would have to leave his silks, velvets, golden ornaments, spices, and display of every kind unbought. This traffic has not existed much longer than a hundred years, and it has already brought almost all princes, endowed institutions, cities, nobles, and their heirs to poverty, misery, and ruin. If it goes on for another hundred years, Germany will not have a penny left, and the chances are we shall have to eat one another. The devil invented the practice, and by confirming it[238] the pope has brought woe upon the whole world.

Therefore, I beg and pray at this point that everyone open his eyes and see the ruin of his children and heirs. Ruin is not just at the door, it is already in the house. I pray and beseech emperor, princes, lords, and city councilors to condemn this trade as speedily as possible and prevent it from now on, regardless of whether the pope with all his law—"unlaw" rather—objects or whether benefices or monasteries are based upon it. It is better for a city to have one benefice supported by honest legacies or revenue than to have a hundred benefices supported by *zynskauf*. Indeed, a benefice supported by a *zynskauf* is more grievous and oppressive than twenty supported by legacies. In fact, the *zynskauf* must be a sign and proof that the world has been sold to the devil because of its grievous

sins and that at the same time we are losing both temporal and spiritual possessions. And yet we do not even notice it.

In this connection, we must put a bit in the mouth of the Fuggers and similar companies. How is it possible in the lifetime of one man to accumulate such great possessions, worthy of a king, legally and according to God's will? I don't know. But what I really cannot understand is how a man with one hundred gulden can make a profit of twenty in one year. Nor, for that matter, can I understand how a man with one gulden can make another—and all this not from tilling the soil or raising cattle, where the increase of wealth depends not on human wit but on God's blessing. I leave this to men who understand the ways of the world. As a theologian I have no further reproof to make on this subject except that it has an evil and offending appearance, about which St. Paul says, "Avoid every appearance or show of evil" [I Thess. 5:22]. I know full well that it would be a far more godly thing to increase agriculture and decrease commerce. I also know that those who work on the land and seek their livelihood from it according to the Scriptures do far better. All this was said to us and to everybody else in the story of Adam, "Cursed be the ground when you work it; it shall bear you thistles and thorns, and in the sweat of your face you shall eat your bread" [Gen. 3:17–19]. There is still a lot of land lying unworked and neglected.

Next comes the abuse of eating and drinking,[240] which gives us Germans a bad reputation in foreign lands, as though it were a special vice of ours. Preaching cannot stop it, so deeply is it rooted and so firmly has it got the upper hand. The waste of money would be its least evil, were it not followed by all the vices that accompany it—murder, adultery, stealing, blasphemy, and every other form of immorality. Government can do something to prevent it; otherwise, what Christ says will come to pass, that the last day shall come like a secret snare, when they shall be eating and drinking, marrying and wooing, building and planting, buying and selling.[241] It is so much like what is now going on that I sincerely hope the day of judgment is at hand, although very few people give it any thought.

Finally, is it not lamentable that we Christians tolerate open and common brothels in our midst, when all of us are baptized unto chastity? I know perfectly well what some say to this, that is, that it is not a custom peculiar to one nation, that it would be difficult to put a stop to it, and, moreover, that it is better to keep such a house than that married women, or girls, or others of still more honorable estate should be outraged. Nevertheless, should not the government, which is temporal and also Christian, realize that such evil cannot be prevented by that kind of heathenish practice? If the children of Israel could exist without such an abomination, why cannot Christians do as much? In fact, how do so many cities, country towns, market towns, and villages do without such houses? Why can't large cities do without them as well?

In this matter of brothels, and in other matters previously mentioned, I have tried to point out how many good works the temporal government could do, and what the duty of every government should be, so that everyone may learn what an awful responsibility it is to rule and sit in high places. What use would it be if an overlord were as holy in his own life as St. Peter, if he did not diligently try to help his subjects in these matters? His very authority will condemn him. It is the duty of authorities to seek the best for those they govern. But if the authorities were to give some thought to how young people might be brought together in marriage, the hope of marriage would greatly help every one of them to endure and resist temptation.

But today everybody is attracted to the priesthood or the monastic life, and among them, I am sorry to say, there is not one in a hundred who has any other reason than that he seeks a living and doubts that he will ever be able to support himself and a family. Therefore, they live wildly enough beforehand, and wish, as they say, to get it out of their system, but experience shows that it is only more deeply embedded in them. I find the proverb true, "Despair makes most monks and priests."[242] That is what happens and that is how it is, as we see.

I will, however, sincerely advise that to avoid the many sins which entice so shamelessly, neither youth nor maid should be bound by the vow of chastity or a vow to adopt the religious life before the age of thirty.[243] Chastity, as St. Paul says, is a special gift [I Cor. 7:7]. Therefore, I would advise those upon whom God has not conferred his special gift

not to enter religious orders or take the vows. Furthermore, I say that if you trust God so little that you cannot support yourself as a married man and wish to become a religious only because of this distrust, then I beg you for your own soul's sake not to become a religious at all, but rather a farmer or anything you like. For where a single measure of faith in God is needed to earn your daily bread, there must be ten times that amount of faith to remain a religious. If you do not trust God to support you in temporal things, how will you trust him to support you in spiritual things? Alas, unbelief and distrust spoil everything and lead us into all kinds of misery, as we see in all walks of life.

Much more could be said of this pitiable state of affairs. The young people have nobody to look after them. They all do as they please, and the government is as much use to them as if it never existed. And yet the care of young people ought to be the chief concern of the pope, bishops, the ruling classes, and of the councils. They want to exercise authority far and wide, and yet they help nobody. For just this reason a lord and ruler will be a rare sight in heaven, even though he build a hundred churches for God and raise up all the dead!

That is enough for the moment. [I think I have said enough in my little book *Treatise on Good Works* about what the secular authorities and the nobility ought to do. There is certainly room for improvement in their lives and in their rule, yet the abuses of the temporal power are not to be compared with those of the spiritual power, as I have shown in that book.][245]

I know full well that I have been very outspoken. I have made many suggestions that will be considered impractical. I have attacked many things too severely. But how else ought I to do it? I am duty-bound to speak. If I had the power, these are the things I would do. I would rather have the wrath of the world upon me than the wrath of God. The world can do no more to me than take my life. In the past I have made frequent overtures of peace to my enemies, but as I see it, God has compelled me through them to keep on opening my mouth wider and wider and to give them enough to say, bark, shout, and write because they have nothing else to do. Well, I know another little song about Rome and the Romanists.[246] If their ears are itching to hear it, I will sing that one to them, too—and pitch it in the highest key! You understand what I mean, dear Rome.

Moreover, many times have I offered my writings for investigation and hearing, but to no avail. Nevertheless, I know full well that if my cause is just, it must be condemned on earth and be justified only by Christ in heaven, for all the Scriptures show that the cause of Christians and of Christendom must be judged by God alone. Moreover, no cause has ever yet been justified on earth by men because the opposition has always been too great and too strong. It is still my greatest concern and anxiety that my cause may not be condemned, by which I would know for certain that it is not yet pleasing to God.

Therefore, just let them go hard at it, pope, bishop, priest, monk, or scholar. They are just the ones to persecute the truth, as they have always done.

God give us all a Christian mind, and grant to the Christian nobility of the German nation in particular true spiritual courage to do the best they can for the poor church. Amen.

Wittenberg, in the year 1520.

-----

[6] Charles V, who had been elected emperor in 1519 when only twenty years of age, and whom Luther appeared before at the Diet of Worms in 1521.

[14] Cf. Josh. 6:20.

[15] I.e., confers tonsure.

[17] *Ehelich. PE* and other English translations also render this word as "married." It can, however, also mean "legitimately born." Karl Benrath notes that according to canon law only one born in wedlock may receive ordination as a priest. Cf. *An den christlichen Adel deutscher Nation von des christlichen Standes Besserung. . . . Bearbeitet, sowie mit Einleitung und Erläuterungen versehen von Karl Benrath* (Halle: Verein für Reformationsgeschichte, 1884), p. 83, n. 7.

[18] Canon law, which Luther throughout this treatise and elsewhere calls the "spiritual law," is a general name for the decrees of councils and the decisions of the popes collected in the *Corpus Iuris Canonici*. It comprised the whole body of church law and embodied in legal forms the medieval theory of papal absolutism, which accounts for the bitterness with which Luther speaks of it, espec-ially in this treatise. Cf. *PE* 2, 67, n. 2.

[19] Augustine, bishop of Hippo (395–430).

[20] Ambrose, bishop of Milan (374–397), was elected to

the office by the people of Milan, even though he was not yet baptized.

[21] Cyprian, bishop of Carthage (247–258), was also elected to the episcopate by the laity.

[22] The *character indelebilis* or "indelible mark," was given authoritative formulation in the bull *Exultate Deo* (1439). Eugene IV, summing the decrees of the Council of Florence, wrote: "Among these sacraments there are three—baptism, confirmation, and orders—which indelibly impress upon the soul a character, i.e., a certain spiritual mark which distinguishes them from the rest" (Carl Mirbt, *Quellen zur Geschichte des Papstums* [2nd ed.], No. 150). The Council of Trent, in its twenty-third session, July 15, 1563 (Mirbt, *op. cit.*, No. 312), defined the correct Roman teaching as follows: "Since in the sacraments of orders, as in baptism and confirmation, a character is impressed which cannot be destroyed or taken away, the Holy Synod justly condemns the opinion of those who assert that the priests of the New Testament have only temporary power, and that those once rightly ordained can again be made laymen, if they do not exercise the ministry of the Word of God." Cf. *PE* 2, 68, n. 5.

[23] *Schwetzen*; literally, "to chatter nonsense."

[24] The sharp distinction drawn by the Roman church between clergy and laity made possible the contention that the clergy was exempt from the jurisdiction of the civil courts. This is known as *privilegium fori,* i.e., "benefit of clergy." It was further claimed that the governing of the clergy and the administration of church property were matters for church authorities, and that lay rulers could not make or enforce laws which affected the church in any way. Cf. *PE* 2, 70, n. 1.

[25] I.e., temporal.

[26] Church authorities insisted that clergy charged with infractions of the laws of the state first be tried in ecclesiastical courts. Priests found guilty by such courts were deprived of their priesthood and were surrendered to the temporal authorities. *PE* 2, 71, n. 1.

[27] The interdict prohibits the administration of the sacraments and the other rites of the church within a given territory. Its use was not uncommon in the Middle Ages, and at the height of papal power it proved an effective means of bringing rulers to terms. Innocent III imposed the interdict upon England in 1208, during the reign of King John. Interdicts of more limited local extent were quite frequent. The use of the interdict for trifling infractions of church law was a subject of complaint at the Diet of Worms in 1521 and of Nürnberg in 1524. Cf. *PE* 2, 72, n. 1.

[29] Gregory the Great (590–604), in *Regula pastoralis*, II, 6. *MPL* 77, 34.

[30] Antichrist is the incarnation of all that is hostile to Christ and his kingdom and whose appearance is prophesied in II Thess. 2:3–10; I John 2:18, 22; 4:3; and Revelation 13.

[31] The doctrine of papal infallibility was never officially sanctioned in the Middle Ages, but the claim was repeatedly made by the champions of papal power, e.g., Augustinus Triumphus (d. 1328) in his *Summa de potestate Papae*. In his attack on the *Ninety-five Theses* (*Dialogus de potestate Papae,* December, 1517) Sylvester Prierias had asserted, 'The supreme pontiff cannot err when giving a decision as pontiff, i.e., when speaking officially [*ex officio*]"; and also, "Whoever does not rest upon the teaching of the Roman church and the supreme pontiff as an infallible rule of faith, from which even Holy Scripture draws its vigor and authority, is a heretic" (*EA Var. arg.* 1, 348). In the *Epitome* Prierias had said, "Even though the pope as an individual [*singularis persona*] can do wrong and hold a wrong faith, nevertheless as pope he cannot give a wrong decision" (*WA* 6, 337). Cf. *PE* 2, 73, n. 5.

[32] I.e., a single letter of Scripture to support their claim.

[34] Matt. 16:19, 18:18, and John 20:23. Throughout his career Luther dealt with the office of the keys. He first mentioned it in 1517 in his *Ninety-five Theses* (*LW* 31, 27, 31) and devoted a substantial portion of his last treatise, *Against the Roman Papacy, An Institution of the Devil* (1545) to a discussion of the keys (*LW* 41, 315–320 *passim*). His clearest and most extensive treatment was set forth in his 1530 treatise *The Keys* (*LW* 40, 321–377).

[35] Literally, "the creed," referring to the Apostles' Creed.

[36] *Beten*; literally, "to pray."

[37] Luther means baptism. See p. 127.

[38] This is another contention of Prierias. On November 28, 1518, Luther appealed his cause from the decision of the pope, which he could foresee would be adverse, to the decision of a council to be held at some future time. In the *Epitome* Prierias discusses this appeal, asserting among other things that "when there is one undisputed pontiff, it belongs to him alone to call a council," and that "the decrees of councils neither bind nor hold [*nullum ligant vel astringunt*] unless they are confirmed by authority of the Roman pontiff." *WA* 6, 335; *PE* 2, 77, n. 1.

[39] A mere gathering of people as opposed to a *concilium*, i.e., a valid council.

[40] The Council of Nicaea (325), the first general council, was convened by Constantine to settle the Arian controversy on the relation of Christ to God. Luther's contention is historically correct.

[41] Luther is referring to the first four ecumenical councils: Nicaea, Constantinople (381), Ephesus (431), and Chalcedon (451).

[42] A council free of papal control. Cf. p. 126, n. 12.

[43] *Kunst*; literally, "skill."

[115] The complaint against these judges was that they assumed jurisdiction over cases which belonged in the secular courts and enforced their decision through ecclesiastical censure. The *Gravamina* of 1521 specify the charges against these episcopal courts. Cf. *PE* 2, 103, n. 2.

[126] Since the coronation of Charlemagne in 800 the German Empire had been regarded as the continuation of the Roman Empire, a fiction fostered by the popes. The right to crown an emperor was held to be the prerogative of the pope. Cf. *PE* 2, 108, n. 2.

[132] A decree of Pope Clement V issued in 1313 and subsequently incorporated into canon law in *Clementinarum,* lib. ii, tit. XI, C. II. *CIC* 2, cols. 1151–1153.

[133] This document purported to be the testament of Emperor Constantine (306–337). It conveyed to the pope title to the city of Rome, certain lands in Italy, and "the islands of the sea." Medieval pontiffs used the document to support their claims to temporal power. In 1440 Laurentius Valla, an Italian humanist, exposed the *Donation* as an eighth-century forgery. Ulrich von Hutten's 1517 republication of Valla's exposé came to Luther's attention just before he wrote the present treatise. Luther published an annotated translation of the *Donation* in 1537. *WA* 50, 60–89. Cf. *PE* 2, 109, n. 4.

[134] The papal claim to sovereignty over this little kingdom which, comprised the island of Sicily and certain territories in southern Italy, goes back to the eleventh century. This claim was steadily asserted during the later Middle Ages and was one of the issues in the conflict between Emperor Frederick II (1200–1260) and the popes. The popes claimed the right to award the kingdom to a ruler who would swear allegiance to the Holy See. At the time Luther wrote this treatise, sovereignty over this kingdom was contested by the royal houses of France and of Spain, of which latter house Charles V was head. Cf. *PE* 2, 110, n. 1.

[139] There were other famous shrines, but the holy places at Rome had long been favorite destinations of pilgrimages, and this practice had been zealously fostered by the popes through the institution of the "golden" or "jubilee" years. Cf. p. 171, n. 142.

[140] Cf. Ulrich von Hutten's remark in *Vadiscus*, "Three things there are which those who go to Rome usually bring back with them: a bad conscience, a ruined stomach, and an empty purse." Eduard Böcking, *Ulrichs von Hutten-Schriften* (Leipzig, 1860), IV, 169. Erasmus was another critic of pilgrimages. Cf. *PE* 2, 113, n. 3. Cf. also *Erasmi Colloquia,* Vol. II, *Encomium Moriae* (Leipzig, n.d.), pp. 341 ff.

[141] *Die einfeltigen menschen*; literally, the simple, or those of untrained mind.

[142] The "golden" or "jubilee" years were inaugurated by Boniface VIII in 1300. Originally every hundreth year was to be a jubilee, but by 1473 this was reduced to every twenty-fifth year. During these jubilee years indulgences were granted to those who visited the churches of St. Peter and St. Paul in Rome. These indulgences were extended on a limited scale by Clement VI in 1350 to those who could not make the pilgrimage to Rome. Still later Boniface IX sent commissioners throughout Europe to dispense the indulgences for the cost of a journey to Rome and back. In a great many instances these indulgences were represented as offering pardon without penitential or sacramental formality. For this representation as well as for irregularity of their financial accounts a great many of these commissioners were punished by the pope. Cf. Lea, *A History of Auricular Confession and Indulgences in the Latin Church*, III, 63–66. Benrath notes that very large numbers of Germans participated in the pilgrimages of 1500. Cf. Benrath, *op. cit.*, p. 101, n. 59.

[150] Cf. Luther's understanding of I Cor. 4:1 expressed in *Concerning the Ministry* (LW 40, 35). The reference is to Jerome's *Commentary on Titus* [1:7]. MPL 26, 562; cf. also 22, 656.

[151] The first definitive and documented canon to prescribe and enforce clerical celibacy was that of Pope Siricius in 385. Cf. Henry Charles Lea, *History of Sacerdotal Celibacy in the Christian Church* (revised 3rd ed.; New York: The Macmillan Co., 1907), I, 64.

[152] The controversy over celibacy was involved in the schism between the Greek and Roman churches. Cf. *PE* 2, 120, n. 1.

[153] Luther had cast himself in this role in the introduction. Cf. p. 123

[154] Cf. Exod. 12:35–36.

[157] Irregulars are monks who have violated the rules of their order and in consequence have been deprived of the benefits enjoyed by those living within the *regula* or rule of the order; cf. Benrath, *op. cit.*, p. 102, n. 65. Among the violations is the concealing of sins in confession; cf. MA³ 2, 398.

[158] *Jartag, begencknis, seelmessen,* translated here as "endowed masses for the dead," were masses endowed either by the descendants of the deceased or by testamentary bequest. The terms by which Luther referred to these masses indicate the occasion of their celebration: *jartag*, the annual anniversary of the beneficiary's death; *begencknis*, the appointed day of the year when all the benefactors of a religious order were commemorated; and *seelmessen*, the masses regularly offered in behalf of souls in purgatory. Cf. Adolph Franz, *Die Messe im Deutschen Mittelalter* (Freiburg im Breisgau: Herdersche Verlagshandlung, 1902), pp.

243–244; cf. also Benrath, *op. cit.*, p. 102, n. 67.

[159] Originally the term "vigil" was applied to the night before a major festival. Gradually the term came to include the entire day, and finally was applied to the particular liturgical offices connected with the festivals. Luther probably was thinking of vigils in this liturgical sense. Cf. Benrath, *op. cit.*, p. 103, n. 68.

[165] Luther refers here to the numerous saints' days and minor religious holidays which fell on weekdays. These observances not only interfered with the working week but led to gambling, drinking, and vice. Cf. *Treatise on Good Works*, in this volume, p. 55.

[166] The feast day of this obscure saint is observed in the territory of Strassburg on December 13. Cf. *The Roman Martyrology* (London: Burns Oates and Washbourne, Ltd., 1937), p. 342.

[168] *Kirchweye,* the anniversary celebration of the consecration of a church. These days had become feast days in the parish. Cf. *PE* 2, 128, n. 1.

[170] Dispensations from the marriage laws were issued by the *Datarius*. Cf. p. 151, n. 83.

[171] On the *confessionalia*, see p. 155, n. 103, on butter letters, see pg. 155, n. 102. Mass letters were certificates entitling the holder to the benefits of masses celebrated by sodalities (cf. p. 192, n. 94). Cf. Benrath, *op. cit.*, p. 103, n. 75.

[172] Here Luther makes a pun on *geistliche netz,* i.e., spiritual snares, and *geystlich gesetz,* i.e., spiritual or canon law.

[173] Cf. Matt. 15:11.

[174] I Cor. 10:23; Col. 2:16.

[190] Franciscans, Dominicans, Augustinians, Carmelites, and Servites.

[191] I.e., wandering beggars who acted as ambassadors or messengers of a particular saint. Their practice was to enrol their benefactors on the list of beneficiaries of the saint they claimed to represent. This enrolment, they claimed, provided immunity from particular diseases, accidents, and other misfortunes. Protests were raised against this practice at the diets of Worms (1521) and Nürnberg (1523). Included in this protest were the *terminarii,* the collectors of alms sent out by these mendicants. Cf. the extensive note in Benrath, *op. cit.*, p. 105, n. 79; cf. also WA 6, 451, n. 1.

[192] I.e., men who spent their lives wandering from one place of pilgrimage to another subsisting on the alms of the faithful. Cf. *PE* 2, 135, n. 3.

[194] The brotherhoods flourished in the sixteenth century. Members of brotherhoods were obligated to recite certain prayers and to attend certain masses at appointed times. Membership in the association meant that each member participated in the benefits accruing from the good works of all the members. In

the case of most of the brotherhoods, the membership enjoyed certain indulgences. In 1520 Wittenberg boasted of twenty such fraternities; Cologne, eighty; Hamburg, more than one hundred. In 1519 Degenhard Peffinger of Wittenberg was a member of eight such fraternities in his hometown and of twenty-seven in other places. Luther had expressed his views on these groups more fully in his *The Blessed Sacrament of the Holy and True Body of Christ, and the Brotherhoods* (1519). *LW* 35, 47–73 (*WA* 2, 742–758). Cf. the detailed footnote in Benrath, *op. cit.,* p. 106 n. 80.

[210] I.e., places for the training of youth in the fashions of Greek culture. Cf. II Macc. 4:9.

[211] Scholars other than Luther were and had been against the Aristotelian domination in the medieval universities, e.g., Roger Bacon and Erasmus. In brief, Luther's animadversion sprang mainly from Aristotle's baleful effect on Christian soteriology. Aristotle taught that a man becomes good by doing good, and ultimately led theologians to a belief in man's power to save himself. Luther taught that it was only when a man lost all belief in himself that he ever knew what it was to have faith in Christ. Luther had no objection to heathen philosophy as such and saw its value in the discipline of logical reasoning, but his main objection to Aristotle was that he served to displace Christ who alone could save a man and give him true knowledge of natural and spiritual things.

[212] Luther lectured on Aristotle's *Nicomachean Ethics* four times a week during his first year in Wittenberg (1508–1509).

[213] Duns Scotus (d. 1308) was highly regarded in the fifteenth and sixteenth centuries as a rival to Thomas for first place among theologians.

[234] This section followed immediately after section 25 in the first edition and was numbered 26. Cf. *WA* 6, 465, n. 2.

[235] Such a law was proposed to the Diet of Worms in 1521. Cf. *PE* 2, 158, n. 2.

[236] Spices were one of the chief articles of foreign commerce in the sixteenth century. The discovery of the Cape route to India had given the Portuguese a practical monopoly of this trade. A comparative statement of the cost of spices over a period of years was reported to the Diet of Nürnberg (1523). Cf. *PE* 2, 159, n. 1.

[237] Cf. p. 98, n. 61 Cf. also Benrath's extensive discussion of the significance of this passage in *op. cit.,* p. 109, n. 99.

[238] The *zynskauf* was legalized by the Fifth Lateran Council in 1512. Cf. Benrath, *op. cit.,* 109, n. 99, and *MA*³ 2, 401.

[240] The diets of Augsburg (1500) and Cologne (1512) had passed edicts against drunkenness. The Diet of Worms (1521) adjourned before a recommendation that these earlier edicts be reaffirmed could be acted upon. Cf. *PE* 2, 161, n. 1.

[241] Luther may have had in mind such passages as Luke 21:34, 12:45, and Matt. 24:36–44.

[242] *Desperatio facit monachum.* Cf. Burton Stevenson (ed.), *The Home Book of Proverbs, Maxims, and Familiar Phrases* (New York: The Macmillan Company, 1948), p. 1619.

[243] In the *Discussion of Confession* (*Confitendi Ratio*) (1520) Luther sets the minimum age for men at eighteen or twenty, and for women at fifteen or sixteen (*WA* 6, 159–169). Cf. *PE* 1, 100. In *The Judgment of Martin Luther on Monastic Vows* (1521) Luther sets the minimum age at sixty. Cf. in this volume, pp. 387–388.

[245] The bracketed sentences did not appear in the first edition.

[246] This little song is *The Babylomian Captivity of the Church* (1520), written shortly after the present treatise was published. *LW* 36, 3–126.

CHAPTER 14

THE SCIENTIFIC REVOLUTION: GALILEO GALILEI

BACKGROUND AND BEGINNINGS

The Scientific Revolution was a series of causally connected events whose immediate impact was confined to a relatively small geographical area and time period—Britain and Western Europe about 1550–1650. The beginnings of the Scientific Revolution are not at all obvious and have given rise to considerable scholarly debate. With respect to consequences, on the other hand, the Scientific Revolution had, and continues to have, dramatic repercussions. Because of its implications for nearly all aspects of modern life, that sequence of events was quickly recognized, even if not always welcomed, as something new and immeasurable in its potential. The Scientific Revolution must therefore rank alongside the prehistoric Agricultural or Neolithic Revolution of around 10,000 BCE and the Industrial Revolution of the eighteenth and nineteenth centuries as one of the most significant changes in human cultural evolution.

The term "Scientific Revolution" has come to describe a unique and complex set of events, the most obvious of which is the introduction of a method of inquiry in which the role of experiment is central. An experimental method of studying nature is considerably different from the methods employed in two earlier periods of Western civilization in which attempts were made to understand nature: classical antiquity and the late Middle Ages. Although the methods and results of both ancient and medieval science profoundly influenced the shape that the Scientific Revolution would eventually assume—both positively and negatively—the latter is *sui generis* (self-generated). One indication of the vast differences that separated the Scientific Revolution from the earlier forms of

science is that they did not disrupt the fabric of the culture that fostered them. In neither of the earlier cases, moreover, was there a belief that nature was to be understood in order to be used for human benefit. These characteristics of modern science have become so ingrained in our culture that it requires considerable effort to visualize a culture in which science is not a model in terms of which other forms of inquiry are patterned and measured.

In an overview of the Scientific Revolution, only the highlights can be considered, along with a brief examination of some of the men and women who were both pioneers of the Scientific Revolution itself and authors of texts that sought to explain it or to defend it. In order to appreciate the revolutionary nature of the beginnings of modern science, it is necessary to go back briefly to the late Middle Ages and examine the climate of inquiry that came to be displaced by new methods of investigating nature and the human place in it.

With a few noteworthy exceptions, such as the thirteenth-century Franciscan scholar Roger Bacon, medieval methods of investigating natural phenomena resulted in elaborate, sometimes convoluted answers to questions the answers to which were already known. That may appear paradoxical, but there were two recognized sources of authority in the late Middle Ages: principally Aristotle's writings, including his immensely influential *Physics*, and Christian theology. Thomas Aquinas' synthesis of Aristotelian philosophy and Christian theology in the thirteenth century is a well-known and influential example of this approach. Inquiry was often little more than confirmation of received opinion or new modes of explaining the essential compatibility between the

Aristotelian worldview and Scripture. In the process, empirical data were rarely examined and almost never subjected to experiments. Instead the terms that denoted natural objects were defined and redefined and the arguments in their support searchingly examined for logical consistency and scriptural harmony. Even the simpler quantitative techniques such as counting, weighing, and measuring were ignored on the grounds that the nature or properties of discrete natural objects could not contravene theories supported by the christianized Aristotelianism best typified by scholasticism. And it was the later medieval forms of scholasticism against which many of the forerunners and makers of the Scientific Revolution were reacting when they insisted upon methods that directly investigated nature.

The scholastic approach toward understanding nature by logically defining and hierarchically ranking its component members within a static universe weathered many challenges, and vestiges of it lasted through the early nineteenth century (notably in biology). Its end was hastened, however, by a combination of forces, not easily foreseen as late as 1500, and by the positive results of workers in fields that were all but ignored by scholasticism. These were the artisans and craftspeople—metal workers, tool makers, dyers, painters, tanners and the like—who had long recognized, and taken advantage of, the physical and behavioral properties of natural objects. These they counted, weighed and measured, and otherwise analyzed in an effort to explain and understand them. In this sense, they took the lead in reestablishing a relationship with nature and her products that could be, and in many cases was, of considerable usefulness and benefit to people. Because many of these craftspeople committed the techniques and results of their professional expertise to writing, they provided a valuable source of technical information not otherwise obtainable. The technical manuals which they wrote, while unprepossessing and of little literary pretense, were valued by some contemporary scholars in their attempt to provide a more generalized explanation and understanding of nature that was consistent with nature itself, if not necessarily consistent with the prevailing intellectual authorities.

The readers of such technical manuals were mainly urban, like-minded members of the middle class: merchants, burghers, and, of course, other craftspeople. They were eager to exploit a new understanding of nature but were unable to read scholarly books written in Latin for other scholars. In time this body of technical manuals, usually written in the vernacular and conveniently known today as *Fachliteratur* (technical literature), reached an even more important audience. By a process known today as "technology transfer," members of three other groups studied, and, in turn, wrote similar texts: physicians, apothecaries (pharmacists), and "gentleman and lady" scholars—members of the aristocracy who pursued learning of various sorts. These *literati*, many of whom had only a tenuous connection with the universities, often established informal societies or associations where topics of mutual interest were debated, sometimes even experimentally tested, without much concern for scholastic or ecclesiastical authority. One of the most important episodes in this series of secular, non-academic bases of the Scientific Revolution was the invention by Johann Gutenberg, about 1450–1455, of printing with moveable type. By the institution of a new, mechanical process, identical multiple copies of a text could be inexpensively produced. With respect to technical details, the consequences of disseminating such information quickly over long distances were unparalleled in Western culture.

Now at just this time the effects of the Renaissance were being experienced and its message assimilated in academic quarters. Originally the Renaissance had been primarily a literary and artistic response to the "rediscovery" of classical antiquity. Its most notable exponents, the humanists, had been generally oblivious to *Fachliteratur* and to the slowly developing interest in examining nature. But despite their indifference to what later became known as science, they advocated something that was as influential as the artisans' desire to unlock the secrets of nature in simple but utilitarian terms. This was the humanists' insistence on a fluent command of Greek and Latin, without which the newly discovered ancient texts could not be understood. Among the classical texts rediscovered during the fifteenth century, and hence unencumbered by scholastic commentary, were a number of Greek and Roman technical treatises on mathematics, astronomy, zoology, botany, medicine, agriculture, and architecture. Each of these texts presented new data and, in many instances, new ways of looking at a nature that had been so overcoated with exegetical commentary as to have been forgotten—not by the craftspeople, or indeed by the peasants, but by those for whom scholasticism provided the only link with nature. Thus the humanism of the Renaissance joined forces with the artisans' less polished attempts to understand and to explain a physical world that had been obscured and whose details had been regarded as unworthy of study.

FOUR MODELS IN THE DEVELOPMENT OF THE NEW SCIENCE

Having sketched the intellectual background of the Scientific Revolution, we shall now turn to its makers and their principal contributions. Not only because of the enormous amount of material available—both primary sources and secondary studies—but also because of the many issues and allegiances professed by the pioneers of the Scientific Revolution, neither a biographical procedure nor one in terms of different fields of investigation is entirely satisfactory. In place of those approaches, we have chosen to organize the data in terms of *models of inquiry* adopted by the major scientific revolutionaries. Admittedly, this is not as tidy a method as a series of biographies of scientific heroes, and it is rather more removed from the modern compartmentalization of scientific disciplines and sub-disciplines. But the procedure we have adopted here does have one outstanding advantage: It is an attempt to recognize, and to identify, the sources and the stimuli, not all of which would be recognized as "scientific" today, that underlay the several approaches of the founders of modern science.

By the mid-sixteenth century, and certainly as a result of both the success of the Renaissance and public recognition of the importance of the several craft-traditions, there were at least four alternative models for studying nature. Each of these could be, and sometimes was, capable of being reconciled to scholasticism, but they owed little to, and often ignored, its methods. I have identified the four models with the most descriptive label available,

although not in all cases would these labels have been as meaningful or as identifiable then as they are today. But that, of course, is just another index of the success enjoyed by the Scientific Revolution and its overwhelming drive to examine, to understand, and to explain nature.

Major scientific figures made use of more than one of our four models at various places and times in their research. But that is precisely what one should expect of pioneers, seeking the best means to achieve a distant goal. Hardly less important is the fact that the various scientific disciplines and sub-disciplines came into being at different times and often as the result of stimuli, issues, and accidents perhaps unforeseen and certainly not readily apparent several centuries later. Moreover, the growth rates of the various scientific disciplines varied considerably: sometimes in accordance with socio-economic and other non-scientific issues that retarded their growth, and at other times in response to successful solutions of problems that accelerated their growth.

With these reservations in mind, we may now proceed to examine the formation and growth of modern science in terms of the thematic models that shaped its early development. The four themes or models in terms of which Nature was first successfully investigated in a way that can be recognized as "scientific" today are as follows:

1) The Platonic-Pythagorean Model

Definition: The belief that the universe is mathematically constituted and can be numerically described has its ancient roots in Pythagoras, to whom was attributed the saying that "All is number," and the Pythagoreans. Plato was influenced by this emphasis of Pythagoreanism, and influentially expressed his metaphysical interest in mathematics in dialogues such as the *Timaeus* and portions of the *Republic*. The Renaissance brought a renewed interest in Plato and Platonism, and some saw in Plato's views of mathematics a guide to nature. For the advocates of this model, chiefly the astronomers, the task was to explain celestial phenomena in terms of geometrical harmonies, mathematically calculated orbits, ratios and distances, and to establish, wherever possible, harmonies and commensurabilities between objects. But above all, it was the formulation of mathematical law that not only described, but, in a peculiar sense, determined the behavior of objects.

Application: It was by its undoubted power of ordering, extrapolating, and predicting that the first signals of the Scientific Revolution were sounded. These were, first and foremost, epitomized by a series of astronomers who provided an unbroken tradition from 1543 to 1687, all consciously building on the more limited work of their predecessors. But it also must be noted that the Renaissance humanist Marsilio Ficino's translation of all of Plato's writings in 1482, followed by translations and editions of several ancient mathematical and philosophical texts, suddenly presented scholars with a radically new way of explaining one very obvious part of nature: the heavens above.

For over a thousand years the astronomical theory of Ptolemy (second century CE), who built largely on Aristotle's important work on physics, had gone virtually unchallenged. The Ptolemaic universe was *geocentric*, with a stationary earth at the center of the universe and all the planets and stars revolving around it. The earth (*terra* in Latin) consists of the "terrestrial" or "sub-lunar" elements: fire, air, water, and earth. The rest of the universe, from the moon outward, is the "celestial" realm (from *caelum*, the heavens), pervaded by the fifth and lightest element, the Aether. The terrestrial contains the "dross" of the universe; it is the sphere of imperfection. The celestial—the moon, sun, planets, and stars—are perfect beings rotating on perfect crystalline spheres. Ptolemy developed an elaborate system to account for all observed celestial movement, notably a system of "epicycles" or "circles upon circles" to account for the eccentric movement of the planets. The Ptolemaic system enjoyed unrivalled success for so long because it seemed to accord with common observation and seemed able to account—however elaborately—for the various movements of celestial bodies. For a Western world dominated by Christianity, it also appeared to be the view that was in harmony with the biblical account of nature. But there were persistent problems with the Ptolemaic system, which was progressively modified over the centuries in the light of continuing observation of the heavens into an even more complex and cumbersome explanation of celestial movement.

Credit for what later was regarded by many as the opening round of the Scientific Revolution belongs to the Polish astronomer, Nicolaus Copernicus (1473-1543), whose four years in Italy brought him into touch with the literary productions of the Renaissance. In the year of his death, Copernicus published his *De revolutionibus orbium coelestium*. (*On the Revolution of the Heavenly Spheres*). Retaining a belief in the uniform, circular motion of the planets, and only modifying the epicycles and other legacies from Ptolemy, Copernicus nevertheless substituted a *heliocentric* or sun-centered universe for a geocentric universe. The full implications of this move were not immediately recognized, probably because Copernicus regarded the new heliocentric model as a hypothesis, mathematically interesting but not a physical rival to the older cosmological theories noted above.

The revolutionary character of Copernicus' heliocentric hypothesis became apparent with the work of the German astronomer Johannes Kepler (1571–1630). Kepler's writings, much more influential in his time than those of Copernicus, equally well illustrate the appeal and usefulness of mathematical modeling. In his early work, *Mysterium Cosmographicum* (*Cosmographic Mystery*) (1596), he sought to demonstrate the validity of a planetary system composed of the five known planets. He reasoned that the five regular or Platonic solids (tetrahedron, cube, octahedron, dodecahedron, and icosahedron) could be so arranged, one inside the other, as to define the spaces, in harmonious, geometrical ratios, between the planetary spheres. The universe, he concluded, was constructed according to geometrical principles. Although this kind of reasoning may seem far removed from modern science, Kepler, who greatly admired Copernicus' work, recognized a major flaw in Copernicus' hypothesis and sought to correct it. For Kepler the issue was twofold: not only must an astronomical system be mathematically sound, it must also possess physical reality. This left Kepler with no alternative but to replace the Copernican circular orbits with elliptical orbits. In the process of calculating the orbits described by the planets, he noted and corrected a second flaw in Copernicus' system, arguing that planetary motion is not uniform. This led Kepler to formulate his laws of planetary motion. Although later modified by Galileo and

Based on his own experiments, Galileo published support of the Copernican theory that the sun, not the earth, was the center of the universe. Catholic church officials subsequently accused him of heresy for his heliocentric views. Galileo's book, *Dialogue on the Two Chief World Systems,* was banned in 1632; the following year, he was brought before the Inquisition at the Vatican. Fleury's painting captures a moment of Galileo's trial, where the accused stands with one hand on a book and the other at his chest. The trial ended with Galileo's sentence of life imprisonment and a forced recantation of earlier beliefs.

Figure VI-6 Joseph Nicolas Robert-Fleury. *Galileo Galilei Before the Inquisition.* 1847. Oil on canvas (1.96 x 3.08 m). Musée du Louvre, Paris. Courtesy of Erich Lessing/Art Resource, NY.

Newton, the mere establishment of such laws provided evidence for the necessity of demonstrating a mathematical basis for astronomy. Later, of course, the mathematical model would be fundamental in the other physical sciences as well.

Kepler was not the only admirer of Copernicus. Galileo, though he corresponded with Kepler, retained the circular orbits of the Copernican system. But this was only an apparent step backward, because Galileo Galilei (1564–1642), Italian mathematician, physicist, and astronomer, by his many contributions placed the heliocentric system on firm footing. This was made possible in part by the tele-

scope, invented some time after 1600. Galileo was not the first to use that newly developed instrument, but he was the first to demonstrate by its use that other celestial bodies, invisible to the naked eye, were rotating about the sun. Even more revolutionary was the fact that by being the first to describe the satellites of Jupiter (unknown to Aristotle and Ptolemy), Galileo established a physical analogue, not just a mathematical construct, to the earth's satellite, the moon, both of which revolved about the sun. An equally important issue was raised by Galileo when he described the surface of the moon. It was pitted and irregular, and hence similar to the earth's surface, whereas, according to the Aristotelian-scholastic model, it was supposed to be smooth and immaculate because it was exempt from the kinds of changes defining the sub-lunar world. In this way, together with his analysis of the Milky Way galaxy into countless stars too far away to detect stellar parallax, Galileo believed he had demonstrated the infinity of the universe.

Such conclusions seriously challenged the orthodox Christian view of the universe, and for years Galileo's hypotheses were debated and investigated not only by scientists but also by clergy up to and including the pope. As with later turning points or "paradigm shifts" in science such as Darwinian evolutionary theory, when a whole view of nature and the human place in it was fundamentally challenged both scientifically and theologically, there were clergy—some quite prominent—who defended Galileo's Copernicanism and scientists who rejected it. But there were very powerful Catholic clergy, notably Cardinal Robert Bellarmine (1542–1621) and the Holy Office of the Inquisition, who considered Galileo's views not only scientifically unproven but also heretical, contrary to the teachings of the Bible. Galileo's trial in 1632, leading to his humiliation, recantation, and confinement the rest of his life under house arrest, was followed with concerned interest by intellectuals throughout Europe, and has its own very special place in the Scientific Revolution. It brought home to the educated layperson, no less than to the scientist, the fact that the findings of science cannot be dictated by authority, whether ecclesiastical or political.

The almost legendary name of the Englishman Sir Isaac Newton (1642–1727), astronomer, mathematician, and physicist, is a fitting capstone to this section. His *Mathematical Principles of Natural Philosophy* (1687), better known simply as the *Principia* from its Latin title, was at once an announcement that the Scientific Revolution had ended *and* that modern science had begun. But Newton's contributions were not confined to astronomy, nor did his use of mathematics, consummate as it was, fully indicate all of his sources. As I noted earlier in this study, the makers of the Scientific Revolution cannot be neatly categorized with respect to their reliance upon or allegiance to a single model. Depending upon the nature of the problem to be solved, at different stages in a productive career or as a result of new information, the same scientist might make use of a mathematical, a mechanistic, and a Hermetic model. Newton was no exception, for while the *Principia* is the outstanding example of following the mathematical model, his great work *Optics* (1704) depended upon a mechanistic model based on atoms, while his alchemical studies reveal that Hermeticism appealed strongly to the mystical side of Newton's complex personality.

Thanks to the excellent library resources at Cambridge University, Newton was well-read in the writings of his predecessors. We know that he was acquainted with the writings of Kepler, Galileo, and Descartes and, predictably, he recognized their deficiencies. What set Newton apart from the many other investigators who, working along similar lines, also recognized the inadequacies of their predecessors, was that he sought to do more than rectify mathematical errors or modify the accounts of others regarding the physical nature of the objects whose behavior was mathematically calculated. After many years of study and meditation, he proposed a *synthesis* of previous thought.

It was a grand synthesis that included and accounted for the behavior of both celestial and terrestrial objects under the same universal laws. But unlike any of the many rival "world systems" then competing for scientific approbation, Newton's system mathematically demonstrated, experimentally proved, and made physically acceptable, that freely falling bodies and projectiles, planets revolving about the sun, the moon revolving about the earth, and the daily tides were all subject to the same universal law of gravitation. Going a step farther, he proposed his justly famous three laws of motion which, in many respects, still provide the bases for understanding the mathematical framework of physical reality: (1) "Every body continues in its state of rest, or of uniform motion in a right line, unless it is compelled to change that state by forces impressed upon it." (2) "The change of motion is proportional to the motive force impressed; and is made in the direction of the right line in which that force is impressed." (3) "To every action there is always opposed an equal reaction: or, the mutual actions of two bodies upon each other are always equal, and directed to contrary parts."

2) The Mechanical or Mechanistic Model

Definition: In this model, the forces of nature were regarded as similar to mundane domestic activities magnified to cosmic dimensions. As such, the activities that took place in the cosmos were modeled after mechanical activities while the objects of nature were the result of these mechanical processes. Atoms moving through a void or the alternation of the heating and cooling of liquids, including the four "humors" that were believed to constitute—and explain—mammalian physiology, are alike instances of how this model won acceptance by its reasonable, easily visualizable analogies with domestic and mechanical processes known to all.

Application: There never was a lack of advocates of a mechanistic conception of nature, a tradition that can be traced back to some of the Pre-Socratic "nature philosophers" of ancient Greece and notably to the atomists such as Democritus and Leucippus. The mechanical model of explanation found a ready acceptance in the seventeenth century largely because understanding it did not require advanced education or mathematical training, but also because of the ease with which it could be applied to the solution of problems which did not, at that time, lend themselves to the kind of analysis associated with, and required by, a mathematical model. Whereas the mathematical model was first, and most successfully, applied to the solution of astronomical problems, the mechanical model, almost from the beginning of the Scientific Revolution, was applied to the elucidation of a wide range of problems in a variety of different areas of scientific investigation.

Basically, there were two strands to the "mechanical philosophy," the seventeenth century phrase used to describe those attempts to understand nature by means of likening its workings to machines, using mechanical analogies and materialist assumptions. This approach is exemplified by the writings of Gilbert, Boyle and Harvey, though of course other scientists such as Galileo and Newton also made use of mechanistic explanations.

The English scientist William Gilbert (1540–1603), trained as a physician, has been described as the discoverer of magnetism because of his book *De magnete* (*On the Magnet*) (1600). But as he himself admitted, the behavior of the loadstone was known already in antiquity, though the explanations for what came to be known as magnetism were little more than combinations of occultism and guesswork. What Gilbert accomplished was to synthesize and explain, under one general heading, the behavior of a wide range of objects; this was his "magnetical philosophy." Among the objects he brought together and gave a unified explanation were loadstones, iron magnets, and the mariner's compass. These and other objects upon which Gilbert performed a long series of experiments led him to conclude that the earth itself is a huge magnet, thus strengthening the views of the mathematical astronomers that the earth, like any other object, is an appropriate object of scientific inquiry.

As might be suggested by Gilbert's work, mechanical explanations could be offered for a variety of other natural processes. That is in fact exactly what occurred. Robert Boyle (1627–1691), English philosopher and investigator, for example, adopted the old atomistic philosophy of classical antiquity and adapted it so as to provide the foundations of what later became chemistry, as distinct from alchemy. Alchemy, the forerunner and source of chemistry, was in the Middle Ages devoted to efforts to turn base metals into gold and to find a universal solvent and a universal medicine (panacea). In his book *The Sceptical Chemist* (1661) Boyle hypothesized that atoms of one universal kind of matter constitute all substances. Different substances are produced by different arrangements and movements of atoms. He developed what became known as Boyle's law, that the volume of a gas varies inversely as the pressure.

The mechanistic and materialistic model provided the scientific and philosophic bases for explanations of natural processes of both inanimate and animate nature. In this way those processes could be studied experimentally and the variables isolated so that they, in turn, could be independently examined. This is no better exemplified than by the epoch-making discoveries of William Harvey (1578–1657), English physician and the founder of modern physiology. Although Harvey made little direct use of the atomic model in his book *De Motu Cordis et Sanguinis* (*On the Motion of the Heart and the Blood*) (1628), the mechanistic basis is evident throughout his small book. Leaving aside the technical, anatomical details of the mammalian heart, concerning which Harvey had accumulated much data through numerous well-designed experiments, and also leaving aside some 1500 years of speculation about human physiology, Harvey demonstrated two simple truths: that the only function of the heart is to pump blood throughout a closed system in a continuous cycle; and that the heart can be understood, and its function explained, by viewing it as a machine which can thus be quantitatively and mechanically described.

3) The Hermetic Model

Definition: This model of scientific investigation takes its name from Hermes Trismegistus, a Greek god identified with the Egyptian god Thoth and considered in the ancient world the founder of occult sciences, especially alchemy. At first sight, anything smacking of magic and occult causes might be dismissed as prescientific. Nonetheless, the recognition that there were causes that could be described but not explained, and that the results of many processes often contained unexpected results, was common to most forms of inquiry. By postulating that the cosmos was filled with animate forces and powers, by openly admitting the existence of many of nature's secrets, and by arguing that those secrets could be studied if only suitable methods were available, the advocates of the Hermetic model attempted to make sense of processes not explicable by either mathematical or mechanistic means.

Application: While the principal components of this model can be established with some certitude, they may not strike the modern reader as in any way relevant to science. But from the early sixteenth century onward, an appeal to what we might call "magical" and "supernatural" elements had a great vogue, especially in the biological sciences and medicine, where the explanation of processes peculiar to the living body had lagged behind the explanation of inanimate nature. In explaining this model it is important to bear in mind that, despite the emphasis on magic, this is a secular and not a religious model. As such, it was designed to call attention to, and to supplement the inadequacies of, theological explanation (in which supernatural agencies played a key role). It was claimed, moreover, by its advocates that it could account for the behavior of various objects ignored by a mechanistic explanation and bypassed by the mathematicians.

Undoubtedly the principal figure in the Hermetic tradition was the Swiss physician and alchemist Philip Bombastus von Hohenheim, known as Paracelsus (c. 1493–1541). An angry man throughout his eventful career, he was alternately vilified as a magician and charlatan and lionized as a genius of true Hermetic lineage. Paracelsus left behind a large body of writings covering most of the scientific and medical topics debated during his lifetime. He also left behind a group of disciples who sought to explain and defend his pronouncements and to extend them, often by supplementing Paracelsus' insights with experimentally derived data. Together, his writings and those of his followers added a significant stimulus to a better understanding of natural, especially biological processes. Many of those processes, to be sure, had been discussed by Aristotle and the medieval Scholastics, but by virtue of their reliance on non-experimental methods and their almost complete ignorance of chemistry, many questions were left unanswered. Some of these Paracelsus addressed by viewing the human body as a chemical laboratory and the bodily processes as so many chemical reactions.

It is difficult to summarize the main tenets of the Hermetic model, if only because many of them, when shorn of the mysticism and obscurity of Paracelsian terminology, were assimilated by later writers in an effort to explain biological phenomena. For example, the concept of "specific virtue"—forces that give particular substances their character and power to act—was to play an important role in pharmacology. Nonetheless, certain key concepts can be isolated from the Hermetic philosophy of nature. Chief among them was the belief in the importance of a bonding between the macrocosm and the microcosm by means of occult, vital, yet impersonal forces. This millennium-old belief was given a new meaning by Paracelsus and those whom he influenced. They sought to establish, in different contexts, by the use of experimental data, interconnections between animate nature and the larger inanimate world, celestial as well as terrestrial.

The two areas where the application of Hermetic philosophy is most evident were themselves ancient. Paracelsus gave new importance to alchemy and astrology, making these two subjects carry the burden of Paracelsian inquiry. In time, of course, both alchemy and astrology became thoroughly discredited. But in that very process, positive results were achieved. For one thing, the lively, sometimes acrimonious debate between the Paracelsians and their opponents conditioned investigators to examine and to confirm—or disconfirm—by experimental means, precisely those interconnections called for by the Paracelsians. Because Paracelsus called attention to the complex nature of chemical processes (albeit under the guise of astral influences upon the human body), these processes began to receive the attention previously given to problems that were more amenable to mathematical analysis and mechanistic solutions.

One of Paracelsus' goals was to explain chemically the workings of the human body. By extension that meant a radical reformation of medicine and especially pharmacology. Scholars are still divided as to the merits of Paracelsus' claims, yet there appears to be little doubt that by his attacks on tradition, the grounds were established for trying to understand what we would term the biochemical mechanisms of the mammalian body.

Jean Baptiste van Helmont (1577–1644), Belgian physician, extended the Paracelsian model by suggesting various ways in which Paracelsus' program could be applied in medicine. Despite his mystical outlook, van Helmont succeeded in translating some of the vague ideas of Paracelsus into doctrines that could be studied experimentally. One example was the process of fermentation, central to which is the recognition, if not the identification, of the liberation and exchange of gases of various kinds. In fact, the very word "gas" was coined by van Helmont in his efforts to understand biochemical processes. The latter remained almost as mysterious as they had been for the physicians of antiquity. They recognized, of course, the processes of digestion and respiration but were unable to provide explanations that could be experimentally tested.

4) The Empirico-Descriptive Model

Definition: As the name suggests, this was a method of describing or cataloguing objects without the necessity of having to explain them or to account for variations, abundance (or rarity), geographical distribution, and the like. It was employed with considerable success by the early naturalists, and is the approach to nature we still associate with the word "naturalist." In fact, this

kind of activity has not completely ended, though the heyday of the collector-naturalist is all but over.

Application: In the process of explaining nature in terms of the mathematical and mechanistic models, much of organic nature had been ignored. The Hermeticists, to be sure, partially rectified this by including human beings within the new framework provided by science. But that still left unaccounted and unexplained, except by reference to the Genesis account of creation, the other living inhabitants of nature. Already in the last quarter of the fifteenth century, attempts had been made to describe some of the better-known plants, animals, and minerals in terms of their usefulness in the preparation of drugs. But the anonymous herbals (books about herbs or plants), for example the *Gart der Gesundheit* (*Garden of Health*), printed in Mainz in 1485, were only forerunners of more revolutionary books to follow. It was not until the mid-sixteenth century that a sharp break can be detected between the medieval encyclopedic account (based largely on extracts from Scripture and classical Greco-Roman sources), and a new approach to nature for which empirical data supplied the bases for understanding. Until an inventory was made of the plants, animals, and minerals, there could be no progress in theorizing about their behavior or distribution. Once that was accomplished, humans could be fitted into the world of animate nature and their behavior appropriately described and naturalistically explained.

Pride of place thus belongs to the first modern description of human anatomy, *De Humani Corporis Fabrica* (*On the Construction of the Human Body*), written by the Belgian physician Andreas Vesalius (1514–1564). Published the same year as Copernicus' *De Revolutionibus* (1543), it is a fitting counterpart to the latter's cosmological focus. Vesalius was conscious of the need to correct the errors and lacunae in ancient and medieval anatomical texts and prints. He accomplished this by a method that today seems obvious, but at the time it was another shocking and controversial aspect of the scientific revolt against tradition. He himself dissected the human body and, no less importantly, he supervised the preparation of the illustrations for his *Fabrica*. In short, he described what he observed, and for the most part he resisted the temptation to philosophize about the purpose and functions of the various organs that he described. No better testimony to the revolutionary character of the *Fabrica* is that upon its publication, all previous anatomical studies were immediately superseded. Moreover, the *Fabrica* was quickly adapted and plagiarized by lesser scientific investigators who recognized its superiority.

Once the fabric of the human body had been literally opened to public inspection, similar examinations of plants and animals followed suit. However, descriptions of plants, based on empirical observation, had already begun to appear a decade prior to the publication of the *Fabrica*. More specifically three men, closely linked professionally and geographically, had begun to study plants in terms of the same empirico-descriptive model that Vesalius shortly thereafter would employ—a model that others would use to study animals and minerals.

These three botanists, all of whom were also physicians and were collectively known as the *Patres rei herbariae* (fathers of herbal science), were Otto Brunfels (1488–1534), Hieronymus Tragus (1498–1554), and Leonhart Fuchs (1501–1566). By publishing their realistically illustrated herbals they demonstrated conclusively that descriptive studies of plants—and the same applies as well to animals—must begin with empirical observation. They also demonstrated that accurate illustrations and precise identifications are the steps necessary for more detailed studies of the behavior and habitat of plants and animals. By thus describing the flora of Western Europe, to which for the most part they wisely restricted themselves, they put botany on a footing that was certainly different from, say, astronomy, but no less scientific. The herbals of the three *patres* provided a basis for extending botanical studies to the flora of newly-discovered lands in America, Africa, and Asia.

Much the same pattern was followed by those who, in studying animals, created the discipline later known as zoology. First the organisms must be described and identified. Then, and only then, can serious studies of their natural history replace the fabulous accounts of medieval bestiaries and credulous travellers. The two most notable practitioners of the empirico-descriptive method as applied to the investigation of animals were the Swiss polymath Conrad Gesner (1516–1565) and the Italian biologist Ulisse Aldrovandi (1522–1606). To

their great credit, each tried to include in their multi-volume studies all the animals then known. Quite naturally, the quality of their descriptions varied in accordance with the availability of specimens and the size of the organisms; hence the accounts of whales and fleas, for example, leave much to be desired. Quadrupeds, birds, and fish fared better than arthropods, reptiles, and echinoderms, though there were still many uncertainties and some fabulous accounts were treated as if they had been field reports. But the shortcomings of these and other pioneer zoologists must not obscure the soundness of the method they adopted nor the model in terms of which their method was justified. To this day—now supported by a vast array of instruments, photography, and statistical means—new organisms are still being described and classified in an effort to catalogue completely our non-human companions.

Methods to describe some of the smaller organisms were devised by two other investigators whose role in the Scientific Revolution is as secure as that of Gesner and Aldrovandi. Anton van Leeuwenhoek (1632–1723) and Robert Hooke (1635–1703) were largely responsible for opening up the invisible microscopic world and describing some of its inhabitants whose existence had been suspected but not known. Leeuwenhoek was a Dutch merchant by profession; Hooke was an English experimentalist and mathematician and a rival of Newton in the Royal Society. Both men tried hard to describe only what they saw: in Leeuwenhoek's case, protozoa, and in Hooke's case, everything from cellular walls to the appendages of fleas. That was made possible by the invention of the microscope, which in its later modified form permitted the viewing of worlds as new and strange in their way as those that Columbus had described.

It remains, finally, to consider the third kingdom of nature and two representative students of it. By adopting the empirico-descriptive model, Agricola and Biringuccio initiated a series of descriptive studies that established the bases of the earth sciences. Georgius Agricola (1490–1555), German physician and geologist, and Vannoccio Biringuccio (1480–1533), Italian engineer, chose, for purely pragmatic reasons, to investigate and to describe the earthly components of creation. In both cases, they described what they perceived, though they were hampered by the undeveloped state of chemistry and consequently the difficulty of making chemical analyses of minerals.

Agricola spent many years collecting the data for his two major publications, *De Natura Fossilium* (*On the Nature of Fossils*) (1546) and *De Re Metallica* (*On Mining*) (1556). Like the humanistically trained scholar he was, he collected the passages from classical Greek and Latin texts relating to gemstones, minerals, and metals. But unlike the typical humanist, he went a step farther. He sought to identify the substances described in the ancient accounts by comparing them with those substances that he personally collected. These could then be taken to his workshop and subjected to physical tests and to the then-rudimentary forms of chemical analysis. Once that was completed, he felt sufficiently armed to consider the usefulness of such substances to the rapidly-growing field of applied science—in other words, technology.

Biringuccio, though not the scholar that Agricola was, nonetheless was as concerned as the latter with practical matters. Holding a number of responsible positions as armourer and foundryman in various Italian municipalities, he recognized the great gulf between alchemical texts and the casting of cannon and cathedral bells. A flaw in either of the latter would make a difference that no amount of theorizing could correct. For such reasons, Biringuccio examined and tested samples of ore before the final casting, and it is the reports of such testing that make up the core of his book *De la Pirotechnia* (*On Pyrotechnics*) (1540).

THE INSTITUTIONALIZATION OF THE SCIENTIFIC REVOLUTION

The Faustian image of the lone scholar, isolated from the mundane world and acquiring arcane knowledge by questionable means, is in many ways not an unfaithful picture of the early scientific pioneers. That image was to undergo a radical transformation with the development and gradual acceptance of the potential of science to answer questions by means of controlling nature. To do that, however, required the patience and dedication of many investigators working toward the same end.

The new image of science as a collective enterprise owes much in theory, if not in practice, to the English philosopher Francis Bacon (1561–1626). In his important book *Novum Organum* (*A New Instru-*

ment or Method [of knowledge]) (1620), he called for a restoration (*instauratio*) of the sciences by a new method, the inductive or experimental method, to replace the deductive analysis of Scholastic Aristotelianism. He envisioned that this new science would be conducted by teams of investigators who worked together—a scientific community.

That Bacon's dream was not an idle one is indicated by the chartering in April 1663 of the Royal Society of London for Improving Natural Knowledge. Such was its success that four years later, Thomas Sprat (1635–1773), future Bishop of Rochester, published his *History of the Royal Society*. Praising its accomplishments, and at the same time defending the role of science against its detractors, Sprat left no doubt that science had become a part of a new society. Although some time would elapse before courses in science were routinely available to university students, all the necessary constituents of the scientific enterprise were available by the beginning of the eighteenth century: scientific instruments, a scientific press, governmental recognition and patronage, and, of course, a growing number of professional scientists. As a result, science became institutionalized. It is the early stages of that institution that I have tried to reconstruct, albeit summarily, in the present chapter.

GALILEO GALILEI

Galileo (1564–1642) stands as one of the great pioneers of modern science, not only for his discoveries in astronomy and physics, but also for his important role in the development of the methods of science. He was born in Pisa in 1564, the son of a well-known composer and musician. In 1574 the family moved to Florence. Galileo studied at the University of Pisa, and began teaching there in 1589. From 1592–1610 he taught mathematics at the University of Padua, in the Venetian Republic. Galileo was truly a "Renaissance man": artist, musician, lover of literature, and excellent writer as well as a scientist. While in Padua he met and entered into a long-term relationship with Marina Gamba, with whom he had three children: two daughters, Virginia and Livia, and a son, Vincenzo. These were also fruitful years intellectually for Galileo, when he was establishing a reputation as a brilliant and creative scientist. In 1597 he invented a military compass. In 1602 he began experiments on magnetism.

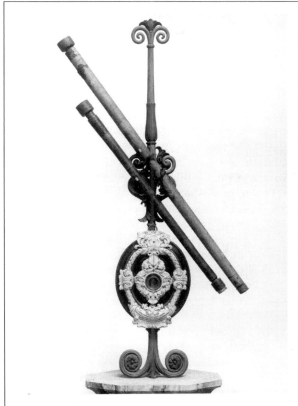

This collection of instruments represents Galileo's many scientific achievements. Galileo used the lens shown here to observe the moons of Jupiter, which he called the "Medicean Planets." Years after Galileo's discovery, the Medici family commissioned the oval ebony frame to house the lens. The telescopes pictured are just two of the many devices produced by Galileo between 1610 and 1640. Galileo designed a host of accessories for the telescope's various applications. One of these, the micrometer, measured distances between Jupiter and its moons. Another, the helioscope, made it possible to observe sunspots without risking eye damage.

Figure VI-7 Two of Galileo's Telescopes and a Lens. ca. 1609–10. Museo di Storia della Scienza, Florence. Wood, leather, 980 mm in length. Courtesy of the Granger Collection, New York.

In 1604 he made an initial attempt at formulating the law of falling bodies, and also declared himself a Copernican. In 1609, after hearing of the invention of the telescope, he constructed the first telescope to be used for astronomical purposes, with which he carried out the observations and made the discoveries that led to the publication of his first important book, *The Starry Messenger*, in 1610. We will examine this book in more detail below. He dedicated the book to Cosimo II di Medici, Grand Duke of Florence, in the hope of getting the job of "resident scientist" at court, and was duly rewarded with the position. Galileo moved to Florence in 1610 as tutor to the prince and Chief Mathematician and Philosopher to the Grand Duke.

In Florence Galileo continued actively to pursue experimental research in physics and observation in astronomy. He also argued publicly and actively for the acceptance of Copernicus's heliocentric world system, believing that his own observations provided empirical proof of its correctness. In 1611 Galileo published *Discourse on Bodies in Water*, and in 1613 another astronomical work, *Letters on Sunspots*. By this time his advocacy of Copernican theory, which he pursued with great self-assurance and ill-concealed disdain for his opponents, was becoming the focus of ecclesiastical as well as scientific controversy. Some church leaders supported the new theory while others attacked it on biblical grounds. Many astronomers were far from persuaded that Galileo had provided sufficient reasons to abandon long-established astronomical theory. Galileo was particularly exasperated by theologians who used biblical passages to support their Aristotelian view of science. In 1615 he defended his views theologically as well as scientifically in a letter he wrote to the Grand Duchess Christina, mother of Duke Cosimo II, who had expressed interest in the controversy. The *Letter to the Grand Duchess Christina*, which we will discuss in more detail below, is one of the first great modern essays on the relationship between science and religion.

In 1616 Galileo was summoned to Rome to respond to the accusations of his theological enemies. He met with Cardinal Robert Bellarmine, a learned theologian and head of the Holy Office of the Inquisition. Bellarmine was not unsympathetic to Galileo's arguments for Copernicanism, but the

Church had decided to condemn Copernican theory. Bellarmine, profoundly obedient to Church teaching and authority, insisted that the heliocentric theory must be used purely heuristically, as a useful hypothesis in doing mathematical calculations about the sun and planets, but not as a factual description of the nature of the universe. Bellarmine ordered Galileo not to "hold, teach and defend in any manner, in words or in print," the Copernican system as the truth about the relations among the sun and the planets, but only as a mathematical hypothesis. Galileo politely submitted to the cardinal's directive, but was inwardly resolved to interpret it with the widest possible latitude—much wider, as it turned out, than the official Catholic position would allow. Minutes were kept of the meeting between the two, but not officially signed. Years later, when Galileo was on trial before the Inquisition and the Cardinal was dead, the Jesuits in the Vatican who were prosecuting him produced the minutes and used them against him.

In 1620 Cardinal Maffeo Barberini was elected to be Pope Urban VIII. He had long been on good terms with Galileo, and admired his scientific work. They had had lively but inconclusive discussions about Copernican theory. Galileo, who had continued brashly to argue for Copernicanism as a demonstrably true theory and not simply a mathematical hypothesis, now had some hope that Copernicanism would have ecclesiastical support "at the top" and get a fair hearing. Emboldened by what he thought was a more congenial atmosphere for his ideas, in 1632 he published, in Italian rather than in the usual Latin of scholars, his *Dialogue Concerning the Two Chief World Systems*. The book was a supremely confident argument for the heliocentric theory and a contemptuous dismissal of its Ptolemaic opponents, in some cases presenting tentative hypotheses as if they were proven conclusions. The characters in the dialogue are Salviati, the voice of Galileo himself, Sagredo, his witty friend who raises questions and objections to sharpen the discussion, and a third person named "Simplicio" (which means "simpleton" in Italian), a stubbornly uncomprehending representative of the conventional Aristotelian science of Galileo's enemies. Upon reading it, Urban VIII was angered not only by the tone and content of the book, but also by what he believed

was Galileo's personal satirizing of his views in the character of Simplicio.

In 1632 publication of the *Dialogue* was ordered to be stopped, and Galileo was summoned to Rome—this time to stand trial for heresy before inquisitors of the Church. By this time he was sixty-eight years old, frail, and going blind. Among other features of his trial he was shown the instruments of torture. Faced with a foregone conclusion and the threat of excommunication and torture, Galileo, humiliated and defeated, read aloud and signed a formal statement in which he abjured the Copernican theory and affirmed his adherence to the teachings of the Church. He was placed under house arrest, first in Siena and then, for the rest of his life, in the village of Arcetri in the hills south of Florence.

Despite his infirmities, Galileo carried out many physical experiments and formulated the law of falling bodies during those last years in Arcetri. His book *Two New Sciences* (1638), published in The Netherlands, was the first great work of modern physics, establishing the sciences of mechanics and optics. By 1637 he was completely blind. Galileo was not closely guarded at his home, and he received visitors from Italy and beyond, including two famous Englishmen, the philosopher Thomas Hobbes and the poet John Milton. Galileo died in 1642, the year Isaac Newton was born.

An intimate and poignant personal aspect of Galileo's story is his relationship with his daughter Virginia, who in 1614 at the age of thirteen had become a nun in the Order of Poor Clares, taking the name of Suor Maria Celeste and living in the Convent of San Matteo in Arcetri until her death in 1634. (Her younger sister Livia entered the same order and convent at the same time, taking the name of Sister Arcangela.) During his years in Florence Galileo lived not far from the convent, and of course in Arcetri he was just down the road. Suor Maria Celeste and her father carried on correspondence, and also saw each other periodically, over a period of several years. Her letters to Galileo survived, and in 2001 were published in English translation. Life in the convent was marked by extreme austerity and poverty. Suor Maria Celeste's contact with her famous father was a window on a world of which she otherwise knew nothing. Father and daughter made jam and mixed medicines together, and she mended his clothes. Galileo repaired the convent clock, sent the nuns music and plays to perform, and helped them with food and clothing. Suor Maria Celeste died, at the age of thirty-four, only a short time after Galileo was moved to Arcetri.

While Galileo is famously known for his challenge to the Catholic Church and his subsequent trial, there is an interesting contemporary footnote: Although Catholic scientists and Catholic teaching have long accepted the heliocentric theory of Copernicus and Galileo, the Catholic Church did not officially reopen the "Galileo case" until 1979, when Pope John Paul II appointed a commission to study the case. In 1992 the pope publicly "absolved" Galileo and said that the theologians of his day had erred in thinking that the "literal sense of sacred Scripture" explains the physical world.

The Starry Messenger (1610) Galileo published *The Starry Messenger* (in Latin) in 1610, dedicating it to Cosimo II de Medici, Grand Duke of Tuscany. Cosimo II was one of a long line of Medicis who dominated the city-state of Florence. In studying the Renaissance we learned about his ancestor Lorenzo the Magnificent in the fifteenth century, to whose grandson Machiavelli dedicated *The Prince*. The Grand Duchess Christina, to whom Galileo later addressed his *Letter*, was the mother of Cosimo II. *The Starry Messenger*, with its fulsome praise of Cosimo II, got Galileo the job he had sought as Chief Mathematician and Astronomer to the Grand Duke. Galileo even christened the moons of Jupiter, which he discovered, the "Medicean stars" (in Galileo's time, the term "stars" was used for both stars and planets).

Reading *The Starry Messenger* is an exciting "you are there" kind of experience. Almost 400 years later we can still "look over the shoulder" of the man who revolutionized our view of the universe as he reports on the first discoveries about the heavens he has made with a new invention called the telescope. Notice how he uses hypothesis, mathematics, and observation, and reports step-by-step on his procedures in good scientific fashion. With a telescope less powerful than you can buy at Wal-Mart, Galileo saw things about the moon and the planets, and saw many stars, that no one had ever seen before. Notice that in his conclusion Galileo states that the moon is not smooth and polished (as befits the perfection celestial bod-

ies are supposed to manifest in the Ptolemaic system), but very much like the earth. That was a revolutionary and potentially dangerous view to hold after 1500 years of Ptolemaic astronomy. Galileo promised a future book called *System of the World*. This book, published in 1632 in Italian as *Dialogue Concerning the Two Chief World Systems, Ptolemaic and Copernican*, brought him before the Inquisition.

Letter to the Grand Duchess Christina (1615) In *Letter to the Grand Duchess Christina* (1615) Galileo shows that he can outthink the theologians as well as the scientists—and on their own terms, with references to and quotations from the Church Fathers, notably Augustine. This is one of the great early writings on the relationship between science and religion, an issue posed by the Scientific Revolution and still debated and written about. There were clergy—some of them prominent in the church—who supported Galileo's Copernican views and even wrote books defending them theologically, just as there were scientists who rejected and attacked his views. The common reference to the "conflict between science and religion" is an oversimplification. Whenever revolutionary new ideas in modern science have appeared—the great examples are the Copernican theory of the universe and Darwin's theory of evolution—they have split *both* the scientific community *and* the religious community.

Letter to the Grand Duchess Christina merits careful reading to see what Galileo was arguing. His opponents claimed that the Copernican theory of a sun-centered universe and a moving earth contradicted Scripture. Galileo considered himself a good Catholic, and makes it clear in the *Letter* that he accepts the divine authority of the Bible. He holds the standard view of the time that the biblical writers, such as Moses, David, and Solomon, were all-wise and communicated under the inspiration of the Holy Spirit. The issue for Galileo was: how is sacred Scripture to be *interpreted* when it speaks of natural phenomena?

Galileo summarizes his view: God's primary purpose in giving us the Bible is to lead humans to salvation, but he has given us reason and our senses to gain knowledge of nature. Since both reason and revelation come from God, they cannot conflict when they are rightly used and understood. Galileo appeals, with some justification, to Thomas Aquinas, who held the same view at an earlier stage of scientific knowledge. The inspired writers of the Bible, including the author of the Book of Joshua, adapted their language to the understanding of ordinary people of their time when they were referring to nature. To our ordinary observation the sun *does* rise and set and move across the heavens. Having cited the leading authorities on Christian doctrine and biblical interpretation, from the Church Fathers to the Council of Trent, Galileo dramatically concludes by showing how Joshua's command to the sun to stand still makes sense only on the *Copernican* theory, not the Ptolemaic!

A final note: When Galileo wrote his *Dialogue Concerning the Two Chief World Systems*, he ignored an important third alternative to both the Ptolemaic and the Copernican systems, the *Tychonic theory*, which was popular with scientists of the day and dealt effectively with the problems of the Ptolemaic astronomy. It is named for the Danish astronomer Tycho Brahe (1546–1601), who, with the assistance of his sister Sofie, spent years in his observatory making the most meticulous and accurate observations and calculations of planetary and stellar motion that anyone had made before the invention of the telescope. Tycho's observations of comets persuaded him that the Ptolemaic theory could not be right, but he did not accept Copernicus' alternative. Tycho developed his own theory: a stationary earth at the center of the universe with the other planets revolving around the sun, which in turn orbited around the earth. With his careful observations and calculations to back it up, the Tychonic theory was more attractive than the Copernican theory to those astronomers who were having trouble with the Ptolemaic theory, since it preserved a stationary earth at the center of the universe while permitting accurate calculations of the movement of sun, moon, planets, and stars. Although Copernicus and Galileo were right and Tycho was wrong, Galileo made it easier for himself by ignoring the Tychonic theory.

FIGURES OF IMPORTANCE IN THE SCIENTIFIC REVOLUTION

Roger Bacon (ca. 1214–1294). English scholastic scientist and philosopher; Franciscan.

Johann Gutenberg (ca. 1398–1498). German inventor and printer.

Nicolaus Copernicus (1473–1543). Polish astronomer, mathematician and economist.

Paracelsus (ca. 1493–1541). Swiss physician and alchemist.

Andreas Vesalius (1514–1564). Flemish anatomist.

Johannes Kepler (1571–1630). German astronomer.

Galileo Galilei (1564–1642). Tuscan astronomer, philosopher, and physicist.

William Gilbert (1540–1603). English scientist and physician.

William Harvey (1578–1657). English physician.

Jean Baptiste van Helmont (1577–1644). Belgian physician.

Robert Boyle (1627–1691). Anglo-Irish physicist and chemist.

Isaac Newton (1642–1727). English mathematician, natural philosopher and physicist.

QUESTIONS FOR STUDY AND REFLECTION

1. What were the main differences between the new science emerging in the sixteenth and seventeenth centuries and the science of the late Middle Ages? What ideas from the ancient Greeks played a role in shaping the new science?

2. Describe the four main models in the development of modern science, and give one example for each of a distinguished scientific pioneer who used that model.

3. In *The Starry Messenger* how does Galileo express characteristics of what "science" has come to mean in the modern world? What findings of Galileo about the heavens, reported in this book, would have been shocking or unsettling to many readers?

4. What was the issue between Galileo and his opponents in the church? Was it a matter of "science versus religion"? Why or why not? How did he respond to his opponents in *Letter to the Grand Duchess Christina*? Do you find any permanent insights in his approach to the relationship between science and faith? If so, what?

5. Summarize Newton's achievements.

SUGGESTIONS FOR FURTHER READING

Briggs, Robin. *The Scientific Revolution of the Seventeenth Century*. New York: Harper and Row, 1969.

Dekosky, Robert K. *Knowledge and Cosmos: Development and Decline of the Medieval Perspective*. Washington, D.C.: University Press of America, 1979.

Hall, A.R. *The Scientific Revolution 1500–1800. The Formation of the Modern Scientific Attitude*. Boston: Beacon Press, 1956.

Kearney, Hugh. *Science and Change, 1500–1700*. New York: McGraw-Hill, 1971.

Rossi, Paolo. *Philosophy, Technology, and the Arts in the Early Modern Era*. Translated by Salvator Attanasio. New York: Harper and Row, 1970.

Reston, James, Jr. *Galileo, A Life*. New York: Harper-Collins, 1995.

Sobel, Dava. *Galileo's Daughter*. New York: Walker & Co., 1999.

Westfall, Richard. *The Construction of Modern Science: Mechanisms and Mechanics*. New York: John Wiley & Sons, Inc., 1971.

Wightman, W. P. D. *Science and the Renaissance*. 2 volumes. New York: Hafner, 1962.

SUGGESTED READINGS ON GENERAL THEMES IN WESTERN CIVILIZATION

Armstrong, Karen. *A History of God: The 4,000-Year Quest of Judaism, Christianity and Islam.* York: Ballantine, 1994.

Barzun, Jacques. *From Dawn to Decadence: 500 Years of Western Cultural Life. 1500 to the Present.* New York: HarperCollins, 2000.

Bloom, Harold. *The Western Canon: The Books and Schools of the Ages.* New York: Riverhead Books, 1994.

Boorstin, Daniel. *The Discoverers: A History of Man's Search to Know His World and Himself.* New York: Vintage, 1983. *The Creators: A History of Heroes of the Imagination.* New York: Vintage, 1992. *The Seekers: The Story of Man's Continuing Quest to Understand His World.* New York: Vintage, 1998.

Denby, David. *Great Books: My Adventures with Homer, Rousseau, Woolf and Other Indestructible Writers of the Western World.* New York: Simon & Schuster, 1996.

Hourani, Albert. *A History of the Arab Peoples.* Cambridge, MA: Belknap/Harvard University Press, 1991.

Magee, Bryan. *The Great Philosophers: An Introduction to Western Philosophy.* London: Oxford University Press, 1987.

Moynahan, Brian. *The Faith: A History of Christianity.* New York: Doubleday, 2002.

Tarnas, Richard. *The Passion of the Western Mind: Understanding the Ideas That Have Shaped Our World.* New York: Ballantine Books, 1991.

INDEX

W

wahy, 291

Wartburg Castle, 381, 390

Western Empire, 163, 207, 212–214, 216, 299

Westminster Confession, 387

Wife of Bath, 335–336, 338

William the Conqueror, 298, 302, 309

Wittenberg, 378–379, 382–383, 385, 406, 409

Word *[Logos}*, 11

Worms, 306, 308–309, 381, 406, 408–409

Writings, 5, 13–14, 16, 25–26, 28–29, 410

Wyclif, John, 356

X

Xerxes, 102

Y

Yahweh, 15, 26, 28, 30–31, 34

Yathrib, 285

Yom Kippur, 293

Z

Zakat, 293

Zealots, 164–165, 357, 360

Zeno of Citium, 189

Zeno's Paradoxes, 131

Zeus, 99, 106, 113, 123, 156, 181–182

ziggurat, 4–5

zoology, 412, 419

Zurich, 383, 385

Zwingli, Ulrich, 383, 384

Playlist for accompanying compact disc

MUSIC FOR PATTERNS IN WESTERN CIVILIZATION, VOLUME I, FOURTH EDITION

TRACK	TITLE	Time
[1]	*PSALM 93* Congregation of the Ioanina Synagogue, Jerusalem (s)	2:07
[2]	*I GOT UP EARLY* H. Borbolis, vocal (s)	2:38
[3]	Seikilos: *SONG* Ensemble De Organographia (p)	2:04
[4]	Euripides: *CHORAL ODE* from *Orestes* Ensemble De Organographia (p)	1:13
[5]	Anonymous: *Instrumental Exercises* Ensemble De Organographia (p)	2:37
[6]	*POMPA GLADIATORUM* Praecones Provinciae Britanniae (r)	2:20
[7]	*COPA* Praecones Provinciae Britanniae (r)	6:03
[8]	*ANTIPHONAE CUM PSALMIS: A summo caelo; Dominus dixit;* *Notum fecit; Laetare nunc; Descendit sicut pluvia; Tu es via* Schola Hungarica, Janka Szendrei and Lásló Dobszay, conductors (q)	6:09
[9]	*GLORIA – KYRIE* Schola Hungarica, Janka Szendrei and Lásló Dobszay, conductors (q)	2:14
[10]	*CALL TO PRAYER* Mustafa Ozcan Gunesdogdu (w)	3:59
[11]	SURAT AL-INFITAR Muhammad Khalil al-Husari (w)	3:04
[12]	*KYRIE* from *Hodie Christus Resurrexit* Schola Hungarica, Lásló Dobszay, conductor (d)	1:46
[13]	*AVE, GENEROSA, GLORIOSA* Schola der Benediktinerinnenabtei (q)	5:02
[14]	*SALTARELLO* Sine Nomine Ensemble for Medieval Music (q)	5:00
[15]	*JE NE VIS ONCQUES LA PAREILLE* Sine Nomine Ensemble for Medieval Music (q)	4:13
[16]	Josquin Desprez: *KYRIE* from *Missa Pange Lingua* Spandauer Kantorei, Martin Behrmann, conductor (z)	3:04
[17]	Martin Luther: *EIN FESTE BURG IST UNSER GOTT* Westfälische Kantorei, Wilhem Ehmann, conductor (q)	4:03
[18]	Giovanni Pierluigi da Palestrina: *KYRIE* from *Pope Marcellus Mass* Vienna Motenttenchor, Bernhard Klebel, conductor (q)	3:14
[19]	Claudio Monteverdi: *IO NON DIRO* from *L'Orfeo* Cyrille Gerstenhaber, La Grande Ecurie et la Chambre du Roy Jean-Claude Malgoire, conductor (q)	1:01
	(Approx) Total Time	**61:51**

RECORDING CREDITS

(d) Laserlight Records, Courtesy of Delta Entertainment
(p) Courtesy of Pandourion Records
(q) Courtesy of Qualiton Imports, Ltd.
(r) Courtesy of Riverrun Records
(s) Courtesy of Smithsonian Folkways Recordings
(w) Courtesy of White Cloud Press
(z) Courtesy of SPJ Music

PRODUCED BY SILVERDISC
White Plains, New York 10601

SCD 570